ETHICAL ISSUES

A SEARCH FOR THE CONTEMPORARY CONSCIENCE

EDITED BY
WILLIAM R. DURLAND
AND
WILLIAM H. BRUENING
Purdue University, Fort Wayne, Indiana

MAYFIELD PUBLISHING COMPANY

Copyright © 1975
by William R. Durland and William H. Bruening
First edition 1975

All rights reserved. No portion of this book may be reproduced in any form or by any means without written permission of the publisher.

Library of Congress Catalog Card Number: 74-33868
International Standard Book Number: 0-87484-328-6

Manufactured in the United States of America
Mayfield Publishing Company
285 Hamilton Avenue, Palo Alto, California 94301

This book was set in Galaxy Medium and Trump Medieval by Computer Typesetting Services and was printed and bound by the George Banta Company. Sponsoring editor was Alden C. Paine, Carole Norton supervised editing, and manuscript editors were Fiorella and Bengt Ljunggren. Michelle Hogan supervised production, and the book and cover were designed by Nancy Sears.

CONTENTS

SUBJECT GUIDE TO CONTENTS vi

PREFACE ix

INTRODUCTION 1

Ethics and Morality 1
 William H. Bruening

Ethics and Legality 13
 William R. Durland

1 RELIGION AND MORALITY 31

The Sermon on the Mount 36
 Matthew 5:21-48

Situation Ethics versus Rule Ethics 37
 Luther J. Binkley

Christian Ethics and Moral Philosophy   61
   George Finger Thomas

The Sacrifice of Isaac   73
   Genesis 22:1-19

Is There Such a Thing As a Teleological Suspension of the Ethical?   75
   Sören Kierkegaard

On the Suspension of the Ethical   87
   Martin Buber

Ethics and Faith Again: Prolegomena to the End of a Debate   91
   William H. Bruening

2 LAW AND MORALITY   99

Morals and the Criminal Law   104
   Patrick Devlin

Immorality and Treason   113
   H.L.A. Hart

On Punishment   118
   A. M. Quinton

Punishment: For and Against   127
   Arthur Lelyveld

3 PACIFISM AND VIOLENCE   141

Pacifism: A Philosophical Analysis   145
   Jan Narveson

The Moral Equivalent of Violence   160
   William R. Durland

Concerning Violence   176
   Frantz Fanon

Black Power   188
   Martin Luther King, Jr.

4 MEDICAL AND ENVIRONMENTAL ETHICS   199

Abortion and the Sanctity of Human Life   205
   Baruch A. Brody

Euthanasia: Our Right to Die   220
   Joseph Fletcher

Our Destruction of Tomorrow: A Philosophical Reflection
on the Ecological Crisis 247
   Norbert O. Schedler

Where Are We Now and Where Are We Headed? 269
   Erich Fromm

5 GOVERNMENT AND BUSINESS   287

Will It Play in Peoria? 291
   David L. Fairchild

Reply to Critics: A Letter Addressed to
The Daily Chronicle 306
   Leo Tolstoy

Truth in the Marketplace: Advertisers, Salesmen,
and Swindlers 310
   Burton M. Leiser

What Is Property? 336
   Pierre-Joseph Proudhon

6 SEX AND LIBERATION   347

Playboy's Doctrine of Male 352
   Harvey Cox

Marriage and Morals 357
   Bertrand Russell

Myth and Reality 375
   Simone de Beauvoir

7 RIGHTS, RACE, AND HUMAN DIGNITY   385

Rights: Legal and Moral Parameters 389
   William H. Bruening

The Differences Are Real: Race, Intelligence,
and Genetics 403
   Arthur Jensen

The Silent Mugging of the Black Community:
Scientific Racism and IQ 414
   Robert L. Williams

Bury My Heart at Wounded Knee 424
   Dee Alexander Brown

INDEX   **437**

SUBJECT GUIDE TO CONTENTS

PHILOSOPHY AND LAW

Bruening Ethics and Morality
Durland Ethics and Legality   13
Devlin Morals and the Criminal Law   104
Hart Immorality and Treason   113
Quinton On Punishment   118
Lelyveld Punishment: For and Against   127
Fletcher Euthanasia: Our Right to Die   220
Fairchild Will It Play in Peoria?   291
Leiser Truth in the Marketplace   310
Bruening Rights: Legal and Moral Parameters   385

RELIGION AND ETHICS: THEORY AND PRACTICE

Bruening Ethics and Morality   1
The Sermon on the Mount   36
Binkley Situation Ethics versus Rule Ethics   37
Thomas Ethics and Christian Philosophy   61
The Sacrifice of Isaac   73
Kierkegaard . . . Teleological Suspension of the Ethical?   75
Buber On the Suspension of the Ethical   87
Lelyveld Punishment: For and Against   127
Durland The Moral Equivalent of Violence   160
King Black Power   188
Brody Abortion and the Sanctity of Human Life   205
Fletcher Euthanasia: Our Right to Die   220
Schedler Our Destruction of Tomorrow   247
Tolstoy Reply to Critics   306
Cox *Playboy*'s Definition of Male   352

CHRISTIAN ETHICS

Binkley Situation Ethics versus Rule Ethics   37
Thomas Ethics and Christian Philosophy   61
Kierkegaard . . . Teleological Suspension of the Ethical?   75
Durland The Moral Equivalent of Violence   160
King Black Power   188
Tolstoy Reply to Critics   306
Cox *Playboy*'s Definition of Male   352

JEWISH ETHICS

Buber On the Suspension of the Ethical   87
Lelyveld Punishment: For and Against   127
Brody Abortion and the Sanctity of Human Life   205

EXISTENTIAL ETHICS

Kierkegaard . . . Teleological Suspension of the Ethical?   75
Buber On the Suspension of the Ethical   87

Fromm Where Are We Now . . . 269
deBeauvoir Myth and Reality 375

ETHICS AND MINORITIES

Fanon Concerning Violence 176
King Black Power 188
deBeauvoir Myth and Reality 375
Bruening Rights: Legal and Moral Parameters 385
Jensen The Differences Are Real 403
Williams The Silent Mugging of the Black Community 414
Brown Bury My Heart at Wounded Knee 424

ABORTION

Brody Abortion and the Sanctity of Human Life 205
Fletcher Euthanasia: Our Right to Die 220
Bruening Rights: Legal and Moral Parameters 385

WAR

Narveson Pacifism: A Philosophical Analysis 145
Durland The Moral Equivalent of Violence 160
Fanon Concerning Violence 176
King Black Power 188
Bruening Rights: Legal and Moral Parameters 385

RIGHTS

Devlin Morals and the Criminal Law 104
Hart Immorality and Treason 113
Narveson Pacifism: A Philosophical Analysis 145
Brody Abortion and the Sanctity of Human Life 205
Fletcher Euthanasia: Our Right to Die 220
Fairchild Will It Play in Peoria? 291
Leiser Truth in the Marketplace 310
Proudhon What Is Property? 336
deBeauvoir Myth and Reality 375
Bruening Rights: Legal and Moral Parameters 385

CONSUMERISM AND TECHNOLOGY

Schedler Our Destruction of Tomorrow 247
Fromm Where Are We Now . . . 269
Leiser Truth in the Marketplace 310
Proudhon What Is Property? 336

KILLING

The Sacrifice of Isaac 73
Kierkegaard . . . Teleological Suspension of the Ethical? 75
Buber On the Suspension of the Ethical 87
Lelyveld Punishment: For and Against 127

vii
SUBJECT GUIDE
TO CONTENTS

Narveson Pacifism: A Philosophical Analysis   145
Durland The Moral Equivalent of Violence   160
Fanon Concerning Violence   176
King Black Power   188
Brody Abortion and the Sanctity of Human Life   205
Fletcher Euthanasia: Our Right to Die   220
Bruening Rights: Legal and Moral Parameters   385

ETHICAL THEORY

Bruening Ethics and Morality   1
Durland Ethics and Legality   13
Binkley Situation Ethics versus Rule Ethics   37
Devlin Morals and the Criminal Law   104
Hart Immorality and Treason   113
Quinton On Punishment   118
Bruening Rights: Legal and Moral Parameters   385

ETHICS AND SCIENCE

Schedler Our Destruction of Tomorrow   247
Fromm Where Are We Now . . .   269
Jensen The Differences Are Real   403
Williams The Silent Mugging of the Black Community   414

PREFACE

Charles Dickens's *A Tale of Two Cities* begins with the following paragraph: "It was the best of times, it was the worst of times, it was the age of wisdom, it was the age of foolishness, it was the epoch of belief, it was the epoch of incredulity, it was the season of Light, it was the season of Darkness, it was the spring of hope, it was the winter of despair, we had everything before us, we had nothing before us, we were all going direct to Heaven, we were all going direct the other way—in short, the period was so far like the present period that some of its noisiest authorities insisted on its being received, for good or for evil, in the superlative degree of comparison only." Dickens indicates that the eighteenth-century revolutionary France and his own nineteenth-century England were very much alike. We believe that Dickens's words also serve to describe the time of this book.

To say that we live in troubled times sounds like a cliché. Yet, can it be denied that wherever we look—at society, the economy, the political scene—our times appear troubled indeed? In the face of the staggering decisions we are called to make day by day, both as individuals and as a society, our personal and collective equilibriums often seem threatened. Our personal decisions may range from the issue of abortion to questions about euthanasia. The decisions of our society range from issues of institutional violence to questions about the very future of our planet.

Many of our twentieth-century problems did not exist in eighteenth-century France or nineteenth-century England, but moral problems are present in all societies and in all historical epochs. The selections in this book address a small area of the moral problems of our own time. We feel that part of our present difficulties—be they in the political, social, economic, or any other arena—stems from a general lack of understanding of the very nature of morality and from the failure of many to think of contemporary issues in terms of morality.

Thus we see an urgent need to assess and to reassess in moral terms the many issues and problems facing us. But to satisfy this need we would not ignore the legal ramifications of the same issues and problems. In fact, it seldom occurs that a moral problem is not also a legal problem, and vice versa. And it is also quite evident that moral and legal problems often turn out to be religious problems as well.

We have divided the following readings into seven sections, each devoted to one general topic. Yet a quick reading of the selections will show that all the topics are interrelated, and the issues discussed in one section bear on those discussed in another. We urge the reader to draw out these various relationships among the issues treated and to see how taking a position on one issue entails certain consequences when discussing another.

Space considerations have forced us to exclude much material worthy of inclusion. To some degree the suggested additional reading alleviates this ineluctable problem, and we hope that the reader will find the time to investigate these additional readings on any issue of particular interest and concern.

Editors always have difficult choices to make about what to include and what to leave out in a book of this nature. We have spent considerable time agonizing over the final selections and we can only hope that our choices were the best ones. Yet we are very conscious of our fallibility, and we hope that those who know of better or more readable selections will write us and offer their suggestions.

The introductions to each section are written in dialogue form with a mythical Professor Malcolm Edwards teaching his class in a modified Socratic manner. Professor Edwards's students, however, are far less pliable and far more contumacious than those Socrates is reported to have taught. These introductions are not meant to set up any ideal of what should happen in any particular classroom, but they are intended to communicate a basic principle that the editors hold —that learning takes place only when there is interchange of ideas. Students must take an active part in the learning process. Since students have made, and will make, moral decisions, they must develop or continue to develop the ability to think in moral terms and make moral decisions. If this book is of any value at all, it will be as a facilitator to assist students to extend, and hopefully improve, their grasp on the ability to make moral decisions.

If it is true that the students must take an active part in the learning process, it is equally true that the teacher has to create an atmosphere that encourages the students to participate, that allows them what Carl Rogers calls "the freedom to learn." One of the ways to create such an atmosphere is for the teacher to communicate indirectly *à la* Socrates or Kierkegaard by actions the extent of his or her concern with the issues discussed. Students are among the most perceptive of people (little children are the only ones who are more perceptive), and it is of little or no value to discuss, for example, human rights in the classroom if, in the process, the teacher tramples on the rights of the students by allowing the teacher-student relationship to deteriorate into the master-slave relationship characteristic of some traditional pedagogical settings. One's philosophy of education will determine the failure or success of this book and books like it. If the editors have made a successful effort to pick the readings, and if the teacher and students use the readings not as an infallible guide nor as a rigid agenda of the topics to be discussed in each class but as a catalyst for learning, then our effort as editors will be rewarded, and the students and teachers will experience real learning, real communication, and something that in our own experience as students was very rare—the joy of learning. Thus, perhaps far more than most editors, we depend a great deal on others to determine the final impact and significance of this book.

As usual, there are a number of people who had a great deal to do with the development of this book whose names do not appear on the cover. It is virtually impossible to mention all of them by name. The students in our ethics classes here at Purdue are, in many respects, the real editors of the book. They have read the articles that follow and many others that we have used over a period of five years and have been very definite about what they liked and did not like. Their views have been one criterion, and the most important criterion, for our final selection.

Special thanks are due to Dave Fairchild and Norb Schedler for their original articles on specific topics that we wanted discussed. We were particularly fortunate in being able to work directly with these two excellent writers.

Mayfield Publishing Company has been all that we could hope for in a publisher. Alden Paine assisted us tremendously by making suggestions, encouraging us, and, in general, just being there when we needed him. Michelle Hogan, Pam Trainer, and Carole Norton, among others, helped us with the text organization and the selections and kept the more business-like aspects of the book in order. Fiorella and Bengt Ljunggren edited the manuscript with great skill and perception.

Jan Hoagburg has been of tremendous importance to this book. She typed all of the manuscript at least once and—since the editors, as editors will, made several major changes—parts of it as many as three times. This she did cheerfully and unbelievably quickly, and thereby removed many burdens from our sometimes bowed shoulders. She still likes roses, too.

The patience of our families has been tried by this book, and their fortitude and understanding should not go unnoticed. Lee Durland and her children Michael, Patrick, and Jenifer have witnessed their husband-father turn from lawyer to philosopher and theologian. They offered only encouragement and support as he left the arena of politics to teach in the halls of academia. Sheila Bruening and her children Jennifer and Willie have also witnessed a transformation as their husband-father turned from philosopher to amateur lawyer. Most importantly, Sheila has borne him a second son, Sean, in the interim.

We would hope and pray that our children grow into mature human beings, that they develop moral sensitivity, that they help create a moral and humane world, and that, most of all, they create themselves along the principles that they deem most important. With deep fatherly love and joyful anticipation, we dedicate this book to them.

William R. Durland
January 10, 1975   *William H. Bruening*

INTRODUCTION

William H. Bruening
ETHICS AND MORALITY

THIS ESSAY does not attempt to be a definitive exposition of the nature of moral philosophy. Rather, it is a brief and somewhat bold attempt to sketch in broad strokes an introduction to the underlying structure of the discipline known as moral philosophy. In addition, this essay seeks to provide a theoretical framework for the more practical moral issues treated in the article that follows. To that end, it focuses on two fundamental questions: (1) What is moral philosophy? and (2) What is the structure of a moral code?

Let us suppose that we are observing the first session of an ethics class, and see how one particular teacher introduces his students to the topics to be considered in the course.

"I am Professor Malcolm Edwards. This course is Philosophy 101, Introduction to Ethics. These typed sheets I am handing out contain all pertinent information about office hours, texts, exams, and so on." In most courses the teacher will now launch into a brief résumé of the technical aspects of the course, perhaps followed by a few bits of information about himself—information that he considers relevant or, possibly, simply impressive. So, while the sheets are being passed out, Professor Edwards' students sit back, comfortably secure in the belief that, for now at least, they have nothing to do but listen to a lecture.

Certainly there is nothing unusual in this scene; it is repeated endlessly on the first day of term in countless courses. But our fictional Professor Edwards does not begin with a lecture. Instead, he disturbs the slightly bored tranquillity of his class with a query, "What do you think ethics is all about?"

A ripple of mild consternation and indignation spreads through the class. What is this? Suddenly the burden is being shifted from where it belongs to the students and, as might be expected, many students don't like it. Not unreasonably, they expect the professor to tell them, not the other way around.

Finally, a brave student drowns out the silence by asking, "Isn't it about what is good and bad?"

Professor Edwards nods. "Certainly ethics concerns itself with issues of good and bad. But what kind of good and bad?" Then he adds with a smile, "For example, are we talking about good and bad steaks or good and bad basketball players?"

"No, about good and bad actions," the student replies.

"All right, but don't basketball players make good plays and bad plays? And how can we relate that to ethics?" asks Edwards.

"I mean right and wrong actions," the student amends desperately.

To his relief, Edwards says, "That's as good a place to start as any—right and wrong actions. Now a reasonable question might be, What right and wrong actions? How do we tell them apart?"

A student slouched in the back of the room, fingering what he hopes will become a beard, picks up the ball. "Whatever anybody does is right just as long as it doesn't hurt anyone else," he declares.

"Are you saying that the wrongness of an action is determined solely by the consequences of that action, specifically by the consequences on another?" Professor Edwards sounds puzzled.

The barely bearded student clearly has some definitive views on ethics because he asserts rather defiantly, "Yeah, that's the way it is!"

To his surprise, Edwards merely nods and smiles. "You are not alone in that belief. What about the rest of you? Any comments?"

An unusually neat, rather prim-looking coed joins in, "I can't agree that everything is OK as long as you don't hurt anybody. When I think of what is right or wrong, I think of what my religion tells me is God's will, and then I do what is God's will. Sometimes that means I have to help people as well as not hurt them."

"Are you saying that right, or right actions, is something more than just the absence of wrong, or wrong actions?" asks Edwards.

"How can you talk of right or wrong actions in the abstract?" asks another coed. "I mean, it's all relative, isn't it?"

"You seem to be suggesting that ethics is relative to the culture in which one lives. Am I talking to a budding anthropologist or sociologist?" Professor Edwards asks.

The girl nods. "Well, the Eskimos put their old people on ice floes to die. They think it's all right, so it's all right for them. Some Oriental mystics think smoking hash is helpful in religious meditation. So it's OK for them."

"Come off it!" calls an intense-looking young man from the other side of the room. "Eskimos and mystics," he snorts, "what do they have to do with the problems of our society?"

"What problems are those?" asks the professor.

"Well, for one thing, the whole idea of moral laws. Like all laws, they are nothing but another Establishment gimmick to keep the people in line. Right is what is best for the elite and vice versa—that's what they try to get us to believe! What's right for the people comes second, if ever."

Professor Edwards raises a clenched fist in a mock salute. "All power to the people! Right?" The militant student frowns and shrugs with a grin. "Fine, we have a political activist among us," says Edwards. "That can be useful. Now, just for the sake of argument, let's say that our society does get its moral laws from the elite, from what you call the Establishment. You obviously don't approve of that source; so tell me, from where should our moral laws come?"

"God," murmurs the first coed.

"The people," shouts the activist.

"Are you saying that what the people think or, rather, what most people think is what we should call right?" Professor Edwards asks.

The militant student nods, though somewhat uncertainly. To the surprise of the rest of the class, Edwards nods in return. "All right, asking what people think is right is certainly one way of investigating what ethics is all about."

"Just what is ethics all about anyway?" wails a frustrated, rather inattentive student.

Professor Edwards looks around in seeming confusion and asks, "Uh, isn't this the part where we all came in?"

Professor Edwards has begun his class with the fairly unorthodox pedagogical technique of asking questions without answering them. So far the class appears to be generating little more than confusion. This may seem somewhat strange because normally subject matter treated by a course is clearly defined, and the course proceeds along the lines of explaining the whys and wherefores of the subject. But ethics is not such a subject. There is no agreed-upon subject matter. Indeed, part of the study of ethics is deciding what the subject matter of ethics is. So the students of Professor Edwards' class will not be able to decide what ethics is or answer the question, What is ethics all about? by referring to the works of moral philosophers.

They, like you, will learn that those who write about ethics do not agree on the subject matter of ethics. They, like you, will have to decide "what ethics is all about," and that is what this book is all about—helping the reader make his-her own determination.

The divergence of views concerning the definition of ethics can be clearly seen by looking at the disparate approaches offered by various ethics books and ethics courses. Some concentrate solely on practical problems such as, Should I sleep with my neighbor's wife? Should I fight or refuse to fight in a war? Others go to the other extreme and address themselves almost solely to the speculative issues of what is 'right' or what is 'justice'.

WHAT IS MORAL PHILOSOPHY?

Having essentially stated that there is no clear-cut, simple answer to the question of what the study of ethics, or moral philosophy, is all about, we shall nevertheless attempt a partial answer. For this purpose we should like to define three kinds of ethics: descriptive, normative, and metaethics.

The first, descriptive ethics, concerns itself solely with studying the actual moral beliefs of a person or group of persons; with what the individual or society considers to be right or wrong. Descriptive ethics is not concerned with whether the individual or the group is right or wrong; it merely studies the views held, for better or worse. It is a study more commonly pursued by psychologists, psychiatrists, anthropologists, or sociologists. It is not, generally, the primary interest of the moral philosopher.

Instead of asking about the views of right or wrong that people hold, the moral philosopher is more likely to be interested in questions behind these views—questions such as, How do you evaluate the various and multifarious ethical views that people have? What is the moral theory, or moral code, on which these ethical views are based? What constitutes a moral code? How does one set up a moral code?

Traditionalists tend to define moral philosophy as "a discipline concerned with good and bad conduct." Like many simple definitions of complex subjects, this one offers little enlightenment. At the risk of casting more darkness on the subject, we suggest that moral philosophy is defined by the questions raised by moral philosophers. This may cause the reader to curse the darkness but we can light a candle by asking, Just what are the questions raised by moral philosophers? Historically some of these questions have been: What is the ultimate good? What ought one to do? How should one order one's life? How should society be formed in order to function properly? All of these questions relate to setting up certain kinds of norms by which one can judge the rightness or wrongness, the goodness or badness of certain actions, persons, or institutions. Questions of this type are all related to a second type of ethics, called normative ethics.

But in order to establish norms for rightness or wrongness of specific actions or objects, there are other underlying questions that deserve attention. What does it mean to say that something is good, that it is right? How does one define 'good' or 'right' within and without the moral context? To what principle can I appeal when I want to justify my conduct? These questions are not directly concerned with norms of behavior, but they demand answers that must be given before the normative questions can be answered with any finality. Such questions are called metaethical, and indicate the third kind of ethics, metaethics.

Thus we have three distinct kinds of ethics: descriptive ethics, normative ethics, and metaethics. How these three are related will become clear as we proceed. It might be well here to give a sample list of a few of the more traditional questions of normative ethics and metaethics.

Normative questions

1. What ought I to do? (in general or with respect to some specific issue)
2. What makes a person good?
3. Is homicide, for instance, moral or immoral?
4. What is my ultimate normative principle?
5. Do I have any middle-range principles? What are they?
6. How does one solve conflicts in one's moral code?
7. What determines what makes an action good or bad?

Metaethical questions

1. How do I define basic moral terms like 'good', 'bad', 'right', 'wrong'?
2. How do these words function in a specifically moral context? How is this different in a nonmoral context?
3. How do I define other related terms like 'freedom', 'conscience', 'responsibility'?
4. What kind of justification can I give for my moral code? Can any justification be given?

WHAT IS THE STRUCTURE OF A MORAL CODE?

Earlier we suggested that one way to describe moral philosophy is to investigate the questions raised by moral philosophers. An excellent example of such investigation is provided by Socrates when he confronted his last, and perhaps most celebrated, moral conflict.

This story of Socrates as related by Plato is rather famous, but some details concerning his life may be appropriate here.[1] Socrates was a philosopher whose main interest seems to have been in moral matters and in their definition. How he discovered his vocation of moral philosopher is in itself a rather interesting story. According to Socrates, a friend of his went to the Oracle of Apollo at Delphi and asked who was the most knowledgeable person. The oracle answered that no one was smarter than Socrates. When he heard this statement, Socrates was somewhat surprised since he knew he was not so gifted. However, the oracle was famous for giving ambiguous statements, so Socrates set out to discover what the oracle meant. He questioned many people as to their wisdom and, to his surprise, he found many who claimed wisdom but no one who actually possessed it. This led him to the conclusion that his wisdom lay not in the fact that he possessed great knowledge, but rather in the fact that he was honest enough with himself to see that he lacked wisdom. When confronted by Socrates, all those who claimed knowledge were eventually forced to admit that they knew little or nothing.

Now, going around questioning prominent and powerful people and demonstrating that they are not even intelligent enough to know that they know nothing can well lead to trouble. Certainly in the case of Socrates it did, and he was brought to trial on two specific charges: being irreligious and corrupting the youth of Athens.[2] The ruling powers at Athens demanded that Socrates refrain from his lifelong activity of seeking the truth wherever he found it and at whatever cost to the sensibilities of the elite. Socrates refused to be silent, and he gave two reasons why he could not. One reason was that he claimed to have a divine mission from Apollo—the god related to the oracle.[3] The other reason he gave was that his teaching was for the state's own benefit.

All this makes Socrates a social critic whose main occupation was to be a sort of unofficial state nuisance. Indeed Socrates referred to himself as a gadfly. But this alone does not provide material for a moral conflict. What does set the stage for a conflict is the fact that Socrates was also an extreme patriot. Socrates was found guilty of both charges and was sentenced to death, though a series of circumstances delayed his execution. During his imprisonment, one of Socrates' friends, Crito, tried to convince him to escape. Crito argued that the charges were trumped up and that everyone knew it. Moreover, as he pointed out, there was nothing wrong in escaping; as a matter of fact, it was rather expected that a convicted person would escape and go into exile. To Crito, Socrates had every logical justification for refusing to abide by an obviously unjust verdict. But Socrates argued that escape was not available to him for three reasons. First, he suggested that doing harm to anyone is wrong and that escape would harm the state by breaking one of its laws. Second, he suggested that the state functions as a parent and teacher and must therefore be obeyed. And thirdly, he suggested that by staying in Athens for seventy or so years, he had obviously committed himself to obey its laws and that if he had some difficulties in obeying these laws, he should have left much sooner.

This is the basic information we need about Socrates and his conflict. When Socrates was ordered to keep quiet, he refused to obey the state; but when the state said he should be put to death, he obeyed the state. Each decision considered separately gives rise to no conflict.[4] It is only when we compare the two decisions that the conflict appears. How could he obey the state in one case and not in the other? Clearly, Socrates made two definite moral judgments: one judgment that it was right to disobey the state and teach; another judgment that it was wrong to disobey the state and live. Was he just being inconsistent? Or did the two, apparently inconsistent, moral judgments derive from some moral structure or moral code that Socrates espoused?

Socrates gave two reasons to justify his original refusal to obey the state, and he gave three reasons why he felt that he would not be justified in disobeying the state when escape was suggested. These two sets of reasons—the reasons to disobey and the reasons to obey the state—are the key to the resolution of the apparent inconsistency of his judgments and the apparent conflict in his moral code. The reasons are not all of the same order; they are not all of equal force. The way out of the apparent conflict is to suggest that the first set of reasons (i.e., to obey the state is inconsistent with my conscience and/or sense of duty) was more important to Socrates than the second set (i.e., to obey the state is consistent with my belief that it has a right to punish malfeasance). Thus, the apparent logical inconsistency (i.e., I shall not obey the state/I shall obey the state) over the same issue vanishes when one considers that Socrates was consistent as far as his moral code was concerned. Socrates was saved from what we might call moral inconsistency because his moral principles were structured in some hierarchial way such that conflicts between them could be settled. We might point out in passing that only in cases of conflict is it necessary for higher-level principles to take precedence over lower-level principles. Clearly, if there is no conflict, higher-level and lower-level principles can both be obeyed.

It was mentioned in passing that Socrates had a moral code. Now, most people asked to write out their own moral code probably wouldn't know where to begin. In fact, most people don't even know what a moral code looks like. The story of Socrates does, however, provide some clues. First, it suggests that one of the requirements of a moral code is that it contains moral principles that can be ranked in some sort of hierarchial order. We have also seen that conflict between different levels of this hierarchy can be settled by letting the higher level take precedence over the lower one; or if the conflict is about principles on the same level, then the governing principle is justified by appealing to a higher-level principle. Perhaps another example will be helpful. Suppose that I have the two following principles among others in my moral code: I ought to return borrowed goods, and I ought to prevent unjust killing whenever possible. Suppose also that a friend of mine comes charging into my house cursing a neighbor, threatening to shoot this neighbor, and demanding that I return his shotgun which I had borrowed for a hunting trip. My friend is clearly indicating that he has some immediate use for the gun on this mutual neighbor. I have a conflict here. I borrowed the shotgun, and my moral code includes the moral principle that

I return it. But, on the other hand, the highly agitated state of my friend suggests that returning the shotgun puts our neighbor in rather immediate peril. If I keep my promise to return the gun, I am not preventing unjust killing whenever possible. And, if I try to prevent the killing, I must violate my principle concerning return of borrowed goods.

An ethical code needs to be able to handle such conflicts, and the suggestion we get from Socrates' example is that the principles here are either on different rungs in my hierarchical ladder of values, in which case the higher rung takes precedence, or, if the two principles are on the same rung, I must justify holding one and breaking the other by appeal to some higher rung which tells me which to choose in this case.

As we all know, ladders come in various sizes. There is no set number of rungs that our moral codes or theories should have. But all moral codes should have a top rung representing the highest principle that we hold. This rung is what is often called our ultimate principle and represents, if you like, the Supreme Court of our ethical code. Usually an ethical theory or code has only one such principle.

Below is a tentative schema for a moral code.

A MORAL CODE

Name	Examples	Characteristics
Ultimate moral principle	1. Do God's will	1. always holds and always applies
	2. Promote the greatest good for the greatest number	2. usually just one—if more than one, they can never be in conflict
Moral laws	1. Murder is wrong	1. always hold but do not always apply
	2. Lying is wrong	2. cannot conflict with ultimate or corollaries or other moral laws
Moral rules	1. Lying is wrong	1. usually hold but do not always apply
	2. Return borrowed goods	2. violation must be justified
	3. Thou shalt not kill	3. can conflict with higher principles
Legal rules[5] (local rules)	1. Pay your income tax	1. applicable only in locale where they are part of legal/social system and only during effective dates
	2. Register for the draft	2. can conflict

Clearly it is not necessary that every moral code has all four of the rungs proposed here. Some codes may have no principles which fit at certain levels. Instead of our ladder, a moral code might be a stepladder with only three rungs. For example, Moral Laws and Moral Rules could be combined or one of the two could be dropped in other schemas. What does appear absolutely necessary for any moral code is that the top level has something that qualifies. The reason for this seems to be that the top level is what justifies all of the levels below it, and if the top level were not present, nothing could be justified. Indeed, without an ultimate moral principle or principles, normative ethics could not survive.

THE TWO CLASSES OF ULTIMATE MORAL PRINCIPLES

Much of traditional moral philosophy has been devoted to debating what qualifies as an ultimate moral principle. Given our earlier comments about the diversity of opinion about the nature of moral philosophy, it would be too much to expect that moral philosophers agreed on the first principle of morals, or ultimate moral principle.[6]

There is, however, agreement among some moral philosophers concerning the classification of ultimate moral principles. Traditionally such principles have been characterized as belonging to one of two classes. The first class of ultimate principles stresses the consequences of certain actions, focusing on what effects the action will have on what is considered good. The second class of ultimate principles stresses the nature of the action itself, focusing on the inherent quality of the action regardless of its consequences in attaining what is considered good. Adherence to moral principles of this class is considered a duty—one which is to be followed without exceptions if the action is to be regarded as good. Technically the first class defines right in terms of good, and the second class defines right independently of good. Moral philosophers label the consequence-oriented theory *teleology*, from the Greek word meaning "end or purpose"; the duty-oriented theory is called *deontology*, from a Greek word meaning "ought."[7] . . .

Teleological theories determine the morality or immorality of any action in light of its effect in producing a desired end or goal. If the action leads to the realization of this end, it is good; and, if it does not lead to such a realization, it is not good. What constitutes the end to be sought is not well agreed upon by teleologists. Some say that the end to be sought is pleasure and the avoidance of pain; others offer somewhat less hedonistic goals such as the pursuit of truth. Teleologists also are not in agreement as to the number of people to be taken into consideration when deciding which action brings about the desired end. For example, if I personally get some benefit out of an action which is detrimental to many others, some teleologists will say that considerations concerning my own benefit take precedence over any consideration for the consequences of the action on others. This type of teleology is often called egoism. Other teleologists will say that the benefit must be judged in light of what is the effect of an action on the greatest number of people. This type of teleology is often called ethical universalism or, more commonly, utilitarianism.

Deontological theories are quite clearly at odds with teleological theories (at least as they are described here). Deontologists assert that certain actions are right or wrong not because they have good or bad consequences, but because they are right or wrong in and of themselves. For instance, a teleologist might condone homicide if it led to a greater realization of the end, but a deontologist would presumably say that homicide is wrong no matter what benefit accrues to a further realization of the end.

We do not mean to imply that teleologists and deontologists must necessarily disagree on all practical questions about lying, or stealing, or what have you. It is even possible that they could agree on what belongs on levels two and three of our schema. Further, they need not disagree on any or all of the moral principles regarding specific actions. But they certainly will disagree on how one justifies an act or determines what is moral or immoral.

A final comment on the structure of a moral code as exemplified in the proposed schema above. There is a considerable difference between a moral theory or code based on rules which are developed from tradition, experience, and critical analysis and a moral code which denies that such rules can be formulated. The latter position argues that each situation is unique and that rules of the type offered in our schema under the rubric Moral Laws are impossible to discover. There are even a few of those stressing the uniqueness of each act who suggest that the Moral Rules in our schema are impossible to define. These people are act-theorists as opposed to the former group who are called rule-theorists. There are act-theorists and rule-theorists in both the teleologists' camp and the deontologists' camp.

Now that we have touched on a few of the technical distinctions that moral philosophers make in defining the subject matter of their discipline, we shall return to Professor Edwards' class to see how they are progressing.

"Are there any questions?" Professor Edwards inquires for perhaps the twentieth time.

One student who has been silently following the endless questions with obvious irritation blurts out, "What good is it asking questions? All one gets is questions in return."

"Are you objecting to the fact that questions aren't being answered?" asks Professor Edwards. The student nods. "All right, now let me ask the whole class: How many of you here can remember at least one question being answered during this class?"

Eventually about a third of the class raise their hands.

"Good!" says Edwards. "Now think carefully. How many of those questions did *I* answer?"

At first only a couple of hands go down, then several drop. Professor Edwards surveys the class in obvious satisfaction. "Those two brave souls who still have their hands up may possibly be right. Maybe I slipped up and answered one or two questions. [*laughter*] But that's not what I'm here for. I'm here to work with you so that *you* will find the answers. I'm not here to hand them to you."

The prim, neatly dressed coed raises her hand, and Professor Edwards acknowledges it. "If that's true, how come you seem to be shooting down everybody's beliefs and making fun of their religion and their ideas about politics and things?" she inquires.

"Am I doing that or am I simply asking why you hold a particular belief or why you feel as you do about religion or politics?" Edwards answers.

"Another question," groans a student in back, and the class laughs.

"All right," says Edwards with a smile. "Now a statement, not a question. What I'm interested in is what *you* believe. And I'm interested in *why* you believe as you do. Also, I'm interested in discovering whether you can see if some of your beliefs or the reasons behind them may be wrong. And, finally, if you see that they are wrong, are you able to admit it—to yourself if to no one else?"

"Are you willing to admit the same thing?" the coed asks.

"Why not? We must all come to grips with the fact that this course may change our positions on some issues, mine as well as yours. Although I may have studied more about the topics we shall cover, and have presumably spent much more time on them than anyone else in the class, the whole thrust of the course is not for me to convince you that I am right. The odds are surely on the side that I might be mistaken *some* time." The class laughs. "What I shall do and shall expect you to do is offer positions and defend them. It does not matter whether we are right or even whether we believe we are right. When we argue a position, what does matter is that we develop an argument so as to discover what, if anything, is wrong."

"I don't understand," says the coed. "I mean, a thing is either right or wrong."

Professor Edwards shakes his head with a smile. "In this class something may be right on Monday, wrong on Wednesday, and right again on Friday."

As the bell rings, he adds, "Besides your reading, I want everyone to write down at least five beliefs you hold and explain why you hold them. Then write a reason why you shouldn't hold each belief. Class dismissed."

"I believe I should take another course," a voice cries from the back of the room.

"Fine," calls Edwards as he passes through the doorway. "Now work out why you should not take another course!"

Professor Edwards' class illustrates how one particular philosophy teacher handles an Introduction to Ethics. Though the methods used and the topics covered might vary greatly from teacher to teacher, the philosophical approach—specifically the Socratic method—is, or at least should be, employed in teaching ethics. Edwards, as we shall see, exemplifies this method by his technique of asking questions, probing for answers, rejecting pat answers, being open to conflicting views, being willing to change a position when and if necessary.

Unlike most academic subjects, the subject matter of this book and of Professor Edwards' course calls for some kind of existential commitment on the part of the student. Professor Edwards would doubtless affirm that moral sensitivity is in fact the real thing to be learned in his course. But he, like most of us, would be quick to admit that he does not know how to teach such a sensitivity (though there are those who claim they can). He would hope that his course would be an aid for the students' developing such a sensitivity, although he knows that this, perhaps more often than not, fails to occur.

NOTES

1. Our knowledge of Socrates and his teachings is indirect since Socrates himself never wrote anything. What we know of him is mostly what his disciple Plato has told us, and Plato sometimes put his own words in Socrates' mouth.
2. These were the stated charges. One can only speculate that calling the Athenian rulers fools might very well, from their point of view, be considered irreligious and a corrupting influence.
3. Whether or not this reason had any validity as far as Socrates was concerned is debatable since there are indications that Socrates did not accept the orthodox Greek gods. What Socrates might have been saying is that he had a personal vocation and dedication, and not to follow them would constitute a violation of his own conscience.
4. Clearly Socrates is not suggesting that a citizen can disobey the state anytime he wants to. On the contrary, he is suggesting that obedience is the rule rather than the exception and that the exception occurs only when the state commands the citizen to do something that the citizen thinks is immoral.
5. It may disturb some people that legal rules (laws, in the civil sense) appear at the bottom of this proposed moral code ladder. We should point out that legal rules may also be moral rules or moral laws. That is, a particular society may make it illegal to do that which is also immoral. What is important to keep in mind is that what is illegal is not necessarily immoral. If one wants civil disobedience and/or revolution to be possible, then the status quo laws of a society cannot be such that they always hold. If legal rules always hold (because they are legal and not because they are moral), then no dissent for the purpose of changing or disobeying the law is morally possible.
6. Such agreement would make any exposition on ethics much easier. But even if such agreement existed, a consensus of this type could not guarantee that such a proposed first principle was in fact a valid first principle. Agreement is not a logically compelling reason for accepting any moral principle as valid.
7. We are not suggesting that all ultimate moral principles fit neatly into these two classes or that such principles can be "fudged" so they fit. Moreover, if one examines the moral codes that people actually espouse, it may be quite difficult to determine whether a particular code is either deontological or teleological.

William R. Durland
ETHICS AND LEGALITY

AS THIS COUNTRY prepares to celebrate its 200th anniversary, America's young people are showing an interest in morality as it relates to legal and political processes that is unparalleled at any time in the nation's history since the early days of its founding. In the late fifties, Sputnik, the starting gun of the space race, awakened a renewed interest in science and technology. Though the sixties saw rapid technological developments culminating in man's first trip to the moon, another subject was to replace technology as a focus of attention—the Vietnam War. In the early part of the decade, questions were already being raised concerning the legality of America's involvement in the Vietnam struggle. The second half of the decade saw rapidly mounting concern about the morality of American intervention in Vietnam, a concern that eventually led to campus riots and waves of national protest. In the seventies, it has been the Watergate issue with its questions concerning ethics and morality in high office, its revelation of the strengths and weaknesses of America's legal and political institutions and processes that has claimed our attention and concern.

In less than two decades, the doors of Congress, the courts, and the ivory towers have been forced open and political, legal, and moral issues have entered America's living rooms over the major television networks. For weeks Senator Sam Ervin's moral homilies replaced the ethics of "Guiding Light" and "Edge of Night." For days the lawyers of the House Judiciary Committee replaced the fictional legal legerdemain of Perry Mason with the real drama of politicians grappling with the thorny issues of legality and morality.

The events of recent years are likely to cause profound changes in the way Americans perceive the relationship between morality and the law. We feel it not only appropriate but necessary that any anthology on Ethics investigate this relationship.

In his introductory article, Professor Bruening proposes a schema for a moral code which includes legal rules. He observes that what is illegal is not necessarily immoral, and we may readily infer the obverse, namely, that what is legal is not necessarily moral. Obviously there is some definite connection between morality and the law, and it is the intent of this essay to investigate that connection.

One link between law and morality is provided by the concept of justice. Justice—what the ancients defined as "giving each man his due"—can quite properly be considered a moral concept implying that each man has a right to something. Like other moral concepts, justice will be accepted voluntarily by the moral person. But what chance is there that each man will get his due unless all men accept the moral principle of justice? In the real world, little or no chance; and it is here that the concepts and institutions of law enter in. Law is often defined as enforced justice. Under law, it is not necessary to accept the moral principle of justice, but it is necessary to abide by it (or, failing to do so, to suffer the consequences).

Another link between morality and the law is found in their respective approaches to actions and attitudes. While morality is by no means indifferent to a person's actions, conduct, or behavior, its primary focus is on the attitudes and motives behind the actions. Though the enforcement of a law requiring or prohibiting a certain conduct may well influence a person's attitudes and motives, the law, on the other hand, deals essentially with actions, not attitudes. The justice of the law is the justice of one's conduct, the conforming of one's behavior and conduct to the requirements of what the law considers to be just.

Such concern as the law does have for attitudes and motives is indirect and, as we shall see, inferential. Law speaks of intent, and in the criminal law a *mens rea,* or guilty mind, is a necessary element in holding one responsible for the commission of a crime. A guilty mind, however, usually must be deduced from the act of the crime. Unless a person who has committed a crime admits to having a guilty mind, there is no way that the law can delve into subjective considerations of attitude, and it must determine by the objective empirical facts whether a guilty mind exists or not.[1] Thus, the law must look to the action and not to the attitude or intent. Usually the law presumes that a person intends the natural and probable consequences of his act.

To delineate the law's approach to actions and motives, let us take an example where A kills B under circumstances where the first presumption—that A intended B to die as a result of his act—is not in question. If the act takes place in a war authorized by A's country, and the killing conforms to the constitutional and military law of that country, the second presumption—that of a guilty mind—is of no consequence. Even if the killing was done out of motives of revenge and an attitude of hatred, as long as B is an enemy, A is not a criminal under his country's law regardless of his state of mind. Even if A loudly proclaims a guilty mind, he would not be held responsible because his conduct was legal. However, if A kills B under circumstances in which his country has established that the act constitutes a crime, the mere statement of the defendant that he does not have a guilty mind is of no defense. He must prove it from objective or empirical facts. All this is not to say that the law ignores motives and attitudes. Both are taken into consideration in the mitigation of legal sanctions, but the sanctions themselves stand.

For a further investigation of the law's emphasis on action rather than on attitude or intent, an example from civil law may be instructive. In civil law, the law of agency treats, among other relationships, that of master and servant. Under this law, if a servant (or employee) commits a negligent act which results in actionable injury to another, and that act is within the scope of his duties to his master (or employer), the injured party may elect whether to sue the servant or the master. Since the servant is the employee of the master and since the master may be presumed to possess a greater net worth than his employee, an injured party has a right to sue the master even though it is established that an action by the servant and not by the master is the direct cause of the injury. Not only is it unnecessary for the master to have a guilty mind as it is contemplated in the criminal law, but under civil law he need not be the individual who physically caused the injury. The injured party may recover damages in a civil suit simply because the master hired the servant who caused the injury. Here the law obviously does not contemplate any moral consideration, as far as the servant or malefactor is concerned, but addresses itself to the practical consideration of where an injured party can best recover damages. Since most employees cannot pay, the employer is required to pay.

In a sense, the law can never really be concerned with attitudes or motives because the law must make judgments grounded in empirical evidence alone. Motive may be inferred from conduct, but it can never be definitively established. So, if the law cannot judge a person's moral aims or attitudes, is it possible for law to enforce morality (which itself must be concerned with attitudes)? It would seem not. It is only possible for law to enforce the *appearance* of morality based on one's conduct. It then follows that law enforces only one aspect of moral behavior, man's conduct, but not his attitudes, not the reasons and motives which prompted that conduct. Do not attitudes, reasons, and motives—the question of why we do as we do—form the core of morality? If so, what is the relationship between law and morality exactly? Is it that law is, in effect, a device for coercing moral conduct without regard for one's attitude? And if so, should it be so?

This anthology will examine some of the moral and legal implications of such issues as violence, civil disobedience, pacifism, abortion, euthanasia, technology versus ecology, obscenity, homosexuality, women's rights, minority rights, and consumer rights. Each of these essentially moral issues has a connection with law. For example: The state claims the legal right to authorize violence. Does it also have the moral right and, if so, under what conditions? Should an individual have the right not to follow the dictates of the state in every particular? Does the legal right of freedom of worship carry any moral implications? Is abortion moral because the state allows it? Is euthanasia immoral because the state disallows it? If the law no longer declares marijuana illegal, what, if any, are the moral implications of selling marijuana? Assuming it is immoral for two members of the same sex to display their affections publicly, should it also be illegal?

This country was started and expanded by taking land from the previous tenants. Was there any justification—either legal or moral—

for depriving the Indian of his property? Was the "justification" one of race? Is freedom from discrimination a moral as well as a legal right? How have changes in our moral stand with regard to racial, and more recently sexual, discrimination affected our legal posture? In the last few years, the law has been called in to protect the consumer against the businessman, the environment against the exploiters of natural resources. Do laws protecting the consumer and the environment have any moral component? Is there any moral reason for also extending legal protection to the businessman?

It would appear that, to an increasing extent, the law is considered as the one sure objective mechanism for bringing morality back into our world by enforcing morality through the institutions of the state. Clearly a relationship between the law and the morally loaded issues treated in this book, to which we have referred, does exist. Moreover, the relationship between law and morality is, as we have just observed, an important one and deserves some more specific clarification.

Though it would seem that many legal issues have a moral component and that many moral issues are in some manner reflected in the law, what about the law in and of itself? Is the law itself intrinsically moral? Is it immoral? Or is it perhaps simply amoral? Finally, if the law is, to a greater or less extent, either immoral or amoral, should it instead be moral? To answer these questions we shall examine the following four theories: (1) the law as moral; (2) the law as ought to be moral; (3) the law as amoral; and (4) the law as immoral.[2]

We could examine the relationship between these four theories in many ways, but perhaps the most useful approach might be to reintroduce the concept of justice. Since justice may be considered a moral concept, it follows that the law is moral because law is actualization of justice. Alternatively, law is in fact not synonymous with justice, but perfection of the law would make it synonymous with justice. Thus, accepting the theory that the law ought to be just, once the law becomes synonymous with justice we then have law as moral. Or, to restate the third theory, the law has nothing to do with justice or injustice. Law is simply a set of rules designed to be enforced and is in fact amoral—divorced from any concepts of morality. Or, lastly, the law is basically unjust and therefore immoral.

If, as we said earlier, law may be defined as enforced justice, then all theories concerning the relationship between law and morality must, in some way, address themselves to the matter of enforcing the law. But the law and its enforcement are not synonymous, and the relationship between morality and the law is not synonymous with the relationship between morality and the enforcement of the law.

For centuries much has been said concerning the morality of justice and of laws embodying the concept of justice. Less has been said about the morality or immorality of enforcement, and it is at this point that the essence of law must be examined. For justice is a moral as well as a legal concept, but enforcement lies at the very heart of what law is all about—a judgment, a condemnation, a penalty. And so, in order to discuss the first of the above four theories on the relationship between law and morality, we believe it necessary to undertake an examination of another fundamental distinction between law and morality—the necessity of enforcement for law to be law as distinct from morality.

THE LAW AS MORAL

A suitable introduction to this theory is provided by Messner who says:

> The specific character of law lies in this, that it constitutes a rule of external conduct and provides the power to insure this conduct by force. Hence law differs from morality in two respects: first, it has regard only to external relations; secondly, it empowers the community to enforce compliance with its claims. Law, then, is directed only towards external conduct, not toward inner attitudes. Morality, on the contrary, is also concerned with man's intentions. Social order must establish ordered autonomy of action in accordance with responsibilities for existential ends. Such order is guaranteed when the external actions of the members of society are in harmony with law. The social order is not directly affected by the fact that the motive for these actions is respect for others or is fear of punishment. . . . The external conduct demanded by law must be realized if social order is to exist. Hence law is essentially bound up with the power to secure this conduct by the application of physical force through social cooperation. St. Thomas and Hegel agree that the title to compulsion is then an essential and necessary constituent of law, both for the same reason, that it is so because of the unsocial element in society.[3]

It should be noted that Hegel does not find compulsion a primary concept of law because he looks upon compulsion coming into play only as the result of injustice. But he does see that compulsion must be part of the law if only to meet acts of injustice. In his *Philosophy of Right* Hegel admits that coercion is self-destructive, but he says: "That coercion is in its conception self-destructive is exhibited in the world of reality by the fact that coercion is annulled by coercion; coercion is thus shown to be not only right under certain conditions but necessary, i.e., as a second act of coercion which is the annulment of one that has preceded."[4]

In his examination of law, morals, and what he describes as ethics, Hegel views the state as the culmination of all three, as the "realization of ethics in the community."[5] According to Friedrich, "Hegel's state is the ethical community. It is not an institution for the realization of ethics but is this realization itself. . . . [Ethics] can be realized only through or in the state."[6] Later, Friedrich adds, "Hegel insists upon the veneration of the law as the basis of all true ethics when he says 'How infinitely important, how divine it is, that the duties of the state and the rights of the citizens, just as the rights of the state and the duties of the citizen, are legally determined.' "[7] Commenting on civil society, Hegel says: "The principle of rightness becomes the law . . . when, in its objective existence, it is posited . . . i.e., when thinking makes it determinate for consciousness and makes it known as what is right and valid; and in acquiring this determinate character, the right becomes positive law in general . . ."[8]

So for Hegel the ideal state is the moral state and morality can be achieved by man in a society wherein the state becomes the chief vehicle for community cohesiveness, order, and justice. According to Hegel, then, law is morality—either actually or potentially—and morality can be discovered by examining the institution of the state and its laws or requirements upon its individuals. Hegel doesn't seem to be saying that the institution of the state determines morality, but that the institution is the embodiment of the morality of its constituents.[9] This interpretation of Hegel is acceptable to many of his critics because in a sense Hegel holds that only as part of the state can the individual actualize freedom.[10] Other critics disagree. It is not necessary for our purpose to resolve Hegel's meaning irrevocably. His analysis simply tends to illustrate that, for some, morality is ultimately to be found in the state. And this is also true for Thomas Hobbes, Austin, and others.

The concept of law as moral has its shortcomings. For example, such a theory tends to stifle inquiry or change. If the law as we see it and as it affects us is synonymous with morality, we do not further question what morality is. It is simply the law. Also, the concept of law as moral elevates enforcement to great heights so that those who do not adhere to the public morality are forced to adhere through punishment and penalty and are, at the same time, severely discourged from attempting to change public morality. Moreover, for those who look upon law as the expression of morality, when the institution does change its laws, that change represents automatically a change of morality as well. For example, abortion has only recently been made legal in certain states. Does this mean that, for those affected, abortion is now moral whereas in the past it was immoral? For some people this is exactly what it means. The institution determines our morality for us and, whether or not this would be Hegel's viewpoint, the positing of morality as being entirely within the concept of the law may make this conclusion inevitable for some.

THE LAW AS OUGHT TO BE MORAL

The theory that the law ought to be moral presupposes, or at least suggests, a model for the positive law (law established or recognized by governmental authority).

The idea of a higher moral law towards which the positive law should gravitate is described as "the natural law." Legal philosophers such as Aquinas and Locke have been influential in developing this concept which in turn influenced the authors of the U. S. Constitution.

To investigate the theory of the law as ought to be moral, consider the plight of Mr. and Mrs. Poor People. They lived in the county of Rich in the state of Plenty in the year 1971. The county was noted for its comparative affluence. It had only a few pockets of poverty, and our Mr. and Mrs. Poor People lived in one of them. In an affidavit filed as a part of a petition in a court proceeding they had this to say: "We are adult citizens of the United States, and residents of Rich County where we have lived for more than three years. Two of our five children live with us at home, the other three having been taken from us by Rich County. The apartment is entirely too small for our needs. There are only a small living room and one bedroom in addition to a tiny kitchen which one must pass through to enter the apartment. We sleep with our two children in the one bedroom. All of our children are under the control of the welfare department. Judge Helpful has told us that as soon as we obtain an apartment large enough to house all five of our children and submit a receipt for the first month's rent for such an apartment to the county officials, Rich County will return our three other children. We have looked all over Rich County, but there is just no housing we can afford that will meet county requirements for all five children. In view of the fact that the county has done everything to see to it that people of low income such as us cannot obtain decent housing, we think it unjust that the county will not let us have our children until we obtain decent housing."

Mr. and Mrs. Poor People are in effect charging the county with immorality by suggesting that its laws are unjust. According to the theory that the law ought to be moral, what should be done? The facts behind the couple's argument are simple. They are residents of the county and they are poor. They have a large family and the laws of the county require that a family their size must live in a dwelling that has more than one bedroom. Until they find such a dwelling, the county has exercised its authority to take away some of their children. But Rich County does not have adequate housing for its low-income residents, thereby making it impossible for Mr. and Mrs. Poor People to abide by county laws and thus keep their children. This, the couple charges, is unjust. Should there be a moral-legal requirement that the county provide adequate housing or return the children? Those who adhere to the proposition that the law ought to be moral would question the moral content of the Rich County laws in this case.

But to what extent should the law incorporate morality? Adherents to the philosophy that the law ought to be moral do not necessarily suggest that law is identical with morality.[11] Instead, they would examine the law to see to what extent morality should or should not influence it. But any determination on the extent to which morality should influence the law must depend on what we mean by morality. Some would take a limited view of morality's influence on the law because they see the guarantee of "liberty" and "freedom" as more important than the guarantee of "equality."

First let us discuss the extent to which morality should be enforced by the state through its laws. This will go a long way to resolving questions concerning the extent to which the law ought to be moral or more moral. Any question about whether the law ought to be moral or more moral begs the issue of the extent to which morals should be enforced by the law, since to say that the law ought to become more moral means that the law must enforce more morality. This philosophical problem has been described as "the enforcement of morals by the law." The modern debate on this problem began in 1859 with John Stuart Mill's essay *On Liberty*. Mill said ". . . that the sole end for which mankind are warranted, individually or collectively, in interfering with the liberty of action of any of their number, is self-protection; that the only purpose for which power can be rightfully exercised over any member of a civilized community, against his will, is to prevent harm to others."[12] Mill's position was immediately criticized as too restrictive.[13] Since the mid-nineteenth century the trend toward more legal and governmental regulation has brought with it increasing criticism of this position.

In 1954 a committee headed by John Wolfenden was created in England to examine the existing criminal law concerning homosexuality and prostitution and to make recommendations. In 1957 the Wolfenden Report was released. It recommended that homosexual behavior conducted privately between consenting adults should no longer be a crime. The report further recommended that the laws concerning prostitution should not be changed. The committee's recommendations were based on a distinction between matters of private morality and matters of public morality: criminal law should not regulate in the first category, but should regulate matters in the second. The recommendation was based on a determination that matters of public morality might involve harm to others.

In 1958 Lord Patrick Devlin, in a lecture entitled "The Enforcement of Morals," criticized the theory behind the Wolfenden Committee's recommendations as being essentially Millian in character. Devlin saw a much broader area of morality with which the law should be concerned and proposed a countertheory to the effect that morality is essential to the very existence of society. Therefore society has a right to legislate against immorality as such, even in the absence of offense to others. Since any immorality is, at least potentially, injurious to society, the enforcement of morality should extend to anything that may represent a threat to the preservation of society's moral code. Sexual behavior, Devlin maintains, is no exception and, as a potential threat to morality, should come under legal regulation.

In America today we see legal enforcement of morality extending far beyond sexual offenses to drug offenses and to numerous areas commonly regarded as potentially violative of the public interest such as ecology and the exploitation of natural resources, civil rights, racial and sexual bias. Mill presumably would see this as an unwarranted "interfering with the liberty of action," unless we could convince him that deprivation of one class or group by another is harmful and it exists because there is no law to prevent it. And what would Mills say to laws protecting consumer interests? Is there a need to pass legislation which will protect the consumer who in a vast and technologically complex society cannot protect himself? Or is this type of governmental interference beyond the pale of protection in the Millian concept?

Let us return to the issue raised above concerning the right to adequate housing. Does such a right fall within the Millian concept or the Devlin concept? In recent years, the defensive cry "we cannot enforce morality" has been heard in connection with the civil rights movement. It has been said that we cannot legislate morality by a law that seeks to bring races together. Yet the United States Supreme Court decision in 1954 seemed to seek just that. Only history can attest to the benefits and detriments of changing the behavior of one race toward another through the broadening of the moral base on which legislation rests. But this, in fact, has happened. A whole series of legal cases, many on the constitutional level, have expanded the spectrum of legal regulation of "morality" in such diverse areas as voting rights, housing, marriage, and jobs.

In the case of our couple living without adequate housing, a "Good Guys and Girls" coalition of public-spirited citizens tried to resolve the problem of inadequate housing in Rich County. The coalition did not concern itself so much with the subject of moral attitudes as it did with the practical accomplishment of its task. The result of its efforts was an attempt to change the conduct of the county and its residents with regard to providing adequate low-income housing. The coalition argued that it was in the self-interest of the county residents to provide such housing because police, firemen, house helpers, and other service people from whom the richer people benefited were unable to live in the county. Consequently, they argued, some very valuable services were being reduced or lost to the county. This combination of egoistic and altruistic motives formed a strong coalition which demanded that every builder who chose to build within the county provide a minimum of 15 percent low- and moderate-income housing in any apartment dwelling thereafter built. Hundreds of people representing dozens of interest groups appeared before the local county government and a law to that effect was passed. In the eyes of many, a more moral situation was created by the extension of moral concepts into the area of adequate housing for the poor and lower-income groups. Of course the law required enforcement. The justice of "equality" as envisaged by this law had to be enforced at the cost of coercing those who did not see this as a moral question or who, in fact, saw it as an act of immorality limiting the "freedom" of builders to build where and what they chose.

Mr. and Mrs. Poor People were happy. The new law offered the promise of adequate housing that they could afford and the possibility of getting their children back. The builders, however, were not to be so easily controlled by the legislators. They appealed the legislative decision to the courts whereupon Mr. and Mrs. Poor People, with the aid of Attorney Righteous, filed an affidavit as intervening petitioners (a group of people who wish to join a suit, after it commences, either as plaintiffs or defendants, in this instance, as plaintiffs). Along with others, Mr. and Mrs. Poor People stated that they were persons of low or moderate incomes who, together with their respective families, were eligible to benefit directly as the result of the new legislation. In support thereof, the intervening petitioners presented to the court affidavits stating that (1) all petitioners were living in dwelling units for which they paid more than they could afford, (2) these dwelling units were substandard, and (3) their living space was greatly overcrowded. The petitioners said they would be directly and adversely affected if the legislation were declared invalid by the court. The petitioners asked the court to allow them to become part of the case on the basis of their stated belief that they might be advancing positions which differed from those advanced by others in the case.

A group of landowners also applied to become part of the case saying that they too had a direct interest in the case because they owned land in Rich County and would be affected by the legislation insofar as it dealt with rezoning and property values. Judge Blinders decided that the landowners could become part of the case but that the poor people could not. The judge declared that the landowners had a direct interest in the new law but that the poor people did not have a direct interest in the new law because whether or not these poor people would ever move into housing was contingent on the housing being built. As for the owners, Judge Blinders considered their interest to be direct rather than contingent because land values in Rich County would be directly affected by the new law. If the court allowed the legislation to stand, any owner whose land would be built upon thereafter would be subject to the 15-percent rule which might cause builders to build elsewhere, with the result that land owned by county residents would be more difficult to sell. Therefore Judge Blinders ruled in favor of the economic interest and not the human interest, in effect declaring human interest indirect (not a subject for the law), and economic interest direct.

The case illustrates three aspects of the theory that law ought to become moral. First, the law ought to regulate activities that may result in harm to others. In the case of Mr. and Mrs. Poor People, the "harm" is economic. When Mill talks of harm, is he talking only about physical harm or is he talking about economic harm as well? Proponents of a free, unregulated economy in the last century cited Mill as a source for their position. Second, the case illustrates that the resolution of a moral problem by means of the law calls for increased enforcement. And third, it illustrates a situation where a court may find that it is not appropriate for the law to resolve a moral problem (in the case, the possible moral question related to providing adequate housing to the poor). And this perhaps can serve as an entree into our third category—that law is amoral.

THE LAW AS AMORAL

In reexamining the problem of law and morality, some legal writers in the early part of this century concluded that law and morality ought to be separated rather than combined. In his work *The Pure Theory of Law,* Hans Kelsen wrote:

> The validity of the legal norm cannot be questioned on the ground that its contents are incompatible with some moral or political value. A norm is a valid legal norm by virtue of the fact that it has been created according to a definite rule and by virtue thereof only . . . Law is always positive law, and its positivity lies in the fact that it is created and annulled by acts of human beings, thus being independent of morality and similar norm systems. This constitutes a difference between positive law and natural law, which like morality, is deduced from a presumably self-evident basic norm which is considered to be the expression of the "will of nature" or of "pure reason."[14]

So for Kelsen law is quite distinct from morality. Moreover, he states that "law is a coercive order, that is, a normative order that attempts to bring about a certain behavior by attaching to the opposite behavior a socially organized coercive act, whereas morals is a social order without such sanctions."[15] Such reasoning expresses the view that law is independent of morality and that it should be obeyed simply because it is the law. Kelsen's brand of legal reasoning is generally described as "positivism."[16]

It may certainly be possible to act as if law did not possess morality, but in the last analysis can such a separation actually be made? Let us examine an illustrative case wherein a judge attempted to abstract morality from law. The case that was brought on appeal had been decided in Kansas in 1903[17] and it is a good example of how a Kelsenian judge might act. The original case was brought by Adeline Cappier, mother of Ervin Ezelle, to recover damages resulting from the death of her son who was run over by a car of the Union Pacific Railway, and it was decided in her favor. According to the appellate judge, evidence at the original trial had indicated that "no careless act of the railway company's servants in the operation of the car was shown," though Ezelle had one leg and one arm cut off by the car wheels, and the servants of the railway company failed to call a surgeon or to render the injured man any assistance after the accident, but permitted him to remain by the side of the tracks and to bleed to death.

The facts of the case were stated as follows. While attempting to cross the railway tracks, Ezelle was struck by a moving freight car pushed by an engine. A yardmaster riding on the end of the car nearest the victim gave warning by shouting, but it was either too late or Ezelle did not hear it. The engine stopped until the injured man was clear of the track and then proceeded to move ahead with the freight car, it being feared that a scheduled passenger train would overtake them. The general yardmaster was then informed of the accident. An ambulance was called, and the yardmaster went to where Ezelle was lying and found three switchmen binding his limbs to stop the flow of blood. The ambulance arrived about thirty minutes later, and Ezelle died a few hours afterward. The issue of the case was whether there was a legal duty owed to the injured man by the railway company.

The appellate judge in presenting his decision cited Beach on *Contributory Negligence* (paragraph 215) wherein it said, "When a trespasser has been run down, it is the plain duty of the railway company to render whatever service is possible to mitigate the severity of the injury. The train that has an occasion to harm must be stopped and the injured person looked after, and, when it seems necessary, removed to a place of safety and carefully nursed until other relief can be brought to the disabled person." The judge stated that authority cited to support the above contention in the legal treatise was the case of *North Central Railway Co.* v. *The State*. In that case train operators were negligent in running a train too fast without sounding a whistle over a road crossing. That court also said that it thereupon became the duty of the servants of the company to remove the injured man "with proper regard to his safety and the laws of humanity."

The appellate judge decided as follows:

> We are unable, however, to approve the doctrine that when acts of a trespasser himself result in his injury, those in charge of the instrument which inflicted the hurt, being innocent of wrongdoing, are to blame if they neglect thereafter to administer to him whose wounds were self-imposed. With the humane side of the question courts are not concerned. It is the negligent discharge of legal duties only which come within the judicial cognizance. For withholding relief from the suffering, for failure to respond to the calls of worthy charity, or for faltering in the bestowment of brotherly love on the unfortunate penalties are not found in the laws of men but in that higher law the violation of which is condemned by the voice of conscience whose sentence of a punishment for the recreant act is swift and sure.

The judge concluded that Ezelle's injuries were not inflicted by the company. The railway company was no more responsible than it would have been had the deceased been run down by the cars of another company. His injuries were deemed to have been inflicted by himself, not the company.

The judge analyzed the case on the basis of a legal duty, without respect to morality. Legal duty only attached when the company could be found to be at fault prior to the negligence of the trespasser. No such fault on the part of the company was found in this case. Therefore there was no legal duty, although it would seem that a moral duty was owed to the trespasser as a human being over and above any economic considerations involving the company. But the judge summarized: "The moral law would obligate . . . but the law of the land does not . . . ." This case illustrates the failure of the law to enforce what might be considered a moral right owed an injured party by the company.

If we abstract all morality from law, and if we believe that law does not constitute a depository of morality, have we any reason for failing to honor the requirements of the law? If the law attempts to enforce upon us an order, are we not then bound to obey that order because the law is the depository of enforcement and what it is attempting to enforce upon us is a lawful order? What would emerge from such reasoning would be the most efficient, orderly legal system in the world—a system devoid of justice and the concerns of morality, of the balancing of good and evil, and of the necessities of considering "oughtness" as far as morality and the law are concerned. We could imagine as a result an extremely efficient penal code unencumbered by warrants and prohibitions against unreasonable search and seizure and protections against self-incrimination. But would we find this type of law acceptable? Under such system, if the law said abortion was legal, the question of whether or not abortion were moral would be irrelevant.[18] In any system where we abstract all morality from the law, what the law says is legal must be obeyed regardless of any moral consideration. Such a theory seems to license the law to do what it will and we reach the heights of enforcement, the grandeur of condemnation. The law then becomes synonymous with enforcement, and justice becomes irrelevant. Or is this theory really proposed to prevent the problems of the Hegelian thesis—one being that the only morality which exists and which one is obliged to obey is not codified in law? In the last analysis, if you disagree with the law, does it really make much practical difference whether you must obey it because it is "moral" or, in the case of the law as amoral, because you are coerced?

THE LAW AS IMMORAL

We come now to the fourth theory on the relationship of law and morality. It is well that it follows the extremes of enforcement inherent in the theory of the law as amoral, because the theory of law as immoral addresses itself to the immorality *per se* of enforcement and is less concerned with the concept of justice except insofar as enforcement *per se* constitutes injustice. Here the concept of law defined as enforced justice is inappropriate because enforced justice is immorality.

Examples of this theory are found in the words and deeds of Leo Tolstoy. Tolstoy was a prolific writer of the nineteenth century, perhaps best known for his novels *War and Peace* and *Anna Karenina*. He is less known for his writings on religion and morals. Tolstoy was born into Russian aristocracy, and his family attended the Russian

Orthodox church. He grew up honoring the institutions of his time, including the Russian Orthodox church, the czar and the czarina, and the practice of owning serfs. Further, he evinced no objection to war, gambling, and prostitution. In later life, however, he underwent a spiritual conversion and came to see these institutions and practices as corrupt in substance and form.

Tolstoy found his inspiration in the words of Jesus in the Sermon on the Mount to resist not the evil doers, to turn the other cheek, to love one's enemies. He studied the lives of the early Christians and found that their version of Christianity, which he was later to accept as the true version, was indeed quite different from what he had been forced to practice. The Russian Church was a national church which permeated the political institutions, and vice versa. Tolstoy's analysis of the underlying premise of the legal institution, whether that of the church or that of the state, necessitates the use of force, and ultimately of violence, to support whatever concepts it deems to be just. The very fact that law is and must of necessity be enforced made it immoral as far as Tolstoy was concerned. First of all, Tolstoy saw force as generally requiring man to kill or to enslave or to do violence, be that violence psychological, economic, political, religious, or any other. Further, he noted that justice, although a moral virtue, is not the highest virtue, love being the ultimate; and Tolstoy interpreted that no government can love. He concluded that, at its best, the government can do justice and, at its worst, it does much less than this—and generally it operates far below its best.

Tolstoy believed that attitudes and motivations count far more than behavior and conduct, and that a change in behavior and conduct caused by laws and penalties constitutes no change at all morally speaking. He therefore concluded that the law is morally ineffective and noted that, to the extent that all law is based on force, law becomes essentially immoral. His answer was for each man to follow his spirit, and for Tolstoy the guiding light of that spirit was the teachings of Jesus Christ in the Sermon on the Mount. He saw that one who would voluntarily practice these moral teachings would in effect be able to live with his neighbor in peace and love; that the Christian would turn the other cheek and suffer the blows and resist not the evil doer if necessary, but do him no harm; and that he would free all from jail, make war against none, and practice only the law of love towards his fellow man.

According to Tolstoy:

> Governmental power, even if it suppresses private violence, always introduces fresh forms of violence into the lives of men and does this increasingly as it continues and grows stronger. So that though governmental violence (being expressed not in strife but in submission) is less noticeable than individual violence committed by members of a society against one another, it nevertheless exists and generally to a greater degree than in former times. And it could not be otherwise since apart from the fact possession of power corrupts men, the interest or even the

unconscious tendency of those employing force will always be to reduce those subjects of violence to the greatest degree of weakness, for the weaker the oppressed the less effort is needed to keep them in subjugation.[19]

For Tolstoy force (law) is used to create justice and injustice, and as such is a bad means to a questionable end. For freedom, he said, should be our means and love our end. Tolstoy was an anarchist, but unlike some of his secular counterparts his primary concern was not the attempt to transfer political power from the state to the individual but, rather, that of putting an end to political power altogether.

So ends our discussion of the four theories of law in its relation to morality. Before proceeding to examine the various ethical problems treated in the articles of this anthology, we should make clear two points: one, that ethical questions should be examined in a totally ethical framework and propositions of law should not *determine* our ethical positions. For example, because the law says that abortion is legal, we must not assume that abortion is morally right. And two, we should remember that, in the final analysis, ethics or morality cannot be divorced from the law. Even those who claim that we can separate the two, those who view the law as amoral, talk about the end of law being "happiness" (a teleological concept) or law as "order" which is in a sense a moral concept replacing the moral concept of justice.[20]

Felix Cullen tells us that "the relevance of ethics to the philosophy of law would be clear even if it were not unconsciously assumed by those who appear to deny or to ignore the connection. For ethics is the study of the meaning and the application of judgments of good, bad, right, wrong, etc., and every final evaluation of law involves an ethical judgment. When we say, for instance, that a given law is bad, that one judicial decision is better than another, that the United States Constitution ought to be revised, or that laws ought to be obeyed, we are passing judgments whose truth or falsity cannot be established without a consideration of ethics. . . . There is no way of avoiding this ultimate responsibility of law to ethics."[21] (We do not, however, affirm the converse. Ethics does not owe an ultimate responsibility to law.)

In conclusion, we might return to the example provided by Socrates when he seemed to act under the proposition "Do not obey the state when you think what it does is immoral." For the theorist who believes that law is synonymous with morality there is no problem; he would obey the state for the state can do nothing immoral. For the theorist who believes that law ought to become moral, there would also be no problem. He would simply follow the statement of Socrates that in the event the law is not moral it need not be obeyed. The third theorist, who views law as amoral, would also have no problem. Since he conceives that the state acts neither morally nor immorally, the question of morality does not arise; the law is to be obeyed without reference to morality. And the fourth theorist who views law as immoral and sees that in all instances the state acts immorally since it uses force would simply not obey the state unless the commandments of the law coincided with his moral commandments.

When you examine the forthcoming ethical issues, ask yourself, Is this an example where law and morality may be equated? Is this an example where the law is becoming more moral or ought to become more moral? Is this simply a question which has the appearance of morality but does not involve any question of morality and is in essence amoral? Or, finally, is this an ethical issue that has really been decided by the law through the use of force and therefore does not require an assent? These are some of the questions which deserve attention when we consider the relationship of law and morality.

NOTES

1. This is also true of other attitudes such as "malice" or "willfulness," which under the law must be determined largely by inference from the act itself.
2. It should be understood that the law as it relates to morality may not be explained comfortably or completely in any one of these theories, but they will serve as an introduction to the subject.
3. J. Messner, *Social Ethics* (London: B. Herder & Co., 1952), p. 160.
4. Clarence Morris, ed., *The Great Legal Philosophers* (Philadelphia: University of Pennsylvania Press, 1971), p. 309.
5. Carl J. Friedrich, *The Philosophy of Law in Perspective* (Chicago: The University of Chicago Press, 1963), p. 131.
6. Ibid., pp. 131–32.
7. Ibid., p. 133.
8. Morris, op. cit., p. 320.
9. Extensions of this concept might be seen in a Calvinist theocracy, in a communal society living apart from the world, or in the folk-race concept of Nazi Germany. In all these instances, the institutions are believed to embody morality, and the acts of the institution are invoked as morality itself.
10. See Jacques Maritain, *Moral Philosophy* (1964), pp. 169–70.
11. One might concede that there is always an element of the law which coincides with morality, overlaps it, or is coextensive; but it is not necessary to assume that all the law may be related to morality. Indeed, as we shall see when we complete this discussion, there is a theory that presents the argument that law is immoral *per se* because enforcement is immoral. But for the moment we are concerned with the absence of morality in a particular situation in a particular legal action.
12. Richard Wasserstrom, *Morality and the Law* (Belmont, Calif.: Wadsworth, 1971), p. 2.
13. Mill's position may be less restrictive than the above quotation suggests, for later he said that persons may be required to help others because to do otherwise in certain circumstances may also be a form of harm.
14. George Christie, *Jurisprudence* (St. Paul, Minn.: West Publishing Co., 1973), p. 624.
15. Ibid., p. 631.
16. Although other legal philosophers, such as Austin and Hart, have been described as positivists, their jurisprudence could be distinguished from Kelsenism in many particulars. For instance, they disagree with Kelsen when he says that one must obey the law simply because it is the law. They are positivists, however, because they agree that a law need not be moral to be a valid law.

17. *Union Pacific Ry.* v. *Cappier,* 73 Pac. 281 (Kansas 1903).
18. By way of contrast, recall that an Hegelian system states that if the law says that something is legal, *ipso facto* it is moral.
19. Marshall Shatz, ed., *The Essential Works of Anarchism* (New York: Bantam, 1971), p. 236.
20. When the law says that a woman should have the sole right to determine whether to abort a fetus, and the law does not consider the father or the fetus as possessing any rights, is that law orderly? Is that law just? That is, is there some reason why a father or a fetus should not be considered in determining the issue? Are these not, in a sense, moral questions looking for a moral answer? And if the answer is that the woman alone should have the right, is not that answer couched in moral terms which, though they justify the existing legal order, are nonetheless determined from a moral base?
21. Bishin and Stone, eds., *Law, Ethics, and Language* (Mineola, N.Y.: The Foundation Press, 1972), p. 33.

1 ⁂ RELIGION AND MORALITY

PREDICTABLY, Professor Malcolm Edwards begins his class with a question, "How many of you claim a belief in God?" Well over half the class raise their hands. "All right. Now, how many of you feel that we cannot effectively continue this course unless we bring religion into our discussions?"

Most of the hands remain raised. "Excellent!" says Edwards. "Not only do I think that a discussion of religion is important to any investigation of morality, but religion and morality is what I had planned to discuss with you today, and I don't know what we would have talked about if I hadn't had so many takers."

"Can we have another vote?" calls a voice from the back. [*Laughter*]

Edwards shakes his head with a smile. "Too late. All right, let me ask you this: can you suggest what, if any, is the relationship between religion and morality?" This time only one hand is offered. "Cheri, isn't it?"

"Yes. Well, I don't know if this is an answer to your question, but it has to do with what I think is right for me. I wouldn't want to claim that everyone has to believe just as I do. Still, I have my own religious beliefs and they are very important to me. I just couldn't give them up and be the same person. I don't know exactly how this is related to morality, except that if others have different beliefs I think that's fine, and I certainly don't think that makes them immoral."

"Jeff. You have a question?"

"Well, Mr. Edwards. I used to accept the idea of everybody doing his own thing when it comes to religion. That's what Cheri is saying, and I don't agree with that any more. I mean, if all religions are equally OK, then my own religious beliefs seem to get watered down. Cheri is talking as if choosing a religion is like picking out the ice cream flavor of the month at Baskin-Robbins."

"That's ridiculous," cries Cheri. "There's no comparison, and you know it! What about that story in the Bible where God tells Abraham to take his son Isaac and sacrifice him? How can you compare his choice with deciding between fudge ripple and butter-pecan ice cream?"

"If God asked you to sacrifice your son, what would be your decision? What would you do?" Edwards asks. "Jeff?"

"Well, if it was really God, what else could I do?"

"Cheri?"

"If it were really God, I don't know. I'm a member of a peace church and we don't believe in killing. I guess the God I believe in wouldn't ask that of anyone."

"How could you tell if it were God asking you to do it?" asks Edwards. But this typically philosophical puzzler doesn't even slow down the dialogue.

"I'd know if it was God," Jeff declares immediately.

"Me, too," says Bob.

"But *how?*" demands Cheri.

"God would let me know," says Bob.

Before Cheri has a chance to ask the obvious question, Don breaks in. "What does he do, call you up on a 'hot line'? Look, I don't want to put down anybody's religion, but what tees me off are people who run around doing what they want and then pray to God to straighten things out."

"Why? Do you object to people asking for help?" asks Edwards.

"No way. But what gets me are people who think they can do any immoral act they like and then act as if all they have to do is believe like hell and yell to God to make it right. But what they do is still wrong!"

"You have a rather colorful way of putting it, but what I think I hear you saying is that morality takes precedence over religion. Am I right?" Don nods, and Edwards continues. "Recalling our moral-code ladder, we may then be looking at an instance where a higher-level principle takes precedence over a lower-level principle." Edwards has been hoping to work this into the discussion, but he has no such luck.

"If you don't have faith, you're lost," says Cloteal in obvious irritation. "If you want to be saved, you must accept Jesus, and He will take care of you no matter what; and that has nothing to do with higher- and lower-level principles."

"Even if you kill your son when the devil asks you to do it? What kind of morality is that?" Don asks.

"Only believers can be saved, and it doesn't matter what they do; they're saved. And it doesn't matter what nonbelievers do; as long as they don't accept Jesus, they're damned."

A few members of the class groan and then laugh as a voice calls out in a high falsetto whine, "The devil made me do it!"

Edwards ignores the interruption and asks, "What if they accept Jehovah or Mohammed or Buddha? Or what if they don't believe in any religion in the sense we use the term, yet still do the right thing as far as they can determine? What happens to them?"

"They get a one-way ticket to hell," Cloteal declares, and Bob nods in agreement.

"What kind of God is it that you believe in who can condemn people for doing the moral thing and save those who do immoral things just because they say that they believe?" asks Don.

"I think we're getting off the point here," Cheri says. "I don't care what religion we believe in; many of us can't even agree what is right or wrong according to our own religion. For example, a friend of mine claims to be a Christian too, but she says her church allows killing in war or in self defense and so on. Well, my church says that killing is wrong no matter what."

Professor Edwards tries again. "Cheri, would you say that killing, or, rather, not killing, is a moral law as we defined it last week?"

"Yes, I guess you could say that. And then I guess my friend's position makes not killing only a moral rule."

Edwards nods in manifest satisfaction. "You say there are no exceptions to the rule, and she says that there are exceptions. Right?"

"Yes, but how do we decide who is right?"

"I'm not so sure that question can be answered, although our discussions here may eventually suggest an answer that you might accept," Edwards responds.

"Professor Edwards, how can you talk about what you call moral laws and moral rules without first talking about where and when those rules or laws, or whatever, are going to be used? It seems to me that what's right or wrong depends first on the situation. What might be right in one situation might be wrong in another, so how can you make up a moral code ahead of time?"

"Example, Doug?" asks Edwards.

33
Chapter 1
RELIGION AND
MORALITY

"Well, take killing and what we were talking about before. Sure, killing is normally wrong. But what if you love God and He tells you to kill? What good are moral laws or rules then?"

"Love God and do what you will?" asks Edwards.

"I don't know about other religions, but the Christians here ought to say something like that. Jesus claims that love of God and love in general is the big thing in a moral person. I'll buy that, but I won't buy anything else unless I know what the situation is."

"If love is your ultimate principle, then I can't see how any other principles can be derived from it. But wouldn't that mean going right from the ultimate principle to the individual case?" asks Edwards. "And wouldn't the lack of any intermediate moral laws or rules make it very difficult to determine whether what one does is moral or immoral?"

"Maybe, but I still think it doesn't matter what you do as long as you don't hurt anybody," says Don. "Anyway I agree with Doug. You just can't sit around dreaming up some sort of moral code that will fit real life situations. I think sitting in a classroom making up a bunch of rules and laws is just some kind of intellectual game. I mean, you can't decide before you get into a situation, and what you decide in one case may be different from what you decide in another."

"So what do you suggest we do?" asks Edwards.

Don pauses for a moment and then says, "Well, my second answer to that is, Just take one ultimate principle, like love, and leave it at that."

"Love is the answer," Bob states. Cloteal and Jeff nod in vigorous agreement.

"What is the question?" Edwards asks with a grin.

FOR FURTHER READING

Bruening, William H. "The Existence of God and Ethics." *Proceedings of The American Catholic Philosophical Association* 46 (1972): 133–140. This short paper argues that there is no logical relationship between the existence, or nonexistence, of God and any moral principle. The author discusses other possible relationships and wonders why ethics is so often taught in the context of religion.

Buber, Martin. *Between Man and Man.* New York: Macmillan, 1965. A collection of five essays that apply the principles outlined in Buber's famous *I and Thou* to practical problems of modern life.

──────────. *Eclipse of God: Studies in the Relation between Religion and Philosophy.* New York: Harper & Row, 1952. See especially chapter 6, "Religion and Ethics" and chapter 7, "On the Suspension of the Ethical."

Cox, Harvey, ed. *The Situation Ethics Debate.* Philadelphia: Westminster, 1968. A collection of short reviews and longer essays on the work of Joseph Fletcher. A reply by Fletcher is included.

Cunningham, Robert, ed. *Situationism and the New Morality.* New York: Appleton, Century, Crofts, 1970. Another collection of essays on situation ethics, but somewhat broader in scope than the Cox collection. The editor's introductory essay is particularly helpful.

Fackenheim, Emil. *Encounters between Judaism and Modern Philosophy.* New York:

Basic Books, 1972. Written by one of the best-known living Jewish philosophers, this book covers a broad range of topics. Of particular interest is the chapter entitled "Abraham and the Kantians: Moral Duties and Divine Commandments."

Fletcher, Joseph. *Moral Responsibility: Situation Ethics at Work.* Philadelphia: Westminster, 1967. Fletcher, one of the most noted exponents of the situational theory, demonstrates the practical application of this theory by employing it in the resolution of a number of practical moral problems.

———. *Situation Ethics: The New Morality.* Philadelphia: Westminster, 1966. This is the theoretical counterpart to *Moral Responsibility* and, as such, somewhat more technical and abstract than the former.

Girvetz, Harry K., ed. *Contemporary Moral Issues.* Belmont, Calif.: Wadsworth, 1968. An anthology of relatively short essays on a wide number of moral issues relevant to contemporary society.

Lehmann, Paul. *Ethics in a Christian Context.* New York: Harper & Row, 1963. A vigorous defense of a position called Christian contextualism.

Nowell-Smith, P.H. "Religion and Morality." In *The Encyclopedia of Philosophy,* edited by Paul Edwards, vol. 7, pp. 150–158. New York: Macmillan, 1967. Written by one of the best-known metaethicists, this essay also contains a short but good bibliography.

Outka, Gene, and Ramsey, Paul, eds. *Norm and Context in Christian Ethics.* New York: Scribner's, 1968. A collection of writings by various Protestant and Catholic theologians on the so-called new morality.

Outka, Gene, and Reeder, John R., Jr., eds. *Religion and Morality.* Garden City, N.Y.: Doubleday, 1973. This book focuses on the central theme of our first section and contains essays by theologians, philosophers, and other thinkers. It is more ecumenical than the previous book.

Ramsey, Paul. *Deeds and Rules in Christian Ethics.* New York: Scribner's, 1967. Ramsey defends his position against Fletcher and other situational theologians. The book ranges over a great number of issues, which are approached from a theoretical rather than a practical angle.

Robinson, John A.T. *Honest to God.* Philadelphia: Westminster, 1963. One of the more popular summaries of what has been happening in theology in the last two decades, this little book is one of the more readable introductions to the "new theology."

Sontag, Frederick. *How Philosophy Shapes Theology: Problems in the Philosophy of Religion.* New York: Harper & Row, 1971. A lengthy and exhaustive study of the relationship between theology and philosophy. It includes discussions of a number of problems which bear on the topics of this section.

Tillich, Paul. *Love, Power, and Justice.* London: Oxford University Press, 1954. A somewhat technical and difficult discussion by perhaps the best-known theologian of the twentieth century. It presupposes some knowledge of philosophy and may be beyond the beginner's grasp.

36 THE SERMON ON THE MOUNT
MATTHEW 5:21-48

> The Sermon on the Mount is found in the Gospels of both Matthew and Luke. The Gospel according to Matthew—one of Jesus' twelve original disciples—was written between A.D. 75 and 100 and is the source of the following excerpt. The Sermon on the Mount, which is believed to be based on oral tradition, is one of the best-known parts of the Scriptures and represents the charter of the New Kingdom. It stands in contrast to the law of justice of the Old Covenant—eye for eye and tooth for tooth—by preaching the law of love of the New Covenant—offer the wicked man no resistance, love your enemies, and pray for those who persecute you. Excerpt from *The Jerusalem Bible,* copyright © 1966 by Darton, Longman & Todd, Ltd. and Doubleday and Company, Inc. Used by permission of the publisher.

You have learnt how it was said to our ancestors: *You must not kill;* and if anyone does kill he must answer for it before the court. But I say this to you: anyone who is angry with his brother will answer for it before the court; if a man calls his brother "Fool" he will answer for it before the Sanhedrin; and if a man calls him "Renegade" he will answer for it in hell fire. So then, if you are bringing your offering to the altar and there remember that your brother has something against you, leave your offering there before the altar, go and be reconciled with your brother first, and then come back and present your offering. Come to terms with your opponent in good time while you are still on the way to the court with him, or he may hand you over to the judge and the judge to the officer, and you will be thrown into prison. I tell you solemnly, you will not get out till you have paid the last penny.

You have learnt how it was said: *You must not commit adultery.* But I say this to you: if a man looks at a woman lustfully, he has already committed adultery with her in his heart. If your right eye should cause you to sin, tear it out and throw it away; for it will do you less harm to lose one part of you than to have your whole body thrown into hell. And if your right hand should cause you to sin, cut it off and throw it away; for it will do you less harm to lose one part of you than to have your whole body go to hell.

It has also been said: *Anyone who divorces his wife must give her a writ of dismissal.* But I say this to you: everyone who divorces his wife, except for the case of fornication, makes her an adulteress; and anyone who marries a divorced woman commits adultery.

Again, you have learnt how it was said to our ancestors: *You must not break your oath, but must fulfil your oaths to the Lord.* But I say this to you: do not swear at all, either by *heaven,* since that is God's throne; or by *the earth,* since that is *his footstool;*

or by Jerusalem, since that is *the city of the great king.* Do not swear by your own head either, since you cannot turn a single hair white or black. All you need say is "Yes" if you mean yes, "No" if you mean no; anything more than this comes from the evil one.

You have learnt how it was said: *Eye for eye and tooth for tooth.* But I say this to you: offer the wicked man no resistance. On the contrary, if anyone hits you on the right cheek, offer him the other as well; if a man takes you to law and would have your tunic, let him have your cloak as well. And if anyone orders you to go one mile, go two miles with him. Give to anyone who asks, and if anyone wants to borrow, do not turn away.

You have learnt how it was said: *You must love your neighbour* and hate your enemy. But I say this to you: love your enemies and pray for those who persecute you; in this way you will be sons of your Father in heaven, for he causes his sun to rise on bad men as well as good, and his rain to fall on honest and dishonest men alike. For if you love those who love you, what right have you to claim any credit? Even the tax collectors do as much, do they not? And if you save your greetings for your brothers, are you doing anything exceptional? Even the pagans do as much, do they not? You must therefore be perfect just as your heavenly Father is perfect.

Luther J. Binkley
SITUATION ETHICS VERSUS RULE ETHICS

Luther J. Binkley is professor and Chairman of the Department of Philosophy at Franklin and Marshall College. He is the author of *Conflict of Ideals: Changing Values in Western Society* (1969) from which the following selection is taken. He is also the author of *Contemporary Ethical Theories* (1961). In this article Binkley examines the similarities and contrasts between rule ethics and situation ethics. He uses Joseph Fletcher to illustrate the position of the situation ethicists. According to Fletcher, a Christian who practices situation ethics grounds all his decisions on *agapē*—Christian love in its highest manifestations. All other rules or principles are valid only if they serve love in a particular situation. Binkley has chosen Paul Ramsey as an illustration of rule ethics. Like Fletcher, Ramsey considers *agapē* as the basic norm of Christian ethics. But, unlike Fletcher, he is concerned with finding the general rules for human behavior that express and embody what love requires. Binkley's analysis is very meaningful to the ongoing dialogue between the rule ethicists and the situation ethicists. It also raises some

Chapter 1
RELIGION AND MORALITY

fundamental questions for all of us: If we accept love as the guiding principle of our lives, can we—and how do we—decide what is a loving action and what is not? If we believe that our conduct should be predicated upon the effects of our actions on others, can we—and how do we—know what these consequences will really be? And, finally, is it in fact possible at all for us to find general rules of ethics to guide our conduct and help us decide our actions? From *Conflict of Ideals: Changing Values in Western Society* by L. Binkley. © 1969. Reprinted by permission of D. Van Nostrand Company.

The present trends in theology have tended to reflect a greater interest in ethics than in previous more theologically oriented periods of Christian history. Generally, almost all of the contemporary theologians stress Christian love, *agapē*, as the distinctive motivation for their ethical positions. They differ in the extent, however, to which they believe that *agapē* can be expressed in general rules or principles for human behavior. Bishop Robinson and Joseph Fletcher are the best known advocates of a situational approach to ethics; they claim that one ought always to ask what would be the loving thing to do in this situation for the persons involved. Emil Brunner, Reinhold Niebuhr and Paul Ramsey, while they do not deny that love may sometimes have to override traditional morality, firmly insist that *agapē* can be expressed in some general rules or principles which will give the Christian guidance for the specific situations he is likely to face in the world.

This difference of viewpoint concerning the place of love in Christian ethics is somewhat like the debate between the teleologists and deontologists in philosophical discussions of normative ethics. The teleologists maintain that acts are right if and only if their consequences are desirable, that is, if they produce the greatest amount of good possible for that particular situation. The deontologists, on the other hand, hold that there are some acts which are always right independently of the likely consequences of those acts in particular situations producing or not producing the greatest possible amount of good. The teleologists have often adopted some form of utilitarianism and have held that those acts are right which tend to produce the greatest amount of happiness for the greatest number of people. The deontologists have often appealed to some general principles, such as justice, or to general rules, such as one's obligation toward a benefactor, or the obligation not to harm another person, as providing *prima facie* moral rules which can be seen to be fitting and appropriate principles or rules for human behavior.

William Frankena in a very perceptive essay, "Love and Principle in Christian Ethics," tends to interpret Christian ethicists as usually holding to some form of teleological ethics. Christian love, or *agapē*, in this interpretation is concerned with advocating those acts which will produce the greatest possible amount of love-fulfillment or benevolence. Most of the writers whom we are discussing advocate a teleological ethic, although some, such as Paul Ramsey, seem to also stress a deontological aspect to the Christian ethic. In terms of a deontological interpretation, some acts are seen to be right because they always express *agapē*, while others are seen to be wrong because they never can express *agapē*. Many traditional interpretations of the Christian ethic which have literally identified it with obedience to the Ten Commandments and to the Sermon on the Mount would appear to be deontological.

In recent philosophical writing, there has not been quite the extreme disagreement between teleologists and deontologists which we have sketched. Instead, the debate has focused on two possible interpretations of utilitarianism: act-utilitarianism and rule-utilitarianism. The pure act-utilitarian maintains that in a specific situation one ought to explore the likely consequences of one's actions and then choose to act so as to bring about the greatest amount of happiness possible. The important point here is that the pure act-utilitarian holds that one ought not to ask about the likely consequences which might ensue "if the same thing we done in similar situations (i.e., if it were made a rule to do that act in such situations)."[1] At issue for the act-utilitarian is only the specific contemplated act for a particular circumstance; it is held to be irrelevant to inquire as to whether one ought to act that way in future situations which might be similar. In contrast to the act-utilitarian, the rule-utilitarian maintains that in a particular situation one ought to appeal to some set of general rules, such as "Tell the truth," "Do not commit murder," etc., rather than attempt to calculate the likely consequences of the contemplated action. The rule-utilitarian is not a deontologist, however, for he maintains that these general rules, such as "Tell the truth," are justified because acting in accordance with these rules always produces the greatest good or the greatest happiness. In short, he is a utilitarian because his ultimate justification for the general rules he advocates is based on the greatest good for the greatest number of people, and not upon the rules simply being seen to be appropriate or fitting to the situation. For the rule-utilitarian it may be one's duty to follow the rule "Tell the truth" even if in a particular situation more good would apparently be produced by lying. Rule-utilitarians would justify the rule even in the exceptional case by pointing out that in the last analysis more good is achieved for everyone by always upholding the moral rules. While a lie in a specific situation might produce more immediate good for those directly concerned, it would tend to break down the moral fabric of our society and encourage lying in other situations which might be less justifiable. Therefore, the greatest amount of good in the long run for the greatest number of people would be obtained by an undeviating adherence to the moral rule.

There is, however, a third possibility: modified act-utilitarianism. This interpretation recognizes elements of strength in both rule- and act-utilitarianism. The modified act-utilitarian admits that rules can be formulated for moral action, but he insists that these rules are not absolute; they are only generally binding. Thus in most cases, "Tell the truth" will produce the greatest amount of good, but one is justified, for the sake of the ultimate principle of utility itself, in disobeying the rule in a particular situation where more good is likely to be achieved by such disobedience.

Frankena suggests that the debate concerning the status of rules or principles in Christian ethics parallels the above debate between the act and the rule utilitarians. The Christian ethic is often interpreted as asserting *agapē*, or the "law of love," as its highest and only ultimate principle. In the light of this ultimate commitment to *agapē*, however, the Christian ethic can be developed in terms of pure act-agapism, modified act-agapism, or pure rule-agapism. These distinctions are not sharply drawn in most of the writings on Christian ethics, but we shall attempt to suggest some ethicists of this century who seem to fit fairly well into this classificatory scheme.

Situation Ethics by Joseph Fletcher comes extremely close to being a perfect illustration of pure act-agapism; certainly the main drift of his position is toward the specific situation in which the person is acting and away from any general or summary rules for moral behavior. Fletcher holds that there are only three main approaches to the making of moral decisions: (1) the legalistic which always insists that the moral rules must be obeyed—they are absolute laws; (2) the antinomian or existentialist which maintains that there are no guidelines whatsoever for ethical choices since each situation is so unique that one must in each case make a new decision; and (3) the situational approach, which falls somewhere between these two other approaches, but comes down closer to the existentialist side than to the legalistic side. It is Christian situation ethics which Fletcher himself wishes to defend as the best approach to the making of moral decisions.

Fletcher maintains that a Christian practicing situation ethics approaches "every decision-making situation fully armed with the ethical maxims of his community and its heritage, and he treats them with respect as illuminators of his problems."[2]* Nevertheless, in any particular situation Fletcher holds that it is best to set aside

---

*From *Situation Ethics: The New Morality*, by Joseph Fletcher. Copyright © MCMLXVI, W.L. Jenkins. This and succeeding quotations from the same source used by permission of The Westminster Press.

the inherited moral principles "if love seems better served by doing so."³ He thus calls his version of the Christian ethic "principled relativism."⁴ Rules or principles are valid only if they serve love in a particular situation. The most important factors in ethical decision-making would involve knowing the facts of the case, calculating the likely consequences of the alternative possibilities for action, and then choosing that act which will best serve love. In this preliminary discussion of the position Fletcher wishes to defend, he appears to be putting forth a version of modified act-agapism: principles are generally valid but one ought to set them aside in any instance in which love would be better served by not following them. In fact in one of his illustrations, he suggests that ethical rules are like the instructions in football, "Punt on fourth down. . . . The best players are those who know when to ignore them."⁵ Fletcher holds that there is only one unexceptionable principle in Christian ethics—love. "Everything else without exception, all laws and rules and principles and ideals and norms, are only *contingent*, only valid *if they happen to serve love in any situation*."⁶ The principles or rules of moral behavior then are, at best, cautious generalizations. In almost all of the illustrations which he uses throughout his book it is difficult to find him making any constructive use of the existing moral principles. Perhaps this is because all of his illustrations deal with exceptional cases, situations in which he believes love is best served by going against moral conventions. Despite his protest to the contrary, his ethics appears to be one of pure act-agapism, or act-agapism modified by rational calculation as to the likely consequences of a chosen action. In this respect he appears much closer to the radical existentialist ethic than he wishes to admit. Fletcher says *"only* love and reason really count when the chips are down!"⁷ His extreme emphasis upon the uniqueness of each case, and the necessity for making a new decision in each case, undoubtedly derives from his conviction that Christian ethics has too often been identified with an unbending legalism.

Fletcher states the main propositions upon which his interpretation of Christian ethics rests as follows:

1. Only one "thing" is intrinsically good, namely, love; nothing else at all.
2. The ruling norm of Christian decision is love; nothing else.
3. Love and justice are the same, for justice is love distributed; nothing else.
4. Love wills the neighbor's good whether we like him or not.
5. Only the end justifies the means; nothing else.
6. Love's decisions are made situationally, not prescriptively.⁸

The opposite of love, according to Fletcher, is not hate but indifference, for even hate treats the other person as a "thou" while indifference reduces the other to a thing. To be filled with Christian love is to care for persons, and to do what one can for them in their specific situations. Fletcher adheres to a personalist interpretation of Christian ethics and hence asserts boldly: "There *are* no 'values' at all; there are only things (material and nonmaterial) which *happen* to be valued by persons."[9] Something becomes a value only if it becomes worth something to some person. Despite his initial exposition of his position, it thus appears that there are no principles or rules in Fletcher's ethic, except love in terms of which we are to do the greatest amount of good we can. That Fletcher does not shrink from this conclusion is evident in the following quotation from *Situation Ethics:*

> If a lie is told unlovingly it is wrong, evil; if it is told in love it is good, right. Kant's legalism produced a "universal"—that a lie is always wrong. But what if you have to tell a lie to keep a promised secret? Maybe you lie, and if so, good for you if you follow love's lead. . . . If love vetoes the truth, so be it. . . . *The situationist holds that whatever is the most loving thing in the situation is the right and good thing.* It is not excusably evil, it is positively good.[10]

Many Christian moralities, such as that of the Roman Catholic Church, have combined love with an ethic of natural law. In such positions justice is often used as an additional principle in determining one's actions. Fletcher not only rejects this approach, but even holds that the Ten Commandments and the injunctions in the Sermon on the Mount are not absolutely binding upon the Christian. In referring to the Ten Commandments Fletcher comments:

> Situation ethics has good reason to hold it as a *duty* in some situations to break them, *any or all of them.* We would be better advised and better off to drop the legalist's love of law, and accept only the law of love.[11]

Despite the fact that Fletcher, like most modern Protestant theologians, finds Bonhoeffer to be one of his forerunners, he objects to Bonhoeffer's belief that "all deliberate killing of innocent life is arbitrary," and therefore wrong, since Bonhoeffer believes that whatever is arbitrary is wrong. This for Fletcher is to put another norm alongside love; it is not to be fully situational. A situationist suggests Fletcher would protest "that, in principle, even killing 'innocent' people might be right."[12]

Tillich, as we have seen, found that there were aspects of all kinds of love present in every human instance of love. Fletcher disagrees with this analysis because he wants to separate *agapē* from all other kinds of love which have an aspect of desire in them:

Agapē is giving love—non-reciprocal, neighbor-regarding—"neighbor" meaning "everybody," even an enemy. . . . Erotic and philic love are emotional, but the effective principle of Christian love is *will*, disposition; it is an *attitude*, not feeling.[13]

Fletcher's affinity with existentialist ethics comes through even here, as he claims that each man must take the risk of making his own decisions in the light of his understanding of the facts of the case and his loving attitude: "Decision is a 'risk rooted in the courage of being' free."[14]

While Fletcher insists that there is only one principle in Christian ethics, namely love, he wants to make it very clear that the love he is talking about is not to be identified with sentimentality. Prudence and careful calculation are the ways by which Christian love works, so that justice is included within love and is not a separate principle from it. He admits that love including justice must give every man his due; since in most situations we are faced with a complex network of claims and duties, "love is compelled to be calculating, careful, prudent, distributive."[15] The Christian love ethic "needs to find *absolute love's relative course*. The what and the why are given but the how and the which must be found."[16] Fletcher insists that to separate justice from love tends to make love sentimental and justice impersonal and legalistic; furthermore, if they are separated neither *agapē* nor justice is satisfied. Hence, he maintains that "*agapē* is what is due to all others," and that "justice is nothing other than love working out its problems."[17] Even if it is maintained that justice is concerned with seeing to it that each man gets his rights, Fletcher claims that *agapē* is the only norm which can validate any human rights whatsoever:

> You have a right to anything that is loving; you have no right to anything that is unloving. All alleged rights and duties are as contingent and relative as all values. The right to religious freedom, free speech, public assembly, private property, sexual liberty, life itself, the vote—*all* are validated only by love.[18]

In the Christian's attempt to search for social policies he should unite with the utilitarian in seeking for the greatest good of the greatest number. The hedonistic calculus of the utilitarian thus becomes "the agapeic calculus, the greatest amount of neighbor welfare for the largest number of neighbors possible."[19] Fletcher does not shrink from admitting that the Christian seeks happiness as his end, indeed he insists that "all ethics are happiness ethics." There are different schools of ethics because not all men find happiness in the same things, but the Christian ethic *à la* Fletcher attempts to unite the best of naturalistic, self-realization and hedonistic positions. Thus Fletcher says:

The Christian situationist's happiness is in doing God's will as it is expressed in Jesus' Summary. [Love God, and love your neighbor as yourself.] And his utility method sets him to seeking his happiness (pleasure, too, and self-realization!) by seeking his neighbors' good on the widest possible scale.[20]

If a particular situation arises in which the Christian finds himself confronted with a law which in all honesty he considers to be morally unjust, that is unloving, then he should not hesitate to disobey openly that particular law. Perhaps the situationist should do all that he can to get the law thrown out by the courts, or repealed by the legislature, but if he fails in these attempts then he decides to abide by the higher law of love and break the particular unjust law confronting him. This ought not to be a rash decision, for the Christian values civil law since it provides order within a society. Yet in the last analysis, "neither the state nor its laws is boss for the situationist; when there is a conflict, he decides for the higher law of love."[21]

We have already noted that Fletcher insists that *agapē* is not emotional love; it is not liking but it is an attitude of goodwill or benevolence toward all men, including those who are not likeable. It is not looking for reciprocity; it gives, expecting nothing in return, even if it hopes for a positive response. *Agapē* is not opposed to loving oneself in the right way; that is, loving oneself for the sake of others. It seeks to do the most useful thing in any concrete situation. Its ultimate justification is that it loves the neighbor or oneself for the sake of God, not for the sake of the neighbor or for the sake of oneself. As Fletcher explains:

> To love is not necessarily to please. *Agapē* is not gratification. . . . For *agapē* is concerned for the neighbor, ultimately, for God's sake; certainly not for the self's, but not even for the neighbor's own sake only. Christian love, for example, cannot give heroin to an addict just because he wants it. Or, at least, if the heroin is given, it will be given as part of a cure. And the same with all pleas—sex, alms, food, anything.[22]

Fletcher uses a rather extreme case to illustrate the difference he finds between *philia* (love as liking each other) and *agapē*:

> A young unmarried couple might decide, if they make their decisions Christianly, to have intercourse (e.g., by getting pregnant to force a selfish parent to relent his over-bearing resistance to their marriage). But as Christians they would never merely say, "It's all right if we *like* each other!" Loving concern can make it all right, but mere liking cannot.[23]

Fletcher's radical commitment to the new morality, in which each situation differs radically from all other situations, is frankly admitted by him when he discusses the relationships of means to ends. After insisting that the means chosen should be as appropriate to the end as possible, for unloving means could well distort the loving end, he says:

> The new morality, situation ethics, declares that anything and everything is right or wrong, according to the situation. And this candid approach is indeed a revolution in morals![24]

Love viewed as *agapē* is the only principle which makes any acts right or wrong. Thus, Fletcher continues:

> Theodore Roosevelt was either not altogether honest (candid) or altogether thoughtful when he said, "No man is justified in doing evil on the ground of expediency." He was mired down in intrinsicalist legalism. Love could justify anything. There is no justification other than love's expedients. What else? In a particular case, why should not a single woman who could not marry become a "bachelor mother" by natural means or artificial insemination, even though husbandless, as a widow is?[25]

Thus, although one ought to seek for appropriate means, one ought not to fail to realize that sometimes an evil means can bring about a good end. If this happens, then the evil means is fully justified by the end realized. Hence, even "paid sex" might be justified if a good result were achieved by it. Fletcher thus justifies the prostitute in the movie *Never on Sunday:*

> We could, we might, decide that the whore in the Greek movie *Never on Sunday* was right. In Piraeus near Athens, she finds a young sailor who is afraid he cannot function sexually as an adult and virile man, and suffers as a prey to corrosive self-doubt and nonidentity. She manages things deliberately (i.e., responsibly) so that he succeeds with her and gains his self-respect and psychic freedom from a potential fixation on sex itself.[26]

Fletcher in his discussion of the ethics of sex objects to the *Playboy* argument that anything sexual is all right if it is practiced by consenting adults and does not hurt anybody. Not hurting anybody is not a sufficient criterion for Fletcher, for "Christians say that nothing is right unless it *helps* somebody."[27]* Thus, the prostitute in the movie *Never on Sunday* did the right thing—she did some good for the young man; she helped him to discover his sexual identity. Hence, the Christian is fully justified in doing "what would be evil in some contexts if in *this* circumstance love gains the balance. It is love's business to calculate gains and losses, and to act for the sake of its success."[28] Thus, if for the emotional and spiritual welfare of all the parties concerned, a divorce appears to be the best solution to

---

*From *Moral Responsibility: Situation Ethics at Work*, by Joseph Fletcher. Copyright © MCMLXVII, The Westminster Press. This and succeeding quotations from the same source used by permission.

an unhappy marriage, then "getting a divorce is sometimes like David's eating the reserved Sacrament; it is what Christ would recommend."[29] To will the end of loving welfare is to will whatever means are necessary to achieve that end.

Fletcher poses some interesting cases for his readers to think through for themselves, using his method of situation ethics. In one of these cases he describes a dilemma put to him by a young woman of about twenty-eight years of age who sat next to him on an airline flight. One of the American intelligence agencies had asked her to use her sex to lure an enemy spy into blackmail. When she protested that she couldn't violate her personal integrity in such a manner, they said, " 'We understand. It's like your brother risking his life or limb in Korea. We are sure this job can't be done any other way. It's bad if we have to turn to somebody less competent and discreet than you are.' "[30] The issue was "how was she to balance loyalty and gratitude as an American citizen over against her ideal of sexual integrity?"[31] Fletcher in a later essay indicates that he would have approved if the girl had said "Yes" to the intelligence agency. He flatly remarks, "Is the girl who gives her chastity for her country's sake any less approvable than the boy who gives his leg or his life? No!"[32] Again the existentialist emphasis in Fletcher's view comes to the foreground. Speaking of any sexual acts outside of marriage, he says:

> The personal commitment, not the county clerk, sanctifies sex.... In this kind of Christian sex ethic the essential ingredients are caring and commitment. Given these factors, the only reason for disapproving sexual relations would be situational, not legal or principled.... There is nothing against extramarital sex as such, in this ethic, and in *some* cases it is good.[33]

Only in a concrete situation, when the facts are known and the persons involved are considered as persons, can one give moral advice. Fletcher rejects such questions as "Is adultery wrong?" They are too general to call for a serious answer. He says:

> One can only respond, "I don't know. Maybe. Give me a case. Describe a real situation." Or perhaps somebody will ask if a man should ever lie to his wife, or desert his family, or spy on a business rival's design or market plans, or fail to report some income item in his tax return. Again, the answer cannot be an answer, it can only be another question. "Have you a *real* question, that is to say, a concrete situation?" If it has to do with premarital sex or libel or breach of contract or anything else ("you name it"), the reply is always the same: "You are using words, abstractions. What you are asking is without substance; it has no living reality. There is no way to answer such questions."[34]

Although no prefabricated moral system can be offered, the situationist can tell people to make the best decisions in concrete situations and then "sin bravely."[35] Love must decide in a concrete case and at a specific moment of time. Legalistic moral codes simply do not fit our present society, nor are they applicable to the real decisions most people are called upon to make. The professed sexual code of most Americans is so openly flouted in practice, that Fletcher holds we would be better off to junk it rather than to pay lip service to it. Repressive legalism has been most damaging to individuals precisely at this point of the ethics of sexual behavior. Fletcher holds that rather than try to construct a network of moral rules regulating sexual behavior, we would be far more ethical if we admitted that "whether any form of sex (hetero, homo, or auto) is good or evil depends on whether love is fully served."[36] We are moving into an age of honesty, Fletcher believes, and our age is allergic to legalism. The time is ripe, therefore, for his tactical formula for making moral decisions:

> Love, in the imperative mood of neighbor-concern, examining the relative facts of the situation in the indicative mood, discovers what it is obliged to do, what it should do, in the normative mood. What is, in the light of what love demands, shows what ought to be.[37]

Fletcher admits that many secular men who do not call themselves Christians may actually advocate and practice the ethic he recommends better than do many Christians. Why then does he call it a Christian ethic? His answer is that "we understand love in terms of Jesus Christ. This is the Christian faith ethic."[38]

Fletcher's interpretation of Christian ethics, despite his early insistence upon coming fully equipped with the moral baggage of our culture when we face an actual situation, turns out to be very close to the radical existential freedom of decision advocated by Sartre and other existentialists. In few, if any, of the actual cases which he discusses in his books and articles does he ever invoke a moral principle generally held to be correct by our society, unless it be to oppose it to what the right act would be for the particular situation he is discussing. In fact, his summary of what he understands situation ethics to be as he presented it in a paper called "Situation Ethics for Business Management" sounds like another American version of Sartre's position:

> Finally, in a situational approach, the decision must be made not only *in* the situation but also *by* the decider in the situation! It is an ethic of deliberate responsibility, based on the need for stoutly embracing "the burden of freedom" like men, not mice. The burden is only added to, not lightened, by the understanding that the decisions we make will rarely if ever be "correct." Its very relativism compels it to acknowledge that finite men will never fully foresee all of the consequences, never "objectively" assess all of the motives and means and ends at stake.[39]

It does not seem to bother Fletcher to admit that the decisions one makes by using situational ethics "will rarely if ever be 'correct.'" Instead, he concludes his advice to business managers by saying: "In all humility, knowing that he cannot escape the human margin of error, he will—to use Luther's phrase—'Sin bravely.'"[40] If, in Frankena's terminology, there is an exponent of pure act-agapism today it is Joseph Fletcher.

Bishop John A. T. Robinson prefers to link himself with the new morality or situation ethics, but it is clear from his presentations that he represents a modified act-agapism. He is just as opposed as is Joseph Fletcher to the old traditional ethic of prohibitions and legalism. Robinson holds that since people today no longer believe in the old supernatural God it is inevitable that they will not believe that the Ten Commandments or any other moral code represent God's absolute rules. As Robinson interprets the moral dilemma, he finds that:

> 'Why shouldn't I?' or 'What's wrong with it?' are questions which in our generation press for an answer. And supranaturalist reasons—that God or Christ has pronounced it a 'sin'—have force, and even meaning, for none but a diminishing religious remnant.[41]

Bishop Robinson, like Fletcher, maintains that Christian love is not only the one absolute principle in ethics, but also that it can be relied upon to find the right answer in a specific situation. He does, however, make much more of guiding rules for this love, and insists that without them, love could not even find its way:

> Such an ethic cannot but rely, in deep humility, upon guiding rules, upon the cumulative experience of one's own and other people's obedience. It is this bank of experience which gives us our working rules of 'right' and 'wrong,' and without them we could not but flounder.[42]

Robinson, therefore, has much more respect for the moral rules and principles than does Fletcher, even though in the last analysis he suggests that they may be violated if love were better served.

The old morality, as Robinson calls it, tended to locate the unchanging element in Christian ethics in the contents of the moral commands, while the new morality finds in the attitude of "unselfregarding *agapē*"[43] the one unchanging element in Christian ethics. What the contents are of the Christian ethic will differ with every period of history, every group, and indeed even with every individual. Changing nonmoral factors inevitably affect the moral scope of any generation. Thus in the modern world the new atomic and biological weapons which can be used in war profoundly affect any discussion of the morality of war. Sociological investigations which have shown the ineffectiveness of capital punishment as a deterrent to crime also suggest radical changes in the old moral commands. But, unlike

Fletcher, he insists that there are some actions which are always wrong. We had better let him speak for himself here, so that we can see that he really represents a modified act-agapism:

> I would, of course, be the first to agree that there are a whole class of actions—like stealing, lying, killing, committing adultery—which are so fundamentally destructive of human relationships that no differences of century or society can change their character. But this does not, of course, mean that stealing or lying can in certain circumstances never be right. All Christians would admit that they could be.[44]

If there are any absolutely unbreakable moral rules, however, they obtain their status because it is inconceivable how violating them could ever be an expression of love. He suggests that "cruelty to children or rape" are always wrong, but the reason they are wrong is because they never can be conceived to be commanded by love. In addition to these more absolute moral prohibitions, there are a whole host of "working rules" which can be laid down as practical guides to Christian conduct. But these working rules can be broken by love, if need be. This "moral net" of working rules is so important for the ordering of any society that Robinson is convinced that the Christian should be in the forefront to help repair the net when circumstances require that particular moral principles or rules be modified or replaced.

Robinson insists that his version of the Christian ethic begins with the primacy of persons and personal relationships. For this reason he holds that principles are not absolutely binding for men, "however much they may help them (and often, indeed, save them) in their moral choices."[45] Yet, he does admit that moral rules or principles are needed as guideposts for action, and that therefore the Christian is concerned with helping to create a just moral and legal code. Robinson remarks:

> The deeper one's concern for persons, the more effectively one wants to see love buttressed by law. But if law usurps the place of love because it is safer, that safety is the safety of death.[46]

Thus, the Christian should work to help create an ethos in his society which will support the development of human personality and eliminate exploitation and destructiveness. In this respect, Robinson insists Christian ethics is a form of humanism—the difference with most types of humanism is that Christianity has added to it an element of mystery.

Two other theologians, however, provide even better illustrations of the Christian ethic interpreted as a modified act-agapism. They are Emil Brunner and Reinhold Niebuhr. Both stress justice as a moral principle in addition to *agapē;* both attempt to avoid legalism in their concern to speak directly to our present human situation.

Emil Brunner, the Swiss theologian, has expressed his basic conviction concerning Christian ethics in *The Divine Imperative*. That which is good, that which we should do, is that which God wills. But God who is Love wills always that we should love the neighbor; only this is not a general commandment but a supremely personal existence communication (*à la* Kierkegaard) from God to the individual. As Brunner states it:

> The Good is simply what *God* wills that we should do, not that which we would do on the basis of a principle of love. God wills to do something quite definite and particular through us, here and now, something which no other person could do at any other time.[47]

In terms of this general statement Brunner's position does not seem to be far from that of situation ethics; even Fletcher himself says that Brunner almost made it to the situational approach, but then he backed away, since he admitted rules and principles to govern the social order. In fact, Brunner goes so far as to insist that the love God expects of us implies all the virtues of which the classical moralists spoke. "Each virtue, one might say, is a particular way in which the person who lives in love takes the other into account, and 'realizes' him as 'Thou.' "[48] Thus, although the Christian will reflect the virtues of honesty, justice, temperance, and wisdom in his actions he will do so because he is living a life of obedient love to God. Brunner insists that there can never be any inhuman commands in God's dealing with us; there can never be a suspension of ethics for a supposedly higher category as Kierkegaard had thought.

The basic difference between Brunner and Fletcher concerns the status of justice. Brunner would not agree that love and justice are the same. Brunner's discussion of *agapē* is basically in agreement with what Fletcher says about it. The love of God is *agapē*, that is, self-giving concern for others not limited by the worth of the person upon whom the love is bestowed. This kind of love is incomprehensible to human reason but is most clearly seen in Jesus Christ:

> This love is known only where God is revealed as He Who does not judge the sinner according to his deserts, but incomprehensibly forgives his sin and so heals the breach in communion. This love is therefore only to be comprehended and won by faith. For to possess this love is the same thing as to possess God—the God who "first loved us," and reveals Himself as that loving God in His acts of revelation and reconciliation.[49]*

---

*From Emil Brunner, *Justice and the Social Order*, transl. by Mary Hottinger (1945). This and succeeding quotations from the same source used by permission of Harper & Row Publishers, Inc.

Justice for Brunner is an entirely different thing from Christian *agapē*. In justice we give the other person his due—no more and no less. He gets what he deserves, based on a sober, rational, and realistic appraisal of the facts of the case. Justice is comprehensible to every one's reason and completely impersonal. It does not regard the person, but sees only what is right. As Brunner puts it:

> The just man recognizes in the other the same dignity which he finds in himself, the same quality as a person, the same general law of being. ... Justice is never concerned with the human being as such, but only with the human being in relationships. Justice belongs to the world of systems, not to the world of persons.[50]

In its own sphere, justice is supreme. This has often led to misunderstanding, for it has been claimed that the Christian must cease to love in the realm of social relationships. Brunner insists that this cannot be true if the person is a true Christian.

How is this possible? How can one be just in his dealings in society and yet not relinquish his obligation to love? Brunner answers by saying that in the realm of systems love compels the Christian to be just. In other words, in the realm of impersonal relationships, the Christian must attempt to recoin love into justice. Thus, justice is not an inferior way of acting, but rather is as indispensable as love!

> This can be seen by the fact that the man of love, as soon as he has to act in the world of institutions, turns his love into justice. He knows that if he did otherwise, he would ruin, destroy, the world of institutions. Love which is not just in the world of institutions is sentimentality. And sentimentality, feeling for feeling's sake, is the poison, the solvent which destroys all just institutions.[51]

Does this mean that according to Brunner the Christian cannot display love in any of his relationships without recoining it into justice? No, in extremely close personal relationships, such as those of marriage, the Christian can show love directly to another person. Brunner proposes his law of the closeness of relationship to give a relative standard for determining when love is indeed possible: "The more closely an institution approaches the personal sphere, the smaller the number of human beings it embraces, and the less things in it predominate over persons, the greater is the scope it gives to love."[52] In the orders of life between marriage and the state one finds many social relationships in which one is involved. If in these relationships persons predominate, then love rules; while if things are primary, justice holds sway. But even in the most impersonal institutions love can be shown indirectly in attitude and in criticism.

It is important to note that Brunner insists that while love transcends justice, it can never do less than justice demands. As Brunner points out in a pertinent example, "A citizen who falsifies his income-tax return in order to practise charity cannot appeal to love in exculpation; love of that kind is sheer sentimentality."[53] It is always the responsibility of love to see that justice is done, and then the real work of love actually begins. Justice can be achieved fully, but not love. "Only the love which is without measure fulfills itself—the love of God."[54] Love is always doing more; it is never finished, but in its eagerness to act it must be careful to fulfill the demands of justice lest, according to Brunner, it becomes irrational and sentimental.

Reinhold Niebuhr, one of the great Protestant ethicists of this century, stressed "the impossible possibility" of Christian love, particularly in the area of social ethics, and suggested that in the context of actions between groups or nations love must be recoined into justice. Love seeks to do more than justice, but it ought, according to Niebuhr, never to do less than, or other than, justice. The moral goals of the individual (love and unselfishness) cannot be applied to society. This is one of the themes running throughout Niebuhr's many books and articles.[55] We must get rid of the illusion which regards society as an "individual writ large." Action in society requires coercion, along with reason and cooperation among individuals, if we are to achieve a tolerable amount of justice. The religious fanatic and the moralistic idealist who attempt to apply love uncritically to social groups will either be destroyed by society or taken advantage of by others. We must be realistic; we must acquire some of the wisdom of the children of this world in our application of Christian love and moral ideals to social living. Niebuhr therefore calls for the Christian to work in and through the existing power structures in order to create justice within groups and between groups in society.

Thus, both Brunner and Reinhold Niebuhr introduce justice as an additional principle alongside of Christian *agapē*. If this interpretation of their thought is correct, then they represent modified act-agapism. Although they both stress *agapē* as the distinctive norm of Christian ethics, they insist that *agapē* cannot often be directly fulfilled in our world. Love must, therefore, serve as the motivating force for the Christian working in society to achieve justice for all mankind.

The best example of a Christian ethic which holds to general rules, and is therefore, largely an ethic of rule-agapism, or mixed agapism, is to be found in Paul Ramsey's recent treatment of ethics in *Deeds and Rules in Christian Ethics*. Indeed, Ramsey, who is Professor of Religion at Princeton University, is well acquainted with the writers in philosophical ethics, and is far more concerned with developing a Christian ethic which will meet the canons of consistency and validity than are either Fletcher or Robinson. His book also contains excellent criticisms of Fletcher's position, based partly on showing that Fletcher cannot avoid slipping into some summary or general rules even in what he directly says in *Situation Ethics*. This book by Ramsey will provide the reader with an excellent example of responsible ethical and philosophical thinking today by a Christian theologian, and is, therefore, well worth detailed study.

Ramsey takes his stand, along with Fletcher and Bishop Robinson, on the primacy of *agapē* as the basic norm of Christian ethics. Furthermore, he agrees with them that we begin with persons and take full cognizance of the facts which are applicable to any moral decision. Ramsey has, however, profited from his study of the philosopher John Rawls' provocative paper "Two Concepts of Rules," and thus asks if Christian love should not also be concerned with evolving some general rules expressing what love requires to be practiced.[56] As he puts it: "The question is simply whether there *are* any general rules or principles or virtues or styles of life that embody love, and if so what these may be."[57]* He agrees with the situation ethicists that the Christian ought to always seek to act so as to fulfill what love requires, but he objects to their belief that from the requirements of love no general rules for human behavior can be found. Let us see how Ramsey develops his position that *agapē* does in fact lead to general rules of practice for the Christian ethicist.

The interpretation which Ramsey gives of Christian ethics is primarily deontological. In this respect he differs with Frankena's identification of agapism with a teleological ethic.

> *Agapē* defines for the Christian what is right, righteous, obligatory to be done among men; it is not the Christian's definition of the good that better be done and much less is it a definition of the right way to be good.[58]

The Christian ethic is based on obedience to God as presented in Christ and the Kingdom of God. Hence, any teleological calculus, such as that advocated by Fletcher, must be subordinated to the Christian's "ready obedience to the *present* reign of God, the alignment of the human will with the Divine will that men should live together in covenant-love no matter what the morrow brings. . . ."[59]

While act-agapism may be adopted theoretically, Ramsey holds that in practice it is almost impossible for the ethicist to avoid making some general claims for human action which at least surreptitiously introduce principles or rules into the ethical system. Thus, he finds that Fletcher does make some general claims which would be wholly

---

*From *Deeds and Rules in Christian Ethics*, by Paul Ramsey (1967). This and succeeding quotations from the same source used by permission of Charles Scribner's Sons.

inconsistent with a pure situation ethics. Despite his insistence that no two situations are alike enough to allow for general statements of conduct, Fletcher himself claims that *"no unwanted and unintended* baby should ever be born"[60] is a general justification for abortion. In fact, Fletcher explicitly supports Kant's second version of the categorical imperative:

> Kant's second maxim holds: Treat persons as ends, never as means. Even if in some situations a material thing is chosen rather than a person, it will be (if it is Christianly done) for the sake of the person, not for the sake of the thing itself. If a man prefers to keep his money invested instead of giving it to his son who needs it, it could only be because he believes his son will need it far more urgently later on. . . . Things are to be used; people are to be loved. It is "immoral" when people are used and things are loved. Loving actions are the *only* conduct permissible.[61]

Exploitation of persons is always wrong, according to Fletcher, because it is unloving: hence, he condemns prostitution and the exploitation of the laborer in the early nineteenth-century form of capitalism as "sins." While his book his filled with extreme cases in which he can justify adultery, pre-marital sexual encounters, and so on, nevertheless, he insists that sex is wrong unless love is present between the persons. He makes clear in the context that he is referring to *agapē* and not to *eros*:

> The point is that, Christianly speaking, sex which does not have love as its partner, its *senior* partner, is wrong. If there is no responsible concern for the *other* one, for the partner as a subject rather than a mere object, as a person and not a *thing*, the act is immoral.[62]

It would appear clear, therefore, that *agapē*, even for Fletcher's radical situational approach, does lead to at least some summary rules governing human behavior. If Fletcher's above comment is interpreted as holding that sex is always wrong unless it is done with love as its partner, then he has even, although unwittingly, proposed a general ethical rule.

We should clarify a distinction which Ramsey and Frankena make between summary rules and general rules in agapistic ethics. A summary rule is one which holds that following the practice advocated is generally best, or that avoiding the kind of behavior prohibited should prove in the majority of cases to be the right way of acting. Thus, a summary rule would have the form of "keeping promises is 'generally' love-fulfilling," while a general rule would maintain that "keeping-promises-always is love-fulfilling."[63] The difference is clarified by Frankena as follows:

> The difference is that on the latter view we may and sometimes must obey a rule in a particular situation even though the action it calls for is seen not to be what love itself would directly require. . . . "Summary

rule" agapism . . . admits rules but regards them as summaries of past experience, useful, perhaps almost indispensable, but only as rules of thumb. It cannot allow that a rule may ever be followed in a situation when it is seen to conflict with what love dictates in that situation.[64]

Ramsey thinks that Frankena has drawn the distinction too sharply, for if Frankena's distinction is correct, then the most a Christian could follow in his moral decisions would be summary rules, "since he should always do what love requires."[65] Ramsey's proposal is that there may be some kinds of situations in which Christians can appeal to no more than summary rules, while there may be other kinds of situations in which they could appeal to general rules of universal validity. Beginning with persons, Ramsey believes that some rules of ethical conduct can be discerned which become more than summary rules. Asking what does love require may lead to some rules of general validity. It is to cut off the investigation too soon, before it has gotten under way, if writers such as Fletcher simply deny that love can ever discern any general rules of universal validity. True to the spirit of much contemporary philosophical investigation, Ramsey suggests we must look and see whether or not love leads to any general rules embodying what love itself directly requires. He thus draws the following distinction between general and summary rules:

> If it could be shown that to act in accord with one of these love-formed principles of conduct is in a particular situation not what love itself directly requires, then that was not a general principle of conduct but a summary rule only.[66]

The Christian should be very careful, however, so that he does not confuse the demands of sentimental love with what *agapē* directly requires.

One of the dangers in situation ethics, as Ramsey sees it, is its attempt to limit the calculations of *agapē* to the direct consequences of the particular action under consideration. That is, it asks if it is the loving thing to lie, or to steal, or to engage in premarital sex, in this particular situation. How will it affect the other person? Will this action tend to bring more good into the lives of the people immediately concerned? Part of the difficulty encountered in any ethical calculus, including an agapistic one, lies in knowing exactly where to draw the line between those who are likely to be affected by the act, and those who will not be affected by it. Will the exceptional act which one believes justifiable for the two persons immediately involved really not have any effect upon others? Will it not affect one's parents or one's friends? How can one be sure? Furthermore, how can one tell how the act will really affect the other person? Ramsey makes this point even more strongly:

But one way or another the Christian will know that an exceptional action of his (which may be the most loving thing to do in all its own *direct* consequences and probable consequences) may still as a side-effect tend to break down the social practice of a rule of behavior which "generally" embodies love, and thus lead in the end and on balance to a totality of less loving actions than if he had not made an exception of himself and his single action (which, however, it cannot be denied, *was* justified in terms of an individualistic act-calculus).[67]

The Christian should have a concern for the indirect effect of his actions upon the social order. Will his telling a justified lie tend to break down the fabric of truth-telling? If so, then this concern must also be taken into his calculations. As Ramsey puts it: "Order and justice are both 'values'; both are rules of love."[68] Order and justice are two of the social needs of men for which *agapē* should always strive. Ramsey suggests that a mixed agapism might be the best version of Christian ethics, that is, an ethic in which although love is the primary norm there are other norms such as man's natural sense of justice and order. Such an approach would stress the need for much careful thought before justifying the breaking of "unjust laws."

Following John Rawls' distinction of two concepts of rules, Ramsey proposes that some general rules in Christian ethics are based on the consequences of the acts, while the other type of general rules are rules of social practice. As examples of the first type he suggests that cruelty and rape are always wrong, because of the lovelessness that inheres in these acts, and breaking promises is always wrong, because they are never love-fulfilling in a personal sense. These general rules are justified because obeying them results in good consequences for persons. When love is not served by obeying these general rules, then the general rules should be modified and stated more precisely. Ramsey's interpretation of how general rules get revised is in agreement with the basic thesis of R. M. Hare, a contemporary British philosopher, whose ethical theory we shall examine in detail in the next chapter. Hare insists that on the basis of moral experience one formulates the general ethical rules more precisely, so that instead of "Never break a promise," one more correctly spells out the rule as, "Never break a promise except in cases where it is necessary to save a life, and so on."[69] This way of modifying general principles allows for both moral experience and for moral guidance.

Ramsey, however, is more interested in defending the general rules which are practices, a justification which is made independently of the consequences of observing the practice.

> Rules of practices . . . specify that to engage in a practice demands the performance of those actions required by the practice. The *practice*

itself is to be justified by a direct application of Christian love. One asks *which practice* most embodies or fulfills love. But then one justifies an action falling under it by appeal to the practice.[70]

Ramsey, following Rawls' lead, explains what is meant by a practice by referring to the rules of games such as baseball and football. Thus, if while playing a football game, the captain of the team asked the officials if his team could not have five downs instead of four, he would be assumed to be joking. Among the rules of the game called football there is one which states that a team has four downs (tries) in which to make ten yards. If it does not make at least the required yardage it must surrender the ball to the other team. As long as the game of football is being played, this is among the rules of the game. One could attempt to reform the game by trying to get the officials of the league to change the rules, or one might even choose to construct a different ball game. But if he chose the latter course, he would have to specify some rules under which the new game were to be played. Now, according to Ramsey, rules of practice function in society very much like the rules of football function when that game is being played:

> Rules of practice necessarily involve the abdication of full liberty to guide one's actions case by case by making immediate appeals to what love (or utility) requires in each particular case. The point of a practice is to annul anyone's title to act, on his individual judgment, in accordance with ultimate utilitarian or prudential considerations, or from considerations of Christian love in that one instance alone.[71]

The practice itself, not a specific action falling under it, may be justified by an appeal to *agapē*. As long as the practice is part of the socially accepted and most love-fulfilling ethic, no individual has the right to claim to be an exception to the practice. He is only justified in trying to get the practice itself modified or replaced by one which he believes will more fully embody *agapē*.

Following a practice, however, does not mean that the individual may not have to deliberate in certain difficult cases which call upon him to make decisions. Ramsey is not defending the hard and fast legalism which situationist ethics criticizes. Instead he insists that in many instances the individual must ask what the practice really means, and try to understand the "qualifications and exceptions that should be understood to fall under the rules themselves."[72] We are born into a society in which there are certain moral practices, and part of our acquiring moral wisdom is our learning what these practices mean and in what circumstances qualifications are built into the practices themselves. Thus, to use a simple illustration, if someone under duress utters the words, "I promise," the simple uttering of the words does not in fact constitute a promise. If someone points a gun at you and forces you to promise to aid him in robbing a bank, no one would claim that you had made a promise which you were obligated to keep because it is an accepted social practice. Likewise if someone twists your arm, literally or figuratively, in order to get you to say that you promise to forgive him for what he has done, it seems clear that no genuine promise was made and that no real forgiveness was given. You must in the first place understand what it means to promise (a little baby cannot therefore promise anybody anything); you must make the decision freely (that is, not under compulsion); and you should be in a position to carry out your promise (you cannot promise to loan someone a thousand dollars if you do not have the money). Many moralists who defend a deontological ethic have maintained that there is a kind of hierarchy among the justified social practices, so that, for example, not taking a life is more binding than speaking the truth. W. D. Ross, a British moralist, has tried to establish some rough rules of preference among what he calls *prima facie* duties.[73] At any rate, a refinement of what exactly is meant by a moral rule, indicating the exceptions and qualifications which are built into the rule itself, might present a viable alternative to situation ethics.

Perhaps the case for general moral rules could be strengthened by continuing our comparison with the rules of games, such as football. Every year the Football Rules Committee of the National Collegiate Athletic Association approves the specific rules for that year. Hence, some years unlimited substitution has been allowed, while in other years limitations have been placed upon substitutions. Now there is no comparable body which decides the interpretation of and the specific moral rules for a society—there the parallel apparently ends. A study of the history of morals, however, shows that changes, even if they have been gradual, have occurred in both social mores and moral rules. An inspection of some of the accepted social rules for gracious behavior advocated by an etiquette book of fifty years ago would show that our patterns of acceptable etiquette are quite different today. Furthermore, both with respect to moral rules and the civil laws we now take far more cognizance of the psychological state of the person before we find him either morally or legally guilty of wrong-doing than was the case fifty years ago. Unofficially, but by a kind of general consensus, the moral rules get changed over the generations. The result of this may be a refinement of the moral rules, or a replacement of old rules by new rules which are more love-fulfilling, or which tend to produce greater good than the old ones. Ramsey has shown that this kind of an interpretation is a real alternative to a radical situation ethic which tends to treat the exceptional case as though it were the only type of case one ever encountered. The reader should recall that Ramsey is not denying that we may face some cases in which we must appeal to the general utility of the action to promote more good than any viable alternative. What he wishes to insist upon is that in addition to this type of example, there are a whole host of occasions for which our moral duty is more easily spelled out as acting in conformity with the accepted moral practice.

NOTES

1. William K. Frankena, "Love and Principle in Christian Ethics," in *Faith and Philosophy: Philosophical Studies in Religion and Ethics*, ed. by Alvin Plantinga (Grand Rapids, Mich.: William B. Eerdmans Publishing Co., 1964), p. 207.
2. Joseph Fletcher, *Situation Ethics: The New Morality* (Philadelphia: The Westminster Press, 1966), p. 26.
3. Ibid., p. 26.
4. Ibid., p. 31.
5. Ibid., p. 28.
6. Ibid., p. 30.
7. Ibid., p. 31.
8. Ibid., Chapter headings for chs. III, IV, V, VI, VII, VIII.
9. Ibid., p. 58.
10. Ibid., p. 65.
11. Ibid., p. 74.
12. Ibid., p. 75.
13. Ibid., p. 79.
14. Ibid., p. 84.
15. Ibid., p. 89.
16. Ibid., p. 90.
17. Ibid., p. 95.
18. Ibid., p. 95.
19. Ibid., p. 95.
20. Ibid., p. 96.
21. Ibid., p. 101.
22. Ibid., p. 117.
23. Ibid., p. 104.
24. Ibid., p. 124.
25. Ibid., pp. 125-126.
26. Ibid., pp. 126-127.
27. Joseph Fletcher, *Moral Responsibility: Situation Ethics at Work* (Philadelphia: The Westminster Press, 1967), p. 40.
28. Fletcher, *Situation Ethics*, p. 132.
29. Ibid., p. 133.
30. Ibid., p. 164.
31. Ibid., p. 164.
32. Fletcher, *Moral Responsibility*, p. 39.
33. Ibid., pp. 39-40.
34. Fletcher, *Situation Ethics*, pp. 142-143.
35. Ibid., p. 135.
36. Ibid., p. 139.
37. Ibid., p. 151.
38. Ibid., p. 157.
39. Fletcher, *Moral Responsibility*, p. 181.
40. Ibid., p. 181.
41. John A. T. Robinson, *Honest to God* (London: SCM Press Ltd., 1963), pp. 109-110.

42. Ibid., pp. 119-120.
43. John A. T. Robinson, *Christian Morals Today* (Philadelphia: The Westminster Press, 1964), p. 12.
44. Ibid., p. 16.
45. Ibid., p. 42.
46. Ibid., p. 26.
47. Emil Brunner, *The Divine Imperative: A Study in Christian Ethics*, trans. by Olive Wyon (Philadelphia: The Westminster Press, 1947), p. 117.
48. Ibid., p. 167.
49. Emil Brunner, *Justice and the Social Order*, trans. by Mary Hottinger (New York: Harper and Brothers, Publishers, 1945), pp. 126-127.
50. Ibid., pp. 127-128.
51. Ibid, pp. 128-129.
53. Ibid., p. 129.
54. Ibid., p. 130.
55. See Reinhold Niebuhr, *An Interpretation of Christian Ethics* (New York: Harper and Brothers, Publishers, 1935); Reinhold Niebuhr, *Moral Man and Immoral Society: A Study in Ethics and Politics* (New York: Charles Scribner's Sons, 1948); Reinhold Niebuhr, *The Nature and Destiny of Man: A Christian Interpretation*, One Volume Edition: I. Human Nature, II. Human Destiny (New York: Charles Scribner's Sons, 1946).
56. John Rawls, "Two Concepts of Rules," *The Philosophical Review*, LXIV (1955), 3–32. Also reprinted in many anthologies.
57. Paul Ramsey, *Deeds and Rules in Christian Ethics* (New York: Charles Scribner's Sons, 1967), p. 112.
58. Ibid., p. 108.
59. Ibid., pp. 108-109.
60. Fletcher, *Situation Ethics*, p. 39.
61. Ibid., p. 51.
62. Fletcher, *Moral Responsibility*, p. 35.
63. Ramsey, *Deeds and Rules in Christian Ethics*, pp. 109-110.
64. Frankena, "Love and Principle in Christian Ethics," in *Faith and Philosophy*, p. 212.
65. Ramsey, *Deeds and Rules in Christian Ethics*, p. 111.
66. Ibid., p. 112.
67. Ibid., p. 115.
68. Ibid., p. 116.
69. See R. M. Hare, *The Language of Morals* (Oxford: Clarendon Press, 1952), chs. 3 and 4; Luther J. Binkley, *Contemporary Ethical Theories* (New York: Philosophical Library, Inc., 1961), pp. 132-140.
70. Ramsey, *Deeds and Rules in Christian Ethics*, p. 134.
71. Ibid., p. 135.
72. Ibid., p. 136.
73. See W. D. Ross, *The Right and the Good* (Oxford: Clarendon Press, 1955), ch. 2; Binkley, *Contemporary Ethical Theories*, pp. 30-34.

George Finger Thomas

CHRISTIAN ETHICS AND MORAL PHILOSOPHY

George Finger Thomas is Chairman of the Department of Religion at Princeton University. He has taught at Southern Methodist University, Swarthmore College, Dartmouth College, and the University of North Carolina. Thomas studied at Oxford as a Rhodes Scholar and received his Ph.D. degree from Harvard University. Among his best-known works are *Philosophy and Religious Belief* (1970) and *Religious Philosophy of the West* (1965). In the following selection, taken from *Christian Ethics and Moral Philosophy* (1955), Thomas asks the fundamental questions of what is the basis for the good life and what represents a valid ethical first principle. Do we have to choose between moral philosophy and Christian ethics? in other words, is there absolute opposition between the autonomy of reason and the authority of revelation? Thomas believes that the attempt by many modern philosophers to separate moral philosophy from Christian ethics is a grave mistake since the two are related to each other and should be regarded as complementary rather than mutually exclusive. Reprinted by permission of Charles Scribner's Sons from *Christian Ethics and Moral Philosophy* by George F. Thomas. Copyright 1955 George F. Thomas.

Is moral philosophy . . . an adequate basis for the good life? Many moral philosophers have thought so, especially in our secular age. But there are *limitations* of moral philosophy which have always prevented most men, even educated men, from regarding it as by itself sufficient. What are these limitations?

First, moral philosophers are concerned with the discovery of what is good for men and right for them to do, but they have seldom been able to awaken in men a love of the good or to stimulate their wills to do the right. This is the familiar problem of moral *incentive* or *motive*. It may be admitted, with Sidgwick,* that there is a desire in man to do that which is right and reasonable. But that desire, by itself, is not strong enough in most men to overcome the natural passions and social forces which are opposed to the right and reasonable. It is not enough to appeal to the reason; the will and the affections must somehow be brought into line with the dictates of reason. Plato realized the importance of moral education through associating pleasure with the good and pain with the evil, and Aristotle emphasized the necessity of forming right habits. But philosophers have seldom probed this problem very deeply. They have tended to assume that if we know our true good we will seek it and if we know our duty we will do it. Therefore, they have thought that when they have defined the good and the right, their task is over. But man's will is divided and he cannot love his true good with

---
*See Henry Sidgwick, *Methods of Ethics* (London, 1874). ED.

all his heart. Again and again, he finds himself in the tragic situation of St. Paul: he knows what is good but he chooses the evil. He is powerless by himself to acquire the virtues or perform the duties which are required of him by moral philosophy. If he is to attain true goodness, he must be radically transformed. His desires must be redirected and his affections fixed firmly upon the good.

Second, man's effort to attain virtue by himself is often a source of *moral dangers.* Although the greatest moral philosophers insist upon a disinterested devotion to the good, the realization of higher values often leads to moral pride and complacency. Man's self-centeredness even perverts his virtues and turns them into means of furthering his own interests. Without faith and love, the attempt to attain virtue and do good works often leads to self-righteousness. Apart from this tendency of natural egoism to corrupt the achievements of the moral will, the excessive dependence upon moral striving is accompanied by serious dangers. It sometimes produces inner tension and anxiety concerning the success of one's efforts. Moralism in the sense of strenuous effort by the will to "live up to" high ethical ideals without the power to do so may be the cause of inner conflict and failure. The result may be psychological frustration or even breakdown. More often moralism leads to a stern, unlovely character with strength but without graciousness and spontaneity. Some of the finest moral qualities cannot be attained by conscious willing at all but must come from the unconscious influence of other persons and from participation in the life of a moral community.

Third, there is no *imaginative vision* in moral philosophy capable of inspiring spontaneous love and devotion. The principles of moral philosophy are expressed in concepts rather than images. This is necessary for the sake of clarity and precision; but it prevents most moral philosophers from moving the heart and stimulating the will. One of the reasons Bergson does not recognize the morality of philosophers as a third type of morality along with "closed" and "open" morality is that its concepts seem to him to have little power over the will.[1] His tendency to anti-intellectualism leads him to minimize unduly the function of reason in morality, for reason can survey the various ends sought by men and organize them into a unified ideal. But it is a timely warning against the opposite tendency to neglect the non-rational factors in the moral life. What is there in moral philosophy which can stimulate aspiration like the Christian vision of a universal community based upon love of God as Father and love of all men as brothers?

Fourth, the ideals of moral philosophers also lack the appeal that comes from the *incarnation* of a way of life in a living person and the inspiration that is derived from *imitation* of him. One of the greatest sources of appeal in Platonism, which is close to religious morality in many ways, is the embodiment of its ideal in Socrates. The power of Buddhist ethics is due largely to the fact that the followers of the Buddha are called upon to "take refuge" in *him* as well as in his *teachings*. Certainly, the reason Christian ethics has been able to transform the lives of men is to be found not only in the teachings of Christ but also in his life and in union with him. While a moral philosophy presents men with an *ideal* to be followed, it seldom offers them the *example* of one who has followed it. Nor is its ideal embodied in the way of life of a *community* or *church*, whose members strengthen and encourage one another in their efforts to realize it. Is this the reason why the greatest rival of Christian ethics in our time is not philosophical ethics but the secularized religious ethics of Communism, with its imaginative vision of a classless society embracing all men, the embodiment of its ideal in great leaders like Lenin, and its dependence upon an organized party to make its vision come true?

While moral philosophy has undoubtedly been one of the major sources of the ethical tradition of the Western world, these limitations force us to raise the question whether the attempt of many modern philosophers to separate moral philosophy from Christian ethics is not a fatal mistake. Should not moral philosophy and Christian ethics be regarded as complementary rather than mutually exclusive? May not the limitations of moral philosophy be overcome and its insights made more effective by the acceptance of Christian faith and love? May not Christians be aided by the insights of moral philosophy to obey God and serve their neighbors more wisely? The purpose of this chapter is to suggest that these questions should be answered in the affirmative, and to indicate a way in which the breach between Christian ethics and moral philosophy can be overcome.

THE AUTHORITY OF REVELATION AND THE AUTONOMY OF REASON

In carrying out this purpose, however, we shall be confronted with *objections* from moral philosophers and Christian theologians. Some moral philosophers repudiate Christian ethics on the ground that it is based on revelation rather than reason and consequently is "authoritarian." Some Christian theologians refuse to accept any of the theories of moral philosophers on the ground that they are useless and unnecessary for men of faith. It is essential to deal with these two objections before we attempt to show how Christian ethics and moral philosophy should be related to each other. We shall begin with the objection of secular moral philosophers that Christian ethics is "authoritarian."

With respect to the source of authority, Christian ethics and moral philosophy seem at first sight to be in absolute opposition to one another. Christian ethics derives its principles from the revelation recorded in the Bible. Liberal as well as orthodox Christians insist upon the authority of this revelation. In contrast, secular moral philosophers seem to reject every authority but that of reason. Moral philosophy, they insist, must be "autonomous"; the moralist must depend upon no source of truth beyond reason. This raises several important questions: In what sense does Christian ethics rest upon the authority of revelation? Insofar as it does so, is it necessarily "authoritarian"? Again, what do moral philosophers mean by the "autonomy" of the reason? Is this autonomy absolute or limited? Finally, is it possible to accept the "authority" of revelation without sacrificing the legitimate "autonomy" of the reason?

First, in what sense does Christian ethics assert the *authority of revelation?* Christians differ in their answer to this question. In Protestantism, Christian ethics is based upon the authority not of the Church but of the Bible. Since the Bible is the record of a divine revelation in history, this means that Christian ethics is ultimately based upon the authority of that revelation. However, the revelation cannot be simply identified with the words of the Bible in which it is expressed; the "Word" of God is not the same as the words in Hebrew and Greek by which it is mediated to us. Moreover, as Temple has said, it does not consist of dogmas and commandments stated in propositional form. It is a revelation of God and His redemptive activity, not of dogmas about God; of new life in love, not rules of conduct. For it is a revelation in historical events as interpreted by prophets and apostles, and the full meaning of historical events can never be exhausted by the words of any of its interpreters.[2] If so, the responsibility for interpreting the meaning of the revelation belongs to the individual person as a member of the Christian community. Does not God address men in the Biblical revelation as beings who can listen, understand, raise questions, and judge for themselves?

When understood in this way, the authority of revelation is wholly inconsistent with religious "authoritarianism." Religious "authoritarianism" is usually based upon belief in a visible authority, e.g., Church or Bible, as the source of dogmas which must be believed and rules which must be obeyed. Moreover, the pronouncements of this authority are unquestioned. They are felt to be binding whether or not they are approved by the reason and conscience of the individual. The free acceptance of revelation, as we have described it, is incompatible with this authoritarianism. According to our view, the acceptance of the authority of revelation by a Christian not only permits but demands that he use his reason fully in determining its meaning and its implications for his life.

This brings us to the question, what is the meaning of *"autonomy"* in moral philosophy? Positively, it asserts that man should determine his moral conduct by laws or principles approved by his own reason. Negatively, it denies the dependence of the rational will upon any external authority such as a church or state. According to Kant, it is "the property of the will to be a law to itself,"[3] and "the will possesses this property because it belongs to the intelligible world, under laws which, being independent of nature, have their foundation not in experience but in reason alone."[4] This view of the "autonomy" of the reason seems to assert that the reason lays down moral laws in complete independence of moral experience. However, Kant argued that his fundamental ethical principle was only a precise formulation of what is presupposed in the common moral consciousness. In any case, the usual method of philosophical ethics is to develop its principles through an examination of the moral experience of men as reflected in their moral judgments. Thus, "autonomy" means only that reason should not passively submit to an external authority, but should derive its ethical principles from reflection upon moral experience. If "autonomy" is interpreted in this way, reason may and should take into account every kind of moral experience, including that of religious men, in formulating its ethical principles.

When the "authority" of revelation and the "autonomy" of reason are interpreted in this way, the absolute opposition between Christian ethics and moral philosophy is seen to be unnecessary. On the one hand, the Biblical revelation of moral truth was not imparted to men whose minds and consciences were passive, but was mediated to them through their moral experience. Moreover, it continues to be accepted by Christians because it seems to be confirmed in their own moral experience. Thus, there is nothing arbitrary or irrational about it. On the other hand, the moral philosopher depends upon the facts of moral experience, and since the value of his conclusions is determined largely by the depth and breadth of the moral experience from which he derives them, it is reasonable for him to take seriously the moral experience recorded in the Bible.

In fact, however, there is a fundamental *difference* between Christian ethics and secular moral philosophy in their interpretation of moral experience. Christian ethics is inseparable from the Christian faith that God has revealed His will in Christ. A philosopher who does not share this faith cannot accept Christian ethics as a whole, although he may incorporate into his own thinking certain ideas derived from it. Consequently, he cannot give the moral experience recorded in the Bible a "privileged position" in his examination of the facts of the moral consciousness. He may acknowledge that important and valid ethical ideas originated in this moral experience, but he cannot acknowledge their primacy in his ethical thinking.

Thus, while there is no logical necessity for an absolute opposition between Christian ethics and moral philosophy *as such*, there is a radical difference between Christian ethics and a *secular* moral philosophy. However, the Christian moralist can do much to bridge the gap. Although the secular moral philosopher refuses to give primacy to ethical insights derived from the Christian moral experience, the Christian moralist should acknowledge the truth of some of the ethical insights of moral philosophers and adapt them for the use of Christians. We shall indicate later in this chapter why he should do so and how he can do so in the most fruitful way.

In addition, he can seek to remove a common misconception from the minds of moral philosophers which stands in the way of their acceptance of the Christian faith and ethic. This is the idea that, while Christian ethics is based upon the moral experience of a particular people in the past, moral philosophy is a product of universal reason reflecting impartially upon the moral experience of all humanity. Because of this supposed difference between them, the secular moral philosopher believes that his method and conclusions are superior to those of the Christian moralist. But is his examination of moral experience as all-inclusive and impartial as he thinks? Does he actually analyze the moral judgments of *all* peoples of every time and place? Does he analyze moral judgments from the perspective of an *impartial* reason unconditioned by his own time and place?

The moral philosopher is incapable of such an analysis. The limitations of his knowledge and the effect of his culture upon him cannot be overcome. In his analysis he usually limits himself to the moral judgments of his own people or civilization. Even when he deals with the moral judgments of other people and other times, he is naturally influenced more deeply by those of his own. The ethical theories of Plato and Aristotle would have been impossible in any country except ancient Greece, and Kant's ethics is clearly a product of the Age of Reason. Thus, the perspective of the moral philosopher is not that of universal reason reflecting impartially upon the *general* moral experience of mankind; it is that of his own reason conditioned by the *particular* moral experience of his time and place. In reality, he accords a "privileged position" to the particular moral experience of ancient Greeks or modern Europeans, as the Christian moralist accords such a position to the experience of Hebrew prophets and Christian apostles.

If so, the moral philosopher should not claim superiority for his method. Like the Christian moralist, he gives the "privileged position" to those whom he believes to have been the wisest and best; and if he is pressed for the reason why he believes them to be so, it will be seen that his belief really rests upon metaphysical and ethical assumptions which he cannot demonstrate but accepts by a kind of faith. In brief, there is no such thing as an ethic which has been developed by pure reason without the aid of presuppositions. The difference between Christian ethics and secular moral philosophy is not that the former has presuppositions while the latter is free from them; it is that they derive their presuppositions from different sources. Can the moral philosopher prove that his presuppositions or the sources from which he draws them are superior to those of the Christian moralist? If the test of ethical presuppositions is their fruitfulness in ethical theory and their value as a guide in moral decisions, Christian ethics has stood this test successfully during many centuries. Can more be said of the ethical presuppositions of any philosopher?

FAITH AND REASON

The preceding argument concerning the relation of Christian ethics to moral philosophy presupposes a certain view of the nature of the Christian faith and its relation to reason. We must now make this view more explicit. Some philosophers suppose that faith has no cognitive value but is a wholly irrational act which springs from the will or the feelings. Now, it is certainly true that faith is not only intellectual assent; it is also a response of the whole self, including the will and heart, to the reality of God. But this does not destroy its *cognitive value*. For faith involves an apprehension of the reality and goodness of God as He has revealed Himself. It is not a blind faith, but a response to God as He has confronted man in his experience. It differs from reason when the latter is conceived as the faculty of discursive thinking. Faith *affirms* the reality and goodness of God as He is experienced and it leads to a commitment to Him. Reason, on the other hand, critically *examines* a judgment to determine whether there are adequate grounds for asserting it and it frequently leads to a refusal of commitment. Thus, faith is more adventurous than reason, reason more cautious than faith. But while faith goes beyond reason, it need not contradict any knowledge which has been definitely established by reason. And reason, which has a constructive as well as a critical task, cannot complete its task unless it is willing to accept premises or presuppositions which it cannot demonstrate. Thus, while faith without reason is uncritical, reason without faith is uncreative.

Of course, reason can attain to knowledge of certain kinds without the aid of faith. In the form of common sense, it can enable men to cope with problems of everyday life. In the form of science, it can describe natural phenomena, make predictions about future events, and design machines for exploiting natural resources. But it cannot attain to wisdom about the world as a whole or the highest good of man without *presuppositions* derived from faith.

The mind can understand reality, says Niebuhr, "only by making faith the presupposition of its understanding."[5] This is the Augustinian view of the relation between faith and understanding. "Credo ut intelligam," "I believe in order that I may understand." Since every world view rests upon presuppositions which cannot be rationally demonstrated, each of us must face the problem as to whether he is to start with presuppositions derived, at least in part, from the religious experience of God as transcendent Reality and Good. If we try to avoid the problem by denying the possibility of a world view and contenting ourselves with the description of relations between natural phenomena, as in Positivism, we refuse to heed the highest demand of reason and to meet the deepest need of life itself. If we try to find the meaning of the whole of reality in some aspect of nature, e.g., matter or life, we are merely explaining the whole by one of its finite parts to which we have arbitrarily accorded a privileged position over other finite parts. But if we have had a vital religious experience, we can never be satisfied with anything less than a religious world view based upon an affirmation of faith in God as transcendent Reality and Good.

Of course, in laying hold of God by faith, man's "reach exceeds his grasp." Though God has revealed Himself in religious experience, He remains hidden in His transcendent otherness. Nevertheless, faith ventures out beyond the world of finite and contingent things and affirms an infinite and supersensible Being as the Ground of its existence, its nature, and its value.

Thus faith is a *source of truth* about reality, not a subjective fancy. As such, it involves not only an act of trust, but also an intellectual act, an act of insight. That is why it is the source not only of religion, but also of any philosophy which does justice to the transcendent element in experience. Every world view, irreligious as well as religious, is based upon a principle of meaning, a vision of truth, which is accepted by a kind of faith as the key to reality as a whole. In the words of Bradley, "metaphysics is the finding of bad reasons for what we believe on instinct."[6] A religious world view differs from naturalistic world views in that the principle of meaning upon which it rests is a transcendent principle, God. The fact that it is transcendent, however, does not mean that it is irrelevant to our understanding of the finite and contingent things of the world in which we live and to our life in that world. Indeed, finite and contingent things, especially the life and spirit of man, find their meaning and explanation only in relation to it, and apart from it they become unintelligible.

This is not a mere dogmatic assertion of religion alone; it can be confirmed by reference to other spiritual activities and values also. Plato points out in the "Symposium" how the experience of beautiful faces and forms leads on to the experience of beautiful souls and finally to the experience of Beauty itself as the transcendent principle which is invisible but is present in all visible things of beauty and is the ultimate source of their beauty. One does not have to accept the Platonic theory of Ideas as universal Forms which subsist in a realm of their own to see that he is describing the experience of all those who love beauty as something more than the "aesthetic surface" of a physical object. The sense of frustration of every great artist because he cannot capture perfectly the vision that hovers before him points in the same direction. Similarly, all moral striving seems to presuppose an absolute and perfect goodness that is never fully realized in men's conduct but that haunts them and beckons them on. Thus, the aesthetic and moral experience of man, like his religious experience, points to a transcendent Reality and Good beyond the natural world. But since religious faith apprehends directly this Reality and Good, it is the source of the highest knowledge. Without faith, all knowledge of finite reality through common sense or science becomes distorted and loses its crown of wisdom.

This is the theoretical significance of faith; its *moral significance* is equally important. Without faith the will of man is directed towards values that are near and immediately accessible because they belong to the world of actuality. He finds it hard, if not impossible, to conceive of a life radically different from his own or values radically different from those of the society in which he lives. But the man of faith has caught a vision of possibilities that go far beyond anything in the world of actuality, of a new life and other values which are richer and more blessed than those he knows around him. Thus, it is faith in the Christian sense which envisages a universal, "open" community in the place of the exclusive, "closed" societies in which men actually live. It sees the possibility of a more perfect love than that of even the best men. Moreover, it trusts in the mercy and power of God to bring into reality that universal community and that perfect love in the lives of men. In this way, faith transforms the moral will by setting before it higher and broader purposes than those of the self or the group and strengthening it in its efforts to realize those purposes. By subjecting the self to the will of God, faith rescues it from its self-centeredness and self-love. It frees the self from its fears and anxieties about itself and enables it to give itself in love to others. Thus, faith not only apprehends God as the transcendent Reality who gives meaning to all existence, but also awakens devotion to Him as the absolute Good which is the source of all the higher values of the moral life. . . .

THE REPUDIATION OF MORAL PHILOSOPHY: EMIL BRUNNER

If this is true, the objection of secular moral philosophers that Christian ethics is authoritarian and that Christian faith is incompatible with reason is unwarranted. But we must also consider the objection of some *Christian theologians* against any attempt of Christian moralists to appropriate the conclusions of moral philosophers. This objection arises in large part out of a reaction against the tendency to accommodate Christian truth to secular thought or to form a synthesis between them.

The reaction against these tendencies in recent Protestant theology has led to a virtual *repudiation of philosophy* by some Christian theologians. Like Tertullian, they ask, "What has Athens to do with Jerusalem?" Perhaps the best example of this attitude in Christian ethics is to be found in Emil Brunner's *The Divine Imperative*. Since Brunner has usually shown himself more hospitable than Barth to secular thought, it might be supposed that he would be sympathetic with the efforts of moral philosophers to deal with problems of conduct. But his conclusions with respect to "philosophical ethics" are almost entirely negative. After a very brief survey of a few systems of "philosophical ethics," he concludes that each system has its values but also its defects and that any kind of "synthetic ethics" is also unsatisfactory.[7] All "natural morality," he says, necessarily leads to contradictions because of the cleavage of human life due to sin. When man makes himself independent of God, God becomes to him an alien power and His commands seem external and arbitrary. Therefore, he tries to free himself from them by means of a purely rational morality of universal laws and falls into ethical legalism. Or he develops an ethic of happiness which regards life as good in itself apart from God. In both cases, "natural morality" is a product of man's sinful rebellion against God's will. Though there are "fragments" of truth in it, each fragment "by its isolation from the whole, is itself twisted, distorted into a caricature of the original," so that "the picture presented by natural ethics is a heap of ruins."[8] Thus, philosophical ethics is virtually useless to the Christian. But this does not matter, since Christian ethics needs no help from any other source. Its own answer to the questions raised by morality is all-sufficient. "Does the Christian faith," Brunner asks, "give *the* answer, the *only* answer, and the *whole* answer to the ethical problem?"[9] His reply is an uncompromising "Yes."

This negative attitude towards "philosophical ethics" is determined, in part, by Brunner's conception of Christian ethics. Obedience to God's will, he holds, requires only one thing: love of God as expressed in love of one's neighbor. But how are we to determine what *duties* love of our neighbor requires? Brunner replies that we cannot be guided by any "principle" in deciding what the divine command of love requires in a situation. In this sense, Christian ethics has no "content." Its "content" must be discovered anew in each situation by listening to the voice of the Spirit. . . .[10]

Now, the real question for the Christian is not whether moral philosophy has the whole truth but whether it has important insights that must be included in the truth. As we have said, secular philosophers have often made exaggerated claims for moral philosophy, insisting that reason can discover the highest good without the aid of faith. Christians must reject these claims. But this does not justify the conclusion that, because moral philosophy does not have *all* the truth, it has *none* of the truth. Although Brunner has pointed out defects or weaknesses in a number of ethical theories, it hardly justifies him in rejecting them altogether. It is also true that there are serious contradictions between the Hedonist's view that pleasure is the only good and Kant's view that the good will is both a good and the only unconditional good. But when we are faced by such a contradiction between two theories are we simply to throw up our hands and refuse to think further about the question? Or are we to try our best to decide whether one theory is right and the other wrong, or whether both are wrong, or whether, as is often the case, one is right in a certain respect and the other is right in another respect? If we take the former course and stop thinking about the problem, we shall never arrive at or even come closer to the truth, for the road to truth lies through the patient and critical examination of opposing views. If we take the latter course, we shall find ourselves involved in philosophical reflection with all its difficulties as well as its rewards. Anyone, Christian or otherwise, may refuse to become involved in it if he wishes, but if he does refuse he has no right to an opinion on the question whether the difficulties can be solved.

Thus, Brunner's criticisms of the weaknesses and contradictions in moral philosophy are not so much false as irrelevant. Like all branches of philosophy, ethics is a continuous, cumulative intellectual enterprise, and those who engage in that enterprise may hope to broaden their understanding of moral truth even if they do not arrive at final solutions of moral problems. The fact that there is error along with truth, chaff among the wheat, does not change this fact. Indeed, not the least fruitful part of philosophical reflection is that which consists in discriminating between error and truth.

THE CHRISTIAN'S NEED FOR MORAL PHILOSOPHY

We have attempted to show that the repudiation of "philosophical ethics" by theologians like Brunner is unjustified and that it is necessary for Christian moralists to appropriate valid insights of moral philosophers concerning duty and value if their interpretation of Christian ethics is to be adequate. "But," it may be asked, "are not Christian faith and love sufficient? If we say that they must be supplemented with principles derived from non-Christian moralists, do we not admit that Christian ethics is imperfect?"

While Christian faith and love are an adequate *basis* for all morality, they do not by themselves provide the whole *content* of morality. This does not imply that Christian ethics is imperfect. Christian ethics was never intended to be an "ethical theory" which would solve in a systematic and comprehensive manner all the problems of morality, as it was not intended to be a new code of laws specifying what men should or should not do in every kind of situation. It is part of the Gospel, and the Gospel came into the world as a religion, not a theory. Unlike Judaism and Hinduism, which are religious cultures, the Gospel was concerned almost exclusively with the relation between man and God and between man and his neighbor in the Kingdom of God. Consequently, its ethic was purely religious and had little or nothing to say about the social institutions, civic virtues, and values of culture. As we have seen, this has been the source of many difficulties and disagreements among Christians who have had to concern themselves with problems of society. If they were not to withdraw from the world, they could not avoid these problems, and yet they could find no solutions of them in the Gospel. Therefore, they were forced to look for solutions wherever they could find them. It was no accident that from the second century they went to the best social and political philosophy which was available to them and that they have continued to do so ever since.

In short, since Christian ethics defines the right relationship between man and God and between man and his neighbor, it provides the *adequate foundation* of any morality which is to stand the test of life. To hear Jesus' words and follow him is to have one's house built upon a rock. But Christians have the *responsibility of building* upon this foundation the best and fullest lives they can, using the materials of human nature and shaping them with the help of reason and experience. In this process of building, moral philosophy, like literature and history, is indispensable to them because it contains the wisdom of serious and thoughtful men during more than two thousand years.

NOTES

1. H. Bergson, *The Two Sources of Morality and Religion* (New York: Holt, 1935), p. 57.
2. William Temple, *Nature, Man and God* (London: Macmillan, 1940), Lecture 12.
3. I. Kant, *The Metaphysics of Morals*, tr. by T. K. Abbott in *Kant's Theory of Ethics* (London: Longmans, Green, 1909), p. 66.
4. Ibid., p. 72.
5. R. Niebuhr, *The Nature and Destiny of Man* (New York: Scribners, 1941) I, p. 158.
6. F. H. Bradley, *Appearance and Reality* (New York: Macmillan, 1893), p. XIV.
7. *The Divine Imperative*, copyright, 1947, by W. L. Jenkins (The Westminster Press), p. 43.
8. Ibid., p. 67.
9. Ibid., p. 51.
10. Ibid., p. 111.

THE SACRIFICE OF ISAAC
GENESIS 22:1-19

The dialogue between Abraham and God is recorded in the Old Testament, *Genesis* 22:1-24. God had promised Abraham that his descendants would occupy the Promised Land, yet God calls upon Abraham to sacrifice his son, Isaac. Abraham does not ask how God will fulfill his promise if his only son is to be sacrificed, but prepares to kill Isaac without question. God, in the form of an angel, intervenes in the last moment telling Abraham that his fear of God is enough, and as a reward for Abraham's unquestioning obedience, God promises that all nations will be blessed by the descendants of Abraham. Excerpt from *The Jerusalem Bible*, copyright © 1966 by Darton, Longman & Todd, Ltd. and Doubleday and Company, Inc. Used by permission of the publisher.

It happened some time later that God put Abraham to the test. 'Abraham, Abraham' he called. 'Here I am' he replied. 'Take your son,' God said, 'your only child Isaac, whom you love, and go to the land of Moriah. There you shall offer him as a burnt offering, on a mountain I will point out to you.'

Rising early next morning Abraham saddled his ass and took with him two of his servants and his son Isaac. He chopped wood for the burnt offering and started on his journey to the place God had pointed out to him. On the third day Abraham looked up and saw the place in the distance. Then Abraham said to his servants, 'Stay here with the donkey. The boy and I will go over there; we will worship and come back to you.'

Abraham took the wood for the burnt offering, loaded it on Isaac, and carried in his own hands the fire and the knife. Then the two of them set out together. Isaac spoke to his father Abraham, 'Father' he said. 'Yes, my son,' he replied. 'Look,' he said 'here are the fire and the wood, but where is the lamb for the burnt offering?' Abraham answered, 'My son, God himself will provide the lamb for the burnt offering'. Then the two of them went on together.

When they arrived at the place God had pointed out to him, Abraham built an altar there, and arranged the wood. Then he bound his son Isaac, and put him on the altar on top of the wood. Abraham stretched out his hand and seized the knife to kill his son.

But the angel of Yahweh called to him from heaven. 'Abraham, Abraham' he said. 'I am here' he replied. 'Do not raise your hand against the boy' the angel said. 'Do not harm him, for now I know you fear God. You have not refused me your son, your only son.' Then looking up, Abraham saw a ram caught by its horns in a bush. Abraham took the ram and offered it as a burnt-offering in place of his son. Abraham called this place 'Yahweh provides,' and hence the saying today: On the mountain Yahweh provides.

The angel of Yahweh called Abraham a second time from heaven. 'I swear by my own self—it is Yahweh who speaks—because you have done this, because you have not refused me your son, your only son, I will shower blessings on you, I will make your descendants as many as the stars of heaven and the grains of sand on the seashore. Your descendants shall gain possession of the gates of their enemies. All the nations of the earth shall bless themselves by your descendants, as a reward for your obedience.'

Abraham went back to his servants, and together they set out for Beersheba, and he settled in Beersheba.

Sören Kierkegaard 75
IS THERE SUCH A THING AS A TELEOLOGICAL SUSPENSION OF THE ETHICAL?

Sören Kierkegaard was born in Copenhagen on May 5, 1813, and died there at the age of 42. He spent most of his life in his native city and studied philosophy and theology at the University of Copenhagen from 1830 to 1840. A philosopher and a Protestant theologian, Kierkegaard is regarded as the founder of modern existentialism. Many of his writings appeared under various pseudonyms. *Fear and Trembling,* from which the following selection is taken, is one such work, written under the name Johannes de Silentio. It contains some of the ideas that are at the center of Kierkegaard's thought: True faith means also the acceptance of what is "absurd" because God may require us to behave in ways that are immoral by rational standards. Abraham, who obeyed without questions and without an attempt to understand God's command to kill his only son, represents Kierkegaard's religious ideal. He is the "knight of faith" because he took the "leap of faith"—a dramatically subjective choice unsupported by either rational understanding or the guarantee that the action reflects God's will. From "Problemata," Problem 1 in Sören Kierkegaard, *Fear and Trembling and The Sickness unto Death,* transl. by Walter Lowrie (copyright 1941, 1954 by Princeton University Press; Princeton Paperback, 1968), pp. 64–77. Reprinted by permission of Princeton University Press.

PROBLEM I

The ethical as such is the universal, and as the universal it applies to everyone, which may be expressed from another point of view by saying that it applies every instant. It reposes immanently in itself, it has nothing without itself which is its *telos*,[1] but is itself *telos* for everything outside it, and when this has been incorporated by the ethical it can go no further. Conceived immediately as physical and psychical, the particular individual is the individual who has his *telos* in the universal, and his ethical task is to express himself constantly in it, to abolish his particularity in order to become the universal. As soon as the individual would assert himself in his particularity over against the universal he sins, and only by recognizing this can he again reconcile himself with the universal. Whenever the individual after he has entered the universal feels an impulse to assert himself as the particular, he is in temptation *(Anfechtung),* and he can labor himself out of this only by penitently abandoning himself as the particular in the universal. If this be the highest thing that can be said of man and of his existence, then the ethical has the same character as man's eternal blessedness, which to all eternity and at every instant is his *telos,* since it would be a contradiction to say that this might be abandoned (i.e. teleologically suspended), inasmuch as this is no sooner suspended than it is forfeited, whereas in other cases what is suspended is not forfeited but is preserved precisely in that higher thing which is its *telos*.[2]

If such be the case, then Hegel is right when in his chapter on "The Good and the Conscience,"[3] he characterizes man merely as the particular and regards this character as "a moral form of evil" which is to be annulled in the teleology of the moral, so that the individual who remains in this stage is either sinning or subjected to temptation *(Anfechtung)*. On the other hand, Hegel is wrong in talking of faith, wrong in not protesting loudly and clearly against the fact that Abraham enjoys honor and glory as the father of faith, whereas he ought to be prosecuted and convicted of murder.

For faith is this paradox, that the particular is higher than the universal—yet in such a way, be it observed, that the movement repeats itself, and that consequently the individual, after having been in the universal, now as the particular isolates himself as higher than the universal. If this be not faith, then Abraham is lost, then faith has never existed in the world . . . because it has always existed. For if the ethical (i.e. the moral) is the highest thing, and if nothing incommensurable remains in man in any other way but as the evil (i.e. the particular which has to be expressed in the universal), then one needs no other categories besides those which the Greeks possessed or which by consistent thinking can be derived from them. This fact Hegel ought not to have concealed, for after all he was acquainted with Greek thought.

One not infrequently hears it said by men who for lack of losing themselves in studies are absorbed in phrases that a light shines upon the Christian world whereas a darkness broods over paganism. This utterance has always seemed strange to me, inasmuch as every profound thinker and every serious artist is even in our day rejuvenated by the eternal youth of the Greek race. Such an utterance may be explained by the consideration that people do not know what they ought to say but only that they must say something. It is quite right for one to say that paganism did not possess faith, but if with this one is to have said something, one must be a little clearer about what one understands by faith, since otherwise one falls back into such phrases. To explain the whole of existence and faith along with it, without having a conception of what faith is, is easy, and that man does not make the poorest calculation in life who reckons upon admiration when he possesses such an explanation; for, as Boileau says, "*un sot trouve toujours un plus sot qui l'admire.*"

Faith is precisely this paradox, that the individual as the particular is higher than the universal, is justified over against it, is not subordinate but superior—yet in such a way, be it observed, that it is the particular individual who, after he has been subordinated as the particular to the universal, now through the universal becomes the individual who as the particular is superior to the universal, for the fact that the individual as the particular stands in an absolute relation to the absolute. This position cannot be mediated, for all mediation comes about precisely by virtue of the universal; it is and remains to all eternity a paradox, inaccessible to thought. And yet faith is this paradox—or else (these are the logical deductions which I would beg the reader to have *in mente* at every point, though it would be too prolix for me to reiterate them on every occasion)—or else there never has been faith . . . precisely because it always has been. In other words, Abraham is lost.

That for the particular individual this paradox may easily be mistaken for a temptation *(Anfechtung)* is indeed true, but one ought not for this reason to conceal it. That the whole constitution of many persons may be such that this paradox repels them is indeed true, but one ought not for this reason to make faith something different in order to be able to possess it, but ought rather to admit that one does not possess it, whereas those who possess faith should take care to set up certain criteria so that one might distinguish the paradox from a temptation *(Anfechtung)*.

Now the story of Abraham contains such a teleological suspension of the ethical. There have not been lacking clever pates and profound investigators who have found analogies to it. Their wisdom is derived from the pretty proposition that at bottom everything is the same. If one will look a little more closely, I have not much doubt that in the whole world one will not find a single analogy (except a later instance which proves nothing), if it stands fast that Abraham is the representative of faith, and that faith is normally expressed in him whose life is not merely the most paradoxical that can be thought but so paradoxical that it cannot be thought at all. He acts by virtue of the absurd, for it is precisely absurd that he as the particular is higher than the universal. This paradox cannot be mediated; for as soon as he begins to do this he has to admit that he was in temptation *(Anfechtung)*, and if such was the case, he never gets to the point of sacrificing Isaac, or, if he has sacrificed Isaac, he must turn back repentantly to the universal. By virtue of the absurd he gets Isaac again. Abraham is therefore at no instant a tragic hero but something quite different, either a murderer or a believer. The middle term which saves the tragic hero, Abraham has not. Hence it is that I can understand the tragic hero but cannot understand Abraham, though in a certain crazy sense I admire him more than all other men.

Abraham's relation to Isaac, ethically speaking, is quite simply expressed by saying that a father shall love his son more dearly than himself. Yet within its own compass the ethical has various gradations. Let us see whether in this story there is to be found any higher expression for the ethical such as would ethically explain his conduct, ethically justify him in suspending the ethical obligation toward his son, without in this search going beyond the teleology of the ethical.

When an undertaking in which a whole nation is concerned is hindered,[4] when such an enterprise is brought to a standstill by the disfavor of heaven, when the angry deity sends a calm which mocks all efforts, when the seer performs his heavy task and proclaims that the deity demands a young maiden as a sacrifice—then will the father heroically make the sacrifice. He will magnanimously conceal his pain, even though he might wish that he were "the lowly man who dares to weep,"[5] not the king who must act royally. And though solitary pain forces its way into his breast, he has only three confidants among the people, yet soon the whole nation will be cognizant of his pain, but also cognizant of his exploit, that for the welfare of the whole he was willing to sacrifice her, his daughter, the lovely young maiden. O charming bosom! O beautiful cheeks! O bright golden hair! (v.687). And the daughter will affect him by her tears, and the father will turn his face away, but the hero will raise the knife.—When the report of this reaches the ancestral home, then will the beautiful maidens of Greece blush with enthusiasm, and if the daughter was betrothed, her true love will not be angry but be proud of sharing in the father's deed, because the maiden belonged to him more feelingly than to the father.

When the intrepid judge[6] who saved Israel in the hour of need in one breath binds himself and God by the same vow, then herocially the young maiden's jubilation, the beloved daughter's joy, he will turn to sorrow, and with her all Israel will lament her maiden youth; but every free-born man will understand, and every stout-hearted woman will admire Jephtha, and every maiden in Israel will wish to act as did his daughter. For what good would it do if Jephtha were victorious by reason of his vow if he did not keep it? Would not the victory again be taken from the nation?

When a son is forgetful of his duty,[7] when the state entrusts the father with the sword of justice, when the laws require punishment at the hand of the father, then will the father heroically forget that the guilty one is his son, he will magnanimously conceal his pain, but there will not be a single one among the people, not even the son, who will not admire the father, and whenever the law of Rome is interpreted, it will be remembered that many interpreted it more learnedly, but none so gloriously as Brutus.

If, on the other hand, while a favorable wind bore the fleet on with swelling sails to its goal, Agamemnon had sent that messenger who fetched Iphigenia in order to be sacrificed; if Jephtha, without being bound by any vow which decided the fate of the nation, had said to his daughter, "Bewail now thy virginity for the space of two months, for I will sacrifice thee"; if Brutus had had a righteous son and yet would have ordered the lictors to execute him—who would have understood them? If these three men had replied to the query why they did it by saying, "It is a trial in which we are tested," would people have understood them better?

When Agamemnon, Jephtha, Brutus at the decisive moment heroically overcome their pain, have heroically lost the beloved and have merely to accomplish the outward sacrifice, then there never will be a noble soul in the world who will not shed tears of compassion for their pain and of admiration for their exploit. If, on the other hand, these three men at the decisive moment were to adjoin to their heroic conduct this little word, "But for all that it will not come to pass," who then would understand them? If as an explanation they added, "This we believe by virtue of the absurd," who would understand them better? For who would not easily understand that it was absurd, but who would understand that one could then believe it?

The difference between the tragic hero and Abraham is clearly evident. The tragic hero still remains within the ethical. He lets one expression of the ethical find its *telos* in a higher expression of the ethical; the ethical relation between father and son, or daughter and father, he reduces to a sentiment which has its dialectic in its relation to the idea of morality. Here there can be no question of a teleological suspension of the ethical itself.

With Abraham the situation was different. By his act he overstepped the ethical entirely and possessed a higher *telos* outside of it, in relation to which he suspended the former. For I should very much like to know how one would bring Abraham's act into relation with the universal, and whether it is possible to discover any connection whatever between what Abraham did and the universal . . . except the fact that he transgressed it. It was not for the sake of saving a people, not to maintain the idea of the state, that Abraham did this, and not in order to reconcile angry deities. If there could be a question of the deity being angry, he was angry only with Abraham, and Abraham's whole action stands in no relation to the universal, is a purely private undertaking. Therefore, whereas the tragic hero is great by reason of his moral virtue, Abraham is great by reason of a purely personal virtue. In Abraham's life there is no higher expression for the ethical than this, that the father shall love his son. Of the ethical in the sense of morality there can be no question in this instance. In so far as the universal was present, it was indeed cryptically present in Isaac, hidden as it were in Isaac's loins, and must therefore cry out with Isaac's mouth, "Do it not! Thou art bringing everything to naught."

Why then did Abraham do it? For God's sake, and (in complete identity with this) for his own sake. He did it for God's sake because God required this proof of his faith; for his own sake he did it in order that he might furnish the proof. The unity of these two points of view is perfectly expressed by the word which has always been used to characterize this situation: it is a trial, a temptation *(Fristelse)*.[8] A temptation—but what does that mean? What ordinarily tempts a man is that which would keep him from doing his duty, but in this case the temptation is itself the ethical . . . which would keep him from doing God's will. But what then is duty? Duty is precisely the expression for God's will.

Here is evident the necessity of a new category if one would understand Abraham. Such a relationship to the deity paganism did not know. The tragic hero does not enter into any private relationship with the deity, but for him the ethical is the divine, hence the paradox implied in his situation can be mediated in the universal.

Abraham cannot be mediated, and the same thing can be expressed also by saying that he cannot talk. So soon as I talk I express the universal, and if I do not do so, no one can understand me. Therefore if Abraham would express himself in terms of the universal, he must say that his situation is a temptation *(Anfechtung)*, for he has no higher expression for that universal which stands above the universal which he transgresses.

Therefore, though Abraham arouses my admiration, he at the same time appalls me. He who denies himself and sacrifices himself for duty gives up the finite in order to grasp the infinite, and that man is secure enough. The tragic hero gives up the certain for the still more certain; and the eye of the beholder rests upon him confidently. But he who gives up the universal in order to grasp something still higher which is not the universal—what is he doing? Is it possible this can be anything else but a temptation *(Anfechtung)*? And if it be possible . . . but the individual was mistaken—what can save him? He suffers all the pain of the tragic hero, he brings to naught his joy in the world, he renounces everything . . . and perhaps at the same instant debars himself from the sublime joy which to him was so precious that he would purchase it at any price. Him the beholder cannot understand nor let his eye rest confidently upon him. Perhaps it is not possible to do what the believer proposes, since it is indeed unthinkable. Or if it could be done, but if the individual had misunderstood the deity—what can save him? The tragic hero has need of tears and claims them, and where is the envious eye which would be so barren that it could not weep with Agamemnon; but where is the man with a soul so bewildered that he would have the presumption to weep for Abraham? The tragic hero accomplishes his act at a definite instant in time, but in the course of time he does something not less significant, he visits the man whose soul is beset with sorrow, whose breast for stifled sobs cannot draw breath, whose thoughts pregnant with tears weigh heavily upon him, to him he makes his appearance, dissolves the sorcery of sorrow, loosens his corslet, coaxes forth his tears by the fact that in his sufferings the sufferer forgets his own. One cannot weep over Abraham. One approaches him with a *horror religiosus,* as Israel approached Mount Sinai.—If then the solitary man who ascends Mount Moriah, which with its peak rises heaven-high above the plain of Aulis, if he be not a somnambulist who walks securely above the abyss while he who is stationed at the foot of the mountain and is looking on trembles with fear and out of reverence and dread dare not even call to him—if this man is disordered in his mind, if he had made a mistake! Thanks and thanks again to him who proffers to the man whom the sorrows of life have assaulted and left naked—proffers to him the figleaf of the word with which he can cover his wretchedness. Thanks be to thee, great Shakespeare, who art able to express everything, absolutely everything, precisely as it is—and yet why didst thou never pronounce this pang? Didst thou perhaps reserve it to thyself—like the loved one whose name one cannot endure that the world should mention? For the poet purchases the power of words, the power of uttering all the dread secrets of others, at the price of a little secret he is unable to utter . . . and a poet is not an apostle, he casts out devils only by the power of the devil.

But now when the ethical is thus teleologically suspended, how does the individual exist in whom it is suspended? He exists as the particular in opposition to the universal. Does he then sin? For this is the form of sin, as seen in the idea. Just as the infant, though it does not sin, because it is not as such yet conscious of its existence, yet its existence is sin, as seen in the idea, and the ethical makes its demands upon it every instant. If one denies that this form can be repeated [in the adult] in such a way that it is not sin, then the sentence of condemnation is pronounced upon Abraham. How then did Abraham exist? He believed. This is the paradox which keeps him upon the sheer edge and which he cannot make clear to any other man, for the paradox is that he as the individual puts himself in an absolute relation to the absolute. Is he justified in doing this? His justification is once more the paradox; for if he is justified, it is not by virtue of anything universal, but by virtue of being the particular individual.

How then does the individual assure himself that he is justified? It is easy enough to level down the whole of existence to the idea of the state or the idea of society. If one does this, one can also mediate easily enough, for then one does not encounter at all the paradox that the individual as the individual is higher than the universal—which I can aptly express also by the thesis of Pythagoras, that the uneven numbers are more perfect than the even. If in our age one occasionally hears a rejoinder which is pertinent to the paradox, it is likely to be the following effect: "It is to be judged by the result." A hero who has become a σκάνδαλον[9] to his contemporaries because they are conscious that he is a paradox who cannot make himself intelligible, will cry out defiantly to his generation, "The result will surely prove that I am justified." In our age we hear this cry rather seldom, for as our age, to its disadvantage, does not produce heroes, it has also the advantage of producing few caricatures. When in our age one hears this saying, "It is to be judged according to the result," a man is at once clear as to who it is he has the honor of talking with. Those who talk thus are a numerous tribe, whom I will denominate by the common name of *Docents*.[10] In their thoughts they live secure in existence, they have a *solid* position and *sure* prospects in a well-ordered state, they have centuries and even millenniums between them and the concussions of existence, they do not fear that such things could recur—for what would the police say to that! and the newspapers! Their lifework is to judge the great, and to judge them according to the result. Such behavior toward the great betrays a strange mixture of arrogance and misery: of arrogance because they think they are called to be judges; of misery because they do not feel that their lives are even in the remotest degree akin to the great. Surely a man who possesses even a little *erectioris ingenii* [of the higher way of thinking] has not become entirely a cold and clammy mollusk, and when he approaches what is great it can never escape his mind that from the creation of the world it has been customary for the result to come last, and that, if one would truly learn anything from great actions, one must pay attention precisely to the beginning. In case he who should act were to judge himself according to the result, he would never get to the point of beginning. Even though the result may give joy to the whole world, it cannot help the hero, for he would get to know the result only when the whole thing was over, and it was not by this he became a hero, but he was such for the fact that he began.

Moreover, the result (inasmuch as it is the answer of finiteness to the infinite query) is in its dialectic entirely heterogeneous with the existence of the hero. Or is it possible to prove that Abraham was justified in assuming the position of the individual with relation to the universal . . . for the fact that he got Isaac by *miracle?* If Abraham had actually sacrificed Isaac, would he then have been less justified?

But people are curious about the result, as they are about the result in a book—they want to know nothing about dread, distress, the paradox. They flirt aesthetically with the result, it comes just as unexpectedly but also just as easily as a prize in the lottery; and when they have heard the result they are edified. And yet no robber of temples condemned to hard labor behind iron bars, is so base a criminal as the man who pillages the holy, and even Judas who sold his Master for thirty pieces of silver is not more despicable than the man who sells greatness.

It is abhorrent to my soul to talk inhumanly about greatness, to let it loom darkly at a distance in an indefinite form, to make out that it is great without making the human character of it evident— wherewith it ceases to be great. For it is not what happens to me that makes me great, but it is what I do, and there is surely no one who thinks that a man became great because he won the great prize in the lottery. Even if a man were born in humble circumstances, I would require of him nevertheless that he should not be so inhuman toward himself as not to be able to think of the King's castle except at a remote distance, dreaming vaguely of its greatness and wanting at the same time to exalt it and also to abolish it by the fact that he exalted it meanly. I require of him that he should be man enough to step forward confidently and worthily even in that place. He should not be unmanly enough to desire impudently to offend everybody by rushing straight from the street into the King's hall. By that he loses more than the King. On the contrary, he should find joy in observing every rule of propriety with a glad and confident enthusiasm which will make him frank and fearless. This is only a symbol, for the difference here remarked upon is only a very imperfect expression for spiritual distance. I require of every man that he should not think so inhumanly of himself as not to dare to enter those palaces where not merely the memory of the elect abides but where the elect themselves abide. He should not press forward impudently and impute to them kinship with himself; on the contrary, he should be blissful every time he bows before them, but he should be frank and confident and always be something more than a charwoman, for if he will not be more, he will never gain entrance. And what will help him is precisely the dread and distress by which the great are tried, for otherwise, if he has a bit of pith in him, they will merely arouse his justified envy. And what distance alone makes great, what people would make great by empty and hollow phrases, that they themselves reduce to naught.

Who was ever so great as that blessed woman, the Mother of God, the Virgin Mary? And yet how do we speak of her? We say that she was highly favored among women. And if it did not happen strangely that those who hear are able to think as inhumanly as those who talk, every young girl might well ask, "Why was not I too the highly favored?" And if I had nothing else to say, I would not dismiss such a question as stupid, for when it is a matter of favor, abstractly considered, everyone is equally entitled to it. What they leave out is the distress, the dread, the paradox. My thought is as pure as that of anyone, and the thought of the man who is able to think such things will surely become pure—and if this be not so, he may expect the dreadful; for he who once has evoked these images cannot be rid of them again, and if he sins against them, they avenge themselves with quiet wrath, more terrible than the vociferousness of ten ferocious reviewers. To be sure, Mary bore the child miraculously, but it came to pass with her after the manner of women, and that season is one of dread, distress and paradox. To be sure, the angel was a ministering spirit, but it was not a servile spirit which obliged her by saying to the other young maidens of Israel, "Despise not Mary. What befalls her is the extraordinary." But the Angel came only to Mary, and no one could understand her. After all, what woman was so mortified as Mary? And is it not true in this instance also that one whom God blesses He curses in the same breath? This the spirit's interpretation of Mary, and she is not (as it shocks me to say, but shocks me still more to think that they have thoughtlessly and coquettishly interpreted her thus) —she is not a fine lady who sits in state and plays with an infant god. Nevertheless, when she says, "Behold the handmaid of the Lord"—then she is great, and I think it will not be found difficult to explain why she became the Mother of God. She has no need of worldly admiration, any more than Abraham has need of tears, for she was not a heroine, and he was not a hero, but both of them became greater than such, not at all because they were exempted from distress and torment and paradox, but they became great through these.[11]

It is great when the poet, presenting his tragic hero before the admiration of men, dares to say, "Weep for him, for he deserves it." For it is great to deserve the tears of those who are worthy to shed tears. It is great that the poet dares to hold the crowd in check, dares to castigate men, requiring that every man examine himself whether he be worthy to weep for the hero. For the waste-water of blubberers is a degradation of the holy.—But greater than all this it is that the knight of faith dares to say even to the noble man who would weep for him, "Weep not for me, but weep for thyself."

One is deeply moved, one longs to be back in those beautiful times, a sweet yearning conducts one to the desired goal, to see Christ wandering in the promised land. One forgets the dread, the distress, the paradox. Was it so easy a matter not to be mistaken? Was it not dreadful that this man who walks among the others—was it not dreadful that He was God? Was it not dreadful to sit at table with Him? Was it so easy a matter to become an Apostle? But the result, eighteen hundred years—that is a help, it helps to the shabby deceit wherewith one deceives oneself and others. I do not feel the courage to wish to be contemporary with such events, but hence I do not judge severely those who were mistaken, nor think meanly of those who saw aright.

I return, however, to Abraham. Before the result, either Abraham was every minute a murderer, or we are confronted by a paradox which is higher than all mediation.

The story of Abraham contains therefore a teleological suspension of the ethical. As the individual he became higher than the universal. This is the paradox which does not permit of mediation. It is just as inexplicable how he got into it as it is inexplicable how he remained in it. If such is not the position of Abraham, then he is not even a tragic hero but a murderer. To want to continue to call him the father of faith, to talk of this to people who do not concern themselves with anything but words, is thoughtless. A man can become a tragic hero by his own powers—but not a knight of faith. When a man enters upon the way, in a certain sense the hard way of the tragic hero, many will be able to give him counsel; to him who follows the narrow way of faith no one can give counsel, him no one can understand. Faith is a miracle, and yet no man is excluded from it; for that in which all human life is unified is passion,* and faith is a passion.

---

*Lessing has somewhere given expression to a similar thought from a purely aesthetic point of view. What he would show expressly in this passage is that sorrow too can find a witty expression. To this end he quotes a rejoinder of the unhappy English king, Edward II. In contrast to this he quotes from Diderot a story of a peasant woman and a rejoinder of hers. Then he continues: "That too was wit, and the wit of a peasant at that; but the situation made it inevitable. Consequently one must not seek to find the excuse for the witty expressions of pain and of sorrow in the fact that the person who uttered them was a superior person, well educated, intelligent, and witty withal, *for the passions make all men again equal*—but the explanation is to be found in the fact that in all probability everyone would have said the same thing in the same situation. The thought of a peasant woman a queen could have had and must have had, just as what the king said in that instance a peasant too would have been able to say and doubtless would have said." Cf. *Sämtliche Werke*, XXX. p. 223[12]

TRANSLATOR'S NOTES

**Chapter 1
RELIGION AND
MORALITY**

1. A Greek word meaning end or goal—which S.K. writes with Greek letters but I transliterate because it is of such common occurrence, and also because it is in the way of becoming an English word.
2. This is the conception of the ethical which is stressed in the Second Part of *Either/Or*. Perhaps Schrempf is right in affirming that what caused S.K. unnecessary agony was his acceptance of the Hegelian notion of the relation between the universal and the particular.
3. Cf. *Philosophie des Rechts*, 2nd ed. (1840) §§129-141 and Table of Contents p. xix.
4. The Trojan war. When the Greek fleet was unable to set sail from Aulis because of an adverse wind the seer Calchas announced that King Agamemnon had offended Artemis and that the goddess demanded his daughter Iphigenia as a sacrifice of expiation.
5. See Euripides, *Iphigenia in Aulis*, v. 448 in Wilster's translation. Agamemnon says, "How lucky to be born in lowly station where one may be allowed to weep." The confidants mentioned below are Menelaus, Calchas and Ulysses. Cf. v. 107.
6. Jephtha. Judges 11:30-40.
7. The sons of Brutus, while their father was Consul, took part in a conspiracy to restore the king Rome had expelled and Brutus ordered them to be put to death.
8. This is temptation in the sense we ordinarily attach to the word. For temptation in a higher sense *(Anfaegtelse)* I have in the translation of other books used the phrase "trial of temptation." Professor Swenson, in an important passage in the *Postscript*, preferred to use the German word *Anfechtung*. In this work I have used "temptation" and added the German word in parentheses. The distinction between the two sorts of temptation is plainly indicated by S.K. in this paragraph.
9. This is the Scriptural word which we translate by "offense" or "stumbling block." Only Mr. Dru has preferred to use the identical word "scandal."
10. *Docents* and *Privatdocents* (both of them German titles for subordinate teachers in the universities) were very frequently the objects of S.K.'s satire. He spoke more frequently of "the professor" after Martensen had attained that title.
11. It would be interesting and edifying to make an anthology of the passages in which S.K. speaks of the Blessed Virgin; for surely no Protestant was ever so much engrossed in this theme, and perhaps no Catholic has appreciated more profoundly the unique position of Mary.
12. In *Auszüge aus den Literatur-Briefen*, 81st letter, in Maltzahn's ed. Vol. vi, pp. 205*ff*.

Martin Buber
ON THE SUSPENSION OF THE ETHICAL

Martin Buber (1878–1965) was an Austrian-born existentialist philosopher and Judaic scholar whose prolific writings on humanism and the cultural significance of Judaism have attracted worldwide readership. In this selection, from his *Eclipse of God: Studies in the Relation Between Religion and Philosophy* (1952), Buber examines Kierkegaard's conclusions about the story of Abraham and Isaac in the light of other Old Testament writings as well as in the context of the twentieth century when "false absolutes rule over the soul" and in their name "honest men lie and compassionate men torture." "On the Suspension of the Ethical" from *Eclipse of God* (hardbound edition) by Martin Buber. Copyright 1952 by Harper & Row, Publishers, Inc. Reprinted by permission of the publisher.

The first book of Kierkegaard's that I read as a young man was *Fear and Trembling*, which is built entirely upon the Biblical narrative of the sacrifice of Isaac. I still think of that hour to-day because it was then that I received the impulse to reflect upon the categories of the ethical and the religious in their relation to each other.

Through the example of the temptation of Abraham this book sets forth the idea that there is a "teleological suspension of the ethical," that the validity of a moral duty can be at times suspended in accordance with the purpose of something higher, of the highest. When God commands one to murder his son, the immorality of the immoral is suspended for the duration of this situation. What is more, that which is otherwise purely evil is for the duration of this situation purely good because it has become pleasing to God. In the place of the universal and the universally valid steps something which is founded exclusively in the personal relation between God and "the Single One." But just through this the ethical, the universal and the universally valid, is relativized. Its values and laws are banished from the absolute into the relative; for that which is a duty in the sphere of the ethical possesses no absoluteness as soon as it is confronted with the absolute duty toward God. "But what is duty?" asks Kierkegaard. "Duty is indeed just the expression for God's will!" In other words, God establishes the order of good and evil, and breaks through it where He wishes. He does so from person to person, that is, in direct personal relation with the individual.

On the deadly seriousness of this "from person to person" Kierkegaard has, it is true, laid the greatest possible stress. He has declared most clearly that this trial will only be laid upon one who is worthy of being called God's chosen one. "But who," he asks, "is such a one?" In particular, he assures us time and again that he himself does not have this courage of faith which is necessary to plunge confidently, with closed eyes, into the absurd. It is impossible for him to perform the paradoxical movement of faith that Abraham performed. One must keep in mind, however, the fact that Kierkegaard also states that he has fought to become "the Single One" in the strictest sense of the term but has not attained it and the fact that he nonetheless once considered having the words "that Single One" placed upon his grave. There are many indications that when he described how Abraham gave up his son and nonetheless believed that he would not lose him (so Kierkegaard understood the event), he had in mind the day, a little more than a year before, when he himself broke his engagement with his beloved and yet thought that he would be able to preserve it in a higher, incomprehensible dimension. In the way of this union (he once explained) "there stood a divine protest"* though he had, to be sure, no lasting confidence in this idea. So little confidence had he, in fact, that in the year of the publication of *Fear and Trembling* he was able to set down the sentence, "Had I had faith, I would have remained with her."

The event is here removed out of the situation between Abraham and God, in which God breaks through the ethical order which He Himself established, into a sphere where what happens takes place in a much less unequivocal fashion than in the Biblical narrative. "That which the Single One is to understand by Isaac," says Kierkegaard, "can be decided only by and for himself." That means, clearly and precisely, that he does not learn it, at least not unmistakably, from God. God demands a sacrifice of him, but it is left to the Single One to interpret what that sacrifice is. His interpretation will always be determined by his life-circumstances in this hour. How differently the Biblical voice speaks here! "Thy son, thine only one, whom thou lovest, Isaac." There is nothing here to interpret. The man who hears learns entirely what is demanded of him; the God who speaks proposes no riddles.

But we still have not arrived at the decisive problematics. This first appears to us when Kierkegaard compares his Abraham with Agamemnon, who is getting ready to sacrifice Iphigenia. Agamemnon is the tragic hero, who is called upon by "the universal" to sacrifice for the welfare of his people. He, therefore, "remains within the borders of the ethical," which Abraham, "the knight of faith," crosses over. Everything depends upon this, that Abraham crosses over them with the paradoxical movement of faith. Otherwise all becomes a demonic temptation (*"Anfechtung"*), the readiness to sacrifice a readiness to murder, and "Abraham is lost." This also is decided

---

*She also stated once, much later, that he had sacrificed her to God.

in "absolute isolation." "The knight of faith," says Kierkegaard, "is left to his own resources, single and alone, and therein lies the dreadful."

This is true insofar as there is no one on earth who can help him to come to a decision and to perform "the movement of infinity." But Kierkegaard here takes for granted something that cannot be taken for granted even in the world of Abraham, much less in ours. He does not take into consideration the fact that the problematics of the decision of faith is preceded by the problematics of the hearing itself. Who is it whose voice one hears? For Kierkegaard it is self-evident because of the Christian tradition in which he grew up that he who demands the sacrifice is none other than God. But for the Bible, at least for the Old Testament, it is not without further question self-evident. Indeed a certain "instigation" to a forbidden action is even ascribed in one place to God (2 Samuel 24:1) and in another to Satan (1 Chronicles 21:1).

Abraham, to be sure, could not confuse with another the voice which once bade him leave his homeland and which he at that time recognized as the voice of God without the speaker saying to him who he was. And God did indeed "tempt" him. Through the extremest demand He drew forth the innermost readiness to sacrifice out of the depths of Abraham's being, and He allowed this readiness to grow to the full intention to act. He thus made it possible for Abraham's relation to Him, God, to become wholly real. But then, when no further hindrance stood between the intention and the deed, He contented Himself with Abraham's fulfilled readiness and prevented the action.

It can happen, however, that a sinful man is uncertain whether he does not have to sacrifice his (perhaps also very beloved) son to God for his sins (Micah 6:7). For Moloch imitates the voice of God. In contrast to this, God Himself demands of this as of every man (not of Abraham, His chosen one, but of you and me) nothing more than justice and love, and that he "walk humbly" with Him, with God (Micah 6:8)—in other words, not much more than the fundamental ethical.

Where, therefore, the "suspension" of the ethical is concerned, the question of questions which takes precedence over every other is: Are you really addressed by the Absolute or by one of his apes? It should be noted in this connection that, according to the report of the Bible, the divine voice which speaks to the Single One is the "voice of a thin silence" (1 Kings 19:21).* The voice of Moloch,

---

*A bold visual metaphor for an acoustical event: It is a silence, but not a thick and solid one, rather one that is of such veil-like thinness that the Word shines through it.

in contrast, usually prefers a mighty roaring. However, in our age especially, it appears to be extremely difficult to distinguish the one from the other.

Ours is an age in which the suspension of the ethical fills the world in a caricaturized form. The apes of the Absolute, to be sure, have always in the past bustled about on earth. Ever and ever again men are commanded from out of the darkness to sacrifice their Isaac. *Here* the sentence is valid, "That which the Single One is to understand by Isaac, can be decided only by and for himself." But stored away in men's hearts, there were in all those times images of the Absolute, partly pallid, partly crude, altogether false and yet true, fleeting as an image in a dream yet verified in eternity. Inadequate as this presence certainly was, insofar as one bore it concretely in mind one only needed to call on it in order not to succumb to the deception of the voices.

That is no longer so since, in Nietzsche's words, "God is dead," that is, realistically speaking, since the image-making power of the human heart has been in decline so that the spiritual pupil can no longer catch a glimpse of the appearance of the Absolute. False absolutes rule over the soul, which is no longer able to put them to flight through the image of the true. Everywhere, over the whole surface of the human world—in the East and in the West, from the left and from the right, they pierce unhindered through the level of the ethical and demand of you "the sacrifice." Time and again, when I ask well-conditioned young souls, "Why do you give up your dearest possession, your personal integrity?" they answer me, "Even this, this most difficult sacrifice, is the thing that is needed in order that. . . ." It makes no difference, "in order that equality may come" or "in order that freedom may come," it makes no difference! And they bring the sacrifice faithfully. In the realm of Moloch honest men lie and compassionate men torture. And they really and truly believe that brother-murder will prepare the way for brotherhood! There appears to be no escape from the most evil of all idolatry.

There is no escape from it until the new conscience of men has arisen that will summon them to guard with the innermost power of their souls against the confusion of the relative with the Absolute, that will enable them to see through illusion and to recognize this confusion for what it is. To penetrate again and again into the false absolute with an incorruptible, probing glance until one has discovered its limits, its limitedness—there is to-day perhaps no other way to reawaken the power of the pupil to glimpse the never-vanishing appearance of the Absolute.

William H. Bruening

ETHICS AND FAITH AGAIN: PROLEGOMENA TO THE END OF A DEBATE

William H. Bruening teaches philosophy at Purdue University at Fort Wayne, Indiana. He is also active in The Center for the Study of the Person at the same university. He is coeditor of this book; editor of *Self, Society, and the Search for Transcendence: An Introduction to Philosophy* (1974); author of *Ludwig Wittgenstein* (forthcoming); and coauthor, with Sheila Bruening, of *Sartre* (forthcoming). He has also published a number of articles in professional journals. Bruening's selection focuses on the debates concerning the relation of ethics to religion and looks at the views of three people who have taken a position on this issue: Bonhoeffer, Fletcher, and Dewey. The author argues that the debate is misplaced because ethics asks different questions than religion. He also argues that ethics has priority over religion when the two conflict, but that such conflict is by no means inevitable.

Philosophers have long been involved in discussing the relationships between philosophy and related disciplines, with the result that we have debates on the viability of traditional philosophy of nature in light of modern physics, of philosophical psychology in light of developments in psychology, or of moral philosophy in light of moral theology. These debates continue year after year with undiminished vigor and one gets the impression that they will never be resolved. To some extent one can tolerate a lack of definitive resolutions, yet it creates a certain uneasiness, especially in regards to the ethical debate. Although we can manage without resolving, for example, the philosophy of nature/modern physics debate, we cannot get along without a resolution to the moral philosophy/moral theology debate. The resolution of this debate seems more pressing because we are all required to make ethical decisions. The other debates, by comparison, tend to be a bit more academic or professional; they do not seem to demand immediate resolution.

The purpose of this paper is: (1) to investigate some views on the relationship between moral philosophy and moral theology; (2) to expose what seems to be the crux of the problem in relating them; and (3) to show that perhaps the debate concerning their relationship is misplaced at the outset.

The men chosen here do not necessarily represent the best defense possible for the views they take; but I think they may be considered as representative.

Dietrich Bonhoeffer's *Ethics*[1] represents what one might call a religious ethics or, more specifically, a Christian ethics. The starting point for such an ethics is the Christian God—the Biblical God.[2] And God is the starting point for man.

> Man at his origin knows only one thing: God. It is only in this unity of his knowledge of God that he knows of other men, of things, and of himself. He knows all things only in God, and God in all things. The knowledge of good and evil shows that he is no longer at one with his origin.[3]

The reference to the Fall as recorded in Genesis and the concomitant introduction of knowledge concerning good and evil are quite clear. Yet all ethical thought is aimed at gaining a knowledge of good and evil.[4] Bonhoeffer's Christian ethics, however, differs in its approach to gaining such knowledge and speaks instead in terms of bringing man back to his origins.

This return, or "reconciliation," Bonhoeffer sees as the message of the New Testament, specifically the message of Christ the Redeemer.

> Now anyone who reads the New Testament even superficially cannot but notice the complete absence of this world of disunion, conflict and ethical problems. Not man's falling apart from God, from men, from things and from himself, but rather the rediscovered unity, reconciliation, is now the basis of the discussion and the "point of decision of the specifically ethical experience." The life and activity of men is not at all problematic or tormented or dark; it is self-evident, joyful, sure and clear.[5]

Thus, unlike many ethical theories, Bonhoeffer's Christian ethics does not start with any "abstract" theory about the definition of 'good'. Indeed, he sees any attempt to define 'good' as always doomed to failure and always leading to formalism or casuistry, with the "conflict between the good and the real."[6] Instead, Christian ethics begins with a "rediscovered unity," a "reconciliation" of man with God—especially through the person of Jesus Christ.[7]

In a chapter of *Ethics* entitled "The Last Things and the Things before the Last," Bonhoeffer develops his views on such practical ethical questions as euthanasia, suicide, and birth control. From the discussion of these issues, one would be inclined to say that his is a "natural law" ethics. There are some references to the Catholic Church as the only institution which still holds the natural in high respect,[8] and the author is highly critical of Protestant ethics for placing the natural in a place of ill repute. Bonhoeffer explains what he means by "natural" in this context:

> The natural is that which after the Fall is directed toward the coming of Christ . . . Formally the natural is determined through God's will to preserve it and through its being directed toward Christ. In its formal aspect, therefore, the natural can be discerned only in its relation to

Jesus Christ Himself. As for its contents, the natural is the form of the preserved life itself, the form which embraces the entire human race.[9]

The implications of this explanation of "natural" are seen in Bonhoeffer's definition of "reason." "Reason" is the vehicle of our knowledge of the natural—it is a natural power and "rests upon what is objectively given."[10] At the same time, he notes that reason has been "entirely involved" in the Fall and, presumably, in the advent of knowledge concerning 'good' and 'evil'.

What is the content of this natural-law ethics? According to Bonhoeffer, the right to life is man's first right and is the foundation for all other rights. Any attack or injury to the body is seen as a violation of this basic right of man.[11] Euthanasia is deemed wrong because it is seen as the destruction of innocent life and, as such, it violates the first right of man. Also forbidden is suicide; Bonhoeffer says that it is wrong because it manifests a "lack of faith" in God.[12] Suicide is viewed as an attempt by man for self-justification.

> God has reserved for Himself the right to determine the end of life, because He alone knows the goal to which it is His will to lead it. It is for Him alone to justify a life or to cast it away. Before God, self-justification is quite simply sin, and suicide is therefore also sin. There is no other cogent reason for the wrongfulness of suicide, but only the fact that over men there is a God. Suicide implies denial of this fact.[13]

Birth control is another moral issue discussed in some detail by Bonhoeffer. He argues that birth control is sinful because it violates the right to live which God has bestowed on the embryo.[14] He adds that any deliberate, constant prevention of birth is also a violation of this right. At the same time, he does see the possibility that some cases will arise where "limitation" may be necessary. Clearly, Bonhoeffer takes a "conservative" view on certain moral issues, viz., killing, euthanasia, suicide, and birth control.[15]

In summary one can say that Bonhoeffer's ethics depends on the Christian view he takes. More specifically, it depends on his view of the New Testament, Christ, and the theology which he develops along Protestant lines in *Ethics* and his other works. One might question whether an ethics which is derived from, and dependent on, the Christian tradition must inevitably, or even ineluctably, offer conservative solutions to ethical problems. In short, need conservatism follow from a Christian ethics?

By way of contrast, Joseph Fletcher in his *Situation Ethics* contends that Christianity demands a very "liberal" ethics. Quite opposed to Bonhoeffer in general, he argues for euthanasia, suicide, and birth control in some situations. What is especially interesting, however, is that he, like Bonhoeffer, quite clearly recognizes his foundations as posited, not proved. Fletcher's ethics has a number of "presuppositions," one of which he calls "positivism."

> A third presupposition is "positivism." In the case of Christian ethics this means theological positivism. When we get right down to it there are really only two ways to approach "religious knowledge" or belief—two kinds of theological epistemology. One is theological *naturalism*, in which reason adduces or deduces faith propositions from human experience and natural phenomena: nature yields the evidence, natural reason grasps them. Natural theology, so called, and "natural law" ethics are examples of this method. The other approach is theological *positivism* (or "positive theology"), in which faith propositions are "posited" or affirmed voluntaristically rather than rationalistically. It is a-rational but not irrational, outside of reason but not against it.[16]

So, for Fletcher, as well as for Bonhoeffer, one must posit certain religious (in this case, Christian) tenets, and if these are not posited, ethics (at least their kind of ethics) is impossible. There is something unsatisfactory with this position for many (including myself). Call it intellectual pride, if you will, yet one wants his ethics to be somehow available to the nonbeliever, at least in some instances. Even if someone does not accept all of the tenets of a religious belief, we would still be inclined to believe that he could share some of our ethical beliefs—especially those which are fundamental. There seem to be other reasons besides a religious faith to hold that murder, for example, is wrong. Religious faith may be a "good reason," but surely not the only "good reason."

Historically there have been a number of ethical theories called "natural law" theories. These theories propose that there are nonreligious grounds for holding some actions to be wrong. Reason is able to give good reasons without any overt aid from religion.[17] It seems quite normal for one to say, "Sure, you're not a Christian (or Jew, or Mohammedan), but can't you understand that action X is still wrong?"

John Dewey, for example, tries to rid ethics of its dependence on religious institutions and beliefs, while holding on to many of the ethical beliefs of such institutions.[18] In his *A Common Faith*, Dewey attempts to distinguish religion from the religious—the noun from the adjective.[19] Religions always link up with the supernatural, with unseen powers, with a "god." But he feels that this linkage is quite unnecessary.

> It is widely supposed that a person who does not accept any religion is thereby shown to be a non-religious person. Yet it is conceivable that the present depression in religions is closely connected with the fact that religions now prevent, because of their weight of historic encumbrances, the religious quality of experience from coming to consciousness and finding the expression that is appropriate to present conditions

intellectual and moral . . . I believe that many persons are so repelled from what exists as a religion by its intellectual and moral implications, that they are not even aware of attitudes in themselves that if they come to fruition would be genuinely religious.[20]

A "religion" is an institution which has certain beliefs and practices, while "religious" describes a certain kind of attitude. To have an "unreligious" attitude, says Dewey, means that one "attributes human achievement and purposes to man in isolation from the world of physical nature and his fellows."[21] The consequence of this separation of "religion" from "religious" leads Dewey to conclude that traditional religions are outdated, so to speak.

Dewey's position is diametrically opposed to Bonhoeffer's. He wants to rid mankind of any traditional religion (at least if it does not foster a religious attitude), while Bonhoeffer sees religion, specifically Christianity, as the salvation of mankind. Bonhoeffer's justification of certain actions rests on theological reasons—e.g., faith or lack of faith in God. Dewey's justification often, if not always, rests on social reasons—e.g., the development of human society. What strikes me as interesting about these two views is that there is no a priori reason why they need disagree about concrete cases, even though the justifications they attempt may be quite antithetical.

Let us relate this to the debate between moral philosophy and moral theology. Bonhoeffer's ethics is meaningless without the theological underpinnings he takes from the Bible and from the Christian (specifically, Lutheran) tradition. One would be inclined to suggest that his ethics is not philosophical, but theological. (What a way to start a debate!) Dewey quite obviously objects to such parochialism. Here is the crux of the debate. Can one be ethical and/or treat ethics without a theology? Dewey says yes, Bonhoeffer says no. But what does this question mean? Does it mean, Can following a non-Christian or nontheological ethics get one to heaven? Or, Can good reasons be given only by a Christian? Or, even more concretely, Can good reasons be given only by a Catholic (or Lutheran, or Jew)? Must we also add, Only by a liberal (or conservative) Catholic, etc.? Don't we eventually end up by asking, Can good reasons be given if and only if they hold what I hold? I trust that most of us would stop well short of asking the last question. But one wonders where to stop.

If we hold certain religious beliefs, and we say that those who do not share our beliefs cannot give good reasons for their views, are we not condemning them as either immoral or unenlightened? Such accusations seem unwarranted. What is a good reason for a Christian may not be a good reason for a Moslem. How can we say which religion gives the "best reason"? Each religion thinks it gives the best reasons. To ask the question about which gives the best reasons seems only to beg the issue behind the debate.

Some suggest that "sincerity" or "honesty" must be taken into account. For instance, a Christian might say that a Moslem, although wrong, may be sincere—honestly believe he is right. A Moslem might say the same about a Christian. And a Communist may be quite sincere in his desire to rule the world. Presumably all sincere believers in a religion or doctrine hold their views to be the best. So, taking sincerity or honesty into account cannot be enough since any sincere belief in certain doctrines can lead one (though not necessarily) to take a superior position and condemn, totally or partially, views that do not stem from such a belief.

But how should we view those with differing beliefs? Their reasons are good reasons for them just as ours are good reasons for us. There seems to be no way to settle the question of who gives "better reasons," and an obvious conclusion would be that only an ethical relativism is possible. But such a resolution is not acceptable to most of us.

Are we at an impasse, unable to give a solution that seems acceptable? I think not. We are faced with a diversity of beliefs. Human nature seems to demand such a diversity and functions in the face of it. We are able to maintain some order in society without infringing on everyone's beliefs (although at times some beliefs may be infringed upon). A pluralistic society can and does exist. The answer to our impasse may be that it is possible to set forth a number of ethical beliefs necessary for the preservation of society and freedom—beliefs that are held by sectarians and nonsectarians alike. From a collection of such commonly held beliefs we might develop a "metaethics" wherein every man is entitled to his beliefs as long as they do not threaten the existence of society and freedom.[22]

What activities might be ruled out by such a metaethics? Surely wars of aggression and suppression of individual freedom. As usual with ethics, though, the more concrete the case, the less one is able to decide beforehand. If such a metaethics does not give all the answers, it may be simply that we do not even know all the questions.

Given such a system of metaethics, what does the believer do with his faith? Is he forced to say that his belief is superfluous? On the other hand, if his metaethics fails to cover certain moral issues of everyday life, is he forced to consider it inadequate? This seems to be the real issue. Certainly the metaethics ought to give the minimum reasons required, not only for his own ethics, but for everyone else's as well. And if his metaethics is not adequate in certain instances, there is no reason why the believer's faith cannot add something to this ethics. At the least, it certainly could make him give a different reason (but not necessarily a better one) than someone who is not a member of his sect, as well as giving him certain moral rules peculiar to his sect (such as dietary laws and rules concerning "holy days" etc.). For those who hold a "natural law" ethics, on the other hand, it may be that no additional reasons or rules can be given beyond those provided by their fundamental metaethics. In any event, the essential point is that holding a metaethics is not necessarily antithetical to holding a particular religious belief nor does it render such belief superfluous.

Let us try to summarize. What we are suggesting here is that there exist certain basic moral principles which are necessary for the preservation of society and freedom—principles that are needed in each and every ethic. At the same time, there also exist a number of other principles which may be justified only within the context of a certain religious belief. Such a differentiation does not suggest that these specifically religious principles are any less or more important than the metaethical ones. It simply emphasizes that a different reason is needed for holding these religious principles, and that the justification of such religious principles must be given in terms of faith, i.e., the belief itself is a "good reason" for holding the principle. It should be stressed, however, that no religious principle can conflict with a metaethical principle and survive.

It becomes clear from the preceding discussion that the basic quarrels between moral philosophy and moral theology are misplaced. Though the two may overlap to some extent, the task of each is quite different: Moral philosophy is interested in the metaethical principles, while moral theology is interested in those principles related to a particular faith.

This all sounds quite easy, perhaps too easy. The subtitle of this paper is "Prolegomena to the End of a Debate"; perhaps it should be simply "Prolegomena to a Debate."

NOTES

1. Dietrich Bonhoeffer, *Ethics* (New York: Macmillan, 1968).
2. Ibid., p. 17.
3. Ibid., p. 17.
4. Ibid., p. 17.
5. Ibid., p. 26.
6. Ibid., p. 86.
7. Bonhoeffer himself recognizes the parochial quality of such an ethic when he says, ". . . we regard the West as the region for which we wish to speak, the world of the peoples of Europe and America, in so far as it is already united through the form of Jesus Christ" (ibid., p. 87). So one may reasonably assume that "Christian ethics" means an ethic for Western cultures (specifically Europe and America), and that to speak of Christian ethics for the East would not be appropriate.
8. Bonhoeffer, op. cit., p. 143.

9. Ibid., pp. 144–46.
10. Ibid., p. 146.
11. Bonhoeffer qualifies this somewhat by noting that "arbitrary" killing is wrong, but that not all killing (e.g., killing in a war) is wrong.
12. Bonhoeffer, op. cit., p. 168.
13. Ibid., p. 168.
14. Ibid., p. 171.
15. Magdalen Goffin, review of *The Life and Death of Dietrich Bonhoeffer* by Mary Bosanquet, *The New York Review of Books*, vol. 13, no. 3, 1969, p. 31.
16. Joseph Fletcher, *Situation Ethics: The New Morality* (Philadelphia: Westminster Press, 1966), pp. 46–47.
17. Compare with Bonhoeffer's definition of "reason" above.
18. Though Dewey did not specifically refer to himself as a natural-law theorist, his views may be taken as representative of natural-law theory for the purposes of this discussion.
19. John Dewey, *A Common Faith* (New Haven, Conn.: Yale University Press, 1966), p. 3.
20. Ibid., p. 9.
21. Ibid., p. 25.
22. What struck me as interesting is that there seems to be a great similarity between such a proposed metaethics and what has sometimes been called natural law. ("Natural law" is here being used to mean "an ethics based on human nature and/or society.")

2 LAW AND MORALITY

THE DEBATE on Abraham's act of faith, with all its implications, has been revived in class after class, generating great heat of friction and little light of understanding.

"But what if I did kill my son and got arrested? Do you think a jury would take a statement that I was acting on the basis of my beliefs as a defense?" Don is asking.

"Probably not in our society," says Professor Edwards. "But let's broaden that question a little. Do you think that the law should provide sanctions against all that our society considers immoral, and enforce all that which is considered moral?"

Don objects. "Come on, professor, you're trying to manipulate me again. We've already stated that there's a difference between what you do when it doesn't harm anyone else and what you do when it involves others."

"Yes. That's generally referred to as private and public morality. At least in a sense."

"Right. But killing your son is a matter of public morality, isn't it?" asks Don.

Out of sheer weariness with the subject, Edwards asks, "Don, did you know that the issue of legal enforcement of public morality versus private morality was debated rather recently in England?"

"You mean the Devlin-Hart debates? I peeked ahead," Don admits. "Isn't Devlin the guy who is uptight about sex?"

"I have no idea what Lord Devlin's problems in this regard are, if any," says Edwards. "The point is that your position—essentially that whatever you do is all right as long as it doesn't hurt anyone—and Cheri's position, who seems to disagree with you on that, represent a difference of opinion that mirrors the Devlin-Hart debates. The essence of those debates concerns the extent to which laws should enforce morality and focuses on the issue of how much protection society should afford its individual members in regard to questions of morality."

"Well, I don't think society has any business interfering with me as long as I don't interfere with it," Don states.

"And you're not alone in that view," says Edwards. "John Stuart Mill said much the same thing in his famous essay *On Liberty*. For those of you who haven't read it, Mill said that the only end for which we are warranted to interfere with the freedom of any member of society is self-protection, that is, when the individual acts so as to harm the collective, the society as a whole."

Alice raises her hand, and Edwards nods to her. "Well, in a way I agree with Mill, and I think our society today interferes too much with individual rights. But, what is worse, it uses a double standard when it interferes."

Edwards stops in the middle of lighting a cigarette. "That's a rather provocative statement, Alice. How about an example?"

"Well, take drinking and smoking pot. Nobody gets arrested if he sits quietly and gets stoned out of his skull on booze. But if another guy gets caught smoking marijuana, what happens?"

"Bang, right into the slammer!" shouts Obie.

"Right. So why should one get jailed and not the other?" asks Alice. "I don't think that's right."

"I tend to agree with you," says Edwards. "And so do a number of state legislators who have passed laws which make possession and use of marijuana no longer a felony. But how does this link into the question of public and private morality? Let's say that someone driving under the influence of alcohol hurts or kills another."

"OK. Driving under the influence of alcohol may be an issue of public morality and *that* the law ought to take care of," says Alice.

"And the same thing would apply to marijuana?"

"Sure, Professor. But what I object to is the law interfering when somebody is smoking pot and not hurting anyone. They don't object to people drinking liquor. Maybe that's because those that make laws drink but don't smoke pot."

"But liquor and marijuana harm the people that use them, and it seems to me that the law ought to do something about that," says Doug.

"But that's just the trouble with having the laws trying to enforce morality—anyway, private morality—if what you're talking about is morality at all. What happens is that we end up with too many laws," Don states.

"That's ridiculous!" Cheri says indignantly. "Not only don't we have enough laws, but the laws we have aren't really concerned with morality. I mean, look at all the criminals running around the streets. Today the law isn't moral, it *helps* the criminal more than it enforces morality!"

"Well, I happen to agree that we have a lot of criminals 'running around the streets,' as you put it. But just who are the criminals?" demands Alice. "Is it just the little guy who rips off the liquor store for a few dollars? What about the politicians who get hundreds of thousands in kickbacks? And have you already forgotten Watergate?"

Cheri breaks in. "All right. I don't care if they're blue-collar criminals or white-collar criminals. The laws should enforce morality."

"Whose morality?" asks Alice. "Yours? Mine? The morality of the state? The morality of a particular religion? Look, you're always talking about being a peace-loving Christian. Well, I'm a Christian too and I happen to think that being a Christian means not to judge or condemn. And my brand of Christianity certainly doesn't try to force a particular morality down anybody's throat."

Don, spotting a place to insert his own commercial, says, "Yeah, and I say that we have too many laws trying to control morality."

"Come on, you guys," calls Bob. "If people won't be moral, then we must force them to be moral. And in order to do that we have to have laws."

Edwards, who is getting a little weary of this wrangling, says, "All right. Let us suppose that we could all agree on what constitutes morality. The question I see as being relevant here is whether or not our laws should enforce that which we agree on as being moral."

"We're getting right back to the public and private morality business. And even there the law isn't consistent," Alice says promptly. "Look at that cigarette you're smoking. If we talk about harm, I guess the only harm being done is to yourself unless one wants to argue that you're harming us by polluting the air. Anyway, the law says that because I'm only seventeen I can't legally buy cigarettes, but you, who are in your thirties, can. So I guess the law is trying to see that I don't harm myself, and it doesn't care about you. But the law doesn't penalize me for smoking, it just says I can't buy cigarettes. That's stupid!"

"I think we can all agree that the law has certain inconsistencies," says Edwards, quietly putting out his cigarette. "But you raised an important point. If the law is going to work, it has to impose some sanctions, some penalties. In looking at the relationship between morality and legality, shouldn't we also investigate the relationship between morality and acts of legal punishment?"

"There's only one way of handling punishment from a moral point of view," Bob states. "If a person takes something, he must be made to return it, and if he causes anybody harm, he should be punished by having the same thing happen to him. Talking from a moral point of view, that's fair. And I think anything more or less than that isn't fair."

"Well, that won't stop anybody," says Cheri. "You can't just punish them for the act alone. You have to punish them for breaking the moral code—that is, supposing we could agree on one, as Mr. Edwards suggested. Law is the only way you can get people to conform to a moral code."

"If that's true, how come so many criminals who know that they're going to get heavy sentences keep going out and committing the same crime over and over again?" Don asks.

"Louis? You seem to have been wanting to say something for a while," Edwards says with a nod.

"Yes. I think the answer to Don's question is simple. The law doesn't work most of the time. Only a small number of criminals get caught, and only a few of those that get caught get a heavy sentence; unless, that is, they happen to be my color. Anyway, when Cheri talks about having the law make us conform, all I see is the majority trying to get a minority group to conform to the majority's beliefs."

"You sound as if you believed that most people in jail were political prisoners," says Edwards.

"I don't know about most. But I do know that a lot of brothers and sisters are doing time because of their color," Louis answers.

"You're not objecting to punishing people who are guilty in the legal sense. You're objecting to punishment by reason of class or race membership. Right?"

"I guess you could put it that way. Anyhow, I think people who are legally guilty should be punished. But only, and I mean *only*, when laws are applied equally to everybody," Louis replies.

Edwards nods. "All right. I think there is no one here that would dispute the idea that laws should treat everybody equally. But I am still interested in the question of morality and legal punishment. Has someone anything to add to Bob's idea of how to determine punishment for the guilty? Anyone?"

Sheila, who spends much of the class hoping she won't be called on, finally volunteers. "I remember reading that the English lords used to execute serfs for poaching on their lands. And the lords were taxing the serfs so hard they didn't have enough to eat. Well, poaching was against the law, so I guess what the serfs were doing was illegal all right. But execution seems a bit much."

"Do you feel that, as the expression goes, the punishment should fit the crime?" Edwards asks.

"Sort of," Sheila agrees. "I don't exactly agree with Bob, but I certainly think a severe penalty for a minor crime is pretty immoral."

"Talking about immorality, look at our penal system," Louis adds. "We've just been talking about punishment. But prisons are supposed to do more than just punish people. They're supposed to teach them something so that they'll be better off once they get out. And anyone who believes that's what they do has got to believe in the tooth fairy. Hell, most guys are worse off after being in the can."

"You sound like you think prisons ought to be some kind of summer camp for delinquents," Cloteal says. "As far as I am concerned, they ought to lock them up and throw away the key."

The class bell adds to the noise of loud groans from Alice and a few others. Edwards steps in briskly. "All right. We've flushed out some questions that should be kept in mind when we read and discuss the next selections. Are morality and legality linked in some way? Should the law enforce morality? Indeed, can the law even avoid enforcing morality? Also, laws do impose penalties on those it finds guilty. How do we determine the penalty? Is guilt alone sufficient, or should we consider the consequences of a particular penalty, both from the point of view of the guilty party and the society as a whole? And, finally, as we just now touched on, should penal systems focus primarily on punishment or should they not seriously consider the problem of rehabilitation? Yes, Don. Make it quick."

"You know, the trouble with this class is that all it does is to raise questions without answering them."

Edwards smiles broadly. "Thank you, Don. If you had said that the trouble with this class is that all it does is to answer questions without raising them, I would have to concern myself with some rehabilitation for us all. Class dismissed."

FOR FURTHER READING

American Friends Service Committee. *Struggle for Justice.* New York: Hill and Wang, 1971. A report on crime and punishment in America discussing, from the Quaker viewpoint, the repressing functions of the current criminal justice system and proposing an alternative role for the criminal law.

Baier, Kurt. "Is Punishment Retributive?" *Analysis* 16 (1955): 25-32. A criticism of Quinton's theory, which should be read in conjunction with Quinton's article—one of this section's selections.

Bedau, Hugo, ed. *The Death Penalty in America: An Anthology.* Garden City, N.J.: Doubleday, 1964. The best anthology of its kind, it discusses the arguments for and against the death penalty and includes articles by Sydney Hook, James McCafferty, and J. Edgar Hoover.

Buckland, William. *Some Reflections on Jurisprudence.* Hamden, Conn.: Archon Books, 1974. A good, concise summary of legal theories concentrating on the writings of Austin.

Cotham, Perry. *Obscenity, Pornography, and Censorship: Where Should Christians Draw the Line?* Grand Rapids, Mich.: Baker Book House, 1973. A discussion of obscenity, pornography, and censorship relating the legal aspects of these practices to morality and religion.

Flew, Antony. "The Justification of Punishment." *Philosophy* 29 (1954). An analysis of the justifications for punishment and of the related moral issues.

McCafferty, James. *Capital Punishment.* Chicago: Aldine-Atherton, 1972. An anthology of recent writings on capital punishment, including articles by Hugo Bedau, Ramsey Clark, and James B. Bennett.

Menninger, Karl. *The Crime of Punishment.* New York: Viking, 1966. A discussion of the injustice of justice questioning whether a desire for vengeance is not at the roots of punishment.

Mill, John Stuart. *On Liberty.* Available in various editions. Mill's famous discussion of the nature and limits of the power that society can properly exercise over the individual.

Morris, Herbert. "Persons and Punishment." *The Monist* 52 (1968). A defense of "law and order" and a critique of its opponents.

Rawls, John. "Justice as Fairness." *Philosophical Review* 64 (1955). An attempt to show that fairness is justice's essential component.

──────────────. *A Theory of Justice.* Cambridge, Mass.: Harvard University Press, 1971. This thought-provoking commentary on the essence of justice has been a center of attention in philosophical circles since its publication.

──────────────. "Two Concepts of Rules." *Philosophical Review* 64 (1955). An article uncovering the logical basis and significance of the distinction between justifying a practice and justifying a particular act that ensues from such practice.

Wasserstrom, Richard, ed. *Morality and the Law.* Belmont, Calif.: Wadsworth, 1971. An excellent anthology that brings together six articles and four legal cases dealing with the enforcement of morality. Articles by Devlin, Mill, Hart, and Dworkin are among the selections.

Patrick Devlin

MORALS AND THE CRIMINAL LAW

Lord Patrick Devlin served as Justice of the High Court Queen's Bench from 1948 to 1960 and as Lord of Appeals from 1961 to 1964. He is the author of *Trial by Jury* (1956), *The Criminal Prosecutor in England* (1957), and *Samples of Lawmaking* (1962). The following selection is taken from Devlin's "Morals and the Criminal Law" (1959), an essay that was reprinted in the collection by the title *Enforcement of Morals* (1965). This famous essay represents the opening statement of what was later to be described as the Devlin-Hart debates on the reform of criminal law in England. In this selection Devlin uses the Wolfenden Report on homosexual offenses and prostitution as a starting point for an inquiry into the connection between crime and sin. The basic question to which Devlin addresses himself is, should the criminal law concern itself with the enforcement of morals and punish sin or immorality as such? Devlin sees only one explanation of what has been and is being considered in our society as the basis of the criminal law: Society itself rests on certain moral principles, and their breach is an offense not merely against the person being injured but against society as a whole. This being so, society has a right to use the law to enforce such moral principles. Edited from Morals and the Criminal Law from *The Enforcement of Morals* by Lord Devlin. © Oxford University Press 1965. Reprinted by permission of the publisher.

**Devlin
MORALS AND
THE CRIMINAL
LAW**

... What is the connection between crime and sin and to what extent, if at all, should the criminal law of England concern itself with the enforcement of morals and punish sin or immorality as such?

The statements of principle in the Wolfenden Report [on homosexual offenses and prostitution] provide an admirable and modern starting-point for such an inquiry ...

Early in the Report the Committee put forward:

> our own formulation of the function of the criminal law so far as it concerns the subjects of this inquiry. In this field, its function, as we see it, is to preserve public order and decency, to protect the citizen from what is offensive or injurious, and to provide sufficient safeguards against exploitation and corruption of others, particularly those who are specially vulnerable because they are young, weak in body or mind, inexperienced, or in a state of special physical, official or economic dependence.
>
> It is not, in our view, the function of the law to intervene in the private lives of citizens, or to seek to enforce any particular pattern of behavior, further than is necessary to carry out the purposes we have outlined.

The Committee preface their most important recommendation

> that the homosexual behavior between consenting adults in private should no longer be a criminal offense, [by stating the argument] which we believe to be decisive, namely, the importance which society and the law ought to give to individual freedom of choice and action in matters of private morality. Unless a deliberate attempt is to be made by society, acting through the agency of the law, to equate the sphere of crime with that of sin, there must remain a realm of private morality and immorality which is, in brief and crude terms, not the law's business. To say this is not to condone or encourage private immorality.

Similar statements of principle are set out in the chapters of the Report which deal with prostitution. ...

These statements of principle are naturally restricted to the subject-matter of the Report. But they are made in general terms and there seems to be no reason why, if they are valid, they should not be applied to the criminal law in general. They separate very decisively crime from sin, the divine law from the secular, and the moral from the criminal. They do not signify any lack of support for the law, moral or criminal, and they do not represent an attitude that can be called either religious or irreligious. There are many schools of thought among those who may think that morals are not the law's business. There is first of all the agnostic or free-thinker.... He cannot accept the divine law; that does not mean that he might not view with suspicion any departure from moral principles that have for generations been accepted by the society in which he lives; but in the end he judges for himself. Then there is the deeply religious person who feels that the criminal law is sometimes more of a hindrance than a help in the sphere of morality, and that the reform of the sinner—at any rate when he injures only himself—should be a spiritual rather than a temporal work. Then there is the man who without any strong feeling cannot see why, where there is freedom in religious belief, there should not logically be freedom in morality as well. All these are powerfully allied against the equating of crime with sin.

I must disclose at the outset that I have as a judge an interest in the result of the inquiry which I am seeking to make as a jurisprudent. As a judge who administers the criminal law and who has often to pass sentence in a criminal court, I should feel handicapped in my task if I thought that I was addressing an audience which had no sense of sin or which thought of crime as something quite different. Ought one, for example, in passing sentence upon a female abortionist to treat her simply as if she were an unlicensed midwife? If not, why not? But if so, is all the panoply of the law erected over a set of social regulations? I must admit that I begin with a feeling that a complete separation of crime from sin (I use the term throughout this [selection] in the wider meaning) would not be good for the moral law and might be disastrous for the criminal. But can this sort of feeling be justified as a matter of jurisprudence? And if it be a right feeling, how should the relationship between the criminal and the moral law be stated? Is there a good theoretical basis for it, or is it just a practical working alliance, or is it a bit of both? That is the problem which I want to examine, and I shall begin by considering the standpoint of the strict logician. It can be supported by cogent arguments, some of which I believe to be unanswerable and which I put as follows.

Morals and religion are inextricably joined—the moral standards generally accepted in Western civilization being those belonging to Christianity. Outside Christendom other standards derive from other religions. . . . It may or may not be right for the State to adopt one of these religions as the truth, to found itself upon its doctrines, and to deny to any of its citizens the liberty to practice any other. If it does, it is logical that it should use the secular law wherever it thinks it necessary to enforce the divine. If it does not, it is illogical that it should concern itself with morals as such. But if it leaves matters of religion to private judgment, it should logically leave matters of morals also. A State which refuses to enforce Christian beliefs has lost the right to enforce Christian morals.

If this view is sound, it means that the criminal law cannot justify any of its provisions by reference to the moral law. It cannot say, for example, that murder and theft are prohibited because they are immoral or sinful. . . .

. . . There is only one explanation of what has hitherto been accepted as the basis of the criminal law and that is that there are certain standards of behavior or moral principles which society requires to be observed; and the breach of them is an offense not merely against the person who is injured but against society as a whole.

Thus, if the criminal law were to be reformed so as to eliminate from it everything that was not designed to preserve order and decency or to protect citizens (including the protection of youth from corruption), it would overturn a fundamental principle. It would also end a number of specific crimes. Euthanasia or the killing of another at his own request, suicide, attempted suicide and suicide pacts, dueling, abortion, incest between brother and sister, are all acts which can be done in private and without offense to others and need not involve the corruption or exploitation of others. Many people think that the law on some of these subjects is in need of reform, but no one hitherto has gone so far as to suggest that they should all be left outside the criminal law as matters of private morality. They can be brought within it only as a matter of moral principle. It must be remembered also that although there is much immorality that is not punished by the law, there is none that is condoned by the law. The law will not allow its processes to be used by those engaged in immorality of any sort. For example, a house may not be let for immoral purposes; the lease is invalid and would not be enforced. But if what goes on inside there is a matter of private morality and not the law's business, why does the law inquire into it at all? . . .

In jurisprudence, as I have said, everything is thrown open to discussion and, in the belief that they cover the whole field, I have framed three interrogatories addressed to myself to answer:
1. Has society the right to pass judgment at all on matters of morals? Ought there, in other words, to be a public morality, or are morals always a matter for private judgment?
2. If society has the right to pass judgment, has it also the right to use the weapon of the law to enforce it?
3. If so, ought it to use that weapon in all cases or only in some; and if only in some, on what principles should it distinguish?

I shall begin with the first interrogatory and consider what is meant by the right of society to pass a moral judgment, that is, a judgment about what is good and what is evil. . . .

. . . What makes a society of any sort is community of ideas, not only political ideas but also ideas about the way its members should behave and govern their lives; these latter ideas are its morals. Every society has a moral structure as well as a political one: or rather, since that might suggest two independent systems, I should say that the structure of every society is made up both of politics and morals. Take, for example, the institution of marriage. Whether a man should be allowed to take more than one wife is something about which every society has to make up its mind one way or the other. In England we believe in the Christian idea of marriage and therefore adopt monogamy as a moral principle. Consequently the Christian institution of marriage has become the basis of family life and so part of the structure of our society. It is there not because it is Christian. It has got there because it is Christian, but it remains there because it is built into the house in which we live and could not be removed without bringing it down. The great majority of those who live in this country accept it because it is the Christian idea of marriage and for them the only true one. But a non-Christian is bound by it, not because it is part of Christianity but because, rightly or wrongly, it has been adopted by the society in which he lives. It would be useless for him to stage a debate designed to prove that polygamy was theologically more correct and socially preferable; if he wants to live in the house, he must accept it as built in the way in which it is.

We see this more clearly if we think of ideas or institutions that are purely political. Society cannot tolerate rebellion; it will not allow argument about the rightness of the cause. Historians a century later may say that the rebels were right and the Government was wrong and a percipient and conscientious subject of the State may think so at the time. But it is not a matter which can be left to individual judgment.

The institution of marriage is a good example for my purpose because it bridges the division, if there is one, between politics and morals. Marriage is part of the structure of our society and it is also the basis of a moral code which condemns fornication and adultery. The institution of marriage would be gravely threatened if individual judgments were permitted about the morality of adultery; on these points there must be a public morality. But public morality is not to be confined to those moral principles which support institutions such as marriage. People do not think of monogamy as something which has to be supported because our society has chosen to organize itself upon it; they think of it as something that is good in itself and offering a good way of life and that it is for that reason that our society has adopted it. I return to the statement that I have already made, that society means a community of ideas; without shared ideas on politics, morals, and ethics no society can exist. Each one of us has ideas about what is good and what is evil; they cannot be kept private from the society in which we live. If men and women try to create a society in which there is no fundamental agreement about good and evil they will fail; if, having based it on common agreement, the agreement goes, the society will disintegrate. For society is not something that is kept together physically; it is held by the invisible bonds of common thought. If the bonds were too far relaxed the members would drift apart. A common morality is part of the bondage. The bondage is part of the price of society; and mankind, which needs society, must pay its price....

You may think that I have taken far too long in contending that there is such a thing as public morality, a proposition which most people would readily accept, and may have left myself too little time to discuss the next question which to many minds may cause greater difficulty: to what extent should society use the law to enforce its moral judgments? But I believe that the answer to the first question determines the way in which the second should be approached and may indeed very nearly dictate the answer to the second question. If society has no right to make judgments on morals, the law must find some special justification for entering the field of morality: if homosexuality and prostitution are not in themselves wrong, then the onus is very clearly on the lawgiver who wants to frame a law against certain aspects of them to justify the exceptional treatment. But if society has the right to make a judgment and has it on the basis that a recognized morality is as necessary to society as, say, a recognized government, then society may use the law to preserve morality in the same way as it uses it to safeguard anything else that is essential to its existence. If therefore the first proposition is securely established with all its implications, society has a prima facie right to legislate against immorality as such.

The Wolfenden Report, notwithstanding that it seems to admit the right of society to condemn homosexuality and prostitution as immoral, requires special circumstances to be shown to justify the intervention of the law. I think that this is wrong in principle and that any attempt to approach my second interrogatory on these lines is bound to break down. I think that the attempt by the Committee does break down and that this is shown by the fact that it has to define or describe its special circumstances so widely that they can be supported only if it is accepted that the law *is* concerned with immorality as such.

The widest of the special circumstances are described as the provision of "sufficient safeguards against exploitation and corruption of others, particularly those who are specially vulnerable because they are young, weak in body or mind, inexperienced, or in a state of special physical, official or economic dependence." The corruption of youth is a well-recognized ground for intervention by the State and for the purpose of any legislation the young can easily be defined. But if similar protection were to be extended to every other citizen, there would be no limit to the reach of the law. The "corruption and exploitation of others" is so wide that it could be used to cover any sort of immorality which involves, as most do, the cooperation of another person. . . .

I think, therefore, that it is not possible to set theoretical limits to the power of the State to legislate against immorality. It is not possible to settle in advance exceptions to the general rule or to define inflexibly areas of morality into which the law is in no circumstances to be allowed to enter. Society is entitled by means of its laws to protect itself from dangers, whether from within or without. Here again I think that the political parallel is legitimate. The law of treason is directed against aiding the king's enemies and against sedition from within. The justification for this is that established government is necessary for the existence of society and therefore its safety against violent overthrow must be secured. But an established morality is as necessary as good government to the welfare of society. Societies disintegrate from within more frequently than they are broken up by external pressures. There is disintegration when no common morality is observed and history shows that the loosening of moral bonds is often the first stage of disintegration, so that society is justified in taking the same steps to preserve its moral code as it does to preserve its government and other essential institutions. The suppression of vice is as much the law's business as the suppression of subversive activities; it is no more possible to define a sphere of private morality than it is to define one of private subversive activity. It is wrong to talk of private morality or of the law not being concerned with immorality as such or to try to set rigid bounds to the part which the law may play in the suppression of vice. There are no theoretical limits to the power of the State to legislate against treason and sedition, and likewise I think there can be no theoretical limits to legislation against immorality. You may argue that if a man's sins affect only himself it cannot be the concern of society. If he chooses to get drunk every night in the privacy of his own home, is any one except himself the worse for it? But suppose a quarter or a half of the population got drunk every night, what sort of society would it be? You cannot set a theoretical limit to the number of people who can get drunk before society is entitled to legislate against drunkenness. . . .

In what circumstances the State should exercise its power is the third of the interrogatories I have framed. But before I get to it I must raise a point which might have been brought up in any one of the three. How are the moral judgments of society to be ascertained? By leaving it until now, I can ask it in the more limited form that is now sufficient for my purpose. How is the lawmaker to ascertain the moral judgments of society? It is surely not enough that they should be reached by the opinion of the majority; it would be too much to require the individual assent of every citizen. English law has evolved and regularly uses a standard which does not depend on the counting of heads. It is that of the reasonable man. He is not to be confused with the rational man. He is not expected to reason about anything and his judgment may be largely a matter of feeling. It is the viewpoint of the man in the street—or to use an archaism familiar to all lawyers—the man in the Clapham omnibus. He might also be called the right-minded man. For my purpose I should like to call him the man in the jury box, for the moral judgment of society must be something about which any twelve men or women drawn at random might after discussion be expected to be unanimous. . . .

Immorality then, for the purpose of the law, is what every right-minded person is presumed to consider to be immoral. Any immorality is capable of affecting society injuriously and in effect to a greater or lesser extent it usually does; this is what gives the law its *locus standi*. . . .

I do not think that one can talk sensibly of a public and private morality any more than one can of a public or private highway. Morality is a sphere in which there is a public interest and a private interest, often in conflict, and the problem is to reconcile the two. . . .

. . . Nothing should be punished by the law that does not lie beyond the limits of tolerance. It is not nearly enough to say that a majority dislikes a practice; there must be a real feeling of reprobation. . . . It would be possible no doubt to point out that until a comparatively short while ago nobody thought very much of cruelty to animals and also that pity and kindliness and the unwillingness to inflict pain are virtues more generally esteemed now than they have ever been in the past. But matters of this sort are not determined by rational argument. Every moral judgment, unless it claims a divine source, is simply a feeling that no right-minded man could behave in any other way without admitting that he was doing wrong. It is the power of a common sense and not the power of reason that is behind the judgments of society. But before a society can put a practice beyond the limits of tolerance there must be a deliberate judgment that the practice is injurious to society. . . .

I return now to the main thread of my argument and summarize it. Society cannot live without morals. Its morals are those standards of conduct which the reasonable man approves. A rational man, who is also a good man, may have other standards. If he has no standards at all he is not a good man and need not be further considered. If he has standards, they may be very different; he may, for example, not disapprove of homosexuality or abortion. In that case he will not share in the common morality; but that should not make him deny that it is a social necessity. A rebel may be rational in thinking that he is right but he is irrational if he thinks that society can leave him free to rebel.

A man who concedes that morality is necessary to society must support the use of those instruments without which morality cannot be maintained. The two instruments are those of teaching, which is doctrine, and of enforcement, which is the law. If morals could be taught simply on the basis that they are necessary to society, there would be no social need for religion; it could be left as a purely personal affair. But morality cannot be taught in that way. Loyalty is not taught in that way either. No society has yet solved the problem of how to teach morality without religion. So the law must base itself on Christian morals and to the limit of its ability enforce them, not simply because they are the morals of most of us, nor simply because they are the morals which are taught by the established Church—on these points the law recognizes the right to dissent—but for the compelling reason that without the help of Christian teaching the law will fail.

IMMORALITY AND TREASON

H.L.A. Hart is a senior research fellow at the Nuffield Foundation and has been a research fellow of University College, Oxford, England. From 1952 to 1968 he was Professor of Jurisprudence at Oxford University. His major works include *The Concept of Law* (1961), *Punishment and Responsibility* (1968), and *Law, Liberty, and Morality* (1963), from which the following selection is taken. The publication in 1957 of the Wolfenden Report, which recommended liberalizing British law concerning homosexuality and prostitution, precipitated what became known as the Devlin-Hart debates. The position taken by Lord Patrick Devlin in the preceding selection is rebutted by Hart in the following article. Hart warns that "when morality is enforced, individual liberty is cut down." He finds that the morality which Devlin seeks to enforce does not justify making it subject to criminal law "with all the misery which criminal punishment entails." To those who seek to invoke criminal law to preserve morality without careful scrutiny of the implications, Hart says, "Morality, what crimes may be commited in thy name!" "Immorality and Treason" originally appeared in *The Listener*, July 30, 1959 (pp. 162–63). Reprinted by permission of the author.

The most remarkable feature of Sir Patrick's lecture is his view of the nature of morality—the morality which the criminal law may enforce. Most previous thinkers who have repudiated the liberal point of view have done so because they thought that morality consisted either of divine commands or of rational principles of human conduct discoverable by human reason. Since morality for them had this elevated divine or rational status as the law of God or reason, it seemed obvious that the state should enforce it, and that the function of human law should not be merely to provide men with the opportunity for leading a good life, but actually to see that they lead it. Sir Patrick does not rest his repudiation of the liberal point of view on these religious or rationalist conceptions. Indeed much that he writes reads like an abjuration of the notion that reasoning or thinking has much to do with morality. English popular morality has no doubt its historical connection with the Christian religion: "That," says Sir Patrick, "is how it got there." But it does not owe its present status or social significance to religion any more than to reason.

What, then, is it? According to Sir Patrick it is primarily a matter of feeling. "Every moral judgment," he says, "is a feeling that no right-minded man could act in any other way without admitting that he was doing wrong." Who then must feel this way if we are to have what Sir Patrick calls a public morality? He tells us that it is "the man in the street," "the man in the jury box," or (to use the phrase so familiar to English lawyers) "the man on the Clapham omnibus." For the moral judgments of society so far as the law is concerned are to be ascertained by the standards of the reasonable man, and he is not to be confused with the rational man.

Indeed, Sir Patrick says "he is not expected to reason about anything and his judgment may be largely a matter of feeling."

INTOLERANCE, INDIGNATION, AND DISGUST

But what precisely are the relevant feelings, the feelings which may justify use of the criminal law? Here the argument becomes a little complex. Widespread dislike of a practice is not enough. There must, says Sir Patrick, be "a real feeling of reprobation." Disgust is not enough either. What is crucial is a combination of intolerance, indignation, and disgust. These three are the forces behind the moral law, without which it is not "weighty enough to deprive the individual of freedom of choice." Hence there is, in Sir Patrick's outlook, a crucial difference between the mere adverse moral judgment of society and one which is inspired by feeling raised to the concert pitch of intolerance, indignation, and disgust.

This distinction is novel and also very important. For on it depends the weight to be given to the fact that when morality is enforced individual liberty is necessarily cut down. Though Sir Patrick's abstract formulation of his views on this point is hard to follow, his examples make his position fairly clear. We can see it best in the contrasting things he says about fornication and homosexuality. In regard to fornication, public feeling in most societies is not now of the concert-pitch intensity. We may feel that it is tolerable if confined: only its spread might be gravely injurious. In such cases the question whether individual liberty should be restricted is for Sir Patrick a question of balance between the danger to society in the one scale, and the restriction of the individual in the other. But if, as may be the case with homosexuality, public feeling is up to concert pitch, if it expresses a "deliberate judgment" that a practice as such is injurious to society, if there is "a genuine feeling that it is a vice so abominable that its mere presence is an offense," then it is beyond the limits of tolerance, and society may eradicate it. In this case, it seems, no further balancing of the claims of individual liberty is to be done, though as a matter of prudence the legislator should remember that the popular limits of tolerance may shift: the concert pitch feeling may subside. This may produce a dilemma for the law; for the law may then be left without the full moral backing that it needs, yet it cannot be altered without giving the impression that the moral judgment is being weakened.

A SHARED MORALITY

If this is what morality is—a compound of indignation, intolerance, and disgust—we may well ask what justification there is for taking it, and turning it as such, into criminal law with all the misery which criminal punishment entails. Here Sir Patrick's answer is very clear and simple. A collection of individuals is not a society; what makes them into a society is among other things a shared or public morality. This is as necessary to its existence as an organized government. So society may use the law to preserve its morality like anything else essential to it. "The suppression of vice is as much the law's business as the suppression of subversive activities." The liberal point of view which denies this is guilty of "an error in jurisprudence": for it is no more possible to define an area of private morality than an area of private subversive activity. There can be no "theoretical limits" to legislation against immorality just as there are no such limits to the power of the state to legislate against treason and sedition.

Surely all this, ingenious as it is, is misleading. Mill's formulation of the liberal point of view may well be too simple. The grounds for interfering with human liberty are more various than the single criterion of "harm to others" suggests: cruelty to animals or organizing prostitution for gain do not, as Mill himself saw, fall easily under the description of harm to others. Conversely, even where there is harm to others in the most literal sense, there may well be other principles limiting the extent to which harmful activities should be repressed by law. So there are multiple criteria, not a single criterion, determining when human liberty may be restricted. Perhaps this is what Sir Patrick means by a curious distinction which he often stresses between theoretical and practical limits. But with all its simplicities the liberal point of view is a better guide than Sir Patrick to clear thought on the proper relation of morality to the criminal law: for it stresses what he obscures—namely, the points at which thought is needed before we turn popular morality into criminal law.

SOCIETY AND MORAL OPINION

No doubt we would all agree that a consensus of moral opinion on certain matters is essential if society is to be worth living in. Laws against murder, theft, and much else would be of little use if they were not supported by a widely diffused conviction that what these laws forbid is also immoral. So much is obvious. But it does not follow that everything to which the moral vetoes of accepted morality attach is of equal importance to society; nor is there the slightest reason for thinking of morality as a seamless web: one which will fall to pieces carrying society with it, unless all its emphatic vetoes are enforced by law. Surely even in the face of the moral feeling that is up to concert pitch—the trio of intolerance, indignation, and disgust—we must pause to think. We must ask a question at two different levels which Sir Patrick never clearly enough identifies or separates. First, we must ask whether a practice which offends moral feeling is harmful, independently of its repercussion on the general moral code. Secondly, what about repercussion on the moral code? Is it really true that failure to translate this item of general morality into criminal law will jeopardize the whole fabric of morality and so of society?

We cannot escape thinking about these two different questions merely by repeating to ourselves the vague nostrum: "This is part of public morality and public morality must be preserved if society is to exist." Sometimes Sir Patrick seems to admit this, for he says in words which both Mill and the Wolfenden Report might have used, that there must be the maximum respect for individual liberty consistent with the integrity of society. Yet this, as his contrasting examples of fornication and homosexuality show, turns out to mean only that the immorality which the law may punish must be generally felt to be intolerable. This plainly is no adequate substitute for a reasoned estimate of the damage to the fabric of society likely to ensue if it is not suppressed.

Nothing perhaps shows more clearly the inadequacy of Sir Patrick's approach to this problem than his comparison between the suppression of sexual immorality and the suppression of treason or subversive activity. Private subversive activity is, of course, a contradiction in terms because "subversion" means overthrowing government, which is a public thing. But it is grotesque, even where moral feeling against homosexuality is up to concert pitch, to think of the homosexual behavior of two adults in private as in any way like treason or sedition either in intention or effect. We can make it *seem* like treason only if we assume that deviation from a general moral code is bound to affect that code, and to lead not merely to its modification but to its destruction. The analogy could begin to be plausible only if it was clear that offending against this item of morality was likely to jeopardize the whole structure. But we have ample evidence for believing that people will not abandon morality, will not think any better of murder, cruelty, and dishonesty, merely because some private sexual practice which they abominate is not punished by the law.

Because this is so the analogy with treason is absurd. Of course "No man is an island": what one man does in private, if it is known, may affect others in many different ways. Indeed it may be that deviation from general sexual morality by those whose lives, like the lives of many homosexuals, are noble ones and in all other ways exemplary will lead to what Sir Patrick calls the shifting of the limits of tolerance. But if this has any analogy in the sphere of government it is not the overthrow of ordered government, but a peaceful change in its form. So we may listen to the promptings of common sense and of logic, and say that though there could not logically be a sphere of private treason there is a sphere of private morality and immorality.

Sir Patrick's doctrine is also open to a wider, perhaps a deeper, criticism. In his reaction against a rationalist morality and his stress on feeling, he has I think thrown out the baby and kept the bath water; and the bath water may turn out to be very dirty indeed. When Sir Patrick's lecture was first delivered *The Times* greeted it with these words: "There is a moving and welcome humility in the conception that society should not be asked to give its reason for refusing to tolerate what in its heart it feels intolerable." This drew from a correspondent in Cambridge the retort: "I am afraid that we are less humble than we used to be. We once burnt old women because, without giving our reasons, we felt in our hearts that witchcraft was intolerable."

This retort is a bitter one, yet its bitterness is salutary. We are not, I suppose, likely, in England, to take again to the burning of old women for witchcraft or to punishing people for associating with those of a different race or color, or to punishing people again for adultery. Yet if these things were viewed with intolerance, indignation, and disgust, as the second of them still is in some countries, it seems that on Sir Patrick's principles no rational criticism could be opposed to the claim that they should be punished by law. We could only pray, in his words, that the limits of tolerance might shift.

CURIOUS LOGIC

It is impossible to see what curious logic has led Sir Patrick to this result. For him a practice is immoral if the thought of it makes the man on the Clapham omnibus sick. So be it. Still, why should we not summon all the resources of our reason, sympathetic understanding, as well as critical intelligence, and insist that before general moral feeling is turned into criminal law it is submitted to scrutiny of a different kind from Sir Patrick's? Surely, the legislator should ask whether the general morality is based on ignorance, superstition, or misunderstanding; whether there is a false conception that those who practice what it condemns are in other ways dangerous or hostile to society; and whether the misery to many parties, the blackmail and the other evil consequences of criminal punishment, especially for sexual offenses, are well understood. It is surely extraordinary that among the things which Sir Patrick says are to be considered before we legislate against immorality these appear nowhere; not even as "practical considerations," let alone "theoretical limits." To any theory which, like this one, asserts that the criminal law may be used on the vague ground that the preservation of morality is essential to society and yet omits to stress the need for critical scrutiny, our reply should be: "Morality, what crimes may be committed in thy name!"

As Mill saw, and de Tocqueville showed in detail long ago in his critical but sympathetic study of democracy, it is fatally easy to confuse the democratic principle that power should be in the hands of the majority with the utterly different claim that the majority, with power in their hands, need respect no limits. Certainly there is a special risk in a democracy that the majority may dictate how all should live. This is the risk we run, and should gladly run; for it is the price of all that is so good in democratic rule. But loyalty to democratic principles does not require us to maximize this risk: yet this is what we shall do if we mount the man in the street on the top of the Clapham omnibus and tell him that if only he feels sick enough about what other people do in private to demand its suppression by law no theoretical criticism can be made of his demand.

A.M. Quinton
ON PUNISHMENT

Anthony Quinton is a fellow of New College, University of Oxford. He is the author of *Utilitarian Ethics* (1973), the editor of *Political Philosophy* (1967), and has contributed numerous articles to professional journals. In the following selection, first published in 1959, Quinton discusses the two major theories on the philosophical justification of punishment—the retributive and the utilitarian. Is punishment only justified by guilt, as retributivists contend, or by the value of its consequences, as held by utilitarians? Is the retributionists' charge that utilitarianism permits the punishment of the innocent valid? Can the utilitarian's countercharge that retribution is essentially "pointless and vindictive barbarity" be sustained? These are some of the fundamental questions that Quinton examines and tries to answer in his article. Reprinted from *Analysis* 14 (1954) by permission of Basil Blackwell, Publisher.

INTRODUCTORY

There is a prevailing antinomy about the philosophical justification of punishment. The two great theories—retributive and utilitarian—seem, and at least are understood by their defenders, to stand in open and flagrant contradiction. Both sides have arguments at their disposal to demonstrate the atrocious consequences of the rival theory. Retributivists, who seem to hold that there are circumstances in which the infliction of suffering is a good thing in itself, are charged by their opponents with vindictive barbarousness. Utilitarians, who seem to hold that punishment is always and only justified by the good consequences it produces, are accused of vicious opportunism. Where the former insists on suffering for suffering's sake, the latter permits the punishment of the innocent. Yet, if the hope of justifying punishment is not to be abandoned altogether, one of these apparently unsavory alternatives must be embraced. For they exhaust the possibilities. Either punishment must be self-justifying, as the retributivists claim, or it must depend for its justification on something other than itself, the general formula of "utilitarianism" in the wide sense appropriate here.

In this [selection] I shall argue that the antinomy can be resolved, since retributivism, properly understood, is not a moral but a logical doctrine, and that it does not provide a moral justification of the infliction of punishment but an elucidation of the use of the word. Utilitarianism, on the other hand, embraces a number of possible moral attitudes toward punishment, none of which necessarily involves the objectionable consequences commonly adduced by retributivists, provided that the word "punishment" is understood in the way that the essential retributivist thesis lays down. The antinomy arises from a confusion of modalities, of logical and moral necessity and possibility, of "must" and "can" with "ought" and "may." In brief, the two theories answer different questions: retributivism the question "when (logically) *can* we punish?," utilitarianism the question "when (morally) *may* we or *ought* we to punish?" I shall also describe circumstances in which there is an answer to the question "when (logically) *must* we punish?" Finally, I shall attempt to account for this difference in terms of a distinction between the establishment of rules whose infringement involves punishment from the application of these rules to particular cases.

THE RETRIBUTIVE THEORY

The essential contention of retributivism is that punishment is only justified by guilt. There is a certain compellingness about the repudiation of utilitarianism that this involves. We feel that whatever other considerations may be taken into account, the primary and indispensable matter is to establish the guilt of the person to be punished. I shall try to show that the peculiar outrageousness of the rejection of this principle is a consequence, not of the brutality that such rejection might seem to permit, but of the fact that it involves a kind of lying. At any rate the first principle of retributivism is that it is necessary that a man be guilty if he is to be punished.

But this doctrine is normally held in conjunction with some or all of three others which are logically, if not altogether psychologically, independent of it. These are that the function of punishment is the negation or annulment of evil or wrongdoing, that punishment must fit the crime (the *lex talionis*) and that offenders have a right to punishment, as moral agents they ought to be treated as ends not means.

The doctrine of "annulment," however carefully wrapped up in obscure phraseology, is clearly utilitarian in principle. For it holds that the function of punishment is to bring about a state of affairs in which it is as if the wrongful act had never happened. This is to justify punishment by its effects, by the desirable future consequences which it brings about. It certainly goes beyond the demand that only the guilty be punished. For, unlike this demand, it seeks to prescribe exactly what the punishment should be. Holding that whenever wrong has been done it must be annulled, it makes guilt—the state of one who has done wrong—the sufficient as well as the necessary condition of punishment. While the original thesis is essentially negative, ruling out the punishment of the innocent, the annulment doctrine is positive, insisting on the punishment and determining the degree of punishment of the guilty. But the doctrine is only applicable to a restricted class of cases, the order of nature is inhospitable to attempts to put the clock back. Theft and fraud can be compensated, but not murder, wounding, alienation of affection, or the destruction of property or reputation.

Realizing that things cannot always be made what they were, retributivists have extended the notion of annulment to cover the infliction on the offender of an injury equal to that which he has caused. This is sometimes argued for by reference to Moore's theory of organic wholes, the view that sometimes two blacks make a white.*
That this, the *lex talionis*, revered by Kant, does not follow from the original thesis is proved by the fact that we can always refrain from punishing the innocent but that we cannot always find a punishment to fit the crime. Some indeed would argue that we can never fit punishment to wrongdoing, for how are either, especially wrongdoing, to be measured? (Though, as Ross has pointed out, we can make ordinal judgments of more or less about both punishment and wrongdoing.**)

---

*G.E. Moore, *Principia Ethica* (Cambridge at the University Press, 1968), Sections 18-19.
**David W. Ross, *The Right and the Good* (Oxford: Clarendon Press, 1930).

Both of these views depend on a mysterious extension of the original thesis to mean that punishment and wrongdoing must necessarily be somehow equal and opposite. But this is to go even further than to regard guilt and punishment as necessitating one another. For this maintains that only the guilty are to be punished and that the guilty are always to be punished. The equal and opposite view maintains further that they are to be punished to just the extent that they have done wrong.

Finally retributivism has been associated with the view that if we are to treat offenders as moral agents, as ends and not as means, we must recognize their right to punishment. It is an odd sort of right whose holders would strenuously resist its recognition. Strictly interpreted, this view would entail that the sole relevant consideration in determining whether and how a man should be punished is his own moral regeneration. This is utilitarian and it is also immoral, since it neglects the rights of an offender's victims to compensation and of society in general to protection. A less extreme interpretation would be that we should never treat offenders merely as means in inflicting punishment but should take into account their right to treatment as moral agents. This is reasonable enough; most people would prefer a penal system which did not ignore the reformation of offenders. But it is not the most obvious correlate of the possible view that if a man is guilty he ought to be punished. We should more naturally allot the correlative right to have him punished to his victims or society in general and not to him himself.

THE RETRIBUTIVIST THESIS

So far I have attempted to extricate the essentials of retributivism by excluding some traditional but logically irrelevant associates. A more direct approach consists in seeing what is the essential principle which retributivists hold utilitarians to deny. Their crucial charge is that utilitarians permit the punishment of the innocent. So their fundamental thesis must be that only the guilty are to be punished, that guilt is a necessary condition of punishment. This hardly lies open to the utilitarian countercharge of pointless and vindictive barbarity, which could only find a foothold in the doctrine of annulment and in the *lex talionis*. (For that matter, it is by no means obvious that the charge can be sustained even against them, except in so far as the problems of estimating the measure of guilt lead to the adoption of a purely formal and external criterion which would not distinguish between the doing of deliberate and accidental injuries.)

Essentially, then, retributivism is the view that only the guilty are to be punished. Excluding the punishment of the innocent, it permits the other three possibilities: the punishment of the guilty, the nonpunishment of the guilty, and the nonpunishment of the innocent. To add that guilt is also the sufficient condition of punishment, and thus to exclude the nonpunishment of the guilty, is another matter altogether. It is not entailed by the retributivist attack on utilitarianism and has none of the immediate compulsiveness of the doctrine that guilt is the necessary condition of punishment.

There is a very good reason for this difference in force. For the necessity of not punishing the innocent is not moral but logical. It is not, as some retributivists think, that we *may* not punish the innocent and *ought* only to punish the guilty, but that we *cannot* punish the innocent and *must* only punish the guilty. Of course, the suffering or harm in which punishment consists can be and is inflicted on innocent people, but this is not punishment, it is judicial error or terrorism or, in Bradley's characteristically repellent phrase, "social surgery."* The infliction of suffering on a person is only properly described as punishment if that person is guilty. The retributivist thesis, therefore, is not a moral doctrine, but an account of the meaning of the word "punishment." Typhoid carriers and criminal lunatics are treated physically in much the same way as ordinary criminals; they are shut up in institutions. The essential difference is that no blame is implied by their imprisonment, for there is no guilt to which the blame can attach. "Punishment" resembles the word "murder"; it is infliction of suffering on the guilty and not simply infliction of suffering, just as murder is wrongful killing and not simply killing. Typhoid carriers are no more (usually) criminals than surgeons are (usually) murderers. This accounts for the flavor of moral outrage attending the notion of punishment of the innocent. In a sense a contradiction in terms, it applies to the common enough practice of inflicting the suffering involved in punishment on innocent people and of sentencing them to punishment with a lying imputation of their responsibility and guilt. Punishment *cannot* be inflicted on the innocent; the suffering associated with punishment *may* not be inflicted on them, firstly, as brutal and secondly, if it is represented as punishment, as involving a lie.

This can be shown by the fact that punishment is always *for* something. If a man says to another "I am going to punish you" and is asked "what for?" he cannot reply "nothing at all" or "something you have not done." At best, he is using "punish" here as a more or less elegant synonym for "cause to suffer." Either that or he does not understand the meaning of "punish." "I am going to punish you for something you have not done" is as absurd a

---
*Francis H. Bradley, *Ethical Studies* (New York: Oxford University Press, 1927).

statement as "I blame you for this event for which you were not responsible." "Punishment implies guilt" is the same sort of assertion as "ought implies can." It is not *pointless* to punish or blame the innocent, as some have argued, for it is often very useful. Rather the very conditions of punishment and blame do not obtain in these circumstances.

AN OBJECTION

But how can it be useful to do what is impossible? The innocent can be punished and scapegoats are not logical impossibilities. We do say "they punished him for something he did not do." For A to be said to have punished B it is surely enough that A thought or said he was punishing B and ensured that suffering was inflicted on B. However innocent B may be of the offense adduced by A, there is no question that, in these circumstances, he has been punished by A. So guilt cannot be more than a *moral* precondition of punishment.

The answer to this objection is that "punish" is a member of that now familiar class of verbs whose first-person-present use is significantly different from the rest. The absurdity of "I am punishing you for something you have not done" is analogous to that of "I promise to do something which is not in my power." Unless you are guilty I am no more in a position to punish you than I am in a position to promise what is not in my power. So it is improper to say "I am going to punish you" unless you are guilty, just as it is improper to say "I promise to do this" unless it is in my power to do it. But it is only *morally* improper if I do not *think* that you are guilty or that I can do the promised act. Yet, just as it is perfectly proper to say of another "he promised to do this," whether he thought he could do it or not, provided that he *said* "I promise to do this," so it is perfectly proper to say "they punished him," whether they thought him guilty or not, provided that they *said* "we are going to punish you" and inflicted suffering on him. By the first-person-present use of these verbs we prescribe punishment and *make* promises; these activities involve the satisfaction of conditions over and above what is required for *reports* or *descriptions* of what their prescribers or makers represent as punishments and promises.

Understandably "reward" and "forgive" closely resemble "punish." Guilt is a precondition of forgiveness, desert—its contrary—of reward. One cannot properly say "I am going to reward you" or "I forgive you" to a man who has done nothing. Reward and forgiveness are always *for* something. But, again, one can say "they rewarded (or forgave) him for something he had not done." There is an interesting difference here between "forgive" and "punish" or "reward." In this last kind of assertion "forgive" seems more peculiar, more inviting to inverted commas, than the other two. The three undertakings denoted by these verbs can be divided into the utterance of a more or less ritual formula and the consequences authorized by this utterance. With punishment and reward the consequences are more noticeable than the formula, so they come to be sufficient occasion for the use of the word even if the formula is inapplicable and so improperly used. But, since the consequences of forgiveness are negative—the absence of punishment, no such shift occurs. To reward involves giving a reward, to punish inflicting a punishment, but to forgive involves no palpable consequence, e.g., handing over a written certificate of pardon.

Within these limitations, then, guilt is a *logically* necessary condition of punishment and, with some exceptions, it might be held, a morally necessary condition of the infliction of suffering. Is it in either way a sufficient condition? As will be shown in the last section there are circumstances, though they do not obtain in our legal system, nor generally in extralegal penal systems (e.g., parental), in which guilt is a logically sufficient condition of at least a sentence of punishment. The parallel moral doctrine would be that if anyone is guilty of wrongdoing he ought morally to be punished. This rather futile rigorism is not embodied in our legal system with its relaxations of penalties for first offenders. Since it entails that offenders should never be forgiven it is hardly likely to commend itself in the extralegal sphere.

THE UTILITARIAN THEORY

Utilitarianism holds that punishment must always be justified by the value of its consequences. I shall refer to this as "utility" for convenience without any implication that utility must consist in pleasure. The view that punishment is justified by the value of its consequences is compatible with any ethical theory which allows meaning to be attached to moral judgments. It holds merely that the infliction of suffering is of no value or of negative value and that it must therefore be justified by further considerations. These will be such things as prevention of and deterrence from wrongdoing, compensation of victims, reformation of offenders, and satisfaction of vindictive impulses. It is indifferent for our purposes whether these are valued as intuitively good, as productive of general happiness, as conducive to the survival of the human race or are just normatively laid down as valuable or derived from such a norm.

Clearly there is no *logical* relation between punishment and its actual or expected utility. Punishment *can* be inflicted when it is neither expected, nor turns out, to be of value and, on the other hand, it can be foregone when it is either expected, or would turn out, to be of value.

But that utility is the morally necessary or sufficient condition, or both, of punishment are perfectly reputable moral attitudes. The first would hold that no one should be punished unless the punishment would have valuable consequences; the second that if valuable consequences would result punishment ought to be inflicted (without excluding the moral permissibility of utility-less punishment). Most people would no doubt accept the first, apart from the rigorists who regard guilt as a morally sufficient condition of punishment. Few would maintain the second except in conjunction with the first. The first says when you may not but not when you ought to punish, the second when you ought to but not when you may not.

Neither permits or encourages the punishment of the innocent, for this is only logically possible if the word "punishment" is used in an unnatural way, for example as meaning any kind of deliberate infliction of suffering. But in that case they cease to be moral doctrine about punishment as we understand the word and become moral doctrines (respectively, platitudinous and inhuman) about something else.

So the retributivist case against the utilitarians falls to the ground as soon as what is true and essential in retributivism is extracted from the rest. This may be unwelcome to retributivists since it leaves the moral field in the possession of the utilitarians. But there is a compensation in the fact that what is essential in retributivism can at least be definitely established.

RULES AND CASES

So far what has been established is that guilt and the value or utility of consequences are relevant to punishment in different ways. A further understanding of this difference can be gained by making use of a distinction made by Sir David Ross in the appendix on punishment in *The Right and the Good*. This will also help to elucidate the notion of guilt which has hitherto been applied uncritically.

The distinction is between laying down a rule which attaches punishment to actions of a certain kind and the application of that rule to particular cases. It might be maintained that the utilitarian theory was an answer to the question "What kinds of action should be punished?" and the retributive theory an answer to the question "On what particular occasions should we punish?" On this view both punishment and guilt are defined by reference to these rules. Punishment is the infliction of suffering attached by these rules to certain kinds of action, guilt the condition of a person to whom such a rule applies. This accounts for the logically necessary relation holding between guilt and punishment. Only the guilty can be punished because unless a person is guilty, unless a rule applies to him, no infliction of suffering on him is properly called punishment, since punishment is infliction of suffering as laid down by such a rule. Considerations of utility, then, are alone relevant to the determination of what in general, what *kinds* of action, to punish. The outcome of this is a set of rules. Given these rules, the question of whom in particular to punish has a definite and necessary answer. Not only will guilt be the logically necessary but also the logically sufficient condition of punishment or, more exactly, of a sentence of punishment. For declaration of guilt will be a declaration that a rule applies and, if the rule applies, what the rule enjoins—a sentence of punishment—applies also.

The distinction between setting up and applying penal rules helps to explain the different parts played by utility and guilt in the justification of punishment, in particular the fact that where utility is a moral, guilt is a logical, justification. Guilt is irrelevant to the setting up of rules, for until they have been set up the notion of guilt is undefined and without application. Utility is irrelevant to the application of rules, for once the rules have been set up, punishment is determined by guilt; once they are seen to apply, the rule makes a sentence of punishment necessarily follow.

But this account is not an accurate description of the very complex penal systems actually employed by states, institutions, and parents. It is, rather, a schema, a possible limiting case. For it ignores an almost universal feature of penal systems (and of games, for that matter, where penalties attend infractions of the rules)—discretion. For few offenses against the law is one and only one fixed and definite punishment laid down. Normally only an upper limit is set. If guilt, the applicability of the rule, is established no fixed punishment is entailed but rather, for example, one not exceeding a fine of forty shillings or fourteen days' imprisonment. This is even more evident in the administration of such institutions as clubs or libraries and yet more again in the matter of parental discipline. The establishment of guilt does not close the matter; at best it entails some punishment or other. Precisely how much is appropriate must be determined by reference to considerations of utility. The variety of things is too great for any manageably concise penal code to dispense altogether with discretionary judgment in particular cases.

But this fact only shows that guilt is not a logically *sufficient* condition of punishment; it does not affect the thesis that punishment entails guilt. A man cannot be guilty unless his action falls under a penal rule and he can only be properly said to be punished if the rule in question prescribes or permits some punishment or other. So all applications of the notion of guilt necessarily contain or include all applications of the notion of punishment.

Arthur Lelyveld
PUNISHMENT: FOR AND AGAINST

Arthur Lelyveld is President of the American Jewish Congress and the rabbi of Fairmont Temple in Cleveland, Ohio. He has been a minister-counselor for the National Council of Churches and holds a degree of Doctor of Divinity from the Hebrew Union College. In his selection, which concludes this section on law and morality, Rabbi Lelyveld examines the question of punishment. After asking whether punishment effectively serves its alleged goals of deterrence and correction, and after coming to a negative answer, Rabbi Lelyveld calls for alternative positive measures to punishment, which he sees as having no place in enlightened criminology. In a conclusion that reflects the "compassionate rabbinic mind," the author says, "That God will repay is the answer given by Scripture. We imperfect mortals with our hang-ups, our blind-spots, and our less-than-balanced scales, would do well to leave it to Him." Reprinted from *Punishment: For and Against,* ed. by Harold H. Hart (New York: Hart Publishing Co., 1972), pp. 57-81, by permission of the publisher.

There is no denying the aesthetic satisfaction, the sense of poetic justice, that pleasures us when evil-doers get the comeuppance they deserve. The impulse to punish is primarily an impulse to even the score—to be able to say with sardonic glee, "Good for you! You had it coming."

That satisfaction is heightened when it becomes possible to measure out punishment in exact proportion to the size and shape of the wrong that has been done. This is the ancient quest of *"mida k'neged mida*—measure for measure," that underlies the often-quoted and much misunderstood *lex talionis*: "an eye for an eye and a tooth for a tooth." The connoisseurship of W.S. Gilbert's *Mikado* is above reproach from traditional sources when he confides that his "object all sublime" is "to make the punishment fit the crime."

Punishment in this context is the infliction of pain and suffering upon the wrong-doer as a direct result of his wrong-doing.

The urge to punish is so deep-seated and so vicious, so id-like, that it has to be dressed in the concealing garments of pious purpose. Essentially and primarily, it is anger, vindictiveness and consequent cruelty. It reflects the dark abysses of our own evil fantasies and it is never the one who is without sin who throws the first stone.

Says Dr. Karl Menninger:[1]

> Criminals represent our alter egos—our 'bad' selves—rejected and projected. They do for us the forbidden illegal things we wish to do, and like scapegoats of old, they bear the burdens of our displaced guilt and punishment.

We prefer, as did our fathers, the repenting sinner over a hundred who are wholly righteous: "In the place where penitents stand," says the Talmud, "the wholly righteous cannot stand"; and Franz Aleander[2] says that this is because the penitent is "a living and instructive example of the victory of the super-ego over the instinctual drives of man."

When we demand expiation through punishment, we are taking action against our own hidden and forbidden drives. When we seek revenge, we are responding to an instinctual impulse to strike back.

The fact that through the ages a conscious counteraction to these emotional and unconscious foundations of punishment has developed is a marvelous example of the power of man to rationalize and control his instincts. Except for certain backwaters and lapses, Western society has done exactly that. Punishment has been limited more and more by that Western conscience or super-ego, until today it has been reduced to two forms: imprisonment and monetary compensation or fines. Capital punishment, which cannot be defended as a means of correction and which has fallen into disrepute as an effective deterrent, is outlawed in many civilized countries and practiced less and less in others.

When it is intended to be the means of achieving public justice or of protecting the community, punishment is administered by society through its corporate organs designed to determine guilt or innocence and to sentence the guilty. The highest authority is the possessor of the greatest physical power. The punisher himself, if he acts only according to his own canons, stands in danger of being punished. A telling example of this was once cited by the great Warden Lewis E. Lawes:[3]

> An Eskimo murderer, after the appropriate tribal ceremonies and forms, is sentenced to death and two of his fellow-tribesmen carry out the sentence. In due course, the two executioners are arrested by the Canadian Mounted Police, tried and sentenced to death because as executioners they had acted according to tribal law in conflict with Canadian law.

Continuing, Warden Lawes further reflects:

Vengeance again becomes decorous and legal and there seems to be no higher power ready to swing the British executors of the Eskimo executors off into the Arctic darkness of eternity.

This is where doubt begins to creep in. Man is compassionate as well as vengeful. In his calm and rational moments he asks himself, "Who really has the right to inflict pain and suffering upon another?" Presumably such an instrument of justice would himself have to be wholly without sin. Probably, were the purity of the relationship between punisher and punished to be strictly maintained, nobody would be qualified to throw the first stone. Even to test or try the accused, says Rabbi Akiba in the Talmud, the accuser must needs be free of guilt.

Compassion breeds ambivalence about punishment and frequently creates irrational procedures. Thus, when a condemned man becomes ill, society ironically prescribes that he must be treated and restored to health before he may be appropriately punished, possibly even killed.

Of course, our ambivalence renders us ingenious in the production of rationalizations. The most favored rationalization from ancient times on has been that punishment is really loving correction. This is going to hurt me more than it hurts you! It is for your own good! "He that spareth the rod," says the Book of Proverbs, "hateth his son, but he that loveth him chasteneth him betimes."

Actually, punishment, if we "tell it like it is," is never administered in the spirit of love. The two are contradictory. The emotions that accompany the meting out of punishment are anger and vindictiveness. The parent who, without anger, coldly inflicts physical punishment on a child "for his own good" is inhuman. When he strikes a child, the parent is displaying his own feelings about what the child has done. This probably achieves a modicum of catharsis for the parent, but it is doubtful that it does anything to correct the child.

To be effective, punishment as a means of training must be swift, severe and inevitable with each repetition of the offense. This is the basis of the validity of the "hot stove" idea. A child who is burned learns not to touch it. But the difficulty of applying this test of immediateness, severity and inevitability to every infraction of household rules or family codes is obvious, and a child may play the odds by choosing the immediate satisfaction he seeks over the possibility of punishment if caught. The same balancing of desire against fear operates to some degree within the older malefactor. Therefore, modern child psychologists tend to emphasize the value of rewarding approved conduct over punishing that which is disapproved. This is the way one authority formulates that judgment:

Unless we are in a position to punish the activity every time it appears, it will soon reinstate itself.[4]

The condemned activity brings a gratification of impulse which operates as a positive reinforcement that outweighs the inconsistent and weak negative reinforcement of the punishment.

Society, in the form of tribes, kingdoms and governments of all forms, has been limitlessly inventive in devising punishments deemed just or appropriate to the condemned deed.

The mildest of these punishments took the form of exposing the offender to public obloquy by displaying him in the stocks or the pillory, or hanging him in an iron cage for the delectation of the general public. Stocks are a very old form of punishment, for Jeremiah experienced them as a penalty for his outspoken opposition to the Establishment of his time. This technique of punishment is not to be found in Mosaic legislation and was evidently imported from one of the more "advanced" civilizations.

Other techniques achieved the double effect of obloquy and pain, through branding or mutilation, cutting off ears or slicing nostrils—a relatively recent practice in western civilization. In this category, too, we can place public whipping or flogging. Sometimes this was made more exquisite by special devices such as the "cat" or the "knout," the purpose of which was to add the pain of laceration to the pain of the beating. Whipping, it should be added, was practiced in Great Britain and in the United States until only yesterday, and it is still authorized in Delaware and elsewhere. Another ingenious device was the "brank," an iron-spiked bridle used to punish a "scold." The ducking-stool was contrived to deal with the same kind of offense and, along with tumbrels and the gallows itself, it was often elaborately made and decorated. "Indecent" women were sometimes paraded about the town in the seat of the ducking-stool, indecently exposed, "on the time-honored principle," says Margaret Wilson, "that if an offender is anti-social the thing to do is to make him more anti-social."[5]

These are but a few examples of the inventiveness displayed in devising forms of punishment that were said to be intended to achieve the correction of the offender. While equally impressive ingenuity was applied to the mechanisms for executing the death penalty, they were deprived of the rationalization of benefiting the offender. Here retribution or vindictiveness could only be given an acceptable facade by saying that the viciousness of the forms of execution was intended as a warning and a deterrent to others. Indeed, if deterrence *is* the genuine purpose of the death penalty, the more frightening forms of execution could be considered far more effective than the gas chamber. Western society has much to offer in the way of techniques, some of them used until quite recently: burning in oil, breaking at the wheel, interment alive in a spiked iron coffin, impaling and immuring, drawing and quartering. This last, which persisted into the nineteenth century, involved cutting down the hanged offender while he was still alive, disemboweling him and cutting his body in quarters.

Obviously, the logic of deterrence leads to absurdities which are intolerable to the normal mind today!

Imprisonment, which is the most prevalent form of punishment today, was in the past not usually the punishment itself but an interim practicality used until the authorities could determine what to do with the offender, or until the offender should see the light and repent. Imprisonment was also a means of protecting the offender from the vengeance that would be sought by the kinsmen of his victim: such were the Biblical cities of refuge for those guilty of unpremeditated murder.

Joseph was put in ward by the Egyptians; and from the fate of the chief baker who was imprisoned with him, it seems that the prisoners were being held until Pharoah determined what to do with them. Dungeons, dank and dark and suited for durance vile, are found in almost every medieval castle. Chains, and bread and water as the common fare were their hallmark, as in the case of a 13th century Brother John who, having bitten his prior's finger, was condemned by the bishop to be kept "under iron chains in which he shall be content with bread, indifferent ale, pottage and a pittance of meat or fish (which on the sixth day he shall do without) until he is penitent."[6] Except for the chains, these procedures persist to this day in our contempt of court decrees which are intended to force compliance—the offender shall be held "in durance vile" until he is penitent and relents.

Reviewing the forms of punishment men have devised in the past should make clear the nature of our dilemma. We are modern, civilized human beings. We have proscribed cruelty—or so we want to believe. The prohibition of "cruel and unusual punishment" is written into our Bill of Rights. Therefore, we must deny or repress the retributive or vengeful aspects of punishment. Whatever else it may be, we say, punishment for us is not a means of getting even.

Our only objectives we claim are:

1. Publicly displaying the wages of sin so as to warn others against the commission of the same act.
2. Effecting a change of heart in the offender, leading him to "penitence" (hence, "penitentiaries") so that he may be corrected ("correctional facilities").

For our ancestors, expiation or propitiation was inextricably bound up with deterrence. ". . . so shalt thou put away the evil from the midst of thee," the Bible says of the sentence of death by stoning, "and all Israel shall hear, and fear.'" The land and the community had to be protected against defilement, and the people had to see that they should "henceforth commit no more any such evil." Therefore, retaliation was necessary: "Thine eye shall not pity: life for life, eye for eye, tooth for tooth, hand for hand, foot for foot."[8]

We are told that the intention of these Biblical sanctions was to impose restraint upon punishment: no *more* than an eye for an eye. It is also highly probable that these severe acts of retaliation were rarely interpreted literally—the Talmudic interpretation of paying monetary damages equivalent to the damage inflicted was more than likely an alternative adopted even in prerabbinic times. Nevertheless, the talionic principle of "measure for measure" persists in Western tradition and in our society today. Just recently in Nevada, a twenty-three-year-old man who had whipped the four-year-old daughter of his girl friend with a leather belt was sentenced to be whipped with a similar belt on the steps of the city hall. The offender "called the sentence just." Evidently there is some correspondence between the retaliation principle and the psychological needs of both the offender and the community.

But that the *lex talionis* was never literally and officially carried out in post-Biblical times is a certainty. The mood of the rabbinic tradition with respect to punishment makes such a harsh act inconceivable, for the major characteristic of that mood is compassion. However, since the development of rabbinic Judaism coincided with the end of Jewish statehood, the Talmudic teachers were dealing with theoretical rather than actual situations. Their decisions flowed from their obligation to interpret Scripture and from their debates about the demands of justice. This, it might be said, gave their compassionate views free rein. But there is also evidence that the Jewish propensity for mercy antedated the end of Jewish criminal jurisdiction. Discussions about capital punishment make this clear.

The Mishnah, the body of rabbinical tenets that formed the basis of the Talmud, looks back at a Sanhedrin (tribunal) which had real jurisdiction, and says that any court which executed one man in seven years could be called a murderous or destructive court. Whereupon one rabbinic authority declared that it would be murderous if it had executed one man in 70 years. And Rabbi Tarfon and Rabbi Akiba, scholars whose word carried great weight, added, "If we had been in the Sanhedrin, no man would ever have been put to death." (But a sour die-hard, in a modern-sounding aside, said, "and so murderers would have multiplied in the land!")

The above quotation comes from the tractate of the Talmud known as *Makkot*, which means *flogging*, or literally *stripes*. This was the one form of punishment, apart from monetary fines, with which the rabbinic authorities did have practical experience. *Makkot* as a form of punishment, therapy, or prophylaxis, has persisted among traditional Jews up to modern times. But what a gentle form of whipping it was, in contrast with the use of the knout to inflict pain. In the first place, the rabbinical authorities held that the officer of the court who was to administer the flogging had to be *superior* in rabbinic scholarship and *inferior* in bodily strength! Secondly, if at any time the floggee exhibited pain or terror, the remainder of the sentence was to be immediately remitted.

The Biblical warrant for whipping says:

> If the wicked man deserve to be beaten, the judge shall cause him to lie down, and to be beaten before his face, according to the measure of his wickedness, by number. Forty stripes he may give him, he shall not exceed; lest, if he should exceed, and beat him above these many stripes, then thy brother should be dishonored before thine eyes.⁹

The interpretation of this passage provides a beautiful insight into the compassionate rabbinic mind. In the first place, "according to the measure of his wickedness" was with complete ingenuousness replaced by "according to the measure of his strength." The court was now obliged to examine the offender in order to determine how many lashes he could stand. If his physical condition was such that he could not safely take any beating, then he was discharged without having been beaten. Secondly, the maximum number of lashes was reduced to thirty-nine, on the principle of acting *"lifnim mi-shurat ha-din,* within the line of the law," so that the Biblical prohibition against exceeding forty might not be accidentally violated. And, third, Rabbi Chananya ben Gamliel interpreted "lest . . . thy brother should be dishonored" to mean that after he has been whipped he must be received as your brother, having fully expiated the sin with which he had been charged.

In striving constantly to mitigate and limit punishment, the rabbis were following the injunction of Beruriah, the saintly and scholarly wife of the eminent second-century sage Rabbi Meir, to "hate the sin but love the sinner," reading the verse from Psalms which says "Let sinners perish from the earth," as "Let sin perish . . ."

The mood of the classical school of penology in Western thought is worlds apart from all this. The modern campaign against barbarism in penological practices which was launched by the eighteenth-century treatise of Cesare Bonesana, Marchese di Beccaria, sought to make the prevention of crime the major goal of a new penological "science."

It created a calculus of pleasure and pain whose objective was to make the pain of punishment *exactly* great enough to outweigh the pleasure of the criminal act. Since the potential offender would have to have the opportunity to figure this out for himself in advance, the punishment, which would be made public, would have to be the same for all, without regard to physical condition, age, intellectual attainments or any other individual circumstances. Indeed, Jeremy Bentham tried to work out "precise mathematical laws for the infliction of punishment."

The humanitarian purpose of this kind of calculus was to eliminate from the purview of criminal law the complicating and non-objective factors of expiation and vengeance. Expiation is properly in the domain of religion, not of criminal law, says Sheldon Glueck, and as for retribution:

> Official social institutions should not be predicated upon the destructive emotion of vengeance, which is not only the expression of an infantile way of solving a problem but unjust and destructive of the purpose of protecting society.[10]

Punishment now bids for acceptance in modern penology in a carefully tailored new guise. It is objectified, presumably stripped of its vindictive emotional overtones, divested of intentional cruelty, and serves only as an instrument for the correction of criminals and for the deterrence of others from the commission of criminal acts.

We ought, then, to ask whether punishment effectively serves these goals of deterrence and correction. These questions are germane even if the rational approach to punishment is, as psychological authorities suggest, only a facade behind which lurk the old motivations of retaliation and enforced atonement. Punishment will deter, says one commonly held opinion, if it is severe enough. This view is based on the classical risk-and-reward calculus, and holds that society must do the calculating, the criminal need only be aware of the risk.

This approach, which calls for the kind of police efficiency which will apprehend the largest percentage of offenders in every offense, and the kind of court efficiency which will try and punish every malefactor without delay, make deterrence dependent upon the allocation of an inordinate portion of society's resources to police-judicial activity. It does not deal with the effect of such an allocation of time, energy and finances upon the society which does this, nor does it evaluate the chances for success in such an effort.

The fact is that there is no evidence that stiffer sentences prevent or diminish the incidence of crime. One highly-touted effort "to stand up against lawlessness" with severe penalties is associated with the name of Judge Lester H. Loble of Helena, Montana. Judge Loble has allowed full publicity for his court procedures dealing with juvenile offenders charged with felonies. Typical of his harsh sentences was the one which sent a 17-year-old to the state prison for ten years after the young malefactor had pleaded guilty to "slugging a gas-station attendant during an armed robbery." But the National Council on Crime and Delinquency has attacked the claim that these tactics have brought about a drop in the number of felonies. The Council reports:

> Such figures as we have been able to obtain, indicate that juvenile offenses have substantially increased not only in Helena but throughout the state of Montana since the passage of the Loble Law.[11]

The classic and most-often-cited example of the failure of punishment to deter is drawn from the time when pickpockets were publicly hung in England. The hangings attracted large crowds of spectators. During these spectacles, we are told, the pickpockets who were being hung were honored by their brother pickpockets who would pass through the crowd taking advantage of the glorious opportunity to ply their trade successfully.

As for correction, the figures on recidivism support the view that prison has a hardening effect, confirming the criminal in his criminal ways. Karl Menninger reports a case he saw in 1967 in which a check forger was sentenced to the penitentiary for thirty years! "The judge's rationalization," says Dr. Menninger, "was that the man had offended in this way twice before and had served shorter sentences without reforming!"[12]

The penitentiary, as indicated earlier, was intended to lead the convicted person to penitence and hence to reform. But what is too frequently overlooked is the hard fact that our prisons generate far more anger than remorse. Recently, the word Soledad has become a common-place in the headlines. The full name of this institution is the *Soledad Correctional Training Facility*. The purpose of that high-sounding name has been frustrated by the actual conditions which have converted Soledad into a "pressure cooker for rage."

We cannot change the reality by changing labels. Ramsey Clark writes:

> Correctional facilities, so-called, place young first offenders among hardened criminals, brutalize them, and send them forth to offend again as more effectively trained criminals.[13]

He adds that most of our modern penal institutions are "warehouses of degradation."

Soledad, California, offers vivid proof that the charge is accurate.

All the evils that plague the prison system are concentrated and magnified in the Soledad Correctional Facility: over-crowding, inadequately trained and overworked staff, too few professional social and psychiatric workers, too little rehabilitation, too much enforced idleness, accompanied by homosexuality, brutality and brutalized actions, futile acts of desperation by prisoners with faeces and urine. The prison is a witches' cauldron ready at every moment to boil up in fierce violence.

Since incarceration is almost the only form of punishment practiced by our society, and the Soledad example is too typical of our prison system—destructive, warping the souls of inmates, confirming them in their anger and frustrations—the implications strongly urge a review of concepts of punishment.

George Jackson describes the effect of the maximum security isolation unit called "O Wing."[14]

> It destroys the logical processes of the mind, a man's thoughts become completely disorganized. The noise, madness streaming from every throat, frustrated sounds from the bars, metallic sounds from the walls, the steel trays, the iron beds bolted to the wall, the hollow sounds from a cast-iron sink or toilet.
>
> The smells, the human waste thrown at us, unwashed bodies, the rotten food. When a white con leaves here, he's ruined for life. No black leaves Max Row (the maximum security section) walking. Either he leaves on the meat wagon or he leaves crawling, licking at the pig's feet. In two weeks that little average man who may have ended up on Max Row for suspicion or attempted escape is so brutalized, so completely without holds, that he will never heal again. It's worse than Vietnam.

And Dr. F. L. Rundle, the Chief Psychiatrist at Soledad, agrees in great part, according to Steven Roberts:

> O Wing is like a pressure cooker for human emotions. They put the fire up on high and there isn't any safety valve. There has to be a change in the philosophy of the people who run these places. They believe that the way to get a man's behavior to change is to impose very strict controls and take away everything he values and make him work to get it back. But that doesn't make him change. It just generates more and more rage and hostility.[15]

The prison system takes no account of differences in personality, education or temperament among its inmates. For the most part, all are thrown together in a situation ripe for the development of a special prison subculture, made even more possible by the absence of adequate or effective staffing. What results is a prison hierarchy in which the most aggressive prisoners take control, with the consequent growth of rackets and coerced homosexuality in a brutal power pattern.

These evils are intensified by the fact that institutions are overloaded and many of them housed in obsolete or positively antiquated structures. There are some new and well-conceived facilities designed with modern correctional objectives in mind, but they are few in number and the problem grows faster than the remedy. It is sad to note that much of this overcrowding is an unnecessary result of an unfair bail system which favors the mobsters and the rich over the poor and uninfluential. On a single census day during 1970, according to a Federal Justice Department report, 52% of the 160,863 persons in city and county jails had not been convicted of any crime.[16]

But the plight of imprisoned men was much worse just a few years ago: flogging for rules infraction; damp, underground, solitary cells; reduction of food rations; routine use of high-pressure water hoses against refractory prisoners—all are gradually disappearing. Enforced silence and hard labor have been in retreat—but much too often they are replaced not by enlightened correctional procedures but by debilitating and mind-warping idleness.

Modern criminology tells us that we must resort to punishment *when we are at a loss as to what to do* to control the offender. And of punishment, John Conrad tells us:

> It is enormously expensive. It gets in the way of our positive measures of resocialization . . . The task of correctional advance is clear: to reduce to an absolute minimum the use of punishment through alternative positive measures.[17]

How do we go about the task and what are the possible alternative measures?

What is called for is a radical change of attitude. If we truly want to correct and to rehabilitate, and not to get even with the offender, then past forms and stereotypes will have to be scrupulously reexamined. We will have to be disposed to respond with openness and receptivity to the kind of plea that Father Daniel Berrigan[18] made in his great letter to Federal Judge Roszel C. Thomsen after he had been sent to Danbury prison in 1968:

> We must spend time, money, talent, in the dismemberment of the prison empire. We must substitute for it humane groupings of inmates, and dedicated specialists—instead of the conglomerates of low talent and special interest who presently, in such abundance, batten off the misery of others, and seem adamant against all or any change. We need to substitute for the crime of punishment a sense of the true potential of man.

The same spirit resides—and not strangely so—in one who in antithesis to Father Berrigan is representative of the Establishment—Warren E. Burger, now Chief Justice of the Supreme Court, who

Whether we find it palatable or not, we must proceed, even in the face of bitter contrary experiences, in the belief that every human being has a spark somewhere hidden in him that will make it possible for redemption and rehabilitation. If we accept the idea that each human, however "bad," is a child of God, we must look for that spark.

Chief Justice Burger found that this basic Judaeo-Christian conviction is being put into practice in the little country of Denmark. There, he said, the evils of our adversary system of criminal justice are avoided and, instead, the process is marked by a "humane and compassionate disposition and treatment of the offender." A typical case, he notes, is disposed of in about six weeks—far less than in the prolonged and creaky procedures of our courts—"and the first offender is almost always placed on probation under close supervision and free to return to a gainful occupation and normal family life." For offenders for whom institutionalization is deemed necessary, they will find in the normal prison one psychiatrist for every 100 prisoners; and in the maximum-security prison, there is one psychiatrist for every 50 prisoners. Our own ratio of psychiatrists or psychologists to prisoners is one for every 1,500 in the federal prisons; and this figure drops to one for every 5,000 inmates in state prisons; and in some states, to zero.

We not only need vastly increased numbers of social workers and psychological counselors; we also need new approaches that will reduce the number of the institutionalized by returning to the community under probationary supervision those who are diagnosed as capable of profiting from such a regimen.

To that end, we need diagnostic centers, such as those that have been established in Kansas where the court's sentence is tentative until the judge receives the center's full report.

We need adequate hospital facilities for the neurotic offender.

We need to limit institutionalization or imprisonment strictly to those cases where there is no alternative, and to the period which is judged essential for the rehabilitation of the offender. The purpose of imprisonment may be the protection of society, or the providing of an opportunity for rehabilitation. When its purpose is vindictive punishment, it serves no socially acceptable need.

We need major changes in court procedures and in types and numbers of court personnel in order to avoid inordinate delay in trial procedures, and to eliminate the unfair and destructive practice of imprisoning accused individuals awaiting trial. We need a thorough revision of our antiquated and inequitable bail procedures.

We need, above all, to give far more attention to prevention of crime by attacking its causes and breeding-grounds through an intensified battle to eliminate poverty, unemployment, inadequate housing, inferior education. We need to do something about the frustration and alienation that produces a situation in which three-quarters of all those who commit the "index offenses" of burglary, larceny, murder, rape and aggravated assault are less than twenty-five years of age!

We need . . . we need! . . . What we need is to build the good society. But while we're building we need to move away from the punishment ideology and objective.

For what we are left with is the conviction that the concept of punishment has no place in enlightened criminology. Dress it up as you will, it is an expression of vindictiveness and a projection of guilt upon others. It is ineffective as a means of preventing crime. It is even of doubtful value in the training of children where positive reinforcement or reward can be used with far less character damage to parent and child and with far greater consistency and effectiveness.

Punishment may remain an aspect of theological or philosophical speculation: to what extent does a wicked action visit evil results upon the malefactor as well as upon his victims? In what sense can it be said that God punishes, or that life itself, with the mills grinding slowly and exceeding small, will in the long run reward goodness and provide a built-in retribution for wickedness? That God will repay is the answer given by Scripture. We imperfect mortals with our hang-ups, our blindspots, and our less-than-balanced scales, would do well to leave it to Him.

NOTES

1. Karl Menninger, *The Crime of Punishment* (Viking Press, 1968), pp. 153 f.
2. Franz Alexander, *The Criminal, The Judge and the Public*, with Hugo Staub, tr. Gregory Zilboorg (Macmillan, 1931), p. 217.
3. Lewis E. Lawes, *Man's Judgment of Death* (Putnam, 1924), p. 3.
4. G. C. Homans, *Social Behavior in Its Elementary Forms* (Harcourt, Brace and World, 1961), p. 26.
5. Margaret Wilson, *The Crime of Punishment* (1931), p. 41.
6. E. H. Sutherland and D. R. Cressey, *Principles of Criminology* (Lippincott, 1966), p. 324.
7. Book of Deuteronomy 21:21.
8. Ibid. 19:19-21; Leviticus 24:17-21.
9. Deuteronomy 25:2-3.
10. Sheldon Glueck, *Crime and Correction: Selected Papers* (Addison-Wesley, 1952), pp. 75 f.
11. Samuel Grafton, *Crime and Its Prevention*, ed. Stephen Lewin, vol. 40, no. 4 (Wilson, 1968), p. 188.
12. Menninger, op. cit., p. 203.
13. Ramsey Clark, *Crime in America* (Simon and Schuster, 1970).
14. George Jackson, *A Soledad Brother: The Prison Letters of George Jackson* (Holt, 1970).

15. Steven Roberts, Article in *New York Times*, Feb. 7, 1971.
16. *New York Times*, April 7, 1970.
17. John Conrad, *Crime and Its Correction* (University of California, 1965).
18. *New York Times*, December 14, 1970.
19. *Crime and Its Prevention*, p. 199.

3 ※ PACIFISM AND VIOLENCE

PROFESSOR Malcolm Edwards's class is still locked in battle over the type of harm the law should act to prevent and the extent to which the law should interfere with individual rights in order to prevent harm. Since the discussion is moving effectively and productively, Edwards is off thinking about Terri O'Neill who is apparently asleep in the back row. Terri has apologized to Edwards, claiming she enjoys the class and that it keeps her awake most of the time, which is more than she can say for some of her other classes. She has told Edwards that she doesn't know why she needs so much sleep and admitted to even falling asleep while driving to school. After cautioning her about the likely consequences, as well as the morality, of driving under those conditions, Edwards has advised her to get medical help. Now he is wondering whether he should call the university health service to see if she has taken his advice.

"Hello. Anybody at home?" a voice calls.

"I'm sorry, Alice. I was pondering a question involving the ethics of interference," Edwards says with a smile.

"I was saying that we have all heard about that firefight between the police and the so-called People's Liberation group—you know, that group that did all that killing and kidnapping some time back."

"Yes. That sort of news is hard to miss," says Edwards.

"Well, it seems to me that the police really overreacted. I mean, they blew that house those guys were hiding in all apart. It was like the police were in a war. Now, I can't see how the law is justified in doing that kind of thing. I mean, how can you justify violence by the police, which is really violence by the law?"

"All right. Let me ask you whether you think violence is ever justified and, if so, under what circumstances."

"There you go again, answering a question with a question," Alice says in obvious disgust. "Can't you ever answer a question?"

"Yes. I'll answer the one you just asked. Most people are primarily concerned with finding the right answers. Well, I am certainly concerned with your finding the answers that are right for you. And it is for that reason that I am even more concerned with finding the right questions."

While Alice is digesting this, Bob says, "If you want an example of when violence is justified, I think that when the police have to use violence to control a mob that's going crazy looting and burning buildings and cars, that's justified. That is just violence being used in self-protection, and that's particularly true when the police themselves are being attacked."

"I don't think you can even call what the police do in a case like that violence," says Cloteal. "I don't think what a person does to protect himself against violence can be called violence at all. And if you have a violent mob running around like they did in Detroit and Watts a few years back, they have to be stopped. If you're fighting violence, you have to use it—only, I think, it should have another name. And even if it is violence, it's justified. It's self-defense, and that's a moral right."

"Now that's real honky talk," says Louis disgustedly. "You talk about Watts as if you knew something about it. Do you have any idea what ghetto life is like? The dehumanizing, humiliating, crummy feeling of hopelessness? Hell, that's just something for you to read about and see on TV, safe in your pretty white suburb. Well, if you think self-defense is so moral, Cloteal, why do you people object to us defending ourselves when we are attacked?"

"What are you talking about?" asks Cloteal. "Nobody went in and attacked the people in Watts. They started the violence there!"

"Started it? Hell, we've had two hundred years of violence. You think violence is just physical? There's violence to a person's spirit and mind, and that's the worst kind of violence. And that's what's happened to us. We've been dumped on, our humanity has been violated."

"Right on!" Obie calls. "Whites can use violence; only, when they use it, it's not really violence, it's self-defense. Let Blacks, Chicanos, Indians, or anyone else try defending their rights, and it's just naughty old violence. Some morality!"

"You, Louis, and you, Obie, only seem to question the justification of violence when used by one group and not another," notes Edwards. "But let me repeat my question: Is violence ever justifiable?"

"When a society is attacked by rebels, it has a right to defend itself, even if that means using violence," states Bob.

"Hold on!" Cheri calls. "You all seem to end up agreeing that violence is all right. All you're disagreeing about is who should have the right to use that violence. Can't you see that violence is wrong no matter who uses it and whether you call it self-defense or something else? Cloteal, Bob, can't you see that if the violence Louis and Obie are talking about is wrong, so is yours? And can't you two see the same thing?" she asks turning to Louis and Obie.

The four look at each other uncertainly. Terri yawns and says sleepily, "Why can't we just be nonviolent?"

"Why not indeed?" says Cheri.

"So what do you expect us to do when the pigs come in and hassle us?" Obie asks Cheri. "Turn the other cheek? It's easy to ask the other guy to be nonviolent. Why don't you people start by being nonviolent?"

"But that's just what I am," says Cheri. "But the four of you all seem to be going along with the idea that you should match others' violence with violence of your own. Why are you guys arguing anyway? You really agree on everything except who has the right to commit violence. Boy! This is some kind of ethics discussion."

Bob, who can't quite figure out how he got into this alliance, says, "Man is a violent animal. It's his nature. Look at history. Man has always been violent, it's innate." Cloteal murmurs agreement, but both Louis and Obie are quiet. They too are wondering how they could agree with Bob and Cloteal on anything.

"Don, do you mean innately violent, or innately aggressive?" asks Edwards, but he is ignored.

Cheri says almost pleadingly, "Look. Can't you guys see that the question isn't the right of one group to use violence versus the right of another group to use violence? And I mean 'right' in the moral sense."

"What is the question?" asks Bob unconsciously copying one of Professor Edwards' favorite queries.

"Well, you all talk as though the way to settle injustice is by violence. But all violence gets you is more violence. What you need is another way to stop injustices. You have to find some nonviolent way. I believe that's the only moral thing to do."

"You expect us to be nice moral sheep and let them run all over us?" asks Cloteal. Bob nods his agreement with her question.

"I dig that question," says Louis and Obie seems to agree. "Of course, I don't know if Cloteal and I would exactly agree on the color of the sheep," he adds with a grin.

"You guys are too much," says Cheri, "all four of you agreeing on something like this. Doesn't that make you wonder? Anyway, I don't think you have to be run all over. There are people who are pacifists, who practice passive resistance to violence. And I don't mean that passivism and pacifism are the same thing. Take Martin Luther King, for example."

"*You* take him. He was an Uncle Tom," says Obie. Louis nods tentatively.

"Look what it got him," Bob and Cloteal say almost in unison.

"It got him a lot," Cheri states emphatically. "Maybe not so much personally, but a lot for what he was fighting for. And there are many others who have been militant without being violent. They've demonstrated, and boycotted, and done a lot of things that have caused changes without using violence."

"But it doesn't really work," objects Bob. "Anyway, very few people have enough discipline to take getting beaten up and jailed without reacting violently."

"Right on, man!" Obie calls out and then says to himself, "A lot you know about it." Louis keeps quiet trying to figure out why he agrees with both Bob and Cheri.

Edwards finally asserts himself. "The bell rang, five minutes ago, and there's another class due in here. For those of you who can, and want to, drop over to my office. We can have some coffee and continue this discussion, and maybe you'll even let me say a word or two. Class dismissed."

FOR FURTHER READING

Bondurant, Joan V. *Conquest of Violence: The Gandhian Philosophy of Conflict.* Berkeley: University of California Press, 1969. Including an analysis of Hindu traditions, this book examines Gandhi's philosophy of conflict and the method of social action *(satyagraha)* he developed.

Brock, Peter. *Pacifism in the United States: From the Colonial Era to the First World War.* Princeton, N.J.: Princeton University Press, 1968. Tracing the history of pacifism, Brock's work offers a unique study of this subject.

Day, Dorothy. *Loaves and Fishes.* New York: Harper & Row, 1963. Dorothy Day discusses her life and dedication to nonviolence through her experiences in Friendship Houses, at Tivoli Farm, and with the Catholic Worker.

Douglass, James W. *The Non-Violent Cross.* London: Macmillan, 1968. One of the first books on nonviolence that emerged from the Vietnam War, tracing the significance of the symbol of the cross to the world, the church, and history.

Durland, William. *No King but Caesar.* Scottsdale, Pa.: Herald Press, 1975. The author questions, in the light of the Gospel, whether one who accepts Christianity may at any time practice violence and asks the church to return to the original, pacifistic teachings of Jesus.

Eller, Vernard. *King Jesus' Manual of Arms for the Armless: War and Peace from Genesis to Revelation.* Nashville, Tenn.: Abingdon Press, 1973. Eller's "with it" personality permeates this analysis of war and peace. He reconciles the Old Testament's stance of retribution with the New Testament's teachings of nonviolence.

Gandhi, Mohandas K. *Non-Violent Resistance.* New York: Schocken, 1970. A one-volume collection of Gandhi's works that includes his description of *satyagraha*, the method of direct social action based on courage, nonviolence, and truth, which Gandhi developed and used.

Guinan, Edward, ed. *Peace and Non-Violence: Basic Writings.* New York: Paulist Press, 1973. An anthology of writings from many of the leading exponents and practitioners of nonviolence including Adin Ballou, Vinoba Bhave, Danilo Dolci, Cesar Chavez, Dorothy Day, George Fox, and Leo Tolstoy.

King, Martin Luther, Jr. *Strength to Love.* New York: Pocket Books, 1968. A collection of sermons on love and nonviolence. King discusses the imperative of loving one's enemies.

McSorley, Richard. *Kill for Peace.* New York: Corpus Papers, 1970. A work written by a Catholic priest-pacifist urging the necessity of pursuing peace in a world threatened by nuclear disaster.

Ramsey, Paul. *War and the Christian Conscience: How Shall Modern War Be Conducted Justly?* Durham, N.C.: Duke University Press, 1961. The author discusses the "just war" in context of Protestant-Roman Catholic thought. Noting the universalism of the early Christians' pacifism, he concludes by formulating a limited just-war theory for contemporary Christians.

Shaffer, Jerome A., ed. *Violence: Award Winning Essays in the Council for Philosophical Studies Competition.* New York: McKay, 1971. This collection of award-winning essays discusses the concepts of force, coercion, justification, and law.

Sharp, Gene. *The Politics of Non-Violent Action.* Boston: Porter Sargent, 1973. A political, nontheological analysis of violence and nonviolence discussing the concept and control of political power. It reviews the methods and successes of nonviolent action and emphasizes the effectiveness of the nonviolent approach.

Wasserstrom, Richard, ed. *War and Morality.* Belmont, Calif.: Wadsworth, 1970. An anthology examining the morality of war and including articles by William James, Elizabeth Anscombe, Jan Narveson, and Gunter Lewy.

Yoder, John H. *The Politics of Jesus.* Grand Rapids, Mich.: Eerdmans, 1972. Writing from a Mennonite background, the author shows how the contemporary biblical realist revolution, in which ecclesiology and eschatology are given a new import, is reflected in the field of ethics.

Jan Narveson

PACIFISM:
A PHILOSOPHICAL ANALYSIS

Professor Narveson is the author of several articles on moral and social philosophy and on pacifism, including "Pacifism: A Philosophical Analysis," presented below, and "Is Pacifism Consistent?" (1966). He is also the author of a book, *Morality and Utility* (1967). In the article that follows, Narveson examines the doctrine of pacifism from a philosophical point of view with the intent of showing that if pacifism is advanced as a moral doctrine, it is logically untenable. To call himself a pacifist, the author maintains, a person must believe that it is wrong to use violence to prevent, resist, or punish violence against oneself or others. In other words, a pacifist must deny the right of defense in general. This, Narveson says, results in a self-contradictory position: "In saying that violence is wrong, one is at the same time saying that people have a right to its prevention, by force if necessary." What about the conscientious objectors? Narveson's answer to this question may seem surprising, as he says himself, in view of his argument about pacifism: The only justifiable means of getting a conscientious objector to comply with conscription is rational persuasion. From *Ethics* 75: 259-71. Copyright 1965 by The University of Chicago Press. Reprinted by permission of Jan Narveson and The University of Chicago Press.

Several different doctrines have been called "pacifism," and it is impossible to say anything cogent about it without saying which of them one has in mind. I must begin by making it clear, then, that I am limiting the discussion of pacifism to a rather narrow band of doctrines, further distinctions among which will be brought out below. By "pacifism," I do *not* mean the theory that violence is evil. With appropriate restrictions, this is a view that every person with any pretensions to morality doubtless holds: Nobody thinks that we have a right to inflict pain wantonly on other people. The pacifist goes a very long step further. *His* belief is not only that violence is evil but also that it is morally wrong to use force to resist, punish, or prevent violence. This further step makes pacifism a radical moral doctrine. What I shall try to establish below is that it is in fact, more than merely radical—it is actually incoherent because self-contradictory in its fundamental intent. I shall also suggest that several moral attitudes and psychological views which have tended to be associated with pacifism as I have defined it do not have any necessary connection with that doctrine. Most proponents of pacifism, I shall argue, have tended to confuse these different doctrines, and that confusion is probably what accounts for such popularity as pacifism has had.

It is next in order to point out that the pacifistic attitude is a matter of degree, and this in two respects. In the first place, there is the question: How much violence should not be resisted, and what degree of force is one not entitled to use in resisting, punishing, or preventing it? Answers to this question will make a lot of difference. For example, everyone would agree that there are limits to the kind and degree of force with which a particular degree of violence is to be met: we do not have a right to kill someone for rapping us on the ribs, for example, and yet there is no tendency toward pacifism in this. We might go further and maintain, for example, that capital punishment, even for the crime of murder, is unjustified without doing so on pacifist grounds. Again, the pacifist should say just what sort of a reaction constitutes a forcible or violent one. If somebody attacks me with his fists and I pin his arms to his body with wrestling holds which restrict him but cause him no pain, is that all right in the pacifist's book? And again, many non-pacifists could consistently maintain that we should avoid, to the extent that it is possible, inflicting a like pain on those who attempt to inflict pain on us. It is unnecessary to be a pacifist merely in order to deny the moral soundness of the principle, "an eye for an eye and a tooth for a tooth." We need a clarification, then, from the pacifist as to just how far he is and is not willing to go. But this need should already make us pause, for surely the pacifist cannot draw these lines in a merely arbitrary manner. It is his reasons for drawing the ones he does that count, and these are what I propose to discuss below.

The second matter of degree in respect of which the pacifist must specify his doctrine concerns the question: Who ought not to resist violence with force? For example, there are pacifists who would only claim that they themselves ought not to. Others would say that only pacifists ought not to, or that all persons of a certain type, where the type is not specified in terms of belief or non-belief in pacifism, ought not to resist violence with force. And, finally, there are those who hold that everyone ought not to do so. We shall see that considerations about this second variable doom some forms of pacifism to contradiction.

My general program will be to show that (1) only the doctrine that everyone ought not to resist violence with force is of philosophical interest among those doctrines known as "pacifism"; (2) that doctrine, if advanced as a moral doctrine, is logically untenable; and (3) the reasons for the popularity of pacifism rest on failure to see exactly what the doctrine is. The things which pacifism wishes to accomplish, insofar as they are worth accomplishing, can be managed on the basis of quite ordinary and conservative moral principles.

Let us begin by being precise about the kind of moral force the principle of pacifism is intended to have. One good way to do this is to consider what it is intended to deny. What would non-pacifists, which I suppose includes most people, say of a man who followed Christ's suggestion and, when unaccountably slapped, simply turned the other cheek? They might say that such a man is either a fool or a saint. Or they might say, "It's all very well for him to do that, but it's not for me"; or they might simply shrug their shoulders and say, "Well, it takes all kinds, doesn't it?" But they would *not* say that a man who did that ought to be punished in some way; they would not even say that he had done anything wrong. In fact, as I have mentioned, they would more likely than not find something admirable about it. The point, then, is this: The non-pacifist does *not* say that it is your *duty* to resist violence with force. The non-pacifist is merely saying that there's nothing wrong with doing so, that one has every right to do so if he is so inclined. Whether we wish to add that a person would be foolish or silly to do so is quite another question, one on which the non-pacifist does not *need* to take any particular position.

Consequently, a genuine pacifist cannot merely say that we may, if we wish, prefer not to resist violence with force. Nor can he merely say that there is something admirable or saintly about not doing so, for, as pointed out above, the non-pacifist could perfectly well agree with that. He must say, instead, that, for whatever class of people he thinks it applies to, there is something positively wrong about meeting violence with force. He must say that, insofar as the people to whom his principle applies resort to force, they are committing a breach of moral duty—a very serious thing to say. Just how serious, we shall ere long see.

Next, we must understand what the implications of holding pacifism as a moral principle are, and the first such implication requiring our attention concerns the matter of the size of the class of people to which it is supposed to apply. It will be of interest to discuss two of the four possibilities previously listed, I think. The first is that in which the pacifist says that only pacifists have the duty of pacifism. Let us see what this amounts to.

If we say that the principle of pacifism is the principle that all and only pacifists have a duty of not opposing violence with force, we get into a very odd situation. For suppose we ask ourselves, "Very well, which people are the pacifists then?" The answer will have to be, "All those people who believe that pacifists have the duty not to meet violence with force." But surely one could believe that a certain class of people, whom we shall call "pacifists," have the duty not to meet violence with force without believing that one ought not, oneself, to meet violence with force. That is to say, the "principle" that pacifists ought to avoid meeting violence with force, is circular: It presupposes that one already knows who the pacifists are. Yet this is precisely what that statement of the principle is supposed to answer! We are supposed to be able to say that anybody who believes that principle is a pacifist; yet, as we have seen, a person could very well believe that a certain class of people called "pacifists" ought not to meet violence with force without believing that he himself ought not to meet violence with force. Thus everyone could be a "pacifist" in the sense of believing that statement and yet no one believe that he *himself* (or anyone in particular) ought to avoid meeting violence with force. Consequently, pacifism cannot be specified in that way. A pacifist must be a person who believes either that he himself (at least) ought not to meet force with force or that some larger class of persons, perhaps everyone, ought not to meet force with force. He would then be believing something definite, and we are then in a position to ask why.

Incidentally, it is worth mentioning that when people say things such as "Only pacifists have the duty of pacifism," "Only Catholics have the duties of Catholicism," and, in general, "Only *X*-ists have the duties of *X*-ism" they probably are falling into a trap which catches a good many people. It is, namely, the mistake of supposing that what it *is* to have a certain duty is to *believe* that you have a certain duty. The untenability of this is parallel to the untenability of the previously mentioned attempt to say what pacifism is. For, if having a duty is believing that you have a certain duty, the question arises, "*What* does such a person believe?" The answer that must be given if we follow this analysis would then be, "He believes that he believes that he has a certain duty"; and so on, ad infinitum.

On the other hand, one might believe that having a duty does not consist in believing that one has and yet believe that only those people really have the duty who believe that they have it. But in that case, we would, being conscientious, perhaps want to ask the question, "Well, *ought* I to believe that I have that duty, or oughtn't I?" If you say that the answer is "Yes," the reason cannot be that you already do believe it, for you are asking whether you *should*. On the other hand, the answer "No" or "It doesn't make any difference—it's up to you," implies that there is really no reason for doing the thing in question at all. In short, asking whether I ought to believe that I have a duty to do x, is equivalent to asking whether I should *do* x. A person might very well believe that he ought to do x but be wrong. It might be the case that he really ought *not* to do x; in that case the fact that he believes he ought to do x, far from being a reason why he ought to do it, is a reason for us to point out his error. It also, of course, presupposes that he has some reason other than his belief for thinking it is his duty to do x.

Having cleared this red herring out of the way, we must consider the view of those who believe that they themselves have a duty of pacifism and ask ourselves the question: What general kind of reason must a person have for supposing a certain type of act to be *his* duty, in a moral sense? Now, one answer he might give is that pacifism as such is a duty, that is, that meeting violence with force is, as such, wrong. In that case, however, what he thinks is not merely that *he* has this duty, but that *everyone* has this duty.

Now he might object, "Well, but no; I don't mean that everyone has it. For instance, if a man is defending not himself, but *other* people, such as his wife and children, then he has a right to meet violence with force." Now this, of course, would be a very important qualification to his principle and one of a kind which we will be discussing in a moment. Meanwhile, however, we may point out that he evidently still thinks that, if it weren't for certain more important duties, everyone would have a duty to avoid meeting violence with force. In other words, he then believes that, other things being equal, one ought not to meet violence with force. He believes, to put it yet another way, that if one does meet violence with force, one must have a special excuse or justification of a moral kind;

then he may want to give some account of just which excuses and justifications would do. Nevertheless, he is now holding a general principle.

Suppose, however, he holds that no one *else* has this duty of pacifism, that only he himself ought not to meet force with force, although it is quite all right for others to do so. Now if this is what our man feels, we may continue to call him a "pacifist" in a somewhat attenuated sense, but he is then no longer holding pacifism as a *moral* principle or, indeed, as a principle at all.* For now his disinclination for violence is essentially just a matter of taste. I like pistachio ice cream, but I wouldn't dream of saying that other people have a duty to eat it; similarly, this man just doesn't *like* to meet force with force, although he wouldn't dream of insisting that others act as he does. And this is a secondary sense of "pacifism," first, because pacifism has always been advocated on moral grounds and, second, because non-pacifists can easily have this same feeling. A person might very well feel squeamish, for example, about using force even in self-defense, or he might not be able to bring himself to use it even if he wants to. But none of these has anything to do with asserting pacifism to be a duty. Moreover, a mere attitude could hardly license a man to refuse military service if it were required of him, or to join ban-the-bomb crusades, and so forth. (I fear, however, that such attitudes have sometimes caused people to do those things.)

And, in turn, it is similarly impossible to claim that your support of pacifism is a moral one if your position is that a certain selection of people, but no one else, ought not to meet force with force, even though you are unprepared to offer any reason whatever for this selection. Suppose, for example, that you hold that only the Arapahoes, or only the Chinese, or only people more than six feet high have this "duty." If such were the case, and no reasons offered at all, we could only conclude that you had a very peculiar attitude toward the Arapahoes, or whatever, but we would hardly want to say that you had a moral principle. Your "principle" amounts to saying that these particular individuals happen to have the duty of pacifism just because they are the individuals they are, and this, as Bentham would say, is the "negation of all principles." Of course, if you meant that somehow the property of being over six feet tall *makes* it your duty not to use violence, then you have a principle, all right, but a very queer one indeed unless you can give some further reasons. Again, it would not be possible to distinguish this from a sheer attitude.

Pacifism, then, must be the principle that the use of force to meet

---

*Compare, for example, K. Baier, *The Moral Point of View* (Cornell, 1958), p. 191.

force is wrong *as such*, that is, that nobody may do so unless he has a special justification.

There is another way in which one might advocate a sort of "pacifism," however, which we must also dispose of before getting to the main point. One might argue that pacifism is desirable as a tactic: that, as a matter of fact, some good end, such as the reduction of violence itself, is to be achieved by "turning the other cheek." For example, if it were the case that turning the other cheek caused the offender to break down and repent, then that would be a very good reason for behaving "pacifistically." If unilateral disarmament causes the other side to disarm, then certainly unilateral disarmament would be a desirable policy. But note that its desirability, if this is the argument, is due to the fact that peace is desirable, a moral position which anybody can take, pacifist or no, plus the purely contingent fact that this policy causes the other side to disarm, that is, it brings about peace.

And, of course, that's the catch. If one attempts to support pacifism because of its probable effects, then one's position depends on what the effects are. Determining what they are is a purely empirical matter, and, consequently, one could not possibly be a pacifist as a matter of pure principle if his reasons for supporting pacifism are merely tactical. One must, in this case, submit one's opinions to the governance of fact.

It is not part of my intention to discuss matters of fact, as such, but it is worthwhile to point out that the general history of the human race certainly offers no support for the supposition that turning the other cheek always produces good effects on the aggressor. Some aggressors, such as the Nazis, were apparently just "egged on" by the "pacifist" attitude of their victims. Some of the S.S. men apparently became curious to see just how much torture the victim would put up with before he began to resist. Furthermore, there is the possibility that, while pacifism might work against some people (one might cite the British, against whom pacifism in India was apparently rather successful—but the British are comparatively nice people), it might fail against others (e.g., the Nazis).

A further point about holding pacifism to be desirable as a tactic is that this could not easily support the position that pacifism is a *duty*. The question whether we have no *right* to fight back can hardly be settled by noting that not to fight back might cause the aggressor to stop fighting. To prove that a policy is a desirable one because it works is not to prove that it is *obligatory* to follow it. We surely need considerations a good deal less tenuous than this to prove such a momentous contention as that we have no *right* to resist.

It appears, then, that to hold the pacifist position as a genuine, full-blooded moral principle is to hold that nobody has a right to fight back when attacked, that fighting back is inherently evil, as such. It means that we are all mistaken in supposing that we have a right of self-protection. And, of course, this is an extreme and extraordinary position in any case. It appears to mean, for instance, that we have no right to punish criminals, that all of our machinery of criminal justice is, in fact, unjust. Robbers, murderers, rapists, and miscellaneous delinquents ought, on this theory, to be let loose.

Now, the pacifist's first move, upon hearing this, will be to claim that he has been misrepresented. He might say that it is only one's *self* that one has no right to defend, and that one may legitimately fight in order to defend other people. This qualification cannot be made by those pacifists who qualify as conscientious objectors, however, for the latter are refusing to defend their fellow citizens and not merely themselves. But this is comparatively trivial when we contemplate the next objection to this amended version of the theory. Let us now ask ourselves what it is about attacks on *other* people which could possibly justify *us* in defending them, while we are not justified in defending ourselves. It cannot be the mere fact that they are other people than ourselves, for, of course, everyone is a different person from everyone else, and if such a consideration could ever of itself justify anything at all it could also justify anything whatever. That mere difference of person, as such, is of no moral importance, is a presupposition of anything that can possibly pretend to be a moral theory.

Instead of such idle nonsense, then, the pacifist would have to mention some specific characteristic which every *other* person has which we lack and which justifies us in defending them. But this, alas, is impossible, for, while there may be some interesting difference between *me*, on the one hand, and everyone else, on the other, the pacifist is not merely addressing himself to me. On the contrary, as we have seen, he has to address himself to everyone. He is claiming that each person has no right to defend himself, although he does have a right to defend other people. And, therefore, what is needed is a characteristic which distinguishes *each* person from everyone else, and not just *me* from everyone else—which is plainly self-contradictory.

If the reader does not yet see why the "characteristic" of being identical with oneself cannot be used to support a moral theory, let him reflect that the proposition "Everyone is identical with himself" is a trivial truth—as clear an example of an analytic proposition as there could possibly be. But a statement of moral principle is not a trivial truth; it is a substantive moral assertion. But non-tautologous statements, as everyone knows, cannot logically be derived from tautologies, and, consequently, the fact that everyone is identical with himself cannot possibly be used to prove a moral position.

Again, then, the pacifist must retreat in order to avoid talking idle nonsense. His next move, now, might be to say that we have a right to defend all those who are able to defend themselves. Big, grown-up men who are able to defend themselves ought not to do so, but they ought to defend mere helpless children who are unable to defend themselves.

This last, very queer theory could give rise to some amusing logical gymnastics. For instance, what about groups of people? If a group of people who cannot defend themselves singly can defend themselves together, then when it has grown to that size ought it to stop defending itself? If so, then every time a person *can* defend someone else, he would form with the person being defended a "defensive unit" which was able to defend itself, and thus would by his very presence debar himself from making the defense. At this rate, no one will ever get defended, it seems: The defenseless people by definition cannot defend themselves, while those who can defend them would enable the group consisting of the defenders and the defended to defend themselves, and hence they would be obliged not to do so.

Such reflections, however, are merely curious shadows of a much more fundamental and serious logical problem. This arises when we begin to ask: But why should even defenseless people be defended? If resisting violence is inherently evil, then how can it suddenly become permissible when we use it on behalf of other people? The fact that they are defenseless cannot possibly account for this, for it follows from the theory in question that everyone ought to put himself in the position of people who are defenseless by refusing to defend himself. This type of pacifist, in short, is using the very characteristic (namely, being in a state of not defending oneself) which he wishes to encourage in others as a reason for denying it in the case of those who already have it (namely, the defenseless). This is indeed self-contradictory.

To attempt to be consistent, at least, the pacifist is forced to accept the characterization of him at which we tentatively arrived. He must indeed say that no one ought ever to be defended against attack. The right of self-defense can be denied coherently only if the right of defense, in general, is denied. This in itself is an important conclusion.

It must be borne in mind, by the way, that I have not said anything to take exception to the man who simply does not wish to defend himself. So long as he does not attempt to make his pacifism into a principle, one cannot accuse him of any inconsistency, however much one might wish to say that he is foolish or eccentric. It is solely with moral principles that I am concerned here.

We now come to the last and most fundamental problem of all. If we ask ourselves what the point of pacifism is, what gets it going, so to speak, the answer is, of course, obvious enough: opposition to violence. The pacifist is generally thought of as the man who is so much opposed to violence that he will not even use it to defend himself or anyone else. And it is precisely this characterization which I wish to show is far from being plausible, morally inconsistent.

To begin with, we may note something which at first glance may seem merely to be a matter of fact, albeit one which should worry the pacifist, in our latest characterization of him. I refer to the commonplace observation that, generally speaking, we measure a man's degree of opposition to something by the amount of effort he is willing to put forth against it. A man could hardly be said to be dead set against something if he is not willing to lift a finger to keep it from going on. A person who claims to be completely opposed to something yet does nothing to prevent it would ordinarily be said to be a hypocrite.

As facts, however, we cannot make too much of these. The pacifist could claim to be willing to go to any length, short of violence, to prevent violence. He might, for instance, stand out in the cold all day long handing out leaflets (as I have known some to do), and this would surely argue for the sincerity of his beliefs.

But would it really?

Let us ask ourselves, one final time, what we are claiming when we claim that violence is morally wrong and unjust. We are, in the first place, claiming that a person *has no right* to indulge in it, as such (meaning that he has no right to indulge in it, *unless* he has an overriding justification). But what do we mean when we say that he has no right to indulge in it? Violence, of the type we are considering, is a two-termed affair: one does violence *to* somebody, one cannot simply "do violence." It might be oneself, of course, but we are not primarily interested in those cases, for what makes it wrong to commit violence is that it harms the people to whom it is done. To say that it is wrong is to say that those to whom it is done have a right *not* to have it done to them. (This must again be qualified by pointing out that this is so only if they have done nothing to merit having that right abridged.)

Yet what could that right to their own security, which people have, possibly consist in, if not a right at least to defend themselves from whatever violence might be offered them? But lest the reader think that this is a gratuitous assumption, note carefully the reason why having a right involves having a right to be defended from breaches of that right. It is because the prevention of infractions of that right is precisely what one has a right to when one has a right at all. A right just *is* a status justifying preventive action. To say that you have a right to X but that no one has any justification whatever for preventing people from depriving you of it, is self-contradictory. If you claim a right to X, then to describe some action as an act of depriving you of X, is logically to imply that its absence is one of the things that you have a right to.

Thus far it does not follow logically that we have a right to use force in our own or anyone's defense. What does follow logically is that one has a right to whatever may be necessary to prevent infringements of his right. One might at first suppose that the universe *could* be so constructed that it is never necessary to use force to prevent people who are bent on getting something from getting it.

Yet even this is not so, for when we speak of "force" in the sense in which pacifism is concerned with it, we do not mean merely physical "force." To call an action a use of force is not merely to make a reference to the laws of mechanics. On the contrary, it is to describe whatever is being done as being a means to the infliction on somebody of something (ordinarily physical) which he does not want done to him; and the same is true for "force" in the sense in which it applies to war, assault and battery, and the like.

The proper contrary of "force" in this connection is "rational persuasion." Naturally, one way there *might* be of getting somebody not to do something he has no right to do is to convince him he ought not to do it or that it is not in his interest to do it. But it is inconsistent, I suggest, to argue that rational persuasion is the only morally permissible method of preventing violence. A pragmatic reason for this is easy enough to point to: Violent people are too busy being violent to be reasonable. We cannot engage in rational persuasion unless the enemy is willing to sit down and talk; but what if he isn't? One cannot contend that every human being can be persuaded to sit down and talk before he strikes, for this is not something we can determine just by reasoning: it is a question of observation, certainly. But these points are not strictly relevant anyway, for our question is not the empirical question of whether there is some handy way which can always be used to get a person to sit down and discuss moral philosophy when he is about to murder you. Our question is: *If* force is the only way to prevent violence in a given case, is its use justified *in that case?* This is a purely moral question which we can discuss without any special reference to matters of fact. And, moreover, it is precisely this question which we should have to discuss with the would-be violator. The point is that if a person can be rationally persuaded that he ought not to engage in violence, then precisely what he would be rationally persuaded of if we were to succeed would be the proposition that the use of force is justifiable to prevent him from doing so. For note that if we were to argue that only rational persuasion is permissible as a means of preventing him, we would have to face the question: Do we mean *attempted* rational persuasion, or *successful* rational persuasion, that is, rational persuasion which really does succeed in preventing him from acting? Attempted rational persuasion might fail (if only because the opponent is unreasonable), and then what? To argue that we have a right to use rational persuasion which also succeeds (i.e., we have a right to its success as well as to its use) is to imply that we have a right to prevent him from performing the act. But this, in turn, means that, if attempts at rational persuasion fail, we have a right to the use of force. Thus what we have a right to, if we ever have a *right* to anything, is not merely the use of rational persuasion to keep people from depriving you of the thing to which you have the right. We do indeed have a right to that, but we also have a right to anything else that might be necessary (other things being equal) to prevent the deprivation from occurring. And it is a logical truth, not merely a contingent one, that what *might* be necessary is *force*. (If merely saying something could miraculously deprive someone of the ability to carry through a course of action, then those speech-acts would be called a type of force, if a very mysterious one. And we could properly begin to oppose their use for precisely the same reasons as we now oppose violence.)

What this all adds up to, then, is that *if* we have any rights at all, we have a right to use force to prevent the deprivation of the thing to which we are said to have a right. But the pacifist, of *all* people, is the one most concerned to insist that we do have some rights, namely, the right not to have violence done to us. This is logically implied in asserting it to be a duty on everyone's part to avoid violence. And this is why the pacifist's position is self-contradictory. In saying that violence is wrong, one is at the same time saying that people have a right to its prevention, by force if necessary. Whether and to what extent it may be necessary is a question of fact, but, since it is a question of fact only, the *moral* right to use force on some possible occasions is established.

We now have an answer to the question. How much force does a given threat of violence justify for preventive purposes? The answer, in a word, is "Enough." That the answer is this simple may at first sight seem implausible. One might suppose that some elaborate equation between the aggressive and the preventive force is needed: the punishment be proportionate to the crime. But this is a misunderstanding. In the first place, prevention and punishment are not the same, even if punishment is thought to be directed mainly toward prevention. The punishment of a particular crime logically cannot prevent *that* instance of the crime, since it presupposes that it has already been performed; and punishment need not involve the use of any violence at all, although law-enforcement officers in some places have a nasty tendency to assume the contrary. But preventive force is another matter. If a man threatens to kill me, it is desirable, of course, for me to try to prevent this by the use of the least amount of force sufficient to do the job. But I am justified even in killing him *if* necessary. This much, I suppose, is obvious to most people. But suppose his threat is much smaller: suppose that he is merely pestering me, which is a very mild form of aggression indeed. Would I be justified in killing him to prevent this, under any circumstances whatever?

Suppose that I call the police and they take out a warrant against him, and suppose that when the police come, he puts up a struggle. He pulls a knife or a gun, let us say, and the police shoot him in the ensuing battle. Has my right to the prevention of his annoying me extended to killing him? Well, not exactly, since the immediate threat in response to which he is killed is a threat to the lives of the policemen. Yet my annoyer may never have contemplated real violence. It is an unfortunate case of unpremeditated escalation. But this is precisely what makes the contention that one is justified in using enough force to do the job, whatever amount that may be, to prevent action which violates a right less alarming than at first sight it seems. For it is difficult to envisage a reason why extreme force is needed to prevent mild threats from realization except by way of escalation, and escalation automatically justifies increased use of preventive force.

The existence of laws, police, courts, and more or less civilized modes of behavior on the part of most of the populace naturally affects the answer to the question of how much force is necessary. One of the purposes of a legal system of justice is surely to make the use of force by individuals very much less necessary than it would otherwise be. If we try to think back to a "state of nature" situation, we shall have much less difficulty envisaging the need for large amounts of force to prevent small threats of violence. Here Hobbes's contention that in such a state every man has a right to the life of every other becomes understandable. He was, I suggest, relying on the same principle as I have argued for here: that one has a right to use as much force as necessary to defend one's rights, which include the right of safety of person.

I have said that the duty to avoid violence is only a duty, other things being equal. We might arrive at the same conclusion as we have above by asking the question: Which "other things" might count as being unequal? The answer to this is that whatever else they may be, the purpose of preventing violence from being done is necessarily one of these justifying conditions. That the use of force is never justified to prevent initial violence being done to one logically implies that there is nothing wrong with initial violence. We cannot characterize it as being wrong if preventive violence is not simultaneously being characterized as justifiable.

We often think of pacifists as being gentle and idealistic souls, which in its way is true enough. What I have been concerned to show is that they are also confused. If they attempt to formulate their position using our standard concepts of rights, their position involves a contradiction: Violence is wrong, *and* it is wrong to resist it. But the right to resist is precisely what having a right of safety of person is, if it is anything at all.

Could the position be reformulated with a less "committal" concept of rights? I do not think so. It has been suggested* that the pacifist need not talk in terms of this "kind" of rights. He can affirm, according to this suggestion, simply that neither the aggressors nor the defenders "have" rights to what they do, that to affirm their not having them is simply to be against the use of force, without this entailing the readiness to use force if necessary to protect the said rights. But this will not do, I believe. For I have not maintained that having a right, or believing that one has a right, entails a *readiness* to defend that right. One has a perfect right not to resist violence to oneself if one is so inclined. But our question has been whether self-defense is justifiable, and not whether one's belief that violence is wrong entails a willingness or readiness to use it. My contention has been that such a belief does entail the justifiability of using it. If one came upon a community in which no sort of violence was ever resisted and it was claimed in that community that the non-resistance was a matter of conscience, we should have to conclude, I think, not that this was a community of saints, but rather that this community lacked the concept of justice—or perhaps that their nervous systems were oddly different from ours.

The true test of the pacifist comes, of course, when he is called upon to assist in the protection of the safety of other persons and not just of himself. For while he is, as I have said, surely entitled to be pacific about his own person if he is so inclined, he is not entitled to be so about the safety of others. It is here that the test of principles comes out. People have a tendency to brand consci-

---
*I owe this suggestion to my colleague, Leslie Armour.

entious objectors as cowards or traitors, but this is not quite fair. They are acting as if they were cowards or traitors, but claiming to do so on principle. It is not surprising if a community should fail to understand such "principles," for the test of adherence to a principle is willingness to act on it, and the appropriate action, if one believes a certain thing to be grossly wrong, is to take steps to prevent or resist it. Thus people who assess conscientious objection as cowardice or worse are taking an understandable step: from an intuitive feeling that the pacifist does not really believe what he is saying they infer that his actions (or inaction) must be due to cowardice. What I am suggesting is that this is not correct: The actions are due, not to cowardice, but to confusion.

I have not addressed myself specifically to the question whether, for instance, conscription is morally justifiable, given that the war effort on behalf of which it is invoked is genuinely justifiable. Now, war efforts very often aren't justifiable (indeed, since at least one of the parties to each war must be an aggressor, a minimum of 50 per cent of war efforts must be unjustifiable); but if they ever are, is it then justifiable to conscript soldiers? In closing, I would suggest an answer which may seem surprising in view of my arguments a few pages back. My answer is that it is, but that in the case of conscientious objectors, the only justifiable means of getting them to comply is rational persuasion.

The reason is that, in showing that self-defense is morally justifiable, one has not simultaneously shown that the defense of other people is morally *obligatory*. The kinds of arguments needed to show that an act is obligatory are quite different from those which merely show that it is justified. And, since what has been shown is that self-defense is justifiable and not obligatory, the only conclusion that can be immediately inferred from this is that defense of others is also justifiable and not obligatory. Would it be possible to show that the defense of others (at least in some circumstances) is obligatory and not merely justifiable, without at the same time showing that self-defense is obligatory and not merely justifiable?

The only thing I can suggest here is that the answer requires us to speculate about the obligations of living in a community. If a community expects its members to assist in the common defense when necessary, it can make this clear to people and give them their choice either to be prepared to meet this obligation or to live somewhere else. But a community of pacifists would also be quite conceivable, a community in which no citizen could expect the others to defend him as a part of their community responsibilities. One might not care to live in such a community, but then, a pacifist might not care to live in our sort. When the community is a whole nation of present-day size, it is much more difficult to put the issue clearly to each citizen in advance. But the upshot of it is that (1) the issue depends upon what sort of community we conceive ourselves to have; (2) we do not have clearly formed views on this point; (3) there is no basic moral duty to defend others; (4) we therefore have no direct right to force people to become soldiers in time of justified wars; (5) but we do have the right to deny many basic community services to people who will not assist us in time of need by contributing the force of their arms; and so (6) the only thing to do is to try to argue conscientious objectors into assistance, pointing to all of the above factors and leaving them their choice.

Too much can easily be made of the issue of conscription *versus* voluntary service in time of war. (In time of peace, we have another issue altogether; my arguments here apply only when there is clear justification for defensive measures.) It must be remembered that there is a limit to what law can do in "requiring" compliance, and the pacifist is precisely the person who cannot be reached by the ordinary methods of the law, since he has made up his mind not to be moved by force. The philosophical difference lies not in the question of whether compliance is ultimately voluntary, since with all laws it to some extent must be, but in the moral status which military service is presumed to have. The draft is morally justifiable if the defense of persons is considered a basic obligation of the citizen. In contemporary communities, it seems to me that there is good reason for giving it that status.

Many questions remain to be discussed, but I hope to have exposed the most fundamental issues surrounding this question and to have shown that the pacifist's central position is untenable.

William R. Durland

THE MORAL EQUIVALENT OF VIOLENCE

William R. Durland, coeditor of this volume, is an Associate Professor of Philosophy at Purdue University, Fort Wayne, Indiana. His early career was in law and politics. He was a member of the bar in Virginia and the District of Columbia and a Virginia State legislator. Active in the civil rights movement of the sixties, he is Christian pacifist and has taught courses on social ethics, philosophy of law, and the philosophy of nonviolence at Georgetown University, the University of Virginia, and the University of Notre Dame. He is the author of *No King but Caesar* (forthcoming). In the following selection, Durland searches for a moral equivalent to violence and finds it in certain practices of nonviolence. He sees that a combination of James's concept of discipline and Tolstoy's "law of love" offers a framework for developing a moral equivalent of violence. The article examines the spectrum of nonviolent practices, from the least to the greatest use of force. Durland concludes that the power of nonviolence provides a way for us all to "win our humanity."

Two giants of the nineteenth century, one a psychologist turned philosopher, and the other an author turned itinerant theologian, died in the year 1910, shortly before the first of the world wars. The theologian, Leo Tolstoy, wrote, preached, and practiced his belief that violence only begets violence, and that humankind must, and will, return to the nonviolent teachings of the Sermon on the Mount. At approximately the same time, the philosopher William James, also a pacifist, searched for the "moral equivalent of war" in his famous essay of the same name.

James wrote:

> So long as anti-militarists propose no substitute for wars' disciplinary function, no *moral equivalent* of war, analogous, as one might say, to the mechanical equivalent of heat, so long they fail to realize the full inwardness of the situation. And as a rule they do fail. The duties, penalties, and sanctions pictured in the utopias they paint are all too weak and tame to touch the military-minded. Tolstoi's pacifism is the only exception to this rule, for it is profoundly pessimistic as regards all this world's values, and makes the fear of the Lord furnish the moral spur provided elsewhere by the fear of the enemy. But our socialistic peace-advocates all believe absolutely in this world's values; and instead of the fear of the Lord and the fear of the enemy, the only fear they reckon with is the fear of poverty if one be lazy.[1]

James and Tolstoy had much in common. They were both accused of being socialistic.[2] Both were theists, and both exhibited great professional discipline. Tolstoy's road led him to search for the eventual reign of peace by imitating and following the life and teachings of Jesus Christ, particularly as set forth in the Sermon on the Mount. Tolstoy's nonviolence was grounded in a very personal Christian ethic of love. He saw a "law of love" which, when multiplied person by person, would engulf the world. James, on the other hand, looked forward to "a future when acts of war shall be formally outlawed as between civilized peoples." But he did not believe that "peace either ought to be, or will be, permanent on this globe, unless the states pacifically organized preserve some of the old elements of army-discipline."[3] It seems that James' suggestion of discipline and Tolstoy's law of love complement each other and constitute the ingredients for a moral equivalent of violence; that is, the power of disciplined love provides an equivalency for the power of violence.[4]

Tolstoy's ethic derives from the words of Jesus that we should love one another as He has loved us. And the army discipline of James is reminiscent of Paul's letter to the Ephesians:

> Finally, grow strong in the Lord, with the strength of His power. Put God's armour on so as to be able to resist the devil's tactics. For it is not against human enemies that we have to struggle, but against the Sovereignties and the Powers who originate the darkness in this world, the spiritual army of evil in the heavens. That is why you must rely on God's armour, or you will not be able to put up any resistance when the worst happens, or have enough resources to hold your own ground.
> So stand your ground with truth buckled around your waist and integrity for a breastplate, wearing for shoes on your feet the eagerness to spread the gospel of peace, and always carrying the shield of faith so that you can use it to put out the burning arrows of the evil one. And then you must accept salvation from God to be your helmet and receive the word of God from the Spirit to use as a sword.[5]

Perhaps before proceeding it would be appropriate to comment on what might be described as a holy alliance operating within the philosophy and practice of nonviolence, an alliance between revelationists and rationalists, theologians and philosophers, theists and humanists. Tolstoy and Christians like him do not resist the evil doer but turn the other cheek, walk the extra mile, give to anyone who wishes to borrow, and practice love of their friends and enemies alike. The revelationists do not concern themselves with the "justice" or "injustice" of such ethical attitudes and actions; rather, they strive to love one another as Jesus loved them. (It was He who did not resist the evil doer, who turned the other cheek, who walked the extra mile, who loved his enemies and suffered for others.) The humanist approach in this holy alliance is exemplified by the following passage on the right to life as it relates to the rationales for war and violence:

> To say that the right to life is an unconditioned right entails that this right must be respected in all circumstances. Even the person who denies my right to life must not be denied his right to life. Even if the "enemy" destroys my life, I must respect his right to life.
> Another way of phrasing this . . . is to say that man is always an end in himself and never merely a means. This requires treating every human being—your enemies, your friends, and yourself—with human dignity. The right to be treated with human dignity presupposes the right to life and thus pacifism. To say that humans do not have the right to be treated with human dignity flies in the face of Kant's categorical imperative, Socrates' dictum in the *Crito*, not to mention the basic tenets of Christian ethics.[6]

But these are statements of theory. How does the power of nonviolence work in practice, that is, when one's guts are involved? A personal example—Joan Baez talks of her nonviolent attempt to stop a fight between two girls in prison:

> She was a black girl, and one time she picked a fight with a white girl from the kitchen. I knew the white girl was a non-fighter, so I went over to try to talk to the black girl. "Get out of my way," she said. But I stayed where I was standing, so that she couldn't move unless she kicked me aside. She didn't want to kick me. She had hold of the white girl's hair and was trying to kick her in the stomach, and there I was—in the way. Finally, her kicks got milder and then she exploded in tears. And I hugged her.[7]

A public example:

> The outbreak of the French and Indian War—"the commencement of a war with the most barbarious and savage enemy in this our late peaceful colony"—began a period of renewed trials for Virginia Quakers, as it did for some of their brethren in other provinces, as well as for members of the German peace sects. . . . But most Quakers living in the exposed frontier areas held their ground, though appearing "to the outward eye to be in imminent danger. . . . No Friend is known to have been attacked or killed by the Indian raiders."[8]

What was the Indians' attitude towards Quakers and Shakers? The Indians said, "We warriors meddle with a peaceable people. That people we know will not fight—it would be a disgrace to hurt such a people." The Indians left a white feather at the home of Shakers as a sign of peace.[9] The Quakers and the Indians lived in enduring peace for over seventy years while the Quakers governed Pennsylvania.[10]

The power of nonviolence was forceably stated by Martin Luther King, Jr. Speaking to the Detroit Council on Human Rights in 1963, he said:

> We've come to see the power of nonviolence. We've come to see that this method is not a weak method. For it's a strong man who can stand up amid opposition, who can stand up amid violence being inflicted upon him and not retaliate with violence. You see, this method has a way of disarming the opponent. It exposes his moral defenses . . . and he just doesn't know what to do. If he doesn't beat you, wonderful; but if he beats you, you developed a quiet courage of accepting blows without retaliating. If he doesn't put you in jail, wonderful; nobody with any sense likes to go to jail. But if he puts you in jail, you go in that jail and transform it from a dungeon of shame to a haven of freedom and unity. And I submit to you that if a man hasn't discovered something that he will die for, he isn't fit to live;[11]

The reader may question the necessity for searching out a moral equivalence to violence. The reader may say, "I consider myself to be moral. I'm a pacifist and a believer in nonviolence in general. I don't like any war unless it's necessary, and I certainly don't believe in doing violence to others except to defend myself. Self-defense is not even a matter of violence, it's a right we all have." It is toward such an attitude that much of the following discussion is directed.

For many, human violence is not considered a good in itself but a necessary means to achieve a good end—peace, justice, or some other noble goal. Human violence, though seldom considered moral, is often accepted simply because it is powerful, whereas nonviolence, though generally considered moral, is rejected because it is seen as lacking power, as even being passive. It is this point of view that is being challenged by this article and, more specifically, by the question, Is there a moral equivalent to the power of violence? That human violence is powerful is unquestionable. But what else is human violence?

WHAT IS VIOLENCE?

Perhaps any discussion that undertakes to examine the essence and experience of nonviolence must first make an attempt at reaching an understanding on what is meant by violence.

The *World Book Dictionary*, which should be considered an important and significant source since it is designed for use by the maturing adolescent and the young adult, defines violence in several ways, one being ". . . the illegal or unjust use of physical force to injure or damage persons or property."[12] *Black's Law Dictionary* defines violence as "unjust or unwarranted use of force."[13] *Webster's Third New International Dictionary* and the *American Heritage Dictionary* do not define violence in terms of its unjustified, illegal, or unwarranted use. Rather, they define violence as "exertion of any physical force as to injure or abuse"[14] or "physical force exerted for the purpose of violating, damaging, or abusing.[15]

The reader will note that all these definitions of violence employ the word *force*. To begin with, there is no doubt that violence requires force, particularly in physical relationships. But is it true that all force is violent? Only if we are willing to agree that all coercion is violent, can we legitimately state that all force is violent.

Now let us investigate some of the ways in which the words *force* and *violence* are employed. Violence is a word we tend to use when describing what someone else or some other country or some other organization is doing to us. Force is a word we tend to use when describing our reaction to an opponent's violence. For example, regarding the Vietnam War, it has been said that this country had a right to use whatever *force* was necessary to repel the *violence* of communism or of North Vietnam or of the Viet Cong. Now, the force that this country employed in Vietnam was the same force our opponents in that conflict used, namely physical violence. When we use it, we prefer to call it force; when they use it, we prefer to call it violence. Why? Presumably because violence has a negative connotation that force does not have. That type of semantic trickery only blocks our understanding of the meaning of violence. On a more personal level, if I physically harm another human being to the point of causing injury, I must recognize that I am not only forceful, I am violent. So, the first step in examining the meaning of violence is to recognize and admit that we, as well as our opponents, can be violent. Having taken that step, we can then take up the perennial question of whether the use of violence is justified.

With that question in mind, let us contend with violence as illegal, unjust, or unwarranted use of physical force, as defined by the *World Book* and *Black's Law* dictionaries. Such definitions suggest that as long as the act of force is justified, legalized, or warranted, that act is not violent (presumably because of the justice and legality innate in the force). The use of these modifiers of force only serve to obfuscate the meaning of violence. Violence is violence whether or not it is justified or legalized. And justice and authority cannot change violence into something such as "justified force" or "legalized force." If violence is determined on the basis of authorization, then any act, be that torturing, executing, or making war, would not be considered violent if the one committing such acts or causing them to be committed—be he a Roman Caesar or an American president—did so in the duly authorized execution of his office. (This could lead us to the curious conclusion that the obliteration of Carthage or the destruction of Viet Cong villages were not acts of violence.) Similarly, because an act is considered justified, it does not follow that it is nonviolent. In short, it is necessary to examine what we mean by violence before we employ such terms as "just" or "legal."

There are those who say that unless violence is intended it is not violence. What they usually mean is that one is not violent unless he wills the violence that results from his act, be that an act of commission or omission. But violence may exist independent of intent, though lack of intent may render the actor blameless. (Intentionality *is* relevant to an evaluation of the moral consequences of being or doing violence, and as such is properly a matter for our concern.)

Thus, to answer the question, What is violence? we must first recognize that violence is violence regardless of who employs it, and that justification, authorization, and lack of intent do not transform it into something else. With that in mind, let us work toward formulating our own tentative definition of violence. The *American*

Heritage Dictionary and the *Webster's Third New International Dictionary* definitions of violence are unacceptable because they limit violence to simply physical force.

But isn't there still some question as to the amount of force necessary to constitute violence? Are we violent if our use of physical force stops short of causing physical injury or when we cause hurt or damage to another's feelings? Does violence require a kind of permanent damage or injury, or are we in fact violent when we have caused only temporary pain or hurt? If we inflict physical pain and mental anguish on a mental patient with the intent of curing him, are we committing violence? It is a violent act to physically restrict that patient and deprive him of his freedom?

Any attempt to formulate a legalistic statement that would define exactly what constitutes violence in all its particulars is probably fruitless. However, we should have a working definition—what perhaps we might describe as a *prima facie* definition—for the purposes of investigating and discussing specific examples and situations. Only with some working definition, however tentative, can we investigate with any coherence and consistency the validity of such familiar views as war is violent but abortion is not. So let's try. Violence is the exercise of such force as to destruct the spirit, body, or environment of human life. It is immaterial whether the destruction is intended or whether the act is authorized or justified. Instead, the emphasis is on the result of the exercise of force—spiritual, physical, or environmental destruction.[16]

Perhaps a few examples would serve to test the definition of violence as the destruction of the spirit, body, or environment of a human life. The first type of violence inherent in this definition would involve an injury to the spirit (also described as mental or psychological injury) leading to destruction. An example of such injury would be the dehumanization intrinsic to segregation practices. Similarly, deep permanent spiritual injury could result from the use of racist or bigoted terminology, such as kike, nigger, spic, pig, etc. The second type of violence contemplated in our proposed definition would involve manifest physical injury to the body and could include such forms of destruction as maiming or killing. Under killing we would have to list suicide and all forms of homicide. Though arguments are advanced to justify certain types of killing, such as killing in war, capital punishment, euthanasia, and abortion, they are all forms of homicide and as such, together with suicide, constitute violence by our definition, regardless of justification. However, since euthanasia and abortion may be more difficult to picture as acts of violence, these forms of homicide require further comment.

There are cases where it is difficult to define euthanasia because of disagreement about what constitutes "human life." For instance, an individual may be damaged in an automobile accident so that his brain no longer functions, and his heart can only function with outside assistance. In such case, if we define life as requiring viable brain cells, the termination of the heartbeat would not be destroying human life for there could be no killing of a person already dead. But it should be noted that this and similar examples are very particular cases involving a definition of clinical death. In general, however, euthanasia must, by our definition, be classified as an act of violence.

A similar situation obtains in connection with abortion. There are those who argue that an embryo or fetus is not in fact a human being, and therefore the abortion of a fetus would not constitute violence as we have defined it. But if we accept the presence of brain waves as indicative of human life, then as soon as brain waves are exhibited by a fetus (some six to eight weeks after conception), we would be dealing with human life and, therefore, a human being. This is not meant to preclude the existence of other moral questions militating against the destruction of the embryo prior to the advent of brain waves.[17]

The last part of our definition of violence involves destruction of the environment of human life. What is meant here is the destruction of things of value to human life such as land, air, water, animals, etc. Uncontrolled fishing and strip-mining are clearly acts of violence. But destruction by pollution, though not so obvious, is also an act of violence. Finally let us remember that we are not only clearly capable of polluting the outside environment (air, water, land) with the wastes of homes and industry, but we also have the capacity of polluting our inside environment (lungs, liver, genes) with alcohol, tobacco or drugs; and perhaps this, too, constitutes acts of violence.

WHAT IS NONVIOLENCE?

Having developed and discussed a *prima facie* definition of violence, let us undertake an examination of nonviolence. To open our discussion, an investigation of the limited and specialized form of nonviolence known as pacifism is appropriate.[18] There are various types of pacifism, but all are directed against one kind of violence, physical violence, specifically that which results in killing and, more specifically, physical violence in the context of war. Pacifism, then, is not usually concerned with violence to the spirit or violence to the environment (except insofar as violence to the spirit or environment ensues from the violence of war).

There are three types of pacifism. Type one is theoretical, or what might be called idealistic, pacifism. It opposes war but not participation in it. It is characterized by those who are pacifists in peacetime and militarists in wartime in order to become pacifists again in peacetime. This kind of pacifist doesn't like war, doesn't desire war, doesn't justify war *per se*, but will make war for some "good" end. The second type of pacifism is called selective pacifism. Pacifists of this type oppose some wars and not others. Those that they oppose, they oppose absolutely, and will not participate in them for any reason regardless of the consequences, e.g., the Vietnam War pacifists. (There is an interesting variant of selective pacifism known as nuclear pacifism. The nuclear pacifists oppose all nuclear wars and participation in such wars on the basis that no good can be achieved in a war where the end can only be total destruction.) The third type is absolute pacifism, which opposes all war and all participation in war. Generally, pacifists of this type are totally nonviolent, though there are exceptions. A person, for example, may oppose the waging of war and refuse to participate in waging war, but may at the same time feel entirely justified in defending himself and others from violence.

Nonviolence falls into the same three categories—idealistic, selective, and absolute—although its scope is far wider. It is not limited to physical killing alone, as our definition indicates. The essential interrelationship of these three categories pivots around the use of force. There is in fact a continuum ranging from denying that the use of force has any validity to espousing the use of considerable force.

Leo Tolstoy's practice of nonviolence was powered by the concept of persuasive love—a force flowing out of the New Testament ethics which preached the loving of one another in imitation of Jesus. For Tolstoy belief in the power of persuasive love meant total rejection of the use of physical force of any type. Wherever he looked, Tolstoy saw physical force being used in extreme measure: in despotic governments, in the riotous and rebellious revolutionaries opposing these governments, and in the Russian Orthodox Church which preached the message of Jesus and, at the same time, blessed the guns of the czar. He rejected them all, believing that the prohibition against resistance found in the New Testament teachings militated against the use of any physical restraint whatsoever, whether by government, law, or police. But Tolstoy went even further. He would not restrain a mental patient, nor would he even spank a child. He epitomized the practice of complete and absolute nonviolence and declared that no physical force is justified at any time whatsoever. Tolstoy's brand of nonviolence is grounded in a negative, in a refraining from action, on the principle that one will not be violent or do violence to anyone or anything. He leaves us with a problem of developing a positive, of gathering together in a disciplinary fashion that bundle of love described in the New Testament and transforming it into the positive power needed to establish a moral equivalent of violence.

Adin Ballou, a contemporary of Tolstoy and an American Universalist clergyman, also practiced Christian nonviolence. Ballou, however, recognized that there was a type of noninjurious force which was at the same time loving and disciplined, and which could be powerfully active. Ballou said:

> But I go further, and disclaim using the term to express absolute passivity, even towards human beings. I claim the right to offer the utmost moral resistance, not sinful, of which God has made me capable, to every manifestation of evil among mankind. Nay, I hold it my duty to offer such moral resistance. In this sense my very non-resistance becomes a highest kind of resistance to evil . . .[19]

And with this Tolstoy would agree. But Ballou continues:

> There is an uninjurious, benevolent physical force. There are cases in which you would not only be allowable, but in the highest degree commendable to restrain human beings by this kind of force. Thus maniacs, the insane, the delirious sick, the ill natured children, the intellectually or immorally *non-compos mentis*, the intoxicated and the violently passionate, are frequently disposed to perpetrate outrage and inflict injuries, either on themselves or others, which ought to be kindly and uninjuriously prevented by the muscular energy of their friends.[20]

With this Tolstoy would clearly disagree.

Both Tolstoy and Ballou practiced a form of theological nonviolence that is described as nonresistance.[21] Others have employed certain aspects of nonresistance, developing a type of nonviolence called militant nonviolence or nonviolent direct action. Mahatma Gandhi and Martin Luther King, Jr. practiced this type of nonviolence which relies on coercive techniques such as boycotts and sit-ins. On the outer fringes of what might still be called nonviolence, the Fathers Berrigan practiced a form of limited violence—violence to property, in the form of seizing and burning draft records in protest against the Vietnam War—and Daniel Berrigan recommended the sparing use of sabotage. The antiwar May Day demonstrations of 1971, which planned to block all entrances to Washington, D.C. and close down the city, was another example of what we have called militant nonviolence.[22]

The practitioners of nonviolence we have just adverted to represent what might be described as a spectrum of force employed in nonviolence, ranging from refusing to spank a child to plotting the blockade of a city. Let us investigate this spectrum of force in nonviolence from a more systematic perspective by examining the relationships between passivism, passive resistance, nonresistance, noncooperation, nonviolent resistance, and civil disobedience. The type of nonviolence known as pacifism is often confused with passivism. Passivism may result from apathy or coercion and, of course, does not employ force in any form. Though the behavior exhibited by the passive person could be identical with that exhibited by the nonviolent person, the motivation or attitude would be quite different. Nonviolence is, of course, not motivated by apathy or coercion, but is active and freely chosen behavior, as we shall see.

The next category in our spectrum of force is a form of nonviolence called passive resistance. This brand of nonviolence offers no active resistance to the politically powerful primarily because those who are passively resistant lack any power—political or otherwise. However, when the passive resistant does gain power, he may quickly resort to violence. Lacking power, particularly political power, he is generally content with negative approaches such as noncooperation. By way of contrast, the nonresistant may be described as one who has found a nonpolitical source of power. The Christian version of nonresistance is based on the Gospel of Matthew where Jesus says "that of old it was said an eye for an eye and a tooth for a tooth but I say unto you resist not the evil doer but turn the other cheek, walk the extra mile . . ." Nonviolence of this type supports a very loving nonresistance to violence. It calls for loving one's enemies, for exercising great care in dealing with them so as to avoid any kind of hostility. This approach rejects the idea of coercion in any form and does not countenance such techniques as boycotts, strikes, and other nonviolent yet coercive activities.[23] Though Christian nonresistance shuns any type of violence even when violence is done to the nonresistant, it is by no means passive. It requires an active affirmation of love of enemy and an active attempt to change the heart of the enemy through the good witness of the Christian believer. This type of loving persuasion calls for the use of teaching, prayer, and noncoercive displays, marches, demonstrations, and petitions. But it also requires that one lay down one's life before using violence against an enemy.[24]

The relationship between Christian nonresistance and nonviolence in general might be described as follows. Christian nonresistance is essentially nonviolence based on the teachings of Jesus and is therefore theistic, which, of course, is not true of all forms of nonviolence. Its force is directed toward a change of attitude rather than a change of behavior which is where the emphasis lies in other forms of nonviolence. Christian nonresistance is nonpolitical—attempts to change behavior and conduct through the nonviolent but coercive implementation of new laws is beyond its scope. It shuns coercion and looks only to persuasion as a means towards change. It does not necessarily believe that change is inevitable or that nonviolence will work or be efficacious in creating a change. It is therefore reconciled to the possibility that universal peace and justice may not be attainable simply through the good works of nonviolent people; but for the Christian nonresistant material failure is irrelevant. The mere practice of Christian nonresistance insures a spiritual triumph greater than any which would result through political change.

The fourth category of nonviolence may be described as noncooperation. This category encompasses such actions as boycotts, withdrawals from social institutions, strikes, and refusals to pay war taxes or to go to war. In a sense, noncooperation may not constitute a separate category since its practices are characteristic of several types of nonviolence.

A fifth type of nonviolence, nonviolent resistance, would also utilize the techniques of noncooperation such as boycotts, strikes, etc., but in a far more active sense than that employed by practitioners of noncooperation.[25] Indeed, this is the least passive category of nonviolence and, in addition to employing the approaches of nonresistance and noncooperation, it is also characterized by nonviolent resistance, nonviolent direct action, and militant nonviolence. In fact, nonviolent resistance is often called nonviolent direct action or militant nonviolence, and in a sense the terms are interchangeable. This brand of nonviolence typically employs the physical intervention of sit-ins or nonviolent obstruction such as the attempted closedown of Washington, the take-over of university offices, the blocking off of military installations, etc. Within this category of nonviolence there exists a serious controversy between two extremes—the Gandhi-King approach and the Berrigan-New Left approach.

Basic differences between these two approaches are seen in the reluctance of Gandhi and King to break laws prohibiting burglary or sabotage, or guaranteeing free access, and the willingness of the Berrigans and the New Left to do just that in order to dramatize the violence being perpetrated elsewhere, for example, in Vietnam.[26] Secondly, the Gandhi-King approach, unlike that of the New Left, is reluctant to form coalitions with admittedly violent organizations for the purpose of gaining a stronger power base for social change.[27]

A further difference between the Berrigan-New Left brand of antiwar nonviolence and the more traditional nonviolent resistance of Gandhi and King lies in their use of discipline as opposed to the New Left's espousal of a modern freedom ethic. This ethic, which is based on what is called the freedom to do your own thing, is an essential component of the New Left movement. The youth engaged in antiwar demonstrations were simply demonstrating one application of that ethic. Emphasis on the value of doing one's own thing often conflicts with the value of discipline. It is essentially at this point that the traditional nonviolent ethic of Gandhi and King, with its emphasis on discipline, breaks down in the eyes of the more militant New Left youth. One may also observe that the very basic elements of that disciplined love proposed at the beginning of this selection by combining James's and Tolstoy's approaches (the disciplined love that is so highly developed in Christian forms of nonresistance) is lacking in the militant nonviolent freedom ethic. Eventually this lack contributed to some of the failures of the antiwar movement.

King and Gandhi formulated some very specific rules of discipline which guided their nonviolent demonstrations.[28] Rules of discipline they saw as necessary to maintain the power of nonviolence and the motivating force of love and respect for human life. Though they accepted that violence may erupt at a nonviolent demonstration (for example, where police resort to violence to stop a nonviolent demonstration) Gandhi and King were concerned that the proximate cause of any violence not be a result of a breakdown in discipline among those attempting to practice nonviolence. They recognized fully that the end result of such a breakdown would be the loss of the moral equivalent of violence—the power of nonviolence.[29]

Finally we should touch upon the concept of civil disobedience, which is related to all the above categories and is characterized by the examples of nonresistance, noncooperation and nonviolent resistance we mentioned before. The label "civil disobedience" simply designates a specific expression of nonviolence—a deliberate act of disobeying laws or legal authorities coupled with a willingness to submit to the legal consequences of such disobedience.[30]

ETHICAL CONSIDERATIONS

As societies were developed in various places and at various times throughout history, the law of the jungle, which allowed the physically powerful to rule the physically weak, was gradually replaced by some form of tribal, and later governmental, laws. But, though these laws prohibited, or at least abated, the violent use of individual power against another, they did not prohibit all forms of violence. Instead, parameters for the use of violence were established, such parameters being dictated by the current concept of justice. Initially this concept of justice was heavily couched in terms of revenge; still it formed a framework for laws that restricted the use of violence, particularly the practice of retributive justice. By the time of Christ, the code of Hammurabi and the Mosaic law—both of which were essentially grounded in retributive justice—had been refined, and the old law of eye for eye was under serious criticism. But retributive justice still reigned, though not as securely.

Then a new law was proclaimed—the law of love, which denied the justice of "eye for eye and tooth for tooth" and declared henceforth there would be no retaliation, neither for revenge nor for justice. It asked that man turn the other cheek, walk the extra mile, give away his cloak, love his enemies, and by so doing change his enemy's heart. This law embodied the spirit of nonresistance. It forbore the use of violence whether justified or not. Coupled with an affirmative, disciplined love, it gave rise to an equivalent of political power which was efficacious, spiritually if not materially. Very few, however (including those who call themselves Christians) followed this new law and new spirit of love. Most seemed content to remain under the old laws of retributive justice.

Some seventeen hundred years after Christ, a new look was cast in the direction of retributive justice. Jeremy Bentham, the eighteenth-century English jurist and philosopher, said that we should look at the consequences of a particular act, and from these consequences determine what is ethical. This approach, known as teleological utilitarianism, called for the greatest good for the greatest number. It gained a host of adherents in the English-speaking world and still probably predominates in our politics and ethics of today. So, in addition to the nonviolence ethics of the New Testament which revolutionized the deontological characteristics of retributive justice, we must also deal with the teleological questions of utilitarian goodness. Today some deontologists tell us we have a *just* obligation to defend ourselves and our country from aggressors, invoking the time-worn theory that it is just to use violence when violence is exercised by legitimate authority with just cause, with right intention, and with the probability of success. And today the utilitarians tell us that not only must we consider the probabilities of success but also the consequences of failing to defend ourselves and ask us, "Does not the greater good require that we defend ourselves, and is it not the lesser of two evils to kill the guilty who most probably will take the life of the innocent if we do not kill him?" (To that last query we may answer with Tolstoy who suggested that to make the assumption that the innocent life will indeed be taken is to make a certainty that which is only a probability.)

Let us regard a specific example of consequences. What are the consequences of failing to use violence to defend an innocent and defenseless person who is in imminent danger of being shot by a third party? Should we not consider the probable consequences of the situation, and is not the probable consequence of the situation, as we have described it, that an innocent person will be in fact shot?

But is this not also an assumption? Tolstoy says we should never make such an assumption because if we were to act on it and kill the third party before he has shot our innocent person, we become the murderer. We have murdered the probable murderer who then remains innocent of murder (albeit dead). If we are loving, as Tolstoy would have us to be, if we believe in the power of nonviolence, we must stand in the way of the bullets, we must defend the innocent and defenseless party with our bodies, with our spirit, with our person, but without violence. And thus we return to our starting point: James says we must have discipline, and Tolstoy says we must have love. And this love and discipline together constitute a power—a moral equivalent of violence—and with that power we can practice nonviolence regardless of the consequences. We may not win wars this way; we may, however, win our humanity!

THE MORAL EQUIVALENT OF VIOLENCE: THE POWER OF NONVIOLENCE

Whence comes the power of nonviolence? For the theist—whether he be Gandhi, the Hindu, or King, the Christian—it comes from God. The theist loves God and loves humankind seeing God therein. Therefore (s)he cannot kill man and woman, no matter how evil, no matter how unjust they be. (S)he hears the plea of the advocates of just war and just violence. But (s)he has learned that God is above the state, and it is in that authority that (s)he finds power. (S)he learns that there is a higher law than justice, one of love, which requires a forebearance of justice, the turning of the other cheek, and the giving of love to one's enemies. Legitimate authority, just cause, right intention, or probability of success can never be an excuse to kill an enemy once (s)he has learned that (s)he must love the enemy.

The humanist, instead, transcends not vertically but horizontally, and finds himself or herself in other men and women. (S)he finds in other men and women the same innate rights, and therefore (s)he reasons that to destroy the rights of other men and women would be to destroy his or her own rights. And so (s)he can never destroy the rights of others—the right to human life being the highest right —even to the extent that so as not to violate that highest right (s)he permits those who wish to destroy him or her to do so. (S)he will not destroy their rights even at the cost of his or her own life, although (s)he will use whatever rights (s)he possesses to avoid that possibility.

One may *do* nonviolence from time to time when it is tactically advantageous, where it may be more practical or realistic in the face of overwhelming power, or when because of passiveness or cowardliness there is no motivation or possibility to do otherwise; but one will never *be* nonviolent unless (s)he has found a moral equivalent to violence. This equivalent is found in the love for human life, one's own and that of others, and in the discipline to forebear one's own justice and practice nonviolence in the face of violence, in spite of the consequences. From this will come a power equivalent to, yet even greater than, the power of violence—the power of nonviolence.

NOTES

1. William James, *The Moral Equivalent of War* (Nyack, N.Y.: Fellowship Publications, 1960), p. 7.
2. Tolstoy was in fact much more the anarchist, as we shall see. He opposed organized government because of its coercive powers and was against private property because it was secured by force.
3. William James, op. cit., p. 9.
4. Though James's optimism concerning the outlawing of war seems as utopian as the utopians he criticized, his concept of discipline hardly deserves that label. Instead, the Jamesian concept of discipline might be said to provide the missing link in Tolstoy's almost perfect nonviolent ethic. The power of Tolstoy's ethic buttressed by James's discipline is witnessed in the lives and practices of Martin Luther King, Jr., Mahatma Gandhi, and Dorothy Day, among others.
5. Eph. 6:10-25, JB.
6. William Bruening, "In Defense of Pacifism," in *Self, Society, and the Search for Transcendence. An Introduction to Philosophy*, ed. William Bruening (Palo Alto, Cal.: Mayfield Publishing, formerly National Press Books, 1974), p. 302.
7. Joan Baez, "Playboy Interviews," *Playboy*, July 1970.
8. Peter Brock, *Pacifism in the United States* (Princeton, N.J.: Princeton University Press, 1968), p. 60.
9. Adin Ballou, *Christian Non-Resistance* (Philadelphia: Universal Peace Union, 1910), p. 193.
10. It was not until after the Pennsylvania legislature was grasped from the control of the Quakers that Pennsylvania voted with other colonies to arm in anticipation of a future war. Then the relationship between the Indians and the whites deteriorated, and violence came to Pennsylvania, just as it had come to the other colonies before.
11. William R. Miller, *Martin Luther King, Jr.* (New York: Avon Books, 1968), p. 168.
12. *World Book Dictionary* (1967).
13. *Black's Law Dictionary*, 4th ed. (1951).
14. *Webster's Third New International Dictionary* (1961).
15. *American Heritage Dictionary* (1973).
16. Destruction is defined in *Webster's Third International Dictionary* as "the action or process of destroying a material . . . object." It is synonymous with impairment and disintegration.
17. The embryo and the fetus are so identified with human life and human personality that the concept of human life can very easily be applied to the entire developmental process of the embryo and fetus from conception to birth.
18. Quite often people treat pacifism and nonviolence as synonymous. *Webster's New International Dictionary*, 2d ed., defines pacifism as "opposition to war or to the use of military force for any purpose; especially an attitude of mind opposing all war." This definition has the advantage of pointing up the proper focus of pacifism—war and acts connected with war.

19. Adin Ballou, op. cit., p. 2.
20. Ibid., p. 3.
21. The essence of nonresistance will be discussed later.
22. One might question whether such tactics are indeed beyond the pale of nonviolence. At best they may be considered as standing at the very outer fringe of nonviolent resistance.
23. See note 13.
24. The practice of this "loving persuasion" is typified by Mennonites, Brethren, and Quakers.
25. Compare also nonviolent nonresistance, where the emphasis in, say, refusing to go to war is placed on avoiding violence to others.
26. As a caveat to discussing the Berrigans and the New Left under one category, it should be noted that the New Left movement tends to look at nonviolence as a tactic rather than a philosophy of life. The approach of the Berrigan movement (if it can be so described) is similar to that of other groups espousing nonviolence in that nonviolence is seen not as a tactic but as a philosophy of life, albeit one which can afford violence to things and perhaps to institutional power (but never to persons).
27. Gandhi and King would probably reject the development of coalitions solely for such purpose because they would tend to erode group discipline.
28. Mohandas K. Gandhi, *Non-Violent Resistance* (New York: Schocken Books, 1951), pp. 87-88. Kenneth Slack, *Martin Luther King* (London: SCM Press, 1970), pp. 76-77.
29. Gandhi believed that discipline could not be maintained in the face of (1) the use of drugs, (2) the willingness to destroy property, (3) the use of obscenities, (4) the use of such violent techniques as forming a living wall of pickets, and, most of all, (5) the failure to believe in God, who is truth.
30. As in the case of passivism, civil disobedience of a violent nature cannot properly be considered nonviolence as we have described it. Such violent civil disobedient conduct as homicide, burglary, etc. is clearly outside the confines of the nonviolent ethic.

Frantz Fanon
CONCERNING VIOLENCE

Frantz Fanon was born in 1925 in Martinique, West Indies. He studied psychiatric medicine in France and in his late twenties wrote *Black Skin, White Masks,* where he described his experiences as a black psychiatrist. He died of cancer in 1961, soon after writing *The Wretched of the Earth,* from which this selection is taken. *The Wretched of the Earth* has become a vademecum and a declaration of independence not only for the revolutionists of the Third World about which it was written, but for the Black Power movement in the United States as well. Fanon argues both the necessity and inevitability of violence as a means for the oppressed to gain their freedom. Violence he sees as a "cleansing force," as a force that frees the oppressed from despair and inaction and "makes him fearless and restores his self-respect." In direct conflict with

King's view on nonviolence in the next article, Fanon views violence as investing the user with "positive and creative qualities." Reprinted by permission of Grove Press, Inc. Copyright © 1963 by Presence Africaine.

Fanon
CONCERNING VIOLENCE

National liberation, national renaissance, the restoration of nationhood to the people, commonwealth: whatever may be the headings used or the new formulas introduced, decolonization is always a violent phenomenon. At whatever level we study it—relationships between individuals, new names for sports clubs, the human admixture at cocktail parties, in the police, on the directing boards of national or private banks—decolonization is quite simply the replacing of a certain "species" of men by another "species" of men. Without any period of transition, there is a total, complete, and absolute substitution. It is true that we could equally well stress the rise of a new nation, the setting up of a new state, its diplomatic relations, and its economic and political trends. But we have precisely chosen to speak of that kind of *tabula rasa* which characterizes at the outset all decolonization. Its unusual importance is that it constitutes, from the very first day, the minimum demands of the colonized. To tell the truth, the proof of success lies in a whole social structure being changed from the bottom up. The extraordinary importance of this change is that it is willed, called for, demanded. The need for this change exists in its crude state, impetuous and compelling, in the consciousness and in the lives of the men and women who are colonized. But the possibility of this change is equally experienced in the form of a terrifying future in the consciousness of another "species" of men and women: the colonizers.

Decolonization, which sets out to change the order of the world, is, obviously, a program of complete disorder. But it cannot come as a result of magical practices, nor of a natural shock, nor of a friendly understanding. Decolonization, as we know, is a historical process: that is to say that it cannot be understood, it cannot become intelligible nor clear to itself except in the exact measure that we can discern the movements which give it historical form and content. Decolonization is the meeting of two forces, opposed to each other by their very nature, which in fact owe their originality to that sort of substantification which results from and is nourished by the situation in the colonies. Their first encounter was marked by violence and their existence together—that is to say the exploitation of the native by the settler—was carried on by dint of a great array of bayonets and cannons. The settler and the native are old acquaintances. In fact, the settler is right when he speaks of knowing "them" well. For it is the settler who has brought the native into existence and who perpetuates his existence. The settler owes the fact of his very existence, that is to say, his property, to the colonial system.

Decolonization never takes place unnoticed, for it influences individuals and modifies them fundamentally. It transforms spectators crushed with their inessentiality into privileged actors, with the grandiose glare of history's floodlights upon them. It brings a natural rhythm into existence, introduced by new men, and with it a new language and a new humanity. Decolonization is the veritable creation of new men. But this creation owes nothing of its legitimacy to any supernatural power; the "thing" which has been colonized becomes man during the same process by which it frees itself.

In decolonization, there is, therefore, the need of a complete calling in question of the colonial situation. If we wish to describe it precisely, we might find it in the well-known words: "The last shall be first and the first last." Decolonization is the putting into practice of this sentence. That is why, if we try to describe it, all decolonization is successful.

The naked truth of decolonization evokes for us the searing bullets and bloodstained knives which emanate from it. For if the last shall be first, this will only come to pass after a murderous and decisive struggle between the two protagonists. That affirmed intention to place the last at the head of things, and to make them climb at a pace (too quickly, some say) the well-known steps which characterize an organized society, can only triumph if we use all means to turn the scale, including, of course, that of violence.

You do not turn any society, however primitive it may be, upside down with such a program if you have not decided from the very beginning, that is to say from the actual formulation of that program, to overcome all the obstacles that you will come across in so doing. The native who decides to put the program into practice, and to become its moving force, is ready for violence at all times. From birth it is clear to him that this narrow world, strewn with prohibitions, can only be called in question by absolute violence.

The colonial world is a world divided into compartments. It is probably unnecessary to recall the existence of native quarters and European quarters, of schools for natives and schools for Europeans; in the same way we need not recall apartheid in South Africa. Yet, if we examine closely this system of compartments, we will at least be able to reveal the lines of force it implies. This approach to the colonial world, its ordering, and its geographical layout will allow us to mark out the lines on which a decolonized society will be reorganized.

The colonial world is a world cut in two. The dividing line, the frontiers are shown by barracks and police stations. In the colonies it is the policeman and the soldier who are the official, instituted go-betweens, the spokesmen of the settler and his rule of oppression. In capitalist societies the educational system, whether lay or clerical, the structure of moral reflexes handed down from father to son, the exemplary honesty of workers who are given a medal after fifty years of good and loyal service, and the affection which springs from harmonious relations and good behavior—all these aesthetic expressions of respect for the established order serve to create around the exploited person an atmosphere of submission and of inhibition which lightens the task of policing considerably. In the capitalist countries a multitude of moral teachers, counselors, and "bewilderers" separate the exploited from those in power. In the colonial countries, on the contrary, the policeman and the soldier, by their immediate presence and their frequent and direct action maintain contact with the native and advise him by means of rifle butts and napalm not to budge. It is obvious here that the agents of government speak the language of pure force. The intermediary does not lighten the oppression, nor seek to hide the domination; he shows them up and puts them into practice with the clear conscience of an upholder of the peace; yet he is the bringer of violence into the home and into the mind of the native.

The zone where the natives live is not complementary to the zone inhabited by the settlers. The two zones are opposed, but not in the service of a higher unity. Obedient to the rules of pure Aristotelian logic, they both follow the principle of reciprocal exclusivity. No conciliation is possible, for of the two terms, one is superfluous. The settlers' town is a strongly built town, all made of stone and steel. It is a brightly lit town; the streets are covered with asphalt, and the garbage cans swallow all the leavings, unseen, unknown, and hardly thought about. The settler's feet are never visible, except perhaps in the sea; but there you're never close enough to see them. His feet are protected by strong shoes although the streets of his town are clean and even, with no holes or stones. The settler's town is a well-fed town, an easygoing town; its belly is always full of good things. The settlers' town is a town of white people, of foreigners.

The town belonging to the colonized people, or at least the native town, the Negro village, the medina, the reservation, is a place of ill fame, peopled by men of evil repute. They are born there, it matters little where or how; they die there, it matters not where, nor how. It is a world without spaciousness; men live there on top of each other, and their huts are built one on top of the other. The native town is a hungry town, starved of bread, of meat, of shoes, of coal, of light. The native town is a crouching village, a town on its knees, a town wallowing in the mire. It is a town of niggers and dirty Arabs.

The look that the native turns on the settler's town is a look of lust, a look of envy; it expresses his dreams of possession—all manner of possession: to sit at the settler's table, to sleep in the settler's bed, with his wife if possible. The colonized man is an envious man. And this the settler knows very well; when their glances meet he ascertains bitterly, always on the defensive, "They want to take our place." It is true, for there is no native who does not dream at least once a day of setting himself up in the settler's place.

This world divided into compartments, this world cut in two is inhabited by two different species. The originality of the colonial context is that economic reality, inequality, and the immense difference of ways of life never come to mask the human realities. When you examine at close quarters the colonial context, it is evident that what parcels out the world is to begin with the fact of belonging to or not belonging to a given race, a given species. In the colonies the economic substructure is also a superstructure. The cause is the consequence; you are rich because you are white, you are white because you are rich. This is why Marxist analysis should always be slightly stretched every time we have to do with the colonial problem.

Everything up to and including the very nature of precapitalist society, so well explained by Marx, must here be thought out again. The serf is in essence different from the knight, but a reference to divine right is necessary to legitimize this statutory difference. In the colonies, the foreigner coming from another country imposed his rule by means of guns and machines. In defiance of his successful transplantation, in spite of his appropriation, the settler still remains a foreigner. It is neither the act of owning factories, nor estates, nor a bank balance which distinguishes the governing classes. The governing race is first and foremost those who come from elsewhere, those who are unlike the original inhabitants, "the others."

The violence which has ruled over the ordering of the colonial world, which has ceaselessly drummed the rhythm for the destruction of native social forms and broken up without reserve the systems of reference of the economy, the customs of dress and external life, that same violence will be claimed and taken over by the native at the moment when, deciding to embody history in his own person, he surges into the forbidden quarters. To wreck the colonial world is henceforward a mental picture of action which is very clear, very easy to understand and which may be assumed by each one of the individuals which constitute the colonized people. To break up the colonial world does not mean that after the frontiers have been abolished lines of communication will be set up between the two zones. The destruction of the colonial world is no more and no less than the abolition of one zone, its burial in the depths of the earth, or its expulsion from the country.

The natives' challenge to the colonial world is not a rational confrontation of points of view. It is not a treatise on the universal, but the untidy affirmation of an original idea propounded as an absolute. The colonial world is a Manichaean world. It is not enough for the settler to delimit physically, that is to say with the help of the army and the police force, the place of the native. As if to show the totalitarian character of colonial exploitation the settler paints the native as a sort of quintessence of evil.[1] Native society is not simply described as a society lacking in values. It is not enough for the colonist to affirm that those values have disappeared from, or still better never existed in, the colonial world. The native is declared insensible to ethics; he represents not only the absence of values, but also the negation of values. He is, let us dare to admit, the enemy of values, and in this sense he is the absolute evil. He is the corrosive element, destroying all that comes near him; he is the deforming element, disfiguring all that has to do with beauty or morality; he is the depository of maleficent powers, the unconscious and irretrievable instrument of blind forces. Monsieur Meyer could thus state seriously in the French National Assembly that the Republic must not be prostituted by allowing the Algerian people to become part of it. All values, in fact, are irrevocably poisoned and diseased as soon as they are allowed in contact with the colonized race. The customs of the colonized people, their traditions, their myths—above all, their myths—are the very sign of that poverty of spirit and of their constitutional depravity. That is why we must put the DDT which destroys parasites, the bearers of disease, on the same level as the Christian religion which wages war on embryonic heresies and instincts, and on evil as yet unborn. The recession of yellow fever and the advance of evangelization form part of the same balance sheet. But the triumphant communiqués from the missions are in fact a source of information concerning the implantation of foreign influences in the core of the colonized people. I speak of the Christian religion, and no one need be astonished. The Church in the colonies is the white people's Church, the foreigner's Church. She does not call the native to God's ways but to the ways of the white man, of the master, of the oppressor. And as we know, in this matter many are called but few chosen.

At times this Manichaeism goes to its logical conclusion and dehumanizes the native, or to speak plainly, it turns him into an animal. In fact, the terms the settler uses when he mentions the native are zoological terms. He speaks of the yellow man's reptilian motions, of the stink of the native quarter, of breeding swarms, of foulness, of spawn, of gesticulations. When the settler seeks to describe the native fully in exact terms he constantly refers to the bestiary. The European rarely hits on a picturesque style; but the native, who knows what is in the mind of the settler, guesses at once what he is thinking of. Those hordes of vital statistics, those hysterical masses, those faces bereft of all humanity, those distended bodies which are like nothing on earth, that mob without beginning or end, those children who seem to belong to nobody, that laziness stretched out in the sun, that vegetative rhythm of life—all this forms part of the colonial vocabulary. General de Gaulle speaks of "the yellow multitudes" and François Mauriac of the black, brown, and yellow masses which soon will be unleashed. The native knows all this, and laughs to himself every time he spots an allusion to the animal world in the other's words. For he knows that he is not an animal; and it is precisely at the moment he realizes his humanity that he begins to sharpen the weapons with which he will secure its victory.

As soon as the native begins to pull on his moorings, and to cause anxiety to the settler, he is handed over to well-meaning souls who in cultural congresses point out to him the specificity and wealth of Western values. But every time Western values are mentioned they produce in the native a sort of stiffening or muscular lockjaw. During the period of decolonization, the native's reason is appealed to. He is offered definite values, he is told frequently that decolonization need not mean regression, and that he must put his trust in qualities which are well-tried, solid, and highly esteemed. But it so happens that when the native hears a speech about Western culture he pulls out his knife—or at least he makes sure it is within reach. The violence with which the supremacy of white values is affirmed and the aggressiveness which has permeated the victory of these values over the ways of life and of thought of the native mean that, in revenge, the native laughs in mockery when Western values are mentioned in front of him. In the colonial context the settler only ends his work of breaking in the native when the latter admits loudly and intelligibly the supremacy of the white man's values. In the period of decolonization, the colonized masses mock at these very values, insult them, and vomit them up. . . .

Let us return to considering the single combat between native and settler. We have seen that it takes the form of an armed and open struggle. There is no lack of historical examples: Indochina, Indonesia, and, of course, North Africa. But what we must not lose sight of is that this struggle could have broken out anywhere, in Guinea as well as Somaliland, and moreover today it could break out in every place where colonialism means to stay on, in Angola, for example. The existence of an armed struggle shows that the people are decided to trust to violent methods only. He, of whom *they* have never stopped saying that the only language he understands is that of force, decides to give utterance by force. In fact, as always, the settler has shown him the way he should take if he is to become free. The argument the native chooses has been furnished by the settler, and by an ironic turning of the tables it is the native who now affirms that the colonialist understands nothing but force. The colonial regime owes its legitimacy to force and at no time tries to hide this aspect of things. Every statue, whether of Faidherbe or of Lyautey, of Bugeaud or of Sergeant Blandan—all these conquistadors perched on colonial soil do not cease from proclaiming one and the same thing: "We are here by the force of bayonets. . . ."[2] The sentence is easily completed. During the phase of insurrection, each settler reasons on a basis of simple arithmetic. This logic does not surprise the other settlers, but it is important to point out that it does not surprise the natives either. To begin with, the affirmation of the principle "It's them or us" does not constitute a paradox, since colonialism, as we have seen, is in fact the organization of a Manichaean world, a world divided up into compartments. And when in laying down precise methods the settler asks each member of the oppressing minority to shoot down 30 or 100 or 200 natives, he sees that nobody shows any indignation and that the whole problem is to decide whether it can be done all at once or by stages.[3]

This chain of reasoning which presumes very arithmetically the disappearance of the colonized people does not leave the native overcome with moral indignation. He has always known that his duel with the settler would take place in the arena. The native loses no time in lamentations, and he hardly ever seeks for justice in the colonial framework. The fact is that if the settler's logic leaves the native unshaken, it is because the latter has practically stated the problem of his liberation in identical terms: "We must form ourselves into groups of two hundred or five hundred, and each group must deal with a settler." It is in this manner of thinking that each of the protagonists begins the struggle.

For the native, this violence represents the absolute line of action. The militant is also a man who works. The questions that the organization asks the militant bear the mark of this way of looking at things: "Where have you worked? With whom? What have you accomplished?" The group requires that each individual perform an irrevocable action. In Algeria, for example, where almost all the men who called on the people to join in the national struggle were condemned to death or searched for by the French police, confidence was proportional to the hopelessness of each case. You could be sure of a new recruit when he could no longer go back into the colonial system. This mechanism, it seems, had existed in Kenya among the Mau Mau, who required that each member of the group should strike a blow at the victim. Each one was thus personally responsible for the death of that victim. To work means to work for the death of the settler. This assumed responsibility for violence allows both strayed and outlawed members of the group to come back again and to find their place once more, to become integrated. Violence is thus seen as comparable to a royal pardon. The colonized man finds his freedom in and through violence. This rule of conduct enlightens the agent because it indicates to him the means and the end. . . .

It is understandable that in this atmosphere, daily life becomes quite simply impossible. You can no longer be a fellah, a pimp, or an alcoholic as before. The violence of the colonial regime and the counterviolence of the native balance each other and respond to each other in an extraordinary reciprocal homogeneity. This reign of violence will be the more terrible in proportion to the size of the implantation from the mother country. The development of violence among the colonized people will be proportionate to the violence exercised by the threatened colonial regime. In the first phase of this insurrectional period, the home governments are the slaves of the settlers, and these settlers seek to intimidate the natives and their home governments at one and the same time. They use the same methods against both of them. The assassination of the Mayor of Evian, in its method and motivation, is identifiable with the assassination of Ali Boumendjel. For the settlers, the alternative is not between *Algérie algérienne* and *Algérie française* but between an independent Algeria and a colonial Algeria, and anything else is mere talk or attempts at treason. The settler's logic is implacable and one is only staggered by the counterlogic visible in the behavior of the native insofar as one has not clearly understood beforehand the mechanisms of the settler's ideas. From the moment that the native has chosen the methods of counterviolence, police reprisals automatically call forth reprisals on the side of the nationalists. However, the results are not equivalent, for machine-gunning from airplanes and bombardments from the fleet go far beyond in horror and magnitude any answer the natives can make. This recurring terror demystifies once and for all the most estranged members of the colonized race. They find out on the spot that all the piles of speeches on the equality of human beings do not hide the commonplace fact that the seven Frenchmen killed or wounded at the Col de Sakamody kindle the indignation of all civilized consciences, whereas the sack of the douars[4] of Guergour and of the dechras of Djerah and the massacre of whole populations—which had merely called forth the Sakamody ambush as a reprisal—all this is of not the slightest importance. Terror, counterterror, violence, counterviolence: that is what observers bitterly record when they describe the circle of hate, which is so tenacious and so evident in Algeria.

In all armed struggles, there exists what we might call the point of no return. Almost always it is marked off by a huge and all-inclusive repression which engulfs all sectors of the colonized people. This point was reached in Algeria in 1955 with the 12,000 victims of Philippeville, and in 1956 with Lacoste's instituting of urban and rural militias.[5]

Then it became clear to everybody, including even the settlers, that "things couldn't go on as before." Yet the colonized people do not chalk up the reckoning. They record the huge gaps made in their ranks as a sort of necessary evil. Since they have decided to reply by violence, they therefore are ready to take all its consequences. They only insist in return that no reckoning should be kept, either, for the others. To the saying, "All natives are the same," the colonized person replies, "All settlers are the same."[6]

When the native is tortured, when his wife is killed or raped, he complains to no one. The oppressor's government can set up commissions of inquiry and of information daily if it wants to; in the eyes of the native, these commissions do not exist. The fact is that soon we shall have had seven years of crimes in Algeria and there has not yet been a single Frenchman indicted before a French court of justice for the murder of an Algerian. In Indochina, in Madagascar, or in the colonies the native has always known that he need expect nothing from the other side. The settler's work is to make even dreams of liberty impossible for the native. The native's work is to imagine all possible methods for destroying the settler. On the logical plane, the Manichaeism of the settler produces a Manichaeism of the native. To the theory of the "absolute evil of the native" the theory of the "absolute evil of the settler" replies.

The appearance of the settler has meant in the terms of syncretism the death of the aboriginal society, cultural lethargy, and the petrification of individuals. For the native, life can only spring up again out of the rotting corpse of the settler. This then is the correspondence, term by term, between the two trains of reasoning.

But it so happens that for the colonized people this violence, because it constitutes their only work, invests their characters with positive and creative qualities. The practice of violence binds them together as a whole, since each individual forms a violent link in the great chain, part of the great organism of violence which has surged upward in reaction to the settler's violence in the beginning.

The groups recognize each other and the future nation is already indivisible. The armed struggle mobilizes the people; that is to say, it throws them in one way and in one direction.

The mobilization of the masses, when it arises out of the war of liberation, introduces into each man's consciousness the ideas of a common cause, of a national destiny, and of a collective history. In the same way the second phase, that of the building-up of the nation, is helped on by the existence of this cement which has been mixed with blood and anger. Thus we come to a fuller appreciation of the originality of the words used in these underdeveloped countries. During the colonial period the people are called upon to fight against oppression; after national liberation, they are called upon to fight against poverty, illiteracy, and underdevelopment. The struggle, they say, goes on. The people realize that life is an unending contest.

We have said that the native's violence unifies the people. By its very structure, colonialism is separatist and regionalist. Colonialism does not simply state the existence of tribes; it also reinforces it and separates them. The colonial system encourages chieftaincies and keeps alive the old Marabout confraternities. Violence is in action all-inclusive and national. It follows that it is closely involved in the liquidation of regionalism and of tribalism. Thus the national parties show no pity at all toward the caids and the customary chiefs. Their destruction is the preliminary to the unification of the people.

At the level of individuals, violence is a cleansing force. It frees the native from his inferiority complex and from his despair and inaction; it makes him fearless and restores his self-respect. Even if the armed struggle has been symbolic and the nation is demobilized through a rapid movement of decolonization, the people have the time to see that the liberation has been the business of each and all and that the leader has no special merit. From thence comes that type of aggressive reticence with regard to the machinery of protocol which young governments quickly show. When the people have taken violent part in the national liberation they will allow no one to set themselves up as "liberators." They show themselves to be jealous of the results of their action and take good care not to place their future, their destiny, or the fate of their country in the hands of a living god. Yesterday they were completely irresponsible; today they mean to understand everything and make all decisions. Illuminated by violence, the consciousness of the people rebels against any pacification. From now on the demagogues, the opportunists, and the magicians have a difficult task. The action which has thrown them into a hand-to-hand struggle confers upon the masses a voracious taste for the concrete. The attempt at mystification becomes, in the long run, practically impossible.

NOTES

1. We have demonstrated the mechanism of this Manichaean world in *Black Skin, White Masks* (New York: Grove Press, Inc., 1967).
2. This refers to Mirabeau's famous saying: "I am here by the will of the People; I shall leave only by the force of bayonets."—Trans.
3. It is evident that this vacuum cleaning destroys the very thing that they want to preserve. Sartre points this out when he says: "In short by the very fact of repeating them [concerning racist ideas] it is revealed that the simultaneous union of all against the natives is unrealizable. Such union only recurs from time to time and moreover it can only come into being as an active groupment in order to massacre the natives—an absurd though perpetual temptation to the settlers, which even if it was feasible would only succeed in abolishing colonization at one blow." *(Critique de la Raison Dialectique,* p. 346.)
4. Temporary village for the use of shepherds.—Trans.
5. We must go back to this period in order to judge the importance of this decision on the part of the French government in Algeria. Thus we may read in "Résistance Algérienne," No. 4, dated 28th March 1957, the following:

    "In reply to the wish expressed by the General Assembly of the United Nations, the French Government has now decided to create urban militias in Algeria. 'Enough blood has been spilled,' was what the United Nations said; Lacoste replies, 'Let us form militias.' 'Cease fire,' advised UNO; Lacoste vociferates, 'We must arm the civilians.' Whereas the two parties face to face with each other were on the recommendation of the United Nations invited to contact each other with a view to coming to an agreement and finding a peaceful and democratic solution, Lacoste decrees that henceforward every European will be armed and should open fire on any person who seems to him suspect. It was then agreed (in the Assembly) that savage and iniquitous repression verging on genocide ought at all costs to be opposed by the authorities: but Lacoste replies, 'Let us systematize the repression and organize the Algerian manhunt.' And, symbolically, he entrusts the military with civil powers, and gives military powers to civilians. The ring is closed. In the middle, the Algerian, disarmed, famished, tracked down, jostled, struck, lynched, will soon be slaughtered as a suspect. Today, in Algeria, there is not a single Frenchman who is not authorized and even invited to use his weapons. There is not a single Frenchman, in Algeria, one month after the appeal for calm made by UNO, who is not permitted, and obliged, to search out, investigate, and pursue suspects.

    "One month after the vote on the final motion of the General Assembly of the United Nations, there is not one European in Algeria who is not party to the most frightful work of extermination of modern times. A democratic solution? Right, Lacoste concedes; let's begin by exterminating the Algerians, and to do that, let's arm the civilians and give them *carte blanche.* The Paris press, on the whole, has welcomed the creation of these armed groups with reserve. Fascist militias, they've been called. Yes; but on the individual level, on the plane of human rights, what is fascism if not colonialism when rooted in a traditionally colonialist country? The opinion has been advanced that they are systematically legalized and commended; but does not the body of Algeria bear for the last one hundred and thirty years wounds which gape still wider, more numerous, and more deep-seated than ever? 'Take care,' advises Monsieur Kenne-Vignes, member of parliament for the MRP, 'do we not by the creation of these militias risk seeing the gap widen between the two communities in Algeria?' Yes; but is not colonial status simply the organized reduction to slavery of a whole people? The Algerian revolution is precisely the affirmed contestation of that slavery and that abyss. The Algerian revolution speaks to the occupying nation and says: 'Take your fangs out of the bleeding flesh of Algeria! Let the people of Algeria speak!'

    "The creation of militias, they say, will lighten the tasks of the Army. It will free certain units whose mission will be to protect the Moroccan and Tunisian borders. In Algeria, the army is six hundred thousand strong. Almost all the Navy and the Air Force are based there. There is an enormous, speedy police force with a horribly good record since it has absorbed the ex-torturers from Morocco and

Tunisia. The territorial units are one hundred thousand strong. The task of the Army, all the same, must be lightened. So let us create urban militias. The fact remains that the hysterical and criminal frenzy of Lacoste imposes them even on clearsighted French people. The truth is that the creation of militias carries its contradiction even in its justification. The task of the French Army is never-ending. Consequently, when it is given as an objective the gagging of the Algerian people, the door is closed on the future forever. Above all, it is forbidden to analyze, to understand, or to measure the depth and the density of the Algerian revolution: departmental leaders, housing-estate leaders, street leaders, house leaders, leaders who control each landing. . . . Today, to the surface checkerboard is added an underground network.

"In 48 hours two thousand volunteers were enrolled. The Europeans of Algeria responded immediately to Lacoste's call to kill. From now on, each European must check up on all surviving Algerians in his sector; and in addition he will be responsible for information, for a 'quick response' to acts of terrorism, for the detection of suspects, for the liquidation of runaways, and for the reinforcement of police services. Certainly, the tasks of the Army must be lightened. Today, to the surface mopping-up is added a deeper harrowing. Today, to the killing which is all in the day's work is added planified murder. 'Stop the bloodshed,' was the advice given by UNO. 'The best way of doing this,' replied Lacoste, 'is to make sure there remains no blood to shed.' The Algerian people, after having been delivered up to Massu's hordes, is put under the protection of the urban militias. By his decision to create these militias, Lacoste shows quite plainly that he will brook no interference with HIS war. It is a proof that there are no limits once the rot has set in. True, he is at the moment a prisoner of the situation; but what a consolation to drag everyone down in one's fall!

"After each of these decisions, the Algerian people tense their muscles still more and fight still harder. After each of these organized, deliberately sought after assassinations, the Algerian people build up their awareness of self, and consolidate their resistance. Yes; the tasks of the French Army are infinite: for oh, how infinite is the unity of the people of Algeria!"

6. This is why there are no prisoners when the fighting first starts. It is only through educating the local leaders politically that those at the head of the movement can make the masses accept (1) that people coming from the mother country do not always act of their own free will and are sometimes even disgusted by the war; (2) that it is of immediate advantage to the movement that its supporters should show by their actions that they respect certain international conventions; (3) that an army which takes prisoners is an army, and ceases to be considered as a group of wayside bandits; (4) that whatever the circumstances, the possession of prisoners constitutes a means of exerting pressure which must not be overlooked in order to protect our men who are in enemy hands.

Martin Luther King, Jr.

BLACK POWER

Martin Luther King, Jr. was born on January 15, 1929 in Atlanta, Georgia, and died on April 4, 1968 at the hands of an assassin. He was awarded the Nobel Peace Prize in 1964 as a leader of the nonviolent struggle for racial equality in the United

States. His numerous works include *Stride toward Freedom* (1958), *Strength to Love* (1963), and *Where Do We Go from Here: Chaos or Community?* (1967) from which this selection is taken. King argues for the use of nonviolence in the Negro struggle for racial equality on both pragmatic and moral grounds. Speaking out against violence which "deepens the brutality of the oppressor and increases the bitterness of the oppressed," King states that the Black Power violence can only result in a battle that the Negro cannot hope to win. Nonviolence—which involves "love in its strong and commanding sense"—he sees as the only "morally excellent" means by which the Negro can win his freedom and the only approach that will allay the irrational fears that foster the white community's practices of racial segregation. From pp. 54–66 *Where Do We Go From Here: Chaos or Community?* by Martin Luther King, Jr. Copyright © 1967 by Martin Luther King, Jr. By permission of Harper & Row, Publishers, Inc.

Probably the most destructive feature of Black Power is its unconscious and often conscious call for retaliatory violence. Many well-meaning persons within the movement rationalize that Black Power does not really mean black violence, that those who shout the slogan don't really mean it that way, that the violent connotations are solely the distortions of a vicious press. That the press has fueled the fire is true. But as one who has worked and talked intimately with devotees of Black Power, I must admit that the slogan is mainly used by persons who have lost faith in the method and philosophy of nonviolence. I must make it clear that no guilt by association is intended. Both Floyd McKissick and Stokely Carmichael have declared themselves opponents of aggressive violence. This clarification is welcome and useful, despite the persistence of some of their followers in examining the uses of violence.

Over cups of coffee in my home in Atlanta and my apartment in Chicago, I have often talked late at night and over into the small hours of the morning with proponents of Black Power who argued passionately about the validity of violence and riots. They don't quote Gandhi or Tolstoy. Their Bible is Frantz Fanon's *The Wretched of the Earth*.[1] This black psychiatrist from Martinique, who went to Algeria to work with the National Liberation Front in its fight against the French, argues in his book—a well-written book, incidentally, with many penetrating insights—that violence is a psychologically healthy and tactically sound method for the oppressed. And so, realizing that they are a part of that vast company of the "wretched of the earth," these young American Negroes, who are predominantly involved in the Black Power movement, often quote Fanon's belief that violence is the only thing that will bring about liberation. As they say, "Sing us no songs of nonviolence, sing us no songs of progress, for nonviolence and progress belong to middle-class Negroes and whites and we are not interested in you."

As we have seen, the first public expression of disenchantment with nonviolence arose around the question of "self-defense." In a sense this is a false issue, for the right to defend one's home and one's person when attacked has been guaranteed through the ages by common law. In a nonviolent demonstration, however, self-defense must be approached from another perspective.

The cause of a demonstration is the existence of some form of exploitation or oppression that has made it necessary for men of courage and goodwill to protest the evil. For example, a demonstration against *de facto* school segregation is based on the awareness that a child's mind is crippled by inadequate educational opportunities. The demonstrator agrees that it is better to suffer publicly for a short time to end the crippling evil of school segregation than to have generation after generation of children suffer in ignorance. In such a demonstration the point is made that the schools are inadequate. This is the evil one seeks to dramatize; anything else distracts from that point and interferes with the confrontation of the primary evil. Of course no one wants to suffer and be hurt. But it is more important to get at the cause than to be safe. It is better to shed a little blood from a blow on the head or a rock thrown by an angry mob than to have children by the thousands finishing high school who can only read at a sixth-grade level.

Furthermore, it is dangerous to organize a movement around self-defense. The line of demarcation between defensive violence and aggressive violence is very thin. The minute a program of violence is enunciated, even for self-defense, the atmosphere is filled with talk of violence, and the words falling on unsophisticated ears may be interpreted as an invitation to aggression.

One of the main questions that the Negro must confront in his pursuit of freedom is that of effectiveness. What is the most effective way to achieve the desired goal? If a method is not effective, no matter how much steam it releases, it is an expression of weakness, not of strength. Now the plain, inexorable fact is that any attempt of the American Negro to overthrow his oppressor with violence will not work. We do not need President Johnson to tell us this by reminding Negro rioters that they are outnumbered ten to one. The courageous efforts of our own insurrectionist brothers, such as Denmark Vesey and Nat Turner, should be eternal reminders to us that violent rebellion is doomed from the start. In violent warfare one must be prepared to face the fact that there will be casualties by the thousands. Anyone leading a violent rebellion must be willing to make an honest assessment regarding the possible casualties to a minority population confronting a well-armed, wealthy majority with a fanatical right wing that would delight in exterminating thousands of black men, women and children.

Arguments that the American Negro is a part of a world which is two-thirds colored and that there will come a day when the oppressed people of color will violently rise together to throw off the yoke of white oppression are beyond the realm of serious discussion. There is no colored nation, including China, that now shows even the potential of leading a violent revolution of color in any international proportions. Ghana, Zambia, Tanganyika and Nigeria are so busy fighting their own battles against poverty, illiteracy and the subversive influence of neo-colonialism that they offer little hope to Angola, Southern Rhodesia and South Africa, much less to the American Negro. The hard cold facts today indicate that the hope of the people of color in the world may well rest on the American Negro and his ability to reform the structure of racist imperialism from within and thereby turn the technology and wealth of the West to the task of liberating the world from want.

The futility of violence in the struggle for racial justice has been tragically etched in all the recent Negro riots. There is something painfully sad about a riot. One sees screaming youngsters and angry adults fighting hopelessly and aimlessly against impossible odds. Deep down within them you perceive a desire for self-destruction, a suicidal longing. Occasionally Negroes contend that the 1965 Watts riot and the other riots in various cities represented effective civil rights action. But those who express this view always end up with stumbling words when asked what concrete gains have been won as a result. At best the riots have produced a little additional antipoverty money, alloted by frightened government officials, and a few water sprinklers to cool the children of the ghettos. It is something like improving the food in a prison while the people remain securely incarcerated behind bars. Nowhere have the riots won any concrete improvement such as have the organized protest demonstrations.

It is not overlooking the limitations of nonviolence and the distance we have yet to go to point out the remarkable record of achievements that have already come through non-violent action. The 1960 sit-ins desegregated lunch counters in more than 150 cities within a year. The 1961 Freedom Rides put an end to segregation in interstate travel. The 1956 bus boycott in Montgomery, Alabama, ended segregation on the buses not only of that city but in practically every city of the South. The 1963 Birmingham movement and the climactic March on Washington won passage of the most powerful civil rights law in a century. The 1965 Selma movement brought enactment of the Voting Rights Law. Our nonviolent marches in Chicago last summer brought about a housing agreement which, if implemented, will be the strongest step toward open housing taken in any city in the nation. Most significant is the fact that this progress occurred with minimum human sacrifice and loss of life. Fewer people have been killed in ten years of nonviolent demonstrations across the South than were killed in one night of rioting in Watts.

When one tries to pin down advocates of violence as to what acts would be effective, the answers are blatantly illogical. Sometimes they talk of overthrowing racist state and local governments. They fail to see that no internal revolution has ever succeeded in overthrowing a government by violence unless the government had already lost the allegiance and effective control of its armed forces. Anyone in his right mind knows that this will not happen in the United States. In a violent racial situation, the power structure has the local police, the state troopers, the national guard and finally the army to call on, all of which are predominantly white.

Furthermore, few if any violent revolutions have been successful unless the violent minority had the sympathy and support of the nonresisting majority. Castro may have had only a few Cubans actually fighting with him, but he would never have overthrown the Batista regime unless he had had the sympathy of the vast majority of the Cuban people. It is perfectly clear that a violent revolution on the part of American blacks would find no sympathy and support from the white population and very little from the majority of the Negroes themselves.

This is no time for romantic illusions and empty philosophical debates about freedom. This is a time for action. What is needed is a strategy for change, a tactical program that will bring the Negro into the mainstream of American life as quickly as possible. So far, this has only been offered by the nonviolent movement. Without recognizing this we will end up with solutions that don't solve, answers that don't answer and explanations that don't explain.

Beyond the pragmatic invalidity of violence is its inability to appeal to conscience. Some Black Power advocates consider an appeal to conscience irrelevant. A Black Power exponent said to me not long ago: "To hell with conscience and morality. We want power." But power and morality must go together, implementing, fulfilling and ennobling each other. In the quest for power I cannot by-pass the concern for morality. I refuse to be driven to a Machiavellian cynicism with respect to power. Power at its best is the right use of strength. The words of Alfred the Great are still true: "Power is never good unless he who has it is good."

Nonviolence is power, but it is the right and good use of power. Constructively it can save the white man as well as the Negro. Racial segregation is buttressed by such irrational fears as loss of preferred economic privilege, altered social status, intermarriage and adjustment to new situations. Through sleepless nights and haggard days numerous white people struggle pitifully to combat these fears. By following the path of escape, some seek to ignore the questions of race relations and to close their minds to the issues involved. Others, placing their faith in legal maneuvers, counsel massive resistance. Still others hope to drown their fears by engaging in acts of meanness and violence toward their Negro brethren. But how futile are all these remedies! Instead of eliminating fear, they instill deeper and more pathological fears. The white man, through his own efforts, through education and goodwill, through searching his conscience and through confronting the fact of integration, must do a great deal to free himself of these paralyzing fears. But to master fear he must also depend on the spirit the Negro generates toward him. Only through our adherence to noviolence—which also means love in its strong and commanding sense—will the fear in the white community be mitigated.

A guilt-ridden white minority fears that if the Negro attains power, he will without restraint or pity act to revenge the accumulated injustices and brutality of the years. The Negro must show that the white man has nothing to fear, for the Negro is willing to forgive. A mass movement exercising nonviolence and demonstrating power under discipline should convince the white community that as such a movement attained strength, its power would be used creatively and not for revenge.

In a moving letter to his nephew on the one hundredth anniversary of emancipation, James Baldwin wrote concerning white people:

> The really terrible thing, old buddy, is that *you* must accept *them.* And I mean that very seriously. You must accept them and accept them with love. For these innocent people have no other hope. They are, in effect, still trapped in a history which they do not understand; and until they understand it, they cannot be released from it. They have had to believe for many years, and for innumerable reasons, that black men are inferior to white men. Many of them, indeed, know better, but, as you will discover, people find it very difficult to act on what they know. To act is to be committed, and to be committed is to be in danger. In this case, the danger, in the minds of most white Americans, is the loss of their identity.... But these men are your brothers—your lost, younger brothers. And if the word *integration* means anything, this is what it means: that we, with love, shall force our brothers to see themselves as they are, to cease fleeing from reality and begin to change it....²

The problem with hatred and violence is that they intensify the fears of the white majority, and leave them less ashamed of their prejudices toward Negroes. In the guilt and confusion confronting our society, violence only adds to the chaos. It deepens the brutality of the oppressor and increases the bitterness of the oppressed. Violence

**Chapter 3
PACIFISM AND
VIOLENCE**

is the antithesis of creativity and wholeness. It destroys community and makes brotherhood impossible.

My friend John Killens recently wrote in the *Negro Digest:* "Integration comes after liberation. A slave cannot integrate with his master. In the whole history of revolts and revolutions, integration has never been the main slogan of the revolution. The oppressed fights to free himself from his oppressor, not to integrate with him. Integration is the step after freedom when the freedman makes up his mind as to whether he wishes to integrate with his former master."[3]

At first glance this sounds very good. But after reflection one has to face some inescapable facts about the Negro and American life. This is a multiracial nation where all groups are dependent on each other, whether they want to recognize it or not. In this vast interdependent nation no racial group can retreat to an island entire of itself. The phenomena of integration and liberation cannot be as neatly divided as Killens would have it.

There is no theoretical or sociological divorce between liberation and integration. In our kind of society liberation cannot come without integration and integration cannot come without liberation. I speak here of integration in both the ethical and the political senses. On the one hand, integration is true intergroup, interpersonal living. On the other hand, it is the mutual sharing of power. I cannot see how the Negro will be totally liberated from the crushing weight of poor education, squalid housing and economic strangulation until he is integrated, with power, into every level of American life.

Mr. Killens' assertion might have some validity in a struggle for independence against a foreign invader. But the Negro's struggle in America is quite different from and more difficult than the struggle for independence. The American Negro will be living tomorrow with the very people against whom he is struggling today. The American Negro is not in a Congo where the Belgians will go back to Belgium after the battle is over, or in an India where the British will go back to England after independence is won. In the struggle for national independence one can talk about liberation now and integration later, but in the struggle for racial justice in a multiracial society where the oppressor and the oppressed are both "at home," liberation must come through integration.

Are we seeking power for power's sake? Or are we seeking to make the world and our nation better places to live. If we seek the latter, violence can never provide the answer. The ultimate weakness of violence is that it is a descending spiral, begetting the very thing it seeks to destroy. Instead of diminishing evil, it multiplies it. Through violence you may murder the liar, but you cannot murder the lie, nor establish the truth. Through violence you may murder the hater, but you do not murder hate. In fact, violence merely increases hate. So it goes. Returning violence for violence multiplies violence, adding deeper darkness to a night already devoid of stars. Darkness cannot drive out darkness: only light can do that. Hate cannot drive out hate: only love can do that.

The beauty of nonviolence is that in its own way and in its own time it seeks to break the chain reaction of evil. With a majestic sense of spiritual power, it seeks to elevate truth, beauty and goodness to the throne. Therefore I will continue to follow this method because I think it is the most practically sound and morally excellent way for the Negro to achieve freedom.

In recent months several people have said to me: "Since violence is the new cry, isn't there a danger that you will lose touch with the people in the ghetto and be out of step with the times if you don't change your views on nonviolence?"

My answer is always the same. While I am convinced the vast majority of Negroes reject violence, even if they did not I would not be interested in being a consensus leader. I refuse to determine what is right by taking a Gallup poll of the trends of the time. I imagine that there were leaders in Germany who sincerely opposed what Hitler was doing to the Jews. But they took their poll and discovered that anti-Semitism was the prevailing trend. In order to "be in step with the times," in order to "keep in touch," they yielded to one of the most ignominious evils that history has ever known.

Ultimately a genuine leader is not a searcher for consensus but a molder of consensus. I said on one occasion, "If every Negro in the United States turns to violence, I will choose to be that one lone voice preaching that this is the wrong way." Maybe this sounded like arrogance. But it was not intended that way. It was simply my way of saying that I would rather be a man of conviction than a man of conformity. Occasionally in life one develops a conviction so precious and meaningful that he will stand on it till the end. This is what I have found in nonviolence.

One of the greatest paradoxes of the Black Power movement is that it talks unceasingly about not imitating the values of white society, but in advocating violence it is imitating the worst, the most brutal and the most uncivilized value of American life. American Negroes have not been mass murderers. They have not murdered children in Sunday school, nor have they hung white men on trees bearing strange fruit. They have not been hooded perpetrators of violence, lynching human beings at will and drowning them at whim.

This is not to imply that the Negro is a saint who abhors violence. Unfortunately, a check of the hospitals in any Negro community on any Saturday night will make you painfully aware of the violence within the Negro community. By turning his hostility and frustration with the larger society inward, the Negro often inflicts terrible acts of violence on his own black brother. This tragic problem must be solved. But I would not advise Negroes to solve the problem by turning these inner hostilities outward through the murdering of whites. This would substitute one evil for another. Nonviolence provides a healthy way to deal with understandable anger.

I am concerned that Negroes achieve full status as citizens and as human beings here in the United States. But I am also concerned about our moral uprightness and the health of our souls. Therefore I must oppose any attempt to gain our freedom by the methods of malice, hate and violence that have characterized our oppressors. Hate is just as injurious to the hater as it is to the hated. Like an unchecked cancer, hate corrodes the personality and eats away its vital unity. Many of our inner conflicts are rooted in hate. This is why the psychiatrists say, "Love or perish." I have seen hate expressed in the countenances of too many Mississippi and Alabama sheriffs to advise the Negro to sink to this miserable level. Hate is too great a burden to bear.

Of course, you may say, this is not *practical*; life is a matter of getting even, of hitting back, of dog eat dog. Maybe in some distant Utopia, you say, that idea will work, but not in the hard, cold world in which we live. My only answer is that mankind has followed the so-called practical way for a long time now, and it has led inexorably to deeper confusion and chaos. Time is cluttered with the wreckage of individuals and communities that surrendered to hatred and violence. For the salvation of our nation and the salvation of mankind, we must follow another way. This does not mean that we abandon our militant efforts. With every ounce of our energy we must continue to rid our nation of the incubus of racial injustice. But we need not in the process relinquish our privilege and obligation to love.

Fanon says at the end of *The Wretched of the Earth*:

> So, comrades, let us not pay tribute to Europe by creating states, institutions and societies which draw their inspiration from her.
>
> Humanity is waiting for something other from us than such an imitation, which would be almost an obscene caricature.
>
> If we want to turn Africa into a new Europe, and America into a new Europe, then let us leave the destiny of our countries to Europeans. They will know how to do it better than the most gifted among us.
>
> But if we want humanity to advance a step further, if we want to bring it up to a different level than that which Europe has shown it, then we must invent and we must make discoveries.
>
> If we wish to live up to our peoples' expectations, we must seek the response elsewhere than in Europe.

Moreover, if we wish to reply to the expectations of the people of Europe, it is no good sending them back a reflection, even an ideal reflection, of their society and their thought with which from time to time they feel immeasurably sickened.

For Europe, for ourselves and for humanity, comrades, we must turn over a new leaf, we must work out new concepts, and try to set afoot a new man.[4]

These are brave and challenging words; I am happy that young black men and women are quoting them. But the problem is that Fanon and those who quote his words are seeking "to work out new concepts" and "set afoot a new man" with a willingness to imitate old concepts of violence. Is there not a basic contradiction here? Violence has been the inseparable twin of materialism, the hallmark of its grandeur and misery. This is the one thing about modern civilization that I do not care to imitate.

Humanity is waiting for something other than blind imitation of the past. If we want truly to advance a step further, if we want to turn over a new leaf and really set a new man afoot, we must begin to turn mankind away from the long and desolate night of violence. May it not be that the new man the world needs is the nonviolent man? Longfellow said, "In this world a man must either be an anvil or a hammer." We must be hammers shaping a new society rather than anvils molded by the old. This not only will make us new men, but will give us a new kind of power. It will not be Lord Acton's image of power that tends to corrupt or absolute power that corrupts absolutely. It will be power infused with love and justice, that will change dark yesterdays into bright tomorrows, and lift us from the fatigue of despair to the buoyancy of hope. A dark, desperate, confused and sin-sick world waits for this new kind of man and this new kind of power.

NOTES

1. Evergreen, 1966.
2. *The Fire Next Time*, Dial, 1963, pp. 22-23.
3. November, 1966.
4. *Op. cit.*, p. 255.

4 🞂 MEDICAL AND ENVIRONMENTAL ETHICS

AS PROFESSOR Malcolm Edwards has pointed out a couple of times, class discussions on violence have been rather violent themselves—particularly among the advocates of nonviolence. A few students are maintaining that the practice of nonviolence is an absolute.

"I believe in nonviolence, like you guys," says Jeff nodding to Alice and those sitting with her. "But, Professor Edwards, if we define a situation where nonviolence can't be avoided, then we can't make nonviolence an absolute, can we?"

"No, even one exception effectively destroys an absolute," agrees Edwards. "Do you have an example for us?"

"Well, what about abortion? I mean a case where deciding on whether or not to perform an abortion is actually deciding between saving the life of a child or the life of the mother. Then we can't avoid doing violence to one human being or the other."

The very subject of abortion causes immediate tension for several reasons. But, for some, Jeff's question theatens their newly found and neatly built theory that all violence is wrong. Alice is the first to react in defense. "How can you consider an embryo a human being?" she asks

"I should think that would depend on whom you asked," Edwards observes. "I have a feeling that, say, a philosopher, a theologian, a psychologist, and a biologist would all offer different opinions. And most of those opinions might well vary, depending on the age of the embryo."

"Age has nothing to do with it!" Bob calls out. "Every embryo has a soul, and that makes them human beings."

"Here we go again," says Cheri. "Can't we just assume, for the sake of argument, that the embryo is human and then ask ourselves when, and if, we can morally and/or legally take another's life?"

Alice starts to say something but Edwards cuts in. "All right, but can't we try to address ourselves to the dilemma that Jeff has posed?"

Cheri frowns and says slowly, "I can't see how you can kill a child to protect the mother. Violence is violence, and certainly killing a child qualifies as a violent act. Not that I mean to ignore the mother, but I think taking the child's life is immoral."

"But what if, as Jeff said, it's a choice between the mother's life and the child's?" asks Alice. "What's moral about killing the mother to save the child? That's sure violence and just as immoral, it seems to me."

"My point exactly!" says Jeff breaking in. "You can't avoid violence unless you refuse to do anything. And I wonder if that's not also a form of violence," Jeff adds thoughtfully.

"What about the violence and immorality involved in forcing a woman to have a child?" asks Alice, "I mean, refusing to let her have an abortion when she doesn't want the child, particularly a child resulting from rape?"

This provocative question is lost as the class is startled by a loud yawn. Terri looks at Edwards apologetically, but he gives her a sympathetic grin. "I've been listening," she says and shrugs when the class laughs. "One of the things that always interests me about this abortion bit is that it is a form of killing—some people even call it murder—yet it's treated with a sort of legal detachment."

"It *is* murder," says Cloteal.

"OK, but if it is, then legally it should be treated like murder, only we don't. I mean, the legal system doesn't treat abortion on a par with murder, at least not nowadays. In fact, we seem to be decriminalizing abortion. Isn't that the word we used?"

"I regret to say it is," says Edwards with a sigh. "It's one of the several ways we are committing violence to the English language."

"Well, I don't see that a change in the law requires us to change our moral position," says Cheri impatiently. "Are we supposed to get our morals from reading the latest Supreme Court decisions?"

Hands shoot up all over the room, and Professor Edwards steps in, in one of his rare moves to structure the discussion. "We seem to be sitting on a dilemma here, so let's cut away some underbrush. Let us assume that we are seeing a case where, for some of you, legal and moral considerations are in conflict. Let us also assume, for the sake of discussion only, that the fetus, or embryo, is human. Now, Cheri seems to be arguing that killing a human being is always wrong. There are others of you who indicate that taking a human life may, *at times,* be morally and legally defensible. Why don't we address ourselves to that difference of opinion?"

"I happen to think that we should look at more than the question of brute living," says Jeff. "I mean, Cheri seems to think that mere existence is a good, but what about the quality of that existence?"

"How does that relate to abortion?" asks Cheri.

"Actually, I was thinking more about euthanasia, but they're related. One deals with the beginning of life, the other with the end of life, but they still relate to the issue you talked about, Prof. Isn't it important to be consistent about those two issues, Mr. Edwards?"

"I'm not sure—perhaps—as long as we don't end up with the feeling that we are consistently wrong."

"For the record, I happen to believe that euthanasia is wrong too," says Cheri defiantly. "Am I alone?"

"What do you do for a guy who's got some incurable, terminal disease and is in terrible pain that can't be eased?" asks Jeff. "What do you do if he asks you to help him die so he can be free of his agony? For that matter, what if he is in a coma, and someone else begs you to stop the guy's suffering?"

"Yeah, doesn't a doctor have an obligation to help his patient in a case like that?" asks Doug.

"But hasn't he a higher obligation to preserve human life as long as possible?" demands Cheri.

"Not to me, he doesn't," Alice declares. "It's a matter of private morality if I want to die instead of continuing to suffer from a terminal disease. In fact, it's a private matter if I want an abortion. I think people have an obligation to leave my private life alone!"

"That's your problem," snaps Cheri. "But I still say that there is a moral obligation to save human life, and I don't approve of doctors practicing so-called mercy killing."

"Well, I wish we'd practice more abortion and euthanasia," says Doug suddenly. "Even though population growth is slowing down here, worldwide it's growing so fast we'll soon be up to our tails in people."

"You could use the same argument to support waging nuclear war," Edwards observes. "Surely that would be a more efficient way of reducing our population."

"OK, you made your point; it's a dumb solution. But what I'm really concerned about is not just the expanding population, but the expanding technology that goes with it, and the expanding pollution that goes with *that.* Our technology is running wild. And if you talk about war, I read that we have an overkill capacity in the range of 30 to 40. Talk about technology run wild! We're even conspicuous consumers when it comes to buying nuclear hardware."

"Being able to wipe out the earth 30 or 40 times over isn't conspicuous consumption; it's conspicuous destruction," says Terri closing her eyes again.

"Let's get back to your problem with technology and pollution," says Edwards with a smile.

"I think pollution is simply the result of technology run wild," says Doug. "Today we're talking about shortage of energy sources. By the year 2000 we have be short of even air to breathe and water to drink. We practice planned obsolescence not only in products but in building, and we leave a trail of junk and destruction behind us. If something can be built or made, we seem to think it has to be built or made, and we never ask what the human and environmental price tag will be. Come to think of it, you can't separate those two really. Sure, they talk about environmental protection; but big business makes big money by polluting and big government encourages it, and technology keeps running wild."

"Debbie? We haven't heard from you for a while."

"I think Doug forgets what technology has done for us. Our food supplies have been doubled, tripled, maybe more, by machines and other technological know-how. People complained about DDT, but the use of insecticides has also increased food output. And what about technical advances in medicine and sanitation that increase our life expectancies and improve our health? And what about all the labor-saving devices our technology has given us that increase our leisure time and improve our quality of life?"

"Come off it, Debbie!" says Don. "Leisure to do what? I wanted to drive around and see some of this country last summer, but with gas prices and shortages I couldn't get out of the backyard. The government and the oil and power companies have manipulated prices, and we little guys get ripped off. Technology is supposed to give us all the good life. But who can afford it? And, what's worse, as Doug says, technology is crapping up our environment."

"Well, if it's so bad, why do you depend on technology? Instead of driving your car, why don't you walk, why don't you back-pack into the mountains?" asks Debbie sweetly.

"I tried that, but I kept stumbling over empty pop bottles and plastic plates," snaps Don.

"Maybe it might be worthwhile thinking about why we got into this mess in the first place," Sheila suggests. "We seem to think we're lords of nature and maybe we aren't. Maybe our way of looking at the relationship between man and the rest of nature lets us think we can do what we want with nature without considering the consequences."

"Now we've come to something I can really talk about," says Roger softly. Since Roger seems to spend most of his class time either meditating or zonked out—depending on who is expressing an opinion—the class quiets down to hear him talk. "I'm into Eastern philosophy, and it seems to me that Western thought and Western religions are responsible for our ecological crisis. The East doesn't have any ecological problems like we do, except where Western technology has been introduced. I think technology is immoral and we should abandon it." Turning to Debbie, he adds, "I agree with you that technology does offer some benefits, but the benefits are killing us. I think the East can show us the way out of our mess."

"What do the rest of you think about Roger's suggestion that our Western way of looking at the world is the source of our technological and environmental problems?" asks Edwards.

"We're talking as if technology is some kind of independent Frankenstein monster," Cheri says promptly. "Technology isn't wrong in and of itself. It's us. We can use it to help us or hurt us. In some cases maybe we should curb its use or eliminate it. But I can see there are some areas where we can even use more technology, for example, in fighting pollution."

Cloteal, after having remained silent despite obvious irritation, breaks in. "I don't see anything wrong with technology either. I think those people who cry about environmental side effects are alarmist nuts. Anyway, as Cheri says, we can use technology to clean up pollution. We can build machines to clean up all the air and water we need. Think of that!"

"Right on!" says Louis. "Then we could build machines to clean up the pollution left by the machines cleaning up pollution, then we could . . ." The class laughs as Bob breaks in singing, "And the thigh bone connected to the hip bone . . ."

"This is ridiculous," snaps Bob. "You people talk about how wrong or abusive technology is, or how good it is. I agree with Cheri. It's how people use technology that makes it immoral or moral. My father has a plastic manufacturing plant that makes disposable bottles. Some ecology nuts say he's polluting the air. Well, if people didn't want the bottles, he wouldn't be making them. And he doesn't make people dump them around as litter. My father's not to blame, it's the people who want to use what he makes."

Just then the class bell rings, so Edwards steps in. "Bob has just opened an interesting area for discussion which, unfortunately, we don't have time to treat now. But let us assume that we do have problems in the area of technology and environment and that these problems affect us all to some extent and, to some extent, we are all responsible for these problems. Can we offer any solutions?"

"Why don't we just lead a simpler life?" Roger asks. "We don't need all the gadgets and gimmicks of technology. The East has shown us that."

"At least we could pool our resources and make more efficient use of them," Cheri suggest, "for example, car pools. There we use technology, but we limit its use."

Obie, with a broad grin on his face, says, "I'm worried about all the trees we're cutting down for paper. What about book pools?"

"I'm not sure I know what you mean," says Edwards.

"Sharing books, like cars. For example, when your book you told us about comes out next year, why don't you tell the publisher to print fewer copies and have him tell people to share them instead? What do you say to that?"

"I say, class dismissed."

FOR FURTHER READING

Baier, Kurt, and Rescher, Nicholas, eds. *Values and the Future.* New York: Free Press, 1969. A good reader analyzing values in the context of technology. Articles by Alvin Toffler, Kenneth Boulding, and J. Kenneth Galbraith are included.

Bruening, William H. "The Ambiguity of Abortion." In *Self, Society, and the Search for Transcendence,* edited by William H. Bruening. Palo Alto, Ca.: Mayfield Publishing, formerly National Press Books, 1974. An unusual essay that argues against both the proabortionist position and the antiabortionist position. The author presents his views in a Socratic fashion.

Callahan, Daniel. *Abortion: Law, Choice, and Morality.* New York: Macmillan, 1970. One of the best books available on the subject of abortion. The volume of statistics is overwhelming, and the author argues his own position well.

Carson, Rachel. *Silent Spring.* Boston: Houghton Mifflin, 1962. The book that gave the first warning of an impending environmental crisis. The author wrote about pollutants and pesticides, the "elixirs of death" that would destroy our air and water.

Cutler, Donald, ed. *Updating Life and Death.* Boston: Beacon, 1968. An anthology of articles offering an interdisciplinary view of crucial problems in medical ethics. It is well worth reading and not too difficult, even for the beginner.

Douglas, William O. *A Wilderness Bill of Rights.* Boston: Little, Brown, 1965. About a decade ago, Justice Douglas composed a "wilderness bill of rights." He examines population, pollution, and the rights of man, and advocates a land-conservation ethic.

Feinberg, Joel. *The Problem of Abortion.* Belmont, Ca.: Wadsworth, 1973. A valuable anthology containing some of the more popular philosophical essays on the subject of abortion by Noonan, Callahan, Thomson, Tooley, and others.

Hamilton, Michael, ed. *The New Genetics and the Future of Man.* Grand Rapids, Mich.: Eerdmans, 1972. An anthology that focuses on medical issues arising out of the field of genetics. The approach is interdisciplinary and the book is well organized.

Institute of Society, Ethics, and the Life Sciences. *The Hastings Center Studies* and *The Hastings Center Report.* Hastings-On-Hudson, N.Y.: Institute of Society, Ethics, and the Life Sciences. These two publications should be available in every college library, and readers are encouraged to ask librarians to obtain them if they are not already available. Not only are the articles well written, but the bibliographical work is invaluable.

Noonan, John, Jr., ed. *The Morality of Abortion: Legal and Historical Perspectives.* Cambridge, Mass.: Harvard University Press, 1970. An anthology of well-written essays offering some legal matter rarely included in anthologies. A table of statutes and a table of cases make interesting bibliography for those interested in the legal aspects of abortions.

Ramsey, Paul. *The Patient as Person: Exploration in Medical Ethics.* New Haven, Conn.: Yale University Press, 1970. The author treats a wide range of topics seldom covered in medical ethics books. He also focuses on a number of problem areas relating to the making and breaking of ethical codes.

Reich, Charles. *The Greening of America.* New York: Bantam, 1971. In this highly popular work, Reich writes about the growing consciousness of environmental crises in America.

Roszac, Theodore. *The Making of a Counter-Culture.* Garden City, N.Y.: Doubleday, 1969. The author reflects on a technocratic society and the opposition to such a society among the young. He examines the thoughts of Marcuse, Watts, Ginsberg, Goodman, Brown, and others.

_____, ed. *Sources: An Anthology of Contemporary Materials Useful for Preserving Personal Sanity While Braving the Great Technological Wilderness.* New York: Harper & Row, 1972. An anthology described as a compilation of "contemporary materials useful for preserving personal sanity while braving the great technological wilderness," and offering a diversity of views in articles by poets, psychiatrists, philosophers, and natural scientists.

Teich, Albert, ed. *Technology and Man's Future.* New York: St. Martin, 1972. Teich examines four aspects of technology: (1) scientific views of advancing technology, (2) the philosophy of the technological age, (3) synthesizing technological developments, and (4) movements toward controlling technology. Articles by McLuhan, Marcuse, and Ferkiss are included.

Theobald, Robert. *An Alternative Future for America.* Chicago: Swallow Press, 1968. The author is one of the best known "futurists" in America. He suggests initiatives for solving the problems of hunger, poverty, the ecology crisis, and technology—initiatives which, if implemented, would, in Theobald's opinion, change the present technocratic scene.

Toffler, Alvin. *Future Shock.* New York: Bantam, 1971. This book, written at a time when affluence and growth were thought to be here to stay, is perhaps not quite so relevant today. The author's analysis is, however, thought-provoking for anyone interested.

_____, ed. *The Futurists.* New York: Random House, 1972. This well-known anthology examines the future for technology and the environment as viewed by social critics, scientists, philosophers, and planners. Articles by Margaret Mead, Arthur Waskow, and R. Buckminster Fuller are included.

Truitt, Willis, and Solomons, T. W. G., eds. *Science, Technology, and Freedom.* Boston: Houghton-Mifflin, 1974. This anthology discusses science, technology and culture; the origins and history of science; and the moral and political issues arising from science and technology. It includes articles by Jacques Ellul, C. P. Snow, Aldous Huxley, and René Dubos.

Baruch A. Brody

ABORTION AND THE SANCTITY OF HUMAN LIFE

Baruch A. Brody, coeditor (with Nicolas Capaldi) of *Science, Men, Methods and Goals* (1969) and editor of *Moral Rules and Particular Circumstances* (1970), teaches at the Massachusetts Institute of Technology. In the following selection Brody poses the question, "If a foetus is a human being the destruction of which is wrong as the taking of any human life, are there any extreme circumstances in which an abortion would still be morally permissible?" Arguing by analogy from a series of hypothetical case histories, Brody finds only one, extremely limited, set of circumstances in which abortion could be morally justifiable. "Abortion and the Sanctity of Human Life" was originally published in *American Philosophical Quarterly* 10 (April 1973), pp. 133-40, and it is reprinted here by permission of the publisher and the author.

One of our most fundamental moral intuitions is that, except in the most extreme circumstances, it is wrong to take a human life. This intuition is, however, not very precise, partially because of the vagueness of "extreme circumstances" and partially because of the unclarity about what is a human life. The problem about abortion is a difficult one just because of this latter unclarity. There are those who, with good reason, claim that a foetus is a human being the taking of whose life is, except in the most extreme circumstances, wrong; destroying a foetus, according to this position is just as wrong as the taking of any other human life. There are, however, others who claim, with equally good reason, that a foetus is not a human being and that, therefore, its destruction is permissible in many cases in which it would be wrong to take a human life. Because it is so difficult, given the vagueness of "human life," to decide which of these claims about the foetus is correct, it is very difficult to decide when, if ever, an abortion is morally[1] permissible.

I should like, in this [selection], to consider the following issue: if a foetus is a human being the destruction of which is as wrong as the taking of any human life, are there any extreme circumstances in which an abortion would still be morally permissible? In particular, would it be permissible in order to save the life of the mother?

There are three reasons for being concerned with this question: (a) it just may be the case that a foetus is a human being. If so, then an answer to our question will be the answer to the question as to whether it actually is permissible to perform an abortion in order to save the life of the mother; (b) given that we do not know whether the foetus is a human being, it would be helpful to have an answer to our question for if (as seems possible) it is that it would still be permissible to perform the abortion, then we will at least know that an abortion is permissible in some of the cases in which the need for it is greatest; (c) a consideration of this issue may shed some light upon what are the extreme circumstances in which it is permissible to take a human life.

I

The most obvious reason for supposing that it is permissible to perform an abortion in order to save the life of the mother, even though the foetus is a human being, is that such an abortion would be a permissible act of defending oneself. After all, the foetus's continued existence poses a threat to the life of the mother which she can meet, if necessary, by taking the life of the foetus.[2]

This simple argument from the right to kill the pursuer will not do for there is an important difference between the case of an abortion and the normal case of killing the pursuer. In the normal case of killing the pursuer, B is attempting to take A's life and is responsible for that attempt. It is this guilt which, together with the fact that A will die unless B is stopped, seems to justify the taking of B's life. In the case of an abortion, however, the situation is quite different. Leaving aside for now—we shall return to it later on—the question as to whether the foetus is attempting to take the mother's life, we can certainly agree that the foetus is not responsible for such an attempt (if it is occurring), that the foetus is therefore totally innocent, and that the taking of his life cannot therefore be compared to the ordinary case of killing the pursuer.[3]

Let us put this point another way. Consider the following case: there is just enough medicine to keep either A or B alive; B legitimately owns it, and will not give it to A. In this case, the continued existence of B certainly poses a threat to the life of A; A can survive only if B does not survive. Still, one would not say that it is permissible for A to kill B in order to save A's life. Why not? How does this case differ from the ordinary case of killing the pursuer? The simplest answer is that in this case, while B's continued existence poses a threat to the life of A, B is not guilty of attempting to take A's life; he is not even attempting to do so. On the other hand, in the ordinary case of a pursuer, B is guilty of attempting to kill A. Now if we consider the case of a foetus whose continued existence poses a threat to the life of the mother, we see that it is like the medicine-case and not like the ordinary case of killing the pursuer. The foetus does pose a threat to the life of its mother, but it is not guilty of attempting to take its mother's life. Consequently, analogously to the medicine-case, the mother (or her agent) could not justify destroying the foetus on the ground that it is a permissible act of killing the pursuer.

This objection, while persuasive, is not entirely convincing, and something more must be said about the whole matter of pursuers before we can definitely decide whether an abortion to save the life of the mother could be viewed as a permissible act of killing the pursuer. If we look again at a normal pursuer case, we see that there are three factors involved:

(1) the continued existence of B poses a threat to the life of A, a threat that can be met only by the taking of B's life,

(2) B is justly attempting to take A's life,

(3) B is responsible for his attempt to take A's life.

In the medicine-case, only condition (1) was satisfied, and our intuitions that it would be wrong for A to take B's life in that case are justified by the fact that the mere satisfaction of (1) does not guarantee that killing B will be a justifiable act of killing a pursuer. But it would be rash to conclude, as we did, that all of conditions (1)-(3) must be satisfied before one has a case in which the killing of B will be a justifiable act of killing a pursuer. What would happen, for example, if conditions (1) and (2), but not (3), were satisfied?

There are good reasons for supposing that the satisfaction of (1) and (2) is sufficient for someone's being justified in taking B's life as an act of killing the pursuer. Consider, for example, a normal case of pursuit (e.g., where B is about to shoot A and the only way in which A can stop him is by killing him first) with the modification that B is a minor who is not responsible for his attempt to take A's life.[4] In this case, conditions (1) and (2) but not (3) are satisfied. Still, despite the fact that (3) is not satisfied, it seems that A may justifiably take B's life because doing so is a permissible act of killing a pursuer. So guilt of the pursuer is not a requirement for legitimate cases of killing the pursuer.[5]

Are there any cases in which the satisfaction of (1) and something weaker than (2) is sufficient for A's justifiably killing B as an act of killing a pursuer? It seems that there are. Consider, for example, the following case: B is about to press a button that apparently turns on a light and there is no reason for him to suspect what is the case, viz., that his doing so will blow up a bomb that will destroy A. Moreover, the only way in which we can stop B and save A's life is by taking B's life (there is no opportunity to warn him, etc.). In such a case, neither conditions (2) nor (3) are satisfied. B is not attempting to take A's life, and, *a fortiori*, he is not responsible for, or guilty of, any such attempt. Nevertheless, one is inclined to say that this is still a case in which one would be justified in taking B's life in order to save A's life, that this is a legitimate case of killing a pursuer.

How does this case differ from the medicine-case? Or, to put our question another way, what condition—other than (2)—in addition to (1) is satisfied in this case, but not in the medicine-case, and is such that its satisfaction—together with the satisfaction of (1)—is sufficient to justify our killing B as an act of killing a pursuer? As we think about the two cases, the following idea seems to suggest itself: there is, in this case, some action that B is doing (pressing the button) that results in A's death and which is such that if B knew about this result and still did the action voluntarily he would be to blame for the loss of A's life. In this case, if B knew that A would die if he pressed the button and still pressed it voluntarily, he would be to blame[6] for the loss of A's life. In the medicine-case, on the other hand, there is no such action. It is true that B's refusing to give A the medicine does result in A's death. But even if he knows that and still voluntarily refuses to give A the medicine, he is not to blame for the loss of A's life. A man is not obligated to give up his life to save the life of another person and he is not to blame for the loss of that other person's life when he does refuse to sacrifice himself. It would seem then that it is sufficient, for A to be justified in taking B's life as an act of killing a pursuer, that, in addition to the satisfaction of condition (1), the following condition be satisfied:

(2') B is doing some action that will lead to A's death and is such that if B is a responsible person who did it voluntarily knowing that this result would come about, B will be to blame for the loss of A's life.

To summarize, then, our general discussion of killing the pursuer, we can say that if conditions (1) and (2) or (2') are satisfied, one would be justified in taking B's life in order to save A's life. The satisfaction of (3) is not required.

Let us return now to the problem of abortion and, working with the assumption that the foetus is human, apply these results to the case of the foetus whose continued existence poses a threat to the life of his mother and see whether, in that case, it would be permissible, as an act of killing a pursuer, to abort the foetus in order to save the mother. The first thing that we should note is that our initial objection to the claim that the foetus could be aborted because its abortion is a permissible act of killing a pursuer is mistaken. Our objection was that the foetus is not responsible for any attempt to take the life of the mother, that the foetus is innocent. But that only means that condition (3) is not satisfied and we have seen that the satisfaction of (3) is not necessary.

Is, then, the aborting of a foetus when necessary to save the life of the mother a permissible act of killing a pursuer? Well, in such cases, condition (1) is satisfied, so the only question that we have to consider is whether (2) or (2') is also satisfied. It is clear that (2) is not satisfied. The foetus, after all, has neither the beliefs nor the intentions that would be necessary for any of his actions (if he does act) to be an attempt, on his part, to take the life of his mother. Nor is (2') satisfied. Even if we endow the foetus with the beliefs and intentions of an adult, none of his actions are such that his doing them would result in his being to blame for the loss of his mother's life. The most that he would then be trying to do is to grow to maturity and be born mortally, and even a superendowed foetus would not, because he tried to do that, be to blame for the resulting loss of his mother's life.^x

We conclude, therefore that the mother cannot justify aborting her foetus, even when its continued existence threatens her life, on the grounds that it is a permissible taking of the life of a pursuer. What we must now consider is the possibility that there could be some other justification for aborting the foetus in that case even if the foetus is human.

II

Are there any cases in which it would be permissible to take one life to save another although they are not cases of killing a pursuer? The following seem to be such cases (even if a bit overdramatic—overdramatic cases are still cases):

(a) By a series of accidents for which no one is to blame, it has come about that the five people in room r_2 and the one person in room r_1 will be blown up by a bomb in the next sixty seconds. The only way to prevent this is to defuse the bomb by blowing up its triggering mechanism which is in room r_1. Unfortunately, this necessarily means that the person in r_1 will also be blown up. He is, however, the only one who will die; if you do nothing, all of the six people in question will die. It does seem that one ought to blow up that triggering mechanism and save those lives even if it does mean taking the life of the person in r_1.

(b) A small village is surrounded by a hostile group of brigands who demand that the villagers kill Joe, an innocent villager whom the brigands dislike. If the villagers do not do this, the brigands threaten to (and the villagers have every reason to believe that they will) destroy the village and everyone in it (including Joe). The village is cut off from outside help and giving in to their demands is the only way to save the village. Again, it does seem that one ought to save the life of the villagers even if it does mean taking Joe's life.

How are we to account for these cases? Why, in these cases, is it permissible (and perhaps even obligatory) to take the life of one person in order to save the life of others? Remember, these are not cases of killing a pursuer; only condition (1) is met in any of them. At least three answers suggest themselves:

(I) In these cases, the person whose life you will be taking is going to die anyway. If you take his life, however, you can save those other lives. Taking his life is an optimal act since no lives are sacrificed and some are gained, and that is why it is okay to take his life. In general, it is permissible to take B's life and to save A's life if B is going to die anyway and taking B's life is the only way of saving A's life.
(II) In these cases, it is a question of sacrificing one life to save many other lives. While the life to be sacrificed is tremendously valuable, so are all the lives that can be saved, and when we weigh them, we find that the many lives outweigh the one. This may, of course, seem like a harsh attitude, but it would be even harsher to forget about the many lives you can save by sentimentally refusing to take one life. In general, it is okay to take B's life to save the lives of A and C (where $A \neq C$) if taking B's life is the only way of saving their lives.
(III) In these cases, one does not intend to take the life of anyone; what one is trying to do is to save some lives. The loss of life is an unintended, although certainly foreseen, consequence of a perfectly permissible (and perhaps even obligatory) action. In general, it is okay to do an action that will result in the taking of A's life if you do not intend that result, although it may be foreseen, and the intended results outweigh this unfortunate unintended result.

Of these three accounts, it seems that the third is the least satisfactory. To begin with, it rests upon the dubious distinction between the intended results of an action and the foreseen inevitable consequences of it. Secondly, and perhaps even more seriously, it supposes that the distinction is relevant to the moral evaluation of the action (and not merely the agent). This seems highly questionable. Finally, it does not really handle the second of our cases. When, in that case, the villagers take Joe's life, the taking of Joe's life is precisely what they intend to bring about by, and is not a mere inevitable consequence of, their action. To be sure, it is not the ultimate purpose of their action, but that is irrelevant. So the third account doesn't even explain why it is permissible for them to take Joe's life.

We turn then to the more plausible accounts, (I) and (II). What is the difference between them? The first says that, in our cases, it is permissible to take someone's life just because he will die anyway. The second says that, in our cases, it is permissible to take someone's life because doing that will result in the saving of the most possible lives. These two accounts will, then, disagree in cases where a person would survive if you did not take his life but the taking of his life would result in the saving of many other lives. According to our first account, it would be wrong for you, in such a case, to take that person's life; one cannot sacrifice someone's life to save the life of some other people. According to our second account, however, it would be permissible, in such cases, to kill that person in order to save the other people. After all, one would still be maximizing the number of lives saved.

Once one sees that this is the fundamental difference between the two accounts, one also sees what is wrong with (II). It, in a way, is very much like standard utilitarian theories. Analogously to the utilitarian maximization of happiness, it claims that, in cases like ours, the right action is the one that maximizes the number of human lives saved. And like standard utilitarian theories, it does not do justice to considerations of fairness. We object, on grounds of lack of fairness, to actions that maximize human happiness by making some few people suffer in order that many will be happy. We should similarly object, on the same grounds of lack of fairness, to actions that maximize the number of lives saved by sacrificing some few lives (that would not otherwise be lost) to save a larger number of lives. (I), in contrast, is not open to such objections. It only allows one to take B's life when not taking it won't make a difference, when he will die anyway. In such cases, B is not being treated unfairly, and given that taking his life will save these other lives, it is permissible (and perhaps even obligatory) to do so.

This point emerges even more clearly if we imagine the following two modifications of cases (a) and (b):

- (a') By a series of accidents for which no one is to blame, it has come about that the five people in room r_2 (and only they) will be blown up by a bomb in the next sixty seconds. The only way to prevent this is to defuse the bomb by blowing up its triggering mechanism in room r_1, but this means that the single person in room r_1 will die.
- (b') A small village is surrounded by a hostile group of brigands who, interested (for their own diabolic reasons) in seeing that the villagers kill an innocent man, demand that the villagers kill Joe. If the villagers do not do this, the brigands threaten to (and the villagers have every reason to believe that they will) kill all of the village leaders (this does *not* include Joe). The village is cut off from outside help and giving in to their demands is the only way to save the village leaders.

The important thing to note here is that, according to (II), we should still blow up the triggering mechanism and the villagers should still kill Joe. After all, it is still a question of taking one life to save others. But this just seems mistaken; the acts in question would be wrong because they would be unfair to the man in r_1 and to Joe. Only account (I) takes this into consideration and says, correctly, that it would be wrong for us, in cases (a') and (b'), to kill the man in r_1 or to kill Joe, although it would be permissible for us to do that in cases (a) and (b). It would seem, therefore, that (I) is to be preferred to (II).

It might be objected that we are introducing, in our objection to (II), an asymmetry between taking lives and saving lives that is not justified. After all, while we have been concerned with the unfairness to the man whose life might be taken by us, we have not, it could be argued, been properly concerned with the unfairness to the men whose lives will be lost if we don't act. Why should their lives be sacrificed in order to spare the life of the other man? Isn't that unfair to them?

In a way, I agree with this objection. I have supposed that there is asymmetry between the two; however, this supposition seems justified. Consider, once more, case (a'). If I destroy the triggering mechanism, then I will not have met an obligation that I have toward the man in room r_1, viz., the obligation not to take his life. And when I try to justify not meeting that obligation by saying that I did so in order to save the lives of some other people, it seems open for someone to object that I am acting unfairly to this man by neglecting this vital obligation I have toward him so that others will benefit. The situation is very different if I don't destroy the triggering mechanism. Then, there is no obligation that I have towards the people in r_2 that I have, unfairly, not met. After all, even if one agrees that a man has an obligation to save the lives of his fellow human beings,[9] that obligation is certainly not present when I can only save their lives by taking other lives. The same point can, of course, be made about (b').

This reply depends, of course, upon the assumption that, in cases like (a') and (b'), the obligation to a man not to take his life remains while the obligation towards a man to save his life does not. But this is quite plausible; the former obligation is clearly more important than the latter and is present in a great many cases in which the latter is not. After all, while I am normally under an obligation to another man not to take his life even though this means my losing my own life (and even more so if it only means a worsening in the quality of my life or a loss of all I possess), I certainly am not normally under an obligation[10] to another man to save his life at the cost of my own life (or even at the cost of a significant lowering in the quality of my life or of the loss of all that I possess).

If, then, we agree[11] to accept (I) rather than (II) as our account of why, in the cases that we are considering, it is permissible to take some lives to save others, how, working upon our assumption that the foetus is human, does that affect what we think about the problem of abortion? It seems that its major effect is the following: we have to distinguish two types of cases in which we might want to abort the foetus to save the mother. In one case, if we do nothing, the foetus will survive and the mother will die. Such cases are, of course, only possible at the very end of pregnancy. In such a case, we ought not to abort the foetus, for taking its life to save the life of the mother would be unfair. On the other hand, we may have a case in which, if we do nothing, neither the mother nor the foetus will survive. In such a case, aborting the foetus is not unfair to it, and given the truth of (I), it follows that it is permissible for us to abort it to save the mother if this is the only way to save her.[12]

We seem to have found one case in which, even if we assume that the foetus is a human being entitled to all of the rights to life had by any other human being, it would be permissible to abort the foetus to save the life of its mother. But our argument for this claim depends upon the truth of (I), and since this principle is not unproblematic, we must turn to a further consideration of it.

III

There is a standard objection against (I) that must be considered first. The rationale behind (I) is that, in such cases, everything is gained and nothing is lost by taking the life of the individual in question. From the point of view of lives saved, this seems correct; no additional lives will be lost, and some will be saved, by taking the life of that individual. But aren't there other respects in which something will be lost, in which something bad will have occurred? Won't a murder be committed by you, one that would not otherwise be committed? Therefore, it is simply not true that nothing is lost by taking that person's life.

Proponents of this objection often embellish it with references to the mortal sin that one would commit by this act of murder and to the punishment which will be forthcoming as a consequence of this. Such embellishments, like the original objection, rest upon the presupposition that some evil act, viz., an act of murder, has been committed. I turn therefore to a consideration of this presupposition.

One obviously has to distinguish four possible descriptions of A's taking the life of B: (1) A has taken B's life, (2) A has taken the life of an innocent man B, (3) A has taken the life of an innocent man B who is not pursuing A, and (4) A has murdered B. There clearly are cases in which (1) and, as we saw in Section I, (2) are correct descriptions of an action but (4) is not. In a way, the question that we considered in the last section was whether there could be cases in which (3) would be a correct description of an act but (4) would not. The defenders of (I) say that there are such cases; these are the cases in which B would die anyway. The proponents of our objection would deny this. But they cannot assume that their denial is correct in the course of their arguments without being circular. This is, however, precisely what they do. In trying to show that it would be wrong, in such cases, for A to take B's life, they assume that doing that would be murder, that doing that would be an unjustified taking of a human life, and by assuming that, they beg the question.

There are, however, more serious objections to (I), ones that can be met only by modifying that principle, and we turn therefore to a consideration of them. To begin with, whenever one takes B's life to save A's life, B is going to die anyway. It's just a matter of time for all of us. So, as (I) now stands, one can always take someone's life if it is the only way of saving the life of someone else, and this is clearly mistaken. Obviously, we need some condition that is stronger than "B is going to die anyway."

Two suggested modifications of (I) seem plausible. They are:

(I') It is permissible to take B's life to save A's life if B is going to die anyway in a relatively short time and taking B's life is the only way of saving A's life.

(I'') It is permissible to take B's life to save A's life if taking B's life is the only way of saving A's life and, if nothing is done, the same event will cause the death of A and B.

Looking at our examples (a) and (b), we see how these modified principles work. (I') allows for the killing of the man in r_1 because he will die anyway in the next sixty seconds and it allows for the killing of Joe because he will die anyway when (in the near future) the brigands destroy the village. (I'') allows for the killing of the man in r_1, because, if nothing is done, he and the people in r_2 will both be killed by the bomb's explosion and it allows for the killing of Joe because, if nothing is done, he and all of the villagers will be killed in the brigands' destruction of the village. On the other hand, neither (I') nor (I'') will allow us to take the life of any B to save the life of any A when that is the only way to do so. After all, in the normal case, B is not going to die anyway in a relatively short period of time, and, if nothing is done, the event that causes B to die (when he does eventually die) will not be the same event as the one that caused A's death.

In trying to decide between (I') and (I''), it will be helpful if we see more clearly the differences in their implications. A consideration of the following two modifications of our original bombing case helps bring out these differences:

(a'') By a series of accidents for which no one is to blame, it has come about that the five people in room r_2 (and only they) will be blown up by a bomb in the next sixty seconds. The only way to prevent this is to defuse the bomb by blowing up its triggering mechanism in room r_1 but this means that the single person in room r_1 will die; however, he will die anyway from cancer within the next few hours.

(a''') By a series of accidents for which no one is to blame, it has come about that the five people in room r_2 (and only they) will be blown up by a bomb in the next sixty seconds. The only way to prevent this is to defuse the bomb by blowing up its triggering mechanism in room r_1 but this means that the single person in room r_1 will die. If nothing is done, he will be wounded by the explosion of the bomb and will even eventually die from these wounds; however, he will live for a few years leading a restricted life.

(I') allows for the killing of the man in r_1 in case (a'') because he will die anyway in a relatively short time, but it does not allow for the killing of the man in r_1 in case (a''') since he will live on for some years. (I''), on the other hand, allows for the killing of the man in r_1 in case (a''') since, if nothing is done, his death will be caused by the same explosion that kills the people in r_2, but it does not allow for the killing of the man in r_1 in case (a'') since, if nothing is done, his death will be caused by his cancer and not by the explosion that will kill the people in r_2.

Which, if either, of these principles is correct? One thing seems pretty clear. The whole rationale, in cases like the ones we are considering, for taking some life to save others is that he whose life will be taken loses nothing of significance and is not therefore being treated unfairly. But if, as in cases like (a'''), he will live if we do nothing for a considerable amount of time, our taking his life now means that we will have unfairly subjected him to a significant loss. Consequently, the whole rationale for the taking of lives in such cases collapses, and, in cases like (a'''), it would be unfair and wrong to take that person's life. Since, however, (I'') allows for the killing of the man in r_1 in case (a'''), it is mistaken.

We see, then, that the question of how long B is going to live is central to the question as to whether we can kill him to save A. What we must now consider is whether anything else plays a role, and, in particular, whether the nature of the cause of B's death if we do nothing is at all relevant. To put the question another way, is (I′) true or must we add to it the additional condition that, if nothing is done, the same event will cause the death of A and B?

It is extremely difficult to answer this question. On the one hand, people (myself, my friends whom I have consulted) have the intuition that this additional requirement is reasonable. For this reason, they are troubled by the idea that it is permissible, in case (a″), to take the life of the man in r_1. On the other hand, this additional requirement is totally unreasonable. After all, if the whole justification for taking a human life in these cases is that nothing is lost by doing so and no one is, therefore, being treated unfairly, then it should be permissible to take that life whenever nothing is lost and no one is treated unfairly. That seems to be the case whenever the person in question will die anyway in the very near future,[13] so why should we be concerned with the nature of the cause of his death if we do nothing? I conclude, therefore, that we should adopt (I′), following here our rationale and not our intuitions.

There are, however, serious problems even with (I′). Consider a case in which both A and B will die in a relatively short time if nothing is done, taking B's life is the only way to save A's life, and taking A's life is the only way to save B's life. According to (I′), it would be permissible for anyone to take B's life in order to save A's life. This, however, seems wrong. Why should B's life be sacrificed to save A's life instead of A's life being sacrificed to save B's? Similarly, according to (I′), it would be permissible for anyone to take A's life in order to save B's. This, too, seems wrong. Why should A's life be sacrificed to save B's life rather than B's life being sacrificed to save A's?

The simplest solution to this problem would be to replace (I′) with:

(I‴) It is permissible to take B's life to save A's life if B is going to die anyway in a relatively short time, taking B's life is the only way of saving A's life, and taking A's life (or doing anything else) will not save B's life. This, however, will not do, for (I‴) does not allow us, in the case we are considering, to save either A or B. We must let them both die since the situation does not favor one over the other. This type of Buridan's Ass conclusion makes (I‴) unattractive.

It would seem far better to replace (I′) with:

(I'''') It is permissible to take B's life to save A's life if B is going to die anyway in a relatively short time, taking B's life is the only way of saving A's life and either (i) taking A's life (or doing anything else) will not save B's life or (ii) taking A's life (or doing anything else) will save B's life but one has, by a fair random method, determined that one should save A's life rather than B's life.

Notice that (I'''') entails that, in the case we are now considering, one should not, because it is not permissible to, simply take the life of one to save the life of the other. Rather, one should choose whose life is to be saved and whose life is to be sacrificed by a fair random method. The rationale for this is pretty straightforward. When (i) is not the case, we face a choice as to whom we should save and whose life we should take (and we clearly should take one to save the other), so the only way that we can avoid being unfair is to use a random device to choose for us.

How do these modifications in our original principle, (I), affect the issue of abortion? Well, since (I'''') places even stronger restrictions on the taking of a human life than does (I), it certainly does not allow as permissible any abortions that were not allowed as permissible under (I). But there are some abortions that are, according to (I), permissible but which are not according to (I''''). According to (I), an abortion is always permissible if both the foetus and mother will die if nothing is done and the only way to save the mother is to abort the foetus. According to (I''''), an abortion is permissible only if, in addition to the satisfaction of those conditions, it is the case that the foetus will die in a relatively short time if nothing is done and either there is no way to save the foetus or there is a way but, by a fair random procedure, we have determined that we should save the mother and not the foetus.

I conclude, therefore, that if the foetus is a human being having the same right to life as does any other human being, then the fact that the mother would die otherwise does not justify an abortion unless the very stringent requirements laid down in (I'''') are met.

NOTES

1. This is a question about morals, not about the legal question of whether there should be laws prohibiting abortion. On that issue, see my "Abortion and the Law," *Journal of Philosophy*, 1971.
2. To be sure, it is the abortionist, and not the mother, who will destroy the foetus, but that is irrelevant. To begin with, in such cases, it is permissible for him whose life is threatened (A) to, if necessary, either take the life of him (B) who threatens him or call upon someone else to do so. And more importantly, it seems permissible (and perhaps even obligatory in some cases) for a third person to take B's life

in order to save A's life even if A has not called upon him to do so (we leave aside the question as to whether it is permissible if A objects). For this reason, it seems better to say that it is permissible to take the life of the pursuer, when necessary to save the life of the pursued, rather than to say that it is permissible to take lives, when necessary for self-defense. On this point, see *Talmud Sanhedrin* 72b-75a.
3. This is, essentially, the argument of Pius XI (in *Casti Connubii*, Section 64).
4. This point, and its significance, was first pointed out by R. Huna when he said (*Talmud Sanhedrin*, 72b) that a pursuer who is a minor can be stopped even by killing him.
5. It should be noted that this point wreaks havoc with a very plausible analysis of why we are justified in taking the life of the pursuer. According to this analysis, B's guilt for his attempt to take A's life together with the threat that his continued existence poses for A's life justifies the taking of B's life. Or, to put this analysis another way, B's guilt makes A's life take precedence over B's. We now see that this intuitively plausible analysis cannot be right. After all, in cases where conditions (1) and (2) but not (3) are satisfied, B has incurred no guilt for his attempt to take A's life and his guilt cannot therefore be used to explain why we are justified in taking B's life in order to save A's life.
6. He need not be the only one to blame. The person who placed the bomb might also be responsible. All that is required is that he be to blame.
7. We leave open the question as to whether the satisfaction of either (2) or (2′) is necessary.
8. This is presumably what the Talmud means when (op. cit.) it rejects the justification of its being a killing of a pursuer because "only heaven is pursuing her." The talmudic justification (in *Ohalot*, 7:2) for abortions in the cases we have been considering is that the foetus does not have the same right to life as an ordinary human being. An examination of that claim, however, lies beyond the scope of this paper.
9. Even this is unclear. It may only be a good thing that one do it; the claim that there is an obligation is, of course, much stronger than that, and it may be too strong.
10. One may suppose, however, that this would be a saintly act. But, especially if one is opposed to suicidal acts or to martyrdom, one may not even suppose this. See, on this point, Zevin's *Le'or HaHalacha* (Tel Aviv: 1957), pp. 14-16.
11. (1) is, essentially, the opinion of R. Yochanan in (*Jerusalem Talmud, Trumah*, chapter 8) his discussion of the biblical case of Sheva ben Bichri. For a full account of the talmudic debate on that case, see Maimonides, *Laws of the Foundations of the Tora*, 5, 5 and the commentaries on his discussion.
12. This point was well made in *Responsa Panim Me'irot* (Sulzbach: 1738), vol. III, no. 8.
13. This point helps to shed light upon what is meant by "in a relatively short time." The important thing is that B should not suffer any significant losses (in terms of unrealized potentialities for the period between the time we take his life and the time at which he would have died anyway) because of the taking of his life. Consequently, we must attend to his expectations for that period as well as to its length. It may, after all, be permissible to take B's life even if, had we done nothing, he would have lived for five years so long as he would live them in a coma. In the case of a person with normal expectations, however, five years would certainly be too long.

220 *Joseph Fletcher*
EUTHANASIA: OUR RIGHT TO DIE

Joseph Fletcher, a leading exponent of what is called "situation ethics," is a former dean of St. Paul's Cathedral in Cincinnati, Ohio, and former Professor of Social Ethics at the Episcopal Theological School at Cambridge, Massachusetts. His works include *Situation Ethics: The New Morality* (1966), *Moral Responsibility: Situation Ethics at Work* (1967), and *Morals and Medicine* (1960), from which the following selection is taken. Fletcher defines euthanasia as a "merciful release from incurable suffering." After reviewing the historical approaches to euthanasia in various cultures, he addresses himself to the current legal, religious, and moral views on euthanasia. He concludes that the essential issue around which the issue of euthanasia pivots is "which kind of death, an agonized or peaceful one. Shall we meet death in personal integrity or in personal disintegration?" "Euthanasia: Our Right to Die," in Joseph Fletcher, *Morals and Medicine* (copyright 1954 by Princeton University Press), pp. 172–210. Reprinted by permission of Princeton University Press.

WHERE IS THE STING OF DEATH?

Euthanasia, the deliberate easing into death of a patient suffering from a painful and fatal disease, has long been a troubling problem of conscience in medical care. For us in the Western world the problem arises, *pro forma*, out of a logical contradiction at the heart of the Hippocratic Oath. Our physicians all subscribe to that oath as the standard of their professional ethics. The contradiction is there because the oath promises two things: first, to relieve suffering and, second, to prolong and protect life. When the patient is in the grip of an agonizing and fatal disease, these two promises are incompatible. Two duties come into conflict. To prolong life is to violate the promise to relieve pain. To relieve the pain is to violate the promise to prolong and protect life.

Ordinarily an attempt is made to escape the dilemma by relieving the pain with an analgesic that does not induce death. But this attempt to evade the issue fails in many cases for the simple reason that the law of diminishing returns operates in narcosis. Patients grow semi-immune to its effects, for example in some forms of osteomyelitis, and a dose which first produces four hours of relief soon gives only three, then two, then almost none. The dilemma still stands: the choice between euthanasia or suffering. Euthanasia may be described, in its broadest terms, as a "theory that in certain circumstances, when owing to disease, senility or the like, a person's life has permanently ceased to be either agreeable or useful, the sufferer should be painlessly killed, either by himself or by another."[1] More simply, we may call euthanasia merciful release from incurable suffering.

Our task in this [essay] is to put the practice under examination in its strictly medical form, carefully limiting ourselves to cases in which the patient himself chooses euthanasia and the physician advises against any reasonable hope of recovery or of relief by other means. Yet even in so narrowly defined an application as this, there are conscientious objections, of the sort applied to broader concepts or usages. In the first place it is claimed that the practice of euthanasia might be taken as an encouragement of suicide or of the wholesale murder of the aged and infirm. Again, weak or unbalanced people may more easily throw away their lives if medical euthanasia has approval. Still another objection raised is that the practice would raise grave problems for the public authority. Government would have to overcome the resistance of time-honored religious beliefs, the universal feeling that human life is too sacred to be tampered with, and the problem of giving euthanasia legal endorsement as another form of justifiable homicide. All of this could lead to an appalling increase of crimes such as infanticide and geronticide. In short, . . . there is a common tendency to cry abuse and to ignore *abusus non tollit usum.*

Prudential and expedient objections to euthanasia quickly jump to mind among many people confronted with the issue. There are few, presumably, who would not be moved by such protests as this one from the *Linacre Quarterly:* "Legalized euthanasia would be a confession of despair in the medical profession; it would be the denial of hope for further progress against presently incurable maladies. It would destroy all confidence in physicians, and introduce a reign of terror. . . . [Patients] would turn in dread from the man on whose wall the Hippocratic Oath proclaims, 'If any shall ask of me a drug to produce death I will not give it, nor will I suggest such counsel.' "[2]

However, it is the objection that euthanasia is inherently wrong, that the disposition of life is too sacred to be entrusted to human control, which calls for our closest analysis. . . . We shall be dealing [here] with the *personal* dimensions of morality in medical care. The social ethics of medical care, as it is posed to conscience by proposals to use euthanasia for eugenic reasons, population control, and the like, have to be left for another time and place.

Not infrequently the newspapers carry stories of the crime of a spouse, or a member of the family or a friend, of a hopelessly stricken and relentlessly tortured victim of, let us say, advanced cancer. Desperate people will sometimes take the law into their own hands and administer some lethal dose to end it all. Sometimes the euthanasiast then commits suicide, thus making two deaths instead of one. Sometimes he is tried for murder in a court of law, amid great scandal and notoriety. But even if he is caught and indicted, the judgment never ends in conviction, perhaps because the legalism of the charge can never stand up in the tested conscience of a sympathetic jury.

For the sake of avoiding offense to any contemporaries, we might turn to literary history for a typical example of our problem. Jonathan Swift, the satirist and Irish clergyman, after a life of highly creative letters ended it all in a horrible and degrading death. It was a death degrading to himself and to those close to him. His mind crumbled to pieces. It took him eight years to die while his brain rotted. He read the third chapter of Job on his birthday as long as he could see. "And Job spake, and said, Let the day perish when I was born, and the night in which it was said, There is a man child conceived." The pain in Swift's eye was so acute that it took five men to hold him down, to keep him from tearing out his eye with his own hands. For the last three years he sat and drooled. Knives had to be kept entirely out of his reach. When the end came, finally, his fits of convulsion lasted thirty-six hours.[3] Now, whatever may be the theological meaning of St. Paul's question, "O death, where is thy sting?"[4] the moral meaning—in a word, the evil—of a death like that is only too plain.

We can imagine the almost daily scene preceding Swift's death. (Some will say we should not imagine such things, that it is not fair to appeal to emotion. Many good people cannot willingly accept the horrendous aspects of reality as a factor of reasoning, especially when reality cuts across their customs and commitments. The relative success with which we have repressed the reality of atomic warfare and its dreadful prospects is an example on a wider scale.) We can easily conceive of Dean Swift grabbing wildly, madly, for a knife or a deadly drug. He was *demoralized*, without a vestige of true self-possession left in him. He wanted to commit what the law calls suicide and what vitalistic ethics calls sin. Standing by was some good doctor of physick, trembling with sympathy and frustration. Secretly, perhaps, he wanted to commit what the law calls murder. Both had full knowledge of the way out, which is half the foundation of moral integrity, but unlike his patient the physician felt he had no freedom to act, which is the other half of moral integrity. And so, meanwhile, necessity, blind and unmoral, irrational physiology and pathology, made the decision. It was in reality no decision at all, no moral behavior in the least, unless submission to physical ruin and spiritual disorganization can be called a decision and a moral choice. For let us not forget that in such tragic affairs there is a moral destruction, a spiritual disorder, as well as a physical degeneration. As Swift himself wrote to his niece fully five years before the end: "I am so stupid and confounded that I cannot express the mortification I am under both of body and soul."[5]

The story of this man's death points us directly to the broad problem of suicide, as well as to the more particular problem of euthanasia. We get a glimpse of this paradox in our present customary morality, that it sometimes condemns us to live or, to put it another way, destroys our moral being for the sake of just *being*. This aspect of suicide makes it important for us to distinguish from the outset between voluntary and involuntary euthanasia. They are by no means the same, either in policy or ethical meaning. Those who condemn euthanasia of both kinds would call the involuntary form murder and the voluntary form a compounded crime of murder and suicide if administered by the physician, and suicide alone if administered by the patient himself. As far as voluntary euthanasia goes, it is impossible to separate it from suicide as a moral category; it is, indeed, a form of suicide. In a very proper sense, the case for medical euthanasia depends upon the case for the righteousness of suicide, given the necessary circumstances. And the justification of its administration by an attending physician is therefore dependent upon it too, under the time-honored rule that what one may lawfully do another may help him to do.

"UNTOUCHABILITY"

Felo de se—literally, being a criminal toward oneself, but in common usage meaning to take one's own life—is, of course, as old as mankind and human pain. This is true in spite of the valid generalization that the wish to live is among the strongest instinctual drives in the higher animals, including men. It is true regardless of the reasons we may offer, psychological or otherwise, to explain the frequent occurrence of exceptions to the rule. Some savage tribes laugh at suicide; some practice it freely. Others believe it earns a terrible punishment in the next world, and, like some Christian churches, deny all suicides a religious burial. Many of the Eastern religions allow it without censure, and even encourage it ceremonially. We find this to be true in the ancient Aztec and Inca cultures, but also more recently in the traditional Hindu practice of *suttee*, in which a widow throws herself onto the funeral pyre alongside her husband's body. The Japanese, of Buddhist and Shinto belief, have committed *hara-kiri* after losing face or suffering loss of prestige, or as a remarkably unaggressive reply to insult, as compared, for example, to the dueling code in Western manners. The Greeks and Romans were divided in their opinions about suicide, and therefore about euthanasia. If there were those among them who condemned it rigidly and absolutely, they were few and not given to publishing their views. Some moralists repudiated it as a general practice. For example, Pythagoras, Plato, and Aristotle held that suicide was a crime against the community because it robbed society of a resource, and Plato added that it was a like crime against God. But all of these were willing to justify suicide in cases calling for a merciful death.[6] Stoics usually, but not always, approved of suicide. Cicero, for example, condemned it, whereas Seneca praised it. Epictetus sided with Seneca. But they *all* favored euthanasia. Valerius Maximus said that magistrates at Marseilles kept a supply of poison on hand for those who could convince them that there was a good reason for them to die.

The Semitic religions, Judaism and Mohammedanism, were opposed consistently to suicide. Being more Oriental than the Hellenic doctrines, they tended to regard physiological life as sacrosanct and untouchable, and they also tended to be more materialistic in their conception of the vital principle, so that Jews located life in the blood—and thus their rules about kosher meat. The Christians, as a Jewish sect, went even further with a belief in physical or bodily resurrection to eternal life. Nevertheless, neither the Bible nor the Koran actually set forth an explicit condemnation of suicide, in any form, even though Jewish and Moslem commentators generally were against it. There is a tradition that Mohammed himself refused to bury a suicide. Certainly under the Hebrew influence, which put a heavier stamp of approval and meaning upon historical existence, being this-worldly rather than other-worldly, there was little philosophical ground in the West for the *tedium vitae* of Hinduism. A practice such as *suttee* was simply not within its ideological orbit.

The early Christians, like Chrysostom, followed the rabbis for the most part. A great many of the patristic writers allowed for suicide in certain forms, however, usually to achieve martyrdom, to avoid apostasy, or to retain the crown of virginity. Thus Lactantius declared that it is wicked to bring death upon oneself voluntarily, unless one was "expecting all torture and death" at the hands of the pagan persecutors.[7] Unfortunately for the precedent moralists he never bothered to apply his logic about torture and death to incurable diseases.

But once Christianity and the Roman government joined forces, the authority permitting suicide in persecution was withdrawn. We find St. Jerome allowing it only as a defense of chastity.[8] And then St. Augustine swept away even that exception by announcing that chastity, after all, is a virtue of the soul rather than of the body, so that physical violation did not touch it. St. Augustine cast aside the observation that the Scriptures nowhere condemned suicide, and that they even reported without comment or condemnation the suicides of Ahithophel by hanging, Zimri by fire, Abimelech by sword, Samson by crushing, and Saul by sword. He said with fine simplicity that the Scriptures nowhere *authorized* us to eliminate ourselves.[9] This became the conventional Christian position, and St. Thomas Aquinas gave it its classical form in the saying, "Suicide is the most fatal of sins, because it cannot be repented of."[10] We find that Christian burial was denied to suicides as early as A.D. 563.[11] The Roman Church to this day, by canonical prohibition, refuses to bury a suicide.

Unlike Judaism and Catholicism, Protestantism does not unanimously outlaw suicide, although various bodies will from time to time condemn euthanasia, or call it into question. As recently as 1951 the General Assembly of the Presbyterian Church in the U.S.A. resolved that suicide is contrary to the Sixth Commandment. In the Renaissance the reverence of West Europeans for the Greeks and Romans led to some easing of the old prohibition of suicide, especially in favor of euthanasia, but this was in tension with the Semitic attitude in Christianity. Here and there, occasionally, but almost always outside the Roman jurisdiction, there were testimonies to a new attitude. Thomas More, whose Utopia included euthanasia, was reflecting a new evaluation of human worth and integrity.[12] Lord Francis Bacon in his *New Atlantis* said, "I esteem it the office of a physician not only to restore the health, but to mitigate pains and dolors; and not only when such mitigation may conduce to recovery, but when it may serve to make a fair and easy passage." It was more commonly the Protestant and humanist moralists who relaxed the old prohibition. A typical effort was made in a little book called *Biathanatos* by John Donne, the Anglican priest and poet, dean of St. Paul's, a book which he described on the title page as a "Declaration of that paradoxe, or thesis, that Self-homicide is not so naturally sin, that it may never be otherwise."[13] John Donne was a man who knew what death could be, because he lived for so long in its shadow and marked its many turns. His lines will always live, "Send not to ask for whom the bell tolls; it tolls for thee."[14] It is possible, but not certain, that Jeremy Taylor's *Holy Dying* favored merciful release in somewhat equivocal terms. At any rate, even theologians were beginning to doubt that Hamlet was altogether correct in supposing that "the everlasting" had "fixed his canon 'gainst self-slaughter."

The common civil law has always followed the line of the moral theologians. For centuries suicides were refused last rites by the church and their property impounded by the state. The English law about staking out a suicide's body at the crossroads—a law due partly to Christian theory and partly to fear of ghosts—was not abolished until the reign of George IV. The first really sharp break came with the French Revolution, when France abolished her old laws about suicide, especially the more grotesque priestly features. Then other Continental countries began to follow suit. The churches had held to their absolute prohibition, except for sporadic practices like that of the seventeenth-century people of Brittany, who allowed an incurable sufferer to appeal to the parish priest for the Holy Stone. The family gathered, the patient received the viaticum and last rites, and the oldest living relative raised the heavy stone above the patient's head and let it fall.

England moved very slowly in the matter, thus being very English about it! Her legal prohibition of suicide in any form continued in force, even though there were still a hundred and fifty crimes punishable by death, but it became the custom of juries to presume "absence of mind" or mental derangement in those who attempted or succeeded at *felo de se*. The standard verdicts of "suicide while of unsound mind" or "temporary insanity" had two motives: to remove any stigma from the memory of the deceased, and to prevent confiscation by the state of his property as a post-mortem punishment. As Jeremy Bentham said in his *Principles of Penal Law*, this evasion of the issue by juries meant that perjury became the penance with which they prevented an outrage on humanity. Perhaps, among moralists, the utilitarians like Bentham have been most favorable to the notion of justifiable homicide. When Bentham died, consistent to the last, he asked his doctor to "minimize pain" with his dying breath. The last of the great English philosophers to pay any attention to the old theological arguments, even by way of opposing them, was David Hume in his essay *On Suicide* in 1777.[15] Hume crystallized the issue for medical ethics with his formulation that if our shortening lives interferes with Providence, medical services are already interfering by lengthening them.

It may be worthwhile to recall that the early church condemned the taking of life in military service, and yet it finally consented to it when a political concordat became a strong enough inducement.[16] It also condemned capital punishment as the taking of life, insisting that life is the sole property of God and at his sole disposition, and yet finally agreed to it when the church and state became partners. This double standard is now a part of our established mores or customary morality. We are, by some strange habit of mind and heart, willing to impose death but unwilling to permit it: we will justify humanly contrived death when it violates the human integrity of its victims, but we condemn it when it is an intelligent voluntary decision. If death is not inevitable anyway, not desired by the subject, and not merciful, it is righteous! If it is happening anyway and is freely embraced and merciful, then it is wrong! In the Roman communion the prohibition of suicide is presupposed in certain canonical regulations."[17] There is, however, no clear and certain united front of opinion among Catholic moralists on *medical* euthanasia, apparently because of the difficulties created by the death-inducing effects of anesthesia. Thus Father Davis says if the drugs "shorten life . . . euthanasia is murder, and indefensible."[18] But Koch-Preuss says, "To hasten death artificially . . . *can be regarded as permissible* only if the drugs employed *for this purpose* do not entirely deprive the sufferer of consciousness."[19] Thus it becomes clear that the concern of this moralist is not with life qua life and its sacrosanctity, but with *consciousness*, which is needed for the patient's cooperation in last rites. And of course there is the further complication or confusion of an opinion like St. Alphonsus Liguori's that a man would be justified in taking his own life to escape death in a more painful form, e.g., by leaping from a window to get out of a burning building.[20] Yet even St. Alphonsus' opinion is not left without doubt. Lehmkuhl goes only so far as to say that if a man is condemned by the state to die at his own hand, as in Socrates' case, he would be allowed to obey, although not obliged to since it could be defended as a probable opinion that the act is forbidden by natural law.[21] We are left, therefore, to suppose that we may not choose to die decently instead of living indecently, but if we are to die horribly—through a necessity imposed upon us by a pathology or some other tragic cause—then we are free to exercise a preference between the kind of horror we undergo, just so we are sure to be fully conscious of our suffering! As yet mercy has failed to exert an influence upon many Christians equal to the pull or pressure of power.

This is still the case among Christian moralists generally, and even among some pagan moralists. They are ready to justify the taking of the lives of others but balk at any reason for taking their own! A commission of American Protestants recently concluded that the mass extermination of civilians by atom-bomb blasts can be "just," although many of the members of the commission would hesitate to agree that fatal suffering could be ended righteously for one of the victims burned and charred externally and internally, not even as a response to the victim's plea. But the beatitude "Blessed are the merciful, for they shall obtain mercy" is still in the New Testament, as a part of the divine law. And the New Testament is still in the churches, and the churches are still based for authority on the New Testament. Therefore, as they have changed in some other things, so they may change in this too.[22] Some may come to feel that the divine law takes priority. Among many Christians the line of distinction between natural and divine often appears to be blurred or even erased, with no preference as to the claims of nature and the claims of grace. But most certainly if there is any provision in the divine law or revealed will of God as found in the Bible, it is the fifth beatitude calling for mercy. This is, ethically speaking, a great leap from the *talion* of the Semitic code and the ruthlessness of nature. Mercy cannot by any stretch of the imagination be found to be a plausible statistical average of events or behavior in the natural creation. Natural reason applied to nature could never deduce that mercy is "intended" or "in the mind" of the created physical order. Mercy is a value or virtue born of personal growth and moral stature, a thing of the spirit altogether. By itself nature cannot produce it.

LAW AND MALICE

The present-day legal status of euthanasia, the one form of taking life with which we are concerned in medical morals, is neither ethically clear nor satisfactory to conscience. This is the situation everywhere in the Western world, not only in our own country but in Latin America and Europe, including Soviet Russia. The law of murder fails to take any account of the physical and mental, and hence of the spiritual, condition of the victim or subject of the murder action. Suicide is always a legal felony. As moralists, those who would justify euthanasia have to ask the lawyers and lawmakers to recognize it as justifiable homicide rather than a felony, whether it is merciful death self-administered by the patient, with medical advice, or administered by the physician. There is, at bottom, no real moral difference between self-administered euthanasia and the medically administered form when it is done at the patient's request. Legally, of course, there is a difference. An insurance company might refuse to pay off on a life policy in the case of self-administered euthanasia, calling it suicide. This fact is often presented as a legal-economic objection to euthanasia. It is not at all certain that because a coroner's jury finds a suicide was done "while of unsound mind" that the insurance benefits are thereby preserved. With the present moral philosophy of the law, wherein physical existence is the *summum bonum*, the higher intelligence which subordinates corrupted flesh to moral integrity will always appear unsound, so perhaps concern for insurance equities need not stay the patient's decision nor alarm his beneficiaries.

Bills to legalize euthanasia have been introduced without success in the British Parliament in 1936 and in the state legislatures of Nebraska in 1937 and New York in 1947. The hurdle, of course, is partially ethical inertia and the cake of custom, partially legal prudence and timidity. The biggest issue is drawn around our ideas of murder. By general agreement murder is defined as "the killing of one human being by another *with malice aforethought*."[23] This definition is applied to condemn euthanasia when medically administered in just the same way that the concept of suicide is applied, as self-murder, when euthanasia is self-administered. The legal difficulty with any form of suicide, naturally, is that no sanction or penalty can be applied when the crime is successful. The law can operate only as a deterrent, since an attempt might be unsuccessful. "Although suicide is deemed a grave public wrong, yet from the impossibility of reaching the successful perpetrator, no forfeiture is imposed."[24] (Blackstone had approved burial in the highway, with a stake through the body and forfeiture of goods and chattels to the king.) Hence the remark of one Catholic moralist that euthanasia "is less honorable than the murder committed by a thug; the latter takes a chance on being caught and convicted."[25] But no such escape from penalty is open to the cooperating physician or friend in medical euthanasia. In the United States, at present, euthanasia is nowhere allowed by statute or by judicial decision. Some states, e.g., New York, hold that assisting a suicide is criminal. In Kansas, "every person deliberately assisting another in commission of self-murder shall be guilty of manslaughter in the first degree."[26] This reasoning is generally applied, equally, to those who help self-euthanasiasts, partake in suicide pacts, and make themselves parties to duels.

Moralists would contend that malice is not present as a motive in mercy-killings; that they are mercy-aforethought, not malice-aforethought. But a court, in Turner v. State, has ruled that hatred and malevolence are not necessary to express malice.[27] There need be only "an actual and deliberate intention to take the life of another." This makes malice in the law take on a technical meaning of premeditation, and when unqualified it makes euthanasia not only a felonious homicide but murder. For, unlike manslaughter, euthanasia is certainly a deliberated deed. The issue here is not a mere matter of legal precedents; it goes much deeper, to the philosophy of law and therefore to ethics and to our beliefs about human nature. As far as the law is concerned the problem may well center around the issue whether, ethically, the philosophy of law can rightly be satisfied with the doctrine that malice is implicit in the action of *felo de se*. This is a very questionable assumption indeed. There is some encouragement, therefore, in the recent discussions of English lawyers—precipitated by episodes of euthanasia—considering the advisability of making a rule that *express* malice must be established in order to determine guilt of murder.

Our courts already recognize and allow what they call justifiable homicide in some circumstances when we are attacked by other human beings. What the lawyers have not explained to the satisfaction of many interested moralists is why the same ethical elasticity may not be applied in cases of attack by disease and incurable suffering. Certainly the right to take life in self-defense is at stake in either situation. If it is replied that in self-defense against human attack we are seeking to preserve our life, whereas in euthanasia we are seeking to destroy our life, then we can and must call into question any such pure vitalism. We must deny that "life" is adequately understood as mere vital existence or breathing! For the man of moral integrity and spiritual purpose, the mere fact of being alive is not as important as the terms of the living. As every hero and every martyr knows, there are some conditions without which a man refuses to continue living. Surely among these conditions, along with loyalty to justice and brotherhood, we can include self-possession and personal integrity. Incurable pain destroys self-possession and disintegrates personality, as any wide acquaintance with sickbeds will teach us. Our medical servants know this only too well.

Furthermore, the law usually stipulates that murder is killing from a deliberate and premeditated design "unless it is excusable and justified."[28] Here is a legal qualification of the principle of malice which is highly apropos of euthanasia. It is a qualification made necessary in the law by such cases as the man who has had to plan his self-defense against someone with continuing but as yet unfulfilled designs on his life. Euthanasia is obviously planned and deliberate. It is precisely this that gives it its ethical quality! But it is also "excusable and justified" unless, of course, the law chooses to accept a purely vitalistic doctrine of man's being.

Perhaps the model legislation is to be found in a bill proposed in New York State by a committee of 1,776 physicians who want legislation to make euthanasia lawful, so that they and their patients may be protected from possible prosecution for a practice which, as everyone knows, goes on anyway. The bill is backed by the Euthanasia Society of America and by thousands of doctors. It provides three things, essentially: (1) any sane person over twenty-one years old, suffering from an incurably painful and fatal disease, may petition a court of record for euthanasia, in a signed and attested document, with an affadavit from the attending physician that in his opinion the disease is incurable; (2) the court shall appoint a commission of three, of whom at least two shall be physicians, to investigate all aspects of the case and to report back to the courts whether the patient understands the purpose of his petition and comes under the provisions of the act; (3) upon a favorable report by the commission the court shall grant the petition, and *if it is still wanted by the patient* euthanasia may be administered by a physician or any other person chosen by the patient or by the commission.

There are elements in this proposal that deserve our thoughtful attention. The bill is permissive, not mandatory. Neither patient nor physician is compelled to act. The request for euthanasia must originate with the patient. The patient's freedom to change his mind at any time is fully guaranteed. Disinterested parties inquire into the whole matter. The permit is used only if and when the patient chooses. The proposal leaves aside the whole question of eugenic euthanasia for solution by some other legal instrument, since the merits of medical euthanasia are not inherently tied to the case for eugenic euthanasia.

Now that the United Nations has come into being, protagonists of euthanasia have carried their cause to that authority too. The terms of their appeals are much like those of the proposal to the New York State Assembly. They usually ask for an amendment to the Declaration of Human Rights which would include "the right of incurable sufferers to voluntary euthanasia," referring especially to Article Five of the Declaration, which states that "No one shall be subjected to torture." It is also pointed out that Articles Three and Eighteen declare that "everyone has the right to life, liberty, and *the security of person. . . .*" The right to life does not necessarily entail the obligation to live, especially when continued existence is so hideous and demoralizing that the *person* is blotted out and reduced to coma or ungovernable nerve reactions. English advocates, who are in the thousands, have signed a petition to the United Nations. The list includes such persons as Sir J. J. Conybeare of Guy's Hospital, London; Dr. Ernest Jones, president of the International Psychoanalytic Association; Julian Huxley, H. J. Fleure, G. E. Moore, Dean Inge, Canons Peter Green[29] and J. S. Bezzant; the Rev. Messrs. A. Herbert Gray, Donald Frazer, G. H. C. Macgregor and Hugh Martin; G. B. Shaw, Augustus John, Clifford Bax, Vera Brittain, Louis Golding, Kenneth Ingram, A. A. Milne, and R. Seebohm Rountree. Another recent convert to their ranks is Dean W. R. Matthews of St. Paul's, Inge's successor. Catholics are as clear as are non-Catholics that as far as law is concerned the issue of medical euthanasia is really one of judicial philosophy, not of mere precedent. In opposing legal euthanasia they would describe it as a question of theocentric versus anthropocentric morality. Those who use such question-begging neologisms (for such they really are, with or without any intention to avoid questions) would very probably characterize the freedom ethic running throughout this [essay] as anthropocentric, although the correct problem is: given a theocentric context for the analysis of these matters, "What doth God require of thee?" how is that to be determined? In this particular case it is plain that many Christians do not find any theological logic (natural reason) or revelation to condemn euthanasia.

PRO AND CON

It is at this point that we can turn to the definitely moral arguments for and against euthanasia. Our aim here is to be as orderly as possible in the discussion, and to forsake any *argumentum ad misericordiam*. We must try to avoid the penny-dreadful type of treatment Richard Cabot had in mind when he spoke of euthanasia as "that ancient and reliable novelty . . . which the newspapers trick out afresh each year in August when politics are dull and there is a dearth of copy."[30] In a limited space, perhaps the best procedure will be to speak directly to the ten most common and most important objections. Therefore, suppose we deal with them as if they stood one by one in a bill of particulars.

1. It is objected that euthanasia, when voluntary, is really suicide. If this is true, and it would seem to be obviously true, then the proper question is: have we ever a right to commit suicide? Among Catholic moralists the most common ruling is that "it is never permitted to kill oneself intentionally, without explicit divine inspiration to do."[31] Humility requires us to assume that divine inspiration cannot reasonably be expected to occur either often or explicitly enough to meet the requirements of medical euthanasia. A plea for legal recognition of "man's inalienable right to die" is placed at the head of the physicians' petition to the New York State Assembly. Now, has man any such right, however limited and imperfect it may be? Surely he has, for otherwise the hero or martyr and all those who deliberately give their lives are morally at fault. It might be replied that there is a difference between the suicide, who is directly seeking to end his life, and the hero or martyr, who is seeking directly some other end entirely, death being only an undesired by-product. But to make this point is only to raise a question as to what purposes are sufficient to justify the loss of one's life. If altruistic values, such as defense of the innocent, are enough to justify the loss of one's life (and we will all agree that they are), then it may be argued that personal integrity is a value worth the loss of life, especially since, by definition, there is no hope of relief from the demoralizing pain and no further possibility of serving others. To call euthanasia egoistic or self-regarding makes no sense, since in the nature of the case the patient is not choosing his own good rather than the good of others.

Furthermore, it is important to recognize that there is no ground, in a rational or Christian outlook, for regarding life itself as the *summum bonum*. As a ministers' petition to buttress the New York bill puts it, "We believe in the sacredness of *personality*, but not in the worth of mere existence or 'length of days.' . . . We believe that such a sufferer has the right to die, and that society should grant this right, showing the same mercy to human beings as to the sub-human animal kingdom." (The point might be made validly in criticism of this statement that society can only recognize an "inalienable right," it cannot confer it. Persons are not mere creatures of the community, even though it is ultimately meaningless to claim integrity for them unless their lives are integrated into the community.) In the personalistic view of man and morals, asserted throughout these pages, personality is supreme over mere life. To prolong life uselessly, while the personal qualities of freedom, knowledge, self-possession and control, and responsibility are sacrificed is to attack the moral status of a person. It actually denies morality in order to submit to fatality. And in addition, to insist upon mere "life" invades religious interests as well as moral values. For to use analgesic agents to the point of depriving sufferers of consciousness is, by all apparent logic, inconsistent even with the practices of sacramentalist Christians. The point of death for a human person *in extremis* is surely by their own account a time when the use of reason and conscious self-commitment is most meritorious; it is the time when a responsible competence in receiving such rites as the viaticum and extreme unction would be most necessary and its consequences most invested with finality.

2. It is objected that euthanasia, when involuntary, is murder. This is really an objection directed against the physician's role in medical euthanasia, assuming it is administered by him rather than by the patient on his own behalf. We might add to what has been said above about the word "murder" in law and legal definition by explaining that people with a moral rather than a legal interest— doctors, pastors, patients, and their friends—will never concede that malice means only premeditation, entirely divorced from the motive and the end sought. These factors are entirely different in euthanasia from the motive and the end in murder, even though the means—taking life—happens to be the same. If we can make no moral distinction between acts involving the same means, then the thrifty parent who saves in order to educate his children is no higher in the scale of merit than the miser who saves for the sake of hoarding. But, as far as medical care is concerned, there is an even more striking example of the contradictions which arise from refusing to allow for anything but the consequences of a human act. There is a dilemma in medication for terminal diseases which is just as real as the dilemma posed by the doctor's oath to relieve pain while he also promises to prolong life. As medical experts frequently point out, morphine, which is commonly used to ease pain, also shortens life,

i.e., it induces death. Here we see that the two promises of the Hippocratic Oath actually conflict at the level of means as well as at the level of motive and intention.

3. What of the common religious opinion that God reserves for himself the right to decide at what moment a life shall cease? Koch-Preuss says euthanasia is the destruction of "the temple of God and a violation of the property rights of Jesus Christ."[32] As to this doctrine, it seems more than enough just to answer that if such a divine-monopoly theory is valid, then it follows with equal force that it is immoral to lengthen life. Is medical care, after all, only a form of human self-assertion or a demonic pretension, by which men, especially physicians, try to put themselves in God's place? Prolonging life, on this divine-monopoly view, when a life appears to be ending through natural or physical causes, is just as much an interference with natural determinism as mercifully ending a life before physiology does it in its own amoral way.

This argument that we must not tamper with life also assumes that physiological life is sacrosanct. But as we have pointed out repeatedly, this doctrine is a form of vitalism or naturalistic determinism. Dean Sperry of the Harvard Divinity School, who is usually a little more sensitive to the scent of antihumane attitudes, wrote recently in the *New England Journal of Medicine* that Albert Schweitzer's doctrine of "reverence for life," which is often thought to entail an absolute prohibition against taking life, has strong claims upon men of conscience.[33] Perhaps so, but men of conscience will surely reject the doctrine if it is left unqualified and absolute. In actual fact, even Schweitzer has suggested that the principle is subject to qualification. He has, with apparent approval, explained that Gandhi "took it upon himself to go beyond the letter of the law against killing. . . . He ended the sufferings of a calf in its prolonged death-agony by giving it poison."[34] It seems unimaginable that either Schweitzer or Gandhi would deny to a human being what they would render, with however heavy a heart, to a calf. Gandhi did what he did in spite of the special sanctity of kine in Hindu discipline. In any case Dr. Schweitzer in his African hospital at Lambaréné is even now at work administering death-inducing-because-pain-relieving drugs. As William Temple once pointed out, "The notion that life is absolutely sacred is Hindu or Buddhist, not Christian." He neglected to remark that even those Oriental religionists forget their doctrine when it comes to *suttee* and *hara-kiri*. He said further that the argument that it cannot ever be right to kill a fellow human being will not stand up because "such a plea can only rest upon a belief that life, physiological life, is sacrosanct. This is not a Christian idea at all; for, if it were, the martyrs would be wrong. If the sanctity is *in* life, it must be wrong to give your life for a noble cause as well as to take another's. But the Christian must be ready to give life gladly for his faith, as for a noble cause. Of course, this implies that, *as compared with some things,* the loss of life is a small evil; and if so, then, *as compared with some other things,* the taking of life is a small injury."[35]

Parenthetically we should explain, if it is not evident in these quotations themselves, that Dr. Temple's purpose was to justify military service. Unfortunately for his aim, he failed to take account of the ethical factor of free choice as a right of the person who thus loses his life at the hands of the warrior. We cannot put upon the same ethical footing the ethical right to take our own lives, in which case our freedom is not invaded, and taking the lives of others in those cases in which the act is done against the victim's will and choice. The true parallel is between self-sacrifice and a merciful death provided at the person's request; there is none between self-sacrifice and violent or coercive killing. But the relevance of what Dr. Temple has to say and its importance for euthanasia is perfectly clear. The nontheological statement of the case agrees with Temple: "Are we not allowing ourselves to be deceived by our self-preservative tendency to rationalize a merely instinctive urge and to attribute spiritual and ethical significance to phenomena appertaining to the realm of crude, biological utility?"[36]

4. It is also objected by religious moralists that euthanasia violates the Biblical command, "Thou shalt not kill." It is doubtful whether this kind of Biblicism is any more valid than the vitalism we reject. Indeed, it is a form of fundamentalism, common to both Catholics and reactionary Protestants. An outspoken religious opponent of euthanasia is a former chancellor to Cardinal Spellman as military vicar to the armed forces, Monsignor Robert McCormick. As presiding judge of the Archdiocesan Ecclesiastical Tribunal of New York, he warned the General Assembly of that state in 1947 not to "set aside the commandment 'Thou shalt not kill.'"[37] In the same vein, the general secretary of the American Council of Christian Churches, an organization of fundamentalist Protestants, denounced the fifty-four clergymen who supported the euthanasia bill, claiming that their action was "an evidence that the modernistic clergy have made further departure from the eternal moral law."[38]

Certainly those who justify war and capital punishment, as most Christians do, cannot condemn euthanasia on this ground. We might point out to the fundamentalists in the two major divisions of Western Christianity that the beatitude "Blessed are the merciful" has the force of a commandment too! The medical profession lives by it, has its whole *ethos* in it. But the simplest way to deal with this

Christian text-proof objection might be to point out that the translation "Thou shalt not kill" is incorrect. It should be rendered, as in the responsive decalogue of the *Book of Common Prayer*, "Thou shalt do no murder," i.e., unlawful killing. It is sufficient just to remember that the ancient Jews fully allowed warfare and capital punishment. Lawful killing was also for hunger-satisfaction and sacrifice. Hence, a variety of Hebrew terms such as *shachat, harag, tabach*, but *ratsach* in the Decalogue (both Exodus 20:13 and Deut. 5:17), clearly mean *unlawful* killing, treacherously, for private vendetta or gain. Thus it is laid down in Leviticus 24:17 that "he who kills a man shall be put to death," showing that the lawful forms of killing may even be used to punish the unlawful! In the New Testament references to the prohibition against killing (e.g., Matt. 5:21, Luke 18:20, Rom. 13:9) are an endorsement of the commandments in the Jewish law. Each time, the verb *phoneuo* is used and the connotation is *unlawful* killing, as in the Decalogue. Other verbs connote simply the fact of killing, as *apokteino* (Luke 12:4, "Be not afraid of them that kill the body") and *thuo* which is used interchangeably for slaughter of animals for food and for sacrifice. We might also remind the Bible-bound moralists that there was no condemnation either of Abimelech, who chose to die, or of his faithful sword bearer who carried out his wish for him.[39]

5. Another common objection in religious quarters is that suffering is a part of the divine plan for the good of man's soul, and must therefore be accepted. Does this mean that the physicians' Hippocratic Oath is opposed to Christian virtue and doctrine? If this simple and naive idea of suffering were a valid one, then we should not be able to give our moral approval to anesthetics or to provide any medical relief of human suffering. Such has been the objection of many religionists at every stage of medical conquest, as we pointed out in the first chapter in the case of anesthetics at childbirth. Here is still another anomaly in our mores of life and death, that we are, after much struggle, now fairly secure in the righteousness of easing suffering at birth but we still feel it is wrong to ease suffering at death! Life may be begun without suffering, but it may not be ended without it, if it happens that nature combines death and suffering.

Those who have some acquaintance with the theological habit of mind can understand how even the question of euthanasia may be colored by the vision of the Cross as a symbol of redemptive suffering in Christian doctrine. As Emil Brunner has said of the crucifix, "it is not without its significance that the picture of a dying man is the sacred sign of Christendom."[40] But when it is applied to suffering in general it becomes, of course, a rather uncritical exemplarism which ignores the unique theological claims of the doctrine of the Atonement and the saving power of the Cross as a singular event. It is, at least, difficult to see how any theological basis for the suffering argument against medical euthanasia would be any different or any more compelling for keeping childbirth natural and "as God hath provided it."

It is much more realistic and humble to take as our regulative principle the rule that "Blessed are the merciful, for they shall see mercy," since this moral standard gives more recognition in actual fact to the motive of compassion, which, according to the theology of Atonement, lies behind the crucifixion of Jesus and gave it its power and its *ethos*. "All things whatsoever you would that men should do unto you, do you even so unto them." Mercy to the suffering is certainly the point of Psalm 102, vs. 12: "As a father hath compassion on his children, so hath the Lord compassion on them that fear him: for he knoweth our frame." Let the Biblicist take his position on the story of Job! Job explored the problem of human suffering and left it a mystery for the man of faith. Some have tried to find a recommendation of suicide in Job's wife's advice, but it is hardly more than a warning that he must not curse God.[41] In Job 7:15 there may be a thought of suicide, but nothing more than that. Our point here is that even Job never hinted that euthanasia was wrong; he only wondered, as we all do sometimes, why such a thing is ever needed or desired. The patience of Job is proverbial, but this is the Job of the prose part of the book. The poetry has another Job, a most rebellious and morally disturbed one. He could come to no other conclusion but that suffering is a mystery, as far as God's will and power are concerned. He did not give much attention to man's part in its control, nor to its particular aspect in incurable illness.

6. It is frequently pointed out, as an objection to euthanasia, that patients pronounced incurable might recover after all, for doctors can and do make mistakes. This seems, frankly, like a fundamentally obstructionist argument. It takes us back to the evasion based on fallibility with which we had to deal in the question of truth telling. Doctors are indeed finite creatures. So they may also err in recommending and carrying out operations, or in other forms of treatment. As far as the accuracy of their advice is concerned, we have to trust them, although it is always our right to doubt their advice and to change doctors. If reluctance to trust them were a common attitude pervading medical relationships generally, it would spell the doom of medical care. Also, it is sometimes added that if we will just hang on something may turn up, perhaps a new discovery which will save us after all. Although this objection really evades the point

at issue, it has a very great importance when seen in its own perspective. We always have ground for hope that many of the conditions which have called for euthanasia in the past will no longer do so. Not long ago crippling arthritis was thought almost hopeless, but cortisone and ACTH have offered new hope and success. Medical science is also continuously making discoveries which narrow the range of cases in which the conditions of justifiable euthanasia are apt to occur. Improved narcosis, new healing drugs and treatments, surgical relief of pain by new techniques of chordotomy and lobotomy—these things make news constantly.

And there are, of course, occasional incidents of totally unexpected, last-minute recovery from "hopeless" illnesses. An actual case would be that of the hospital chaplain who once stood by at a "certain" death and a horrible one from pemphigus. The doctors had even advised that the patient's family be called in for a last visit. Then, at the last moment, a new penicillin drug was flown in from another city, and the patient was saved. Such things happen, yes. But all we need to say to this objection to euthanasia is that by no stretch of the imagination, in a typical situation, can we foresee a discovery that will restore health to a life already running out. A patient dying of metastatic cancer may be considered already dead, though still breathing. In advanced cases, even if a cure were to be found, toxemia has in all likelihood damaged the tissues and organs fatally.

7. It is said, with some truth, that patients racked by pain might make impulsive and ill-considered requests for euthanasia, if it were morally and legally approved. To this there are two rejoinders: first, that a careful law, such as that of the Euthanasia Society, would provide that there must be medical advice that death is certain, which rules out any hasty euthanasia in nonfatal illnesses; and, second, that the law would provide an interval between application and administration. The law should not permit euthanasia to be done on the spur of the moment, and the patient should be free to withdraw his request at any time. The requirement that the disease must be of a fatal character is needed to guard against unconscious wishes for destruction which are to be seen sometimes, although rarely, in patients. The confirmation of the patient's and the attending physician's decisions by disinterested parties is a sufficient bulwark against impulsive action. This might also be the place to emphasize that a doctor is always free to refuse to administer medical euthanasia, as a patient ought to be free to request it. In a wide search of the literature, incidentally, only one really *medical* objection to the practice was found, although there are frequent moral objections. Dr. A. A. Brill, of the International Psychoanalytical Association,

has declared that *although doctors are actually doing it they should stop*, because for reasons of depth psychology the practice will demoralize both patients and doctors, fill them with fear that inhibits healing relationships and lowers vitality.[42] As we have already seen, Dr. Brill's colleague in the Association, Dr. Ernest Jones, does not regard this as a real objection to euthanasia, if we may draw that conclusion from his support of it before the United Nations.

Connected with this is this further objection: what if the patient can no longer speak or even gesture intelligibly? Can we be sure we always understand the patient's real desire, his choice for or against death, especially in cases where his condition is nearly unconscious or comatose? We all know that communication is not solely verbal. The provision that the request must come from the patient in a documentary form is introduced in proposals like that of the Euthanasia Society out of great caution, presumably in the fear that a gesture or other sign might be misinterpreted. A restriction like this will also exclude the possibility of a doctor's carrying out euthanasia when the patient had expressed a desire for it but the formalities could not be fulfilled before his physical powers to apply had failed. This would be tragic, but perhaps it is the necessary price exacted for legalization. There is also, of course, the reverse possibility that a patient might make the proper application, then change his mind after his powers of communication had failed. But these seem unreal problems, purely logical in character, if it is held, as we indeed do hold, that a patient who has completely lost the power to communicate has passed into a submoral state, outside the forum of conscience and beyond moral being. Being no longer responsive, he is no longer responsible.

Conscience and consciousness are inseparable and presuppose each other. Their interdependence has always been recognized, since the Stoics first explored the cognitive aspect of conscience as distinct from the judicial, and recognized that to act with *conscientia*, with knowledge, requires consciousness. The Stoics predicated awareness or consciousness of Natural Law insight; the Christians have predicated Natural Law insight plus communion with God and the voice of the Holy Spirit. Some have held that the moral factor in consciousness is innate; others, acquired. Some have thought it to be reason; others, intuition; still others, emotion. In any case, these faculties are parts of consciousness, without which personality is gone and there is no longer a "person" to fulfill even the minimum requirements of moral status, i.e., freedom and knowledge.

8. Sometimes we hear it said that the moral and legal approval of euthanasia would weaken our moral fiber, tend to encourage us to minimize the importance of life. Hence such well-known wit-

ticisms as G. K. Chesterton's, that the proponents of euthanasia now seek only the death of those who are a nuisance to themselves, but soon it will be broadened to include those who are a nuisance to others.[43] It is very hard to find any real hope of taking hold of an objection like this, with its broad value-terms such as "moral fiber" and "the importance of life." It could just as easily be reasoned that to ask for euthanasia, to leave voluntarily for the unknown, would call for courage and resolution and faith, and would encourage us to live with faith and without fear of the unknown. There is great wisdom and moral assurance in the decision of Charlotte Perkins Gilman, one of America's greatest women, who chose self-euthanasia rather than endure a degenerative death by cancer. These were her last words, typed by her own hand: "A last duty. Human life consists in mutual service. No grief, no pain, misfortune or 'broken heart' is excuse for cutting off one's life while any power of service remains. But when all usefulness is over, when one is assured of an imminent and unavoidable death, it is the simplest of human rights to choose a quick and easy death in place of a slow and horrible one. Public opinion is changing on this subject. The time is approaching when we shall consider it abhorrent to our civilization to allow a human being to lie in prolonged agony which we should mercifully end in any other creature. Believing this choice to be of social service in promoting wider views on this question, I have preferred chloroform to cancer."[44]

Our attention should be given particularly to one sentence here: "No grief, no pain, no misfortune or 'broken heart' is excuse for cutting off one's life while any power of service remains." It is a cause for joy that many avenues of service are open, or could be opened, to properly diagnosed terminal patients. Because of its psychological effects, genuine service, or being needed, will postpone the unendurable stages of pain or collapse. Enlightened hospital procedure is making great advances in this respect. One of the most significant services open to terminal patients is willingness to submit to drugs and cures and narcotics of an experimental kind, aimed at eliminating *the very pain and demoralization which is a major justification for euthanasia.* This consideration is certainly a welcome one to the advocates of euthanasia, and is always kept in mind by them. For them the best possible news would be that medicine has at last deprived euthanasia of its *raison d'être.*

Sometimes it is suggested by advocates of euthanasia that those who insist that the suffering go on are unconscious sadists, moved by the wish to make others suffer, or in a voyeurist version actually eager to see them suffer. This is an extremely problematical ground upon which to enter in the discussion, and it tends to "psychologize" all ethical reason out of the picture. It is true, theoretically, that the idea of noble suffering may be, deep down, a reaction formation to rationalize sadistic or masochistic sentiments. But on the other hand, opponents of euthanasia could charge that the advocates are the victims of a death instinct or destruction wishes; or even a sadomasochist syndrome, sadist in the friends of the patient, masochist in the patient. To this, in their turn, the advocates could reply that if they were sadistic in their drives they would *want* the suffering to go on. There are hardly any limits to the kind of woolgathering that could develop along these lines, with little or no possibility of contributing to a solution ethically.

9. It is objected that the ethics of a physician forbids him to take life. We have already recognized that fact *as a fact*, but the issue is raised precisely because there are cases when the doctor's duty to prolong and protect life is in conflict with his equal duty to relieve suffering. As a matter of fact, this dilemma is actually inescapable and inherent in the medical care of many terminal illnesses anyway, at the technical as well as the moral level. If the physician's obligation is both to relieve pain and prolong life, how then can he use analgesics, which bring relief but have the necessary effect of hastening death? Great strides in nontoxemic medications are being made, but it remains true that, for example, prolonged morphine has a lethal effect, especially when finally there is a failure of natural functions such as breathing, salivation, and heat regulation, and when it no longer works intravenously because circulation is ceasing and it has to be injected directly into the heart. Everyone concerned in the care of the sick knows quite well that the medication itself is euthanasia. We hear constantly of overdoses somehow or other taken in terminal cases. There are many cases indeed in which actions are carried out by patients or attendants in the spirit of Socrates, drinking the cup of hemlock, who cried to Crito, "We owe a cock to Aesculapius. . . . Pay the debt and do not forget it."[45]

The dilemma of the physician who takes a contradictory oath could hardly be more evident than in the words of an article in *The New England Journal of Medicine* entitled "The Theology [sic] of Medicine." The author, a physician, declared, "I feel as Dr. Woodward did when he said, 'I have no sympathy with the man who would shorten the death agony of a dog but prolong that of a human being.' "[46] Dr. Woodward had himself advised a class of medical students, "I hold it to be your duty to smooth as much as possible the pathway to the grave even if life is somewhat shortened. Nor is it necessary to talk it over with friends and relatives, nor need you expect them to formally countenance either neglect or expedition. Let that be your affair, settled with your own conscience."[47]

It is a dilemma. The only real problem in conscience is not whether the mystique of vitalism or an ethic of mercifulness should reign, but whether the decision should rest upon the lonely conscience of the doctor without honest approval or responsibility shared fully with patient and family. Dr. Woodward is correct ethically to show mercy, but he is not justified in being so god-like about it. He should be man-like about it, and so should the students to whom he was giving his advice. As long as doctors continue, as at present, making unilateral decisions, they are in the position of needing something stronger than a Rule of Double Effect of their own, whereby they can convince themselves that it is right to do a good thing if they do not intend the evil consequences. Under these circumstances, can they sort out their emotions and motives, and make sure that they do not *want* the luckless patient to reach an end to his sufferings? Under these circumstances, what of the Hippocratic Oath?

Our defense of the right to die, with the doctor's aid, is not made in any kind of illness except the fatal and demoralizing ones. Besides, as we have seen in other questions already discussed, there are common exceptions to the rule against medical homicide. If one can be made at the beginning of life (abortion) why not also at the end of life (euthanasia)? The one situation is no more absolute than the other. There is no more stigma in the one than in the other. On personalistic grounds we could say that there is less question morally in euthanasia, for in euthanasia a merciful death is chosen in cooperation with a person whose integrity is threatened by disintegration, whereas an embryo in therapeutic abortion has no personal value or development at stake and cannot exercise the moral qualities of freedom and knowledge.

10. Finally, it is objected that doctors do not want euthanasia made legal.[48] It is not at all uncommon to hear doctors admit that they generally engage in the practice, in one way or another. Lest any reader be skeptical, he should examine the Cumulative Book Index and the index of periodicals for medical opinion on the subject, and he will find several places in which the admission is candidly made.[49] From time to time there are reports, undocumentable but from usually reliable sources, of medical meetings such as one recently in the Middle West at which a speaker asked for a show of hands from those who have never administered euthanasia. Not a hand was raised.[50] In 1935 great excitement was caused by a doctor's public confession in a London newspaper that he had been practicing euthanasia, and in *Time Magazine* an article reported, "Pungent, voluble Dr. Morris Fishbein, editor of the American Medical Association's *Journal*, observed that the average doctor frequently faces the problem, that when it is a matter between him and his patient he

may decide it in his own way without interference."[51] Many are the uses which we may be sure are made of drugs such as bichloride of mercury, potassium cyanide, and some of the barbiturates. In 1947, when an English doctor publicly announced he too engaged in medical euthanasia, a spokesman for the British Medical Association, in a very oblique but patient *non dixit*, said, "I think a good many doctors feel as Dr. Barton does, that euthanasia ought to be legalized. The association has no objection to doctors saying what they think about law."[52]

There are three other objections closely allied to these we have examined. They may deserve just a word or two. First, it is said that medical euthanasia would weaken medical research, that it would take away the incentive to find cures for painful maladies. This is nonsense because doctors are already practicing euthanasia and yet their fights against fatal diseases is mounting, not flagging. As cancer and malignant tumors, for example, increase (nearly 200,000 Americans will die of them this year) the research in that field increases too. The motive behind medical research is the elimination or control of disease, not merely the avoidance of suffering.[53] Second, it is objected that the heirs or enemies of an invalid might use euthanasia to hasten his death. To this we reply that the legal requirement of a written application by the sufferer, and of both legal and medical investigations, would be a safeguard. He would have far more protection than is provided for many patients now committed for treatment of mental disorder. He would, indeed, have a great deal more protection than he now receives under the present system of clandestine euthanasia being widely practiced. Third, it is claimed that once we legalize mercy deaths the application of the principle will be widened disastrously to cover nonfatal illnesses. But why is it, then, that although legal killing by capital punishment has been in vogue a long time, yet it has been narrowed rather than extended in scope? In fact it has been narrowed a great deal from the days when people were hanged for stealing a few shillings. This alarmist objection is the old red herring against which we have had to aim the rule of *abusus non tollit usum* time and again. It is drawn across many ethical trails.

A TIME TO PLANT, A TIME TO PLUCK

To draw our thinking together, we ought to repeat that there are three schools of thought favoring euthanasia. First, there are those who favor voluntary euthanasia, a personalistic ethical position. Second, there are those who favor involuntary euthanasia for monstrosities at birth and mental defectives, a partly personalistic and partly eugenic position.[54] Third, there are those who favor involuntary euthanasia for all who are a burden upon the community, a purely eugenic position. It should be perfectly obvious that we do not have to endorse the third school of thought just because we favor either the first or the second, or both. Our discussion has covered only the first one—voluntary medical euthanasia—as a means of ending a human life enmeshed in incurable and fatal physical suffering. The principles of right based upon selfhood and moral being favor it.

Defense of voluntary medical euthanasia, it should be made plain, does not depend upon the superficial system of values in which physical evil (pain) is regarded as worse than moral evil (sin) or intellectual evil (error). On the contrary, unless we are careful to see that pain is the least of evils, then our values would tie us back into that old attitude of taking the material or physical aspects of reality so seriously that we put nature or things as they are *out there* in a determinant place, subordinating the ethical and spiritual values of freedom and knowledge and upholding, in effect, a kind of naturalism. C. S. Lewis has described it by saying that, "Of all evils, pain only is sterilized or disinfected evil."[55] Pain cannot create moral evil, such as a disintegration or demoralization of personality would be, unless it is submitted to in brute fashion as opponents of euthanasia insist we should do.

We repeat, the issue is not one of life or death. The issue is which kind of death, an agonized or peaceful one. Shall we meet death in personal integrity or in personal disintegration? Should there be a moral or a demoralized end to mortal life? Surely . . . we are not as persons of moral stature to be ruled by ruthless and unreasoning physiology, but rather by reason and self-control. Those who face the issues of euthanasia with a religious faith will not, if they think twice, submit to the materialistic and animistic doctrine that God's will is revealed by what nature does, and that life, qua life, is absolutely sacred and untouchable. All of us can agree with Reinhold Niebuhr that "the ending of our life would not threaten us if we had not falsely made ourselves the center of life's meaning."[56] One of the pathetic immaturities we all recognize around us is stated bluntly by Sigmund Freud in his *Reflections on War and Death:* "In the subconscious every one of us is convinced of his immortality." Our frantic hold upon life can only cease to be a snare and delusion when we objectify it in some religious doctrine of salvation or, alternatively, agree with Sidney Hook that "the romantic pessimism which mourns man's finitude is a vain lament that we are not gods."[57] At least, the principles of personal morality warn us not to make physical phenomena, unmitigated by human freedom, the center of life's meaning. There is an impressive wisdom in the words of

Dr. Logan Clendenning: "Death itself is not unpleasant. I have seen a good many people die. To a few death comes as a friend, as a relief from pain, from intolerable loneliness or loss, or from disappointment. To even fewer it comes as a horror. To most it hardly comes at all, so gradual is its approach, so long have the senses been benumbed, so little do they realize what is taking place. As I think it over, death seems to me one of the few evidences in nature of the operation of a creative intelligence exhibiting qualities which I recognize as mind stuff. To have blundered onto the form of energy called life showed a sort of malignant power. After having blundered on life, to have conceived of death was a real stroke of genius."[58]

As Ecclesiastes the Preacher kept saying in first one way and then another, "The living know that they shall die" and there is "a time to be born and a time to die, a time to plant and a time to pluck up that which is planted."[59] And in the New Covenant we read that "all flesh is as grass" and "the grass withereth, and the flower thereof falleth away." Nevertheless, "who is he that will harm you, if ye be followers of that which is good?"[60]

Medicine contributes too much to the moral stature of men to persist indefinitely in denying the ultimate claims of its own supreme virtue and ethical inspiration, mercy. With Maeterlinck, we may be sure that "there will come a day when Science will protest its errors and will shorten our sufferings."[61]

NOTES

1. H. J. Rose, "Euthanasia," *Encyc. of Rel. and Ethics*, v, 598–601.
2. Hilary R. Werts, S.J., in April, 1947, 19.2, p. 33.
3. Virginia Moore, *Ho for Heaven*, New York, 1946, pp. 180–182.
4. I Cor. 15:55.
5. Quoted by Richard Garnett, "Jonathan Swift" in *Encyc. Brit.*, 11th ed.
6. Plato, *Laws*, IX, 873 C; Aristotle, *Politics*, 1335 b, 19ff.; for Pythagoras, cf. Cicero, *Cato Major* 20 (72 sq.) and *De Officiis*, i.31 (112).
7. *Divinae institutiones*, vi.17.
8. *Commentarii in Jonam*, i.12.
9. *De civitate dei*, i.16 sq.
10. *Summa Theologica*, ii.-ii 64.5.3.
11. Westermarck, *Christianity and Morals*, New York, 1939, p. 254.
12. *Utopia*, II, viii, "Of bondemen, sicke persons etc."
13. London, 1648.
14. *Sermon on the Bells*.
15. *Essays and Treatises*, London, 1777.
16. C. J. Cadoux, *The Early Christian Attitude to War*, London, 1919, pp. 96–160.
17. *Codex Iuris Can.*, 1240, I, n. 3.
18. Henry Davis, *Moral and Pastoral Theology*, Vol. II, New York, 1943, p. 195.
19. Anthony Koch and Arthur Preuss, *Handbook of Moral Theology*, St. Louis, 1925, p. 91. Italics added.
20. *Theologica Moralis*, III, n. 367. Liguori permits such actions on the principle of double effect, saying that they must be adapted to escape even though they will not succeed: *Theologica Moralis*, III, n. 367. "Licet vero se *indirecte* occidere:

puta, si quis se ejiciat per fenestram, ut effugiat incendium; praesertim si adsit aliqua spes mortem evadendi."
21. *Theologica Moralis*, 11th ed., 1.404.
22. The latest pronouncement of a church body came from the Episcopal Church in 1952. Noting "a growing movement to legalize the practice of Euthanasia," it was resolved that "the members of the General Convention of the Protestant Episcopal Church place themselves in opposition to the legalizing of the practice of Euthanasia, under any circumstances whatsoever." *Journal of the General Convention of the Protestant Episcopal Church*, 1952, p. 216. It should be noted that the resolution actually only opposes making euthanasia legal; it does not oppose the practice. This may be due to poor drafting, and not intentional.
23. 26 *American Jurisprudence*, 161.
24. N.Y., sec. 2301, art. 202, bk. 39, McKinney's *Consolidated Laws of New York*.
25. E. F. Burke, *Acute Cases of Moral Medicine*, Westminster, Md., 1946, p. 55.
26. Sec. 21-408, *General Statutes of Kansas*, 1929.
27. Cited in *Linacre Quarterly*, 19.2, Apr. 1927.
28. Cf. C. F. Potter, *Readers Scope*, May 1947, p. 113.
29. See Canon Green's short discussion in his *Problem of Right Conduct*, New York, 1931, pp. 283-284. This Anglican moralist says of euthanasia, "I have found it impossible to discover any really conclusive argument against suicide under due restrictions." See also in *Moral Problems*, ed. by the Bishop of Croydon, London, 1951, a permissive view taken by Lindsay Dewar, moral theologian of Bishop's College, and by the Bishop of Norwich.
30. *Adventures on the Borderlands of Ethics*, New York, 1926, p. 34.
31. Davis, op. cit., II, 142. This author explains that Jerome and Lessius excused suicide in defense of chastity, but that Aquinas opposed even this exception to the prohibition.
32. Op. cit., II, 76. He cites texts such as I Cor. 3:16-17.
33. Dec. 23, 1948. Incorporated in *The Ethical Basis of Medical Care*, p. 160 sq.
34. *Indian Thought and Its Development*, London, 1930, pp. 225-238.
35. *Thoughts in War Time*, London, 1940, pp. 31-32. Italics in original.
36. H. Roberts, "Two Essays on Medicine," in *Living Age*, Oct. 1934, 347.159-162.
37. Quoted by H. N. Oliphant, *Redbook Magazine*, Sep. 1948.
38. Ibid.
39. Judges 9:54.
40. *Man in Revolt*, New York, 1939, pp. 388-389.
41. Job 2:9-10.
42. *Journ. of Nervous and Mental Diseases*, July 1936, p. 84.
43. Symposium, "Pro and Con," in *The Digest*, Oct. 23, 1937, 124.22-23.
44. Quoted by A. L. Woolbarst, *Medical Record*, May 17, 1939.
45. *Phaedo*, conclusion.
46. R. E. Osgood, M.D., 210.4, 182-192, Jan. 25, 1934.
47. Ibid., 202.18, 843-853.
48. Cf. G. E. Byers, *Ohio Med. Journ.*, 1936, 32.342; J. S. Manson, *Brit. Med. Journ.*, 1936, 1.86; W. W. Gregg, *North Amer. Rev.*, 1934, 237.239; J. J. Walsh, *The Forum*, Dec. 1935, 333-334. The Council of the World Medical Association, at Copenhagen, Apr. 24-28, 1950, *recommended* that "the practice of euthanasia be condemned." Cf. *Journal of the Amer. Med. Assoc.*, June 10, 1950, 143-6, p. 561.
49. E.g., cf. Frank Hinman, M.D., *Journ. of Nervous and Mental Diseases*, 99, 1944.
50. Cf. H. N. Oliphant, op. cit.
51. Nov. 18, 1935, 26.21, pp. 53-54.
52. *New York Herald Tribune*, May 23, 1947.
53. See the thrilling story of vigorous medical progress in an account by the Secretary of the American Medical Association, Stephen M. Spencer, *Wonders of Modern Medicine*, New York, 1953. Between 1900 and 1952 the average life span of Americans has risen from 49 to 69 years, and Louis I. Dublin of the Metropolitan Life Insurance Company estimates it will be 73 within this generation, thus exceeding the threescore and ten allotted in the Bible.

54. It has always been a quite common practice of midwives and, in modern times, doctors, simply to fail to respirate monstrous babies at birth.
55. *The Problem of Pain*, London, 1943, p. 104.
56. *Human Destiny*, New York, 1943, II, 293.
57. Quoted by Corliss Lamont, *The Illusion of Immortality*, New York, 1950, p. 191.
58. *The Human Body*, New York, 1941, 3rd ed., pp. 442-443.
59. Eccl. 9:5 and 3:2.
60. I Pet. 1:24 and 3:13.
61. Quoted by Jacoby, *Physician, Pastor, and Patient*, New York, 1936, p. 206.

Norbert O. Schedler

OUR DESTRUCTION OF TOMORROW: A PHILOSOPHICAL REFLECTION ON THE ECOLOGICAL CRISIS

Norbert O. Schedler is Chairman of the Philosophy Department at Purdue University, Fort Wayne, Indiana. He is the editor of *Philosophy of Religion: Contemporary Perspectives* (1974) and of *A Concise Introduction to the Philosophy of Religion* (forthcoming). His selection points out some of the current criticism of technology and how it causes deterioration of our environment and depletion of our natural resources. Schedler sees war, together with overpopulation, crowding, and hunger, as having caused an ecological crisis of major proportions. He sees us already "west of Eden in a fallen world" and cautions that if we don't act now we may see "the destruction of our tomorrow." Schedler investigates the historical background of the crisis, and finds that the reasons for our technological abuses may be rooted in Western philosophical and religious traditions. Though he does not view Eastern thought as providing final solution to the ecological crisis, he does argue that Eastern philosophies do provide some viable alternatives that may help us to avert disaster. He describes Earth in the terminating years of the twentieth century as a spaceship, and cautions us to treat our world as a closed vehicle with limited resources and space, where the good of all passengers must be considered. Schedler offers some suggestions for saving the future and urges that we implement them today.

I grew up believing only God could end the world. I grew up believing the universe was a garden created for man. I grew up believing hard work was the essence of what it meant to be human. I grew up believing that human progress and growth were unlimited. These beliefs were my Eden. I now live west of Eden in a fallen world.

I still remember the first crack in my early vision. When I was ten years old I saw a science movie about various forms of life that swarmed causing an imbalance in their ecosystem. This imbalance eventually resulted either in the extinction of the species or in that species becoming a minority fighting for its survival. I happened to attend school in a ghetto of a large city. On my way home that day, I passed through the city on a bus. I saw hordes of human beings scurrying over the landscape, and I remembered what happened to the swarming species in the film. I still get prickly heat-like feelings when I think of that bus ride through another swarming species, *homo sapiens.*

Now, at the age of 40, the horrors of that childhood premonition are becoming a reality. The swarming of our species is devastating the earth.[1] We are contaminating our air and water with fumes, chemicals, noise, heat, pesticides, radioactivity, and solid wastes. Our cities are a blight on the land, some observers arguing that they are aproaching uninhabitability. Pictures of the earth from a satellite prompted the famed ecologist-scientist Loren Eiseley to remark:

> Man in space is enabled to look upon the distant earth, a celestial orb, a revolving sphere. He sees it to be green, from the verdure on the land, algae greening the oceans, a green celestial fruit. Looking closely at the earth, he perceives blotches, black, brown, gray and from these extend dynamic tentacles upon the green epidermis. These blemishes he recognizes as the cities and work of man and asks, "Is man but a planetary disease?"[2]

What has happened in the last few decades to so radically change our perspective of man on the earth, from crown of creation to planetary pest? Why is it that so many of us live west of Eden with little hope for human kind? The overwhelming disillusionment that so many now feel has several sources. In this essay I explore the effect of the ecological crisis on our current malaise. Part one deals with the nature of the crisis. Part two deals with the historical roots that contributed to the development of the crisis. Part three attempts to discuss some problems and solutions.[3]

PART ONE: THE CRISIS

Environmental deterioration The quality of our environment is deteriorating at an unprecedented rate. Our food chains all over the world have been infested with poisonous substances such as DDT, mercury, lead, cadmium, and chlorinated compounds. These substances have been found in tissues of animals far from their original point of entry into the ecosystem. DDT has even been found in mother's milk. Industrial refuse, oil spills, human wastes, and other pollutants have affected nearly all the waters of the earth. Paradoxically, the very air we breathe which is necessary for life, has become a potential killer. Our cities have an umbrella of smog and air-borne pollutants. We throw away 28 billion bottles a year. We dispose (?) of 48 billion cans each year, i.e., 91,300 cans *per minute.* The average person in the United States produces 5.3 lbs. of solid waste per day, up from 3.5 lbs. in 1960. While our population has increased 12 percent since 1960, our garbage pile has increased by 80 percent. We are surrounded by filth and ugliness spewed out in the wake of so-called technological advances.

We are operating blindly on the basis of a number of myths—for example, the myth that the "solution to pollution is dilution." This is simply not true. There is a limit to what our air and water can absorb without becoming toxic. Many chemicals cannot be diluted at all or persist for long periods of time, e.g., mercury, DDT, radio-active wastes, etc. We also speak of development as if we were creatively evolving the possibilities of our landscapes. This is another myth. Development actually means more ticky-tacky houses and all the shoddiness of mass-produced suburbia. Indeed, development has actually come to mean destruction and defacement.[4]

Depletion of natural resources Most of us have read the timetables for the depletion of many of the basic raw materials needed to fire our current technological machine. For example, it is widely predicted that we will run out of oil by the turn of the century. We could run out of mercury as soon as 1983. Rather than give a list of the materials and the timetable for their depletion, let me put the problem on a more theoretical base.[5]

What we are really talking about is the depletion of energy of all kinds. The first law of thermodynamics states that energy is neither created nor destroyed, although it may change form. This is comforting since it implies that energy is never lost. But the first law must be coupled with the second law of thermodynamics. In simplified form, this law states that changes in the physical world move from energy in concentrated forms where it is easily converted for use, to diffused forms where it has little practical use. This is why the second law speaks of the "running down" of the universe. Energy can become degraded. The availability of many energy sources that cannot be recycled will be used up within 100 years or less. In short, there is a limit to the usable sources of energy. This problem will become more critical as more energy becomes degraded and increasing population puts more demand on dwindling supplies.[6]

Imagine, for example, that the People's Republic of China miraculously achieved our standard of living with its concomitant demand for energy. The effect on the ecosphere would be devastating. The amount of coal that would be needed to fire her expanded economy for one year would equal the current *total* yearly energy consumption of the world. It is impossible to calculate the other materials China would need with such an economy.

Even the theoretically unlimited resources of the sun pose problems.' An enormous amount of material is required to capture this energy, convert it to a usable form, and transmit it. More materials from the earth will be needed to actually use it. The prospect of energy from the sun allows many to continue to live with the myth that we can keep on growing indefinitely. But where are we going to get the materials to make the machines that this energy from the sun will power?

Then there is a myth about changing the disparity between the have and the have-not nations. The have-nots cannot come up to the standard of living of the haves without destroying the planet. Not acknowledging this is to indulge in what Hardin calls the "fudge factor." We have operated with the myth that the whole system is *open*; that there is always more to come, new lands, new sources of energy, etc. So we fudge on slowing down. But the system is *closed*—just what is and no more! And, given our current population, we may already have exceeded the carrying capacity of the planet. The haves must begin to *lower* their standard of living; there is no other way that the have-nots' standard of living can be raised.

War Although war is universally condemned, it is universally practiced. Although the arms race is denounced, we continue building bigger and better weapons. (Double-talk is very common on all these issues. We make war to win the peace. We exploit the poor to distribute wealth. Think of what we take from other countries every day to fuel our economy. We pollute to increase energy, and then use energy to decrease pollution.) Even if we prevent a major war, the preparation for it uses up human and natural resources that are desperately needed to feed and house the world's deprived people.

But what is even more frightening is that the ecological crisis seems to make future wars inevitable. First, consider the inequality that exists between the haves and the have-nots. The have-nots in their drive for improving their lot will meet the haves head on. The earth is a closed system—a spaceship, if you like—and there is not enough to go around if the have-nots are determined to be equal with the haves. Who is going to back down? If history tells us anything, it tells us that such confrontations end in war. Second, war seems all the more inevitable because we are divided up into nation-states. There seems little likelihood that we will give up sovereignty for the sake of global survival. The United Nations has generally failed for this very reason. The effective negotiations are done by the

Kissingers between nation-states, not at a global level with the good of all in mind.

If we are to survive, limitations on freedom and sovereignty are inevitable and some form of international or, better, transnational control must be adopted. There are few signs that either the haves or the have-nots are willing to reduce their national prestige and surrender sovereignty or, in the case of so-called emerging nations, that they are willing to abandon their nationalistic aims. Both parties fail to see what U Thant said, "90 percent of our problems are world problems." On the spaceship earth we only have *our* problems. Nationalism of the type exemplified by the United States and France can no longer be tolerated. Assuming we have ruled out physical force, what bite can we give to the decision not to "tolerate" in the absence of some political or moral force?[8] Without a moral and political force, all systems are go and the end seems to be "self-destruct" at year _____.

Population, overcrowding, and hunger At the roots of the ecological crisis is population growth. Every 24 hours, 324,000 babies are born while 133,000 persons die. This means 190,000 new passengers join our spaceship and must be supported. "Each week the equivalent of the city of Cleveland is added to the world's population. Each year the increase is more than the entire population of France, Belgium, and Holland."[9] If the population growth of our planet continues at the current pace, doubling every 35 years, by the year 2300 we shall have 3½ trillion people on the globe. Unimaginable! Impossible! Population control is inevitable. It is just a question of whether we control through rational measures, or nature imposes its own controls on another swarming species. Wars for space and resources! Disease, famine, short lives, psychological breakdowns! Can our swarming species survive such threats? Can we still seriously follow the dictum of Genesis to "be fruitful and multiply"? Can we any longer hold the right to breed as an inalienable individual right? Certainly not, but then how do we get today's 3½ billion passengers on the spaceship to agree on procedures for control? What social and political means do we use? Democratic?

To show that the four problem areas discussed are related, notice how population growth leads to issues such as war, pollution, resource depletion. For example, even if we are successful in limiting population we shall still have 7 billion people by the year 2000. Even if we in the industrially advanced West cut back on our standard of living and allow for the underdeveloped nations to increase theirs, we shall have to build houses, hospitals, ports, factories, bridges, etc., in numbers that almost equal all the construction work done by the human race up to now. Where are we doing to get the resources. What will this do to the face of the earth? Ought it even be our goal?

How are we going to feed this swarming species? One billion people suffer from overt hunger or clear-cut starvation. 10 to 20 million people die annually from hunger and starvation-related diseases.[10] 300 to 500 million people get insufficient calories, and nearly half the world's population suffer from protein deficiency. Mind you, we are talking about *now*, not what happens when we are invaded by 3½ billion more by the year 2000. And yet we go to the developing countries and tell them to stop polluting with chemicals to increase crop yield. Until their stomachs are full, they could care less.[11]

The population versus resource depletion ratio is exaggerated in the West. The United States consumes 40 percent (some say 50 percent) of the world's raw materials with only 6 percent of the world's population. This can no longer continue unless we are willing to engage in war for resources, markets, etc. Other countries will refuse to spend their wealth for maintaining our standard of living. Will we agree to lower our standards? Will underdeveloped nations agree to remain *under*developed? The answer is a clear NO! Again, what mechanisms are there for global planning and resolution of this problem? With no such mechanisms, into the vacuum come the horrors of war.

And what about the psychological effects of the loss of space and privacy? Even now one cannot find a place out in nature that is not disturbed by the roar of jets overhead and motor bikes on the surface. Tests with animals show that overcrowding leads to deviate social behavior. I remember a science movie which showed that when rats were placed in an overcrowded environment many could not cope with the resulting stress. They went into catatonic states. What about our cities? We are surrounded by people, yet lonely. We are surrounded by affluence, yet bored to hell. As one psychologist puts it, "There is an overwhelming desire among many to just sleep."[12]

We live west of Eden in a crisis unparalleled since our expulsion from the Garden. Details on the dimensions of the crisis I shall leave to those more qualified in ecology. I turn now to a discussion of the relationship between perspectives and ways of being in the world.

PART TWO: HISTORICAL ROOTS OF THE CRISIS[13]

How a person *acts* in the world follows directly from how one *thinks* about the world. One's fundamental vision of what is real, significant, good, beautiful, and their opposites provide the priorities for meaningful action. Given different perspectives, we interpret the world differently. Note the widely different fundamental outlooks expressed in the following quotes.

> The white people never cared for land or deer or bear. When we Indians kill meat, we eat it all up. When we dig roots, we make little holes. . . . We shake down acorns and pine-nuts. We don't chop down the trees. We only use dead wood. But the white people plow up the ground, pull up the trees, kill everything. The tree says, "Don't. I am sore. Don't hurt me." But they chop it down and cut it up. The spirit of the land hates them. . . . The Indians never hurt anything, but the white people destroy all. They blast rocks and scatter them on the ground. The rock says "Don't! You are hurting me." But the white people pay no attention. When the Indians use rocks, they take little round ones for their cooking. . . . How can the spirit of the earth like the white man? . . . Everywhere the white man has touched it, it is sore.[14]

Contrast the above view with that of a theologian in the Judeo-Christian tradition,

> . . . nature is called into being to serve as a means to God's essential purpose in creating the world of spirits . . . the creation of nature by God . . . a relative necessity, the necessity, namely, of serving as a means to God's previously chosen end of calling into being a multitude of spirits akin to Himself. . . . For the apparatus by which the individual life and all commerce in things spiritual is carried on, presupposes for its permanent existence the whole immeasurable system of the world, mechanical, chemical, organic. . . . The whole universe, therefore, considered thus as the precondition of the moral kingdom of created spirits, is throughout God's creation for this end.[15]

In other words, God created the world for man, a spirit like Himself, and it is only in this world of spirits that value occurs—an obvious case of human chauvinism.

If what I have argued is valid, namely that actions in nature are determined by perspectives about nature,[16] then where we are and where we are going from the standpoint of ecology require making conscious just what this perspective is and subjecting it to evaluation. Is our Western perspective a viable perspective for dealing with the crisis discussed in Part One? My answer is no. What about the Eastern perspective now so popular with the young? While I have deep sympathies with it, I find it also defective as a total perspective.

Western view Why is it that science and technology are almost exclusively a Western phenomenon? White has argued that this is due primarily to the Judeo-Christian view of nature and history. In the West, history is primarily the *human* story, a record of unique and irreversible events. Only in history does real change occur. History, therefore, fills us with anxiety since its outcome is uncertain, and therefore God's direction and promises for a future time are crucial.

Nature, on the other hand, will always be the same, endlessly repeating its divinely ordained patterns. According to the Western view, nature does not play a crucial role in human concern except as the backdrop for the real drama which occurs between man and God.[17] Nature is an artifact of God, and has no freedom of choice or intrinsic value. It has no will of its own, and is therefore seen as inert and impersonal.

God and man are the crucial players. The key words of the Judeo-Christian tradition refer primarily to the relationship between God and man and between man and his fellows, e.g., sin, salvation, repentance, hope, love, faith, righteousness, etc. Only man is created in God's image.[18]

And what is more, man is told to "be fruitful and multiply, and fill the earth and subdue it, and have dominion over the fish of the sea and over the birds of the air and over every living thing" (Gen. 1:28). "Thou hast given him dominion over the works of thy hands; thou hast put all things under his feet" (Ps. 8:6). Here we have a view of man and nature which not only separates man from nature in order of value and separates man's destiny from nature's destiny, but one that gives man the specific injunction to dominate nature as its master. This leads White to remark:

> Especially in its Western form, Christianity is the most anthropocentric religion the world has seen. Christianity, in absolute contrast to ancient paganism and Asia's religions (except perhaps Zorastrianism), not only established a dualism of man and nature but also insisted that it is God's will that man exploit nature for his proper ends.[19]

White's conclusion is that "we shall continue to have a worsening ecologic crisis until we reject the Christian axiom that nature has no reason for existence save to serve man."

The Judeo-Christian tradition is often viewed as a triumph over primitive nature worship. Maybe this so-called triumph ought to be reevaluated. In the primitive perspective every tree, spring, mountain has its own protecting spirit. Before using any natural object one had to ask permission of the spirit. When it was necessary to kill an animal, the tribe asked forgiveness of the animal's spirit. While it seems almost laughable to us, when they hunted and killed an elephant, primitive Kafirs assured its spirit that they had not done so out of malice.

What is central to the primitive perspective is man's unity with nature. He felt guilt whenever he tampered with its processes. Nature, of which he was a part, had a delicate balance, a harmony. Man did not seek dominance over it not because he lacked the intelligence (science) or the tools (technology), but because he had a fundamentally different perspective. Nature was sacred. Therefore he sought to be in tune with it rather than distance himself from it and overpower it.[20] As Ernst Cassirer writes in *An Essay on Man*:

> . . . in his [primitive man] conception of nature and life all these differences are obliterated by a stronger feeling: the deep conviction of a fundamental and indelible solidarity of life that bridges over the multiplicity and variety of its single forms. He does not ascribe to himself a unique and privileged place in the scale of nature.[21]

Nature and all that it contains is seen as a Thou to be respected rather than an It to be exploited. Nature is alive. When Western religionists chased the spirits away from natural objects to reside only in man and a transcendent God, there were no longer any taboos to protect nature from man's technology.

The Judeo-Christian tradition also holds that nature is a creation of God. Indeed, there is no nature as a neutral thing divorced from God's creative purpose.[22] The world is called 'creation', not 'nature'. Since creation was an *act* of God and actions exhibit the intentions of the actor, a study of creation reveals the intentions of God. Science arose in the West then as a *sacred* discipline since its purpose was to know not the nature of natural phenomena, but the nature of God. Science was called natural theology—learning about God through the works of his hands. The great scientist Newton, for example, considered himself a theologian. In Eastern Christianity this view still dominates. Nature is treated more like a work of art which engenders feelings of awe and wonderment, and for just this reason it is to be left as it is. Science is an investigation of the goodness of God.

But, unfortunately, *Western* Christianity developed technology to go along with science. White argues that this happened primarily because two different paradigms of salvation operated. In Eastern Christianity, sin was identified with ignorance and salvation with illumination. The Eastern saint is a person of contemplative bent, mystical in orientation. In Western Christianity sin is seen as immoral *conduct*; salvation as right *action*. Thus, Western Christianity coupled knowing with doing: Knowledge was power to do God's Will; it was not simply knowledge of the inner workings of God's Mind. The passivism of the one outlook and the activism of the other are clear. Technology grew out of the desire to do God's Will on earth. Work had a saving value. And it was nature that must be brought under God's rule through this work. The Puritan work ethic derives in part from this posture.

While our science and technology have been desacralized, many still believe that their assumptions derive from this religious outlook.

We still see man as the center of the universe. We still identify good with right action. We still see work as having a saving value. We still see nature as a commodity to be used. Even humanism and Marxism share these assumptions. Further, expansion of science and technology will not change our outlook. We need a new perspective on nature, and this will require changes in our religion, whether in traditional or desacralized forms.

Eastern view The ecological crisis has shown us the interconnectedness of everything. It has called into question the dualism that characterizes Western religion and philosophy.[23] The growing sense of dependence of one form of life upon all others has been a devastating blow to Western anthropocentrism. This is why many in the West who are disillusioned with Western culture and who take a holistic (the universe as an interlocked community) approach have turned to the East.)[24] A new consciousness, one more in tune with current attitudes toward nature, can be found in the Eastern perspective.[25]

Nature The East denies our presupposition that nature has no claim of its own, only utility for man. In the West, even our concern with ecology is still a concern to save *human* kind. We forget that nature also hurts and dies. The East denies that nature is devoid of purpose and value. We find nature silent, therefore we rush in and put our stamp on it, "Made by Yahweh in 6000 B.C. for you and me." We make it over in our image. The Eastern sage does not find the silence of nature an occasion for anxious activity, but an eloquent silence to be honored and respected. Nature is seen as having rights of its own.

The East also sees few boundaries between plants, animals, etc., rather, a blending of one into another. The epidermis, in the West, is conceptualized much like the shell or boundary that marks the "I" off from everything else. I end or begin at my skin. The East sees the epidermis on the model of the surface of a pond or the soil in the forest, as a delicate membrane through which there is constant traffic. We have here two contrasting perspectives which affect our view of nature.[26] One view stresses our *inness*, the other our *outness*. In the one model, the self is a complex of thoughts and feelings, surrounded by a hard shell—skeleton, organs, clothes, and habits. I am *in* my body as water is in a cup. In the other model the self is extended in all directions, blending *out* into the landscape to such a degree that there seems to be no individual ego.[27] Perhaps a blend of these two views is needed for a balanced ecological perspective.

Humankind A person in the West is seen primarily in terms of *reason* and *action*, as a mind that uses reason to create, refashion, and improve on nature.[28] Reason is a tool to get something done. It provides in-formation (notice the word) which is a process or power to fashion or form; so we have technology as the crown of our activity. The Western God is the Omni-knower and Omni-doer we all seek to emulate. So we make everything into an object and analyze it with the purpose of achieving clarity. Clarity makes possible control. Reason is not receptive as it is in the East, but creative. Reason makes the world what it chooses it to be, a solipsism. D. T. Suzuki summarizes these traits as follows:

Eastern Mind
Silent, humble, synthetic, totalizing, integrative, deductive, nonsystematic, intuitive, nondiscursive, subjective, spiritually individualistic and socially group-minded.

Western Mind
Eloquent, proud, analytical, discriminative, differential, inductive, individualistic, intellectual, objective, scientific, generalizing, conceptual, schematic, impersonal, legalistic, organizing, power-wielding, self-assertive, disposed to impose its will upon others.[29]

It is no wonder that the counterculture finds affinity with the East, and the religion of the American Indian. Our science and technology—the fruits of our perspective—have become our desacralized religion. And it is this religion that many today argue we must dispel. It has led to alienation from the whole, to boredom, and to the destruction of our environmental life-support systems. Technology has become like the ancient god of Western religion. It is subject to no moral strictures but its own capacities. I can! I will! Technology run wild is typified by a test pilot who radioed back from his sleek new jet, "I'm lost, but I'm making record speed." It is this mentality which many of our young in the counterculture have rejected in favor of the Eastern virtues of nonaction, gentleness, humility, simplicity, frugality, and the abandonment of all desire that things be other than they are. Let it be! Get in tune with! Groove! Contentment with life as it is permits the individual to blend into the all-encompassing *Tao*.

Although I have deep sympathies with religious outlooks, both Western and Eastern, I must agree with Rodger Shinn that no traditional religion by itself is adequate to deal with the present crisis. The Eastern dictum, "The world is ruled by letting things take their course; it cannot be ruled by interfering" would be a counsel of despair.[30] The romantic appropriation of the return-to-nature-religions, counseling humankind to drop everything and return to Mother Nature and the forest primeval for solace, would lead to the death of our species. We do need the insights of both East and West, but we also need our science and technology. Destruction comes from nonaction, from a *lack* of foresight and planning as well as an active quest to dominate. If we just let things be, deterioration will continue. As G. P. Marsh said over a hundred years ago, "humankind cannot leave nature to her fate but must . . . become a co-worker with nature in the reconstruction of the damaged fabric which the negligence and wantonness of former lodgers has rendered untenable. He must aid her in reclothing the mountain slopes with forests and vegetable mould, thereby restoring the fountains which she provided to water them."[31]

Some ecologists and counterculture exponents have popularized a nature romanticism which I feel compelled to criticize. Working from various assumptions (God made it! Nature left to herself rights all!), these nature romantics see all civilization as a pollution of nature which by itself is unspoiled and the ultimate criterion of good. What is natural is what is good. So we camp out, eat natural foods, etc. to reintegrate ourselves with nature in pursuit of a kind of nature mysticism. In nature we return to a kind of "innocence" which has been polluted by the city. Our alienation from nature is the source of all our ecological problems. Let nature take its course because nature is wise and compassionate.

But is this true? Has nature been kind to the peoples of the earth? Has nature been our liberator? Our romanticized view of primitive life forgets that such an existence was often hard and cruel. Nature is often hostile, indifferent, and limiting to humankind. The return to nature can be a danger, not a blessing. The biblical writers knew that humankind could be cruel to nature, but they also knew that nature could be cruel to humankind. The biblical writers stressed that humankind was part of nature and yet more. It is in the tension between being in, and yet above, nature in history that we work out our destiny. Our separation from nature can be the occasion for destructive activity toward nature and other selves, but it can also be the occasion for the wise use and control of those aspects of nature that are unfriendly. The human spirit allows humankind to be the stewards of nature. To be civilized is not to destroy unspoiled nature, but to be free from having our fates controlled by natural processes that are often destructive. We are not simply natural entities, but historical entities who, in anxiety, create what is yet to be. We are not just bound to nature in an act of resignation. In freedom we stand apart from nature and choose how to be.[32] In freedom we can destroy our natural habitat or we can be wise stewards. I do not believe that this is human chauvinism, but an awareness of humankind's unique place in the order of things. As unpopular as the thought now is with counterculture groups, nature as well as humankind also needs its redemption.[33]

In fact, would we be human if we simply acted naturally, i.e., without any artifacts? I would argue that the answer is no. In freedom, we create what is not there naturally. Nature did not give us eyeglasses or pacemakers, or electric light, or clothing, or medicine. We are godlike in our very acts of going beyond nature. There is nothing inherently evil about something artificial, just as there is nothing inherently good about something natural.[34] If we acted in a totally natural way, we could not survive. If we acted in a totally artificial way, we could not survive. It is time to do away with this oversimplified dichotomy between natural and artificial. With sensitivity for nature, we must use all the layers of our cerebral cortex to go beyond nature where this serves the needs of the total biotic community. Our survival *and* nature's survival depend on it.

It is time for the West to stop thinking of economically underdeveloped nations as representing a primitive stage of human development on the way to color TV, think-tanks, 747s, and heat-and-serve meals. We must learn from them how to live simply and in tune with nature. Our survival may depend on it. Human history is intimately tied into nature's destiny. But we must not forget in the process that human beings are stewards of their environment and for now, at least, nature's destiny is also intimately tied into human history. "East is East and West is West, and ne'er the twain shall meet" must be changed to "East is East and West is West, and our survival depends on their union." Our science and technology must learn to perceive the interconnectedness of all things (East); care for the earth as stewards (West); search for simplicity, frugality, gentleness and rational love for the earth; and appreciate the importance of inner development.

But isn't it ridiculous to sit here and urge this on humankind? How do people change their outlooks? My only hope is that the momentous character of the crisis will generate this new outlook. I take hope in seeing this new consciousness in the young of our earth.

PART THREE: ETHICS AND THE SPACESHIP EARTH

The seventies will be that decade when we in the West come to realize that our 250-year joyride is over. The end of the era of cheap and abundant resources is over. For these many years the industrial societies of the West have lived on the abundance of the earth and political dominance over its peoples. Now we are moving into a scarcity economy coupled with the increasing demand made upon it by developing countries. These countries can no longer be ignored in world decision making. An example of recognition was seen with the formation of the OPEC (Organization of Petroleum Exporting Countries). Similar resource coalitions will be formed in copper, tin, and bauxite within the next several years. All these materials are crucial to the industrial West. Scarcity and the need for global decision making will seriously challenge many of the following assumptions of Western social and political philosophy.

1. Unlimited progress. Both capitalism and Marxism assume unlimited growth till we reach a society where human beings will achieve economic freedom. All the evils associated with scarcity will then go away—poverty, inequality, injustice, alienation, and fear. The past was barbarous! The present is an improvement! The future will be glorious! Give us time, we will say, to get the kinks out of the technological machine, and we will live happily ever after. As long as we believe in this meliorism (things will get better in the evolutionary process), we will not radically examine the assumption of unlimited progress. We can learn from the east not only that this assumption is false, but its opposite is also false.

Linear views of time lead Western thinkers to predict either utopias or apocalyptic nightmares in some future time. Both these predictions assume time is a straight line going somewhere.[35] Eastern thinkers, instead, are suspicious of straight lines. Drawing on their experience of nature where straight lines are a rarity, they see linear thinking and objects as a sign of man's imposition on nature. When nature is allowed to be, it rounds out humankind's straight lines. The East's preference is for the circle, and their view of time is cyclical. Progress or regress is seen as a Western illusion. Accordingly, they accept the fact that everything keeps coming back to itself only to be repeated over and over again. It is ridiculous, therefore, to speak of things becoming better or worse. "It simply is!"

The American Indian Vine Deloria, Jr. puts this issue in terms of evolution. The theory of evolution has led many to see the evolutionary process in terms of value. We see man as the crown of the evolutionary process. Where does that put other forms of life? We see Western white civilized man as the crown of social evolution. Where does that put everyone else? Again, the linear view of time coupled with Western chauvinism separates us from our natural environment and from other peoples of the earth. We value persons and things in terms of what they are to become rather than what they are. We extol those who alter what is; the American Indian praises one who accepts what is. While this too can be overdone, acceptance of what is must serve as a check on our Promethean urge to make ourselves and our world into an artifact of Western civilization. We need what H. Cox calls a "rebirth of 'Epimethean Man,' the quiet receiver, the unassertive husband of earth, the resigned and ironic refuser of power."[36]

Again, we can learn from other societies, other cultures. When we progress (?) from the simple to the sophisticated, have we really advanced? Does a rich man get more satisfaction from sitting down to a sumptuous, expensive meal than an Indian receives from roasting a buffalo steak after a hard hunt or a peasant from a cool drink of water after a hard day in the field?[37] We praise the sophisticated at the expense of the simple. Our survival may depend on reversing these values.

2. The primacy of the individual and his inalienable rights. As we move into a commodity-deficient economy—what might be called a scarcity economy—realizing that we live in a closed system, group rights will dominate ethical thinking. Restraints on individual rights (including individual nation-states), strict economic and technological controls, and strong political constraints will be the marks of the coming decades. The assumption radically called into question here is individualism. Again the straight-line paradigm operates. A straight line (like an individual) begins somewhere and goes somewhere. It is an independent entity. The West has tended to see everything in terms of these discrete entities. The East sees everything as interconnected, subject to external influence. The *pattern*, or *web*, of life is primary. The parts do not exist separated from the whole. This has led R. Laing and P. Slater to argue that "linearity is pathological."[38]

The ideology of individualism and personal achievement is compared by Slater to cancer cells:

> Imagine a mass of cancerous tissue, the cells of which enjoyed consciousness. Would they not be full of self-congratulatory sentiments at their independence, their more advanced level of development, their rapid rate of growth? Would they not sneer at their more primitive cousins who were bound into a static and unfree existence, with limited aspirations, subject to heavy group constraint, and obviously "going nowhere"? Would they not rejoice in their control over their own destiny, and cheer the conversion of more and more normal cells as convincing proof of the validity of their own way of life? Would they not, in fact, feel increasingly triumphant right up to the moment the organism on which they fed expired?[39]

3. The "let-it-happen" approach. Economic laissez-faire philosophy, which leaves hands off the economic forces allowing them to achieve a balance on their own, is a luxury that in our ecological crisis cannot be allowed. Steady-state or spaceman economics (i.e. strict controls) will dominate economic theory.

4. All persons are basically rational animals acting, if well informed,

for the good of all. This assumption, part of the very base of democracy, is also questionable. We need Plato's notion of "the many" as basically an appetitive group within the body-politic, who use liberty as an excuse for self-indulgence. Viewing people on a Friday night at a shopping center or at a political rally will make Plato's point, namely that people are not all rational, and that where liberty is primary it easily becomes an excuse for self-indulgence. American democracy has usually been based on the principle of competition rather than on that of rational cooperation. Uncontrolled competition is a luxury no longer allowable in the spaceship Earth; rational cooperation will be hard to come by within existing political institutions. Democracy has become a system that allows us individually to gratify our appetitive nature and fulfill our individual rights, rather than one that chooses wise persons who will impose constraints on us.

BUT LIMITATIONS WILL COME. EITHER WE CHOOSE THOSE WHO WILL LIMIT US OR WE WILL BE LIMITED BY THOSE WE DID NOT CHOOSE. This is a strong statement, but I believe that it is valid for the following reason. If predications about the ecological crises in population and resource depletion come true, limitation will occur in one of two ways:

1. Nature left to itself will control the swarming species by disease, famine, etc. We will reach physical limits followed by a Hobbesian universe of war of all against all (anarchy), followed, as anarchy usually is, by a tyrant.
2. If we choose now to impose strict controls in a steady-state economy, then strict controls on human behavior will follow.

To further develop this line of argument let us consider the classic ecological analysis "the tragedy of the commons."[40] Humankind is caught in a situation that resembles a classic tragedy. Although each individual has no ill will toward others, all persons acting in self-interest move inevitably toward destruction of all. The "tragedy" is exemplified in the English villages where animals are kept on a commons, an area to which all villagers have an equal right. There is no problem as long as the number of animals is small enough to be maintained by the size of the commons. But self-interest dictates that each herder enlarge his herd. Thus each herd grows until the number of cattle exceeds the carrying capacity of the commons. The result is that everyone eventually loses as the animals die of starvation. The rational strategy of each individual equals social irresponsibility, leading to disaster for all. The tragedy is that, even though the outcome is perfectly predictable, no one acts to avert the disaster, for this would work only if everyone agreed to limit herd population.

But in a laissez-faire economy there are no constraints placed on individual growth.

Now write this large. The ecosphere is one big, but limited, commons made up of air, water, and mineral resources. Following its own self-interest, each nation attempts to get what it can. For example, the ocean in certain areas has been fished so hard that there are now no fish for anyone. Or take the problem of smog in Los Angeles, which is the result of millions of individuals pursuing private gratification. One individual act of restraint is meaningless. But how do we get everyone to act? We do not have the political and social mechanisms needed to restrain individual or national pursuits. If we are to survive without tragedy—a "tragedy of the commons"—restraints must be placed on individuals and nations, or the restraints will come tragically when, for example, the air in Los Angeles becomes a killer.

Population growth threatens us with the same tragedy. Each individual believes that he or she has the inherent right to breed. But if this right is not limited, all of us will lose that right when the population reaches that point where the "commons" no longer can support all of us. (Some believe that we have already reached that point.) But how are we going to put pressure on couples to limit families to two children? "The community, which guarantees the survival of children, must have the power to decide how many children shall be born."[41] Perhaps we should tax parents for having children, rather than giving them tax breaks.[42] In any case, I agree with Hardin that we must educate our young to think in terms of zero population as we move toward a future stage where limitations on family size will come by coercion—economic, political, or natural. It is inevitable! For the choice before us is not between the freedom to breed or its restraint, but between two kinds of restraint: restraint in breeding versus restraint in all other areas. Each new child brings new pressures on the commons which will result in restraints anyway.

The under-developed countries will see the above argument as another act of "whitey" to limit the power of their increasing numbers. The whites will have their own objection to my argument. As one told me, "If we do not continue to have large families, we will be overrun by niggers and slant-eyes." Unless there is some political process that guarantees equal rights to the commons for all, races will continue to feel threatened and find security in their growing numbers while failing to see the inevitable tragedy of self-destruction for us all.

And what do we do about limiting consumption? It is easy for affluent Westerners to argue a cutback since we already live with an excess. A cutback in consumption will still leave us with a high standard of living. But what about the poor of the world? They too want the good life. They are not going to agree to a cutback or even to maintaining a steady-state economy. They want what we have. "You who are rich and white can afford peace and talk of leveling off. We advocate revolution, even violence, to right the inequalities. This requires an increase in our share of the consumption of resources." But what happens, as surely will happen, when we find that there are not enough resources to maintain a high standard of living for all? Those countries that supply many of the resources for the high standard of living in Europe and North America are beginning to say, "No more! You will have to pay dearly for these resources, so that we can have what you have." To get oil we are going to have to feed the Middle East. And to do this we will have to live with higher costs and less food. What will happen to our own poor? And what happens, again as will surely happen, as population outstrips our capacity to produce? Once more, horrendous ethical dilemmas present themselves. Remember the classical ethical dilemma of people in a life raft with only enough food for a few to survive in the time needed to drift to land? Who lives and who dies? The poor say that this decision is already being made. We are on an Ark with only enough food for a certain population. The powerful West allows millions to die every year and other countless millions to live on a diet that does not provide them with the protein and other nutrients needed for a viable existence. Millions die or are retarded because we in the West are deciding who is to survive. How long will the poor allow this decision to be made against them? I remember speaking with a person from an underdeveloped nation who said that as soon as nuclear weapons are available to smaller, poorer countries, food and resource wars will come. Feed us or we will destroy some of your cities so that there is enough food to go around. Apocalyptic nightmares are not now unimaginable. For example, if population outstrips production, we could have committees deciding who will be allowed to live. If you think this is far-fetched, I repeat, it is already happening. We live well while others die. The poor of the world may soon have the blackmail power to force us to share with them.[43] Then the poor of the West will also die by the millions.

The problem we will face can be put another way. Science and technology have allowed for an increased population which initiates ethical problems for which science and technology can have no solution. The issue again becomes a social or political problem. And we do not now have the institutions necessary for deciding these issues. And, finally, social and political problems are *people* problems.[44] It comes down to fundamental perspectives and life styles.

What should be our ecological attitudes? What life styles are acceptable for the spaceship?

No matter what political structure ensues, there are going to be some serious ethical issues that will result from the development of new research and technology. For a starter, if we are going to limit population, and science provides not only the means for limitation but selective breeding as well, then who decides not only who, but what kind of person we want? If we could soon determine sex, select and modify genes so that we can get exactly what we want in terms of genetic makeup, what kinds of persons would make the best of all possible societies?[45]

Questions like the latter one have led some scientists to argue that our present society is not ready to make use of the attainments of science and technology, that scientists should stop research until our society provides the ethical and political criteria necessary for using the research. "So long as men like Nixon and Agnew determine the direction of society, scientists should stop producing the knowledge that politics will misuse."[46] "Are we to have, in place of Plato's philosopher-king, a geneticist king? And who will be president of the National Sperm Bank and of the National DNA Bank? What checks and balances are to be imposed on the genetic legislature and the genetic executive powers? Who will guard the guardians?"[47] We have reason to fear the political use of scientific research. Some have suggested that the scientific community police itself. But just because someone is scientifically competent, it does not follow that he will be ethically sensitive. Again, we are back to issues raised in social and political philosophy.

Some suggestions I have stated my case in broad strokes; my suggestions will be of a like nature.[48]

1. There is a growing shortage of natural resources, but an even greater shortage of "moral resources." The existing religious and political institutions—at least as they are currently articulated—are not equipped to deal with the problem of life on the spaceship earth. We need a new perspective drawing on the insights of the so-called primitives who offer a new commandment: Love the earth as thyself!

2. We need an environment bill of rights which should begin with Gaylord Nelson's amendment to the Constitution guaranteeing every person an inalienable right to a decent environment.

3. We must begin to give up national sovereignty to a world body under transnational law.

4. Limitation must be placed on progress in the name of generations yet unborn. Technological advances should not be implemented until their ethical and social repercussions are considered. Profit

should not be the first consideration for new technology. A suggested principle by Aldo Leopold could serve as a starter: "A thing is right when it tends to preserve the integrity, stability and beauty of the biotic community. It is wrong when it tends otherwise."[49]

5. We must all begin to make our decisions based on a scarcity economy. Not that we all become ascetics or return to the romantic world of Mother Nature, but that we set policies that keep life styles within the carrying capacity of the earth.

6. We must come to realize that there is no individual acting alone on a spaceship. On the spaceship what each of us does affects the others; group goals must therefore predominate.

7. Nature must be seen as an ally. We are part of nature in an interlocking community. This holistic view sees nature (including humans) as an integrated ecosystem.

8. Technological developments should be pushed in the area of social concerns on the scale of our rush to the moon, i.e., in such areas as public transportation, urban housing, pollution abatement, population control, and the abolition of hunger and poverty.

9. We need a massive drive to limit population coupled with international procedures for distribution of goods. This is the only way the developing nations will agree to population control.

10. A new "religious" perspective centering around cosmic loyalty is needed. Religion must be seen as more than a dialogue between God and man in the latter's search for meaning. A Whiteheadian model seems most promising in the West. The insights of Taoism and the American Indian should also become part of our lore. We need a common ideology coming out of common danger and common experiences.

11. Kenneth Boulding summarizes an experience which should become a shared world perspective:

> We have to visualize the earth as a small, rather crowded spaceship, destination unknown, in which man has to find a slender thread of a way of life in the midst of a continually repeatable cycle of material transformations. In a spaceship, there can be no inputs or outputs. The water must circulate through the kidneys and the algae, the food likewise, the air likewise.... In a spaceship there can be no sewers and no imports.
>
> Up to now the human population has been small enough so that we have not had to regard the earth as a spaceship. We have been able to regard the atmosphere and the oceans and even the soil as an inexhaustible reservoir, from which we can draw at will and which we can pollute at will. There is a writing on the wall, however.... Even now we may be doing irreversible damage to this precious little spaceship.[50]

I once believed only God could end the world. Now I know that is not true. I once believed man was the crown of creation, now I know that humankind may have no more future. Even nature itself no longer seems inevitably there. The prophet's cry that the eschaton (last day) is upon us no longer seems like material for a cartoon. The issue of human survival, along with the great cycle of "seedtime, bloom, and harvest," will be determined within my lifetime and the lifetime of my children. If we are not to see the destruction of our tomorrow, we must act today.[51]

NOTES

1. For a recent article which develops the thesis of what sociologists call the "swarming stage," cf. S. R. Eyre, "Man the Pest: The Dim Chance of Survival," *New York Review* (Nov. 18, 1971): 18-27.
2. From a lecture by Loren Eiseley, "The House We Live In," WCAU-TV, Feb. 5, 1961.
3. An enormous amount of material has been published on the subject of this essay. I will list a few that influenced my discussion, and which the student may wish to consult for a more complete treatment.
    Tom Artin, *Earth Talk: Independent Voices on the Environment* (New York: Grossman Publishers, 1973).
    Ian G. Barbour, editor, *Earth Might Be Fair: Reflections on Ethics, Religion, and Ecology* (Englewood Cliffs, N.J.: Prentice-Hall, 1972).
    John Cobb, Jr., *Is It Too Late?* (Beverly Hills: Bruce, 1972).
    Frederick Elder, *Crisis in Eden* (New York: Abingdon, 1970).
    Richard A. Falk, *This Endangered Planet* (New York: Vintage Books, 1972).
    Garrett Hardin, *Exploring New Ethics for Survival* (Baltimore: Penguin Books, 1973).
    Robert L. Heilbroner, *An Inquiry into the Human Prospect* (New York: W. W. Norton, 1974).
    Dennis C. Pirages and Paul R. Ehrlich, *Ark II* (San Francisco: W. H. Freeman, 1974).
4. Hardin, op. cit., pp. 29 and 70.
5. Pirages, op. cit., p. 26, gives such a timetable. While I have found some variation on the timetables, the range of difference is remarkably small.
6. I will not even deal with so-called thermal pollution—the problem of heat brought about by converting certain energy concentrations into heat and releasing it into the atmosphere. Cf. Pirages, pp. 32-33.
7. It is claimed that energy received from the sun during a period of 40 minutes would meet earth's energy needs for one year. (I'm indebted to David Jacobson for this information, plus a number of other critical suggestions he made in the development of this paper.)
8. See especially Falk, op. cit., passim. "Within the international community there are no effective mechanisms to identify and pursue *world* interests. Perhaps the concern to prevent war is the only example of such activity. But this concern while identifying the issue has not been totally successful in preventing war. The U.N. has provided only background music for real hard government to government bargaining of traditional diplomacy," p. 55.
9. Barbour, op. cit., p. 164.
10. These figures amaze me. Notice that an exact figure is not given. When the swarming species are dropping like flies who can get an accurate count?
11. For the developing countries' point of view see Tom Artin, op. cit., passim.
12. For a good discussion of this issue see Philip Slater's *The Pursuit of Loneliness* (Boston: Beacon Press, 1970).
13. My discussion is dependent on Lynn White, Jr., "The Historical Roots of Our Ecologic Crisis," *Science* 155 (March 10, 1967): 1205 f.

14. T. Roszak, *The Making of a Counter Culture* (Garden City, N.Y.: Doubleday & Co., 1969), p. 245.
15. Albrecht Ritschl, *The Christian Doctrine of Justification and Reconciliation* (Edinburgh: T. & T. Clark, 1900), pp. 279-280.
16. I have used the word "perspective." White, Roszak, Goodman, prefer "religion" which they see as a set of orientating symbols. I have no objection to this word other than that I find "perspective" broad enough to include humanism, Marxism, etc., which are not religious unless you stretch the meaning of the word. "Human ecology is deeply conditioned by beliefs about our nature and destiny—that is, by religion." White, p. 1205.
17. I am using "man" here because there is an element of male chauvinism in the Judeo-Christian tradition, although there are also resources for its elimination.
18. In its rush to imitate the East, many counterculture thinkers fail to see the truth in this position. Human beings are *historical* creatures and cannot simply be united into the flow of nature. Any adequate view must see humankind as a natural-historical being. For an interesting discussion of this issue see Gordon Kaufmann, "A Problem for Theology: The Concept of Nature," *Harvard Theological Review* (July, 1972).
19. White, op. cit., p. 1205. White's position has been attacked by some theologians who argue that the Judeo-Christian tradition was misinterpreted. The Judeo-Christian tradition strongly stresses that man is God's steward of the earth, given the task to care for it. Although this is true, it is beside the point. Even though the stewardship tradition is there, the interpretation White develops was the one used in the West. Most theologians agree. See Elder, op. cit., passim.
20. Cobb, op. cit., ch. 5.
21. (Garden City, N.Y.: Doubleday & Co., Anchor Book, 1953), p. 109.
22. There is no word for nature in classical Hebrew. The word used is "creation."
23. Due to lack of space, I have not developed the influence of Western philosophy on the ecological crisis. The interested student can find materials on this subject in the books mentioned at the beginning of the essay. Some insight into the influence can be found in the contrast below between Eastern and Western outlooks.
24. In speaking of the East I will include insights from the American Indian myths.
25. In what follows I am relying on my former teacher Huston Smith, "Tao Now: An Ecological Testament," in Barbour, op. cit., p. 62 ff.
26. See Paul Shepard's excellent article, "Ecology and Man: A Viewpoint," in *The Subversive Science: Essays Toward an Ecology of Man*, ed. Paul Shepard and Daniel McKinley (Boston: Houghton Mifflin Co., 1969), pp. 1-10.
27. Alan Watts has popularized this Eastern view for Western readers. See especially *The Book on the Taboo Against Knowing Who You Are* (New York: Vintage Books, 1972).
28. Philosophy students study philosophy of mind, but rarely the philosophy of body or nature.
29. D. T. Suzuki, "Lectures on Zen Buddhism" in *Zen Buddhism and Psychoanalysis*, ed. Erich Fromm, D. T. Suzuki and R. DeMartino (New York: Harper & Row, 1960), p. 5.
30. We must remember that nature also suffered at the hands of the Hindus, Taoists, and Buddhists. See Lynton K. Caldwell, *In Defense of Earth* (Bloomington: Indiana University Press, 1972), passim.
31. George Perkins Marsh, *Man and Nature*, ed. David Lowenthal (Cambridge, Mass.: Belknap Press of Harvard University Press, 1965), pp. 35-36. Quoted in John Cobb, Jr., op. cit., p. 46, which has an interesting discussion of the relationship between East and West on the ecology issue.
32. Existentialism stresses this freedom as the essence of what it means to be human.
33. For an excellent discussion of this point of view see Thomas S. Derr, "Man Against Nature," *Cross Currents* (Summer, 1970).
34. Remember that disease, floods, darkness, death, drought, tornados, termites, cabbage worms, etc. are all natural.
35. Philip Slater, *Earthwalk* (Garden City, N.Y.: Doubleday & Co. 1974), pp. 44-45.

36. Harvey Cox, *The Seduction of the Spirit* (New York: Simon & Schuster, 1973), pp. 62-63.
37. See Vine Deloria, Jr., *Toward a Planetary Metaphysics*, unpublished paper.
38. Slater, *Earthwalk*, p. 45.
39. Ibid., p. 40.
40. Garrett Hardin, "The Tragedy of the Commons," *Science* 162 (December 13, 1968): 1243-1248. Reprinted in G. Hardin, *Exploring New Ethics for Survival* (Baltimore: Penguin Books, 1972), pp. 250-263.
41. Ibid., p. 189.
42. This would, of course, be ill-advised at this point because it would penalize the children for the sins of the parents. It would also penalize the poor who frequently have large families. It would only work where everyone was guaranteed a decent living. Hardin and Pirages-Ehrlich have some involved suggestions for dealing with this issue.
43. On the very day I wrote this line, India exploded its first nuclear bomb.
44. Tom Artin, op. cit., p. 77.
45. See the excellent discussion of this and related issues by Roger Shinn in Barbour, op. cit., passim.
46. Barbour, op. cit., p. 132.
47. Theodosius Dobzhansky, quoted in Barbour, op. cit., pp. 130-131.
48. See bibliography in footnote 3 for suggestions about works which treat these issues in more detail.
49. Aldo Leopold, *A Sand County Almanac* (New York: Oxford University Press, 1966), p. 240.
50. *Human Values on the Spaceship Earth* (New York: National Council of Churches, 1966), p. 6.
51. This is not to contradict my earlier remark about predicting apocalyptic nightmares or utopias. I am speaking of creating our *now* as we stand above nature in history.

Erich Fromm

WHERE ARE WE NOW AND WHERE ARE WE HEADED?

Erich Fromm, psychoanalyst and author, views man as a product of his culture who has become increasingly alienated from himself in recent history. Fromm concerns himself with how man, specifically Western man, can come to terms with his current sense of isolation, insignificance, and doubts concerning the meaning of life. His many, well-known works include *Escape from Freedom* (1941), *The Sane Society* (1955), *The Art of Loving* (1956), and *Beyond the Chains of Illusion* (1962). In the following selection taken from *The Revolution of Hope* (1968), Fromm talks of our rapidly developing "technetronic society" (where human thought is being replaced by the thinking of machines)—a society guided by two principles: "the maxim that something *ought* to be done because it is technically *possible* to do it" and *"maximal efficiency and output"* leading to a "requirement of minimal individuality." Fromm sees this society as creating a dehumanizing environment, as leading man to increasing boredom, passivity, alienation, and a form of chronic schizophrenia. From pp. 26-48 *The*

Revolution of Hope by Erich Fromm. World Perspectives Series, Volume Thirty-eight, edited by Ruth Nanda Anshen. Copyright © 1968 by Erich Fromm. Reprinted by permission of Harper & Row, Publishers, Inc.

WHERE ARE WE NOW?

It is difficult to locate our exact position on the historical trajectory leading from eighteenth- and nineteenth-century industrialism to the future. It is easier to say where we are *not*. We are not on the way to free enterprise, but are moving rapidly away from it. We are not on the way to greater individualism, but are becoming an increasingly manipulated mass civilization. We are not on the way to the places toward which our ideological maps tell us we are moving. We are marching in an entirely different direction. Some see the direction quite clearly; among them are those who favor it and those who fear it. But most of us look at maps which are as different from reality as was the map of the world in the year 500 B.C. It is not enough to know that our maps are false. It is important to have correct maps if we are to be able to go in the direction we want to go. The most important feature of the new map is the indication that we have passed the stage of the first Industrial Revolution and have begun the period of the second Industrial Revolution.

The first Industrial Revolution was characterized by the fact that man had learned to replace live energy (that of animals and men) by mechanical energy (that of steam, oil, electricity, and the atom). These new sources of energy were the basis for a fundamental change in industrial production. Related to this new industrial potential was a certain type of industrial organization, that of a great number of what we would call today small or medium-sized industrial enterprises, which were managed by their owners, which competed with each other, and which exploited their workers and fought with them about the share of the profits. The member of the middle and upper class was the master of his enterprise, as he was the master of his home, and he considered himself to be the master of his destiny. Ruthless exploitation of nonwhite populations went together with domestic reform, increasingly benevolent attitudes toward the poor, and eventually, in the first half of this century, the rise of the working class from abysmal poverty to a relatively comfortable life.

The first Industrial Revolution is being followed by the second Industrial Revolution, the beginning of which we witness at the present time. It is characterized by the fact not only that *living energy* has been replaced by mechanical energy, but that *human thought* is being replaced by the thinking of machines. Cybernetics and automation ("cybernation") make it possible to build machines that function much more precisely and much more quickly than the human brain for the purpose of answering important technical and organizational questions. Cybernation is creating the possibility of a new kind of economic and social organization. A relatively small number of mammoth enterprises has become the center of the economic machine and will rule it completely in the not-too-distant future. The enterprise, although legally the property of hundreds of thousands of stockholders, is managed (and for all practical purposes managed independently of the legal owners) by a self-perpetuating bureaucracy. The alliance between private business and government is becoming so close that the two components of this alliance become ever less distinguishable. The majority of the population in America is well fed, well housed, and well amused, and the sector of "underdeveloped" Americans who still live under substandard conditions will probably join the majority in the foreseeable future. We continue to profess individualism, freedom, and faith in God, but our professions are wearing thin when compared with the reality of the organization man's obsessional conformity guided by the principle of hedonistic materialism.

If society could stand still—which it can do as little as an individual—things might not be as ominous as they are. But we are headed in the direction of a new kind of society and a new kind of human life, of which we now see only the beginning and which is rapidly accelerating.

THE VISION OF THE DEHUMANIZED SOCIETY OF A.D. 2000

What is the kind of society and the kind of man we might find in the year 2000, provided nuclear war has not destroyed the human race before then?

If people knew the likely course which American society will take, many if not most of them would be so horrified that they might take adequate measures to permit changing the course. If people are not aware of the direction in which they are going, they will awaken when it is too late and when their fate has been irrevocably sealed. Unfortunately, the vast majority are not aware of where they are going. They are not aware that the new society toward which they are moving is as radically different from Greek and Roman, medieval and traditional industrial societies as the agricultural society was from that of the food gatherers and hunters. Most people still think in the concepts of the society of the first Industrial Revolution. They see that we have more and better machines than man had fifty years ago and mark this down as progress. They believe that lack of direct political oppression is a manifestation of the achievement of personal freedom. Their vision of the year 2000 is that it will be the full realization of the aspirations of man since the end of the Middle Ages, and they do not see that the year 2000 may be not the fulfillment and happy culmination of a period in which man struggled for freedom and happiness, but the beginning of a period in which man ceases to be human and becomes transformed into an unthinking and unfeeling machine.

It is interesting to note that the dangers of the new dehumanized society were already clearly recognized by intuitive minds in the nineteenth century, and it adds to the impressiveness of their vision that they were people of opposite political camps.[1]

A conservative like Disraeli and a socialist like Marx were practically of the same opinion concerning the danger to man that would arise from the uncontrolled growth of production and consumption. They both saw how man would become weakened by enslavement to the machine and his own ever increasing cupidity. Disraeli thought the solution could be found by containing the power of the new bourgeoisie; Marx believed that a highly industrialized society could be transformed into a humane one, in which man and not material goods were the goal of all social efforts.[2] One of the most brilliant progressive thinkers of the last century, John Stuart Mill, saw the problem with all clarity:

> I confess I am not charmed with the ideal of life held out by those who think that the normal state of human beings is that of struggling to get on; that the trampling, crushing, elbowing, and treading on each other's heels, which form the existing type of social life, are the most desirable lot of human kind, or anything but the disagreeable symptoms of one of the phases of industrial progress. . . . Most fitting, indeed, is it, that while riches are power, and to grow as rich as possible the universal object of ambition, the path to its attainment should be open to all, without favour or partiality. But the best state for human nature is that in which, while no one is poor, no one desires to be richer, nor has any reason to fear being thrust back by the efforts of others to push themselves forward.[3]

It seems that great minds a hundred years ago saw what would happen today or tomorrow, while we to whom it is happening blind ourselves in order not to be disturbed in our daily routine. It seems that liberals and conservatives are equally blind in this respect. There are only few writers of vision who have clearly seen the monster to which we are giving birth. It is not Hobbes' *Leviathan*, but a Moloch, the all-destructive idol, to which human life is to be sacrificed. This Moloch has been described most imaginatively by Orwell and Aldous Huxley, by a number of science-fiction writers who show more perspicacity than most professional sociologists and psychologists.

I have already quoted Brzezinski's description of the technetronic society,* and only want to quote the following addition: "The largely humanist-oriented, occasionally ideologically-minded intellectual-dissenter . . . is rapidly being displaced either by experts and house-specialists . . . or by the generalists-integrators, who become in effect ideologues for those in power, providing overall intellectual integration for disparate actions."[4]

A profound and brilliant picture of the new society has been given recently by one of the most outstanding humanists of our age, Lewis Mumford.[5] Future historians, if there are any, will consider his work to be one of the prophetic warnings of our time. Mumford gives new depth and perspective to the future by analyzing its roots in the past. The central phenomenon which connects past and future, as he sees it, he calls the "megamachine."

The "megamachine" is the totally organized and homogenized social system in which society as such functions like a machine and men like its parts. This kind of organization by total coordination, by "the constant increase of order, power, predictability and above all control," achieved almost miraculous technical results in early megamachines like the Egyptian and Mesopotamian societies, and it will find its fullest expression, with the help of modern technology, in the future of the technological society.

Mumford's concept of the megamachine helps to make clear certain recent phenomena. The first time the megamachine was used on a large scale in modern times was, it seems to me, in the Stalinist system of industrialization, and after that, in the system used by Chinese Communism. While Lenin and Trotsky still hoped that the Revolution would eventually lead to the mastery of society by the individual, as Marx had visualized, Stalin betrayed whatever was left of these hopes and sealed the betrayal by the physical extinction of all those in whom the hope might not have completely disappeared. Stalin could build his megamachine on the nucleus of a well-developed industrial sector, even though one far below those of countries like England or the United States. The Communist leaders in China were confronted with a different situation. They had no industrial nucleus to speak of. Their only capital was the physical energy and the passions and thoughts of 700 million people. They decided that by means of the complete coordination of this human material they could create the equivalent of the original accumulation of capital necessary to achieve a technical development which in a relatively short time would reach the level of that of the West.

---

*On p. 1 of *The Revolution of Hope*, the technetronic society is described as ". . . a completely mechanized society, devoted to maximum material output and consumption, directed by computers . . ." ED.

This total coordination had to be achieved by a mixture of force, personality cult, and indoctrination which is in contrast to the freedom and individualism Marx had foreseen as the essential elements of a socialist society. One must not forget, however, that the ideals of the overcoming of private egotism and of maximal consumption have remained elements in the Chinese system, at least thus far, although blended with totalitarianism, nationalism, and thought control, thus vitiating the humanist vision of Marx.

The insight into this radical break between the first phase of industrialization and the second Industrial Revolution, in which society itself becomes a vast machine, of which man is a living particle, is obscured by certain important differences between the megamachine of Egypt and that of the twentieth century. First of all, the labor of the live parts of the Egyptian machine was forced labor. The naked threat of death or starvation forced the Egyptian worker to carry out his task. Today, in the twentieth century, the worker in the most developed industrial countries, such as the United States, has a comfortable life—one which would have seemed like a life of undreamed-of luxury to his ancestor working a hundred years ago. He has, and in this point lies one of the errors of Marx, participated in the economic progress of capitalist society, profited from it, and, indeed, has a great deal more to lose than his chains.

The bureaucracy which directs the work is very different from the bureaucratic elite of the old megamachine. Its life is guided more or less by the same middle-class virtues that are valid for the worker; although its members are better paid than the worker, the difference in consumption is one of quantity rather than quality. Employers and workers smoke the same cigarettes and they ride in cars that look the same even though the better cars run more smoothly than the cheaper ones. They watch the same movies and the same television shows, and their wives use the same refrigerators.[6]

The managerial elite are also different from those of old in another respect: they are just as much appendages of the machine as those whom they command. They are just as alienated, or perhaps more so, just as anxious, or perhaps more so, as the worker in one of their factories. They are bored, like everyone else, and use the same antidotes against boredom. They are not as the elites were of old—a culture-creating group. Although they spend a good deal of their money to further science and art, as a class they are as much consumers of this "cultural welfare" as its recipients. The culture-creating group lives on the fringes. They are creative scientists and artists, but it seems that, thus far, the most beautiful blossom of twentieth-century society grows on the tree of science, and not on the tree of art.

THE PRESENT TECHNOLOGICAL SOCIETY

a. Its principles The technetronic society may be the system of the future, but it is not yet here; it can develop from what is already here, and it probably will, unless a sufficient number of people see the danger and redirect our course. In order to do so, it is necessary to understand in greater detail the operation of the present technological system and the effect it has on man.

What are the guiding principles of this system as it is today?

It is programed by two principles that direct the efforts and thoughts of everyone working in it: The first principle is the maxim that something *ought* to be done because it is technically *possible* to do it. If it is possible to build nuclear weapons, they must be built even if they might destroy us all. If it is possible to travel to the moon or to the planets, it must be done, even if at the expense of many unfulfilled needs here on earth. This principle means the negation of all values which the humanist tradition has developed. This tradition said that something should be done because it is needed for man, for his growth, joy, and reason, because it is beautiful, good, or true. Once the principle is accepted that something ought to be done because it is technically possible to do it, all other values are dethroned, and technological development becomes the foundation of ethics.'

The second principle is that of *maximal efficiency and output.* The requirement of maximal efficiency leads as a consequence to the requirement of minimal individuality. The social machine works more efficiently, so it is believed, if individuals are cut down to purely quantifiable units whose personalities can be expressed on punched cards. These units can be administered more easily by bureaucratic rules because they do not make trouble or create friction. In order to reach this result, men must be de-individualized and taught to find their identity in the corporation rather than in themselves.

The question of economic efficiency requires careful thought. The issue of being economically efficient, that is to say, using the smallest possible amount of resources to obtain maximal effect, should be placed in a historical and evolutionary context. The question is obviously more important in a society where real material scarcity is the prime fact of life, and its importance diminishes as the productive powers of a society advance.

A second line of investigation should be a full consideration of the fact that efficiency is only a known element in already existing activities. Since we do not know much about the efficiency or inefficiency of untried approaches, one must be careful in pleading for things as they are on the grounds of efficiency. Furthermore, one must be very careful to think through and specify the area and time period being examined. What may appear efficient by a narrow definition can be highly inefficient if the time and scope of the discussion are broadened. In economics there is increasing awareness of what are called "neighborhood effects"; that is, effects that go beyond the immediate activity and are often neglected in considering benefits and costs. One example would be evaluating the efficiency of a particular industrial project only in terms of the immediate effects on this enterprise—forgetting, for instance, that waste materials deposited in nearby streams and the air represent a costly and a serious inefficiency with regard to the community. We need to clearly develop standards of efficiency that take account of time and society's interest as a whole. Eventually, the human element needs to be taken into account as a basic factor in the system whose efficiency we try to examine.

Dehumanization in the name of efficiency is an all-too-common occurrence; e.g., giant telephone systems employing Brave New World techniques of recording operators' contacts with customers and asking customers to evaluate workers' performance and attitudes, etc.—all aimed at instilling "proper" employee attitude, standardizing service, and increasing efficiency. From the narrow perspective of immediate company purposes, this may yield docile, manageable workers, and thus enhance company efficiency. In terms of the employees, as human beings, the effect is to engender feelings of inadequacy, anxiety, and frustration, which may lead to either indifference or hostility. In broader terms, even efficiency may not be served, since the company and society at large doubtless pay a heavy price for these practices.

Another general practice in organizing work is to constantly remove elements of creativity (involving an element of risk or uncertainty) and group work by dividing and subdividing tasks to the point where no judgment or interpersonal contact remains or is required. Workers and technicians are by no means insensitive to this process. Their frustration is often perceptive and articulate, and comments such as "We are human" and "The work is not fit for human beings" are not uncommon. Again, efficiency in a narrow sense can be demoralizing and costly in individual and social terms.

If we are only concerned with input-output figures, a system may give the impression of efficiency. If we take into account what the given methods do to the human beings in the system, we may discover that they are bored, anxious, depressed, tense, etc. The result would be a twofold one: (1) Their imagination would be hobbled by their psychic pathology, they would be uncreative, their thinking would be routinized and bureaucratic, and hence they would not come up with new ideas and solutions which would contribute to a more productive development of the system; altogether, their energy would be considerably lowered. (2) They would suffer from many physical ills, which are the result of stress and tension; this loss in health is also a loss for the system. Furthermore, if one examines what this tension and anxiety do to them in their relationship to their wives and children, and in their functioning as responsible citizens, it may turn out that for the system as a whole the seemingly efficient method is most inefficient, not only in human terms but also as measured by merely economic criteria.

To sum up: efficiency is desirable in any kind of purposeful activity. But it should be examined in terms of the larger systems, of which the system under study is only a part; it should take account of the human factor within the system. Eventually efficiency as such should not be a *dominant* norm in any kind of enterprise.

The other aspect of the same principle, that of *maximum output*, formulated very simply, maintains that the more we produce of whatever we produce, the better. The success of the economy of the country is measured by its rise of total production. So is the success of a company. Ford may lose several hundred million dollars by the failure of a costly new model, like the Edsel, but this is only a minor mishap as long as the production curve rises. The growth of the economy is visualized in terms of ever-increasing production, and there is no vision of a limit yet where production may be stabilized. The comparison between countries rests upon the same principle. The Soviet Union hopes to surpass the United States by accomplishing a more rapid rise in economic growth.

Not only industrial production is ruled by the principle of continuous and limitless acceleration. The educational system has the same criterion: the more college graduates, the better. The same in sports: every new record is looked upon as progress. Even the attitude toward the weather seems to be determined by the same principle. It is emphasized that this is "the hottest day in the decade," or the coldest, as the case may be, and I suppose some people are comforted for the inconvenience by the proud feeling that they are witnesses to the record temperature. One could go on endlessly giving examples of the concept that constant increase of quantity constitutes the goal of our life; in fact, that it is what is meant by "progress."

Few people raise the question of *quality*, or what all this increase in quantity is good for. This omission is evident in a society which is not centered around man any more, in which one aspect, that of quantity, has choked all others. It is easy to see that the predominance of this principle of "the more the better" leads to an imbalance in the whole system. If all efforts are bent on doing *more,* the quality of living loses all importance, and activities that once were means become ends.[8]

If the overriding economic principle is that we produce more and more, the consumer must be prepared to want—that is, to consume—more and more. Industry does not rely on the consumer's spontaneous desires for more and more commodities. By building in obsolescence it often forces him to buy new things when the old ones could last much longer. By changes in styling of products, dresses, durable goods, and even food, it forces him psychologically to buy more than he might need or want. But industry, in its need for increased production, does not rely on the consumer's needs and wants but to a considerable extent on advertising, which is the most important offensive against the consumer's right to know what he wants. The spending of 16.5 billion dollars on direct advertising in 1966 (in newspapers, magazines, radio, TV) may sound like an irrational and wasteful use of human talents, of paper and print. But it is not irrational in a system that believes that increasing production and hence consumption is a vital feature of our economic system, without which it would collapse. If we add to the cost of advertising the considerable cost for restyling of durable goods, especially cars, and of packaging, which partly is another form of whetting the consumer's appetite, it is clear that industry is willing to pay a high price for the guarantee of the upward production and sales curve.

The anxiety of industry about what might happen to our economy if our style of life changed is expressed in this brief quote by a leading investment banker:

> Clothing would be purchased for its utility; food would be bought on the basis of economy and nutritional value; automobiles would be stripped to essentials and held by the same owners for the full 10 to 15 years of their useful lives; homes would be built and maintained for their characteristics of shelter, without regard to style or neighborhood. And what would happen to a market dependent upon new models, new styles, new ideas?[9]

b. Its effect on man What is the effect of this type of organization on man? It reduces man to an appendage of the machine, ruled by its very rhythm and demands. It transforms him into *Homo consumens,* the total consumer, whose only aim is to *have* more and to *use* more. This society produces many useless things, and to the same degree many useless people. Man, as a cog in the production machine, becomes a thing, and ceases to be human. He spends his time doing things in which he is not interested, with people in whom he is not interested, producing things in which he is not interested; and when he is not producing, he is consuming. He is the eternal suckling with the open mouth, "taking in," without effort and without inner activeness, whatever the boredom-preventing (and boredom-producing) industry forces on him—cigarettes, liquor, movies, television, sports, lectures—limited only by what he can afford. But the boredom-preventing industry, that is to say, the gadget-selling industry, the automobile industry, the movie industry, the television industry, and so on, can only succeed in preventing the boredom from becoming conscious. In fact, they increase the boredom, as a salty drink taken to quench the thirst increases it. However unconscious, boredom remains boredom nevertheless.

Marx recognized the effect of increasing consumption most clearly. This can be seen in the following statements in his *Economic and Philosophical Manuscripts* 1844:

> ... the production of too many useful things results in too many *useless* people.... Machinery is adapted to the weakness of the human being, in order to turn the weak human being into a machine.
>
> [With the system of private property] every man speculates upon creating a *new* need in another in order to force him to a new sacrifice, to place him in a new dependence and to entice him into a new kind of pleasure and thereby into economic ruin.... With the mass of objects, therefore, there also increases the realm of alien entities to which man is subjected. Every new product is a new potentiality of deceit and robbery. Man becomes increasingly poor as man....

The passiveness of man in industrial society today is one of his most characteristic and pathological features. He takes in, he wants to be fed, but he does not move, initiate, he does not digest his food, as it were. He does not reacquire in a productive fashion what he inherited, but he amasses it or consumes it. He suffers from a severe systemic deficiency, not too dissimilar to that which one finds in more extreme forms in depressed people.

Man's passiveness is only one symptom among a total syndrome, which one may call the "syndrome of alienation." Being passive, he does not relate himself to the world actively and is forced to submit to his idols and their demands. Hence, he feels powerless, lonely, and anxious. He has little sense of integrity or self-identity. Conformity seems to be the only way to avoid intolerable anxiety—and even conformity does not always alleviate his anxiety.

No American writer has perceived this dynamism more clearly than Thorstein Veblen. He wrote:

> In all the received formulations of economic theory, whether at the hands of the English economists or those of the continent, the human

material with which the inquiry is concerned is conceived in hedonistic terms; that is to say, in terms of a passive and substantially inert and immutably given human nature . . . The hedonistic conception of man is that of a lightning calculator of pleasures and pains, who oscillates like a homogeneous globule of desire of happiness under the impulse of stimuli that shift him about the area, but leave him intact. He has neither antecedent nor consequent. He is an isolated, definitive human datum, in stable equilibrium except for the buffets of the impinging forces that displace him in one direction or another. Self-imposed in elemental space, he spins symmetrically about his own spiritual axis until the parallelogram of forces bears down upon him, whereupon he follows the line of the resultant. When the force of the impact is spent, he comes to rest, a self-contained globule of desire as before. Spiritually, the hedonistic man is not a prime mover. *He is not the seat of a process of living, except in the sense that he is subject to a series of permutations enforced upon him by circumstances external and alien to him.*[10]

Aside from the pathological traits that are rooted in passiveness, there are others which are important for the understanding of today's pathology of normalcy. I am referring to the growing split of cerebral-intellectual function from affective-emotional experience; the split between thought from feeling, mind from the heart, truth from passion.

Logical thought is not rational if it is merely logical[11] and not guided by the concern for life, and by the inquiry into the total process of living in all its concreteness and with all its contradictions. On the other hand, not only thinking but also emotions can be rational. *"Le coeur a ses raisons que la raison ne connaît point,"* as Pascal put it. (The heart has its reasons which reason knows nothing of.) Rationality in emotional life means that the emotions affirm and help the person's psychic structure to maintain a harmonious balance and at the same time to assist its growth. Thus, for instance, irrational love is love which enhances the person's dependency, hence anxiety and hostility. Rational love is a love which relates a person intimately to another, at the same time preserving his independence and integrity.

Reason flows from the blending of rational thought and feeling. If the two functions are torn apart, thinking deteriorates into schizoid intellectual activity, and feeling deteriorates into neurotic life-damaging passions.

The split between thought and effect leads to a sickness, to a low-grade chronic schizophrenia, from which the new man of the technetronic age begins to suffer. In the social sciences it has become fashionable to think about human problems with no reference to the feelings related to these problems. It is assumed that scientific objectivity demands that thoughts and theories concerning man be emptied of all emotional concern with man.

An example of this emotion-free thinking is Herman Kahn's book on thermonuclear warfare. The question is discussed: how many millions of dead Americans are "acceptable" if we use as a criterion the ability to rebuild the economic machine after nuclear war in a reasonably short time so that it is as good as or better than before. Figures for GNP and population increase or decrease are the basic categories in this kind of thinking, while the question of the human results of nuclear war in terms of suffering, pain, brutalization, etc., is left aside.

Kahn's *The Year 2000* is another example of the writing which we may expect in the completely alienated megamachine society. Kahn's concern is that of the figures for production, population increase, and various scenarios for war or peace, as the case may be. He impresses many readers because they mistake the thousands of little data which he combines in ever-changing kaleidoscopic pictures for erudition or profundity. They do not notice the basic superficiality in his reasoning and the lack of the human dimension in his description of the future.

When I speak here of low-grade chronic schizophrenia, a brief explanation seems to be needed. Schizophrenia, like any other psychotic state, must be defined not only in psychiatric terms but also in social terms. Schizophrenic experience *beyond* a certain threshold would be considered a sickness in any society, since those suffering from it would be unable to function under any social circumstances (unless the schizophrenic is elevated into the status of a god, shaman, saint, priest, etc.). But there are low-grade chronic forms of psychoses which can be shared by millions of people and which—precisely because they do not go beyond a certain threshold—do not prevent these people from functioning socially. As long as they share their sickness with millions of others, they have the satisfactory feeling of not being alone; in other words, they avoid that sense of complete isolation which is so characteristic of full-fledged psychosis. On the contrary, they look at themselves as normal and at those who have not lost the link between heart and mind as being "crazy." In all low-grade forms of psychoses, the definition of sickness depends on the question as to whether the pathology is shared or not. Just as there is low-grade chronic schizophrenia, so there exist also low-grade chronic paranoia and depression. And there is plenty of evidence that among certain strata of the population, particularly on occasions where a war threatens, the paranoid elements increase but are not felt as pathological as long as they are common.[12]

The tendency to install technical progress as the highest value is linked up not only with our overemphasis on intellect but, most importantly, with a deep emotional attraction to the mechanical, to all that is not alive, to all that is man-made. This attraction to the non-alive, which is in its more extreme form an attraction to death and decay (necrophilia), leads even in its less drastic form to indifference toward life instead of "reverence for life." Those who are attracted to the non-alive are the people who prefer "law and order" to living structure, bureaucratic to spontaneous methods, gadgets to living beings, repetition to originality, neatness to exuberance, hoarding to spending. They want to control life because they are afraid of its uncontrollable spontaneity; they would rather kill it than to expose themselves to it and merge with the world around them. They often gamble with death because they are not rooted in life; their courage is the courage to die and the symbol of their ultimate courage is the Russian roulette.[13] The rate of our automobile accidents and the preparation for thermonuclear war are a testimony to this readiness to gamble with death. And who would not eventually prefer this exciting garble to the boring unaliveness of the organization man?

One symptom of the attraction of the merely mechanical is the growing popularity, among some scientists and the public, of the idea that it will be possible to construct computers which are no different from man in thinking, feeling, or any other aspect of functioning.[14] The main problem, it seems to me, is not whether such a computer-man can be constructed; it is rather why the idea is becoming so popular in a historical period when nothing seems to be more important than to transform the existing man into a more rational, harmonious, and peace-loving being. One cannot help being suspicious that often the attraction of the computer-man idea is the expression of a flight from life and from humane experience into the mechanical and purely cerebral.

The possibility that we can build robots who are like men belongs, if anywhere, to the future. But the present already shows us men who act like robots. When the majority of men are like robots, then indeed there will be no problem in building robots who are like men. The idea of the manlike computer is a good example of the alternative between the human and the inhuman use of machines. The computer can serve the enhancement of life in many respects. But the idea that it replaces man and life is the manifestation of the pathology of today.

The fascination with the merely mechanical is supplemented by an increasing popularity of conceptions that stress the animal nature of man and the instinctive roots of his emotions or actions. Freud's was such an instinctive psychology; but the importance of his concept of libido is secondary in comparison with his fundamental discovery of the unconscious process in waking life or in sleep. The most popular recent authors who stress instinctual animal heredity, like Konrad Lorenz *(On Aggression)* or Desmond Morris *(The Naked Ape)*, have not offered any new or valuable insights into the specific human problem as Freud has done; they satisfy the wish of many to look at themselves as determined by instincts and thus to camouflage their true and bothersome human problems.[15] The dream of many people seems to be to combine the emotions of a primate with a computerlike brain. If this dream could be fulfilled, the problem of human freedom and of responsibility would seem to disappear. Man's feelings would be determined by his instincts, his reason by the computer; man would not have to give an answer to the questions his existence asks him. Whether one likes the dream or not, its realization is impossible; the naked ape with the computer brain would cease to be human, or rather "he" would not *be*.[16]

Among the technological society's pathogenic effects upon man, two more must be mentioned: the disappearance of *privacy* and of *personal human contact*.

"Privacy" is a complex concept. It was and is a privilege of the middle and upper classes, since its very basis, private space, is costly. This privilege, however, can become a common good with other economic privileges. Aside from this economic factor, it was also based on a hoarding tendency in which *my* private life was *mine* and nobody else's, as was *my* house and any other property. It was also a concomitant of *cant*, of the discrepancy between moral appearances and reality. Yet when all these qualifications are made, privacy still seems to be an important condition for a person's productive development. First of all, because privacy is necessary to collect oneself and to free oneself from the constant "noise" of people's chatter and intrusion, which interferes with one's own mental processes. If all private data are transformed into public data, experiences will tend to become more shallow and more alike. People will be afraid to feel the "wrong thing"; they will become more accessible to psychological manipulation which, through psychological testing, tries to establish norms for "desirable," "normal," "healthy" attitudes. Considering that these tests are applied in order to help the companies and government agencies to find the people with the "best" attitudes, the use of psychological tests, which is by now an almost general condition for getting a good job, constitutes a severe infringement on the citizen's freedom. Unfortunately, a large number of psychologists devote whatever knowledge of man they have to this manipulation in the interests of what the big organization considers efficiency. Thus, psychologists become an important part of the industrial and governmental system while claiming that their activities serve the optimal development of man. This claim is based on the rationalization that what is best for the corporation is best for man. It is important that the managers understand that much of what they get from psychological testing is based on the very limited picture of man which, in fact, management requirements have transmitted to the psychologists, who in turn give it back to management, allegedly as a result of an independent study of man. It hardly needs to be said that the intrusion of privacy may lead to a control of the individual which is more total and could be more devastating than what totalitarian states have demonstrated thus far. Orwell's 1984 will need much assistance from testing, conditioning, and smoothing-out by psychologists in order to come true. It is of vital importance to distinguish between a psychology that understands and aims at the well-being of man and a psychology that studies man as an object, with the aim of making him more useful for the technological society.

NOTES

1. Cf. the statements of Burckhardt, Proudhon, Baudelaire, Thoreau, Marx, Tolstoy quoted in *The Sane Society*, (New York: Rinehart, 1955) pp. 184 ff.
2. Cf. Erich Fromm, *Marx's Concept of Man* (New York: Ungar, 1961).
3. *Principles of Political Economy* (London: Longmans, 1929; 1st Edition, 1848).
4. "The Technetronic Society," *Encounter* 30 (1968), p. 19.
5. Lewis Mumford, *The Myth of the Machine* (New York: Harcourt, Brace, 1967 and 1970).
6. The fact that the underdeveloped sector of the population does not take part in this new style of life has been mentioned above.
7. While revising this manuscript I read a paper by Hasan Ozbekhan, "The Triumph of Technology: 'Can' Implies 'Ought.'" This paper, adapted from an invited presentation at MIT and published in mimeographed form by System Development Corporation, Santa Monica, California, was sent to me by the courtesy of Mr. George Weinwurm. As the title indicates, Ozbekhan expresses the same concept as the one I present in the text. His is a brilliant presentation of the problem from the standpoint of an outstanding specialist in the field of management science, and I find it a very encouraging fact that the same idea appears in the work of authors in fields as different as his and mine. I quote a sentence that shows the identity of his concept and the one presented in the text: "Thus, feasibility, which is a strategic concept, becomes elevated into a normative concept, with the result that whatever technological reality indicates we *can* do is taken as implying that we *must* do it." (p. 7).
8. I find in C. West Churchman's *Challenge to Reason* (New York: McGraw-Hill, 1968) an excellent formulation of the problem:

    "If we explore this idea of a larger and larger model of systems, we may be able to see in what sense completeness represents a challenge to reason. One model that seems to be a good candidate for completeness is called an *allocation* model; it views the world as a system of activities that use resources to 'output' usable products.

    "The process of reasoning in this model is very simple. One searches for a central quantitative measure of system performance, which has the characteristic: the more of this quantity the better. For example, the more profit a firm makes, the better. The more qualified students a university graduates, the better. The more food we produce the better. It will turn out that the particular choice of the measure of system performance is not critical, so long as it is a measure of general concern.

    "We take this desirable measure of performance and relate it to the feasible activities of the system. The activities may be the operations of various manufacturing plants, of schools and universities, of farms, and so on. Each significant activity contributes

to the desirable quantity in some recognizable way. The contribution, in fact, can often be expressed in a mathematical function that maps the amount of activity onto the amount of the desirable quantity. The more sales of a certain product, the higher the profit of a firm. The more courses we teach, the more graduates we have. The more fertilizer we use, the more food" (pp. 156-57).
9. Paul Mazur, *The Standards We Raise*, New York, 1953, p. 32.
10. "Why Is Economics Not an Evolutionary Science?," in *The Place of Science in Modern Civilization and Other Essays* (New York: B. W. Huebsch, 1919), p. 73. (Emphasis added.)
11. Paranoid thinking is characterized by the fact that it can be completely logical, yet lack any guidance by concern or concrete inquiry into reality; in other words, logic does not exclude madness.
12. The difference between that which is considered to be sickness and that which is considered to be normal becomes apparent in the following example. If a man declared that in order to free our cities from air pollution, factories, automobiles, airplanes, etc., would have to be destroyed, nobody would doubt that he was insane. But if there is a consensus that in order to protect our life, our freedom, our culture, or that of other nations which we feel obliged to protect, thermonuclear war might be required as a last resort, such opinion appears to be perfectly sane. The difference is not at all in the kind of thinking employed but merely in that the first idea is not shared and hence appears abnormal while the second is shared by millions of people and by powerful governments and hence appears to be normal.
13. Michael Maccoby has demonstrated the incidence of the life-loving versus the death-loving syndrome in various populations by the application of an "interpretative" questionnaire. Cf. his "Polling Emotional Attitudes in Relation to Political Choices" (to be published).
14. Dean E. Wooldridge, for instance, in *Mechanical Man* (New York: McGraw-Hill, 1968), writes that it will be possible to manufacture computers synthetically which are "completely undistinguishable from human beings produced in the usual manner" [!] (p. 172). Marvin L. Minsky, a great authority on computers, writes in his book *Computation* (Englewood Cliffs, N.J.: Prentice-Hall, 1967): "There is no reason to suppose machines have any limitations not shared by man" (p. vii).
15. This criticism of Lorenz refers only to that part of his work in which he deals by analogy with the psychological problems of man, not with his work in the field of animal behavior and instinct theory.
16. In revising this manuscript I became aware that Lewis Mumford had expressed the same idea in 1954 in *In the Name of Socialist Humanism*, ed. Erich Fromm (New York: Doubleday & Co.).

"Modern man, therefore, now approaches the last act of his tragedy, and I could not, even if I would, conceal its finality or its horror. We have lived to witness the joining, in intimate partnership, of the automaton and the id, the id rising from the lower depths of the unconscious, and the automaton, the machine-like thinker and the manlike machine, wholly detached from other life-maintaining functions and human reactors, descending from the heights of conscious thought. The first force has proved more brutal, when released from the whole personality, than the most savage of beasts; the other force, so impervious to human emotions, human anxieties, human purposes, so committed to answering only the limited range of questions for which its apparatus was originally loaded, that it lacks the saving intelligence to turn off its own compulsive mechanism, even though it is pushing science as well as civilization to its own doom" [p. 198].

5 ⚜ GOVERNMENT AND BUSINESS

AS PROFESSOR Edwards's course proceeds and new topics are added in the investigation of ethics, class debates have become increasingly involved and heated. Linda, who has shown little prior interest in discussing moral issues, is fulminating over injustices to consumers.

"So how does the businessman go about, as you put it, ripping off the consumer?" asks Edwards finally.

"You get ripped off every time you buy something in a store, or buy a car, or buy a house. You always have to look out for gimmicks and deals, phoney advertising, and so-called guarantees full of funny little loopholes that take a trained lawyer to catch," says Linda. "Businessmen don't care what they do as long as they make a lousy buck."

"What do you expect out of business?" asks Brock, the only one in the class who reads the Wall Street closings before turning to the headlines. "The whole point of business is to make a profit. It advertises to get people to buy; and the more they buy, the sounder the business. As Bob said a few days ago, if people didn't buy, there wouldn't be any business; so it's up to the consumer to decide what he wants to buy."

"As long as he *gets* what he wants," says Jeff. "I think there is more than money involved in the relationship between businessmen and consumers; I think there are some moral issues. If the only concern of businessmen is profit, then we consumers have to organize to make sure we get a just return for our money. That, or rely on Nader's Raiders or some such group."

"But consumer groups don't really work," Louis objects. "We all know that big business has the money to hire big-time lawyers and lobbyists, and it has the muscle to get legislation and tax laws passed that favor big business against the people. And look at price fixing and all those other conspiracies against the people."

"What we need are more legislators who are on the side of the consumer," Obie says. "But most of those political dudes get payoffs and contributions from big business. Talk about conflict of interest!"

"We've been studying this in my business law class," Linda adds. "The Prof said that when the U.S. Supreme Court ruled that consumers bringing class action suits against businesses must name every single person who will be affected by their case, class action suits were effectively killed. Bang! There went one good way for the little guy to curb big business. I tell you, the courts and the government don't care about us. Sure, they talk a lot, but when it gets right down to it, they favor big business every time."

Even though he knows what will happen, Louis reenters the discussion. "You know, all these problems would be eliminated if we just took the means of production away from private hands and gave it to the little guy. I mean, if money is power and the little guys don't have any money or power, let's eliminate the power base of the big guys; take away their property and their capital and give it to the people."

"First we have a bunch of crazy atheists. Now we've got some kind of a Communist nut!" says Bob irritably.

"Why not? We also have a few religious nuts," somebody remarks.

"All we need now is an argument about capitalism versus communism. Can't we just discuss *one* subject without getting into a lot of irrational haranguing?" asks Linda.

"I don't think it's irrational haranguing to say that big business and big government mean big trouble for the little guy," says Obie. "I think we ought to talk about both business and government and how they affect us. It seems to me that one robs us of our economic rights, and the other one robs us of our political rights."

"Yeah, but I think it starts with government. We ought to do away with the political power structure," Louis declares.

"What are you advocating, anarchy?" Cloteal shouts. "That's a new one, a Communist anarchist."

"Cool it," says Louis patiently. "I'm not advocating no government, only better government. To start with, a legislature that is more responsive to the people and more responsible to them. You know, like of the people, by the people, and for the people? I wonder if the dude who said that was a commie.'' Louis adds with a laugh.

"I'm not sure whether this conversation is going over or under my head," says Edwards. "How many of you feel that some sort of government reforms are needed?" About two-thirds of the class raise their hands. "All right, then perhaps we ought to focus on the problems that you seem to think call for reforms. Cheri?"

"Secrecy is one. I say the people have a right to know what their government is doing. After all, theoretically anyway, the people *are* the government. We claim to be a democracy, but what kind of democracy is it when the people who are supposed to rule don't know what's going on?"

"You and Louis seem to be advocating participatory democracy," says Edwards.

"I guess so," says Cheri. Louis and Obie nod agreement.

"Well I don't know about participatory democracy, but I do know that the government wouldn't be able to operate if the right to know took precedence over the right to withhold information. Politics takes a lot of wheeling and dealing; that's the way the system works, and you can't do that if you air all your dirty laundry," Bob contends. "And what about national security?"

"Sure, we read about national security as an excuse to cover the Watergate mess," says Don quietly.

"Well, you got to admit the whole nation felt pretty insecure when the truth came out," Doug says with a grin.

Ignoring the interruption, Brock says, "The same thing goes for business. Trade secrets, confidential pricing policies, and all that are necessary for our type of economy. Business has to be out to make a profit, and profits are what provide the incentive to invest. That's our system, and I happen to think it's the best in the world."

"All right. Some of you seem to think that the conditions that obtain in business and government are good, or at least necessary," says Edwards. "Yet most of the class have indicated that we need some kind of reforms in government. Our time is getting short, so can we focus on some of the problems calling for reform? Cheri?"

"The government giving property rights to those who never work on the property. The government giving tax breaks that favor the rich and penalize the poor and lower-income groups. The government getting us into wars where the poor die and the rich prosper. I could go on for quite a while."

"No doubt," says Edwards dryly. "Now what can you, or we as individuals, do to effect reforms in the areas you have touched upon?"

"I'm not even sure that we can. I'm not even sure that I can acknowledge the moral or legal legitimacy of such a government. Perhaps the answer is to refuse to participate in such a government.

And that may go for the economic system as well," says Cheri, looking at Brock.

"That sounds like a cop-out, unless you're saying that the whole system is so corrupt it just can't be overhauled from within," Jeff says.

"Any system that lays a lot of illegal and immoral acts on its citizens in the name of national security or executive privilege is in real trouble," says Louis. "Anyway it should be. But it will probably keep happening because most of us are too damn alienated or apathetic to do anything or even care."

"You people really make me sick," says Bob, looking at Cheri and Louis. "You don't seem to want to do anything but criticize. Frankly I think you're being seditious!"

"You mean criticism itself is sedition?" asks Cheri unbelievingly. "What do you think of that, Professor?"

"Well if it is, I'm not saying anything before I consult my attorney. And considering the opinions you have all expressed here at one time or another, may I suggest that all of you exercise the same precaution. To that end, the only thing I will say without benefit of counsel is, class dismissed!"

FOR FURTHER READING

Caplovitz, David. *The Poor Pay More: Consumer Practices of Low Income Families.* New York: Free Press, 1967. An investigation of selling and credit techniques that cause low-income families to pay more for certain products and services than higher-income groups.

Harrington, Michael. *The Other America: Poverty in the United States.* New York: Macmillan, 1963. This book is said to have been most influential in creating the "war on poverty" program of the Johnson administration.

───────────. *Toward a Democratic Left.* Baltimore: Penguin Books, 1968. Writing about the time of the Chicago Democratic Convention, Harrington argues that the American system seems to be breaking down and proposes a New Left movement in which he rejects what he calls the cult of "doing one's thing."

Kelso, L. O., and Adler, M. J. *The Capitalist Manifesto.* New York: Random House, 1958. The Manifesto is, according to its authors, a revolutionary plan for a capitalistic distribution of wealth designed to preserve a free society. It takes the position that to be free one must be a person of property.

Lefcourt, Robert, ed. *Law against the People: Essays to Demystify Law, Order, and Courts.* New York: Vintage, 1971. An anthology that includes articles on the "economic basis of the state" and the "education of the capitalistic lawyer."

Leinwand, Gerald. *The Consumer.* New York: Washington Square, 1970. An informative exposé of fraudulent marketing practices and seductive selling gimmicks.

Lundberg, Ferdinand. *The Rich and the Super Rich.* New York: Bantam, 1968. Who really owns America? How do the rich keep their wealth and power? are questions Lundberg answers. This national bestseller includes chapters on "the Rockefeller monolith," "the Fords of Dearborn," and "the DuPont dynasty."

Luthans, Frederick, and Hogettes, Richard. *Social Issues in Business.* New York: Macmillan, 1972. Designed primarily for business students, this book discusses social and moral problems affecting business. Subjects include poverty, employment discrimination, ecology, and consumerism.

───────────. *Readings on the Current Social Issues in Business: Poverty, Civil*

Rights, Ecology, and Consumerism. New York: Macmillan, 1972. This anthology is a companion reader for *Social Issues in Business.*

Marx, Karl. *Economic and Philosophical Manuscripts of 1844.* New York: International, 1964. This edited translation has an introduction by Durk Struik and includes, among other subjects, Marx's views on wages of labor, profit and rent of land, and the power of money in a bourgeois society.

Marx, Karl, and Engels, Friedrich. "A Manifesto of the Communist Party," in *Marx and Engels: Basic Writings on Politics and Philosophy,* edited by Lewis Feuer. Garden City, N.Y.: Doubleday, 1959. The famous Communist Manifesto expressing Marx's and Engels's views of the class struggle.

New York Times. *The White House Transcripts.* New York: New York Times, 1974. The full text of President Nixon's recorded conversations submitted to the Committee on the Judiciary of the House of Representatives.

Newfield, J., and Greenfield, J. *A Populist Manifesto.* New York: Warner, 1972. Described as a blueprint for creating a new majority in American politics based on populism, the *Manifesto* analyzes land reform, the medical-industrial complex, and foreign policy among other topics.

Schacht, Richard. *Alienation.* Garden City, N.Y.: Doubleday, 1970. A discussion of alienation from a linguistic and analytical viewpoint. The book includes writings of Hegel, Fichte, and Schelling and examines the views of Marx, Fromm, Heidegger, and Tillich among others.

Shatz, Marshall, ed. *The Essential Works of Anarchism.* New York: Bantam, 1971. A good anthology on anarchism containing articles by Proudhon, Bakunin, Kropotkin, and Tolstoy.

David L. Fairchild
WILL IT PLAY IN PEORIA?

David Fairchild, Assistant Professor of Philosophy at Purdue University, Fort Wayne, Indiana, has written *Merleau-Ponty and Austin: A Study in Philosophical Method,* published in 1972. In this selection, Fairchild investigates the sources of, and conflicts between, the public's "right to know" and the government's "right to withhold." Set against the Senate's Watergate investigation, the essay examines the moral and legal underpinnings of these two "rights." Professor Fairchild indicates that the Watergate principals failed to consider the legal and moral implications of their actions. His mordant title "Will It Play in Peoria?" illustrates the essential question governing the White House tactics during the Watergate hearings. His selection deals with the essential issues raised by such hearings—issues that, in Senator Sam Ervin's words, "strike at the very undergirding of our democracy."

RESOLUTION

To establish a select committee of the Senate to conduct an investigation and study of the extent, if any, to which illegal, improper, or unethical activities were engaged in by any persons, acting individually or in combination with others, in the presidential campaign of 1972, or any campaign, canvass, or other activity related to it.[1]

On the face of it, this resolution is not a great deal different from any number of other resolutions which also established investigative committees of the United States Senate. Unique difficulties begin to emerge in the third line, however. From the manner in which the word "or" is used here, it is unclear what types of activities the Senate committee is to investigate: activities that are illegal without being improper or unethical; activities that are improper and unethical without being illegal; or activities that are illegal as well as improper and unethical. That these issues are among the most important that the Senate has been called upon to decide is indicated by Senator Sam Ervin, the committee chairman, who notes that the issues raised by the 1972 election irregularities "strike at the very undergirding of our democracy."[2] The task presented to what became known as the Watergate Committee was not simply to determine whether illegal, improper, or unethical activities had occurred in the 1972 presidential campaign. Such activities alone would hardly justify Senator Ervin's fear that the very foundations of our democracy were threatened. The task, rather, was that of investigating a conflict between rights, and offering some decision as to which rights take precedence over which other rights. Specifically, the conflict is between what is generally known as the public's "right to know," and what has recently been referred to as the government's "right to withhold."

This essay suggests that the conflict between these rights is a genuine conflict, resulting in part from a failure to distinguish between legal rights and moral rights, and in part from a failure to recognize that there is no necessary connection between morality and legality. The first section of the essay offers some brief comments on rights. The second and third sections introduce arguments supportive of the right to know and the right to withhold. The conclusion suggests that the Watergate affair is symptomatic of some confused thinking about morality and legality.

RIGHTS

Even a cursory reading of the daily newspaper reveals frequent and different uses of "rights": civil rights, personal rights, property rights, human rights, legal rights, moral rights, etc. Yet one rarely finds newspapers offering definitions of 'rights', and many writers on rights seem to assume that there is basic agreement about what is meant by 'rights'. That this is an unwarranted assumption can be seen from a consideration of the following partial list of definitions of 'right', all entries in which are for 'right' used as a noun. All nonlegal and nonmoral entries have been omitted.[3]

ENTRY 3: That which is consonant with equity or the light of nature; that which is morally just or due.

ENTRY 4: Just or equitable treatment; fairness in decision; justice.

ENTRY 7: Justifiable claim, on legal or moral grounds, to have to obtain something, or to act in a certain way.

ENTRY 9: A legal, equitable, or moral title or claim to the possession of property or authority, the enjoyment of privileges or immunities, etc.

ENTRY 11: That which justly accrues or falls to any one; what one may properly claim; one's due.

It is interesting that even so authoritative a source as The Oxford English Dictionary manifests the confusion between legal and moral justifications of rights. Three of the five entries cited above (3, 7, 9) state that *moral* considerations are relevant to a determination of what rights are; four of the five (4, 7, 9, 11) state that *legal* considerations are relevant to such a determination; and two of the five (7, 9) state that *either* moral or legal considerations are relevant.

Although this is neither the time nor place to undertake an extended discussion of rights,[4] two comments are appropriate. First, any suggestion of a distinction between moral and legal justifications for rights implies a distinction between at least two kinds of rights. The most frequently mentioned are variously referred to as natural, human, or absolute rights, on the one hand, and civil, legal, or relative rights on the other. Rights in the former category are generally justified on natural or moral grounds, as growing out of the very nature of man, while rights in the second category are justified by law, as growing out of civil societies.[5] We shall refer to these rights as, respectively, moral and legal rights. Within each of these two basic categories, there will normally be some type of hierarchy of specific rights, with each right in the hierarchy taking precedence over any and all rights listed below it. On the moral side, this hierarchy will culminate in an absolute principle, which holds in all cases, conflicts with no other principles, and admits of no exceptions. Conformity with this absolute principle results in an absolute right, which also holds in all cases and admits of no exceptions. Since all rights listed below the absolute right must yield to the absolute right, all other rights may be referred to as relative rights.

The structure is somewhat less clear on the legal side. Although there will probably be a hierarchy here as well, it is unlikely that such a hierarchy will culminate in an absolute right. There may well be one legal right which takes precedence over all other legal rights (such a right being an absolute legal right), but this right would not be an absolute right in the moral sense unless a particular society had made it illegal to do that which was also immoral. There are two reasons for this: First, what is illegal (or legal) is not necessarily immoral (or moral), and conversely. Second, it is clear that (at least at the present time) *no* legal right can be an absolute right, since legal rights are possessed by only those individuals favored by a particular legislative body. Thus, at the risk of oversimplifying, we might say that legal rights as a class are relative to moral rights.[6]

Second, any right, whether moral or legal, absolute or relative, entitles its possessor to the enjoyment thereof without consent of another person. Indeed, Wasserstrom claims that this is perhaps the most obvious thing to be said about rights, and goes on to suggest:

> As long as one has a right to anything, it is beyond the reach of another to properly withhold or deny it. In addition, to have a right is to be absolved from the obligation to weigh a variety of what would in other contexts be relevant considerations; it is to be entitled to the object of the right—at least *prima facie*—without any more ado.[7]

This clearly does *not* mean that rights *cannot* be withheld, denied, or violated. It does mean that the exercise of a right does not need any justification, and that the withholding, denial, or violation of a right does need justification. Reasons for any obstruction of a right must be given. If the obstructed right is a moral one, the justification for the obstruction must be moral; if the obstructed right is a legal one, the justification for the obstruction will generally (but need not) be legal. In those cases in which justification is needed, the burden of justification is on the one who has obstructed the exercise of a right, and not on the one who possesses the right.

THE RIGHT TO KNOW

Abraham Lincoln, in his address at Gettysburg, dedicated himself and his countrymen to the preservation of "government of the people, by the people, for the people." With these words, Lincoln was iterating the sentiments of the framers of the Constitution, for whom there were three axioms of democratic theory: (1) the *people* are the source of power, as that power is wielded by government, (2) without proper and adequate knowledge, the electorate is unable to vote or to express its views intelligently; and (3) if a people are, in the final analysis, to rule themselves, they must be adequately informed to know what they are doing.

The most basic of these principles, that the *people* are the source of government, has gone substantially unchallenged in the nearly two hundred years of our country's existence. If the people *are* the source of government, and if the country is to be governed with the *consent* of the governed, then those who are governed must arrive at opinions about what it is to which their governors would like them to give their consent, and this requires that the people become informed about and by their government. It is this interpretation of the basic axioms of democratic theory that constitutes the public's "right to know." The right to know, therefore, is the result of certain assumptions about democratic forms of government, one of which is that democracy thrives on open discussion.[8] Such assumptions are in turn based on certain epistemological presuppositions, the most interesting of which concerns the nature of truth.

Truth may be viewed either dialectically or dialogically. The dialectical view maintains that truth is a seamless garment, static and of a single piece. In this view, truth is an all-or-nothing affair: one either has it, in which case one has all of it, or one does not have it, in which case one has none of it. The dialectical view is congenial to the idea of a group of expert knowers, an epistemological elite. Truth is not open to the contributions of those who do not have the gnosis. Thus, the knowers, of necessity, are held to enjoy a presumption in their favor. The dialogical view maintains that truth is an open-ended process of attunement to reality, a process that can be aided, at least in principle, by contributions from any source. It maintains that dissenting views provide the motive tension needed for the process of acquiring truth: even an apparently slight insight may be the decisive factor in uncovering the truth. Such a view clearly does not admit of any given presumption.[9] The point of this distinction is that democracy can only be realized by a processional exchange of dialogue, by a dialogical view of truth.

Our initial conclusion, thus, is that the right to know is a right of man, the end product of certain assumptions about the nature of man which prevail in democratic societies such as ours. Even though this right is not specifically articulated in the Constitution, it is a right that has been reinforced in various ways throughout the history of our democracy. The Declaration of Independence suggests that we have a government of, by, and for the people: "Governments are instituted among Men, deriving their just powers from the consent of the governed. . . ." The Tenth Amendment to the Constitution, which has generally been interpreted as stating that the government has *only* those powers explicitly enumerated in the Constitution, together with the Fifth and Fourteenth Amendments (concerning federal and state actions, respectively) are the basic tenets on which the right to know has been argued as a statutory or legal right. As such, the right to know has been upheld by the United States Supreme Court. In the majority opinion on the relevant decision, Justice Douglas wrote: "Secrecy in government is fundamentally undemocratic, perpetuating bureaucratic errors. Open debate and discussion of public issues are vital to our national health."[10]

But the Bill of Rights and the Supreme Court decision against secrecy provide what might be called "passive" justifications for a statutory interpretation of the right to know. That is, they say nothing one way or the other about a right to know: they neither state that the public *has* such a right, nor that the public *does not* have such a right. There is a document, however, written specifically to articulate the right to know. This is the Freedom of Information Act of 1967. Under the provisions of this act, citizens have access to information which was hitherto unavailable to them.[11] The Freedom of Information Act establishes in law an attitude which traces its historical roots back to the basic principles of democracy: the people are the source of power, and they must be informed in order to govern themselves. The act recognizes a point made by Patrick Henry: "The liberties of the people never were, nor ever will be, secure when the transactions of their leaders may be concealed from them."[12]

The point here is that, with the Freedom of Information Act, the right to know, essentially a moral right, has become a legal right. The right to know is based on the principle that democracy *is* government of the people, by the people, and for the people. Consistent with this interpretation of democracy is the principle that the ruler is also the ruled: that he who is responsible *for* us is also responsible *to* us. Consequently, democracy *demands* that rulers educate their citizens, that to the greatest possible extent rulers help us, the citizens, to be our own governors, knowing the "why" as well as the "what" of political decisions.[13]

This means that if the right of the public to know what its government is doing is indeed a right, then there is a corresponding obligation for the government to inform its citizens. Why should the government want to do so? We have already suggested two reasons: so that the citizens may vote and express their ideas intelligently, and so that they may give their consent to governmental policies. There is a third and more important reason: the preservation of the people's ability to rule themselves and the avoidance of what we have introduced as a form of elitism are both contingent on an informed public. This point was well made by former President Nixon: "Fundamental to our way of life is the belief that, when information that properly belongs to the public is systematically withheld by those in power, the people become ignorant of their own affairs, distrustful of those who manage them, and—eventually

—incapable of determining their own destinies."[14] Now, since the passage of the Freedom of Information Act, there is a fourth reason: the government should want to inform its citizens in order not to violate the law. Given the increasing governmental emphasis on "law and order" in recent years, this last reason may ultimately become the most important.

Thus, the right to know is initially a natural right, resulting from certain assumptions about truth and democratic societies. As such, the right to know is implicitly contained in the Constitution and in the Bill of Rights, as is evidenced by the Supreme Court decision mentioned earlier. But the right to know is also a legal right, explicitly articulated in the Freedom of Information Act. Consequently, any obstruction of the right to know must, at the very least, be justified with legal arguments, arguments which suggest that some other law takes precedence over the Freedom of Information Act. Even if such justificatory arguments are provided, however, one could reasonably demand a moral justification for the obstruction of this right as well, since the right to know was initially seen to be a moral right.

This raises an interesting and fairly subtle point that should be noted before we begin a discussion of the right to withhold. We have suggested that the public does have a right to know, and that the government has a corresponding obligation to inform. If this suggestion is correct, then arguments supporting a right to withhold will have to perform two functions: (1) they will have to justify the withholding of information from the public, obviously, and (2) they will, at the same time, have to justify the obstruction of the right to know.

THE RIGHT TO WITHHOLD

If our way of government is that of reason and debate, if the people are the ultimate source of governmental power, and if the people have a right to know, then it is difficult to present arguments designed to justify the withholding of information. This difficulty, at least on the practical level, is compounded by the fact that there has been evidence of fairly widespread distrust by the people of their elected officials.[15] Nonetheless, three general types of arguments are used to justify the withholding of information from citizens. The first is concerned with the complexity of government itself, the second suggests that the withholding of information is for the public's own good, and the third relates to the nature of the presidency itself. We will look first at those arguments concerned with the complexity of government.

The basic "complexity" argument is found in two versions, one of which runs as follows: Irrespective of the degree of nobility and honesty possessed by our national leaders (as measured by their degree of concern over national standards of honesty and integrity), the fact remains that the government must operate within the political system that presently exists, as nasty and uncomfortable as that may be. In such a system, complete openness and candor are impossible. There are areas of concern in which the government's need for secrecy is great, and the public's need to know (and thus its right to know) is marginal or nonexistent. It is, for example, impossible for government officials to conduct frank and open discussions within the government unless they are convinced that what they say will, by and large, remain secret. Thus, as contradictory as it may seem to the uninitiated, it is argued that, if there is to be open communication within the various levels of government, a barrier of sorts must exist between the government and its people. Former President Nixon seemed particularly fond of this argument:

> ... A President must be able to place absolute confidence in the advice and assistance offered by the members of his staff. And in the performance of their duties for the President, those staff members must not be inhibited by the possibility that their advice and assistance will ever become a matter of public debate, either during their tenure in government or at a later date. Otherwise, the candor with which advice is rendered and the quality of such assistance will inevitably be compromised and weakened.[16]

Or, later: "Unless the President protects the privacy of the advice he gets, he cannot get the advice he needs."[17]

Proponents of the complexity approach sometimes resort to a variant of this argument, which runs roughly as follows: A concern for complete candor is all very well when things are being discussed in the abstract, with no direct responsibility for the outcome of events. But this is not the situation in the real world as I know it. Granted that I, as a member of the government, have normal desires for power and success, it cannot be denied that I am also thinking of what is best for the country and the office I hold. I wish I could say the same for my political opponents and the gentlemen of the press, whose primary, if not sole, interest seems to be to advance their own interests by destroying me and the office I hold. This too seemed to be a favorite argument of President Nixon's:

> If I were to make public these tapes, containing as they do blunt and candid remarks on many subjects that have nothing to do with Watergate, the confidentiality of the office of the President would always be suspect. Persons talking with a President would never again be sure that recordings or notes of what they said would not at some future time be made public, and they would guard their words against that possibility. No one would want to risk being known as the person who recommended

a policy that ultimately did not work. No one would want to advance tentative ideas, not fully thought through, that might have possible merit but that might, on further examination, prove unsound. No one would want to speak bluntly about public figures here and abroad. I shall therefore vigorously oppose any actions which would set a precedent that would cripple all future Presidents by inhibiting conversations between them and the persons they look to for advice.[18]

The second major type of argument used to support the withholding of information by government officials is concerned with the public's own good, and is also found in several versions. One version argues that the government is the repository of many kinds of records: social security, tax, personnel, military, etc. Access to these files should be granted only to authorized personnel and only on a "need to know" basis. The computer-born revolution in data processing and retrieval has already led to an unprecedented invasion of privacy which would be even more seriously threatening unless the government continues to restrict access to and release of certain types of information.

Another version of this argument involves the assumption that in a less-than-perfect world the people need to be governed. As Madison said, "If men were angels, no government would be necessary."[19] But as Madison knew only too well, men are far from angelic, and government is needed, at least in part, because without it (or some other recognized force for law and order) men of good will would be at the mercy of those elements of society commonly branded as criminal. Professional organized crime is a major problem, the resolution of which requires the combined efforts of both local and federal agencies. The operations involved in the pursuit of big-time criminals must be kept secret until arrests are made. Information on police activities relating to cases in progress cannot be withheld from criminals without at the same time withholding it from the general law-abiding public.

The final version of this argument in support of withholding information for the public good emphasizes the fact that governments *are* aware of, and sensitive to, their obligation to inform their citizens. In the simplest sense, the obligation to inform *requires* a deception, if only a minor one: oversimplification. If the president himself, who at least theoretically has access to all the information he could possibly want in order to make a decision, must still rely on advisors who interpret this information for him, how can ordinary citizens reasonably be expected to weigh and evaluate all this information even if it were presented to them?[20] The political leader must be a translator, one who changes the language of complex and strange political realities into the comprehensible idiom of the layman. Even purists are unlikely to object when a small child is told the earth is "round," even though such a description is less than accurate.

The third major type of argument used by those who advocate a policy of withholding information from the public is at the same time the most important and the least recognized and admitted argument in political circles (although it is beginning to receive some much deserved attention as a result of the Watergate affair). The power of the executive is a natural subject for myth. Its offices are not simply administratively important, but are also the effective symbols of the nation and its ideals. All political authority lies in that ambiguous world between custom, habit, and convention on the one hand, and the foreign and uncomfortable on the other. Political authority presumes a tension between the familiar (but often false) dogma and the unfamiliar truth, between the apparent and the real. The drama of rulership in this country is that men in authority assume a task they cannot fulfill—knowing the real through the apparent and guiding our conduct by that knowledge to insure the best results for the country.[21]

To put this into a somewhat different perspective: we have but one leader, the president. By virtue of the Constitution, the president is required to be both the political leader of the country and a symbol, a figurehead. In his capacity as a figurehead, the president is expected to host state dinners, meet with visiting dignitaries, carry the symbols and prestige of the country to foreign capitals, etc. Partly as a carryover of our British heritage, we have graced this figurehead with an aura of near-perfection, almost of divinity, and we expect the president to be presented with appropriate accoutrements of the office. But in his capacity as chief administrator and leader of his political party, the president, charged with actually governing the country, is the recipient of none of this majesty and symbolism: he is a mere mortal in a nation and world of mere mortals. Yet—and this is the drama of rulership—were he to divorce himself completely from the symbolism surrounding the office, the president would find his efficacy as chief executive severely hampered. In the attempt to reconcile the opposing attitudes with which the presidency (and thus the president) is regarded, there is often a deliberate attempt to withhold certain types of information dealing with the mundane realities with which the president must concern himself. Thus we find that former President Nixon, in preparing transcripts of some of the tapes that were requested by the Judiciary Committee, edited out some of the more blunt and/or objectionable phrases which the tapes initially contained. To have such language identified with the president would have, in some sense, diminished the stature he enjoyed in the eyes of the public as a figurehead.

What are we to make of these three arguments? Three comments suggest themselves immediately. First, as viewed from the perspective of the president, the question of a right to withhold information from the public becomes a question of executive privilege. According to President Nixon:

> The doctrine of executive privilege is well established. It was first invoked by President Washington, and it has been recognized and utilized by our Presidents for almost 200 years since that time.
> The doctrine is rooted in the Constitution, which vests the "executive power" solely in the President, and it is designed to protect communications within the executive branch in a variety of circumstances in time of both war and peace.[22]

But not all scholars agree with the former president on this question.[23] Nowhere in the Constitution is explicit mention made of the doctrine of executive privilege. Rather, the doctrine in question has been justified on the kinds of pragmatic grounds considered above, and as being of the same general type as other kinds of privileged conversations. Again from President Nixon:

> The law has long recognized that there are many relations sufficiently important that things said in that relation are entitled to be kept confidential, even at the cost of doing without what might be critical evidence in a legal proceeding. Among these are, for example, the relations between a lawyer and his client, between a priest and a penitent, and between a husband and wife . . . the law recognizes that these conversations are "privileged" and that their disclosure cannot be compelled.[24]

One should note that Nixon said nothing about conversations between a president and his advisors. The significance of this omission is that while the right to know is a clearly articulated legal right, the 'right' to withhold is anything but clearly articulated, even on the presidential level. At the very best, the most that can be said for this 'right' is that it has not really been legally denied in the past. At the worst, the right to withhold is not a right at all:

> It is sophistry to pretend that in a free country a man has some sort of inalienable or constitutional right to deceive his fellow men. There is no more right to deceive than there is a right to swindle, to cheat, or to pick pockets.[25]

Second, when the three major types of arguments in support of withholding information are considered in turn, it is clear that those involving the complexity of government and the good of the public are accidental. The fact that our government is so complex and complicated that some information *must* be withheld in the interests of orderly management not only from the general public but from various agencies within the government, even if true, is the result of the contingent or accidental manner in which our government developed. There is nothing in the Constitution, nor is there any natural law, which suggests that governments must be complex. Similar objections can be raised against the argument that it is for the public's own good that information be withheld from it. Perhaps the best response to this second position is that if it is indeed to the good of the public that information be withheld, then that information should not have been collected in the first place. In short, neither one of these arguments establishes the right of the government to withhold information from the public.

Finally, when two positions are the contradictories of each other, one of them *must* be true, the other *must* be false: they cannot both be true (nor, conversely, can they both be false). Thus far we have been introduced to two rights: the right to know (possessed by the public at large in a democracy) and the right to withhold information (possessed by the government). Are these rights contradictories? If both rights are considered from the *same* perspective (whether moral or legal), the inescapable conclusion is yes. If the public does indeed have a right to know, then the government has a corresponding obligation to inform, and does not have a right to withhold. If, on the other hand, the government has a right to withhold information from the public, then the public has no right to know.

In our opening remarks, the following definition of 'right' was suggested: "Justifiable claim, on legal or moral grounds, to have to obtain something, or to act in a certain way." A right is something possessed by someone, something which cannot be obstructed, denied or otherwise violated without justification for the violation. Any justification for the violation of a right should be sensitive to the type of right that has been violated: if the violated right is a moral one, a moral justification for the violation is expected; if the violated right is a legal one, a legal justification is expected. Although it is generally inappropriate to provide a legal justification for the violation of a moral right, it is sometimes appropriate to provide a moral justification for the violation of a legal right. That serious difficulties arise when one fails to maintain the distinction between kinds of rights (moral and legal) or between the kinds of justifications that are appropriate for each of these kinds of rights, is evident in the complex of acts now known as Watergate.

CONCLUDING REMARKS

If the preceding arguments are correct, then the right to know is both a moral right and a legal right. Accordingly, any violation, denial, or obstruction of the right to know will require a complex justification. It will not do simply to articulate some legal provision as justification for the violation of the right to know, for this does not speak to the moral aspects of the right in question; nor does such a legal justification speak to the question of which laws take precedence over which other laws. The Freedom of Information Act has been law since 1967. If one cites some other law as a justification for the violation of *this* law, one must also specify independent criteria in terms of which one can conclude that some laws have priority over other laws. Nor will it suffice for the violator of the right to know to appeal simply to moral justification. He also will need some independent criteria in terms of which he can determine what constitutes a moral law (one which should be obeyed) and what constitutes an immoral law (one which can be violated). The issues involved here are confusing and convoluted, but it is important to note that these are metaethical and metalegal considerations.

Are the arguments offered to justify the withholding of information about the Watergate phenomenon sufficient to justify the obstruction of the right to know?[26] A brief sampling of some of the justifications offered by Watergate principals will suffice to indicate that the answer here is no. When asked for the motivation behind his participation in the cover-up, Jeb Magruder responded:

> Now, here are ethical, legitimate people whom I respected. I respect Mr. Coffin tremendously. He was a very close friend of mine. I saw people I was very close to breaking the law without any regard for any other person's pattern of behavior or belief.
>
> So consequently, when these subjects came up although I was aware they were illegal we had become somewhat inured to using some activities that would help us in accomplishing what we thought was a cause, a legitimate cause.[27]

This is an interesting argument because the question for Magruder was not really a moral one. Though he attempts to raise a moral question and offer a moral justification for a violation of a moral right, he fails, in fact, to actually raise moral issues. What is lacking, of course, is any attempt to argue in terms of a "higher morality" which would justify illegal activity. At best, this position, with its implicit failure to distinguish between overt civil disobedience and clandestine crime, is amoral and hardly relevant to the question asked. President Nixon also seemed to believe that neither moral nor legal questions were relevant, that both must bow to questions of pragmatics:

> I wanted justice done with regard to Watergate, but in the scale of national priorities with which I had to deal . . . I also had to be deeply concerned with insuring that neither the covert operations of the CIA nor the operations of the special investigations unit should be compromised.[28]

Egil Krogh suggested a legal justification for his participation: "... what I undertook was fully authorized and lawful" as a matter of "extraordinary national importance."[29] Krogh was surpassed in this endeavor by Herbert Kalmbach, who wanted both legal and moral authorization, and got it from John Erlichman:

KALMBACH: I said, John, I am looking right into your eyes. I said, ... it is just absolutely necessary, John, that you tell me, first, that John Dean has the authority to direct me in this assignment, that it is a proper assignment, and that I am to go forward with it.

DASH: And did he look you in the eyes?

KALMBACH: Yes, he did.

DASH: What did he say to you?

KALMBACH: He said, Herb, John Dean does have the authority. It is proper, and you are to go forward.[30]

But the extent of the confusion as to what is appropriate in the area of legality/morality is perhaps best summarized by Nixon in remarks made at a news conference held just a few days after the burglary at the Democratic National Office. Nixon is here confronted with a question about law and morality, and from his answer it is clear that he has not given much thought to possible distinctions between the two: "When we talk about the spirit of the law and the letter of the law, my evaluation is that it is the responsibility of all, a high moral responsibility to obey the law and to obey it totally."[31]

There is no question but that the president in his double capacity as chief executive officer and figurehead wields a tremendous amount of power, moral as well as legal and political. By his own frequent admission, former President Nixon set the moral tone of the country: the climate the president fosters in the White House will usually be the climate that is fostered in the rest of the nation as well. It is to the public's credit that the moral climate established by the president for the White House is not *always* accepted by the public as the appropriate moral climate for the nation. The public and congressional outrage in reaction to the "shabby, immoral and disgusting" behavior chronicled in the tape transcripts bears vivid witness to this fact.

The Senate Watergate Committee, in choosing the inclusive use of "or" as delineating its task, raised questions about the relationship between legality and morality as that relationship was understood by various principals in the 1972 presidential campaign. William Sloan Coffin, Jr., on hearing the testimony of one of those principals, remarked: "I guess Magruder failed my ethics course." Part of the reason for this evaluation is that Magruder failed to recognize a difference between the moral and pragmatic questions: "Is it right?" and "Will it play in Peoria?" In this sense, Magruder is joined in failure by a large segment of the general public which accepted an affirmative answer to the second question as precluding the necessity of asking the first. But these questions are not the same, and an answer to one is not an answer to the other. Recognition of this fact, however belated, by the American public is at the same time a recognition that the right to know implies a double obligation: that of the government to inform, and that of the citizen to become informed. With the acceptance of this obligation, the American public will be able to begin providing answers to the difficult questions raised by Watergate.

NOTES

1. Senate Resolution 60 February 7, 1973. *The Watergate Hearings* (New York: Bantam Books, Inc., 1973), p. 131.
2. Senator Sam Ervin, Opening Statement Before the Senate Select Committee on Presidential Campaign Activities, *The Watergate Hearings*, p. 139.
3. *The Oxford English Dictionary* (Oxford: The Clarendon Press, 1933), Vol. VIII, p. 669–670.
4. The interested reader is referred to William Bruening's informative selection "Rights: Legal and Moral Parameters," in this volume, on which part of the following discussion is based.
5. This distinction is preserved in law as well as in philosophy and linguistics. Cf. *Black's Law Dictionary* (St. Paul: West Publishing Co., 1951), p. 1487.
6. A more extended discussion of this point can be found in Professor Bruening's introductory essay "Ethics and Morality," in this volume.
7. Richard Wasserstrom, "Rights, Human Rights, and Racial Discrimination," *The Journal of Philosophy*, 61 (1964). This paper also appears in *Moral Problems*, ed. James Rachels (New York: Harper and Row, 1971). It is to this latter version of Wasserstrom's paper that I refer, p. 112.
8. Cf. William Fulbright, *The Crippled Giant* (New York: Vintage Books, 1972), p. 177.
9. Indeed, a presumption is never *given*, it can only be won. Once having been won, it can be lost by demonstrated unreliability.
10. *New York Times* v. *Sullivan*, 376 U.S. 254.
11. Even under this act, however, there are nine exemptions that may be invoked to withhold information from the public. Classification of "secret" or higher is one of them. Others include "internal" documents, "inter-agency or intra-agency memorandums," and "investigatory files."
12. Cited by J. Murray, *The Bulletin*, American Society of Newspaper Editors, August 1, 1966, p. 3.
13. This position neither demands nor presumes that people are instinctively wise or that the public is guided by some invisible hand in the path of sound public policy. It does presume, however, that the *test* of democratic policy is that it educate and improve the citizen. One of the most visible aspects of this test is that rulers are given the task of winning consent through election.
14. *U.S. News and World Report*, February 15, 1973.
15. Figures released by the Harris organization on April 27, 1974, just three days before President Nixon released his edited transcripts of presidential tapes, indicated that only about 27% of those surveyed believed the president to be telling all he knew about Watergate.

16. President Nixon, Statement of March 12, 1973, *The Watergate Hearings*, p. 677.
17. President Nixon, Nationwide Television Address, April 29, 1974.
18. President Nixon, Statement of August 15, 1973, *The Watergate Hearings*, p. 716.
19. James Madison, "Federalist Paper No. 51," *The Federalist Papers*, ed. Andrew Hacker (New York: Washington Square Press, 1968), p. 117.
20. The president's access to more comprehensive data than is available to the general public is actually irrelevant to the issue: the *kind* of data to which the president has access is the same *kind* of data available to the general public. Cf. George Reedy, *The Twilight of the Presidency* (New York: Mentor Books, 1970), p. 37 ff.
21. Two of the best recent works on this subject are Reedy's *Twilight of the Presidency* and Arthur Schlesinger's *The Imperial Presidency* (Boston: Houghton-Mifflin, 1973).
22. President Nixon, Statement of March 12, 1973, *The Watergate Hearings*, p. 676.
23. Cf. Raoul Berger, *Executive Privilege: A Constitutional Myth* (Cambridge: Harvard University Press, 1974).
24. President Nixon, Broadcast Address of August 15, 1973, *The Watergate Hearings*, p. 716. Interestingly enough, the one type of privileged communication conspicuous by its absence from the president's listing was that involving the doctor/patient relationship, even though there are state laws in all fifty states protecting this type of communication. The few legal precedents to which appeal has been made to justify presidential executive privilege are cited in the attorney general's memorandum to the Senate committee in the McCarthy hearings.
25. Walter Lippmann, cited by David Wise, *The Politics of Lying* (New York: Random House, 1973), p. 367.
26. We are interested here only in the justifications offered for the coverup, not in the justifications offered for the original illegal activities associated with Watergate. Unfortunately, a number of witnesses before the Watergate committee offered exactly the same justifications for both cases. See for example, the testimony of Magruder, Kalmbach, and Erlichman.
27. Jeb Magruder, testimony before the Watergate committee, *The Watergate Hearings*, p. 258.
28. *The Watergate Hearings*, p. 20.
29. *Ibid.*, p. 126.
30. *Ibid.*, p. 48.
31. President Nixon, News Conference of June 22, 1972, *The Watergate Hearings*, p. 669.

Leo Tolstoy

REPLY TO CRITICS: A LETTER ADDRESSED TO *THE DAILY CHRONICLE*

Leo Nikolaevich Tolstoy, born on September 9, 1828 at Yasnaya Polyana where he spent much of his life, died on November 20, 1910. Recognized as one of the world's greatest writers and acclaimed for his novels *War and Peace* and *Anna Karenina*, Tolstoy is less known for his later, philosophical writings, including *A Confession* and *Resurrection*. In the late 1870's Tolstoy was converted to the doctrine of Christian love and the acceptance of the principle of nonresistance to violence. He spent the balance of his life developing a philosophy based primarily on the teachings of Jesus. In the following selection Tolstoy asks, "Shall I form part of a government which recognizes the right to own landed property by men who never work on it, which levies taxes on the poor in order to give them to the rich, . . . which sends out soldiers to commit murder . . . a government the doings of which are contrary to my conscience?" His answer is, "No, I cannot, and will not." The implications of that answer echo through the halls of all governments—of autocracies and democracies, of monarchies and republics alike—shaking the very foundation stones of government itself. This letter first appeared in *The Daily Chronicle* in September 1895 and was later included in *The Novels and Other Works of Lyof N. Tolstoy,* transl. by Aylmer Maude (London: Thomas Crowell & Co., 1899). The present reprint is taken directly from *Tolstoy's Writings on Civil Disobedience and Non-Violence* (New York: Bergman Publishers, 1967).

Since the appearance of my book *The Kingdom of God is within Us* and my article on "Patriotism and Christianity," I often hear and read in articles and letters addressed to me arguments against, I will not say the ideas expressed in those books, but against such misconstructions as are put upon them. This is done sometimes consciously, but very often unwittingly, and is wholly due to a want of understanding of the spirit of the Christian religion.

"It is all very well," they say, "despotism, capital punishments, wars, the arming of all Europe, the precarious state of the working classes are indeed great evils, and you are right in condemning all this; but how can we do without government? What will you give instead of it? Being ourselves men, with a limited knowledge and intellect, have we the right, just because it seems best to us, to destroy that order of things which has helped our forefathers to attain the present state of civilization and its advantages? If you destroy the State, you must put something in its place. How can we run the risk of all the calamities which might ensue if government was abolished?"

But the fact is that the Christian doctrine, in its true sense, never proposed to abolish anything, nor to change any human organization. The very thing which distinguishes Christian religion from all other religions and social doctrines is that it gives men the possibilities of a real and good life, not by means of general laws regulating the lives of all men, but by enlightening each individual man with regard to the sense of his own life, by showing him wherein consists the evil and the real good of his life. And the sense of life thus imparted to man by the Christian doctrine is so simple, so convincing, and leaves so little room for doubt, that if once man understands it and, therefore, conceives wherein is the real good and the real evil of his life, he can never again consciously do what he considers to be the evil of his life, nor abstain from doing what he considers to be the real good of it, as surely as a plant cannot help turning toward light, and water cannot help running downward.

**Chapter 5
GOVERNMENT
AND BUSINESS**

The sense of life, as shown by the Christian religion, consists in living so as to do the will of Him who sent us into life, from whom we are come, and to whom we shall return. The evil of our life consists in acting against this will, and the good in fulfilling it. And the rule given to us for the fulfillment of this will is so very plain and simple that it is impossible not to understand, or to misunderstand, it.

If you cannot do unto others what you would that they should do to you, at least do not unto them what you would not that they should do unto you.

If you would not be made to work ten hours at a stretch in factories or in mines, if you would not have your children hungry, cold, and ignorant, if you would not be robbed of the land that feeds you, if you would not be shut up in prisons and sent to the gallows or hanged for committing an unlawful deed through passion or ignorance, if you would not suffer wounds nor be killed in war—do not do this to others. All this is so simple and straightforward, and admits of so little doubt, that it is impossible for the simplest child not to understand, nor for the cleverest man to refute it. It is impossible to refute this law, especially because this law is given to us not only by all the wisest men of the world, not only by the Man who is considered to be God by the majority of Christians, but because it is written in our minds and hearts.

Let us imagine a servant in his lord's power, appointed by his master to a task he loves and understands. If this man were to be addressed by men whom he knows to be dependent on his master in the same way as he is, to whom similar tasks are set at which they will not work, and who would entreat him for his own good and for the good of other men to do what is directly opposed to his lord's plain commandments, what answer can any reasonable servant give to such entreaties? But this simile is far from fully expressing what a Christian must feel when he is called upon to take an active part in oppressing, robbing people of their land, in executing them, in waging war, and so on, all things which governments call upon us to do; for, however binding the commands of that master may have been to his servant, they can never be compared to that unquestionable knowledge which every man, as long as he is not corrupted by false doctrines, does possess, that he cannot and must not do unto others what he does not wish to be done unto him, and therefore cannot and must not take part in all things opposed to the rule of his Master, which are imposed upon him by governments.

Therefore the question for a Christian does not lie in this: whether or no a man has the right to destroy the existing order of things, and to establish another in its stead, or to decide which kind of government will be the best, as the question is sometimes purposely and very often unintentionally put by the enemies of Christianity (the Christian does not think about the general order of things, but leaves the guidance of them to God, for he firmly believes God has implanted His law in our minds and hearts, that there may be order, not disorder, and that nothing but good can arise from our following the unquestionable law of God, which has been so plainly manifested to us); but the question, the decision of which is not optional but unavoidable, and which daily presents itself for a Christian to decide, is: How am I to act in the dilemma which is constantly before me? Shall I form part of a government which recognizes the right to own landed property by men who never work on it, which levies taxes on the poor in order to give them to the rich, which condemns erring men to gallows and death, which sends out soldiers to commit murder, which depraves whole races of men by means of opium and brandy, etc., or shall I refuse to take a share in a government, the doings of which are contrary to my conscience? But what will come of it, what sort of State will there be, if I act in this way, is a thing I do not know and which I shall not say I do not wish to know, but which I cannot know.

The main strength of Christ's teaching consists especially in this: that He brought the question of conduct from a world of conjecture and eternal doubt down to a firm and indisputable ground. Some people say, "But we also do not deny the evils of the existing order and the necessity of changing it, but we wish to change it not suddenly, by means of refusing to take any part in the government, but, on the contrary, by participating in the government, by gaining more and more freedom, political rights, and obtaining the election of the true friends of the people and the enemies of all violence."

This would be very well, if taking part in one's government and trying to improve it, could coincide with the aim of human life. But, unfortunately, it not only does not coincide, but is quite opposed to it.

Supposing human life to be limited to this world, its aim can consist only in man's individual happiness; if, on the other hand, life does not end in this world, its aim can consist only in doing the will of God. In both cases it does not coincide with the progress of governments. If it lies here, in man's personal happiness, and if life ends here, what should I care about the future prosperity of a government which will come about when, in all probability, I shall be there no more? But if my life is immortal, then the prosperity of the English, the Russian, the German, or any other state, which is to come in the twentieth century, is too paltry an aim for me, and can never satisfy the cravings of my immortal soul. A sufficient aim for my life is either my immediate personal good, which does not coincide with the government measures and improvements, or the fulfillment of the will of God, which also not only cannot be conciliated with the requirements of government, but is quite opposed to them. The vital question not only for a Christian, but, I think, for any reasonable being, when he is summoned to take part in governmental acts, lies not in the prosperity of his state or government, but in this question:

"Wilt thou, a being of reason and goodness, who comes today and may vanish tomorrow, wilt thou, if thou believest in the existence of God, act against His law and His will, knowing that any moment thou canst return to Him; or, if thou dost not believe in Him, wilt thou, knowing that if thou errest thou shalt never be able to redeem thy error, wilt thou, nevertheless, act in opposition to the principles of reason and love, by which alone thou canst be guided in life? Wilt thou, at the request of thy government, take oaths, defend, by compulsion, the owner of land or capital, wilt thou pay taxes for keeping policemen, soldiers, warships, wilt thou take part in parliaments, law courts, condemnations, and wars?"

And to all this—I will not say for a Christian, but for a reasonable being—there can be but one answer: "No, I cannot, and will not." But they say, "This will destroy the State and the existing order." If the fulfillment of the will of God is destroying the existing order, is it not a proof that this existing order is contrary to the will of God, and ought to be destroyed?

Burton M. Leiser

TRUTH IN THE MARKETPLACE: ADVERTISERS, SALESMEN, AND SWINDLERS

Burton M. Leiser, a former member of the Department of Philosophy, State University of New York at Buffalo, is the author of *Liberty, Justice and Morals: Contemporary Value Conflicts* (1973), from which the following selection is taken. Leiser describes tragic cases where the buyer who did not, or could not, heed the warning *Caveat emptor* ("let the buyer beware") suffered greatly. Noting that "one of the state's principal functions is the protection of its citizens against harm that may be done to them by others. . . ." Leiser warns that there is relatively little the government can do to protect the consumer against the "many kinds of fraud and deception in business practices." Addressing himself to both the legal and moral aspects of advertising claims, he shows, with painful and disturbing clarity, how the business community manipulates "truth" to the detriment of the consumer. Reprinted with permission of Macmillan Publishing Co., Inc. from *Liberty, Justice and Morals: Contemporary Value Conflicts* by Burton M. Leiser. Copyright © 1973, Burton M. Leiser.

CAVEAT EMPTOR

The ancient maxim *Caveat emptor* ("Let the buyer beware") was coined, no doubt, because merchants in those days were known for their sharp practices. The meaning of the maxim might have been, "Buyer, be careful, for those from whom you make your purchases are not always truthful. They do not always represent their products as honestly as they might. They have a reputation for charging more than a product is worth. They sometimes sell you one thing and then, in the dark recesses of their stalls, wrap another for delivery to you. Be careful, then, lest you be cheated." This *might* have been the meaning of the maxim at one time. Later, though, it is evident that it acquired a wholly new meaning. It was raised from the status of a *warning* based on general knowledge of certain unsavory practices engaged in by some merchants to that of a *principle:* "In any commercial transaction, if there is a dispute between buyer and seller, the burden of proof shall be upon the buyer. If he has any complaints or reservations about his purchase, let him make them before he signs the sales agreement or takes delivery of the merchandise; for, once the sale is consummated, the purchase is completed, and the officials of the state are obliged to enforce its provisions, whether the customer is satisfied or not."

In all the centuries that men have been selling things to one another, many devices have been perfected for making things appear to be what they are not, and for wording sales pitches and sales contracts so that they seem to say what they do not say—always to the advantage of the seller, for he is the one who writes the agreement or buys pads of printed forms that have been written by his attorneys to afford him the greatest possible protection against any action that might be brought against him by a disgruntled customer. The customer is presented with a printed form and is asked to sign it. He seldom reads it, and if he does read it he does not understand all of its implications, and he hardly ever takes it to his own attorney for advice. If he does and his attorney advises him not to sign it because of possible trouble later on, he is confronted with the choice of complying with the dealer's terms or not having the product that he clearly wants to buy. In almost all cases, then, customers make their purchases on the *seller's* terms, and not on those that would be in their own best interests. In addition, the law has been heavily weighted in the seller's favor; for, until quite recently, the consumer had no advocate to argue for him before the legislatures, there was no organized consumer lobby, and very little publicity was given to any but the most flagrant abuses. Manufacturers and retail associations, on the other hand, sent well-paid lobbyists to work on their behalf at the legislative level, and assured themselves of legislative courtesies by contributing heavily to the election campaigns of those who were sympathetic to their goals.

Case 14. The television set Mrs. Amanda Jones was a poor black woman who lived with her three children in a small rented house in a Midwestern town. She worked as a sorter in a cannery, standing on her feet for eight hours every day. For years she saved a portion of every week's earnings so that her boys could go to college some day.

One day, attracted by an ad in a local newspaper, she went to a discount store to purchase a color television set on very easy terms—$20 down and $20 per month. A few days later the set was delivered, and she and her children sat down to enjoy their new possession. Three weeks later, the set caught fire because of an overheated transformer. When Mrs. Jones called the store the following morning, she was given a long runaround. At last, the manager explained that the store was not responsible for any defect in the merchandise. It was covered by a warranty, he explained, and would be repaired by the manufacturer. The nearest authorized repair station was 300 miles away. Mrs. Jones paid a mover to pack her set and deliver it to the service outlet, and then to return it to her. The service outlet, after examining the set, concluded that it was not authorized to replace the set, but made the necessary repairs. It returned the set to Mrs. Jones at her expense, and enclosed a bill for $125 for the labor, because under the warranty, which Mrs. Jones had not read carefully, only defective parts were covered. By this time, Mrs. Jones had paid nearly $600 for her television set, though she had used it for less than three weeks.

When it was reinstalled, she noticed that human figures had a sickly green cast to them. No amount of dial-twisting and adjusting helped. The set was hopelessly out of adjustment. In anger and frustration, she complained again to the manager of the store from which she had purchased the set and threatened to make no further installment payments unless he repaired the set. (The interest on these installment payments, incidentally, added another $90 to the cost of her set, a fact that she did not fully appreciate because she had never sat down to figure it out.) The manager assured her that he had no responsibility for her problems, that that was for her and the manufacturer to work out, and that she was fully responsible for continued payment of her debt to his firm.

When Mrs. Jones tried her set once more, the green picture faded and the sound went out. She wrote an angry letter to the store and to the manufacturer, and tore up the next bill that came to remind her of the monthly installment that was due. After several reminders from the store, she received a letter from the attorney of a collection agency, informing her that her account had been turned over to him and that if she did not pay the full amount due, she would have to go to court.

Mrs. Jones was only too happy to learn that she would go to court for she felt that at last justice might be done. But to her sorrow, she found that the judge would not listen to her complaints about the set; the only question before him was whether she had failed to make payments in accordance with her contract. Because she admitted that she had failed to make the necessary payments, she was required, under terms of the contract, to make full payment of the entire amount due, plus a 10 percent "service charge," plus court costs and the fees of the finance company's attorneys, as well as her own attorney's fee. Because she could not possibly pay this amount in one lump sum, the judge imposed a garnishment on her wages. Her employer, assuming she must be a "deadbeat," informed her that she was no longer needed. As a result of her continuing inability to pay the judgment, the court ordered the sheriff to seize everything she had that was of any value, except those items that she needed to exist, and to sell them at public auction. At last, the savings account in which she had deposited her sons' future tuition was attached, more than $1,000 was withdrawn from it to pay all the expenses she had incurred, and Mrs. Jones and her children were left with nothing.

Case 14 actually happened and illustrates only a few of the practices engaged in by businesses when the merchandise they sell is defective. Efforts to correct these abuses are often countered by new methods that effectively leave the consumer in the same vulnerable position he had been in prior to the enactment of the legal remedy.

An example of this is the "specious cash sale," a gimmick that was developed by New York merchandisers when the state legislature passed laws designed to protect people like Mrs. Jones from some of the abuses just described.

In the state of New York legislation was passed a few years ago placing some of the responsibility for defective merchandise on the retailer who sold it. In some cases the customer who purchased the item on the installment plan would be permitted to withhold payment until he was given satisfaction for any claims he may have had about defects in the merchandise he had purchased. In order to get around this, merchants assigned the debts to finance companies and banks, who would then collect, regardless of any claims that might be made against the original seller. In 1970 a new law gave the consumer the right to file claims against the bank or finance company in an installment transaction where the dealer failed to make good on any legitimate complaints that the purchaser might have. As a result, these financial institutions refused to deal with retailers who acquired a reputation for being unscrupulous.

The boycotted dealers had to find a way to continue their practices so that they could stay in business and at the same time protect themselves and the finance companies against their customers' complaints. The solution consisted of the "specious cash sale." The retailer, after making the sale, sent his customer to a finance company that lent him the money for the sale. The customer then returned to the merchant and made a "cash" purchase.

Now if the merchant cheated his customer, overcharged him, or refused to replace defective merchandise, the customer was without recourse. He had already paid the merchant for the merchandise and the finance company had lent him the money in a separate transaction. Both the dealer and the finance company were thus in the clear.

In 1971, because of pressure from a million-member consumer lobby and labor unions, the state legislature closed the loophole for some purchases, but not for all. Under the new legislation, where the finance-company personnel are related to the dealer, where the dealer and the finance company are under common control, or where the dealer prepares the forms for paying the loan, the buyer will have the right to redress against the finance company as well as against the dealer.

Four out of five states still adhere to the old doctrine, which gives the finance company or bank that buys an installment contract from a dealer complete immunity against any complaint that the purchaser may have against the dealer. In opposing proposed rulings by the Federal Trade Commission that would do away with these practices, the American Industrial Bankers Association asserted that their practices were "time honored and recognized" and "practiced in the marketplace for many, many years." Consumer groups, on the other hand, have alleged that many cases of consumer fraud would have been impossible were it not for the doctrine that permits such transfers of indebtedness to take place without a corresponding assumption of responsibility for the original sale.[1]

Because there are so many kinds of fraud and deception in business practices, it is impossible to discuss them all here. A few of the more common types, however, will serve to indicate how varied these practices are and how difficult the moral and legal issues involved may be. We shall concentrate on false claims of effectiveness, false claims of need, misleading statements or contexts, the use of illusions, the exploitation of ambiguities, and failure to reveal all relevant information.

It should be noted that not all of these fall under the category of truth telling. In some of the instances to be discussed, it may be argued that no falsehood has been uttered and that the moral issue of truth telling does not arise. If the moral issue of truth telling must be confined within the rigid limits set by the distinction between "stating what is true" and "stating what is false," the discussion that follows clearly goes beyond those limits. But the moral issues surrounding truth telling are actually more subtle than the distinction allows, for the two alternatives set forth—stating what is true and stating what is false—are not exhaustive. In real human discourse there are other possibilities, including telling the truth in a misleading way; not saying anything that is false, but not providing all the information that is needed to make an informed decision; and using various devices to make things seem to be what they are not, without saying anything in words at all. In short, "stating what is true" and "stating what is false" are contraries. "Telling the truth" and "not telling the truth" are contradictories, whose meaning is not exhausted by the contraries just mentioned. Part of the complexity of our problem is bound up with the extremely complicated meanings of these phrases.

FALSE CLAIMS OF EFFECTIVENESS

An ad in a magazine directed at the teen-age market carries a picture of a young girl whose tears are streaming down her cheeks. "Cry Baby!" the ad proclaims.

> That's right, cry if you like. Or giggle. You can even pout. Some things you can do just because you're a woman. And, also because you're a woman, you lose iron every month. The question is, are you putting that iron back? You may be among the 2 out of 3 American women who don't get enough iron from the food they eat to meet their recommended iron intake. . . . But One-A-Day Brand Multiple Vitamins Plus Iron does. . . . One-A-Day Plus Iron. One of the things you should know about, because you're a woman.

Two claims, at least, are made or implied by this advertisement. The first is that most American women do not get enough iron in their diets to make up for the "deficiency" that results from menstruation. The second is that One-A-Day tablets will fill the gap. As for the first claim, the American Medical Association pointed out long ago that "the average diet of Americans is rich in iron." This statement was made during the AMA's campaign against Ironized Yeast, which also claimed to offer beneficial results from the Vitamin B that was included in its compound. The AMA showed that Vitamin B was found in sufficient quantities in the average American diet to require no special supplement.[2] Now, if there is no significant lack of iron in the average person's diet (and this includes the average woman), there is no deficiency for One-A-Day tablets to fill. To be sure, some Americans do suffer from a lack of certain vitamins and minerals because they do not have an adequate diet. But the answer to this is not for them to take One-A-Day pills, but to eat more nutritious food.

Prior to 1922, Listerine had been advertised as "the best antiseptic for both internal and external use." It was recommended for treating gonorrhea and for "filling the cavity, during ovariotomy." During the years that followed, it was also touted as a safe antiseptic that would ward off cold germs and sore throat, and guard its users against pneumonia. Mothers were urged to rinse their hands in Listerine before touching their babies, and, after prayers, to "send those youngsters of yours into the bathroom for a good-night gargle with Listerine." During the Depression the promoters of Listerine warned those who had jobs to hold on to them. To do that it was necessary to "fight colds as never before. Use Listerine."[3] Gerald B. Lambert, a member of the family that manufactured the product, told how Listerine came to be advertised as a mouthwash. He was deeply in debt, and, needing some cash to bail himself out, he decided to move into the family business. In discussing the advertising of the mixture, his brother asked whether it might be good for bad breath. Lambert was shocked at the suggestion that "bad breath" be used in advertising a respectable product. In the discussion that followed, the word *halitosis*, which had been found in a clipping from the British medical journal *Lancet*, was used. The word was unfamiliar to everyone at the meeting, but immediately struck Lambert as a suitable term to use in a new advertising campaign. The campaign caught on, Lambert paid off his debt, and in eight years made $25 million for his company.[4]

Now, how effective is Listerine for the ailments it claimed to cure? The AMA pointed out that the manufacturers of these antiseptics exaggerated the germ-killing powers of their products, that they did not tell of the hazardous germs that were not affected by Listerine, and that they failed to mention that the ability of a compound to kill germs in a test tube or on a glass plate in the laboratory is no indication of its capability of killing them in the mouth, the teeth, the gums, or the throat, let alone in other parts of the body.[5]

A recent case that is merely an echo of similar cases that go back many years is that in which the Federal Trade Commission ordered the ITT Continental Baking Company to stop promoting Profile bread as being less fattening than ordinary bread because it had fewer calories per slice. The advertisers neglected to mention that Profile bread had fewer calories per slice because it was sliced thinner, and that the difference between Profile and other bread slices was 58 as opposed to 63 calories, a rather insignificant amount. In addition, it had been claimed that people could lose weight by eating two slices of Profile before every meal. This was so, the FTC held, only if the consumer ate a lighter meal; and Profile bread had no special virtue, in this respect, over any other brand of bread.[6]

A similar misrepresentation was discovered in ads sponsored by the General Foods Corporation, claiming that two Toast 'ems Pop-Ups contained at least as many nutrients as a breakfast of two eggs, two slices of bacon, and two slices of toast. In a commercial showing a child mulling over such a breakfast, a voice told parents whose children were unhappy at breakfast that "two hot Toast 'ems provide 100 percent of the minimum daily requirements of vitamins and iron. . . . As long as you know that—let them think it's just a big cookie." General Foods signed a consent order prohibiting it from making false nutritional claims for Toast 'ems or any other consumer food product.[7]

I have mentioned only a few of the better-known nationally advertised products that do not do what they claim to do. The reader is no doubt familiar with the claims made by quacks and fakers of all kinds who promise relief from a multitude of ailments through the purchase and use of their nostrums, devices, and treatments. Many people who have not found relief through normal medical channels for such diseases as arthritis, rheumatism, and cancer are prone to take the attitude that they have nothing to lose if they try these cures, particularly when virtually every "doctor" who represents such a nostrum can produce a multidue of written and living testimonials to his success. Such "doctors," whose degrees are seldom medical degrees and are often purchased from mail-order houses or from unknown and unrecognized institutions, never mention their failures, and are unwilling to submit their patients or their treatments to scientifically controlled tests.

One of the most celebrated cases of medical quackery is that of Harry M. Hoxsey, who operated cancer "clinics" for more than a third of a century. He claimed to have received the secret formula for the cure of cancer from his father, but did not disclose the fact that both his parents had died of cancer. He managed to persuade the Taylorville, Illinois, Chamber of Commerce that his "practice" would be good for local business, and thus his advertising directed inquirers to write to the Taylorville Chamber of Commerce. Before long, patients began to come, and some of them died not long after Hoxsey applied his secret paste. One doctor examined such a patient two days before his death and found "necrosis of not only the soft tissue of his face, but a complete destruction of the malar bone. This man died of hemorrhage at the hospital." Analysis at the laboratories of the AMA revealed that the paste Hoxsey used was an escharotic, a corrosive chemical mixture, whose chief active ingredient was arsenic. It ate away the flesh without distinguishing between healthy and cancerous tissue, and sometimes destroyed the blood vessels, causing death through hemorrhage. Hoxsey also prescribed certain medicines that were to be taken internally—one of them consisting of water, potassium iodide (an expectorant), cascara sagrada (a laxative), sugar syrup, prickly ash, buckthorn, alfalfa, and red clover blossoms.

Throughout his long career Hoxsey was arrested and convicted on charges of practicing medicine without a license. He sued numerous people for libel. And he was under constant attack by the AMA and various organs of the government. Pharmacologists and members of the American College of Physicians testified at his various trials to the effect that there was no remedy for cancer among the ingredients that Hoxsey used. Despite countless setbacks in court after court, Hoxsey managed to come back. It is estimated that in 1954, he treated more than 8,000 patients and grossed more than $1.5 million. In 1956 the Food and Drug Administration issued a warning to the public, stating that his methods were worthless and that it was "imminently dangerous to rely on [his treatments] in neglect of competent and rational treatment." This warning was distributed to the press and was contained in a "Public Beware" poster that was sent to 46,000 post offices and postal substations throughout the nation. Finally, by late 1960 the Hoxsey treatment had disappeared. In 1966 the American Cancer Society issued a catalogue of *Unproven Methods of Cancer Treatment* available to the public, containing more than twenty-five major promotions available to Americans who feared they had the disease. After years of battling Hoxsey, the FDA succeeded, in spite of an expenditure of a quarter of a million dollars, in stopping only Hoxsey. Others took over where he left off.[8]

When a false claim of effectiveness is made, it is claimed that a product (treatment, remedy, or whatever) does X, when in fact that product does not do X. This is true of all false claims of effectiveness. But if a product does not do X, it does not follow that it does nothing else. Some products may do nothing; they may give the consumer no benefit, but at the same time do him no harm, other than the financial loss that he has suffered by buying the product. But some products may have *harmful* effects that are ignored in the promotional literature or advertisements that prompt people to buy them. Listerine may be harmless, though it will not prevent colds. Hoxsey's pastes and many other preparations were (and are) harmful. Clearly, though the promoters of both Listerine and Hoxsey's treatments are guilty of false and misleading advertising, there is a further element of guilt in Hoxsey's kind of operation.

Still, the abuses go on, by some of the most respected firms in the food and drug line. In one recent year, the Food and Drug Administration seized shipments of Peritrate SA, a drug prescribed for the massive chest pain of the heart condition known as angina pectoris (Warner-Chilcott Laboratories); Serax, a tranquillizer (Wyeth Laboratories); Lincocin, an antibiotic (Upjohn); Lasix, a diuretic (Hoechst Pharmaceuticals); and Indoklon, an alternative to electroshock in some cases of depression (Ohio Chemical and Surgical Equipment Company)— all for false and deceptive promotion directed to the medical profession. Ayerst Laboratories was required by the FDA to send a "corrective letter" to some 280,000 doctors, retracting a claim that Atromid-S had a "beneficial effect" on heart disease, and the FDA ruled that Searle, Mead-Johnson, and Syntex had sent literature to physicians that misleadingly minimized the hazards of their birth control pills (Ovulen-21, Oracon, Norquen, and Norinyl-1).[9]

Unfortunately, moral suasion is not enough. Many persons, whatever their line of work, are not sufficiently resistant to the temptation to profit at the expense of others, and they are not touched by the moral arguments that might be brought to bear against their practices. One of the state's principal functions is the protection of its citizens against harm that might be done to them by others, even when they are unwitting collaborators in doing harm to themselves. It is the government's duty to require all hazardous substances to be labeled as such, so that everyone can see for himself what dangers he might expose himself to by ingesting them. It is no infringement on the citizen's freedom for the government to require of manufacturers of poisons that they clearly label their products with a warning that everyone may recognize. And the government is not interfering unreasonably with drug manufacturers when it demands that they print only scientifically verifiable facts in the literature that they distribute to the physicians who may be prescribing those products for their patients' use. Nor is it an unconscionable denial of freedom for the government to prevent persons who claim to cure diseases from practicing upon others unless they can offer some proof that the "cures" they offer are efficacious. For the government's right to protect its citizens against physical assault has never been questioned, and the purveyors of false and misleading information about harmful substances are as surely guilty of assault (if not in the legal sense, then at least in the moral sense) as they would have been had they poured their poisons into their victims' morning coffee. To argue that because the consumer has a choice and does not have to buy the product or use it, he is responsible for whatever happens to him, is like arguing that the poison victim had the choice of not drinking his coffee, and that by lifting the cup to his lips, he absolved the poisoner of all responsibility. The law has long maintained that a person who harms another is responsible for the harm that he does, even if he did so at the victim's request and with his active assistance. When a man is seeking relief from pain or illness and in that search relies upon the statements and claims made by drug salesmen, he is certainly entitled to no less protection than is offered to one who is determined to commit suicide.

FALSE CLAIMS OF NEED

Part of the American scheme of things seems to be the creation of needs, the introduction of a conviction into the minds of people that they ought to have something that they had never needed before, often because it had never existed before. Not only Americans, but people the world over today feel that certain items that would have been regarded as luxuries by their grandparents—or even by themselves a few years ago—are necessities today. Yesterday's luxury has become today's necessity. Electric refrigerators, hair driers, canned foods, soup mixes, and instant potatoes are considered by many to be necessities, though the "need" for some of them has been created. The automobile is probably the most outstanding example of a product whose increasing use has in fact created a genuine need for itself by driving all the competition—including not only the horse, but passenger railroads and commuter bus services—out of business. Cosmetics of all kinds are generally regarded by American women as being quite necessary, though women in other countries, including some very advanced nations, feel no particular compulsion about using them, and some American women are now beginning to question the necessity of using them as well. The need for razor blades was created some years ago by clever advertising by the Gillette Company, which convinced men that they were "cleaner" and more attractive if they were "clean-shaven" than if they wore beards or long sideburns. Many members of a new generation have not only called these premises into question, but have acted upon the assumption that it is not necessary to shave in order to be attractive.

The creation of a need is best exemplified by a new line of products that is just emerging. The advertisers have been going all out to convince women of the need for vaginal deodorants. Full-page advertisements have appeared in women's magazines recently, and on television as well, designed to convince women of the need for these deodorants and of the effectiveness of particular brands. A typical ad says:

> Some sprays hide it. Some sprays mask it. But Vespré actually prevents intimate odor.
> *Made especially for the external vaginal area.* Unlike sprays that only hide odor, Vespré feminine hygiene deodorant stops odor-causing bacteria. Contains twice the active odor-fighter of other leading sprays.
> *Tested by gynecologists.* Vespré was tested in leading hospitals. It's so effective it works all day, every day of the month. . . .

Another product, Easy Day, is advertised as "the most effective feminine hygiene deodorant spray you can buy" because "it's the only one with an extra ingredient. . . . This particular combination of ingredients gives you superior protection against odors of the vaginal area. More protection . . . more confidence."

In a recent public discussion on these products and their advertising, one of the commentators, questioning a representative of the firm that produces Vespré, observed that because the pharmaceutical companies had exploited every other part of the body—the head for headache preparations, the eyes, the nose, the throat, the stomach for hyperacidity and a multitude of other ailments, the kidneys, the bowels, and all the rest, nothing was left but the vagina. "Conquer the vagina," she said, "and you conquer the world!"

Another woman on the panel objected to the ad campaigns that were being conducted on behalf of these deodorants on the ground that they were insulting to women. "What you are telling us," she said to the gentleman who represented the pharmaceutical firm, "is that we stink." She had strong doubts about the legitimacy of that claim.[10]

Many gynecologists are opposed to the use of douches because they tend to remove certain bacteria from the vagina that produce a mild acid that protects it against inflammation and infection. Women who douche, it has been observed, have a higher incidence of vaginal infection than women who do not.

The natural odor of vaginal secretions is not widely regarded as offensive, and is considered by some experts on sex to be highly attractive."[11] Offensive odors originate, for the most part, only where disease is present or where foreign matter (including stale perspiration) has been allowed to accumulate. Any artificial attempt to cover natural odors may cause unnecessary delay in consulting a physician in the event of disease that would first be noticed by an abnormal odor. And, where the offensive odor is caused by perspiration, frequent bathing or the application of talcum powder is a good remedy. One of the dangers associated with deodorant sprays is the possibility of sensitive reactions which can be quite troublesome.

Vespré, Easy Day, and similar preparations are totally unnecessary and may be harmful. But a demand is being created for them by extensive advertising campaigns designed to market products that would never have been missed if they had not been produced. In this respect they do not differ at all from many products that we now use regularly without ever wondering whether we really need them, or ought to use them, at all.

We may suppose that nothing false has been stated in these advertisements. But lying behind each of them there is a suppressed premise—one that the reader is expected to supply for herself—namely, the assumption that women need vaginal deodorants. But this suppressed premise is false. To be sure, every woman can consult her physician to find out whether she really needs these products, but few will ever do so. Many, worried about their attractiveness, and insecure, perhaps, over a fear that they may have an unappealing odor that they themselves cannot perceive, will accept the suppressed premise uncritically and, in the process, make the marketers of Vespré and Easy Day and similar products rich.

That is precisely what these advertisers want. The executive vice president of the American Advertising Federation, Jonah Gitlitz, objected to legislation that would require warning signs on poisonous products on the ground that such warnings are "opposed to the whole concept of advertising." "We are opposed to the whole concept of warnings in advertising," he said, "because our primary purpose is to sell. If we do inform, it is only in order to sell."[12]

The principle that the merchant should inform his customer only when it will help him to sell his product, and its corollary—that the customer should not be informed of anything that might deter him from making a purchase, even when such information may be vitally important to him—are just a step from the swindler's principle—that the customer may be told anything, whether it is true or false, so long as he is persuaded to buy.

The swindler's principle operates in much the same way as that of the respectable advertising man. He too is interested in persuading his customer that the latter has a need for a product or service that the swindler is prepared to sell him, even though he knows that the customer does *not* need it, even when he knows that the customer's well-being may be seriously compromised by his purchase. But the principle that the sale must be made, whatever moral principles must be bent, prevails. A few examples may be instructive.

In the 1930's complaints began to pour in to Better Business Bureaus and the Federal Trade Commission about the Holland Furnace Company, a firm that had some 500 offices throughout the United States and employed more than 5,000 persons. Salesmen, misrepresenting themselves as "furnace engineers" and "safety inspectors," gained entry to their victims' homes, dismantled their furnaces, and condemned them as hazardous. They then refused to reassemble them, on the ground that they did not want to be "accessories to murder." Using scare tactics, claiming that the furnaces they "inspected" were emitting carbon monoxide and other dangerous gases, they created, in the homeowners' minds, a need for a new furnace—and proceeded to sell their own product at a handsome profit. They were so ruthless that they sold one elderly woman nine new furnaces in six years for a total of $18,000. The FTC finally forced the company to close in 1965, but in the meantime, it had done some $30 million worth of business per year for many years.

Similar frauds have been perpetrated by home repairmen who climb onto the roof, knock some bricks from the chimney, and persuade the homeowner that he must replace his chimney—at highly inflated prices—or suffer serious consequences. And some automobile repair shops, such as some Aamco Transmission dealers, have been accused in a number of states of declaring that perfectly good transmissions were "burned up" or "shot" and needed replacement or rebuilding at enormous cost.[13] Again, the gimmick is to create a "need" for something when in fact there is no need at all. That is, to persuade the consumer that he ought to buy something that he really ought *not* to buy; to persuade him that it is in his best interests to pay a large sum of money for a given product or service when in fact it is highly detrimental for him to do so, and he gains no benefit whatever from his purchase.

The difference between the cosmetic manufacturer who is trying to persuade women that they need vaginal deodorants and the exterminator who brings his own termites to display to customers whose homes he has inspected, claiming that he found them in the foundation of the home, is one of degree only. To be sure, the advertiser does not victimize any one person to the same degree. He gets rich by extracting a little money from multitudes of women, rather than by taking a lot from a few very gullible people. He has not pulled bricks from his victim's home or dismantled her furnace. But he has produced a pocketful of termites that weren't there when he arrived on the scene.

MISLEADING STATEMENTS OR CONTEXTS

Campbell's Soups concocted a television commercial that showed a thick, creamy mixture that the announcer suggested was Campbell's vegetable soup. Federal investigators, intrigued by the fact that the soup shown in the commercial was much thicker than any Campbell's vegetable soup they had ever seen, discovered that the bowl shown in the commercial had been filled with marbles to make it appear to be thicker than it really was and to make it seem to contain more vegetables than it did. Max Factor promoted a wave-setting lotion, Natural Wave, by showing how a drinking straw soaked in the lotion curled up. The FTC pointed out, however, that it did not logically follow that human hair would react as drinking straws did. The implication left in the viewer's mind, therefore, was false, because, in fact, straight hair did not curl after being soaked in Natural Wave.

Such visual trickery is quite common in television commercials, in newspaper and magazine advertisements, in direct mail advertisements, and on package labels. The bowlful of plump, luscious-looking golden peaches pictured on the label often turns out to be a half-bowl full of sickly looking, stringy brown peaches and a pint of syrup.

Misleading statements are also very common. A number of so-called management companies have been advertising for talented men and women, and especially for children, who would be given an "excellent chance" of being put to work doing television commercials "at no fee." As it turned out, the agencies seldom placed anyone, and, though they charged no fees, they sent their clients to photographers who charge them substantial fees for taking their publicity pictures, or referred them to a firm that took "screen tests," also for lots of money. As it happens, the photographers were always closely allied with the "management" agencies, and the latter always shared a very healthy proportion of the fees charged by the former.[14]

In none of these cases could one say that false statements were made. Strictly speaking, these advertisers are not guilty of lying to the public, if *lying* is defined as the deliberate utterance of an untrue statement. For, taken literally, none of the statements made in these advertisements is untrue. But the messages of the ads are misleading. Because of the pictorial matter in them, the reader or viewer makes inferences that are false; and the advertiser juxtaposes those pictures with the narrative in such a way that false inferences *will* be made. It is through those false inferences that he expects to earn enough money to pay for the ad and to have something left over for himself.

The land promoter who sends a glossy pamphlet advertising his "retirement city" in Arizona may not make a single false statement in the entire pamphlet. But by filling it with beautiful color photographs of swimming pools, golf links, and lush vegetation, none of which exist within 100 miles of the land he is selling, he leads his prospects to believe that certain features exist within that area which do *not* exist. Thus, without uttering or printing a single false statement, he is able to lead his prospects to believe what he knows is not true.

Such deceptions are fraudulent in the moral sense of the word; but unfortunately, in the legal sense of the word, they are very often not considered to be fraudulent. For fraud, legally, is a criminal offense. In order to prove that a man has committed any criminal offense, one must first prove that he did what he did maliciously and with intent to cause injury (financial, mental, physical, or other) to another person. In such cases as these it is almost impossible to prove that such an intent existed, for it is impossible to creep into a man's mind to determine what his intentions or motives really are. It is sometimes possible to gather sufficient evidence to establish, beyond a reasonable doubt, that the accused had the state of mind necessary for a criminal conviction. But in cases of fraud, it is generally impossible to find enough evidence to establish such a proposition satisfactorily. The man accused of fraudulently advertising, promoting, or selling any product whatever can claim that he did not intend to harm anyone through his actions, that he honestly believed in his product, and that he had no idea people would make such false inferences on the basis of the evidence he presented to them. Because it is usually impossible to refute such a stand, very few people are ever convicted of fraud, no matter how much harm they may have done to others as they made themselves rich.

The FTC in the United States has broad powers to deal with perpetrators of fraud when their activity crosses state lines, and the post office has been granted some power to put an end to some of the mail frauds that have been perpetrated upon the public; but these powers are civil rather than criminal in nature, and they consist primarily in the power to stop mail services, to order persons to "cease and desist" from certain practices, and to impose civil fines upon them if they violate such orders. But few states have given their own authorities even that much power, and the federal government is handicapped by a lack of personnel and funds, and is thus unable to handle all the cases that fall within its jurisdiction. As a result, the government is able to exercise very little control over those who publish or write misleading advertisements, and millions of persons are bilked out of billions of dollars every year because of them.[15]

THE EXPLOITATION OF ILLUSIONS

Closely related to misleading pictures and statements is the use made by manufacturers and advertisers of illusions in selling their goods. This is best illustrated by the use merchandisers make of certain optical illusions in their choice of packaging. Cereal boxes would be much more stable, less apt to spill over, if they were short and squat. But the packaging experts at Kellogg's, General Foods, and General Mills know that if housewives are given the choice between two boxes of cereal, one short and squat and the other tall and narrow, they will almost invariably choose the tall and narrow box, *even if it contains less cereal and costs more.* Most housewives judge by the outward appearance of the box and do not look for the net weight and attempt to calculate the price per ounce (a project that is virtually impossible anyway, unless one is equipped with a slide rule). Two lines of equal length, one horizontal and the other vertical, do not *appear* to be of equal length. The vertical line always appears to be longer. Tall boxes appear to be larger than short ones, and the housewife doing her shopping thinks she is getting more in the tall box than she would be getting if she were to purchase the short box.

Bottles follow the same principle. Shampoos, for example, are packaged in tall, narrow bottles—often with the waist pinched to make them even taller—to give the illusion of quantity. Some jars and bottles are manufactured with inner compartments, or double glass walls, so that the actual quantity of goods in the container is much less than it appears to be. Fruit and other goods are canned in large quantities of syrup, and cookies, nuts, and other dry foods are packed in tins or cartons that are stuffed with cardboard—allegedly to prevent breakage, but more realistically to reduce the quantity of goods in the package while giving the customer the illusion that he is purchasing more than is actually to be found in the package.

Manufacturers argue that these stuffings are necessary to prevent breakage, that there is a certain amount of "settling" in some products that results in their packages being a third empty when they reach the consumer, and that their machines have been designed in any case to fill the packages by weight so that the customer always receives an honest measure, regardless of the size or shape of the package. But these explanations do not explain the hiss of air that escapes from my toothpaste tube when I open it (the tube seemed full and firm until then, but turns out to have been full of air); and it does not explain the manufacturers' aversion to standardized weights and their vigorous battle against requirements that the net weight be printed boldly and prominently on the front of the package. Until recent legislation was passed, the net weight of many products was printed in obscure corners of the packages, in microscopic type, and in a color that was just two shades lighter than the background color of the package (e.g., red against a dark red background) so that it was almost impossible for the normal shopper to find out how much merchandise was contained in the package.

However, the producer and the manufacturer may have legitimate excuses for some of these practices. A relatively small macaroni company, for example, may produce a number of different products, in different shapes and with a variety of densities. By standardizing all of its packages by *dimensions* rather than by *weight*, it is able to purchase packages and cases in great quantities and to save considerable money both for itself and, one would hope, for its customers. If it were required to standardize its packages by *weight*, it would have to invest a considerable amount of money in new plant and equipment, and the time during which its plant and equipment were standing idle would be increased significantly, thus raising its costs and, eventually, the cost to the consumer.[16] If standardized packaging were suddenly legislated into existence, it is conceivable that a number of smaller firms would be forced out of business because of their inability to absorb the added costs, and that the giant corporations would be bequeathed an even larger share of the total market than they now have. Still, none of these considerations should apply to a requirement that all packages bear, in clear and unmistakable type, a true and unambiguous statement of the nature of their contents and their weight.

CONCEALMENT OF THE TRUTH

Merchants and producers have many ways of concealing truth from the customers—not by lying to them, but simply by not telling them facts that are relevant to the question of whether they ought to purchase a particular product or whether they are receiving full value for their money. A particularly good example of this is the great ham scandal that broke into the open a few years ago. Major packers, including Swift, Armour, and others, were selling ham that was advertised as being particularly juicy. The consumer was not told, however, that the hams were specially salted and that hypodermic syringes were used to inject large quantities of water into them.

The "juice" was nothing but water that evaporated away during cooking, leaving a ham some 40 percent smaller than the one that had been put into the oven. The housewife purchasing such a ham had no advance warning that she was purchasing water for the price of ham, unless she knew that the words *artificial ham* that were printed in small letters on the seal of the package meant that that was the case. Even that small warning, if it can be called such, was added only because of pressure brought to bear against the packers by the FTC. And there was no publicity to arouse the consumer to the special meaning of that odd term, *artificial ham*.[17]

Probably the most common deception of this sort is price deception, the technique some high-pressure salesmen use to sell their goods by grossly inflating their prices to two, three, and even four times their real worth. Again, there may be no "untruth" in what they say; but they conceal the important fact that the same product, or one nearly identical to it, can be purchased for far less at a department or appliance store. It is not the business of salesmen and businessmen to send their clients to their competitors, but it is certainly unethical for them to fail to tell their customers that they are not getting full value for their money.

Perhaps it may be put as follows: A burglar or a thief may be heavily fined or sent to jail for many months for stealing a relatively small amount of money or valuables from a single person. But a salesman who cheats hundreds of people out of equal sums of money that total, in the aggregate, hundreds of thousands of dollars, is immune to prosecution, and may, in fact, be one of the community's most respected citizens. If Armour and Swift and other large corporations can bilk their customers out of enormous sums of money and do it with impunity, why, one might ask, should the petty thief be subjected to such severe penalties for his activities? He may plead that he desperately needs the money he derives from his dishonest activities, but that excuse would hardly be credible if it was uttered by corporate executives.

OUR DECEPTIVE LANGUAGE

Equivocation was recognized by Aristotle as one of the most deceptive of all logical tricks. The ambiguity of language makes man's most valuable instrument subject to distortion so that it may be used to take advantage of unsuspecting persons who are not familiar with the ways in which seemingly precise terms can actually be used to make considerable profit for those who know how to use them to mean what they want them to mean.

One might suppose that mathematical terms would be the most

precise and unambiguous of all, and that "8 percent of $1,200" would mean the same thing everywhere and at all times. But it is easy to show that this seemingly innocent expression, "8 percent of $1,200," can have a number of meanings and that the precise meaning conferred upon that expression can make a considerable difference to the person who borrows $1,200 for one year at what is said to be 8 percent interest.

Though there are many variations, the following three will serve to illustrate the point.

Case 15. The 8 percent loan Suppose you go to a bank or a finance company and ask for a loan of $1,200. After all the necessary formalities have been completed, you are told that your credit is good, and that the loan will be made "at 8 percent interest." This might mean any of the following things:

1. You are given $1,200 by the banker, and, at the end of each month or whenever you make your payments, you pay interest on the outstanding balance at the rate of 8 percent per year, or .08/12 per month. You will then pay a total of $1,252 and have the use of an average of $650 of the bank's money through the twelve-month period during which you are paying it back, for a true interest rate of 8.05 percent.

2. Eight percent of the total amount of your loan is deducted from the amount given to you when you make the loan. That is, you pay your interest in advance, and then repay the loan in monthly installments. Suppose that you intend to make the loan for one year. Ninety-six dollars will be deducted from the sum given to you, and you then pay the bank $1,200 in monthly installments. Under these circumstances, because you start off with only $1,204 and repay a part of it each month, you would have the use of an average of $554 of the bank's money throughout the loan period. The interest of $96 constitutes 17.3 percent of this amount.

3. Your interest is added to the total amount of the loan you make, and then you pay the amount to the bank in equal installments. Thus, your loan is for the amount of $1,296, but you receive $1,200 cash, and repay the loan in monthly installments of $1,296/12, or $108 per month. Because the average amount of the bank's money in use by the borrower is only $530, he pays a true interest rate of 18.1 percent on his loan.

When the bank or finance company adds "service charges" and insurance charges, the rate can climb considerably higher still. Your friendly neighborhood banker, despite his reputation for honesty in financial affairs, is not above using such verbal trickery to make you believe that you're receiving the prime rate on your loan, when in reality, you're paying two or three times as much for your loan as a wealthy businessman pays for his. A true 8 percent loan on $1,200 would permit the borrower to take $1,200 and keep it for the time agreed—say, one year. At the end of that time, he would return the principal ($1,200) and pay the interest ($96). He would have had the use of the full amount for the full time. When you pay the interest in advance, or have it added to or deducted from the amount of money you receive or the face amount of the loan, you pay considerably more for your use of the money, for you start returning the money to the lender at the end of one month and continue to return it to him throughout the period of the loan, though you have paid interest on it as if you had been able to keep it throughout the period of the loan. The money you have had in your hands during the full period of the loan is not the $1,200 you borrowed, but about half as much—for you must average it out over the number of months that you have been returning it. Thus, in real terms, the money you hold is half as much as you think, and your interest rate is doubled or trebled. Such practices have become more difficult since the United States government passed its truth-in-lending law, but many consumers still don't know how to tell a good loan from a bad one.

A FINAL WORD ON ADVERTISING

Advertising has an important and constructive role to play in the life of the nation. It is not true that all advertising men are unscrupulous or that all businessmen are concerned only with selling, no matter what the cost to their customers. Nor is it true that advertisements are necessarily misleading or fraudulent.

David Ogilvy, one of the most successful advertising executives in the United States, is the creator of such successful advertising images as Schweppes's Commander Whitehead and Hathaway Shirt's man with the eye patch.[18] In his discussion of techniques for building a successful advertising campaign, he says,

> *Give the Facts.* Very few advertisements contain enough factual information to sell the product. There is a ludicrous tradition among copywriters that consumers aren't interested in facts. Nothing could be farther from the truth. Study the copy in the Sears, Roebuck catalogue; it sells a billion dollars' worth of merchandise every year by giving *facts*. In my Rolls-Royce advertisements I gave nothing but facts. No adjectives, no "gracious living."
>
> The consumer isn't a moron; she is your wife. You insult her in-

telligence if you assume that a mere slogan and a few vapid adjectives will persuade her to buy anything. She wants all the information you can give her.[19]

And he adds the following bit of advice that bears directly on our subject:

> You wouldn't tell lies to your own wife. Don't tell them to mine. Do as you would be done by.
> If you tell lies about a product, you will be found out—either by the Government, which will prosecute you, or by the consumer, who will punish you by not buying your product a second time.
> Good products can be sold by *honest* advertising. If you don't think the product is good, you have no business to be advertising it. If you tell lies, or weasel, you do your client a disservice, you increase your load of guilt, and you fan the flames of public resentment against the whole business of advertising.[20]

In short, Ogilvy believes that aside from any ethical reasons that might be advanced for factual, informative, and truthful advertising, it is in the best interests of both the advertising man and his client—from a purely practical point of view—to adhere to these principles, for they keep the attorney general and the FTC away from the door, and in the long run, they are more successful in the marketplace. He claims that the "combative-persuasive" type of advertising that so many people have condemned for its lack of taste is not nearly as profitable as informative advertising.

He argues also that advertising is a force for sustaining standards of quality and service. The advertisement contains a promise that must be fulfilled if the customer is to be satisfied. The public will eventually turn against any advertiser who fails to keep the promises he has made in his public pronouncements. Ogilvy tells of firms that have warned their employees to maintain the standards of service that have been described in their advertising, and of others that have warned that they would move their accounts to other agencies if their commercials were ever cited by government agencies for dishonesty. The fear of exposure by government agencies and consumer groups in the public press, and the adverse publicity that would result, is enough to deter some firms from engaging in deceptive advertising.

As for the charge that advertisers create needs or desires for things that people might well do without, this is what Ogilvy has to say:

> Does advertising make people want to buy products they don't need? If you don't think people need deodorants, you are at liberty to criticize advertising for having persuaded 87 percent of American women and 66 percent of American men to use them. If you don't think people need beer, you are right to criticize advertising for having persuaded 58 percent of the adult population to drink it. If you disapprove of social

mobility, creature comforts, and foreign travel, you are right to blame advertising for encouraging such wickedness. If you dislike affluent society, you are right to blame advertising for inciting the masses to pursue it.

If you are this kind of Puritan, I cannot reason with you. I can only call you a psychic masochist. Like Archbishop Leighton, I pray, "Deliver me, O Lord, from the errors of wise men, yea, and of good men."

Dear old John Burns, the father of the Labor movement in England, used to say that the tragedy of the working class was the poverty of their desires. I make no apology for inciting the working class to desire less Spartan lives.[21]

There is certainly some truth in what Ogilvy says, but at some points he and I must part company. First, he gives the advertisers more credit than may be their due when he asserts that they have persuaded 58 percent of the adult population to drink beer. It is not at all unlikely that some people would be drinking beer even if it were never advertised. The drinking of beer far antedates the modern advertising industry, and may be traced to causes other than the efforts of copywriters. Secondly, the desires for social mobility, creature comforts, and foreign travel are all exploited by advertisers to sell their products, but advertisers did not invent them or create them. The critics of advertising do not believe that social mobility, creature comforts, and foreign travel are wicked, and to say that they do is to evade the issue. The issue is not the advertiser's *encouragement* of these desires, but his *exploitation* of them. Thirdly, unlike beer, social mobility, and foreign travel, there was never a demand for deodorants until the advertisers created it. They did so, not to create a better society, but to make money. Those who object to the exploitation of normal human desires by persons and corporations intent on making money at a great cost to their customers and by utilizing methods that conceal or distort the facts are not psychic masochists (whatever that may be), nor are they Puritans. They are people who are outraged by what they consider to be the unconscionable methods utilized by some businesses to increase their profits at the expense of people who can often ill afford to be exploited.

Some 2,000 years ago there was a debate between the scholars of two great academies as to whether it was proper to praise the beauty of an ugly bride. According to one faction, the principle that one should refrain from uttering any falsehood required that the honest man refrain from praising the ugly bride. The other group, however, insisted that principles of kindness should prevail and that even if one had to lie, one was obliged to add to the newlyweds' happiness rather than to detract from it. They went on to say that in a matter of far less moment to a man than his marriage, the principle of kindness should take precedence, so that if a person had made a bad bargain at the market, one should not rub it in by telling him so.[22] If they were here to participate in a discussion on the issue presently under consideration, it is not hard to imagine what they might say:

> Thousands of men and women are too poor to afford foreign travel, or large and flashy automobiles, or Hathaway shirts, or expensive liquors, or costly cosmetics. What useful purpose is served by dangling these luxuries before their eyes? To some, perhaps, the enticing display of such luxuries may serve as an incentive, spurring them on to greater achievement so that they too many enjoy what their more affluent neighbors take for granted. But to many, and perhaps to most, the display may arouse feelings of frustration, anger, and hurt. "Why," they may ask, "are we unable to have all of these things, when so many others do? Why can we not give our children what those ads show other people giving their children? Why can we not share the happiness that is depicted here?" Before a man is married, it might be appropriate to point out some of his fiancée's faults; but at the wedding, when it's obviously too late, it's unkind to dwell on them. For those who cannot afford the luxuries—and they are luxuries, whatever Ogilvy may say—offered in advertisements that are often directed *specifically at them*, it is cruel to hurt them by offering them what they cannot buy, or to seduce them with false promises of happiness or prestige or success into neglecting their primary obligations in order to seek the fantasy world portrayed in advertisements.

Everyone wants a beautiful bride, I suppose, and it may be good that the working classes no longer desire to live Spartan lives, if they ever did. But some men learn to live very happily with women whose proportions are not even close to those that are currently considered to be the standard of beauty, and it is wrong to jeopardize their happiness by constantly reminding them of that fact; and it would be infinitely worse to parade well-proportioned beauties before them and to urge them to switch. No one is married to a life of poverty. But some people, unable to escape from such a life themselves, have made the adjustment and have found that it is possible to be happy and respectable even on a severely limited income. Is it right to parade the latest fashions in "good living" before their eyes at every opportunity, urging them to buy them *"Now, while our limited supply lasts!"*? Men who have been seduced into discontentment over their wives have been known to commit murder. So have some who have been seduced into dissatisfaction with their style of life. Some of the latter may be partially attributable to advertising.

This is not to say that all advertising is bad; but even when the message is not distorted, those who use the mass media to disseminate it should do so with some sense of social and public responsibility. It is far worse, though, when the message is distorted. And even

David Ogilvy, for all his insistence on honesty in advertising, admits that he is "continuously guilty of *suppressio veri* [the suppression of the truth]. Surely it is asking too much to expect the advertiser to describe the shortcomings of his product? One must be forgiven for putting one's best foot forward."[23] So the consumer is *not* to be told all the relevant information; he is *not* to be given all the facts that would be of assistance in making a reasonable decision about a given purchase. In particular, he will *not* be told about the weaknesses of a product, about its shock hazards, for example, if it is an electrical appliance; about the danger it poses to the consumer's health if it is a cleaning fluid; about the danger it poses to his life if it is an automobile tire that is not built to sustain the heavy loads of today's automobile at turnpike speeds; or, if one carries the doctrine to its final conclusion, about the possibly harmful side effects of a new drug that is advertised to the medical profession. Telling the truth combined with *"suppressio veri"* is *not* telling the truth. It is *not* asking too much of the advertiser to reveal such facts when they are known to him, and he should *not* be forgiven for "putting his best foot forward" at his customer's expense. Ogilvy admits, too, that he sometimes tells the truth about the products he advertises in such a way that it seems to the reader that his product is different, in those respects, from similar products, whereas Ogilvy knows that all other products of the same kind possess the same features. All aspirin is the same, for example, whether it is stamped *Bayer* and sells for $1.95 per hundred or whether it is an unadvertised brand of U.S.P. aspirin that sells for 35 cents per hundred. But the advertiser will try to convince you that what is true of Bayer aspirin is not true of the other product. This is unfair to the consumer, whether he is rich or poor; but it is particularly unfair to the poor consumer, who could use the money he spends paying for Bayer's advertising in other ways.

Advertising has an important role to fill in our society. It is not likely to disappear. But it is not always carried on in the most ethical manner. Its supporters tend to exaggerate the benefits that have flowed from it, and they are not at all shy about boasting about its effectiveness in their trade meetings and in their efforts to win new business. But they often shrug off any suggestion that their efforts may have harmful effects upon some segments of society by denying that they are all *that* effective. They cannot have it both ways. If advertising is as effective as its practitioners claim it to be, then it possesses enormous potential for harm as well as for good. Because many, though not all, advertisers are concerned primarily about selling their products and only secondarily, if at all, about telling the truth, it is reasonable to suggest that some government regulation be exercised over this industry; and in particular, that advertisers —both producers and agencies—be held liable for harm or damage that results to consumers from misleading or false claims in advertisements, and that they be required to make good any financial loss that consumers may suffer as a result of reliance upon any misleading advertisement, whether the advertisement was "fraudulent" in the criminal sense or not. If laws were passed, both on the federal level and at the state or provincial level, making agencies and producers responsible for restitution of damages suffered by customers who relied upon their "messages," there would be a great incentive for those concerned to confine their claims to those that could be substantiated and to resort to fewer misleading gimmicks. Though such legislation would not eliminate all abuses, it would go a long way toward assuring the public that the advertising messages to which it was exposed respected the truth.

NOTES

1. See Robert J. Cole, "New Law Bars Unscrupulous Ruse to Deprive a Debtor of Legal Rights," *New York Times*, August 19, 1971, p. 51.
2. See James G. Burrow, *AMA: Voice of American Medicine* (Baltimore: Johns Hopkins Press, 1963), p. 268, and Arthur J. Cramp, *Nostrums and Quackery and Pseudo-medicine* (Chicago: University of Chicago Press, 1936), Vol. III, pp. 29–31.
3. James H. Young, *The Medical Messiahs* (Princeton, N.J.: Princeton University Press, 1967), pp. 147 f.
4. See David Ogilvy, *Confessions of an Advertising Man* (New York: Atheneum, 1963), p. 86. Also Gerald B. Lambert, "How I Sold Listerine," in *The Amazing Advertising Business*, ed. by the Editors of *Fortune* (New York: Simon & Schuster, 1957), Chapter 5.
5. Young, op. cit., p. 155.
6. *Consumer Reports*, Vol. 36 (September 1971), pp. 525 f.
7. Ibid., p. 561.
8. For the full story of the Hoxsey case, see Young, op. cit., Chapter 17. This is a fully documented account, gleaned from files of the AMA, the FDA, and transcripts of court hearings, as well as from newspapers, journals, and other publications of the period.
9. Mortin Mintz, "Drugs: Deceptive Advertising," in David Sanford (ed.), *Hot War on the Consumer* (New York: Pitman, 1969), pp. 91 ff.
10. CBC, Friday, August 20, 1971.
11. This point, and those below, were made by Dr. Lou Harris of the University of Toronto Medical School on a radio broadcast on the Canadian Broadcasting Company's Consumer Affairs program. See also Th. H. Van de Velde, *Ideal Marriage*, Revised Edition (New York: Random House, 1965), pp. 28 ff.
12. *Consumer Reports*, Vol. 36 (September 1971), p. 526.
13. For a full discussion of the Holland Furnace fraud, the Aamco Transmission fraud, and many others, see Warren G. Magnuson and Jean Carper, *The Dark Side of the Marketplace* (Englewood Cliffs, N.J.: Prentice-Hall, 1968), Chapters 1 and 2 et passim.
14. *Consumer Reports*, Vol. 36 (September 1971), p. 560.
15. For representative figures of financial gains made by persons engaged in fraudulent

deals, see Magnuson and Carper, op. cit.; Max A. Geller, *Advertising at the Crossroads* (New York: Ronald Press, 1952); Dexter Masters, *The Intelligent Buyer and the Telltale Seller* (New York: Knopf, 1966); and other works cited in the bibliography for this section.

16. See "The Consumer," an address by Lloyd E. Skinner, president of the Skinner Macaroni Company, in *Vital Speeches of the Day*, Vol. 33 (January 1, 1967), pp. 189 ff., reprinted in Grant S. McClellan, "The Reference Shelf," Vol. 40, No. 3, *The Consuming Public* (New York: H. W. Wilson Company, 1968), pp. 143 ff. He explains that his company produces some nineteen or twenty different kinds of macaroni products, all packaged in the same containers. If his firm were required to standardize by weight, rather than by volume, he would have to invest $86,000 in new machinery over the $300,000 investment in packaging machinery that he already has, as well as $100,000 in new plant facilities to accommodate the new machines. As opposed to the 90 percent operating time of the packaging machinery that he had at the time, the new machinery would have been operating only 40 to 50 percent of the time, according to his estimates. This would have resulted in an increase of 1 to 2 cents per package in the cost of producing macaroni.
17. Cf. *Consumer Reports*, March and August, 1961; follow-up reports, April and August, 1962.
18. The firm is Ogilvy, Benson and Mather.
19. David Ogilvy, *Confessions of an Advertising Man* (New York: Atheneum, 1963), pp. 95 f.
20. Ibid., p. 99.
21. Ibid., p. 159.
22. Babylonian Talmud, *Ketuvot*, p. 17a. The academies were those that went under the names of Shammai and Hillel, respectively. The "debate" was not comparable to the kind of oratory contest that might be staged by college debating teams. It was a serious discussion on matters of legal and moral principle.
23. Ogilvy, op. cit., pp. 158 f.

Pierre-Joseph Proudhon
WHAT IS PROPERTY?

Pierre-Joseph Proudhon, French journalist, social theorist, and economic reformer, was born in Besançon in 1809 and died in 1865. Proudhon hoped that man's ethical progress would eventually make government unnecessary, and he developed a theory of loosely federated groups that would restrain centralized government, as a compromise between state sovereignty and anarchism. A prolific writer whose many works influenced the French syndicalist movement, Proudhon was catapulted into prominence with the publication of his pamphlet *What Is Property?* (1840), from which this selection is taken. The author answers the question, What is property? with the provocative assertion that "property is robbery" and shows how neither occupancy nor labor can create a right to property—a right which he sees as not being absolute, but as one lying "outside of society." Indeed, contrary to the general view of his day, Proudhon sees property and society as "utterly irreconcilable institutions." From Pierre-Joseph Proudhon, *What Is Property?*, transl. by Benjamin R. Tucker (Princeton, Mass.: Benjamin R. Tucker, 1876).

WHAT PROPERTY IS

If I were asked to answer the following question: *What is slavery?* and I should answer in one word, *It is murder*, my meaning would be understood at once. No extended argument would be required to show that the power to take from a man his thought, his will, his personality, is a power of life and death; and that to enslave a man is to kill him. Why, then, to this other question: *What is property?* may I not likewise answer, *It is robbery*, without the certainty of being misunderstood; the second proposition being no other than a transformation of the first?

I undertake to discuss the vital principle of our government and our institutions, property: I am in my right. I may be mistaken in the conclusion which shall result from my investigations: I am in my right. I think best to place the last thought of my book first: still am I in my right.

Such an author teaches that property is a civil right, born of occupation and sanctioned by law; another maintains that it is a natural right, originating in labor—and both of these doctrines, totally opposed as they may seem, are encouraged and applauded. I contend that neither labor, nor occupation, nor law, can create property; that it is an effect without a cause: am I censurable?

But murmurs arise!

Property is robbery! That is the war-cry of '93! That is the signal of revolutions!

Reader, calm yourself: I am no agent of discord, no firebrand of sedition. I anticipate history by a few days; I disclose a truth whose development we may try in vain to arrest; I write the preamble of our future constitution. This proposition which seems to you blasphemous—*property is robbery*—would, if our prejudices allowed us to consider it, be recognized as the lightning-rod to shield us from the coming thunderbolt; but how many interests, how many prejudices, stand in the way! . . . Alas! philosophy will not change the course of events: destiny will fulfill itself regardless of prophecy. Besides, must not justice be done and our education be finished?

Property is robbery! . . . What a revolution in human ideas! *Proprietor* and *robber* have been at all times expressions as contradictory as the beings whom they designate are hostile; all languages have perpetuated this opposition. On what authority, then, do you venture to attack universal consent, and give the lie to the human race? Who are you, that you should question the judgment of the nations and the ages?

Of what consequence to you, reader, is my obscure individuality? I live, like you, in a century in which reason submits only to fact and to evidence. My name, like yours, is TRUTH-SEEKER. My mission is written in these words of the law: *Speak without hatred and without fear; tell all that which thou knowest.* . . .

Others offer you the spectacle of genius wresting Nature's secrets from her, and unfolding before you her sublime messages; you will find here only a series of experiments upon *justice* and *right*, a sort of verification of the weights and measures of your conscience. The operations shall be conducted under your very eyes; and you shall weigh the result.

Nevertheless I build no system. I ask an end to privilege, the abolition of slavery, equality of rights, and the reign of law. Justice, nothing else; that is the alpha and omega of my argument; to others I leave the business of governing the world. . . .

THE JUSTIFICATION OF PROPERTY

The Declaration of Rights has placed property on its list of the natural and inalienable rights of man, four in all: *liberty, equality, property, security.* What rule did the legislators of '93 follow in compiling this list? None. They laid down principles, just as they discussed sovereignty and the laws; from a general point of view, and according to their own opinion. They did everything in their own blind way. . . .

Nevertheless, if we compare these three or four rights with each other, we find that property bears no resemblance whatever to the others; that for the majority of citizens it exists only potentially, and as a dormant faculty without exercise; that for the others, who do enjoy it, it is susceptible of certain compromises and modifications which do not harmonize with the idea of a natural right; that, in practice, governments, tribunals, and laws do not respect it; and finally that everybody, spontaneously and with one voice, regards it as chimerical. . . .

Liberty is an absolute right, because it is to man what impenetrability is to matter—a *sine qua non* of existence; equality is an absolute right, because without equality there is no society; security is an absolute right, because in the eyes of every man his own liberty and life are as precious as another's. These three rights are absolute; that is, susceptible of neither increase or diminution; because in society each associate receives as much as he gives—liberty for liberty, equality for equality, body for body, soul for soul, in life and in death.

But property, in its derivative sense, and by the definitions of law, is a right outside of society; for it is clear that, if the wealth of each was social wealth, the conditions would be equal for all, and it would be a contradiction to say: *Property is a man's right* to *dispose at will of social property.* Then if we are associated for the sake of liberty, equality, and security, we are not associated for the sake of property; then if property is a *natural* right, this natural right is not social, but *antisocial.* Property and society are utterly irreconcilable institutions. It is as impossible to associate two proprietors as to join two magnets by their similar poles. Either society must perish, or it must destroy property.

If property is a natural, absolute, imprescriptible, and inalienable right, why, in all ages, has there been so much speculation as to its origin?—for this is one of its distinguishing characteristics. The origin of a natural right! Good God! who ever inquired into the origin of the rights of liberty, security, or equality? They exist by the same right that we exist; they are born with us, they live and die with us. With property it is very different, indeed. By law, property can exist without a proprietor, like a quality without a subject. It exists for the human being who as yet is not, and for the octogenarian who is no more. And yet, in spite of these wonderful prerogatives which savor of the eternal and the infinite, they never found the origin of property; the doctors still disagree. In one point only are they in harmony: namely, that the validity of the right of property depends upon the authenticity of its origin. But this harmony is their condemnation. Why have they acknowledged the right before settling the question of origin?

Certain classes do not relish investigations into the pretended titles to property, and its fabulous and perhaps scandalous history. They wish to hold to this proposition: that property is a fact; that it always has been, and always will be. . . .

The titles on which they pretend to base the right of property are two in number: *occupation* and *labor.* I shall examine them successively, under all their aspects and in detail; and I remind the reader that, to whatever authority we appeal, I shall prove beyond a doubt that property, to be just and possible, must necessarily have equality for its condition. . . .

OCCUPATION AS A BASIS FOR PROPERTY RIGHTS

Not only does occupation lead to equality, it *prevents* property. For, since every man, from the fact of his existence, has the right of occupation, and, in order to live, must have material for cultivation on which he may labor; and since, on the other hand, the number of occupants varies continually with the births and deaths, it follows that the quantity of material which each laborer may claim varies with the number of occupants; consequently, that occupation is always subordinate to population. Finally, that, inasmuch as possession, in right, can never remain fixed, it is impossible, in fact, that it can ever become property.

Every occupant is, then, necessarily a possessor or usufructuary; he cannot therefore be a proprietor; he is responsible for the thing entrusted to him; he must use it in conformity with general utility, with a view to its preservation and development; he has no power to transform it, to diminish it, or to change its nature, he cannot so divide the usufruct that another shall perform the labor while he receives the product. In a word, the usufructuary is under the supervision of society, submitted to the condition of labor and the law of equality.

Thus is annihilated the Roman definition of property—*the right of use and abuse*—an immorality born of violence, the most monstrous pretension that the civil laws ever sanctioned. Man receives his usufruct from the hands of society, which alone is the permanent possessor. The individual passes away, society is deathless.

What a profound disgust fills my soul while discussing such simple truths! Do we doubt these things today? Will it be necessary to again take up arms for their triumph? And can force, in default of reason, alone introduce them into our laws?

All have equal right of occupancy.

The amount occupied being measured, not by the will, but by the variable conditions of space and number, property cannot exist.

This no code has ever expressed; this no constitution can admit! These are axioms which the civil law and the law of nations deny! . . .

LABOR AS A BASIS FOR PROPERTY RIGHTS

But I hear the exclamations of the partisans of another system: "Labor, labor! that is the basis of property!"

Reader, do not be deceived. This new basis of property is worse than the first, and I shall soon have to ask your pardon for having demonstrated things clearer, and refuted pretensions more unjust, than any which we have yet considered. . . .

Admit, however, that labor gives a right of property in material. Why is not this principle universal? Why is the benefit of this pretended law confined to a few and denied to the mass of laborers? A philosopher, arguing that all animals sprang up formerly out of the earth warmed by the rays of the sun, almost like mushrooms, on being asked why the earth no longer yielded crops of that nature, replied: "Because it is old, and has lost its fertility." Has labor, once so fecund, likewise become sterile? Why does the tenant no longer acquire through his labor the land which was formerly acquired by the labor of the proprietor?

"Because," they say, "it is already appropriated." That is no answer. A farm yields fifty bushels per hectare; the skill and labor of the tenant double this product: the increase is created by the tenant. Suppose the owner, in a spirit of moderation rarely met with, does not go to the extent of absorbing this product by raising the rent, but allows the cultivator to enjoy the results of his labor; even then justice is not satisfied. The tenant, by improving the land, has imparted a new value to the property; he, therefore, has a right to a part of the property. If the farm was originally worth 100,000 francs, and if by the labor of the tenant its value has risen to 150,000 francs, the tenant, who produced this extra value, is the legitimate proprietor of one-third of the farm. M. Ch. Comte could not have pronounced this doctrine false, for it was he who said: "Men who increase the fertility of the earth are no less useful to their fellowmen, than if they create new land."

Why, then, is not this rule applicable to the man who improves the land, as well as to him who clears it? The labor of the former makes the land worth 1; that of the latter makes it worth 2: both create equal values. Why not accord to both equal property? I defy anyone to refute this argument, without again falling back on the right of first occupancy.

"But," it will be said, "even if your wish should be granted, property would not be distributed much more evenly than it is now. Land does not go on increasing in value forever; after two or three seasons it attains its maximum fertility. That which is added by the agricultural art results rather from the progress of science and the diffusion of knowledge, than from the skill of the cultivator. Consequently, the addition of a few laborers to the mass of proprietors would be no argument against property."

This discussion would, indeed, prove a well-nigh useless one, if our labors culminated in simply extending land privilege and industrial monopoly; in emancipating only a few hundred laborers out of the millions of proletarians. But this also is a misconception of our real thought, and does but prove the general lack of intelligence and logic.

If the laborer, who adds to the value of a thing, has a right of property in it, he who maintains this value acquires the same right. For what is maintenance? It is incessant addition—continuous creation. What is it to cultivate? It is to give the soil its value every year: it is, by annually renewed creation, to prevent the diminution or destruction of the value of a piece of land. Admitting, then, that property is rational and legitimate, admitting that rent is equitable and just, I say that he who cultivates acquires property by as good a title as he who clears, or he who improves; and that every time a tenant pays his rent, he obtains a fraction of property in the land entrusted to his care, the denominator of which is equal to the proportion of rent paid. Unless you admit this, you fall into absolutism and tyranny; you recognize class privileges; you sanction slavery.

Whoever labors becomes a proprietor—this is an inevitable deduction from the acknowledged principles of political economy and jurisprudence. And when I say proprietor, I do not mean simply (as do our hypocritical economists) proprietor of his allowance, his salary, his wages, I mean proprietor of the value which he creates, and by which the master alone profits.

As all this relates to the theory of wages and of the distribution of products—and as this matter never has been even partially cleared up—I ask permission to insist on it: this discussion will not be useless to the work in hand. Many persons talk of admitting working people to a share in the products and profits; but in their minds this participation is pure benevolence: they have never shown—perhaps never suspected—that it was a natural, necessary right, inherent in labor, and inseparable from the function of producer, even in the lowest forms of his work.

This is my proposition: *The laborer retains, even after he has received his wages, a natural right of property in the thing which he has produced.* . . .

The labor of the workers has created a value; now this value is their property. But they have neither sold nor exchanged it; and you, capitalist, you have not earned it. That you should have a partial right to the whole, in return for the materials that you have furnished and the provisions that you have supplied is perfectly just. You contributed to the productions, you ought to share in the enjoyment. But your right does not annihilate that of the laborers, who, in spite of you, have been your colleagues in the work of production. Why do you talk of wages? The money with which you pay the wages of the laborers remunerates them for only a few years of the perpetual possession which they have abandoned to you. Wages is the cost of the daily maintenance and refreshment of the laborer. You are wrong in calling it the price of a sale. The workingman has sold nothing; he knows neither his right, nor the extent of the concession which he has made to you, nor the meaning of the contract which you pretend to have made with him. On his side, utter ignorance; on yours, error and surprise, not to say deceit and fraud. . . .

In this century of bourgeois morality, in which I have had the honor to be born, the moral sense is so debased that I should not be at all surprised if I were asked by many a worthy proprietor what I see in this that is unjust and illegitimate. Debased creature! galvanized corpse! how can I expect to convince you, if you cannot tell robbery when I show it to you? A man, by soft and insinuating words, discovers the secret of taxing others that he may establish himself; then, once enriched by their united efforts, he refuses, on the very conditions which he himself dictated, to advance the well-being of those who made his fortune for him: and you ask how such conduct is fraudulent! Under the pretext that he has paid his laborers, that he owes them nothing more, that he has nothing to gain by putting himself at the service of others, while his own occupations claim his attention, he refuses, I say, to aid others in getting a foothold, as he was aided in getting his own; and when, in the impotence of their isolation, these poor laborers are compelled to sell their birthright, he—this ungrateful proprietor, this knavish upstart—stands ready to put the finishing touch to their deprivation and ruin. And you think that just? Take care! I read in your startled countenance the reproach of a guilty conscience, much more clearly than the innocent astonishment of involuntary ignorance. . . .

FALLACIOUS METHODS OF ESTABLISHING EQUALITY

But, some half-converted proprietor will observe, "Would it not be possible, by suppressing the bank, incomes, farm rent, house rent, usury of all kinds, and finally property itself, to proportion products to capacities? That was Saint-Simon's idea; it was also Fourier's; it is the desire of the human conscience; and no decent person would dare maintain that a minister of state should live no better than a peasant."

O Midas! your ears are long! What! will you never understand that disparity of wages and the right of increase are one and the same? Certainly, Saint-Simon, Fourier, and their respective flocks committed a serious blunder in attempting to unite, the one, inequality and communism; the other, inequality and property: but you, a man of figures, a man of economy—you, who know by heart your logarithmic tables—how can you make so stupid a mistake? Does not political economy itself teach you that the product of a man, whatever be his individual capacity, is never worth more than his labor, and that a man's labor is worth no more than his consumption? . . .

Listen, proprietor. Inequality of talent exists in fact; in right it is inadmissible, it goes for nothing, it is not thought of. One Newton in a century is equal to 30 millions of men; the psychologist admires the rarity of so fine a genius, the legislator sees only the rarity of the function. Now, rarity of function bestows no privilege upon the functionary; and that for several reasons, all equally forcible.

1. Rarity of genius was not, in the Creator's design, a motive to compel society to go down on its knees before the man of superior talents, but a providential means for the performance of all functions to the greatest advantage of all.

2. Talent is a creation of society rather than a gift of Nature; it is an accumulated capital, of which the receiver is only the guardian. Without society—without the education and powerful assistance which it furnishes—the finest nature would be inferior to the most ordinary capacities in the very respect in which it ought to shine. The more extensive a man's knowledge, the more luxuriant his imagination, the more versatile his talent, the more costly has his education been, the more remarkable and numerous were his teachers and his models, and the greater is his debt. The farmer produces from the time that he leaves his cradle until he enters his grave: the fruits of art and science are late and scarce; frequently the tree dies before the fruit ripens. Society, in cultivating talent, makes a sacrifice to hope.

3. Capacities have no common standard of comparison: the conditions of development being equal, inequality of talent is simply speciality of talent.

4. Inequality of wages, like the right of increase, is economically impossible. Take the most favorable case, that where each laborer has furnished his maximum production; that there may be an equitable distribution of products, the share of each must be equal to the quotient of the total production divided by the number of laborers. This done, what remains wherewith to pay the higher wages? Nothing whatever.

Will it be said that all laborers should be taxed? But, then, their consumption will not be equal to their production, their wages will not pay for their productive service, they will not be able to purchase their product, and we shall once more be afflicted with the calamities of property. I do not speak of the injustice done to the defrauded laborer, of rivalry, of excited ambition, and burning hatred—these may all be important considerations, but they do not hit the point.

On the one hand, each laborer's task being short and easy, and the means for its successful accomplishment being equal in all cases, how could there be large and small producers? On the other hand, all functions being equal, either on account of the equivalence of talents and capacities, or on account of social cooperation, how could a functionary claim a salary proportional to the worth of his genius?

But, what do I say? In equality wages are always proportional to talents. What is the economical meaning of wages? The reproductive consumption of the laborer. The very act by which the laborer produces constitutes, then, this consumption, exactly equal to his production, of which we are speaking. When the astronomer produces observations, the poet verses, or the *savant* experiments, they consume instruments, books, travels, etc., etc.; now, if society supplies this consumption, what more can the astronomer, the *savant*, or the poet demand? We must conclude, then, that in equality, and only in equality, Saint-Simon's adage—*To each according to his capacity, to each capacity according to its results*—finds its full and complete application. . . .

Here my task should end. I have proved the right of the poor; I have shown the usurpation of the rich. I demand justice; it is not my business to execute the sentence. If it should be argued—in order to prolong for a few years an illegitimate privilege—that it is not enough to demonstrate equality, that it is necessary also to organize it, and above all to establish it peacefully, I might reply: The welfare of the oppressed is of more importance than official composure. Equality of conditions is a natural law upon which public economy and jurisprudence are based. The right to labor, and the principle of equal distribution of wealth, cannot give way to the anxieties of power. It is not for the proletarian to reconcile the contradictions of the codes, still less to suffer for the errors of the government. On the contrary, it is the duty of the civil and administrative power to reconstruct itself on the basis of political equality. An evil, when known, should be condemned and destroyed. The legislator cannot plead ignorance as an excuse for upholding a glaring iniquity. Restitution should not be delayed. Justice, justice! recognition of right! Reinstatement of the proletarian!—when these results are accomplished, then, judges and consuls, you may attend to your police, and provide a government for the Republic! . . .

6 SEX AND LIBERATION

THE ETHICS CLASS is according sex the same spirited debate with which it has greeted all topics relating to morality. Terri is still struggling against sleep, Roger is still off meditating. Though in view of today's topic someone remarked that he finally knows what Roger is smiling about, it's business as usual in Professor Edwards's class.

Donna has often stopped to talk to Edwards after class, but this is the first time she is thoroughly involved in a class discussion. She has been referring back to the abortion issue and is putting it in a new context.

"What I mean is that the abortion question is handled in sexist terms. The laws, and even our discussions here, have a sexist tone. Abortion seems to be viewed mainly from the male perspective," Donna concludes.

"If I am understanding all that you have said, you seem to be suggesting that a woman, or anyone for that matter, could read prohibitions against abortions as prejudicial to women—another attempt to dehumanize women, as I think you put it. Am I right?" asks Edwards.

"Yes. And I'd like to add something. I think our whole society distorts the nature of sex. And I think men end up no better in it than women. I mean, if our society creates myths and stereotypes of women, it does the same thing to men, either directly or indirectly. I used to read *Playboy,* mainly because my parents didn't want me to. And I used to think that those girls in the centerfold were what I wanted to be. Then I got involved in a women's rights group and I realized that if the *Playboy* ideal was what a woman is supposed to be, I wanted no part of it."

"What are you complaining about, Donna?" asks Brock. "Now you've got *Playgirl,* complete with male fold-outs, to look at."

"Brock, you really are a pompous male chauvinistic ass! Can't you see you're making my point? Both magazines set up stupid cardboard models of what is supposed to be feminine and masculine, and neither show a true picture of real people."

James, who can't seem to say anything without mentioning his army tour of duty in the Far East, says, "Maybe I'm what Donna calls a male chauvinistic ass, but I don't think much of women who send 'Dear John' letters to their guys while they are overseas. A lot of those girls were fooling around at home while the guys were off serving their country, and I think that this whole women's lib business is partly to blame."

"What about your buddies?" asks Edwards. "Didn't they do any fooling around?"

"Sure, they saw a little action," James admits.

"But they expected their wives or girlfriends to remain faithful to them and to the old double standard?" Edwards asks.

"Call it what you like, my buddies never wrote their girls about what they were doing, as far as I know," James replies.

Donna's friend, Reeny, asks, "Are you saying that as long as the girls didn't know what their guys were doing it was OK, but if the girls came up front and admitted what they were doing, it was wrong?"

"Well, not exactly," says James uncomfortably. "But when it comes to sex, men and women are different."

"That's for *sure,*" says Donna warmly. The class applauds and someone yells "Vive la difference!" in a terrible accent.

"I mean besides that. Their needs are different. Women can get by without things that men can't get by without, if you know what I mean," says James.

"I'm afraid I do," says Donna. "Hey man! I think, and I hope, you're a member of an endangered species. I didn't know that there were any young sexual bigots still running loose."

Bob, knowing that he is heading for trouble too, says, "God created Adam first and then Eve as Adam's helpmate. That's the way it is, and women's lib can't change the fact that man is first."

"God simply decided to turn out a better model after seeing the mistakes he made when he created Adam," snaps Reeny. "For once, can't we talk about something without dragging in the Bible?"

"Look, this is supposed to be an ethics class. Can't we talk about sexual morality?" asks Linda.

"Fine, I need all the help I can get to focus these discussions," says Edwards. "What did you have in mind?"

"Well, certainly one common moral issue is that of premarital sex. Many people still believe that sex before marriage is immoral. And by marriage they mean a legal contract," answers Linda.

"Premarital sex is wrong!" declares Cloteal. Bob murmurs agreement.

"Why?" asks Cheri.

"Do you think it's better to be a frustrated virgin?" asks Jeff.

"Morally, yes!" states Cloteal. "Anyway, I am certainly one and not the other."

The class never learns which is which in Cloteal's case because Linda breaks in saying, "I think virginity is overrated." She continues over scattered applause, "I'm not saying that one ought to sleep around just for kicks. But I can see there are a lot of reasons why, at least in some cases, it's not so wrong to have sex with someone before marriage. In fact, in some cases I even think it might be wrong *not* to have sex before marriage. People who are hung up on Victorian ideas about sex and who think that a piece of paper from the county clerk's office is a necessary license to practice sex get some awful rude shocks when they get married."

"Yes, but either way there's as much problem with sex in marriage as there is with sex before or outside marriage," Donna adds. "How can a piece of paper make a relationship good? And how can the lack of a piece of paper make sex wrong if the relationship between two people is good?"

"For some people, perhaps for all of us, Donna, there are times when we are unable to separate the cultural aspects of an issue from the moral aspects. We do still have a certain definite cultural bias in favor of marriage. But it's a little late in the class to start that discussion. Can we return to the models of men and women that somebody mentioned? Reeny?" Edwards smiles at Reeny's intent bid for attention.

"There's this guy who teaches my psych class and admits he's some kind of a freak on Freud. We were talking after class, and he made it sound like I was less than human because I wasn't a male. He says that women ought to become adjusted to what he calls our physiological and psychological realities. He doesn't actually come out and say that we are inferior and ought to be home making babies and meals, but he sure means that. I pity the poor woman he's married to."

"Your pity may be misplaced," notes Edwards. "There are some women who prefer a male-dominated society and actually contribute to sexist biases." Edwards holds up his palm against the many hands raised in the class. "I'm not taking a position, I'm merely stating that such women exist and suggesting that men are not the only ones responsible for sexism. Yes, Bob?"

"Well I wanted to ask Reeny. If she has trouble with traditional sexual morality and with the traditional pictures of the male and female that are implied in such a morality, what does she want to replace them with?"

"Reeny?"

"I'm not sure I can answer the question concerning how I would change traditional sexual morality, because to do that I would have to have some idea of what it is to be male and female in essence. I'm not even sure there is such a thing as female essence or male essence. When we talk about differences and similarities between men and women, I think we are talking about surface things, not the essences of each."

"But if you don't know what the essence of sexual differences are—in your case, what it means to be female in essence—it doesn't seem like you can have any sexual identity. And if that's true, how can you have any personal moral standards about sex?" asks Bob.

"Because my standards are not dependent on my being female; they are dependent on my being Reeny. I'm not denying or ignoring the fact that I am female, but morality is personal, not sexual," Reeny declares, and then adds, "But personal morality does include sexual morality. Does that make any sense?"

For some of the class it does make sense, for a great many it doesn't. The following discussion gets so animated that Edwards has to kick the students out to clear the room for another class.

FOR FURTHER READING

Atkinson, Ronald. *Sexual Morality.* New York: Harcourt, Brace & World, 1965. This book covers a number of topics related to sex and morality, offering the reader some good insights into the arguments for various positions regarding sexual morality.

Brown, Norman O. *Life against Death: The Psychoanalytical Meaning of History.* New York: Modern Library, 1959. A view of history from a psychoanalytic perspective. It is somewhat technical, but offers extensive explanatory notes and a good bibliography.

Committee on Homosexual Offenses and Prostitution. *The Wolfenden Report.* New York: Stein and Day, 1963. This famous report concerning the legal aspects of homosexuality and prostitution was presented to the British Parliament in 1957. Its recommendations created controversy in Great Britain and, later, in the United States—a controversy that is still raging.

Dixon, Marlene. "Why Women's Liberation—2?" *Ramparts* (December 1968): 56-63. Written by a strong supporter of women's liberation, this article criticizes certain aspects of the movement. The author writes from what might be called a Marxist perspective.

Fletcher, Joseph. *Moral Responsibility: Situation Ethics at Work.* Philadelphia: Westminster, 1967. Fletcher applies the "situation ethics" approach to a number of ethical issues including problems of sexual morality.

Friedan, Betty. *The Feminine Mystique.* New York: Dell, 1963. One of the classics of the women's liberation literature and an essential reading for anyone interested in this movement, combining a scholarly approach with a delightful writing style.

Fromm, Erich. *The Art of Loving: An Enquiry into the Nature of Love.* New York: Harper & Row, 1956. This small, highly readable book cannot be recommended highly enough. Fromm, who terms himself a "non-theist mystic," writes with great compassion and insight.

Gornick, Vivian, and Moran, Barbara, eds. *Women in Sexist Society.* New York: Mentor, 1971. An excellent anthology covering a wide range of subjects concerning the place—or lack of place—of women in the world.

Greer, Germaine. *The Female Eunuch.* New York: Bantam, 1972. This humorous, yet very moving book, should be considered essential reading for those interested in the women's liberation movement.

Marcuse, Herbert. *Eros and Civilization: A Philosophical Inquiry into Freud.* New York: Vintage, 1955. A critical and philosophical view of Freud's teachings, which strongly influenced the author's thinking, by one of the most famous spokesmen of the New Left.

May, Rollo. *Love and Will.* New York: Norton, 1969. Based on his experiences as a psychotherapist and his study of modern culture, the author discusses the phenomenon of alienation and how to come to grips with it through a more profound understanding of love and will and their interrelationships.

Mill, John Stuart. *Essay on Liberty.* Available in numerous editions. Written in 1859, this famous work remains a classic, though the views it expresses have come under increasing criticism.

Morgan, Robin, ed. *Sisterhood Is Powerful: An Anthology of Writings from the Women's Liberation Movement.* New York: Random House, 1970. A wide range of essays, poems, and other material relating to women's liberation. Besides offering interesting reading, the anthology provides a very useful bibliography.

Morrison, Eleanor S., and Borosage, Vera, eds., *Human Sexuality: Contemporary Perspectives.* Palo Alto, Ca.: Mayfield Publishing, formerly National Press Books, 1973. An anthology covering a variety of topics including homosexuality, pornography, abortion, and heterosexuality. The editors deliberately chose several articles containing polemical arguments that offer controversial and provocative reading.

Nagel, Thomas. "Sexual Perversion." *Journal of Philosophy* 66 (1969): 5-17. An excellent article offering a phenomenological analysis of sexual relationships. Though, from a phenomenological perspective, the author adjudges certain sexual relationships as being perversions, he does not contend that they are necessarily immoral.

Reich, Wilhelm. *Selected Writings.* New York: Noonday, 1961. Reich, who was imprisoned for violating certain federal statutes in his work, has remained a controversial figure in psychology. Recently his works have received a renewed popularity. This collection includes a biography and a bibliography.

Van Kaam, Adrian. "Sex and Existence." *Review of Existential Psychology and Psychiatry* 3 (1963). An essay that draws upon the teachings of Freud and Merleau-Ponty, the French philosopher. Although the subject matter is difficult, it is an excellently written article that does not presuppose extensive knowledge of the background literature.

Watts, Alan. *Nature, Man, and Woman.* New York: Pantheon, 1958. A discussion of the basic viewpoints of Eastern and Western philosophies as they relate to male/female relationships by a well-known and widely read critic of Western thought and a champion of Eastern thought.

Wilson, John. *Logic and Sexual Morality.* Baltimore: Penguin Books, 1965. Author of several books on morality, Wilson discusses some of the more contemporary issues surrounding the subject of sexual morality.

Harvey Cox
PLAYBOY'S DOCTRINE OF MALE

> Harvey Cox, "one of the nation's most radical and respected young Christian thinkers," according to *Time* magazine, is a former Associate Professor of Church and Society at the Harvard Divinity School. His major works are *The Secular City* and *The Sacred Canopy*. In the following selection Cox describes the *Playboy* magazine approach to sex as "the latest and slickest episode in man's continuing refusal to be fully human." Cox sees *Playboy* defining the successful male as a detached and skillful manipulator of commodities and females as one such commodity. He notes that in such a context, the power and passion of sex is reduced to a packageable and disposable consumer item—a process that dehumanizes both men and women. Reprinted from the April 17, 1961 issue of *Christianity and Crisis*, copyright © 1961 by Christianity and Crisis, Inc.

Sometime this month over one million American young men will place sixty cents on a counter somewhere and walk away with a copy of *Playboy*, one of the most spectacular successes in the entire history of American journalism. When one remembers that every copy will probably be seen by several other people in college dormitories and suburban rumpus rooms, the total readership in any one month easily exceeds that of all the independent religious magazines, serious political and cultural journals, and literary periodicals put together.

What accounts for this uncanny reception? What factors in American life have combined to allow *Playboy*'s ambitious young publisher, Hugh Hefner, to pyramid his jackpot into a chain of night clubs, TV spectaculars, bachelor tours to Europe and special discount cards? What impact does *Playboy* really have?

Clearly *Playboy*'s astonishing popularity is not attributable solely to pin-up girls. For sheer nudity its pictorial art cannot compete with such would-be competitors as *Dude* and *Escapade*. Rather, *Playboy* appeals to a highly mobile, increasingly affluent group of young readers, mostly between eighteen and thirty, who want much more from their drugstore reading than bosoms and thighs. They need a total image of what it means to be a man. And Mr. Hefner's *Playboy* has no hesitancy about telling them.

Why should such a need arise? David Riesman has argued that the responsibility for character formation in our society has shifted from the family to the peer group and to the mass media peer group surrogates. Things are changing so rapidly that one who is equipped by his family with inflexible, highly internalized values becomes unable to deal with the accelerated pace of change and with the varying contexts in which he is called upon to function. This is especially true in the area of consumer values toward which the "other-directed person" is increasingly oriented.

A GUIDEBOOK TO IDENTITY

Within the confusing plethora of mass media signals and peer group values, *Playboy* fills a special need. For the insecure young man with newly acquired time and money on his hands who still feels uncertain about his consumer skills, *Playboy* supplies a comprehensive and authoritative guidebook to this foreboding new world to which he now has access. It tells him not only who to be; it tells him *how* to be it, and even provides consolation outlets for those who secretly feel that they have not quite made it.

In supplying for the other-directed consumer of leisure both the normative identity image and the means for achieving it, *Playboy* relies on a careful integration of copy and advertising material. The comic book that appeals to a younger generation with an analogous problem skillfully intersperses illustrations of incredibly muscled men and excessively mammalian women with advertisements for bodybuilding gimmicks and foam rubber brassiere supplements. Thus the thin-chested comic book readers of both sexes are thoughtfully supplied with both the ends and the means for attaining a spurious brand of maturity. *Playboy* merely continues the comic book tactic for the next age group. Since within every identity crisis, whether in 'teens or twenties, there is usually a sexual identity problem, *Playboy* speaks to those who desperately want to know what it means to be a *man*, and more specifically a *male*, in today's world.

Both the image of man and the means for its attainment exhibit a remarkable consistency in *Playboy*. The skilled consumer is cool and unruffled. He savors sports cars, liquor, high fidelity and book club selections with a casual, unhurried aplomb. Though he must certainly *have* and *use* the latest consumption item, he must not permit himself to get too attached to it. The style will change and he must always be ready to adjust. His persistent anxiety that he may mix a drink incorrectly, enjoy a jazz group that is passé, or wear last year's necktie style is comforted by an authoritative tone in *Playboy* beside which papal encyclicals sound irresolute.

"Don't hesitate," he is told, "this assertive, self-assured weskit is what every man of taste wants for the fall season." Lingering doubts about his masculinity are extirpated by the firm assurance that "real men demand this ruggedly masculine smoke" (cigar ad). Though "the ladies will swoon for you, no matter what they promise, don't give them a puff. This cigar is for men only." A fur-lined canvas field jacket is described as "the most masculine thing since the cave man." What to be and how to be it are both made unambiguously clear.

But since being a male necessitates some kind of relationship to females, *Playboy* fearlessly confronts this problem too, and solves it by the consistent application of the same formula. Sex becomes one of the items of leisure activity that the knowledgeable consumer of leisure handles with his characteristic skill and detachment. The girl becomes a desirable, indeed an indispensable "Playboy accessory."

RECREATIONAL SEX

In a question-answering column entitled "The Playboy Advisor," queries about smoking equipment (how to break in a meerschaum pipe), cocktail preparation (how to mix a "Yellow Fever") and whether or not to wear suspenders with a vest, alternate with questions about what to do with girls who complicate the cardinal principle of casualness, either by suggesting marriage or by some other impulsive gesture toward permanent relationship. The infallible answer from the oracle never varies: sex must be contained, at all costs, within the entertainment-recreation area. Don't let her get "serious."

After all, the most famous feature of the magazine is its monthly fold-out photo of a *play*mate. She is the symbol par excellence of recreational sex. When play time is over, the playmate's function ceases, so she must be made to understand the rules of the game. As the crew-cut young man in a *Playboy* cartoon says to the rumpled and disarrayed girl he is passionately embracing, "Why speak of love at a time like this?"

The magazine's fiction purveys the same kind of severely departmentalized sex. Although the editors have recently dressed up the contents of *Playboy* with contributions by Hemingway, Bemelmans and even a Chekhov translation, the regular run of stories relies on a repetitious and predictable formula. A successful young man, either single or somewhat less than ideally married—a figure with whom readers have no difficulty identifying—encounters a gorgeous and seductive woman who makes no demands on him except sex. She is the prose duplication of the cool-eyed but hot-blooded playmate of the fold-out page.

DON'T GET INVOLVED!

Drawing heavily on the fantasy life of all young Americans, the writers utilize for their stereotyped heroines the hero's school teacher, his secretary, an old girl friend, or the girl who brings her car into the garage where he works. The happy issue is always a casual but satisfying sexual experience with no entangling alliances whatever. Unlike the women he knows in real life, the *Playboy* reader's fictional girl friends know their place and ask for nothing more. They present no danger of permanent involvement. Like any good accessory, they are detachable and disposable.

Many of the advertisements reinforce the sex-accessory identification in another way by attributing female characteristics to the items they sell. Thus a full page for the MG assures us that this car is not only "the smoothest pleasure machine" on the road and that having one is a "love-affair," but most importantly, "You drive it—it doesn't drive you." The ad ends with the equivocal question, "Is it a date?"

Playboy insists that its message is one of liberation. Its gospel frees us from captivity to the puritanical "hat-pin brigade." It solemnly crusades for "frankness" and publishes scores of letters congratulating it for its unblushing "candor." Yet the whole phenomenon of which *Playboy* is only a part vividly illustrates the awful fact of a new kind of tyranny.

Those liberated by technology and increased prosperity to new worlds of leisure now become the anxious slaves of dictatorial tastemakers. Obsequiously waiting for the latest signal on what is cool and what is awkward, they are paralyzed by the fear that they may hear pronounced on them that dread sentence occasionally intoned by "The Playboy Advisor": "you goofed!" Leisure is thus swallowed up in apprehensive competitiveness, its liberating potential transformed into a self-destructive compulsion to consume only what is *au courant*. *Playboy* mediates the Word of the most high into one section of the consumer world, but it is a word of bondage, not of freedom.

Nor will *Playboy's* synthetic doctrine of man stand the test of scrutiny. Psychoanalysts constantly remind us how deeply seated sexuality is in the human self. But if they didn't remind us, we would soon discover it anyway in our own experience. As much as the human male might like to terminate his relationship with a woman as he snaps off the stereo, or store her for special purposes like a camel's hair jacket, it really can't be done. And anyone with a modicum of experience with women knows it can't be done. Perhaps this is the reason why *Playboy's* readership drops off so sharply after the age of thirty.

Playboy really feeds on the presence of a repressed fear of involvement with women, which for various reasons is still present in many otherwise adult Americans. So *Playboy's* version of sexuality grows increasingly irrelevant as authentic sexual maturity is achieved.

A FUTILE DOCTRINE

The male identity crisis to which *Playboy* speaks has at its roots a deep-set fear of sex, a fear that is uncomfortably combined with fascination. *Playboy* strives to resolve this antinomy by reducing the terrible proportions of sexuality, its power and its passion, to a packageable consumption item. Thus in *Playboy's* iconography, the nude woman symbolizes total sexual accessibility, but demands nothing from the observer. "You drive it—it doesn't drive you." The terror of sex, which cannot be separated from its ecstasy, is dissolved. But this futile attempt fails to reduce the *mysterium tremendum* of the sexual fails to solve the problem of being a man. For sexuality is the basic form of all human relationship, and therein lies its terror and its power.

Karl Barth has called this basic relational form of man's life *Mitmensch*, co-humanity. This means that becoming fully human, in this case a human male, necessitates not having the other totally exposed to me and my purposes—while I remain uncommitted—but exposing myself to the risk of encounter with the other by reciprocal self-exposure. The story of man's refusal to be so exposed goes back to the story of Eden and is expressed by man's desire to control the other rather than to *be with* the other. It is basically the fear to be one's self, a lack of the "courage to be."

Thus any theological critique of *Playboy* that focuses on its "lewdness" will misfire completely. *Playboy* and its less successful imitators are not "sex magazines" at all. They are basically antisexual. They dilute and dissipate authentic sexuality by reducing it to an accessory, by keeping it at a safe distance.

It is precisely because these magazines are antisexual that they deserve the most searching kind of theological criticism. They foster a heretical doctrine of man, one at radical variance with the biblical view. For *Playboy's* man, others—especially women—are *for* him. They are his leisure accessories, his playthings. For the Bible, man only becomes fully man by being *for* the other.

Moralistic criticisms of *Playboy* fail because its antimoralism is one of the few places in which *Playboy* is right. But if Christians bear the name of One who was truly man because he was totally *for* the other, and if it is in him that we know who God is and what human life is for, then we must see in *Playboy* the latest and slickest episode in man's continuing refusal to be fully human.

MARRIAGE AND MORALS

Bertrand Russell, philosopher, mathematician, and essayist, was born on May 18, 1872 in Trelleck, England and died on February 2, 1970. Winner of the 1950 Nobel Prize in Literature, he received worldwide recognition for his writings in mathematics, philosophy, psychology, morals, and social reform. Among his better-known works is *Marriage and Morals* (1929) from which the following selection is taken. In the first part, Russell discusses sex in terms of the custom of marriage and the concept of love. Noting the importance of love in a sexual relationship, Russell cautions that "love is an anarchic force which, if left free, will not remain within any bounds set by laws or customs." In the second part, he investigates the dangers of repressive sexual education and discusses the effect of sex and sexual morals on the well-being of the individual. In the last part, Russell places sex in context with other human values, such as the acquisition of power, calling sex "a natural human need like food and drink." Though *Marriage and Morals* was written approximately half a century ago, many of Russell's views are highly relevant to today's societies. Selections reprinted from *Marriage and Morals* by Bertrand Russell, with the permission of the publisher, Liveright Publishing Corporation. Copyright, 1929, by Horace Liveright, Inc. Copyright renewed © 1957, by Bertrand Russell.

MARRIAGE

In this [section] I propose to discuss marriage without reference to children, merely as a relation between men and women. Marriage differs, of course, from other sex relations by the fact that it is a legal institution. It is also in most communities a religious institution, but it is the legal aspect which is essential. The legal institution merely embodies a practice which exists not only among primitive men but among apes and various other animals. Animals practice what is virtually marriage, wherever the cooperation of the male is necessary to the rearing of the young. As a rule, animal marriages are monogamic, and according to some authorities this is the case in particular amongst the anthropoid apes. It seems, if these authorities are to be believed, that these fortunate animals are not faced with the problems that beset human communities, since the male, once married, ceases to be attracted to any other female, and the female, once married, ceases to be attractive to any other male. Among the anthropoid apes, therefore, although they do not have the assistance of religion, sin is unknown, since instinct suffices to produce virtue. There is some evidence that among the lowest races of savages a similar state of affairs exists. Bushmen are said to be strictly monogamous, and I understand that the Tasmanians (now extinct) were invariably faithful to their wives. Even in civilized mankind faint traces of a monogamic instinct can sometimes be perceived. Considering the influence of habit over behavior, it is perhaps surprising that the hold of monogamy on instinct is not stronger than it is. This, however, is an example of the mental peculiarity of human beings, from which spring both their vices and their intelligence, namely the power of imagination to break up habits and initiate new lines of conduct.

It seems probable that what first broke up primitive monogamy was the intrusion of the economic motive. This motive, wherever it has any influence upon sexual behavior, is invariably disastrous, since it substitutes relations of slavery or purchase for relations based upon instinct. In early agricultural and pastoral communities both wives and children were an economic asset to a man. The wives worked for him, and the children, after the age of five or six, began to be useful in the fields or in tending beasts. Consequently the most powerful men aimed at having as many wives as possible. Polygamy can seldom be the general practice of a community, since there is not as a rule a great excess of females; it is the prerogative of chiefs and rich men. Numerous wives and children form a valuable property, and will therefore enhance the already privileged position of their owners. Thus the primary function of a wife comes to be that of a lucrative domestic animal, and her sexual function becomes subordinated. At this level of civilization it is as a rule easy for a man to divorce his wife, though he must in that case restore to her family any dowry that she may have brought. It is, however, in general impossible for a wife to divorce her husband.

The attitude of most semi-civilized communities towards adultery is of a piece with this outlook. At a very low level of civilization adultery is sometimes tolerated. The Samoans, we are told, when they have to go upon a journey, fully expect their wives to console themselves for their absence.* At a slightly higher level, however, adultery in women is punished with death or at best with very severe penalties. Mungo Park's account of Mumbo Jumbo used to be well known when I was young, but I have been pained in recent years to find highbrow Americans alluding to Mumbo Jumbo as a god of the Congo. He was in fact neither a god nor connected with the Congo. He was a pretense demon invented by the men of the upper Niger to terrify women who had sinned. Mungo Park's account of him so inevitably suggests a Voltairean view as to the origins of religion that it has tended to be discreetly suppressed by modern anthropologists, who cannot bear the intrusion of rational scoundrelism into the doings of savages. A man who had intercourse with another man's wife was, of course, also a criminal, but a man who had intercourse with an unmarried woman did not incur any blame unless he diminished her value in the marriage market.

---

*Margaret Mead, *Coming of Age in Samoa*, 1928, p. 104 ff.

With the coming of Christianity this outlook was changed. The part of religion in marriage was very greatly augmented, and infractions of the marriage law came to be blamed on grounds of taboo rather than of property. To have intercourse with another man's wife remained, of course, an offense against that man, but to have intercourse outside marriage was an offense against God, and this, in the view of the Church, was a far graver matter. For the same reason divorce, which had previously been granted to men on easy terms, was declared inadmissible. Marriage became a sacrament and therefore lifelong.

Was this a gain or a loss to human happiness? It is very hard to say. Among peasants the life of married women has always been a very hard one, on the whole it has been hardest among the least civilized peasants. Among most barbarous peoples a woman is old at twenty-five, and cannot hope at that age to retain any traces of beauty. The view of woman as a domestic animal was no doubt very pleasant for men, but for women it meant a life of nothing but toil and hardship. Christianity, while in some ways it made the position of women worse, especially in the well-to-do classes, did at least recognize their theological equality with men, and refused to regard them as absolutely the property of their husbands. A married woman had not, of course, the right to leave her husband for another man, but she could leave him for a life of religion. And on the whole progress towards a better status for women was easier, in the great bulk of the population, from the Christian than from the pre-Christian standpoint.

When we look round the world at the present day and ask ourselves what conditions seem on the whole to make for happiness in marriage and what for unhappiness, we are driven to a somewhat curious conclusion, that the more civilized people become the less capable they seem of lifelong happiness with one partner. Irish peasants, although until recent times marriages were decided by the parents, were said by those who ought to know them to be on the whole happy and virtuous in their conjugal life. In general, marriage is easiest where people are least differentiated. When a man differs little from other men, and a woman differs little from other women, there is no particular reason to regret not having married someone else. But people with multifarious tastes and pursuits and interests will tend to desire congeniality in their partners, and to feel dissatisfied when they find that they have secured less of it than they might have obtained. The Church, which tends to view marriage solely from the point of view of sex, sees no reason why one partner should not do just as well as another, and can therefore uphold the indissolubility of marriage without realizing the hardship that this often involves.

Another condition which makes for happiness in marriage is paucity of unowned women and absence of social occasions when husbands meet other women. If there is no possibility of sexual relations with any woman other than one's wife, most men will make the best of the situation and, except in abnormally bad cases, will find it quite tolerable. The same thing applies to wives, especially if they never imagine that marriage should bring much happiness. That is to say, a marriage is likely to be what is called happy if neither party ever expected to get much happiness out of it.

Fixity of social custom, for the same reason, tends to prevent what are called unhappy marriages. If the bonds of marriage are recognized as final and irrevocable, there is no stimulus to the imagination to wander outside and consider that a more ecstatic happiness might have been possible. In order to secure domestic peace where this state of mind exists, it is only necessary that neither the husband nor the wife should fall outrageously below the commonly recognized standard of decent behavior, whatever this may be.

Among civilized people in the modern world none of these conditions for what is called happiness exist, and accordingly one finds that very few marriages after the first few years are happy. Some of the causes of unhappiness are bound up with civilization, but others would disappear if men and women were more civilized than they are. Let us begin with the latter. Of these the most important is bad sexual education, which is a far commoner thing among the well-to-do than it can ever be among peasants. Peasant children early become accustomed to what are called the facts of life, which they can observe not only among human beings but among animals. They are thus saved from both ignorance and fastidiousness. The carefully educated children of the well-to-do, on the contrary, are shielded from all practical knowledge of sexual matters, and even the most modern parents, who teach children out of books, do not give them that sense of practical familiarity which the peasant child early acquires. The triumph of Christian teaching is when a man and woman marry without either having had previous sexual experience. In nine cases out of ten where this occurs, the results are unfortunate. Sexual behavior among human beings is not instinctive, so that the inexperienced bride and bridegroom, who are probably quite unaware of this fact, find themselves overwhelmed with shame and discomfort. It is little better when the woman alone is innocent but the man has acquired his knowledge from prostitutes. Most men do not realize that a process of wooing is necessary after marriage, and many well-brought-up women do not realize what harm they do to marriage by remaining reserved and physically aloof. All this could be put right by better sexual education, and is in fact very much better with the generation now young than it was with their parents and grandparents. There used to be a widespread belief among women that they were morally superior to men on the ground that they had less pleasure in sex. This attitude made frank companionship between husbands and wives impossible. It was, of course, in itself quite unjustifiable, since failure to enjoy sex, so far from being virtuous, is a mere physiological or psychological deficiency, like a failure to enjoy food, which also a hundred years ago was expected of elegant females.

Other modern causes of unhappiness in marriage are, however, not so easily disposed of. I think that uninhibited civilized people, whether men or women, are generally polygamous in their instincts. They may fall deeply in love and be for some years entirely absorbed in one person, but sooner or later sexual familiarity dulls the edge of passion, and then they begin to look elsewhere for a revival of the old thrill. It is, of course, possible to control this impulse in the interests of morality, but it is very difficult to prevent the impulse from existing. With the growth of women's freedom there has come a much greater opportunity for conjugal infidelity than existed in former times. The opportunity gives rise to the thought, the thought gives rise to the desire, and in the absence of religious scruples the desire gives rise to the act.

Women's emancipation has in various ways made marriage more difficult. In old days the wife had to adapt herself to the husband, but the husband did not have to adapt himself to the wife. Nowadays many wives, on grounds of woman's right to her own individuality and her own career, are unwilling to adapt themselves to their husbands beyond a point, while men who still hanker after the old tradition of masculine domination see no reason why they should do all the adapting. This trouble arises especially in connection with infidelity. In old days the husband was occasionally unfaithful, but as a rule his wife did not know of it. If she did, he confessed that he had sinned and made her believe that he was penitent. She, on the other hand, was usually virtuous. If she was not, and the fact came to her husband's knowledge, the marriage broke up. Where, as happens in many modern marriages, mutual faithfulness is demanded, the instinct of jealousy nevertheless survives, and often proves fatal to the persistence of any deeply rooted intimacy even where no overt quarrels occur.

There is another difficulty in the way of modern marriage, which is felt especially by those who are most conscious of the value of love. Love can flourish only as long as it is free and spontaneous; it tends to be killed by the thought that it is a duty. To say that it is your duty to love so-and-so is the surest way to cause you to hate him or her. Marriage as a combination of love with legal bonds thus falls between two stools. Shelley says:

> I never was attached to that great sect
> Whose doctrine is, that each one should select
> Out of the crowd a mistress or a friend,
> And all the rest, though fair and wise, commend
> To cold oblivion, though it is in the code
> Of modern morals, and the beaten road
> Which those poor slaves with weary footsteps tread,
> Who travel to their home among the dead
> By the broad highway of the world, and so
> With one chained friend, perhaps a jealous foe,
> The dreariest and the longest journey go.

There can be no doubt that to close one's mind on marriage against all the approaches of love from elsewhere is to diminish receptivity and sympathy and the opportunities of valuable human contacts. It is to do violence to something which, from the most idealistic standpoint, is in itself desirable. And like every kind of restrictive morality it tends to promote what one may call a policeman's outlook upon the whole of human life—the outlook, that is to say, which is always looking for an opportunity to forbid something.

For all these reasons, many of which are bound up with things undoubtedly good, marriage has become difficult, and if it is not to be a barrier to happiness it must be conceived in a somewhat new way. One solution often suggested, and actually tried on a large scale in America, is easy divorce. I hold, of course, as every humane person must, that divorce should be granted on more grounds than are admitted in the English law, but I do not recognize in easy divorce a solution of the troubles of marriage. Where a marriage is childless, divorce may be often the right solution, even when both parties are doing their best to behave decently; but where there are children the stability of marriage is to my mind a matter of considerable importance. . . . I think that where a marriage is fruitful and both parties to it are reasonable and decent the expectation ought to be that it will be lifelong, but not that it will exclude other sex relations. A marriage which begins with passionate love and leads to children who are desired and loved ought to produce so deep a tie between a man and woman that they will feel something infinitely precious in their companionship, even after sexual passion has decayed, and even if either or both feels sexual passion for someone else. This mellowing of marriage has been prevented by jealousy, but jealousy, though it is an instinctive emotion, is one which can be controlled if it is recognized as bad, and not supposed to be the expression of a just moral indignation. A companionship which has lasted for many years and through many deeply felt events has a richness of content which cannot belong to the first days of love, however delightful these may be. And any person who appreciates what time can do to enhance values will not lightly throw away such companionship for the sake of new love.

It is therefore possible for a civilized man and woman to be happy in marriage, although if this is to be the case a number of conditions must be fulfilled. There must be a feeling of complete equality on both sides; there must be no interference with mutual freedom; there must be the most complete physical and mental intimacy; and there must be a certain similarity in regard to standards of values. (It is fatal, for example, if one values only money while the other values only good work.) Given all these conditions, I believe marriage to be the best and most important relation that can exist between two human beings. If it has not often been realized hitherto, that is chiefly because husband and wife have regarded themselves as each other's policeman. If marriage is to achieve its possibilities, husbands and wives must learn to understand that whatever the law may say, in their private lives they must be free.

SEX AND INDIVIDUAL WELL-BEING

In the present [section] I propose to [discuss] . . . the effects of sex and sexual morals upon individual happiness and well-being. In this matter we are not concerned only with the actively sexual period of life, nor with actual sex relations. Sexual morality affects childhood, adolescence, and even old age, in all kinds of ways, good or bad according to circumstances.

Conventional morality begins its operations by the imposition of taboos in childhood. A child is taught, at a very early age, not to touch certain parts of the body while grown-up people are looking. It is taught to speak in a whisper when expressing an excretory desire, and to preserve privacy in performing the resultant action. Certain parts of the body and certain acts have some peculiar quality not readily intelligible to the child, which invests them with mystery and a special interest. Certain intellectual problems, such as where babies come from, must be thought over in silence, since the answers given by grown-ups are either evasive or obviously untrue. I know men, by no means old, who, when in infancy they were seen touching a certain portion of their body, were told with the utmost solemnity: "I would rather see you dead than doing that." I regret to say that the effect in producing virtue in later life has not always been all that conventional moralists might desire. Not infrequently threats are used. It is perhaps not so common as it used to be to threaten a child with castration, but it is still thought quite proper to threaten him with insanity. Indeed, it is illegal in the State of New York to let him know that he does not run the risk unless he thinks he does. The result of this teaching is that most children in their earliest years have a profound sense of guilt and terror which is associated with sexual matters. This association of sex with guilt and fear goes so deep as to become almost or wholly unconscious. I wish it were possible to institute a statistical enquiry, among men who believe themselves emancipated from such nursery tales, as to whether they would be as ready to commit adultery during a thunder storm as at any other time. I believe that ninety percent of them, in their heart of hearts, would think that if they did so they would be struck by lightning.

Both sadism and masochism, although in their milder forms they are normal, are connected, in their pernicious manifestations, with the sense of sexual guilt. A masochist is a man acutely conscious of his own guilt in connection with sex. A sadist is a man more conscious of the guilt of the woman as temptress. These effects, in later life, show how profound has been the early impression produced by unduly severe moral teaching in childhood. On this matter, persons connected with the teaching of children, and especially with the care of the very young, are becoming more enlightened. But unfortunately enlightenment has not yet reached the law courts.

Childhood and youth form a period of life when pranks and naughtiness and performance of forbidden acts are natural, spontaneous and not regrettable except when carried too far. But infraction of sex prohibitions is treated by grown-up people quite differently from any other breach of rules, and is therefore felt by the child to belong to a quite different category. If a child steals fruit from the larder you may be annoyed, you may rate the child soundly, but you feel no moral horror, and you do not convey to the child the sense that something appalling has occurred. If, on the other hand, you are an old-fashioned person and you find him masturbating, there will be a tone in your voice which he will never hear in any other connection. This tone produces an abject terror, all the greater since the child probably finds it impossible to abstain from the behavior that has called forth your denunciation. The child, impressed by your earnestness, profoundly believes that masturbation is as wicked as you say it is. Nevertheless, he persists in it. Thus the foundations are laid for a morbidness which probably continues through life. From his earliest youth onward, he regards himself as a sinner. He soon learns to sin in secret, and to find a half-hearted consolation in the fact that no one knows of his sin. Being profoundly unhappy, he seeks to avenge himself on the world by punishing those who have been less successful than himself in concealing a similar guilt. Being accustomed to deceit as a child, he finds no difficulty in practicing it in later life. Thus he becomes a morbidly introverted hypocrite and persecutor as a result of his parents' ill-judged attempt to make him what they consider virtuous.

It is not guilt and shame and fear that should dominate the lives of children. Children should be happy and gay and spontaneous; they should not dread their own impulses; they should not shrink from the exploration of natural facts. They should not hide away in the darkness all their instinctive life. They should not bury in the depths of the unconscious impulses which, even with their utmost endeavors, they cannot kill. If they are to grow into upright men and women, intellectually honest, socially fearless, vigorous in action and tolerant in thought, we must begin from the very beginning to train them so that these results may be possible. Education has been conceived too much on the analogy of the training of dancing bears. Every one knows how dancing bears are trained. They are put on a hot floor, which compels them to dance because their toes are burnt if they remain in contact with it. While this is done, a certain tune is played to them. After a time the tune suffices to make them dance, without the hot floor. So it is with children. While a child is conscious of his sexual organ, grown-ups scold him. In the end, such consciousness brings up a thought of their scolding and makes him dance to their tune, to the complete destruction of all possibility of a healthy or happy sexual life.

In the next stage, that of adolescence, the misery caused by the conventional handling of sex is even greater than in childhood. Many boys do not know at all accurately what is happening to them, and are terrified when they first experience nocturnal emissions. They find themselves filled with impulses which they have been taught to consider extremely wicked. These impulses are so strong as to be an obsession, day and night. In the better sort of boy, there are at the same time impulses of the most extreme idealism towards beauty and poetry, and towards ideal love, which is thought of as wholly divorced from sex. Owing to the Manichaean elements in Christian teaching, the idealistic and the carnal impulses of adolescence are apt, among ourselves, to remain wholly dissociated, and even at war one with the other. On this point I may quote the confession of an intellectual friend, who says: "My own adolescence was, I believe, not untypical, and it exhibited this dissociation in a very marked form. For hours in the day I would read Shelley and sentimentalize over

> The desire of the moth for the star,
> Of the night for the morrow.

Then suddenly I would leave these heights and try to catch a surreptitious glimpse of the housemaid undressing. The latter impulse caused me profound shame; the former had, of course, an element of silliness, since its idealism was the obverse of a foolish fear of sex."

Adolescence, as everyone knows, is a time when nervous disorders are very frequent, and when persons who at all other times are well-balanced may easily be quite the reverse. Miss Mead, in her book called *Coming of Age in Samoa*, asserts that adolescent disorders are unknown in that island, and she attributes this fact to the prevalent sexual freedom. This sexual freedom, it is true, is being somewhat curtailed by missionary activity. Some of the girls whom she questioned lived in the missionary's house, and these, during adolescence, practiced only masturbation and homosexuality, whilst those who lived elsewhere engaged also in heterosexual practices. Our most famous boys' schools are not altogether so very different in this respect from the house of the Samoan missionary, but the psychological effect of behavior which, in Samoa, is harmless, may in an English schoolboy be disastrous, because he probably respects in his heart the conventional teaching, whereas the Samoan regards the missionary merely as a white man with peculiar tastes that have to be humored.

Most young men, in their early adult years, go through troubles and difficulties of a quite unnecessary kind in regard to sex. If a young man remains chaste, the difficulty of control probably causes him to become timid and inhibited, so that when he finally marries he cannot break down the self-control of past years, except perhaps in a brutal and sudden manner, which leads him to fail his wife in the capacity of a lover. If he goes with prostitutes, the dissociation between the physical and the idealistic aspects of love which has begun in adolescence is perpetuated, with the result that his relations with women ever after have to be either platonic or, in his belief, degrading. Moreover, he runs a grave risk of venereal disease. If he has affairs with girls of his own class, much less harm is done, but even then the need of secrecy is harmful, and interferes with the development of stable relations. Owing partly to snobbery and partly to the belief that marriage ought immediately to lead to children, it is difficult for a man to marry young. Moreover, where divorce is very difficult, early marriage has great dangers, since two people who suit each other at twenty are quite likely not to suit each other at thirty. Stable relations with one partner are difficult for many people until they have had some experience of variety. If our outlook on sex were sane, we should expect university students to be temporarily married though childless. They would in this way be freed from the obsession of sex which at present greatly interferes with work. They would acquire that experience of the other sex which is desirable as a prelude to the serious partnership of a marriage with children. And they would be free to experience love without the concomitants of subterfuge, concealment, and dread of disease, which at present poison youthful adventures.

For the large class of women who, as things are, must remain permanently unmarried, conventional morality is painful and, in most cases, harmful. I have known, as we all have, unmarried women of strict conventional virtue who deserve the highest admiration from every possible point of view. But I think the general rule is otherwise. A woman who has had no experience of sex and has considered it important to preserve her virtue has been engaged in a negative reaction, tinged with fear, and has therefore, as a rule, become timid, while at the same time instinctive, unconscious jealousy has filled her with disapproval of normal people, and with a desire to punish those who have enjoyed what she has forgone. Intellectual timidity is an especially common concomitant of prolonged virginity. Indeed, I am inclined to think that the intellectual inferiority of women, in so far as it exists, is mainly due to the restraint upon curiosity which the fear of sex leads them to impose. There is no good reason for the unhappiness and waste involved in the lifelong virginity of those women who cannot find an exclusive husband. The present situation, in which this necessarily occurs very frequently, was not contemplated in the earlier days of the institution of marriage, since in those days the numbers of the sexes were approximately equal. Undoubtedly, the existence of a great excess of women in many countries affords a very serious argument in favor of modifications of the conventional moral code.

Marriage, the one conventionally tolerated outlet for sex, itself suffers from the rigidity of the code. The complexes acquired in childhood, the experiences of men with prostitutes, and the attitude of aversion from sex instilled into young ladies in order to preserve their virtue, all militate against happiness in marriage. A well-brought-up girl, if her sexual impulses are strong, will be unable to distinguish, when she is courted, between a serious congeniality with a man and a mere sex attraction. She may easily marry the first man who awakens her sexually, and find out too late that when her sexual hunger is satisfied she has no longer anything in common with him. Everything has been done in the education of the two to make her unduly timid and him unduly sudden in the sexual approach. Neither has the knowledge on sexual matters that each ought to have, and very often initial failures, due to this ignorance, make the marriage ever after sexually unsatisfying to both. Moreover, mental as well as physical companionship is rendered difficult. A woman is not accustomed to free speech on sexual matters. A man is not accustomed to it, except with men and prostitutes. In the most intimate and vital concern of their mutual life, they are shy, awkward, even wholly silent. The wife, perhaps, lies awake unsatisfied and hardly knowing what it is she wants. The man perhaps has the thought, at first fleeting and instantly banished, but gradually becoming more and more insistent, that even prostitutes are more generous in giving than his lawful wife. He is offended by her coldness, at the very moment, perhaps, that she is suffering because he does not know how to rouse her. All this misery results from our policy of silence and decency.

In all these ways, from childhood through adolescence and youth, and on into marriage, the older morality has been allowed to poison love, filling it with gloom, fear, mutual misunderstanding, remorse, and nervous strain, separating into two regions the bodily impulse of sex and the spiritual impulse of ideal love, making the one beastly and the other sterile. It is not so that life should be lived. The animal and the spiritual natures should not be at war. There is nothing in either that is incompatible with the other, and neither can reach its full fruition except in union with the other. The love of man and woman at its best is free and fearless, compounded of body and mind in equal proportions; not dreading to idealize because there is a physical basis, not dreading the physical basis lest it should interfere with the idealization. Love should be a tree whose roots are deep in the earth, but whose branches extend into heaven. But love cannot grow and flourish while it is hedged about with taboos and superstitious terrors, with words of reprobation and silences of horror. The love of man and woman and the love of parents and children are the two central facts in the emotional life of man. While degrading the one, conventional morality has pretended to exalt the other, but in fact the love of parents for children has suffered through the degradation of the love of parents for each other. Children who are the fruit of joy and mutual fulfilment can be loved in a way more healthy and robust, more in accordance with the ways of nature, more simple, direct, and animal, and yet more unselfish and fruitful, than is possible to parents starved, hungry, and eager, reaching out to the helpless young for some fragment of the nutriment that has been denied them in marriage, and in so doing, warping infant minds and laying the foundation of the same troubles for the next generation. To fear love is to fear life, and those who fear life are already three parts dead.

THE PLACE OF SEX AMONG HUMAN VALUES

The writer who deals with a sexual theme is always in danger of being accused, by those who think that such themes should not be mentioned, of an undue obsession with his subject. It is thought that he would not risk the censure of prudish and prurient persons unless his interest in the subject were out of all proportion to its importance. This view, however, is only taken in the case of those who advocate changes in the conventional ethic. Those who stimulate the appeals to harry prostitutes and those who secure legislation, nominally against the White Slave Traffic, but really against voluntary and decent extra-marital relations; those who denounce women for short skirts and lipsticks; and those who spy upon sea beaches in the hope of discovering inadequate bathing costumes, are none of them supposed to be the victims of a sexual obsession. Yet in fact they probably suffer much more in this way than do writers who advocate greater sexual freedom. Fierce morality is generally a reaction against lustful emotions, and the man who gives expression to it is generally filled with indecent thoughts—thoughts which are rendered indecent, not by the mere fact that they have a sexual content, but that morality has incapacitated the thinker from thinking cleanly and wholesomely on this topic. I am quite in agreement with the Church in thinking that obsession with sexual topics is an evil, but I am not in agreement with the Church as to the best methods of avoiding this evil. It is notorious that St. Anthony was more obsessed by sex than the most extreme voluptuary who ever lived; I will not adduce more recent examples for fear of giving offense. Sex is a natural need, like food and drink. We blame the gormandizer and the dipsomaniac because in the case of each an interest which has a certain legitimate place in life has usurped too large a share of his thoughts and emotions. But we do not blame a man for a normal and healthy enjoyment of a reasonable quantity of food. Ascetics, it is true, have done so, and have considered that a man should cut down his nutriment to the lowest point compatible with survival, but this view is not now common, and may be ignored. The Puritans, in their determination to avoid the pleasures of sex, became somewhat more conscious than people had been before of the pleasures of the table. A a seventeenth-century critic of Puritanism says:

Would you enjoy gay nights and pleasant dinners?
Then must you board with saints and bed with sinners.

It would seem, therefore, that the Puritans did not succeed in subduing the purely corporeal part of our human nature, since what they took away from sex they added to gluttony. Gluttony is regarded by the Catholic Church as one of the seven deadly sins, and those who practice it are placed by Dante in one of the deeper circles of hell, but it is a somewhat vague sin, since it is hard to say where a legitimate interest in food ceases, and guilt begins to be incurred. Is it wicked to eat anything that is not nourishing? If so, with every salted almond we risk damnation. Such views, however, are out of date. We all know a glutton when we see one, and although he may be somewhat despised, he is not severely reprobated. In spite of this fact, undue obsession with food is rare among those who have never suffered want. Most people eat their meals and then think about other things until the next meal. Those, on the other hand, who, having adopted an ascetic philosophy, have deprived themselves of all but the minimum of food, become obsessed by visions of banquets and dreams of demons bearing luscious fruits. And marooned Antarctic explorers, reduced to a diet of whale's blubber, spend their days planning the dinner they will have at the Carlton when they get home.

Such facts suggest that, if sex is not to be an obsession, it should be regarded by the moralists as food has come to be regarded, and not as food was regarded by the hermits of the Thebaid. Sex is a natural human need like food and drink. It is true that men can survive without it, whereas they cannot survive without food and drink, but from a psychological standpoint the desire for sex is precisely analogous to the desire for food and drink. It is enormously enhanced by abstinence, and temporarily allayed by satisfaction. While it is urgent, it shuts out the rest of the world from the mental purview. All other interests fade for the moment, and actions may be performed which will subsequently appear insane to the man who has been guilty of them. Moreover, as in the case of food and drink, the desire is enormously stimulated by prohibition. I have known children to refuse apples at breakfast and go straight out into the orchard and steal them, although the breakfast apples were ripe and the stolen apples unripe. I do not think it can be denied that the desire for alcohol among well-to-do Americans is much stronger than it was twenty years ago. In like manner, Christian teaching and Christian authority have immensely stimulated interest in sex. The generation which first ceases to believe in the conventional teaching is bound, therefore, to indulge in sexual freedom to a degree far beyond what is to be expected of those whose views on sex are unaffected by superstitious teaching, whether positively or negatively. Nothing but freedom will prevent undue obsession with sex, but even freedom will not have this effect unless it has become habitual and has been associated with a wise education as regards sexual matters. I wish to repeat, however, as emphatically as I can, that

I regard an undue preoccupation with this topic as an evil, and that I think this evil widespread at the present day, especially in America, where I find it particularly pronounced among the sterner moralists, who display it markedly by their readiness to believe falsehoods concerning those whom they regard as their opponents. The glutton, the voluptuary, and the ascetic are all self-absorbed persons whose horizon is limited by their own desires, either by way of satisfaction or by way of renunciation. A man who is healthy in mind and body will not have his interests thus concentrated upon himself. He will look out upon the world and find in it objects that seem to him worthy of his attention. Absorption in self is not, as some have supposed, the natural condition of unregenerate man. It is a disease brought on, almost always, by some thwarting of natural impulses. The voluptuary who gloats over thoughts of sexual gratification is in general the result of some kind of deprivation, just as the man who hoards food is usually a man who has lived through a famine or a period of destitution. Healthy, outward-looking men and women are not to be produced by the thwarting of natural impulse, but by the equal and balanced development of all the impulses essential to a happy life.

I am not suggesting that there should be no morality and no self-restraint in regard to sex, any more than in regard to food. In regard to food we have restraints of three kinds, those of law, those of manners, and those of health. We regard it as wrong to steal food, to take more than our share at a common meal, and to eat in ways that are likely to make us ill. Restraints of a similar kind are essential where sex is concerned, but in this case they are much more complex and involve much more self-control. Moreover, since one human being ought not to have property in another, the analogy of stealing is not adultery but rape, which obviously must be forbidden by law. The questions that arise in regard to health are concerned almost entirely with venereal disease, a subject which we have already touched upon in connection with prostitution. Clearly, the diminution of professional prostitution can be best effected by that greater freedom among young people which has been growing up in recent years.

A comprehensive sexual ethic cannot regard sex merely as a natural hunger and a possible source of danger. Both these points of view are important, but it is even more important to remember that sex is connected with some of the greatest goods in human life. The three that seem paramount are lyric love, happiness in marriage, and art. . . . Art is thought by some to be independent of sex, but this view has fewer adherents now than it had in former times. It is fairly clear that the impulse to every kind of aesthetic creation is psychologically connected with courtship, not necessarily in any direct or obvious way, but nonetheless profoundly. In order that the sexual impulse may lead to artistic expression, a number of conditions are necessary. There must be artistic capacity; but artistic capacity, even within a given race, appears as though it were common at one time and uncommon at another, from which it is safe to conclude that environment, as opposed to native capacity, has an important part to play in the development of the artistic impulse. There must be a certain kind of freedom, not the sort that consists in rewarding the artist, but the sort that consists in not compelling him or inducing him to form habits which turn him into a philistine. When Julius II imprisoned Michelangelo, he did not in any way interfere with that kind of freedom which the artist needs. He imprisoned him because he considered him an important man, and would not tolerate the slightest offense to him from anybody whose rank was less than papal. When, however, an artist is compelled to kowtow to rich patrons or town councillors, and to adapt his work to their aesthetic canons, his artistic freedom is lost. And when he is compelled by fear of social and economic persecution to go on living in a marriage which has become intolerable, he is deprived of the energy which artistic creation requires. Societies that have been conventionally virtuous have not produced great art. Those which have, have been composed of men such as Idaho would sterilize. America at present imports most of its artistic talent from Europe, where, as yet, freedom lingers, but already the Americanization of Europe is making it necessary to turn to the Negroes. The last home of art, it seems, is to be somewhere on the Upper Congo, if not in the uplands of Tibet. But its final extinction cannot be long delayed, since the rewards which America is prepared to lavish upon foreign artists are such as must inevitably bring about their artistic death. Art in the past has had a popular basis, and this has depended upon joy of life. Joy of life, in its turn, depends upon a certain spontaneity in regard to sex. Where sex is repressed, only work remains, and a gospel of work for work's sake never produced any work worth doing. Let me not be told that someone has collected statistics of the number of sexual acts *per diem* (or shall we say *per noctem?*) performed in the United States, and that it is at least as great per head as in any other country. I do not know whether this is the case or not, and I am not in any way concerned to deny it. One of the most dangerous fallacies of the conventional moralists is the reduction of sex to the sexual act, in order to be the better able to belabor it. No civilized man, and no savage that I have ever heard of, is satisfied in his instinct by the bare sexual act. If the impulse which leads to the act is to be satisfied, there must be courtship, there must be love, there must be companionship. Without these, while the physical hunger may be appeased for the moment, the mental hunger remains unabated, and no profound satisfaction can be obtained. The sexual freedom that the artist needs is freedom to love, not the gross freedom to relieve the bodily need with some unknown woman; and freedom to love is what, above all, the conventional moralists will not concede. If art is to revive after the world has been Americanized, it will be necessary that America should change, that its moralists should become less moral and its immoralists less immoral, that both, in a word, should recognize the higher values involved in sex, and the possibility that joy may be of more value than a bank account. Nothing in America is so painful to the traveller as the lack of joy. Pleasure is frantic and bacchanalian, a matter of momentary oblivion, not of delighted self-expression. Men whose grandfathers danced to the music of the pipe in Balkan or Polish villages sit throughout the day glued to their desks, amid typewriters and telephones, serious, important and worthless. Escaping in the evening to drink and a new kind of noise, they imagine that they are finding happiness, whereas they are finding only a frenzied and incomplete oblivion of the hopeless routine of money that breeds money, using for the purpose the bodies of human beings whose souls have been sold into slavery.

It is not my intention to suggest, what I by no means believe, that all that is best in human life is connected with sex. I do not myself regard science, either practical or theoretical, as connected with it, nor yet certain kinds of important social and political activities. The impulses that lead to the complex desires of adult life can be arranged under a few simple heads. Power, sex, and parenthood appear to me to be the source of most of the things that human beings do, apart from what is necessary for self-preservation. Of these three, power begins first and ends last. The child, since he has very little power, is dominated by the desire to have more. Indeed, a large proportion of his activities spring from this desire. His other dominant desire is vanity—the wish to be praised and the fear of being blamed or left out. It is vanity that makes him a social being and gives him the virtues necessary for life in a community. Vanity is a motive closely intertwined with sex, though in theory separable from it. But power has, so far as I can see, very little connection with sex, and it is love of power, at least as much as vanity, that makes a child work at his lessons and develop his muscles. Curiosity and the pursuit of knowledge should, I think, be regarded as a branch of the love of power. If knowledge is power, then the love of knowledge is the love of power. Science, therefore, except for certain branches of biology and physiology, must be regarded as lying outside the province of sexual emotions. As the Emperor Frederick II is no longer alive, this opinion must remain more or less hypothetical. If he were still alive, he would no doubt decide it by castrating an eminent mathematician and an eminent composer and observing the effects upon their respective labors. I should expect the former to be nil and the latter to be considerable. Seeing that the pursuit of knowledge is one of the most valuable elements in human nature, a very important sphere of activity is, if we are right, exempted from the domination of sex.

Power is also the motive to most political activity, understanding this word in its widest sense. I do not mean to suggest that a great statesman is indifferent to the public welfare; on the contrary, I believe him to be a man in whom parental feeling has become widely diffused. But unless he has also a considerable love of power he will fail to sustain the labors necessary for success in a political enterprise. I have known many highminded men in public affairs, but unless they had a considerable dose of personal ambition they seldom had the energy to accomplish the good at which they aimed. On a certain crucial occasion, Abraham Lincoln made a speech to two recalcitrant senators, beginning and ending with the words: "I am the President of the United States, clothed with great power." It can hardly be questioned that he found some pleasure in asserting this fact. Throughout all politics, both for good and for evil, the two chief forces are the economic motive and the love of power; an attempt to interpret politics on Freudian lines is, to my mind, a mistake.

If we are right in what we have been saying, most of the greatest men, other than artists, have been actuated in their important activities by motives unconnected with sex. If such activities are to persist and are, in their humbler forms, to become common, it is necessary that sex should not overshadow the remainder of a man's emotional and passionate nature. The desire to understand the world and the desire to reform it are the two great engines of progress, without which human society would stand still or retrogress. It may be that too complete a happiness would cause the impulses to knowledge and reform to fade. When Cobden wished to enlist John Bright in the free trade campaign, he based a personal appeal upon the sorrow that Bright was experiencing owing to his wife's recent death. It may be that without this sorrow Bright would have had less sympathy with the sorrows of others. And many a man has been driven to abstract pursuits by despair of the actual world. To a man of sufficient energy, pain may be a valuable stimulus, and I do not deny that if we were all perfectly happy we should not exert ourselves to become happier. But I cannot admit that it is any part of the duty of human beings to provide others with pain on the off chance that it may prove fruitful. In ninety-nine cases out of a hundred pain proves merely crushing. In the hundredth case it is better to trust to the natural shocks that flesh is heir to. So long as there is death there will be sorrow, and so long as there is sorrow it can be no part of the duty of human beings to increase its amount, in spite of the fact that a few rare spirits know how to transmute it.

Simone de Beauvoir
MYTH AND REALITY

Simone de Beauvoir, the famous French novelist and essayist, is perhaps best known for her book *The Second Sex,* written in 1953. In the following selection, taken from that book, de Beauvoir attacks the practice of defining women in terms of myths and ideals instead of as human beings. Her arguments follow the existentialist principle that essence cannot precede existence, and she contends that woman can only be defined on the basis of what she does, not on the basis of how she is seen in our male-dominated society. De Beauvoir finds that the practice of turning woman into a symbol is founded on its usefulness to men, but compassionately says that man "would have nothing to lose, quite the contrary, if he gave up disguising woman as a symbol," and that "to recognize in woman a human being is not to impoverish man's experience. . . ." From *The Second Sex,* by Simone de Beauvoir, translated by H. M. Parshley. Copyright 1952 by Alfred A. Knopf, Inc. Reprinted by permission of the publisher.

The myth of woman plays a considerable part in literature; but what is its importance in daily life? To what extent does it affect the customs and conduct of individuals? In replying to this question it will be necessary to state precisely the relations this myth bears to reality.

There are different kinds of myths. This one, the myth of woman, sublimating an immutable aspect of the human condition—namely, the "division" of humanity into two classes of individuals—is a static myth. It projects into the realm of Platonic ideas a reality that is directly experienced or is conceptualized on a basis of experience; in place of fact, value, significance, knowledge, empirical law, it substitutes a transcendental Idea, timeless, unchangeable, necessary. This idea is indisputable because it is beyond the given: it is endowed with absolute truth. Thus, as against the dispersed, contingent, and multiple existences of actual women, mythical thought opposes the Eternal Feminine, unique and changeless. If the definition provided for this concept is contradicted by the behavior of flesh-and-blood women, it is the latter who are wrong: we are told not that Femininity is a false entity, but that the women concerned are not feminine. The contrary facts of experience are impotent against the myth. In a way, however, its source is in experience. Thus it is quite true that woman is other than man, and this alterity is directly felt in desire, the embrace, love; but the real relation is one of reciprocity; as such it gives rise to authentic drama. Through eroticism, love, friendship, and their alternatives, deception, hate, rivalry, the relation is a struggle between conscious beings each of whom wishes to be essential, it is the mutual recognition of free beings who confirm one another's freedom, it is the vague transition from aversion to participation. To pose Woman is to pose the absolute Other, without reciprocity, denying against all experience that she is a subject, a fellow human being.

In actuality, of course, women appear under various aspects; but each of the myths built up around the subject of woman is intended to sum her up *in toto*; each aspires to be unique. In consequence, a number of incompatible myths exist, and men tarry musing before the strange incoherencies manifested by the idea of Femininity. As every woman has a share in a majority of these archetypes—each of which lays claim to containing the sole Truth of woman—men of today also are moved again in the presence of their female companions to an astonishment like that of the old sophists who failed to understand how man could be blond and dark at the same time! Transition toward the absolute was indicated long ago in social phenomena: relations are easily congealed in classes, functions in types, just as relations, to the childish mentality, are fixed in things. Patriarchal society, for example, being centered upon the conservation of the patrimony, implies necessarily, along with those who own and transmit wealth, the existence of men and women who take property away from its owners and put it into circulation. The men—adventurers, swindlers, thieves, speculators—are generally repudiated by the group; the women, employing their erotic attraction, can induce young men and even fathers of families to scatter their patrimonies, without ceasing to be within the law. Some of these women appropriate their victims' fortunes or obtain legacies by using undue influence; this role being regarded as evil, those who play it are called "bad women." But the fact is that quite to the contrary they are able to appear in some other setting—at home with their fathers, brothers, husbands, or lovers—as guardian angels; and the courtesan who "plucks" rich financiers is, for painters and writers, a generous patroness. It is easy to understand in actual experience the ambiguous personality of Aspasia or Mme de Pompadour. But if the woman is depicted as the Praying Mantis, the Mandrake, the Demon, then it is most confusing to find in woman also the Muse, the Goddess Mother, Beatrice.

As group symbols and social types are generally defined by means of antonyms in pairs, ambivalence will seem to be an intrinsic quality of the Eternal Feminine. The saintly mother has for correlative the cruel stepmother, the angelic young girl has the perverse virgin: thus it will be said sometimes that Mother equals Life, sometimes that Mother equals Death, that every virgin is pure spirit or flesh dedicated to the devil.

Evidently it is not reality that dictates to society or to individuals their choice between the two opposed basic categories; in every period, in each case, society and the individual decide in accordance with their needs. Very often they project into the myth adopted the institutions and values to which they adhere. Thus the paternalism that claims woman for hearth and home defines her as sentiment, inwardness, immanence. In fact every existent is at once immanence and transcendence; when one offers the existent no aim, or prevents him from attaining any, or robs him of his victory, then his transcendence falls vainly into the past—that is to say, falls back into immanence. This is the lot assigned to woman in the patriarchate; but it is in no way a vocation, any more than slavery is the vocation of the slave. The development of this mythology is to be clearly seen in Auguste Comte. To identify Woman with Altruism is to guarantee to man absolute rights in her devotion, it is to impose on women a categorical imperative.

The myth must not be confused with the recognition of significance; significance is immanent in the object; it is revealed to the mind through a living experience; whereas the myth is a transcendent Idea that escapes the mental grasp entirely. When in *L'Age d'homme* Michel Leiris describes his vision of the feminine organs, he tells us things of significance and elaborates no myth. Wonder at the feminine body, dislike for menstrual blood, come from perceptions of a concrete reality. There is nothing mythical in the experience that reveals the voluptuous qualities of feminine flesh, and it is not an excursion into myth if one attempts to describe them through comparisons with flowers or pebbles. But to say that Woman is Flesh, to say that the Flesh is Night and Death, or that it is the splendor of the Cosmos, is to abandon terrestrial truth and soar into an empty sky. For man also is flesh for woman; and woman is not merely a carnal object; and the flesh is clothed in special significance for each person and in each experience. And likewise it is quite true that woman—like man—is a being rooted in nature; she is more enslaved to the species than is the male, her animality is more manifest; but in her as in him the given traits are taken on through the fact of existence, she belongs also to the human realm. To assimilate her to Nature is simply to act from prejudice.

Few myths have been more advantageous to the ruling caste than the myth of woman: it justifies all privileges and even authorizes their abuse. Men need not bother themselves with alleviating the pains and the burdens that physiologically are women's lot, since these are "intended by Nature"; men use them as a pretext for increasing the misery of the feminine lot still further, for instance by refusing to grant to woman any right to sexual pleasure, by making her work like a beast of burden.[1]

Of all these myths, none is more firmly anchored in masculine hearts than that of the feminine "mystery." It has numerous advantages. And first of all it permits an easy explanation of all that appears inexplicable; the man who "does not understand" a woman is happy to substitute an objective resistance for a subjective deficiency of mind; instead of admitting his ignorance, he perceives the presence of a "mystery" outside himself: an alibi, indeed, that flatters laziness and vanity at once. A heart smitten with love thus avoids many disappointments: if the loved one's behavior is capricious, her remarks stupid, then the mystery serves to excuse it all. And finally, thanks again to the mystery, that negative relation is perpetuated which seemed to Kierkegaard infinitely preferable to positive possession; in the company of a living enigma man remains alone—alone with his dreams, his hopes, his fears, his love, his vanity. This subjective game, which can go all the way from vice to mystical ecstasy, is for many a more attractive experience than an authentic relation with a human being. What foundations exist for such a profitable illusion?

Surely woman is, in a sense, mysterious, "mysterious as is all the world," according to Maeterlinck. Each is *subject* only for himself; each can grasp in immanence only himself, alone: from the point of view the *other* is always a mystery. To men's eyes the opacity of the self-knowing self, of the *pour-soi*, is denser in the *other* who is feminine; men are unable to penetrate her special experience through any working of sympathy: they are condemned to ignorance of the quality of woman's erotic pleasure, the discomfort of menstruation, and the pains of childbirth. The truth is that there is mystery on both sides: as the *other* who is of masculine sex, every man, also, has within him a presence, an inner self impenetrable to woman; she in turn is in ignorance of the male's erotic feeling. But in accordance with the universal rule I have stated, the categories in which men think of the world are established *from their point of view, as absolute:* they misconceive reciprocity, here as everywhere. A mystery for man, woman is considered to be mysterious in essence.

To tell the truth, her situation makes woman very liable to such a view. Her physiological nature is very complex; she herself submits to it as to some rigmarole from outside; her body does not seem to her to be a clear expression of herself; within it she feels herself a stranger. Indeed, the bond that in every individual connects the physiological life and the psychic life—or better the relation existing between the contingence of an individual and the free spirit that assumes it—is the deepest enigma implied in the condition of being human, and this enigma is presented in its most disturbing form in woman.

But what is commonly referred to as the mystery is not the subjective solitude of the conscious self, nor the secret organic life. It is on the level of communication that the word has its true meaning: it is not a reduction to pure silence, to darkness, to absence; it implies a stammering presence that fails to make itself manifest and clear. To say that woman is mystery is to say, not that she is silent, but that her language is not understood; she is there, but hidden behind veils; she exists beyond these uncertain appearances. What is she? Angel, demon, one inspired, an actress? It may be supposed either that there are answers to these questions which are impossible to discover, or, rather, that no answer is adequate because a fundamental ambiguity marks the feminine being; and perhaps in her heart she is even for herself quite indefinable: a sphinx.

The fact is that she would be quite embarrassed to decide *what she is;* but this not because the hidden truth is too vague to be discerned: it is because in this domain there is no truth. An existent *is* nothing other than what he does; the possible does not extend beyond the real, essence does not precede existence: in pure subjectivity, the human being *is not anything.* He is to be measured by his acts. Of a peasant woman one can say that she is a good or a bad worker, of an actress that she has or does not have talent; but if one considers a woman in her immanent presence, her inward self, one can say absolutely nothing about her, she falls short of having any qualifications. Now, in amorous or conjugal relations, in all relations where the woman is the vassal, the other, she is being dealt with in her immanence. It is noteworthy that the feminine comrade, colleague, and associate are without mystery; on the other hand, if the vassal is male, if, in the eyes of a man or a woman who is older, or richer, a young fellow, for example, plays the role of the inessential object, then he too becomes shrouded in mystery. And this uncovers for us a substructure under the feminine mystery which is economic in nature.

A sentiment cannot be supposed to *be* anything. "In the domain of sentiments," writes Gide, "the real is not distinguished from the imaginary. And if to imagine one loves is enough to be in love, then also to tell oneself that one imagines oneself to be in love when one is in love is enough to make one forthwith love a little less." Discrimination between the imaginary and the real can be made only through behavior. Since man occupies a privileged situation in this world, he is in a position to show his love actively; very often he supports the woman or at least helps her; in marrying her he gives her social standing; he makes her presents; his independent economic and social position allows him to take the initiative and think up contrivances: it was M. de Norpois who, when separated from Mme de Villeparisis, made twenty-four-hour trips to visit her. Very often the man is busy, the woman idle: he *gives* her the time he passes with her; she takes it: is it with pleasure, passionately, or only for amusement? Does she accept these benefits through love or through self-interest? Does she love her husband or her marriage? Of course, even the man's evidence is ambiguous: is such and such a gift granted through love or out of pity? But while normally a woman finds numerous advantages in her relations with a man, his relations with a woman are profitable to a man only in so far as he loves her. And so one can almost judge the degree of his affection by the total picture of his attitude.

But a woman hardly has means for sounding her own heart; according to her moods she will view her own sentiments in different lights, and as she submits to them passively, one interpretation will be no truer than another. In those rare instances in which she holds the position of economic and social privilege, the mystery is reversed, showing that it does not pertain to *one* sex rather than the other, but to the situation. For a great many women the roads to transcendence are blocked: because they *do* nothing, they fail to *make themselves* anything. They wonder indefinitely what they *could have* become, which sets them to asking about what they *are*. It is a vain question. If man fails to discover that secret essence of femininity, it is simply because it does not exist. Kept on the fringe of the world, woman cannot be objectively defined through this world, and her mystery conceals nothing but emptiness.

Furthermore, like all the oppressed, woman deliberately dissembles her objective actuality; the slave, the servant, the indigent, all who depend upon the caprices of a master, have learned to turn toward him a changeless smile or an enigmatic impassivity; their real sentiments, their actual behavior, are carefully hidden. And moreover woman is taught from adolescence to lie to men, to scheme, to be wily. In speaking to them she wears an artificial expression on her face; she is cautious, hypocritical, play-acting.

But the Feminine Mystery as recognized in mythical thought is a more profound matter. In fact, it is immediately implied in the mythology of the absolute Other. If it be admitted that the inessential conscious being, too, is a clear subjectivity, capable of performing the *Cogito*, then it is also admitted that this being is in truth sovereign and returns to being essential; in order that all reciprocity may appear quite impossible, it is necessary for the Other to be for itself an other, for its very subjectivity to be affected by its otherness; this consciousness which would be alienated as a consciousness, in its pure immanent presence, would evidently be Mystery. It would be Mystery in itself from the fact that it would be Mystery for itself; it would be absolute Mystery.

In the same way it is true that, beyond the secrecy created by their dissembling, there is mystery in the Black, the Yellow, in so far as they are considered absolutely as the inessential Other. It should be noted that the American citizen, who profoundly baffles the average European, is not, however, considered as being "mysterious": one states more modestly that one does not understand him. And similarly woman does not always "understand" man; but there is no such thing as a masculine mystery. The point is that rich America, and the male, are on the Master side and that Mystery belongs to the slave.

To be sure, we can only muse in the twilight byways of bad faith upon the positive reality of the Mystery; like certain marginal hallucinations, it dissolves under the attempt to view it fixedly. Literature always fails in attempting to portray "mysterious" women; they can appear only at the beginning of a novel as strange, enigmatic figures; but unless the story remains unfinished they give up their secret in the end and they are then simply consistent and transparent persons. The heroes in Peter Cheyney's books, for example, never cease to be astonished at the unpredictable caprices of women: no one can ever guess how they will act, they upset all calculations. The fact is that once the springs of their action are revealed to the reader, they are seen to be very simple mechanisms: this woman was a spy, that one a thief; however clever the plot, there is always a key; and it could not be otherwise, had the author all the talent and imagination in the world. Mystery is never more than a mirage that vanishes as we draw near to look at it.

We can see now that the myth is in large part explained by its usefulness to man. The myth of woman is a luxury. It can appear only if man escapes from the urgent demands of his needs; the more relationships are concretely lived, the less they are idealized. The fellah of ancient Egypt, the Bedouin peasant, the artisan of the Middle Ages, the worker of today has in the requirements of work and poverty relations with his particular woman companion which are too definite for her to be embellished with an aura either auspicious or inauspicious. The epochs and the social classes that have been marked by the leisure to dream have been the ones to set up the images, black and white, of femininity. But along with luxury there was utility; these dreams were irresistibly guided by interests. Surely most of the myths had roots in the spontaneous attitude of man toward his own existence and toward the world around him. But going beyond experience toward the transcendent Idea was deliberately used by patriarchal society for purposes of self-justification; through the myths this society imposed its laws and customs upon individuals in a picturesque, effective manner; it is under a mythical form that the group-imperative is indoctrinated into each conscience. Through such intermediaries as religions, traditions, language, tales, songs, movies, the myths penetrate even into such existences as are most harshly enslaved to material realities. Here everyone can find sublimation of his drab experiences: deceived by the woman he loves, one declares that she is a Crazy Womb; another, obsessed by his impotence, calls her a Praying Mantis; still another enjoys his wife's company: behold, she is Harmony, Rest, the Good Earth! The taste for eternity at a bargain, for a pocket-sized absolute, which is shared by a majority of men, is satisfied by myths. The smallest emotion, a slight annoyance, becomes the reflection of a timeless Idea—an illusion agreeably flattering to the vanity.

The myth is one of those snares of false objectivity into which the man who depends on ready-made valuations rushes headlong. Here again we have to do with the substitution of a set idol for actual experience and the free judgments it requires. For an authentic relation with an autonomous existent, the myth of Woman substitutes the fixed contemplation of a mirage. "Mirage! Mirage!" cries Laforgue. "We should kill them since we cannot comprehend them; or better tranquilize them, instruct them, make them give up their taste for jewels, make them our genuinely equal comrades, our intimate friends, real associates here below, dress them differently, cut their hair short, say anything and everything to them." Man would have nothing to lose, quite the contrary, if he gave up disguising woman as a symbol. When dreams are official community affairs, clichés, they are poor and monotonous indeed beside the living reality; for the true dreamer, for the poet, woman is a more generous fount than is any down-at-heel marvel. The times that have most sincerely treasured women are not the period of feudal chivalry nor yet the gallant nineteenth century. They are the times—like the eighteenth century—when men have regarded women as fellow creatures; then it is that women seem truly romantic, as the reading of *Liaisons dangereuses, Le Rouge et le noir, Farewell to Arms,* is sufficient to show. The heroines of Laclos, Stendhal, Hemingway are without mystery, and they are not the less engaging for that. To recognize in woman a human being is not to impoverish man's experience: this would lose none of its diversity, its richness, or its intensity if it were to occur between two subjectivities. To discard the myths is not to destroy all dramatic relation between the sexes, it is not to deny the significance authentically revealed to man through feminine reality; it is not to do away with poetry, love, adventure, happiness, dreaming. It is simply to ask that behavior, sentiment, passion be founded upon the truth.[2]

"Woman is lost. Where are the women? The women of today are not women at all!" We have seen what these mysterious slogans mean. In men's eyes—and for the legion of women who see through men's eyes—it is not enough to have a woman's body nor to assume the female function as mistress or mother in order to be a "true woman." In sexuality and maternity woman as subject can claim autonomy; but to be a "true woman" she must accept herself as the Other. The men of today show a certain duplicity of attitude which is painfully lacerating to women; they are willing on the whole to accept woman as a fellow being, an equal; but they still require her to remain the inessential. For her these two destinies are incompatible; she hesitates between one and the other without being exactly adapted to either, and from this comes her lack of equilibrium. With man there is no break between public and private life: the more he confirms his grasp on the world in action and in work, the more virile he seems to be; human and vital values are combined in him. Whereas woman's independent successes are in contradiction with her femininity, since the "true woman" is required to make herself object, to be the Other.

It is quite possible that in this matter man's sensibility and sexuality are being modified. A new aesthetics has already been born. If the fashion of flat chests and narrow hips—the boyish form—has had its brief season, at least the overopulent ideal of past centuries has not returned. The feminine body is asked to be flesh, but with discretion; it is to be slender and not loaded with fat; muscular, supple, strong, it is bound to suggest transcendence; it must not be pale like a too shaded hothouse plant, but preferably tanned with a workman's torso from being bared to the open sun. Woman's dress in becoming practical need not make her appear sexless: on the contrary, short skirts made the most of legs and thighs as never before. There is no reason why working should take away woman's sex appeal.[3] It may be disturbing to contemplate woman as at once a social personage and carnal prey: in a recent series of drawings by Peynet (1948), we see a young man break his engagement because he was seduced by the pretty mayoress who was getting ready to officiate at his marriage. For a woman to hold some "man's position" and be desirable at the same time has long been a subject for more or less ribald joking; but gradually the impropriety and the irony have become blunted, and it would seem that a new form of eroticism is coming into being—perhaps it will give rise to new myths.

What is certain is that today it is very difficult for women to accept at the same time their status as autonomous individuals and their womanly destiny; this is the source of the blundering and restlessness which sometimes cause them to be considered a "lost sex." And no doubt it is more comfortable to submit to a blind enslavement than to work for liberation: the dead, for that matter, are better adapted to the earth than are the living. In all respects a return to the past is no more possible than it is desirable. What must be hoped for is that the men for their part will unreservedly accept the situation that is coming into existence; only then will women be able to live in that situation without anguish. Then Laforgue's prayer will be answered: "Ah, young women, when will you be our brothers, our brothers in intimacy without ulterior thought of exploitation? When shall we clasp hands truly?" Then Breton's "Mélusine, no longer under the weight of the calamity let loose upon her by man alone, Mélusine set free . . ." will regain "her place in humanity." Then she will be a full human being, "when," to quote a letter of Rimbaud, "the infinite bondage of woman is broken, when she will live in and for herself, man—hitherto detestable—having let her go free."

NOTES

1. Cf. Balzac: *Physiology of Marriage:* "Pay no attention to her murmurs, her cries, her pains; *nature has made her for our use* and for bearing everything: children, sorrows, blows and pains inflicted by man. Do not accuse yourself of hardness. In all the codes of so-called civilized nations, man has written the laws that ranged woman's destiny under this bloody epigraph: *"Vae Victis!* Woe to the weak!"

2. Laforgue goes on to say regarding woman: "Since she has been left in slavery, idleness, without occupation or weapon other than her sex, she has overdeveloped this aspect and has become the Feminine. . . . We have permitted this hypertrophy; she is here in the world for our benefit. . . . Well! that is all wrong. . . . Up to now we have played with woman as if she were a doll. This has lasted altogether too long! . . ."

3. A point that hardly needs to be made in America, where even cursory acquaintance with any well-staffed business office will afford confirmatory evidence.—Tr.

7 RIGHTS, RACE, AND HUMAN DIGNITY

"BEFORE WE GET too close to the end of our last class, let me remind you that all projects, assignments, and papers have to be turned in at the end of this class or by Friday at the latest. Also, you must hand in a self-evaluation of your performance in this course and the grade that you have earned. Finally, you must sign up for the final conference to be held during exam week. Any questions?"

"Are you really going to give us the grade we ask for, Professor?" Doug asks.

"If you write down a comprehensive and thorough evaluation of your performance in this course and convert that evaluation into a letter grade on the basis of what you believe you deserve—not what you want—then you'll get the grade you ask for. If you stay within the guidelines of ethical behavior as we have discussed it in this class, why shouldn't you be graded in this manner?"

"I'll believe it when I see it," says Bob.

"All right. How shall we spend the rest of our last class together? Sheila?"

"In all the subjects we have talked about—religion, law, violence, sex, and so on—we have been focusing on rights and the conflicts of rights and alleged rights. But I'd like to talk more about what we do, from a practical point of view, when we face a conflict of rights."

"Some conflicts can be resolved by distinguishing one *kind* of right from another kind of right," Edwards replies. "Remember our moral code ladder from the first week of class? Do you see what I am driving at?"

"I think I am way ahead," says Sheila excitedly. "You mean we can treat rights just like we treated various moral principles, and resolve conflicts between rights on the basis of their position in a hierarchy."

"Great, but how do we handle conflicts between legal rights and moral rights or between two legal rights or two moral rights?" Doug asks.

"I don't know much about the law, but I do know that courts distinguish between rights that always hold and rights that usually hold," replies Linda. "And the solution to a conflict is easy. Always-hold rights take precedence over usually-hold rights."

"But what if they are both just usually-hold rights and are in conflict?" Donna asks.

"Then an *always* hold right tells us which of the two conflicting rights wins, if either," Linda answers.

"But how do you structure a hierarchy when the conflict is between a moral and a legal right?" Doug demands.

"We're still talking theory, and Sheila asked about practical examples, about conflicts we face personally every day," says Louis.

"Can you give us an example?" asks Edwards.

"Well, I just read about some KKK bigot sounding off again against Blacks, Jews, Catholics, and Communists. Then the other night I heard a panel show that had that big shot professor who has been preaching a lot of scientific crap about Blacks being biologically inferior. You can argue that they're only exercising their right to freedom of speech, but they are sure tromping on a few other rights in the process."

"Just for the sake of making a point concerning a ladder of rights, would you consider the right to freedom of speech an always hold, or a usually hold right?" asks Edwards.

"Sure, it conflicts with what I think is our right to be treated like human beings," says Linda. "That's basically what Donna and Reeny were talking about last week when we discussed women and sex."

"I think I agree. But how does one resolve a conflict between the right to freedom of speech and what one might call a right not to be dehumanized by what is being said?" Cheri asks.

"Freedom of speech has to be an always hold," says Jeff emphatically.

"Not in our legal system, it isn't," Linda retorts. "Haven't you ever heard of laws against inciting to riot or laws concerning libel? But in terms of what Louis and Cheri are saying, don't people have a right to be treated with human dignity, and doesn't that right take precedence over the right to freedom of speech?"

"Maybe, but who decides what being treated with human dignity means?" asks Doug.

"I'm not sure, but I know what it doesn't mean," says Cheri. "For example, look at the way we treated the Indians in this country. First we stole all their land and then we killed them off or starved them off because they wouldn't accept our ways."

"And then you imported slaves from Africa and kept up the good work," Obie adds.

"But the Indians were savages and uncivilized and also heathens," Bob says.

"Oh, crap! What do you think *we* were?" asks Louis. "I suppose you define Blacks as having a great sense of rhythm and incapable of resisting watermelons."

"So it's not that simple," says Jeff. "But you can't dismiss scientific evidence about racial differences."

"Freud's theory about women was called science too. Well, I can't respect that kind of science; it's just disguised racism or sexism," says Donna. "In fact, what the hell do racial or sexual differences have to do with the rights we're supposed to be discussing?"

"Exactly," says Cheri. "I think we ought to go back to asking what being treated with human dignity really means. For me that means treating each person as a unique individual with unique talents, unique potentials, and even unique faults."

"Well, what if this unique dude you're talking about has the unique fault of wanting to stomp on your unique rights?" asks Obie.

"I must love him no matter what he is or what he does," answers Cheri. "Even if he kills me," she adds.

"Love your enemies," mutters Bob, the Bible quoter who seems bewildered by the quote. "Even Blacks would have a hard time with that. You mean a slave was supposed to love his master? Or a Black today is supposed to love a KKK member?"

"That's exactly what I mean," declares Cheri. "And women have to love their sexist oppressors, and the same goes for men."

"It'll never happen," Jeff says.

"I've heard of idealists, but you're too much," says Brock.

"What do you think, Professor?" asks Sheila.

"I think a number of things," answers Edwards. "First, we have run over time again. Second, I'd rather we discussed this after we have wrapped ourselves around some beer and pizza at my place. Are we all agreed that we'll meet there at 8:30?" He smiles at the chorus of assent. "I do believe this is the first time that everyone in this class has agreed to one thing."

He almost makes it to the door before someone calls, "I don't like anchovies!" So Professor Malcolm Edwards departs his last class of the semester as he has left all the others—shaking his head.

FOR FURTHER READING

Allport, Gordon. *The Nature of Prejudice.* Garden City, N.Y.: Doubleday, 1954. This is *the* classic study of prejudice. Although the data are now somewhat old, the basic conclusion the author reaches is still supported by more recent findings. An absolute must.

Bettelheim, Bruno, and Janowitz, Morris. *Social Change and Prejudice.* New York: Free Press, 1954. Another psychological/sociological investigation into the phenomenon of prejudice, excellent although not as broad in its coverage as Allport's.

Brandt, Richard, and Linde, Hans. "The University of California at Los Angeles: Academic Freedom and Tenure." *AAUP Bulletin* 57 (September 1971): 382-420. Written by a philosopher and a lawyer, this article, which treats the dismissal of Angela Davis from UCLA, is an excellent example of the practical application of philosophy. It is priceless for its depth of detail and objectivity.

Brown, Stuart, Jr. "Inalienable Rights." *Philosophical Review* 64 (1955): 192-211. This article is one of a three-part series on the issue of rights and should be read in conjunction with the articles by Frankena and Hart mentioned below.

Bruening, William H. "Racism: A Philosophical Analysis of a Concept." *Journal of Black Studies* (September 1974). A philosophical analysis of the phenomenon of racism, written from a Marxist/existentialist perspective, offering a few suggestions as to how racism might be curtailed and perhaps eliminated.

Farber, Jerry. *The Student as Nigger.* New York: Pocket Books, 1969. Farber wrote an article entitled "The Student as Nigger" for an underground newspaper, which has since become a classic of its kind. This book, titled after the article, contains other essays on related topics.

Feinberg, Joel. *Social Philosophy.* Englewood Cliffs, N.J.: Prentice-Hall, 1973. This volume is part of a series of books on philosophy published by Prentice-Hall. Of particular interest is Feinberg's discussion of rights.

Frankena, William. "Natural and Inalienable Rights." *Philosophical Review* 64 (1955): Another article of the three-part series on the issue of rights written by one of the most well-known ethicians living today.

Hare, R. M. *The Language of Morals.* New York: Oxford University Press, 1965. This book, which contains a chapter on racism, is somewhat technical for the beginner, but the author is a very good writer, and the rewards of reading him outweigh the effort the beginner may have to make.

Hart, H. L. A. "Are There Any Natural Rights?" *Philosophical Review* 64 (1955): 175-191. The third article in the series mentioned above by a prolific and important writer in the field of rights. Those interested in this subject should be acquainted with Hart's views.

Jacobs, Paul, and Landau, Saul, with Pell, Eve. *To Serve the Devil.* 2 vols. New York: Vintage, 1971. An anthology of writings on various ethnic groups, containing some shocking material, often unbelievable even for those familiar with the history of racism.

Jensen, Arthur. *Educability and Group Difference.* New York: Harper & Row, 1973. A detailed analysis of the evidence supporting, in the author's opinion, his genetic thesis (as opposed to the more popular environmental thesis) concerning racial differences in "intelligence."

_____. *Genetics and Education.* New York: Harper & Row, 1972. This collection contains Jensen's well-known article originally published in *Harvard Educational Review,* wherein he proposes that heredity is responsible for differences in IQ scores between black and white people.

Kovel, Joel. *White Racism: A Psychohistory.* New York: Vintage, 1970. A thought-provoking analysis of the psychology of racism. A very interesting and insightful book.

Mill, John Stuart. *Utilitarianism.* Available in numerous editions. This classic essay in moral philosophy, written in 1863, is remarkable for its lucidity, and any student of ethics should be familiar with it.

Montagu, Ashley, ed. *The Concept of Race.* London: Collier, 1964. An anthology of articles written by authors from various disciplines, arguing that the notion or concept of race cannot be defined with enough precision to be employed for scientific purposes. Although some of the articles may prove difficult to the beginner, others are quite easy.

_____. *Statement on Race.* New York: Oxford University Press, 1972. The author offers a careful and full analysis of the various statements made by UNESCO concerning race, racism, and related issues.

Rawls, John. *A Theory of Justice.* Cambridge, Mass.: Harvard University Press, 1971. This classic in moral and political philosophy may prove difficult for the beginner, but it is extremely worthwhile for those who can master it.

Rogers, Carl. *Freedom to Learn: A View of What Education Might Become.* Columbus, Ohio: Merrill, 1969. This book concerns what might be called a philosophy or psychology of education. The author advances his theories on education and offers practical advice on how to conduct classes. A must.

Schwartz, Barry, and Disch, Robert. *White Racism.* New York: Dell, 1970. A wide-ranging and comprehensive anthology that contains a strong indictment of white racism.

Thomas, Alexander, and Sillen, Samuel. *Racism and Psychiatry.* New York: Brunner/Mazel. Written from a psychiatric perspective, this book indicates how subtle prejudices can enter into medical practice. It also contains a discussion of Jensen's theories on racial differences.

Wasserstrom, Richard. "Rights, Human Rights, and Racial Discrimination." *Journal of Philosophy* 61 (1964). A well-written discussion of some of the topics mentioned in this section. Unfortunately, Wasserstrom's discussion of racial discrimination is not up to the high standards he maintains in his discussion of rights and human rights.

William H. Bruening

RIGHTS: LEGAL AND MORAL PARAMETERS

Many, if not all, moral problems concern themselves with the concept of rights. This article, by one of the editors of this volume, seeks to delineate and define types of rights, such as absolute rights and relative rights, first from a legal viewpoint and then from a moral viewpoint. The author argues that there are absolute, or natural, rights that can never be violated. Positing the existence of absolute rights, he reexamines certain practical moral problems in the context of such rights.

Most practical issues generally discussed and debated in the public forum concern rights: rights of privacy, rights to life, rights to death, rights to property, etc. But rarely does the discussion focus on the concept of rights in and of itself. Usually it is assumed that we all know and agree about what is meant by rights, and that the only controversy concerning rights relates to questions about what rights apply in a particular case or what rights take precedence over others.[1] This paper is an attempt to step back a bit from such debates and focus on a more theoretical discussion of rights in the hope that a conceptual clarification of the underlying concept of "rights" might be helpful in discussing the more practical applications of rights. The last part of the paper will attempt to sketch the implications of this clarification for the debate on practical issues ranging from capital punishment to abortion.

THE LEGAL DEFINITION AND ONE EXAMPLE

Black's Law Dictionary has the following entry under the heading of "right":

> As a *noun*, and taken in an *abstract* sense, justice, ethical correctness, or consonance with the rules of law or the principles of morals. In this signification it answers to one meaning of the Latin *"jus,"* and serves to indicate law in the abstract, considered as the foundation of all rights, or the complex of underlying moral principles which impart the character of justice to all positive law, or give it an ethical content.
>
> As a noun, and taken in a *concrete* sense, a power, privilege, faculty, or demand, inherent in one person and incident upon another. "Rights" are defined generally as "powers of free action." And the primal rights pertaining to men are undoubtedly enjoyed by human beings purely as such, being grounded in personality, and existing antecedently to their recognition by positive law. But leaving the abstract moral sphere, and giving to the term a juristic content, a "right" is well defined as "a capacity residing in one man of controlling, with the assent and assistance of the state, the actions of others." Holl. Jur. 69.[2]

Black's then adds the following:

> There is also a classification of rights, with respect to the constitution of civil society. Thus, according to Blackstone, "the rights of persons, considered in their natural capacities, are of two sorts—*absolute* and *relative;* absolute, which are such as appertain and belong to particular men, merely as individuals or single persons; relative, which are incident to them as members of society, and standing in various relations to each other." 1 Bl. Comm. 123. Johnson v. Johnson, 32 Ala. 637; People v. Berberrich, 20 Barb, (N. Y.) 224.[3]

Natural rights are discussed by Black in the following entry:

> *Natural* rights are those which grow out of the nature of man and depend upon personality, as distinguished from such as are created by law and depend upon civil society; or they are those which are plainly assured

by natural law (Borden v. State, 11 Ark. 519, 44 Am. Dec. 217); or those which, by fair deduction from the present physical, moral, social, and religious characteristics of man he must be invested with, and which he ought to have realized for him in a jural society, in order to fulfill the ends to which his nature calls him. I Woolsey, Polit. Science, p. 26. Such are the rights to life, liberty, privacy, and good reputation. See Black, Const. Law (3rd Ed.) 523.[1]

We have here an introduction to the concepts of absolute and relative rights and to the notion of natural rights. For further discussion of absolute rights, let us look at the *People* v. *Berberrich* case cited above. The court said:

> The right of property is protected against invasion from the legislative, or any other branch of the government, by the express terms of the constitution. (*Constitution*, art. 1, Sects. 1,6.) But aside from this, it is clear that under every free government there are certain fundamental and inherent rights belonging to individuals which are not solely dependent on the will of the legislature; and it is unnecessary to examine the written constitution of the state to ascertain whether they are expressly shielded by that instrument from legislative encroachment. The right of personal security, of personal liberty, and personal property do not depend upon the constitution for their existence. They existed before the constitution was made, or the government was organized. These are what are termed the absolute rights of individuals, which belong to them independently of all government, and which all governments which derive their powers from the consent of the governed, were instituted to protect. They are defined as follows:
> "By the absolute rights of individuals we mean those which are so in their primary and strictest sense, such as would belong to their persons merely in a state of nature, and which every man is entitled to enjoy whether out of society or in it." (1 Black. Com. 123)[5]

This seems to be a clear-cut statement of the legal meaning of 'absolute right,' and had the court stopped here, we might have been content. Unfortunately, the court added the following:

> But while the absolute rights of individuals are better protected, they are not as entirely absolute under government, as in a state of nature. They are subservient to such measures as become necessary for the preservation of the government, its defense against external or internal enemies, or the promotion of the best interests of the whole community. For the protection of the government against external danger, individuals may be compelled to enter into military service, and to subject and expose themselves to the hardships and perils of war. For the protection of society against the consequences of crime, offenders may be deprived of liberty, property or life. Lunatics who become dangerous to others may be imprisoned. Persons sick of contagious diseases may be removed to, and placed in, hospitals. Property may be removed or destroyed, or trades supressed, which endanger the public safety or health. Property may be taken from individuals in the form of taxes, and applied toward the support of the government and its institutions. In short, government is not to be restrained in the exercise of its legitimate powers, which

are essential to the public welfare, because the rights of individuals will be injuriously affected thereby.[6]

This further statement bears some comment. If we assume for the moment that there are absolute rights and that they might be the ones mentioned in the first paragraph,[7] then the second paragraph of the quote causes considerable difficulty from both a logical and a moral point of view. Logically speaking, to call rights absolute and then to say that in a civil society such absolute rights are no longer absolute is either a flat contradiction or a very roundabout way of saying that the rights that appeared to be absolute were in fact relative (call them civil rights if you will). I think that the two paragraphs are simply contradictory.

From a moral point of view, the statement of the court reminds one of Fries' comment on Hegel's philosophy of the state: that it had grown "not in the gardens of science but in the dunghill of servility."[8] The court seems to be saying that whenever the rights of an individual conflict with the rights of the state, the state can summarily deny the rights of the individual. Although it may be true that the state can legally do this, it surely does not follow that it can morally do so. There is a very disturbing ring of totalitarianism in the opinion of the court.

Let us proceed, for sake of further exposition to one recent U.S. Supreme Court decision for a very contemporary view of the legal sense of 'absolute right.' On January 22, 1973 the United States Supreme Court handed down its decision on the constitutionality of certain abortion laws. The two cases considered were *Roe* v. *Wade* and *Doe* v. *Bolton*, but the substance of that decision is not germane to our discussion, at least at this point. For our discussion of the concept of 'rights' the crucial part of the decision is the following:

> ... appellants and some *amici* argue that the women's right is absolute and that she is entitled to terminate her pregnancy at whatever time, in whatever way, and for whatever reason she alone chooses. With this we do not agree. Appellants' arguments that Texas either has no valid interest at all in regulating the abortion decision, or no interest strong enough to support any limitation upon the woman's sole determination, is unpersuasive. The Court's decisions recognizing a right of privacy also acknowledge that some state regulation in areas protected by that right is appropriate. As noted above, a state may properly assert important interests in safeguarding health, in maintaining medical standards, and in protecting potential life. At some point in pregnancy, these respective interests become sufficiently compelling to sustain regulation of the factors that govern the abortion decision. The privacy right involved, therefore, cannot be said to be absolute. In fact, it is not clear to us that the claim asserted by some *amici* that one has an unlimited right to do to one's body as one pleases bears a close relationship to the right of privacy previously articulated in the Court's decisions. The Court

has refused to recognize an unlimited right of this kind in the past. *Jackson v. Massachusetts,* 197 U.S. 11 (1905) (vaccination); *Buck v. Bell,* 274 U.S. 200 (1927) (sterilization).[9]

The full import of the Court's decision is spelled out very simply,

> *Roe v. Wade, ante,* sets forth our conclusion that a pregnant woman does not have an absolute right to an abortion on her demand.[10]

The Court here recognizes the distinction between absolute rights and relative rights as we have mentioned them above. From a legal point of view, then, an absolute right would be a right that no state or civil society can restrict, whatever the interests or reason that state might have; and a relative right is a right that might be called *prima facie,* i.e., a right that the individual can exercise until legally enjoined from so doing.

RIGHTS FROM A MORAL POINT OF VIEW

Having briefly touched on some legal definitions of "rights" and the distinction between absolute and relative rights, I should now like to investigate the concept of 'rights' from a moral point of view. Professor Wasserstrom's discussion of rights serves as an appropriate starting point.[11] In defining rights he says:

> Perhaps the most obvious thing to be said about rights is that they are constitutive of the domain of entitlements. They help to define and serve to protect those things concerning which one can make a very special kind of claim—a claim of right. To claim or to acquire anything as a matter of right is crucially different from seeking or obtaining it as through the grant of privilege, the receipt of favor, or the presence of a permission. To have a right to something is, typically, to be entitled to receive or possess or enjoy it now, and to do so without securing the consent of another. As long as one has a right to anything, it is beyond the reach of another properly to withhold or deny it. In addition, to have a right is to be absolved from the obligation to weigh a variety of what would in other contexts be relevant considerations; it is to be entitled to the object of the right—at least *prima facie*—without any more ado. To have a right to anything is, in short, to have a very strong moral or legal claim upon it. It is the strongest claim that there is.[12]

Wasserstrom's definition (or description, if you prefer) is quite similar to the legal concept of rights developed above.

We can infer from Wasserstrom's discussion that the exercise of a moral right need not be justified—it is assumed to be correctly exercised. Consequently, the burden of justification is on those who prohibit, or seek to prohibit, the exercise of the right. This does not mean that every exercise of right is morally correct, rather, that any violation of rights is a serious matter requiring a very strong and a very persuasive justification. (We must leave open the possibility that some violation of rights may be morally justifiable, since we know that rights conflict and that legally and morally such conflicts can and must be solved.)

Wasserstrom talks of rights as being "at least *prima facie*." *Prima facie* rights, as Wasserstrom defines them, correspond to that rung of a moral-code ladder entitled "moral rules." And if such rights are also legally sanctioned, they also fit on that rung entitled "legal rules."[13]

One difficulty with Wasserstrom's description of rights is that it opens the door to the possibility of treating all rights as *prima facie*. What about the possible existence of absolute rights?[14]

Wasserstrom cites J. B. Mabbott as one of many who deny the existence of absolute, natural, or human, rights (these terms are apparently being used interchangeably). Mabbott argues:

> [T]he niceties of the theory [of natural rights] need not detain us if we can attack it at its roots, and there it is most clearly vulnerable. Natural rights must be self-evident and they must be absolute if they are to be rights at all. For if a right is derivative from a more fundamental right, then it is not natural in the sense intended; and if a right is to be explained or defended by reference to the good of the community or of the individual concerned, then these "goods" are the ultimate values in the case, and their pursuit may obviously infringe or destroy the "rights" in question. Now the only way in which to demonstrate the absurdity of the theory which claims self-evidence for every article of its creed is to make a list of the articles . . .
>
> Not only are the lists indeterminate and capricious in extent, they are also confused in content . . . [T]here is no single "natural right" which is, in fact, regarded even by its own supporters as sacrosanct. Every one of them is constantly invaded in the public interest with universal approval.[15]

It is not clear just what Mabbott means by "self-evident." Aristotle, among others, saw that the meaning of self-evident can vary; it can mean self-evident to everyone, it can mean self-evident to the wise, etc.[16]

Mabbott's difficulty with "natural rights" could be read as a difficulty with the very concept of justification itself, and in particular with justification in ethics and morals. This problem deserves some attention here. All justification has a certain Pandora's box quality. For example, any attempt to justify a particular action or decision by appealing to certain principles as evidence or proof of correctness opens the lid to questions concerning such principles. Higher principles must then be invoked as justification, and so on *ad infinitum*. But it must end somewhere. The place of reasons has to end somewhere.[17] R. M. Hare has made this point quite clearly:

> ... if pressed to justify a decision completely, we have to give a complete specification of the way of life of which it is a part. This complete specification it is impossible in practice to give; the nearest attempts are those given by the great religions, especially those which can point to historical persons who carried out the way of life in practice. Suppose, however, that we can give it. If the inquirer still goes on asking "But why *should* I live like that?" then there is no further answer to give him, because we have already, *ex hypothesi*, said everything that can be included in this further answer. We can only ask him to make up his own mind which way he ought to live; for in the end everything rests upon such decisions of principle. He has to decide whether to accept that way of life or not; if he accepts it, then we can proceed to justify the decisions that are based on it; if he does not accept it, then let him accept some other and try to live by it. The sting is in the last clause. To describe such ultimate decisions as arbitrary, because *ex hypothesi* everything that could be used to justify them has already been included in the decision, would be like saying that a complete description of the universe was utterly unfounded, because no further fact could be called up on corroboration of it. This is not how we use the words 'arbitrary' and 'unfounded.' Far from being arbitrary, such a decision would be based upon a consideration of everything upon which it could possibly be founded.[18]

If what Hare is saying is correct, and I take it that it is, then one could claim that any ultimate principle (one that fits on the top rung of my moral-code ladder) is self-evident in the sense that no further justification of it is possible—and that this impossibility is a *logical* one.

One more comment on Mabbott's troubles with natural rights. The fact that even those who postulate the existence of natural rights have been known to abrogate such rights when they come in conflict with the good of the community suggests one of two things: (1) that natural rights are not in fact absolute or (2) that those who believe in natural rights and yet abrogate them are in error. Mabbot seems to recognize only the first alternative and does not see that the second is also a possibility.

In discussing natural, or human, rights, Wasserstrom makes the following claims:

> If nothing else about the subject is clear, it is evident that one's particular legal rights, as well as some of one's moral rights, are not among one's human rights. If any right is a *human* right, it must, I believe have at least four very general characteristics. First, it must be possessed by all human beings, as well as only by human beings. Second, because it is the same right that all human beings possess, it must be possessed equally by all human beings. Third, because human rights are possessed by all human beings, we can rule out as possible candidates any of those rights which one might have in virtue of occupying any particular status or relationship, such as that of parent, president, or promisee. And fourth, if there are any human rights, they have the additional characteristic

of being assertable, in a manner of speaking, "against the world." That is to say, because they are rights that are not possessed in virtue of any contingent status or relationship, they are rights that can be claimed equally against any and every other human being.[19]

Later, Wasserstrom indicates that he has some qualms about considering human rights as absolute (in the sense that they can never be violated), though he agrees that absolute rights do exist and offers the following example:

> ... the principle that no person should be treated differently from any or all other persons unless there is some general and relevant reason that justifies this difference in treatment is a fundamental principle of morality, if not of rationality itself. Indeed, although I am uncertain how one might argue for this, I think it could well be said that all men do have a "second order" human right—that is, an absolute right—to expect all persons to adhere to this principle.[20]

Wasserstrom's metaprinciple concerning "second order" human rights is, I think, "self-evident" in the sense that Hare talks of decisions of principles. Why Wasserstrom worries about proving it is a matter of speculation.

To summarize this discussion on absolute rights, I should like to relate the positions taken by Wasserstrom and Mabbott to my ladder concept of a moral code.[21] In terms of my moral-code ladder, absolute rights would be those that pertain to either of the top two rungs—ultimate moral principles or moral laws. Wasserstrom's "second order" right obviously pertains only to the top rung since such rights are clearly intended to always hold and always apply. Mabbott, however, would presumably not agree that absolute rights could fit on the second rung—that of moral laws. Since his very denial of the existence of absolute rights is based on the fact that they are derivative, he might say that moral laws, and thus the corresponding rights, seem to be derivative from the top rung of the ladder. Such an objection would be based on a misunderstanding of the relationship between the various rungs of the ladder. To call moral law-rights derivative suggests that one can "deduce" in some way the lower rungs of the ladder once one has selected an ultimate moral principle for the first rung. I do not think that this is possible, and it certainly does not indicate an understanding of the interconnections between the various rungs. In fact, it one speaks of "deducing" or discovering various moral principles, the ultimate moral principle—the one on the highest rung—is probably the last one discovered. (If, on the other hand, one wants to describe an established moral code, then one might begin by talking about the first rung.)

One final comment concerning the concept of absolute rights in context with a moral-code ladder: 'Absolute' in the sense that is being used here describes those laws-rights that always hold; they are not absolute in the sense that they always apply. (It is for this reason that I state that absolute rights pertain to the two top rungs of the ladder.) The source of Mabbott's difficulty [in accepting the existence of absolute rights] stems in part from his apparent failure to make that distinction.

One other comment is also in order. Some discussions of rights seem to argue that rights are things that can be given and taken away from people.[22] This is misleading. Though it may be true that some rights can be granted and taken away, it does not follow that this is true of all rights. Wasserstrom's "second order" right is a good example of a right that can neither be given nor taken away—nor, indeed, can the possessor give it away. One might say that one is stuck with such rights, whether one wants them or not and whether or not others recognize them.

Postulating the existence of absolute rights (variously described as human, natural, or "second order" rights), I shall now investigate the implications of such rights for the resolution of certain practical moral issues. To begin, I should like to make two observations. First, there is a practical moral issue involved in any attempt to deny or abrogate such absolute rights. If such rights exist and accrue to all human beings simply by virtue of the fact that they are human beings, any denial of such rights can only be justified by denying that the one seeking to exercise those rights is human (or, at least, by suggesting that the person is, in some way, less than human). Although not always presented in such a blatant form, this specious justification has been advanced by racists and sexists to deprive certain individuals of their rights. Clearly, the existence of absolute rights has some practical implications concerning discrimination of any kind. Second, the existence of absolute rights has certain implications with regard to the right to life and the derivative practical moral issues of capital punishment, pacifism, and abortion, among others. If absolute rights of any kind exist, then the right to life must be one such right. Rights do not exist *in vacuo*—there must be a bearer of that right. Positing that the right to life exists and then arguing that the bearer of the right may be killed is to engage in logical nonsense.[23]

SOME PRACTICAL CONCERNS

Perhaps the application of my position to some of the practical concerns mentioned at the beginning of this paper will make my position clearer. I am not intending these remarks to be full-blown defenses of the positions taken, but an outline of the way in which a full-blown defense might be made.

Let us consider capital punishment.[24] Since the right to life is absolute, the deliberate taking of a human life by the state or by anyone else is, by definition, immoral, even if in various locales and at various times it is legal.[25]

The immorality of capital punishment is not changed by arguments for deterrence and retribution; it is still taking a human life, and killing is a violation of an absolute right. What a society can morally do to protect itself from crime and criminals is another question and one that I shall not discuss here. I might, however, suggest that imprisonment (under humane conditions) is still a viable alternative to capital punishment since I take the right to physical freedom to be a *prima facie* right and not an absolute right. Given the position I take on the right to life, my position on capital punishment follows.

Another aspect of absolute rights relates to the issues surrounding pacifism and nonviolence. It should be quite obvious that my position concerning the absolute right to life dictates that I be an absolute pacifist.[26] Absolute pacifism has been ridiculed as "naïve, superficial, illogical, and immoral."[27] It has also been contended that pacifism is a "logical muddle" because such a position does not understand that rights themselves are something that may require an active defense. This is quite far from the truth. Although some pacifists are passive, it is by no means necessary to be passive in order to be a pacifist. A pacifist can and, I would argue, must defend rights, but he is bound not to violate any absolute rights in the process. Moreover, even *prima facie* rights can be violated by the pacifist only in exceptional circumstances, and the burden is on the pacifist to justify this exception.

As is true with any moral code that must be applied to real, human moral problems, there are cases where the application of a specific principle to a specific problem is not obvious. It may be quite clear that a pacifist of the type being discussed cannot morally pick up a machine gun and fire into a crowd to stop a runaway criminal. It is not nearly as clear, however, what moral means, if any, the same pacifist can employ in preventing, say, a would-be attacker from charging him with knife in hand. Clearly, the means by which a pacifist defends his right to life are as crucial as the defense of the right itself. Whatever the rights of the would-be assailant, certainly it should be possible to conceive some means whereby the pacifist can defend himself without violating his principles. Though some pacifists of the passive variety may object to any means of defense, I do think that allowing that in this and in similar cases certain means of defense can be justified is not inconsistent with the general pacifist position.

The third practical problem I wish to discuss in connection with absolute rights is abortion, which is also related to the right to life. To posit that the right to life is absolute would seem to dictate that one should oppose abortion in all cases. I do not agree with such a conclusion though, clearly, abortion is a particularly difficult issue for those who hold the right to life as absolute. The question of abortion, in this instance, revolves around the hopeless and thankless task of determining whether or not the fetus is human, especially in the early part of the pregnancy. The logic of the abortion issue is quite clear for those who hold the right to life as absolute. If the fetus is not human, then abortion qua abortion causes no moral problems in regard to the right to life. Since the fetus is not human, it is excluded from the absolute prohibition of not violating the right to life. If, on the other hand, the fetus is human, then no abortion can be accepted as moral since such an abortion clearly violates the right to life.[28]

The case where the fetus is adjudged to be human and the issue is one of taking the life of the unborn child or saving the life of the mother poses a particularly difficult moral dilemma for those who hold the right to life to be absolute. Clearly, a believer in the absolute right to life cannot choose the life of the mother over the life of the child or vice versa. Unfortunately, in this case there may be nothing that can be done that is consistent with the general principle that the right to life is absolute.[29]

The last practical problem that I want to make a few comments on relates to discrimination on the basis of either race or sex. Discrimination in any form would seem to be a clear violation of Wasserstrom's "second order" right. In the specific case of sexual discrimination, if one accepts Wasserstrom's second-order right, then one ought to be in favor of the Equal Rights Amendment[30] unless one wants to contend that there are differences between men and women that are significant and relevant in terms of our moral behavior toward each. Arguments purporting to establish such differences are rather paltry and oftentimes ludicrous. The same can be said about arguments concerning differences in races. I am not arguing that there are no differences between races or sexes.[31] Instead, I am arguing that such differences as may exist are irrelevant from the standpoint of morality. Differences between sexes and between races do not, and should not, result in differences in moral treatment.

Whether or not the reader finds the resolution of specific practical moral issues discussed herein as either acceptable or objectionable is not my primary concern. One of my purposes in writing this article is to demonstrate the existence of forceful arguments in favor of absolute rights; to show that defense of such rights cannot be dismissed as trivial. But beyond questions concerning the existence and application of absolute and other rights there are what Hare calls decisions of principle and the consequences of such decisions. Let us look again at what Hare said about such decisions and their consequences:

> ... if pressed to justify a decision completely, we have to give a complete specification of the way of life of which it is a part. This complete specification it is impossible in practice to give; the nearest attempts are those given by the great religions, especially those which can point to historical persons who carried out the way of life in practice. Suppose, however, that we can give it. If the inquirer still goes on asking "But why *should* I live like that?" then there is no further answer to give him, because we have already, *ex hypothesi*, said everything that can be included in this further answer. We can only ask him to make up his own mind which way he ought to live; for in the end everything rests upon such decisions of principle. He has to decide whether to accept that way of life or not; if he accepts it, then we can proceed to justify the decisions that are based on it; if he does not accept it, then let him accept some other and try to live by it. *The sting is in the last clause.*[32]

Whether or not one must espouse a "great religion" to ultimately justify decisions of principle is open to question[33] and is not germane to this discussion. But Hare's general view about decisions of principle focuses on the real issue involved in any discussion of rights as being ultimately a discussion about a way of life, a Lebensform. This is where the chain of reasons comes to an end.[34]

NOTES

1. Even U.S. Supreme Court holdings do not investigate the concept of rights; rather, they do adjudicate between various claims of rights.
2. *Blacks's Law Dictionary*, 4th rev. ed.
3. Ibid., p. 1487.
4. Ibid. p. 1487.
5. People v. Berberrich, 20 Barb (N.Y.), p. 224.
6. Ibid.
7. The first paragraph, outlining the theory of absolute rights, may be questioned on the grounds that a social contact theory is unacceptable (for a recent discussion of such a theory see John Rawls, *A Theory of Justice*. Cambridge: Harvard University Press, 1971) or that the state of nature concept is unworkable. But for our purposes the origin of the theory used to support the existence of absolute rights is not crucial. As long as one accepts that there are such rights, the other issues are not important for the purposes of this discussion.
8. Quoted by Ernst Cassirer in his *The Myth of the State* (New Haven, Conn.: Yale University Press, 1946), p. 250.
9. *United States Law Week* 41 (January 23, 1973): 4225-4226.
10. Ibid., p. 4236.

11. Richard Wasserstrom, "Rights, Human Rights, and Racial Discrimination," *Journal of Philosophy* 61 (1964). This essay also appears in James Rachels's *Moral Problems* (New York: Harper & Row, 1971), and my references are to this book.
12. Wasserstrom, op. cit., p. 112.
13. For an explanation of the ladder concept of a moral code, see my introductory essay "Ethics and Morality."
14. By 'absolute' I mean a right which holds in all cases and which has no exceptions. Thus, in terms of the ladder concept of a moral code, absolute rights, if such exist, are rights that correspond to either moral laws or to ultimate moral principles.
15. Wasserstrom, op. cit., pp. 110–111. The reference is to Mabbott's *The State and the Citizen* (London: Arrow, 1958), pp. 47–58.
16. G. E. Moore also commented on this in the beginning of *Principia Ethica* (New York: Cambridge University Press, 1959). Though the meaning of self-evident suggests epistemological concerns for some, Moore claimed that some of his propositions were "intuitions" and was very clear that he was not interested in epistemological concerns but with logical ones. I suggest that we adopt a similar attitude with regard to Mabbott since any determination concerning the existence or absence of absolute rights need not involve us in an epistemological debate.
17. Ludwig Wittgenstein, *Philosophical Investigations* (New York: Macmillan, 1968), no. 211–212, 326.
18. R. M. Hare, *The Language of Morals* (New York: Oxford University Press, 1965), p. 69.
19. Wasserstrom, op. cit., p. 114.
20. Ibid., p. 117.
21. Following is a brief summary of the distinctions between ultimate moral principles, moral laws, moral rules, and legal rules, discussed in my introductory essay. An *ultimate moral principle* is an always-hold and always-apply statement, and there is usually only one such absolute in any normative moral code. If there is more than one, there can be no conflict between the various moral absolutes. A *moral law* is an always-hold statement, but not an always-apply statement. If a moral code has more than one moral law, these moral laws cannot conflict with each other or with the moral absolute(s). A *moral rule* is a usually-hold statement, but not an always-apply statement. Moral rules can conflict with each other and with moral laws and moral absolutes, although such conflicts would be rather rare. *Legal rules* are usually-hold, or perhaps even always-hold, statements (depending on whether the political system has always-hold laws) and apply only in the locale where they have been passed by a duly authorized legislative body (or, where such legislative bodies are not part of the culture, they have been generally accepted by the society as a whole). These legal rules can be identical with either moral rules or moral laws, and even moral absolutes. Also, they can conflict with each other and with moral rules, moral laws, or moral absolutes. One other reminder is necessary. Any violation of a moral rule or a legal rule must be justified by appealing to a higher-rung principle—either a moral law or an ultimate moral principle. Since both moral rules and legal rules are usually-holds, the burden of justification is on the one who wants to violate them.
22. The abortion controversy seems to be especially prone to this manner of speaking. For one example of this, see Judith Thomson, "In Defense of Abortion," *Philosophy and Public Affairs* 1 (1971): 47–66. I have discussed her position in some detail in my "The Ambiguity of Abortion," *Self, Society, and the Search for Transcendence: An Introduction to Philosophy*, ed. William Bruening (Palo Alto, Ca.: Mayfield Publishing, formerly National Press Books, 1974).
23. The only alternatives are to argue that the right to life is a *prima facie* right and may be withdrawn under certain circumstances, or, as I have said above, to argue that the bearer of the right is not "really" human or "fully" human, and therefore the concept of absolute human right is not applicable.
24. The recent Supreme Court's decision on capital punishment can be found in *United States Law Week* 40 (1972): 4923 ff.
25. In using the expression "by definition," I am not claiming that *a priori* (in a

pejorative sense of that term) my position is true. Instead, I am saying that once one understands what is meant and implied by the word 'right' in ethics, then one will understand that, given the definition of a right as absolute, my position follows. Of course, one is free to object to my understanding of the meaning of right.

26. I use the expression "absolute pacifist" to distinguish my position from that taken by Wasserstrom and others whom I call "nuclear pacifists" or "modern warfare pacifists." Wasserstrom contends that modern and/or nuclear war violates the canons of morality; I, on the other hand, contend that all wars, modern or not, do so. Wasserstrom's position is conditional upon the historical facts that relate to the way in which modern warfare is conducted. He does not seem to see any particular difficulty in killing in war or elsewhere, just in the *how* of the killing.

27. See William Earle, "In Defense of War," *The Monist* 57 (October 1973); also Jan Narveson, "Pacifism: A Philosophical Analysis," *Ethics* 75 (1965); "Is Pacifism Consistent?" *Ethics* 78 (1968); and a revision of these two articles in Rachels, op. cit.

28. This does not exclude the practice of taking the fetus before term. If the fetus is human, and there is a sound medical reason to take it before term, then, in line with the absolute right to life principle, it should be taken only when it has a reasonable chance to survive, and that chance is balanced against a similar consideration for the mother.

29. One of the objections that can be raised against the general position of the absoluteness of the right to life as it is applied to the abortion question is that such a position is just another brand of male chauvinism. First, it ought to be pointed out that even if the argument is chauvinistic and even if it is male, the objection borders on, if it is not clearly, an *ad hominem* (not an *ad virem* nor an *ad feminem*) since the sex of the arguer has nothing to do with the validity or soundness of the argument. Logical considerations have first priority. If a person continues to hold an illogical position, then psychological considerations are relevant in explaining the arguer's insistence in arguing in an invalid or unsound way.

30. For some discussion of the amendment, see *Congressional Quarterly Almanac* 28 (1972): 199-204; and 26 (1970): 706-709.

31. In the 1972 discussion of ERA, Birch Bayh, a supporter of the amendment, responded to Senator Stennis's concern over military service for women thus: "If a woman wants to volunteer, should she be treated differently from a man?" Sex-neutral standards would probably exempt most women from combat duty "because of the ordinary physical standards required, such as pushups, chinups, running, and other physical and combat characteristics that are necessary for any member of the armed services . . . There is an extremely small likelihood that any will reach combat service" *(Congressional Quarterly Almanac* 28, p. 201). Bayh's comment is surely chauvinistic.

32. Hare, op. cit., p. 69.

33. See my "The Existence of God and Ethics," *The Proceedings of the American Catholic Philosophical Association* 46 (1972): 133-140.

34. Wittgenstein, op. cit., no. 19, 23, 241.

THE DIFFERENCES ARE REAL: RACE, INTELLIGENCE, AND GENETICS

Arthur Jensen, author of *Genetics and Education* (1972), released in 1969 a lengthy report on IQ scores, in which he concluded that American blacks were, on the average, less "intelligent" than American whites by an average of 15 points on the IQ scale. The resulting furor over his findings prompted him to write the following article in which he reaffirms his earlier claims that evidence advanced by environmentalists to explain away the IQ differences between the races is insufficient. Jensen states that intelligence depends upon the physiological structure of the brain and asks, "Since the brain . . . is subject to genetic influence, how can anyone disregard the obvious probability of genetic influence on intelligence?" He refutes traditional environmental theories on lack of racial differences which, he says, are accepted primarily "because they harmonize so well with our democratic belief in human equality." Jensen urges and challenges the scientific community to conduct further research into the area of genetic differences between the races. Reprinted from *Psychology Today* Magazine, December, 1973. Copyright © Ziff-Davis Publishing Company.

In 1969, in the appropriately academic context of *The Harvard Educational Review*, I questioned the then and still prevailing doctrine of racial genetic equality in intelligence. I proposed that the average difference in IQ scores between black and white people may be attributable as much to heredity as environment. Realizing that my views might be wrongly interpreted as conflicting with some of the most sacred beliefs of our democracy, I emphasized the important distinction between individual intelligence and the average intelligence of populations. Moreover, I presented my research in a careful and dispassionate manner, hoping that it would stimulate rational discussion of the issue as well as further research.

Much to my dismay, however, my article set off an emotional furor in the world of social science. Amplified by the popular press, the furor soon spread beyond the confines of academia. Almost overnight I became a *cause célèbre*, at least on college campuses. I had spoken what Joseph Alsop called "the unspeakable." To many Americans I had thought the unthinkable.

Science vs. the fear of racism For the past three decades the scientific search for an explanation of the well-established black IQ deficit has been blocked largely, I feel, by fear and abhorrence of racism. In academic circles doctrinaire theories of strictly environmental causation have predominated, with little or no attempt to test their validity rigorously. The environmentalists have refused to consider other possible causes, such as genetic factors. Research into possible genetic influence on intelligence has been academically and socially taboo. The orthodox environmental theories have been accepted not because they have stood up under proper scientific investigation, but because they harmonize so well with our democratic belief in human equality.

The civil-rights movement that gained momentum in the 1950s "required" liberal academic adherence to the theory that the environment was responsible for any individual or racial behavioral differences, and the corollary belief in genetic equality in intelligence. Thus, when I questioned such beliefs I, and my theories, quickly acquired the label "racist." I resent this label, and consider it unfair and inaccurate.

The real meaning of racism Since the horrors of Nazi Germany, and Hitler's persecution of the Jews in the name of his bizarre doctrine of Aryan supremacy, the well-deserved offensiveness of the term "racism" has extended far beyond its legitimate meaning. To me, racism means discrimination among persons on the basis of their racial origins in granting or denying social, civil, or political rights. Racism means the denial of equal opportunity in education or employment on the basis of color or national origin. Racism encourages the judging of persons not each according to his own qualities and abilities, but according to common stereotypes. This is the real meaning of racism. The scientific theory that there are genetically conditioned mental or behavioral differences between races cannot be called racist. It would be just as illogical to condemn the recognition of physical differences between races as racist.

When I published my article in 1969, many critics confused the purely empirical question of the genetic role in racial differences in mental abilities with the highly charged political-ideological issue of racism. Because of their confusion, they denounced my attempt to study the possible genetic causes of such differences. At the same time, the doctrinaire environmentalists, seeing their own position threatened by my inquiry, righteously and dogmatically scorned the genetic theory of intelligence.

Thankfully, the emotional furor that greeted my article has died down enough recently to permit sober and searching consideration of the true intent and substance of what I actually tried to say. Under fresh scrutiny stimulated by the controversy, many scientists have re-examined the environmentalist explanations of the black IQ deficit and found them to be inadequate. They simply do not fully account for the known facts, in the comprehensive and consistent manner we should expect of a scientific explanation.

The black IQ deficit First of all, it is a known and uncontested fact that blacks in the United States score on average about one standard deviation below whites on most tests of intelligence. On the most commonly used IQ tests, this difference ranges from 10 to 20 points, and averages about 15 points. This means that only about 16 percent of the black population exceeds the test performance of the average white on IQ tests. A similar difference of one standard deviation between blacks and whites holds true for 80 standardized mental tests on which published data exist [see chart, page 412].

A difference of one standard deviation can hardly be called inconsequential. Intelligence tests have more than proved themselves as valid predictors of scholastic performance and occupational attainment, and they predict equally well for blacks as for whites. Unpleasant as these predictions may seem to some people, their significance cannot be wished away because of a belief in equality. Of course, an individual's success and self-fulfillment depends upon many characteristics *besides* intelligence, but IQ does represent an index, albeit an imperfect one, of the ability to compete in many walks of life. For example, many selective colleges require College Board test scores of 600 (equivalent to an IQ of 115) as a minimum for admission. An average IQ difference of one standard deviation between blacks and whites means that the white population will have about seven times the percentage of such potentially talented persons (i.e., IQs over 115) as the black population. At the other end of the scale, the 15-point difference in average IQ scores means that mental retardation (IQ below 70) will occur about seven times as often among blacks as among whites.

The IQ difference between blacks and whites, then, clearly has considerable social significance. Yet the environmentalists dismiss this difference as artificial, and claim it does not imply any innate or genetic difference in intelligence. But as I shall show, the purely environmental explanations most commonly put forth are faulty. Examined closely in terms of the available evidence, they simply do not sustain the burden of explanation that they claim. Of course, they may be *possible* explanations of the IQ difference, but that does not necessarily make them the *most probable*. In every case for which there was sufficient relevant evidence to put to a detailed test, the environmental explanations have proven inadequate. I am not saying that have been proven 100 percent wrong, only that they do not account for *all* of the black IQ deficit. Of course, there may be other possible environmental explanations as yet unformulated and untested.

Arguments for the genetic hypothesis The genetic hypothesis, on the other hand, has not yet been put to any direct tests by the standard techniques of genetic research. It must be seriously considered, however, for two reasons: (1) because the default of the environmentalist theory, which has failed in many of its most important predictions, increases the probability of the genetic theory; (2) since genetically conditioned physical characteristics differ markedly between racial groups, there is a strong *a priori* likelihood that genetically conditioned behavioral or mental characteristics will also differ. Since intelligence and other mental abilities depend upon the physiological structure of the brain, and since the brain, like other organs, is subject to genetic influence, how can anyone disregard the obvious probability of genetic influence on intelligence?

Let us consider some of the genetically conditioned characteristics that we already know to vary between major racial groups: body size and proportions; cranial size and shape; pigmentation of the hair, skin and eyes; hair form and distribution; number of vertebrae; fingerprints; bone density; basic-metabolic rate; sweating; consistency of ear wax; age of eruption of the permanent teeth; fissural patterns on the surfaces of the teeth; blood groups; chronic diseases; frequency of twinning; male-female birth ratio; visual and auditory acuity; colorblindness; taste; length of gestation period; physical maturity at birth. In view of so many genetically conditioned traits that do differ between races, wouldn't it be surprising if genetically conditioned mental traits were a major exception?

The heritability of intelligence One argument for the high probability of genetic influence on the IQ difference between blacks and whites involves the concept of *heritability*. A technical term in quantitative genetics, heritability refers to the proportion of the total variation of some trait, among persons within a given population, that can be attributed to genetic factors. Once the heritability of that trait can be determined, the remainder of the variance can be attributed mainly to environmental influence. Now intelligence, as measured by standard tests such as the Stanford-Binet and many others, does show very substantial heritability in the European and North American Caucasian populations in which the necessary genetic studies have been done. I don't know of any geneticists today who have viewed the evidence and who dispute this conclusion.

No precise figure exists for the heritability of intelligence, since, like any population statistic, it varies from one study to another, depending on the particular population sampled, the IQ test used, and the method of genetic analysis. Most of the estimates for the heritability of intelligence in the populations studied indicate that genetic factors are about twice as important as environmental factors as a cause of IQ differences among individuals.

I do not know of a methodologically adequate determination of IQ heritability in a sample of the U.S. black population. The few estimates that exist, though statistically weak, give little reason to suspect that the heritability of IQ for blacks, when adequately estimated, should differ appreciably from that for whites. Of course the absence of reliable data makes this a speculative assumption.

What implication does the heritability *within* a population have concerning the cause of the difference *between* two populations? The fact that IQ is highly heritable within the white and probably the black population does not by itself constitute formal proof that the difference between the populations is genetic, either in whole or in part. However, the fact of substantial heritability of IQ within the populations does increase the *a priori* probability that the population difference is partly attributable to genetic factors. Biologists generally agree that, almost without exception throughout nature, any genetically conditioned characteristic that varies among individuals within a subspecies (i.e., race) also varies genetically between different subspecies. Thus, the substantial heritability of IQ within the Caucasian and probably black populations makes it likely (but does not prove) that the black population's lower average IQ is caused at least in part by a genetic difference.

What about the purely cultural and environmental explanations of the IQ difference? The most common argument claims that IQ tests have a built-in cultural bias that discriminates against blacks and other poor minority groups. Those who hold this view criticize the tests as being based unfairly on the language, knowledge and cognitive skills of the white "Anglo" middle class. They argue that blacks in the United States do not share in the same culture as whites, and therefore acquire different meanings to words, different knowledge, and a different set of intellectual skills.

Culture-fair vs. culture-biased However commonly and fervently held, this claim that the black IQ deficit can be blamed on culture-biased or "culture-loaded" tests does not stand up under rigorous study. First of all, the fact that a test is culture-*loaded* does not necessarily mean it is culture-*biased.* Of course, many tests do have questions of information, vocabulary and comprehension that clearly draw on experiences which could only be acquired by persons sharing a fairly common cultural background. Reputable tests, called "culture-fair" tests, do exist, however. They use nonverbal, simple symbolic material common to a great many different cultures. Such tests measure the ability to generalize, to distinguish differences and similarities, to see relationships, and to solve problems. They test reasoning power rather than just specific bits of knowledge.

Surprisingly, blacks tend to perform relatively better on the more culture-loaded or verbal kinds of tests than on the culture-fair type. For example, on the widely used Wechsler Intelligence Scale, comprised of 11 different subtests, blacks do better on the culture-loaded subtests of vocabulary, general information, and verbal comprehension than on the nonverbal performance tests such as the block designs. Just the opposite is true for such minorities as Orientals, Mexican-Americans, Indians, and Puerto Ricans. It can hardly be claimed that culture-fair tests have a built-in bias in favor of white, Anglo, middle-class Americans when Arctic Eskimos taking the same tests perform on a par with white, middle-class norms. My assistants and I have tested large numbers of Chinese children who score well above white norms on such tests, despite being recent immigrants from Hong Kong and Formosa, knowing little or no English, and having parents who hold low-level socioeconomic occupations. If the tests have a bias toward the white, Anglo, middle-class, one might well wonder why Oriental children should outscore the white Anglos on whom the tests were originally standardized. Our tests of Mexican-Americans produced similar results. They do rather poorly on the culture-loaded types of tests based on verbal skills and knowledge, but they do better on the culture-fair tests. The same holds true for American Indians. All these minorities perform on the two types of tests much as one might expect from the culture-bias hypothesis. Only blacks, among the minorities we have tested, score in just the opposite manner.

Intelligence tests are colorblind Those who talk of culture bias should also consider that all the standard mental tests I know of are colorblind, in that they show the same reliability and predictive validity for blacks and whites. In predicting scholastic achievement, for example, we have found that several different IQ tests predict equally well for blacks and whites. College-aptitude tests also predict grades equally well for blacks and whites. The same equality holds true for aptitude tests which predict job performance.

We have studied culture bias in some standard IQ tests by making internal analyses to see which kinds of test items produce greater differences in scores between blacks and whites. For example, we made such an item-by-item check of the highly culture-loaded Peabody Picture Vocabulary Test, on which blacks average some 15 points lower than whites. The PPVT consists of 150 cards, each containing four pictures. The examiner names one of the pictures and the child points to the appropriate picture. The items follow the order of their difficulty, as measured by the percentage of the children in the normative sample who fail the item.

California vs. England; boys vs. girls To illustrate the sensitivity of this test to cultural differences in word meanings, we compared the performance of white schoolchildren in England with children of the same age in California. Although the two groups obtained about the same total IQ score, the California group found some culture-loaded words such as "bronco" and "thermos" easy, while the London group found them difficult. The opposite occurred with words like "pedestrian" or "goblet." Thus the difficulty of some items differed sharply depending on the child's cultural background. A similar "cultural" bias shows up when comparing the performance of boys and girls, both black and white. Though boys and girls score about equally well over all, they show significant differences in the rank order of item difficulty; specific items, e.g. "parachute" versus "casserole" reflect different sexual biases in cultural knowledge.

Yet when we made exactly the same kind of comparison between blacks and whites in the same city in California, and even in the same schools, we found virtually no difference between the two groups in the order of items when ranked for difficulty, as indexed by the percent failing each item. Both groups show the same rank order of difficulty, although on each item a smaller percentage of blacks give the correct answer. In fact, even the differences between adjacent test items, in terms of percent answering correctly, show great similarity in both the black and white groups.

If this kind of internal analysis reflects cultural bias between different national groups, and sexual bias *within* the same racial group, why does it not reflect the supposed bias *between* the two racial groups? If the tests discriminate against blacks, why do blacks and whites make errors on the same items? Why should the most and least common errors in one group be the same as in the other?

Another way internal analysis can be used to check for bias involves looking for different patterns of item intercorrelations. For example, if a person gets item number 20 right, he may be more likely to get, say, item 30 right than if he had missed item 20. This follows because the test items correlate with one another to varying degrees, and the amount of correlation and the pattern of intercorrelations should be sensitive to group differences in cultural background. Yet we have found no significant or appreciable differences between item intercorrelations for blacks and whites.

In summary, we have found no discriminant features of test items that can statistically separate the test records of blacks and whites any better than chance, when the records are equated for total number correct. We could do so with the London versus California groups, or for sex differences within the same racial group. Thus, even when using the PPVT, one of the most culture-loaded tests, black and white performances did not differ as one should expect if we accept the culture-bias explanation for the black IQ deficit. I consider this strong evidence against the validity of that explanation.

The effect of the tester What about subtle influences in the test situation itself which could have a depressing effect on black performance? It has been suggested, for example, that a white examiner might emotionally inhibit the performance of black children in a test situation. Most of the studies that have attempted to test this hypothesis have produced no substantiation of it. In my own study in which 9,000 black and white children took a number of standard mental and scholastic tests given by black and white examiners, there were no systematic differences in scores according to the race of the examiners. What about the examiner's language, dialect, or accent? In one study, the Stanford-Binet test, a highly verbal and individually administered exam, was translated into black ghetto dialect, and administered by a black examiner fluent in that dialect. A group of black children who took the test under these conditions obtained an average IQ score less than one point higher than the average IQ score of a control group given the test in standard English.

The question of "verbal deprivation" To test the popular notion that blacks do poorly on IQ tests because they are "verbally deprived," we have looked at studies of the test performances of the most verbally deprived individuals we know of: children born totally deaf. These children do score considerably below average on verbal tests, as expected. But they perform completely up to par on the nonverbal culture-fair type of tests. Their performances, then, turn out to be just the opposite of the supposedly verbally deprived blacks, who score higher on the verbal than on the nonverbal tests.

If one hypothesizes that the black IQ deficit may be due to poor motivation or uncooperative attitudes of blacks in the test situation, then one must explain why little or no difference in scores occurs between blacks and whites on tests involving rote learning and memory. Such tests are just as demanding in terms of attention, effort, and persistence, but do not call upon the kinds of abstract reasoning abilities that characterize the culture-fair intelligence tests. We have devised experimental tests, which look to pupils like any other tests, that minimize the need for reasoning and abstract ability, and maximize the role of nonconceptual learning and memory. On these tests black and white children average about the same scores. Therefore, the racial difference clearly does not involve all mental abilities equally. It involves mainly conceptual and abstract reasoning, and not learning and memory.

Another factor often cited as a possible explanation for the black IQ deficit is teacher expectancy—the notion that a child's test score tends to reflect the level of performance expected by his or her teacher, with the teacher's expectation often based on prejudice or stereotypes. Yet numerous studies of teacher expectancy have failed to establish this phenomenon as a contributing factor to the lower IQ scores of blacks.

Testing the environmental hypothesis To test the environmentalist hypothesis, we have examined the results of those tests that most strongly reflect environmental sources of variance, and they turn out to be the very tests that show the least difference between blacks and whites in average scores. The greatest difference in scores between the two racial groups occurs on the tests we infer to be more strongly reflective of genetic variance. If the cultural-environmental hypothesis were correct, just the opposite would be true.

The "sociologist's fallacy" In an attempt to disprove the genetic hypothesis for the black IQ deficit, environmentalists frequently cite studies that compare IQs of socioeconomically matched racial groups, and find considerably less difference in test scores than the usual 15-point difference between races. Here we have a good example of the "sociologist's fallacy." Since whites and blacks differ in average socioeconomic status (SES), the matching of racial groups on SES variables such as education, occupation, and social class necessarily means that the black group is more highly selected in terms of whatever other traits and abilities correlate with SES, including intelligence. Therefore the two groups have been unfairly matched in terms of IQ.

Those who cite the socioeconomic matching studies also fail to take account of the well-established genetic difference between social classes, which invalidates their comparison. For example, when the two races are matched for social background, the average skin color of the black group runs lighter in the higher SES groups. This difference indicates that genetic characteristics do vary with SES. Thus, SES matching of blacks and whites reduces the IQ difference not only because it controls for environmental differences, but because it tends to equalize genetic factors as well.

Variables that don't behave A host of other environmental variables don't behave as they ought to according to a strictly environmentalist theory of the black IQ deficit. For example, on practically all the socioeconomic, educational, nutritional, and other health factors that sociologists point to as causes of the black-white differences in IQ and scholastic achievement, the American Indian population ranks about as far below black standards as blacks do below those of whites. The relevance of these environmental indices can be shown by the fact that within each ethnic group they correlate to some extent in the expected direction with tests of intelligence and scholastic achievement. Since health, parental education, employment, family income, and a number of more subtle environmental factors that have been studied are all deemed important for children's scholastic success, the stark deprivation of the Indian minority, even by black standards, ought to be reflected in a comparison of the intelligence and achievement-test performance of Indians and blacks. But in a nationwide survey reported in the Coleman Report, in 1966, Indians scored *higher* than blacks on all such tests, from the first to the 12th grade. On a nonverbal test given in the first grade, for example, before schooling could have had much impact, Indian children exceeded the mean score of blacks by the equivalent of 14 IQ points. Similar findings occur with Mexican-Americans, who rate below blacks on socioeconomic and other environmental indices, but score considerably higher on IQ tests, especially on the nonverbal type. Thus the IQ difference between Indians and blacks, and between Mexican-Americans and blacks, turns out opposite to what one would predict from purely environmental theory, which of course, assumes complete genetic equality for intelligence. No testable environmental hypothesis has as yet been offered to account for these findings.

Does malnutrition affect intelligence? What about malnutrition, another factor frequently cited by the environmentalists to disprove the genetic hypothesis? Malnutrition has indeed been found to affect both physical and mental development in a small percentage of children in those areas of the world that suffer severe protein deficiencies: India, South America, South Africa, and Mexico. But

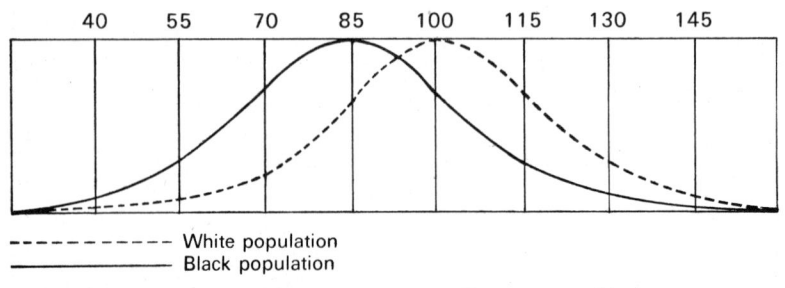

---------- White population
———————— Black population

DISTRIBUTION OF IQ SCORES. *On most intelligence tests, black scores average about 15 points lower than do white scores.*

few blacks in the U.S. show any history or signs of malnutrition, and I have found no evidence that the degree of malnutrition associated with retarded mental development afflicts any major segment of the U.S. population.

Nor do I know of any evidence among humans that maternal malnutrition, by itself, can have pre- or postnatal effects on a child's mental development. The severe famine in the Netherlands during the last years of World War II provided an excellent case study of such a possibility. Thousands of men conceived, gestated, and born during the period of most severe famine, were later tested, as young adults, on Raven's Standard Progressive Matrices, a nonverbal reasoning test. Their scores did not differ significantly from the scores of other Dutch youths of the same age who had not been exposed to such maternal nutritional deprivation.

If further research should definitely establish the existence of genetically conditioned differences in intelligence between certain races, what would be the practical implications? It would take several articles to consider the question adequately, but the only morally tenable position in human relations would remain unchanged: that all persons should be treated according to their own individual characteristics, and not in terms of their group identity. Let me stress that none of the research I have discussed here allows one to conclude anything about the intelligence of any individual black or white person.

Equality of rights and opportunities is clearly the most beneficial condition for any society. Acceptance of the reality of human differences in mental abilities would simply underline the need for equality of opportunity in order to allow everyone to achieve his or her own self-fulfillment. In order to take account and advantage of the diversity of abilities in the population, and truly to serve all citizens equally, the public schools should move beyond narrow conceptions of scholastic achievement. They should offer a much greater diversity of ways for children of whatever aptitude to benefit from their education.

Environment vs. genetics: still an open question I have tried to emphasize the uncertainty of our knowledge of the causes of race differences in mental abilities. I do not claim any direct or definite evidence, in terms of genetic research, for the existence of genotypic intelligence differences between races or other human population groups. I have not urged acceptance of a hypothesis on the basis of insufficient evidence. I have tried to show that the evidence we now have does not support the environmentalist theory, which, until quite recently, has been accepted as scientifically established. Social scientists have generally accepted it without question, and most scientists in other fields have given silent assent. I have assembled evidence which, I believe, makes such complacent assent no longer possible, and reveals the issue as an open question, calling for much further scientific study.

Politicizing a scientific issue Most of the scientists and intellectuals with whom I have discussed these matters in the past few years see no danger in furthering our knowledge of the genetic basis of racial differences in mental or behaviorial traits. Nor do they fear general recognition of genetic differences in such traits by the scientific world, if that should be the eventual outcome of further research. They do see a danger in politicizing a basically scientific question, one that should be settled strictly on the basis of evidence.

Most of the attempts to politicize the issue, I have found, come from the radical left. True liberals and humanists, on the other hand, want to learn the facts. They do not wish to expend their energies sustaining myths and illusions. They wish to face reality, whatever it may be, because only on the level of reality can real problems be effectively confronted. This means asking hard questions, and seeking the answers with as much scientific ingenuity and integrity as we can muster. It means examining all reasonable hypotheses, including unpopular ones. It means maintaining the capacity to doubt what we might most want to believe, acknowledging the uncertainties at the edge of knowledge, and viewing new findings in terms of shifting probabilities rather than as absolute conclusions.

Robert L. Williams

THE SILENT MUGGING OF THE BLACK COMMUNITY: SCIENTIFIC RACISM AND IQ

Robert L. Williams, a founder and former National Chairman of the Association of Black Psychologists, is currently Director of Black Studies and Professor of Psychology at Washington University, Saint Louis. In the following article, Williams defines and describes what he calls scientific racism, noting that the black-white IQ controversy is one of many pernicious examples. He refutes the reliability of IQ and achievement tests as a measure of intelligence, stressing their cultural biases and their failure to recognize the unique cultural traditions of the American black community. Williams argues that reaction to the threat posed by recent social and political gains by blacks and to racial theories advanced by Arthur Jensen and others is starting this country down the road to genocide for the blacks. He calls for stern controls by government and business "to bring about a halt to the continued violation of the civil rights of black people" resulting from the practice of scientific racism. Reprinted from *Psychology Today* Magazine, May, 1974. Copyright © 1974 Ziff-Davis Publishing Company. All rights reserved.

The fundamental, inescapable problem for black people in America is still racism. The civil rights movement of the '60s focused on institutional racism, that oppressive cluster of laws, customs, and practices that systematically support doctrines of superiority and inferiority in America.

Now, blacks suffer another counterforce to survival: scientific racism. It has always been part of the American formula, but recently it has grown more virulent with advances in technology. This cold and inhumane experimentation with, and exclusion of, human beings is insidious because it is housed in universities, nurtured in industry, and cloaked in the language of rational science. An Ashanti proverb warns, "It is the calm and silent waters that drown a man." But the calmness fools no one; scientific racism is part of silent racial war, and the practitioners of it use intelligence tests as their hired guns.

I was almost one of the testing casualties. At 15, I earned an IQ test score of 82, three points above the track of the special education class. Based on this score, my counselor suggested that I take up bricklaying because I was "good with my hands." My low IQ, however, did not allow me to see that as desirable. I went to Philander Smith College anyway, graduating with honors, earned my master's degree at Wayne State University and my Ph.D. at Washington University in St. Louis. Other blacks, equally as qualified, have been wiped out.

The primary issues in the great black-white IQ controversy are not those of cultural test bias, the nature of intelligence, or the heritability of IQ. The issue is admittance to America's mainstream. IQ and achievement tests are nothing but updated versions of the old signs down South that read For Whites Only. University admission policies have required standardized psychological tests such as the Scholastic Aptitude Test (SAT) or the Graduate Record Examination (GRE) as a criterion for admission to colleges, graduate schools, medical or law schools and other professional schools. For blacks, these tests more often mean exclusion.

At the same time, with the help of the federal government, universities have launched research into various aspects of the "black problem." The white belief system has determined their selection of blacks as a problem, how they should be studied, and what the solutions shall be.

Any research that tries to distinguish racial differences, is, as psychologist Charles Thomas puts it, based on ". . . a belief that black people are similar enough to white people to permit measurement by common instruments, and different enough from white people to justify scientific research into the causes of the differences."

Supermarket of oppression The American testing industry goes hand-in-hand with the university in fostering the misuse of tests, and it is no mom-and-pop corner store. It is a multimillion-dollar-a-year supermarket of oppression. If the captains of this industry would admit the truth about testing, they would face bankruptcy. But the economic survival of the testing industry depends upon its symbiotic relationship with educational institutions, and both have constructed elaborate defenses against outside criticism. In spite of arguments to the contrary, test publishers maintain that the tests are neutral. They contend that although test results may be employed in a biased manner, they are not in themselves biased.

The educational institutions argue that testing is the fairest way to determine every child's ability. But no matter which argument one hears or believes, the results are the same. With few recent exceptions, black parents have had no control over whether or not their children were tested and how the test results would be used. Consequently, black children are placed, in disproportionate numbers, in classes for the mentally retarded, special education classes or lower educational tracks.

Such misuse of psychological tests with black children is based upon several misconceptions. First, IQ cannot be inherited. An intelligence quotient (IQ) is nothing more than a score earned on a test. Actual intelligence covers a broad range of human abilities that IQ tests do not even attempt to measure. For example, no test has formally assessed the many verbal and nonverbal skills required to survive in the black community. What we need is a survival quotient (SQ), not an IQ.

Second, IQ tests do not measure the ability to succeed in the world, or even to get along in a different academic environment. Psychologists have designed these tests specifically to predict school success, but children must attend a school that adequately teaches the content of the test in order to score well. Most ghetto schools fail at this task.

A third misconception about the IQ test is its value as a measurement of mental retardation. Illiteracy is frequently equated with mental retardation, but literacy and intellect are not directly correlated. One who is highly literate is not necessarily a wise person or possessed of great intellect. Conversely, an illiterate person is not necessarily mentally retarded. Historical documents have shown that prior to the Civil War, masters often expropriated inventions from their uneducated black slaves. This act robbed the slaves of both their financial rewards and the intellectual credit due them.

Although lack of formal education and other obstacles excluded blacks from fields of science, many patented their inventions. Some of these, such as ice cream, potato chips, lawn mowers, and golf tees are in use today. One black man, Granville T. Woods, who received only a fifth-grade education, obtained about 50 patents, including one for the incubator.

Finally, IQ tests do not measure one's capacity to learn; a low score does not mean low ability. According to Bruno Bettelheim, "One boy who came to us diagnosed as feeble-minded today is a professor at Stanford."[1]

The oral tradition Many white researchers have claimed that black children are nonverbal and lack the ability to reason abstractly. There is irony in that view, since the culture of black people is based upon an oral tradition, dating back before Christ, that abounds in abstractions and symbolism. That tradition predates the Gutenberg press by at least 2,000 years. Proverbs, songs, prayers, myths, stories, and legends were at the heart of formal and informal African educational systems.

Although the slave traders ripped the Africans from their native country, many of their customs and folkways survived the Atlantic passage. The slaves transplanted much of their oral traditions to the plantation, and incorporated them into black culture.

Blacks have maintained this African heritage, although Western chauvinism has isolated and belittled it as childlike and simpleminded. As Edmund Leach, the British anthropologist, has pointed out, the white Westerner is taught to believe that logical, mathematical, Aristotelian statements are the path to communication. This narrow perspective encourages reverence for literature and mathematics, and causes scorn for the metaphysical language of myth, which transcends logic. Westerners believe, says Leach, that they practice Arsitotelian logic all the time. The truth is more complex, and consistent with the African tradition. Human beings communicate on many channels, with messages penetrating us through our eyes, our ears, our noses, our skin. And communication between human beings is not complete without the nuances of tone of voice, gestures, shared visual perceptions, and prior information held in common.

Black scholars are attempting to reconstruct the essence of the African tradition in a concept known as Ebonics. This concept combines linguistic and paralinguistic features that represent the communicative competence of West African, Caribbean, and United States slave descendants of African ancestors. It includes the various idioms, patois, argots, and social dialects of these regions. It also involves nonverbal cues, such as those referred to by Leach. Ebonics should not be confused with so-called Black English. The latter is a common hustle that was created, discussed, and researched almost entirely by whites out of fascination with the ghetto. Black scholars have rejected the concept of Black English because it is simply poor grammar, and not uniquely black. Poor whites of the South speak the same English. Ebonics, unlike Black English, is different, not deficient.

Given these differences in black culture, the rationale for a culture-specific intelligence test is clear. If a child can learn certain familiar relationships in his own culture, he can master similar concepts in the school curriculum, so long as the curriculum is related to his background experiences. For the average black child, there is too often a mismatching or discontinuity between the skills acquired from his culture and those required for successful test-taking and in the school curriculum.

L. Wendell Rivers, a black child psychologist and researcher, and I conducted a study to measure the effects of test instructions written in black dialectal language and in standard English on the performance of black children during intelligence testing. We divided 890 black kindergarten, first- and second-grade children into two groups of 445 each. We controlled for the variables of IQ, age, sex, and grade in both the experimental and control groups. We used the standard version of the Boehm Test of Basic Concepts (BTBC), and a nonstandard version that we developed. The BTBC consists of 50 pictorial multiple-choice items involving concepts of space, quantity, and time. Black teachers and graduate students translated the concepts and objects into the black idiom:

STANDARD VERSION	NONSTANDARD
Mark the toy that is *behind the sofa*.	Mark the toy that is *in back of* the *couch*.
Mark the apple that is *whole*.	Mark the apple that is *still all there*.
Mark the boy who is *beginning* to climb the tree.	Mark the boy who is *starting* to climb the tree. (Variations may be used as: about to, getting ready to.)

Children who took the test that was representative of their cultural background, i.e., the nonstandard version, scored significantly higher than the other group. The language of the standard version penalized the children taking the Boehm test.

That study suggested the need to develop a culture-specific test for black children. I conducted another experiment, this time using the Black Intelligence Test of Cultural Homogeneity (The BITCH Test) that I developed. I took 100 vocabulary items from the *Afro-American Slang* dictionary, my friends, and my personal experiences in working with black people. I gave the test to 100 black and 100 white subjects who were from 16 to 18 years old. Half in each group were from the low socioeconomic level, and half were from the middle. The results showed that blacks scored much higher than whites on a test that was specific to their culture; the black subjects earned a mean score of 87.07, while the whites earned a mean score of 51.07. Clearly, if black children are given a culture-specific test that is representative of their backgrounds, they will do better than white children taking the same test.

The notion of a culture-specific test is not new. The Stanford-Binet, Wechsler Intelligence Scale for Children, and the Peabody Picture Vocabulary Test, among others, are clear examples of culturally specific tests. Representatives of the white middle-class culture contributed the bulk of the test items. White experts determined the correct responses, and all-white populations normalized them. Culture specific tests for *black children* would only continue the tradition. The difference is that those children would not arrive in the classrooms of America with "unteachable" labels pasted, on the bias, to their permanent records.

By focusing closely on children, I do not mean to imply that black people escape scientific racism when they leave grammar school. In July of 1972, 542 people took the Georgia bar exam. Approximately 50 of them were black, and all of them received failing grades. Although these black students had survived the SAT, Law School Admissions Test, and the rigors of law school, the bar fell on them. As my grandfather used to say, "Don't crow till you get out of the woods; the bear might be behind the last tree."

Blacks strike back Black people have begun to strike back at the racism of testing. A suit recently filed in Georgia on behalf of 15 black law school graduates charges that the state exam is prepared and administered in a racially discriminatory manner. The plaintiffs say that the grading system is often the matter of the examiner's judgment rather than a tabulation of technically right or wrong answers. The suit asks that all black law school graduates previously excluded from the bar by the test be allowed to practice. There are similar suits being filed on the national level by the National Bar Association and the American Civil Liberties Union.

Black parents are fighting the same fights on behalf of their children. A class-action suit in San Francisco by parents and the Bay Area Association of Black Psychologists brought a court order that prohibited school officials from using IQ tests as a basis for placing black children in classes for the mentally retarded. The plaintiffs charged, successfully, that the district's placement tests had been standardized on middle-class white students, and were therefore not applicable to blacks. In a Washington, D.C. case, Judge Skelly Wright ordered the public-school system to abolish its educational tracking system, because tests had been used to segregate blacks and whites.

A pattern of dehumanization The implications of the testing controversy should not escape us. Historically, when one group of people has wished to subjugate or exploit another group, they dehumanized them by ascribing derogatory characteristics to the subjects: animalistic, savage, emotional, over-sexed, lazy, unscrupulous, and crazy, to name a few. It was also necessary to impugn the subjects' ability to determine their own destinies; they were described as child-like, immature, backward, simple-minded, illiterate, or of low intelligence.

The black-white IQ controversy presents an analogous situation. When a people is labeled consistently as being of low-intellect or simple-minded, the respect among the general populace for their rights to life can and will erode to nothing. It has happened historically, and it has happened here. The black community has become the white researcher's hunting ground, the ideal experimental laboratory.

What we now know of the Tuskegee syphilis experiment is a shocking disclosure of clear-cut scientific racism. During a 40-year, federally funded study, scientists in Alabama used 600 black men as human guinea pigs. The men, victims of syphilis, were denied treatment even after the discovery of penicillin, so that scientists could study the progress of the disease. There is no moral or medical justification for that act alone, but to make this act of moral pauperism worse, scientists already knew the effects of long-term, untreated syphilis from data obtained from a Norwegian study that was conducted from 1891 to 1910. Syphilis is a highly contagious, dangerous, and debilitating disease, that left untreated, can cause sterility, blindness, deafness, bone deterioration, nervous-system degeneration, heart disease, and eventually death. The experimenters tricked these poor black men into participating in the experiment by offering them transportation to and from the hospital, hot lunches, medical care for ailments other than syphilis, and free burial. Malcolm X reminds us that "a man who tosses worms in the river isn't necessarily a friend to the fish; all the fish who take him for a friend, who think the worm got no hooks in it, usually end up in the frying pan."

Records from the public-health center for disease control in Atlanta disclosed that somewhere between 28 and 100 participants died as a direct result of syphilis. Another 154 persons died of heart disease that may have been caused by syphilis. Unrecorded are the statistics on the many wives and girl friends that the men may have infected.

The Tuskegee experiment underscores the low regard for black lives among some members of the scientific community. This poses a serious threat to the survival of black people in the United States. Approximately 600 psychosurgical operations are performed each year. The subjects are too frequently black and almost invariably poor. Prisoners, especially black ones, seem to be fair game for the psychosurgeon's knife.

Racist research In another exercise in scientific racism, the federal government funded Johns Hopkins University to conduct an experimental program in genetic testing. The program involved 6,000 juvenile delinquents in a Maryland state school, and 7,500 black youths who attended a Baltimore free medical clinic. The purpose of the study was to search for XYY chromosome patterns in delinquents. The XYY pattern is genetically abnormal and is supposedly related to criminal behavior. And suppose they had found the abnormal pattern of genes? What would happen to the carriers? Would they wind up in jail? Or would they be sterilized?

We can ask the same questions in regard to a suggestion by Arnold Hutschnecker, a physician known to the Nixon Administration. In 1969, Hutschnecker suggested mass testing of six- to eight-year-old black ghetto children. Spurred on by the findings of the National Commission on the Causes and Prevention of Violence that black ghetto slums were the breeding ground of violence, he suggested using the Rorschach inkblot and the Sheldon-Glueck Prediction tests, among others, "to detect the children who have violent and homicidal tendencies." (To press his point, Hutschnecker recalled that Lee Harvey Oswald had showed violent tendencies at age 11 but had gone untreated). The logical extension of such a mass testing program could be the mass incarceration of black children. Any child who showed "violent and homicidal tendencies," which is purely a subjective judgment, could be locked up, sterilized, or otherwise isolated from society.

Publicly, at least, Hutschnecker's recommendations were rejected. But experience has taught blacks to be aware of hidden agendas.

American blacks have every right to fear intellectual and physical genocide. In February 1971, 21 states had laws authorizing forced eugenic sterilizations of persons labeled as mentally defective. Minnie and Mary Alice Relf, 14 and 12 years old, are examples of Alabama's interpretation of the law. A white doctor performed tubal ligations on both of them when they went to a clinic, ostensibly for a "shot." Bert Brown, Director of the National Institute of Mental Health, noted that in a recent study of sickle-cell anemia, 22cc of blood were taken from victims, when only one drop of blood is required to make a slide to examine the cells. What else are those blood samples used for? Once again, blacks have no control over how test results are misused, or how their bodies and the bodies of their children are abused. The mother who is notified that her son will be tested may find next week that he is in a class for the mentally retarded. The mother who sends her daughter to a clinic for "immunizations," may find that she has been sterilized.

The road to genocide It is no coincidence that genetic theories of black IQ deficits are being advanced at this time; blacks are making social and political gains that threaten the racist structure of American society. Arthur Jensen has suggested that blacks have an IQ deficit, and that this may be inherited; William Shockley claims that a so-called "dysgenic trend" among blacks threatens to make us a race of idiots. In the minds of black people, both theories lead down one road: genocide. A recent poll conducted by Castellano Turner, an assistant professor of psychology at the University of Massachusetts, and William A. Darity, head of the University's Department of Public Health, found a fear of genocide among blacks. Of 1,890 blacks who were questioned in two cities, 62 percent agreed that, as blacks become more militant, there will be an effort to decrease the black population. And 51 percent agreed that as the need for cheap labor goes down, there will be an effort to reduce the number of blacks. Thirty-nine percent agreed that birth-control programs are a plot to eliminate blacks.

Charles F. Westoff, a professor of sociology at Princeton University, reports that the National Fertility Study conducted in 1970 showed a dramatic drop in unwanted fertility rates during the periods 1961 to 1965, and 1966 to 1970. In the age range, 30 to 44, only 8.4 percent in 1965 and 11.6 percent in 1970 of white married women were sterilized. To the contrary, 21.9 percent in 1965 and 32.5 percent in 1970 of black married women in this age range were sterilized. We can ask how many of these black women were forced to have sterilizations. In Aiken, South Carolina, alone, in the first six months of 1973, 17 pregnant black welfare mothers were forced to undergo sterilization as a condition for delivering their babies.

The statistics cannot be casually dismissed. Although America's handling of the "black problem" may not be as grossly blatant as the Nazi's handling of the "Jewish problem," the signs are there. There is nothing to give assurance that efforts are being made to prevent further ghastly acts like the Tuskegee study. The philosopher George Santayana warned that those who fail to understand the mistakes of history are bound to repeat them. America is a slow learner.

More than a moratorium There must be a major effort made to create the necessary pressure on the corporate structures and the federal government to bring about a halt to the continued violation of the civil rights of black people. The testing arena is the place where blacks are literally thrown to the wolves. We must do more than call for a moratorium on testing:

• A bold, federal regulatory law, a truth-in-testing law must be formulated and enacted through legislation, and vigorously enforced.

• Sanctions, ranging from stiff fines, suspensions, dechartering of the corporations, colleges, or universities, or even more severe criminal penalties should be leveled against the testing corporations, state departments of education, local school districts, colleges, and universities.

• Black communities must establish veto and monitoring groups to assure that unfair testing and exploitive research will be halted immediately.

• Black communities should file class-action law suits that demand an end to testing of black children for whatever reason. Many states have laws requiring testing for various reasons, most of which are questionable. Class-action suits can put an end to these.

• The American Psychological Association and the American Personnel and Guidance Association stance on psychological testing should not be regarded as sufficient to stop abuses. "A Shepherd does not strike his sheep."

• An attempt must be made to reorganize and regulate the corporate structure of the testing industry. At present it is composed of too many people who have a vested interest in maintaining the status quo: eight college presidents, one vice-president, two presidents of foundations, one superintendent of public schools, three presidents of testing corporations, and one congressman.

• Outside agencies, rather than the testing industry itself, must regularly research and assess the tests produced for use in schools. This should include researchers from the populations to be tested. "Never let the fox into the henhouse to feed the chickens."

The issue of scientific racism has affected blacks predominantly because we have been the most vulnerable. But those whites who would dismiss this as a worry solely for blacks should remember that poor whites and unaware whites are equally vulnerable. The forced sterilization of welfare mothers in South Carolina included white mothers as well. And poor white children often wind up in special education classes for reasons that are punitive rather than educational. As with every other manifestation of racism, the scientific variety threatens to destroy us all.

1. See "A Conversation with Bruno Bettelheim," Psychology Today, May 1969.

Dee Alexander Brown
BURY MY HEART AT WOUNDED KNEE

Dee Alexander Brown, author of *Grierson's Raid* (1954), *The Bold Cavaliers* (1959), *The Galvanized Yankees* (1963), and *Fort Phil Kearny: An American Saga* (1971) is an unquestioned leader in the recent movement to expose past and continuing injustices against the American Indian. In his most famous work, *Bury My Heart at Wounded Knee: An Indian History of the American West,* from which the following excerpts are taken, Brown documents the tragic history of the white man's exploitation of the Indian in what has already been acclaimed a classic. Brown writes that, at best, the white man tried to force the Indians to follow his ways; at worst, he treated the Indian as an animal to be hunted down. The result was 400 years of wholesale expropriation of Indian lands and wholesale slaughter of the Indian populations. From *Bury My Heart at Wounded Knee* by Dee Brown. Copyright © 1970 by Dee Brown. Reprinted by permission of Holt, Rinehart and Winston, Publishers.

"Their manners are decorous and praiseworthy"

Where today are the Pequot? Where are the Narragansett, the Mohican, the Pokanoket, and many other once powerful tribes of our people? They have vanished before the avarice and the oppression of the White Man, as snow before a summer sun.

Will we let ourselves be destroyed in our turn without a struggle, give up our homes, our country bequeathed to us by the Great Spirit, the graves of our dead and everything that is dear and sacred to us? I know you will cry with me, "Never! Never!" (Tecumseh of the Shawnees)

It began with Christopher Columbus, who gave the people the name *Indios.* Those Europeans, the white men, spoke in different dialects, and some pronounced the word *Indien,* or *Indianer,* or Indian. *Peaux-rouges,* or redskins, came later. As was the custom of the people when receiving strangers, the Tainos on the island of San Salvador generously presented Columbus and his men with gifts and treated them with honor.

"So tractable, so peaceable, are these people," Columbus wrote to the King and Queen of Spain, "that I swear to your Majesties there is not in the world a better nation. They love their neighbors as themselves, and their discourse is ever sweet and gentle, and accompanied with a smile; and though it is true that they are naked, yet their manners are decorous and praiseworthy."

All this, of course, was taken as a sign of weakness, if not heathenism, and Columbus being a righteous European was convinced the people should be "made to work, sow and do all that is necessary and to *adopt our ways.*" Over the next four centuries (1492-1890) several million Europeans and their descendants undertook to enforce their ways upon the people of the New World.

Columbus kidnapped ten of his friendly Taino hosts and carried them off to Spain, where they could be introduced to the white man's ways. One of them died soon after arriving there, but not before he was baptized a Christian. The Spaniards were so pleased that they had made it possible for the first Indian to enter heaven that they hastened to spread the good news throughout the West Indies.

THE FLIGHT OF THE NEZ PERCÉS

> The earth was created by the assistance of the sun, and it should be left as it was. . . . The country was made without lines of demarcation, and it is no man's business to divide it. . . . I see the whites all over the country gaining wealth, and see their desire to give us lands which are worthless. . . . The earth and myself are of one mind. The measure of the land and the measure of our bodies are the same. Say to us if you can say it, that you were sent by the Creative Power to talk to us. Perhaps you think the Creator sent you here to dispose of us as you see fit. If I thought you were sent by the Creator I might be induced to think you had a right to dispose of me. Do not misunderstand me, but understand me fully with reference to my affection for the land. I never said the land was mine to do with it as I chose. The one who has the right to dispose of it is the one who has created it. I claim a right to live on my land, and accord you the privilege to live on yours. (Heinmot Tooyalaket [Chief Joseph] of the Nez Percés)

In September, 1805, when Lewis and Clark came down off the Rockies on their westward journey, the entire exploring party was halffamished and ill with dysentery—too weak to defend themselves. They were in the country of the Nez Percés, so named by French trappers, who observed some of these Indians wearing dentalium shells in their noses. Had the Nex Percés chosen to do so, they could have put an end to the Lewis and Clark expedition there on the banks of Clearwater River, and seized their wealth of horses. Instead the Nez Percés welcomed the white Americans, supplied them with food, and looked after the explorers' horses for several months while they continued by canoe to the Pacific shore.

Thus began a long friendship between the Nez Percés and white Americans. For seventy years the tribe boasted that no Nez Percé had ever killed a white man. But white men's greed for land and gold finally broke the friendship.

In 1855 Governor Isaac Stevens of Washington Territory invited the Nez Percés to a peace council. "He said there were a great many white people in the country, and many more would come; that he wanted the land marked out so that the Indians and white men could be separated. If they were to live in peace it was necessary, he said, that the Indians should have a country set apart for them, and in that country they must stay."

Tuekakas, a chief known as Old Joseph by the white men, told Governor Stevens that no man owned any part of the earth, and a man could not sell what he did not own.

The governor could not comprehend such an attitude. He urged Old Joseph to sign the treaty and receive presents of blankets. "Take away your paper," the chief replied. "I will not touch it with my hand."

Aleiya, who was called Lawyer by the white men, signed the treaty, and so did several other Nez Percés, but Old Joseph took his people back to their home in Wallowa Valley, a green country of winding waters, wide meadows, mountain forests, and a clear blue lake. Old Joseph's band of Nez Percés raised fine horses and cattle, lived in fine lodges, and when they needed anything from the white men they traded their livestock.

Only a few years after the first treaty signing, government men were swarming around the Nez Percés again, wanting more land. Old Joseph warned his people to take no presents from them, not even one blanket. "After a while," he said, "they will claim that you have accepted pay for your country."

In 1863 a new treaty was presented to the Nez Percés. It took away the Wallowa Valley and three-fourths of the remainder of their land, leaving them only a small reservation in what is now Idaho. Old Joseph refused to attend the treaty signing, but Lawyer and several other chiefs—none of whom had ever lived in the Valley of Winding Waters—signed away their people's lands. The "thief treaty," Old Joseph called it, and he was so offended that he tore up the Bible a white missionary had given him to convert him to Christianity.

WAR COMES TO THE CHEYENNES

When Chivington rode up to the officers' quarters at Fort Lyon, Major Anthony greeted him warmly. Chivington began talking of "collecting scalps" and "wading in gore." Anthony responded by saying that he had been "waiting for a good chance to pitch into them," and that every man at Fort Lyon was eager to joint Chivington's expedition against the Indians.

Not all of Anthony's officers, however, were eager or even willing to join Chivington's well-planned massacre. Captain Silas Soule, Lieutenant Joseph Cramer, and Lieutenant James Connor protested that an attack on Black Kettle's peaceful camp would violate the pledge of safety given the Indians by both Wynkoop and Anthony, "that it would be murder in every sense of the word," and any officer participating would dishonor the uniform of the Army.

Chivington became violently angry at them and brought his fist down close to Lieutenant Cramer's face. "Damn any man who sympathizes with Indians!" he cried. "I have come to kill Indians, and believe it is right and honorable to use any means under God's heaven to kill Indians."

Soule, Cramer, and Connor had to join the expedition or face a court-martial, but they quietly resolved not to order their men to fire on the Indians except in self-defense.

At eight o'clock on the evening of November 28, Chivington's column, now consisting of more than seven hundred men by the addition of Anthony's troops, moved out in column of fours. Four twelve-pounder mountain howitzers accompanied the cavalry. Stars glittered in a clear sky; the night air carried a sharp bite of frost.

For a guide Chivington conscripted sixty-nine-year-old James Beckwourth, a mulatto who had lived with the Indians for half a century. Medicine Calf Beckwourth tried to beg off, but Chivington threatened to hang the old man if he refused to guide the soldiers to the Cheyenne-Arapaho encampment.

As the column moved on, it became evident that Beckwourth's dimming eyes and rheumatic bones handicapped his usefulness as a guide. At a ranch house near Spring Bottom, Chivington stopped and ordered the rancher hauled out of his bed to take Beckwourth's place as guide. The rancher was Robert Bent, eldest son of William Bent; all three of Bent's half-Cheyenne sons would soon be together at Sand Creek.

The Cheyenne camp lay in a horseshoe bend of Sand Creek north of an almost dry stream bed. Black Kettle's tepee was near the center of the village, with White Antelope's and War Bonnet's people to the west. On the east side and slightly separated from the Cheyennes was Left Hand's Arapaho camp. Altogether there were about six hundred Indians in the creek bend, two-thirds of them being women and children. Most of the warriors were several miles to the east hunting buffalo for the camp, as they had been told to do by Major Anthony.

So confident were the Indians of absolute safety, they kept no night watch except of the pony herd which was corralled below the creek. The first warning they had of an attack was about sunrise—the drumming of hooves on the sand flats. "I was sleeping in a lodge," Edmond Guerrier said. "I heard, at first, some of the squaws outside say there were a lot of buffalo coming into camp; others said they were a lot of soldiers." Guerrier immediately went outside and started toward Gray Blanket Smith's tent.

George Bent, who was sleeping in the same area, said that he was still in his blankets when he heard shouts and the noise of people running about the camp. "From down the creek a large body of troops was advancing at a rapid trot . . . more soldiers could be seen making for the Indian pony herds to the south of the camps; in the camps themselves all was confusion and noise—men, women, and children rushing out of the lodges partly dressed; women and children screaming at sight of the troops; men running back into the lodges for their arms. . . . I looked toward the chief's lodge and saw that Black Kettle had a large American flag tied to the end of a long lodgepole and was standing in front of his lodge, holding the pole, with the flag fluttering in the gray light of the winter dawn. I heard him call to the people not to be afraid, that the soldiers would not hurt them; then the troops opened fire from two sides of the camp."

Meanwhile young Guerrier had joined Gray Blanket Smith and Private Louderback at the trader's tent. "Louderback proposed we should go out and meet the troops. We started. Before we got outside the edge of the tent I could see soldiers begin to dismount. I thought they were artillerymen and were about to shell the camp. I had hardly spoken when they began firing with their rifles and pistols. When I saw I could not get to them, I struck out; I left the soldier and Smith."

Louderback halted momentarily, but Smith kept moving ahead toward the cavalrymen. "Shoot the damned old son of a bitch!"a soldier shouted from the ranks. "He's no better than an Indian." At the first scattered shots, Smith and Louderback turned and ran for their tent. Smith's half-breed son, Jack, and Charlie Bent had already taken cover there.

By this time hundreds of Cheyenne women and children were gathering around Black Kettle's flag. Up the dry creek bed, more were coming from White Antelope's camp. After all, had not Colonel

Greenwood told Black Kettle that as long as the United States flag flew above him no soldier would fire upon him? White Antelope, an old man of seventy-five, unarmed, his dark face seamed from sun and weather, strode toward the soldiers. He was still confident that the soldiers would stop firing as soon as they saw the American flag and the white surrender flag which Black Kettle had now run up.

Medicine Calf Beckwourth, riding beside Colonel Chivington, saw White Antelope approaching. "He came running out to meet the command," Beckwourth later testified, "holding up his hands and saying 'Stop! stop!' He spoke it in as plain English as I can. He stopped and folded his arms until shot down." Survivors among the Cheyennes said that White Antelope sang the death song before he died:

Nothing lives long
Only the earth and the mountains.

From the direction of the Arapaho camp, Left Hand and his people also tried to reach Black Kettle's flag. When Left Hand saw the troops, he stood with his arms folded, saying he would not fight the white men because they were his friends. He was shot down.

Robert Bent, who was riding unwillingly with Colonel Chivington, said that when they came in sight of the camp "I saw the American flag waving and heard Black Kettle tell the Indians to stand around the flag, and there they were huddled—men, women, and children. This was when we were within fifty yards of the Indians. I also saw a white flag raised. These flags were in so conspicuous a position that they must have been seen. When the troops fired, the Indians ran, some of the men into their lodges, probably to get their arms. . . . I think there were six hundred Indians in all. I think there were thirty-five braves and some old men, about sixty in all . . . the rest of the men were away from camp, hunting. . . . After the firing the warriors put the squaws and children together, and surrounded them to protect them. I saw five squaws under a bank for shelter. When the troops came up to them they ran out and showed their persons to let the soldiers know they were squaws and begged for mercy, but the soldiers shot them all. I saw one squaw lying on the bank whose leg had been broken by a shell; a soldier came up to her with a drawn saber; she raised her arm to protect herself, when he struck, breaking her arm; she rolled over and raised her other arm, when he struck, breaking it, and then left her without killing her. There seemed to be indiscriminate slaughter of men, women, and children. There were some thirty or forty squaws collected in a hole for protection; they sent out a little girl about six years old with a white flag on a stick; she had not proceeded but a few steps when she was shot and killed. All the squaws in that hole were afterwards killed, and four or five bucks outside. The squaws offered no resistance. Every one I saw dead was scalped. I saw one squaw cut open with an unborn child, as I thought, lying by her side. Captain Soule afterwards told me that such was the fact. I saw the body of White Antelope with the privates cut off, and I heard a soldier say he was going to make a tobacco pouch out of them. I saw one squaw whose privates had been cut out. . . . I saw a little girl about five years of age who had been hid in the sand; two soldiers discovered her, drew their pistols and shot her, and then pulled her out of the sand by the arm. I saw quite a number of infants in arms killed with their mothers."

(In a public speech made in Denver not long before this massacre, Colonel Chivington advocated the killing and scalping of all Indians, even infants. "Nits make lice!" he declared.)

Robert Bent's description of the soldiers' atrocities was corroborated by Lieutenant James Connor: "In going over the battleground the next day I did not see a body of man, woman, or child but was scalped, and in many instances their bodies were mutilated in the most horrible manner—men, women, and children's privates cut out, &c; I heard one man say that he had cut out a woman's private parts and had them for exhibition on a stick; I heard another man say that he had cut the fingers off an Indian to get the rings on the hand; according to the best of my knowledge and belief these atrocities that were committed were with the knowledge of J. M. Chivington, and I do not know of his taking any measures to prevent them; I heard of one instance of a child a few months old being thrown in the feedbox of a wagon, and after being carried some distance left on the ground to perish; I also heard of numerous instances in which men had cut out the private parts of females and stretched them over the saddle-bows and wore them over their hats while riding in the ranks."

RED CLOUD'S WAR

Toward the end of the fighting the Cheyennes and Arapahos on one side and the Sioux on the other were so close together that they began hitting each other with their showers of arrows. Then it was all over. Not a soldier was left alive. A dog came out from among the dead, and a Sioux started to catch it to take home with him, but Big Rascal, a Cheyenne, said, "Don't let the dog go," and somebody shot it with an arrow. This was the fight the white men called the Fetterman Massacre; the Indians called it the Battle of the Hundred Slain.[9]

Casualties were heavy among the Indians, almost two hundred dead and wounded. Because of the intense cold, they decided to take the wounded back to the temporary camp, where they could be kept from freezing. Next day a roaring blizzard trapped the warriors there in improvised shelters, and when the storm abated they went back to their villages on the Tongue.

Now it was the Moon of Strong Cold, and there would be no more fighting for a while. The soldiers who were left alive in the fort would have a bitter taste of defeat in their mouths. If they had not learned their lesson and were still there when the grass greened in the spring, the war would continue.

The Fetterman Massacre made a profound impression upon Colonel Carrington. He was appalled by the mutilations—the disembowelings, the hacked limbs, the "private parts severed and indecently placed on the person." He brooded upon the reasons for such savagery, and eventually wrote an essay on the subject, philosophizing that the Indians were compelled by some paganistic belief to commit the terrible deeds that remained forever in his mind. Had Colonel Carrington visited the scene of the Sand Creek Massacre, which occurred only two years before the Fetterman Massacre, he would have seen the same mutilations—committed upon Indians by Colonel Chivington's soldiers. The Indians who ambushed Fetterman were only imitating their enemies, a practice which in warfare, as in civilian life, is said to be the sincerest form of flattery.

The Fetterman Massacre also made a profound impression upon the United States government. It was the worst defeat the Army had yet suffered in Indian warfare, and the second in American history from which came no survivors. Carrington was recalled from command, reinforcements were sent to the forts in the Powder River country, and a new peace commission was dispatched from Washington to Fort Laramie.

"THE ONLY GOOD INDIAN IS A DEAD INDIAN"

During that autumn Black Kettle established a village on the Washita River forty miles east of the Antelope Hills, and as the young men drifted back from Kansas he scolded them for their errant ways, but like a forgiving father accepted them back into his band. In November, when he heard rumors of soldiers coming, he and Little Robe and two Arapaho leaders made a journey of almost a hundred miles down the valley of the Washita to Fort Cobb, headquarters for their new agency south of the Arkansas. General William B. Hazen was commander of the fort, and on their summer visits the Cheyennes and Arapahos had found him to be friendly and sympathetic.

On this urgent occasion, however, Hazen was not cordial. When Black Kettle asked for permission to move his 180 lodges near Fort Cobb for protection, Hazen refused to grant it. He also refused permission for the Cheyennes and Arapahos to join the Kiowa and Comanche villages. He assured Black Kettle that if his delegation would return to their villages and keep their young men there, they would not be attacked. After issuing his visitors some sugar, coffee, and tobacco, Hazen sent them away, knowing that he would probably never see any of them again. He was fully aware of Sheridan's war plans.

Facing into a raw north wind that turned into a snowstorm, the disappointed chiefs made their way back to their villages, arriving on the night of November 26. Weary as he was from the long journey, Black Kettle immediately called a council of the tribe's leaders.

This time, Black Kettle told his people, they must not be caught by surprise as they had at Sand Creek. Instead of waiting for the soldiers to come to them, he would take a delegation to meet the soldiers and convince them that the Cheyenne village was peaceful. Snow was deep and still falling, but as soon as the clouds left the sky they would start to meet the soldiers.

Although Black Kettle went to bed late that night, he awoke just before dawn as he always did. He stepped outside his lodge, and was glad to see that the skies were clearing. A heavy fog blanketed the valley of the Washita, but he could see deep snow on the ridges across the river.

Suddenly he heard a woman crying, her voice becoming clearer as she came closer. "Soldiers! soldiers!" she was shouting. Reacting automatically, Black Kettle rushed inside his lodge for his rifle. In the few seconds that passed before he was outside again he had made up his mind what he must do—arouse the camp and put everyone to flight. There must not be another Sand Creek. He would meet the soldiers alone at the Washita ford and parley with them. Pointing his rifle skyward, he pulled the trigger. The report brought the village wide awake. As he shouted commands to everyone to mount and ride away, his wife untied his pony and brought it to him.

He was preparing to hurry toward the ford when a bugle blared out of the fog, followed by shouted commands and wild yells of charging soldiers. Because of the snow there was no thunder of hoofbeats, but only a rattle of packs and a jingle of harness metal, a hoarse yelling, and bugles blowing everywhere. (Custer had brought his military band through the snow and had ordered them to play "Garry Owen" for the charge.)

Black Kettle expected the soldiers to come riding across the Washita ford, but instead they were dashing out of the fog from four directions. How could he meet four charging columns and talk to them of peace? It was Sand Creek all over again. He reached for his wife's hand, lifted her up behind him, and lashed the pony into quick motion. She had survived Sand Creek with him; now, like tortured dreamers dreaming the same nightmare over again, they were fleeing again from screaming bullets.

They were almost to the ford when he saw the charging cavalrymen in their heavy blue coats and fur caps. Black Kettle slowed his pony and lifted his hand in the sign gesture of peace. A bullet burned into his stomach, and his pony swerved. Another bullet caught him in the back, and he slid into the snow at the river's edge. Several bullets knocked his wife off beside him, and the pony ran away. The cavalrymen splashed on across the ford, riding right over Black Kettle and his wife, splattering mud upon their dead bodies.

Custer's orders from Sheridan were explicit: "to proceed south in the direction of the Antelope Hills, thence toward the Washita River, the supposed winter seat of the hostile tribes; to destroy their villages and ponies, to kill or hang all warriors, and bring back all women and children."

In a matter of minutes Custer's troopers destroyed Black Kettle's village; in another few minutes of gory slaughter they destroyed by gunfire several hundred corralled ponies. To kill or hang all the warriors meant separating them from the old men, women, and children. This work was too slow and dangerous for the cavalrymen; they found it much more efficient and safe to kill indiscriminately. They killed 103 Cheyennes, but only eleven of them were warriors. They captured 53 women and children.

By this time, gunfire echoing down the valley brought a swarm of Arapahos from their nearby village, and they joined the Cheyennes in a rearguard action. A party of Arapahos surrounded a pursuit platoon of nineteen soldiers under Major Joel Elliott and killed every man. About noontime, Kiowas and Comanches were arriving from farther downriver. When Custer saw the increasing number of warriors on the nearby hills, he rounded up his captives and without searching for the missing Major Elliott started back north in a forced march toward his temporary base at Camp Supply on the Canadian River.

At Camp Supply, General Sheridan was eagerly awaiting news of a Custer victory. When he was informed that the cavalry regiment was returning, he ordered the entire post out for a formal review. With the band blaring triumphantly, the victors marched in, waving the scalps of Black Kettle and the other dead "savages," and Sheridan publicly congratulated Custer for "efficient and gallant services rendered."

In his official report of victory over the "savage butchers" and "savage bands of cruel marauders," General Sheridan rejoiced that he had "wiped out old Black Kettle . . . a worn-out and worthless old cypher." He then stated that he had promised Black Kettle sanctuary if he would come into a fort before military operations began. "He refused," Sheridan lied, "and was killed in the fight."

Tall Chief Wynkoop, who had already resigned in a gesture of protest against Sheridan's policies, was far away in Philadelphia when he heard the news of Black Kettle's death. Wynkoop charged that his old friend had been betrayed, and "met his death at the hands of white men in whom he had too often fatally trusted and who triumphantly report the fact of his scalp in their possession." Other white men who had known and liked Black Kettle also attacked Sheridan's war policy, but Sheridan brushed them aside as "good and pious ecclesiastics . . . aiders and abettors of savages who murdered, without mercy, men, women, and children."

The Great Warrior Sherman gave Sheridan his support, however, and ordered him to continue killing hostile Indians and their ponies, but at the same time advised that he establish the friendly Indians in camps where they could be fed and exposed to the white man's civilized culture.

In response to this, Sheridan and Custer moved on to Fort Cobb, and from there sent out runners to the four tribes in the area, warning them to come in and make peace or else they would be hunted down and killed. Custer himself went out in search of friendly Indians. For this field operation he requisitioned one of the more attractive young women from his Cheyenne prisoners to go with him. She was listed as an interpreter, although she knew no English.

Late in December the survivors of Black Kettle's band began arriving at Fort Cobb. They had to come on foot, because Custer had killed all of their ponies. Little Robe was now the nominal leader of the tribe, and when he was taken to see Sheridan he told the bearlike soldier chief that his people were starving. Custer had burned their winter meat supply; they could find no buffalo along the Washita; they had eaten all their dogs.

Sheridan replied that the Cheyennes would be fed if they all came into Fort Cobb and surrendered unconditionally. "You cannot make peace now and commence killing whites again in the spring," Sheridan added. "If you are not willing to make a complete peace, you can go back and we will fight this thing out."

Little Robe knew there was but one answer he could give. "It is for you to say what we have to do," he said.

Yellow Bear of the Arapahos also agreed to bring his people to Fort Cobb. A few days later, Tosawi brought in the first band of Comanches to surrender. When he was presented to Sheridan, Tosawi's eyes brightened. He spoke his own name and added two words of broken English. "Tosawi, good Indian," he said.

It was then that General Sheridan uttered the immortal words: "The only good Indians I ever saw were dead." Lieutenant Charles Nordstrom, who was present, remembered the words and passed them on, until in time they were honed into an American aphorism: *The only good Indian is a dead Indian.*

MANIFEST DESTINY

The Big Horn Association* was formed in Cheyenne, and its members believed in Manifest Destiny: "The rich and beautiful valleys of Wyoming are destined for the occupancy and sustenance of the Anglo-Saxon race. The wealth that for untold ages has lain hidden beneath the snow-capped summits of our mountains has been placed there by Providence to reward the brave spirits whose lot it is to compose the advance-guard of civilization. The Indians must stand aside or be overwhelmed by the ever advancing and ever increasing tide of emigration. The destiny of the aborigines is written in characters not to be mistaken. The same inscrutable Arbiter that decreed the downfall of Rome has pronounced the doom of extinction upon the red men of America."

---

*This was an association of white frontiersmen who wanted to open the Sioux treaty lands. ED.

INDEX

Abortion, x, 15, 27, 54, 107, 166–67, 199, 206–7, 214, 218, 242, 347, 390–93, 397
Abraham, 32, 74–87
Absolutes, 40, 43, 48, 69, 168, 199, 234, 242, 398; pacifism, 168, 398 (see also Pacifism); principle, 243; right, 293–94, 390–400 (see also Rights)
Absurdity, 77, 79, 87
Abusus non tollit usus, 221, 243
Act: agapism, 40; modified, 40, 41, 48, 49, 52; pure, 40, 41, 48
Act theories, 10, 39
Action, 14, 20
Adultery, 36, 46, 49, 54, 364
Advertising, 311, 330–34
Agape, 38–57. *See also* Love
Alienation, 274, 279, 281

Amorality, 16, 303
Anarchism, 27
Anti-nominianism, 40
Aquinas, Thomas, 17, 225
Arabs, 179
Arbitrariness, 42, 65, 70, 395
Aristotle, 61, 66, 224, 394, 417
Attitudes, 14–15
Autonomy, 64, 65, 384

Baez, Joan, 163
Ballou, Adin, 169
Barth, Karl, 70, 356
Bentham, Jeremy, 173, 226
Bergson, Henri, 62
Berrigan, Philip and Daniel, 169, 171
Bible, 32, 64–65, 87–89, 92, 95, 132–33, 224, 228, 235–37, 426
Bill of Rights, 131, 296–97

437

Birth control 92-93, 319, 422
BITCH test, 419
Black's Law Dictionary, 164-65, 305n5, 390
Blacks, 180, 182, 188-97, 386-87, 403-24
Blackstone, William, 229, 390-91
Bonhoeffer, Dietrich, 42, 91-95
Bradley, F.H., 68
Brunner, Emil, 38, 49-52, 60n47, 60n49, 70-72, 236
Buddha, 33, 63
Buddhists, 63, 223-34
Buyers, 310-11

Cancer, 216, 221, 238, 240, 243, 261, 317, 318
Capital punishment, 48, 166, 235-36, 243, 307, 397-98
Capitalism, 54, 274, 342
Categorical imperative, 54
Catholic, Roman, 42, 92, 95, 148, 225-35, 370, 386
Caveat emptor, 310-11
Chesterton, G.K., 240
Christianity, 33, 34, 38-76, 89-96, 106-8, 112-13, 162, 170, 173-74, 181, 223-39, 307-10, 352, 360, 370, 425-26
Civil disobedience, 15, 170, 172, 303
Civil rights, 292, 293, 392, 404, 415, 423. *See also* Rights
Code of Hammurabi, 374
Coercion, 17, 169
Coffin, William Sloan, 303-4
Columbus, Christopher, 424-25
Communist, 63, 96, 273, 386
Complexity of government, 297, 298, 301
Compulsion, 17
Conduct, 14, 309
Conscience, 220, 228, 234, 239, 242
Constitution, U.S., 18, 265, 294-97, 300-2
Consumer interests, 16
Crime and sin, 105, 358
Criminal law, 106, 114, 134
Crito, 6, 241
Culture:—biased, 407-8, 410;—fair, 407-8, 410;—loaded, 407-9;—specific, 418-19
Custer, George C., 432-34
Cybernation, 270-71

Dean, John, 304
Death, 6, 47, 216-17, 220-27, 238-45, 282, 384-89
Declaration of Rights, 231
Decolonialization, 127, 178, 182, 186
Democracy, 251, 262, 291-92, 295-96, 302, 403-4
Demonstrations, 169, 171
Deontology, 9, 10, 38-39, 53, 58, 173
Descriptive ethics, 4, 5
Deterrence, 131, 134, 398
Devil, 33, 81
Devlin, Lord Patrick, 20-21, 104-11
Dewey, John, 94-95
Dickens, Charles, ix
Disraeli, Benjamin, 272
Divorce, 36, 45-46, 358
Doe v. *Bolton,* 392
Duty (duties), 9, 24, 42-43, 58-62, 71, 78, 80, 87, 150, 157, 220; *prima facie,* 58. *See also* Rights

Ecology, 248, 251-53
Economics, ix, x, 263, 271-72, 275, 278, 281, 290, 416
Embryos, 199-200, 242
Enforcement, 14, 16, 19, 25
Environment, 16-17, 166-67, 202, 248, 403-6, 411-12; environmental hypothesis, 411
Ephesians, Letter to the, 162
Equal Rights Amendment, 399
Equality, 338, 340, 413
Ervin, Samuel, 13, 291-92, 305
Ethics, xi, 1-5, 48, 53, 70, 75, 79, 87, 172-74, 347; descriptive, 4, 5; meta-, 4, 5; normative, 4, 5, 9, 172-74
Euthanasia, x, 15, 92, 93, 107, 166, 200, 220-44
Evidence, 405
Evil, 222, 235, 242, 307, 345
Executive privilege, 301, 306n23
Exploitation, 54, 270, 315, 326, 420, 423
Eye for an eye, 37, 170, 172

Fairness, 212, 218
Faith, 62-72, 76-77, 80, 85-87, 95-96, 235, 240, 254, 271
False claims: of effectiveness, 315, 318-19; of need, 315-20

Fanon, Frantz, 176, 189
Fear, 322
Federal Trade Commission (FTC), 314, 317, 323-25, 328, 331
Felo de se. See Suicide
Fetus (foetus), 167, 199-200, 206-10, 214, 218, 399, 402n28
Fletcher, Joseph, 38, 40-54, 93-94
Forbearance, 174
Force, 27-28, 155-56, 164-66, 178
Frankena, William, 38, 40, 46, 53-55, 59n1
Fraud, 311, 314, 325
Freedom, xi, 5, 96-97, 222, 231, 233, 235, 242, 244, 251, 271-72, 283, 286, 309, 319, 320
Freedom of Information Act, 296-97, 303
Freud, Sigmund, 244, 282-83, 387

Gandhi, Mahatma, 169, 171-72, 174, 189, 234
General rules, 38-39, 53-56. *See also* Rules
Genetic hypothesis, 405, 411
Genetics, 404, 407, 414, 421-22
Genocide, 422
German Peace Sects, 163
God, 2, 3, 8, 31-36, 44, 48-53, 63-74, 80, 84-95, 113, 174, 224, 226, 228, 231, 234, 237, 244, 253-55, 266, 307-10, 349, 358, 427
Gospel according to Matthew, 36, 170
Government, 287, 294-302, 307, 309, 311, 319-20, 326, 330-31, 334-45, 391
Guilt, 57, 78, 207-8, 319, 364

Hare, R. M., 56, 60n69, 394-95
Harm, 22, 26, 115, 319-20
Harvard Educational Review, 403
Hegel, G. W. F., 17, 18, 76
Henry, Patrick, 296
Hereditability, 406-7, 415
Heredity, 403
Hindu, 176, 223, 234
Hinduism, 72, 224
Hippocratic oath, 220-21, 234, 236, 242
Homicide, 5, 10, 166, 221, 226, 228-29, 242, 421

Homosexuality, 15, 105, 107, 114, 116, 136
Housing, 19, 21
Human life, 167, 309; rights, xi, 43, 240, 292-93, 394-97
Humanism (humanists), 47, 134, 173-74, 225, 273, 275, 414
Hume, David, 226
Huxley, Aldous, 272

Idealistic pacifism, 167. *See also* Pacifism
Illegality, 15, 299
Immanence, 25-28, 32, 34, 54, 68, 75, 87, 254
Immorality, 107, 110-11, 199, 255, 294, 398
Inalienable rights, 232, 265. *See also* Rights
Indians, 16, 252, 266, 387, 408, 412, 424, 427-28, 430-31, 434-35
Industrial Revolution, 270-71, 274
Infidelity, 36, 46, 49, 54, 364
Injury, 24, 114, 166
Institutional racism, 415
Intelligence tests (IQ), 403-22
Intent, 14, 209
Iron tablets, 315-16
Isaac, 32, 74, 77-78, 80, 82, 87-88, 90

James, William, 161
Jehovah, 32
Jesus, 26, 33-36, 44-47, 50, 72, 92-93, 147, 161-62, 170, 173, 234, 417
Judaism, 72, 94-95, 224-25, 236, 386, 404, 423
Judeo-Christian tradition, 253-55
Judgment, 107
Judiciary, 13
Justice, 4, 6, 13-16, 25, 38, 42-43, 49-52, 56, 78, 79, 165, 171, 173, 230, 293, 303, 338, 345, 390
Justification, 5, 16, 39, 41, 159, 217, 293-96, 302-4, 338, 345, 393-94

Kalmbach, Herbert, 304, 306n26
Kant, Immanuel, 42, 54, 65-66, 71, 120

439
INDEX

Kierkegaard, Sören, xi, 50, 87-89, 378
Killing, 7, 8, 14, 32-36, 42, 49, 74, 166, 173, 189, 199-200, 208, 210, 215-16, 228, 230, 234-36, 243, 254, 282, 429, 433-34; killing the pursuer, 207-9. *See also* Murder
King, Martin Luther, Jr., 169, 171-74, 188-97
Krogh, Egil, 304

Labor, 314, 337, 339-41, 343
Law, 3, 6, 13-29, 40, 42, 44, 56, 58, 65, 70, 78, 105, 114, 118, 199, 222, 225, 229-31, 233, 238, 243, 265, 282, 296-97, 299, 301, 303-4, 307-8, 312, 337-40, 345, 362, 388, 415, 423; as amoral, 16; as immoral, 16; as moral, 16-18; as ought to be moral, 16, 18-23
Legal rights, 292-95, 297, 301, 386, 395. *See also* Rights
Legal rules, 8, 394. *See also* Rules
Legalism, 40, 43, 47-49, 57, 70, 222
Legality, x, 14, 200, 311, 313, 315, 320
Legislation, 313
Lex talionis, 120-21, 132, 228
Liberation, 384
Liberty, 262, 338, 391
Listerine, 316, 319
Love, 34, 37-57, 61, 64, 70, 72, 161-62, 168, 173, 254, 280, 310, 361, 368, 371; agape, 38-57, 173; philia, 43-44
Lying, 39, 42, 49, 55-56, 324, 327

Mabbott, J. B., 394-96
Madison, James, 299, 300n19
Magruder, Jeb Stuart, 303-5, 306n26
Malcolm X, 420-21
Malice, 228-30, 233, 254
Manicheans, 181, 185, 365
Manslaughter, 229
Marijuana, 15
Marriage, 46, 51, 357, 375, 384
Marx, Karl, 272-74, 279
Marxism, 180
Masochism, 240-41, 364

Master-servant, 15
Master/slave, xi
Mayday, 169
Mead, Margaret, 366
Megamachine, 273-74, 281
Menninger, Karl, 128, 135
Mens rea, 14
Mental retardation, 416
Meta-ethics, 4, 96-97. *See also* Ethics
Militant non-violence, 161-75. *See also* Violence
Mill, John Stuart, 20, 115, 272
Mishnah, 132
Mohammed, 33
Moloch, 89, 272
Moore, G. E., 401n16
Moral code: structure of, 1, 4-10; law, 3, 8-10, 14-29, 33-34; principles, ultimate, 5, 8-9, 34, 47, 396; rights, 292-93, 297, 386, 395 (*see also* Rights); rules, 8-10, 33-34, 38-40, 47, 48, 394, 396 (*see also* Rules)
Morality, x, xii, 1-8, 14-29, 33-34, 46-47, 61, 65-66, 69, 80, 109, 113, 199, 210, 222, 241, 251, 294, 296, 302-5, 311, 315, 319-20, 356, 363-64, 390, 420
Mosaic Law, 174
Moslems (Mohammedans), 94-96, 224
Motives, 14, 15, 47, 61, 226, 229, 233-34, 242-43
Mumford, Lewis, 273
Murder, 8, 14, 39, 76-77, 85, 87-88, 199, 214-15, 221-22, 227-28, 230, 233, 236, 427, 434. *See also* Killing
Myths, 249-50, 300, 384, 414

Narveson, Jan, 145-46, 402
Natural law, 18, 42, 92-94, 97, 227, 239, 302, 391; right, 293, 390-91, 394-95. *See also* Rights
Nazis, 423
Negligence, 23
Negro, 180, 182, 188-97, 386-87, 403-24
New Left, 171
New Testament, 92-93, 168, 173, 227
Niebuhr, Reinhold, 38, 49, 52, 60n55, 68, 244

Nixon, Richard, 296, 298, 300-4, 305n15, 306
Non compos mentis, 169
Non-cooperation, 170-71
Non-resistance, 162, 169-70
Non-violence, 161-63, 167-72, 174-75, 199, 398. *See also* Violence
Non-violent direct action, 171
Non-violent resistance, 170-71
Normative ethics, 4, 5, 9. *See also* Ethics
Norms, 4, 5
Nuclear pacifism, 168. *See also* Pacifism

Obligation to inform, 296-97, 299, 302, 305
Obscenity, 15
Oppression, 416

Pacifism, 141-97, 397; absolute, 168, 398; idealistic, 167; nuclear, 168; selective, 168; theoretical, 167
Pain, 146, 320
Paradox, 76-77, 80-81, 84-86, 225
Passive resistance, 169-70
Passivism, 169, 255, 279
Paul, Saint, 62, 162
Peace, 161, 171, 250, 265, 282, 426, 431-35
People v. *Berberrich*, 390-91, 400n5
Petitions, 22, 170
Philia, 43-44. *See also* Love
Philosophers, xii, 3, 5, 56, 161-62, 199, 340
Plato, 5, 61, 66, 69, 224, 262, 265, 375
Playboy, 45, 352-55
Politics, x, 13, 251, 262-65, 271, 309, 342
Pollution, 167, 200, 202-3, 252, 266
Positivism, 23-25, 68, 94
Power, 111, 161, 175, 294, 296-98, 325, 354
Prayer, 170
Presidency, 298-301, 304, 306
Prima facie rights. *See* Rights, *prima facie*, 38, 58, 166-7
Principle, 7-8, 41-42, 48-49, 53, 65, 97, 214, 230, 293, 311, 332-33, 337

Private morality, 200
Property, 336-43, 358, 391
Prostitutes (prostitution), 54, 105, 107
Protestants, 42, 52, 64, 70, 92, 225, 227, 235
Public good, argument from, 297, 299, 301-2
Punishment, 78, 117-39, 214, 226; retributivist theory of, 119-24, 139; utilitarian theory of, 124-25
Pure Theory of Law, 23

Quakers, 163

Racial (sexual) bias, 387, 409, 424
Racism, 403-4
Racism, institutional, 192
Ramsey, Paul, 38-39, 52-59
Rationalists, 162, 189
Rawls, John, 53, 56-57, 60n56, 400n7
Reason, 6, 7, 62-67, 93, 97, 228, 241, 275, 280, 310
Relative right, 293. *See also* Rights
Religion, 2, 11, 31-33, 68, 92-93, 223, 266, 307, 386, 400
Religiosity, x, 32, 43, 52, 68-69, 72, 87, 91-93, 97, 105-6, 221, 234, 236, 265-66
Responsibilities, 52, 72, 159, 233, 239, 283
Retaliation, 132, 189
Retribution, 119-24, 139, 398
Revelationists, 162
Riesman, David, 352
Right (as opposed to wrong), 2, 4-5, 7, 10-11, 45, 51, 71
Rights, xi, 15, 42-43, 107, 231, 235, 242, 251, 262-63, 292-93, 307, 337-38, 342, 389-97, 413, 425; absolute, 293-94, 337-39, 342, 390-400; civil, 292-93, 392, 404, 415, 423; human, xi, 43, 240, 292-93, 394-97; inalienable, 232, 265, 339; legal, 292, 386, 395; moral, 292, 386, 395; natural, 292-93, 337-39, 342, 390-95; *prima facie*, 393-94, 398; relative, 293, 390-93; second order human, 396-99; to know, 291-305; to life, 214, 218, 232-33, 389, 397-99; to withhold, 291-92,

441
INDEX

297, 301-2; women's, 15, 361-83, 392. See also Duty
Robbery, 337
Robinson, Bishop J. A. T., 38, 48-49, 53, 59n41, 60n43
Roe v. Wade, 392-93
Rogers, Carl, xi
Roman Catholic. See Catholic, Roman
Rule(s), 9-10, 40, 42, 50, 53-57, 64, 97, 394-95; agapism, 55; general, 38-39, 53-56; summary, 53-55; theories, 10, 39

Sabotage, 171
Sadism, 240-41, 364
Safety, 428
Sanctions, 229
Sanhedrin, 36, 132, 219
Sartre, Jean-Paul, 47
Schizophrenia, 280-81
Schweitzer, Albert, 234
Scientific racism, 415, 419-21, 423. See also Racism
Second order human right, 396-99. See also Rights
Security, 338
Selective pacifism, 168. See also Pacifism
Self-defense, 33, 153-55, 159, 163, 189, 230, 427
Seller, 311
Sermon on the Mount, 26, 36, 39, 42
Sex, 15, 20, 44-47, 54-55, 116, 265, 321, 347-49, 352, 354, 357-75, 384, 386, 399
Shakers, 163
Sidgwich, Henry, 61
Sin, 48, 54, 75, 81, 214, 225, 254-55
Sit-ins, 169
Situationalism, 38, 40, 44-45
Slavery, 337-38
Slaves, 417
Social cooperation, 344
Social order, 56
Socialists, 161, 272, 274
Society, x, 6, 56, 58, 61, 95, 251, 262-64, 271, 275, 307, 384, 404-5
Sociological fallacy, 411
Socrates, x, xi, 5-8, 27, 63, 162, 227
Soledad, 135

Spirit, 166, 228, 368
Sputnik, 13
State, 6-7, 44, 65, 82, 225-26, 310-11, 392
Suicide, 92-93, 107, 166, 221-29, 232, 237, 320
Summary rules, 53-55. See also Rules
Summum bonum, 228, 232
Suppressio veri, 334
Supreme Court, U.S., 199, 294-97, 392-93, 400n1, 401n24
Swift, Jonathan, 222

Tale of Two Cities, ix
Talmud, 128-29, 132-33, 219
Technology, 13, 15, 21, 200-3, 249, 264-66, 284
Teleological suspension of the ethical, 75, 77-79, 81, 85, 87, 89-90
Teleology, 9-10, 38-39, 53, 78
Telos, 75, 79
Temple, William, 64, 234-35
Temptation, 75-77, 80, 88
Ten Commandments, 39, 42, 48
Tertullian, 70
Theologians, xii, 47, 70, 199, 225
Theoretical pacifism, 167. See also Pacifism
Tobacco, 432
Tolstoy, Leo, 25-27, 161-62, 168, 172-73, 189
Tragic hero, 77, 79, 85-86
Transcendence, 68, 75, 254. See also Immanence
Trespassor, 24
Truth, 6, 9, 39-40, 56, 58, 68, 71, 237, 295, 297, 300, 310-11, 315, 325, 423
Tuskegee syphilis experiment, 420-23

Unjust, 6-8, 44, 56
Unreasonable search and seizure, 25
Utilitarianism, 10, 38-40, 43, 57, 121, 173, 226

Values, xi, 182, 254, 352, 369
Viet Cong, 164-65
Violation, 427
Violence, x, 15, 26, 141-97, 200, 235, 264, 340, 386, 421. See also Non-violence
Virtue, 50, 53, 62, 72, 80, 228, 236

War, 4, 13-14, 96, 155, 163, 166, 168, 200, 235, 250-52, 262, 282, 307-8, 310, 391, 431-32
Wasserstrom, Richard, 294, 305n71, 393, 397, 399
Watergate, 13, 291-92, 298, 300, 302-3, 305

White, 403-34
Wolfenden Report, 20, 105, 107, 116
Women's rights, 15, 361-83, 392.
See also Rights

Yahweh, 74. *See also* God